D1492686

3102661

Parallel
Computing
Works!

Parallel Computing Works!

Geoffrey C. Fox
Roy D. Williams
Paul C. Messina

Morgan Kaufmann Publishers, Inc.
San Francisco, California

Executive Editor: Bruce M. Spatz
Production Manager: Yonie Overton
Assistant Editor: Douglas Sery
Production Coordinator: Julie Pabst
Cover Design: Studio Silicon
Color Insert Design & Production: Carron Design
Copyeditor: Gary Morris
Printer: R.R. Donnelley & Sons

This book was typeset by the author using laTEX.

Editorial Offices:
Morgan Kaufmann Publishers, Inc.
340 Pine Street, Sixth Floor
San Francisco, CA 94104

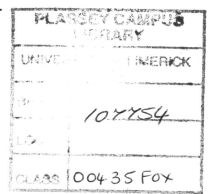

© 1994 by Morgan Kaufmann Publishers, Inc.

All rights reserved
Printed in the United States of America

98 97 96 95 94   5 4 3 2 1

No part of this publication may be reproduced, stored in a retrieval system, or transmitted
in any form or by any means—electronic, mechanical, photocopying, recording, or
otherwise—without the prior written permission of the publisher.

Library of Congress Cataloging-in-Publication Data is available for this book.
ISBN 1-55860-253-4

Contents

Preface

This book describes a set of application and systems software research projects undertaken by the Caltech Concurrent Computation Program (C^{3}P) from 1983–1990. This parallel computing activity is organized so that applications with similar algorithmic and software challenges are grouped together. Thus, one can not only learn that parallel computing is effective on a broad range of problems but also why it works, what algorithms are needed, and what features the software should support. The description of the software has been updated through 1993 to reflect the current interests of Geoffrey Fox, now at Syracuse University but still working with many C^{3}P collaborators through the auspices of the NSF Center for Research in Parallel Computation (CRPC).

Many C^{3}P members wrote sections of this book. John Apostolakis wrote Section 7.4; Clive Baillie, Sections 4.3, 4.4, 7.2 and 12.6; Vas Bala, Section 13.2; Ted Barnes, Section 7.3; Roberto Battitti, Sections 6.5, 6.7, 6.8 and 9.9; Rob Clayton, Section 18.2; Dave Curkendall, Section 18.3; Hong Ding, Sections 6.3 and 6.4; David Edelsohn, Section 12.8; Jon Flower, Sections 5.2, 5.3, 5.4 and 13.5; Tom Gottschalk, Sections 9.8 and 18.4; Gary Gutt, Section 4.5; Wojtek Furmanski, Chapter 17; Mark Johnson, Section 14.2; Jeff Koller, Sections 13.4 and 15.2; Aron Kuppermann, Section 8.2; Paulette Liewer, Section 9.3; Vince McKoy, Section 8.3; Paul Messina, Chapter 2; Steve Otto, Sections 6.6, 11.4, 12.7, 13.6 and 14.3; Jean Patterson, Section 9.4; Francois Pepin, Section 12.5; Peter Reiher, Section 15.3; John Salmon, Section 12.4; Tony Skjellum, Sections 9.5, 9.6 and Chapter 16; Michael Speight, Section 7.6; Eric Van de Velde, Section 9.7; David Walker, Sections 6.2 and 8.1; Brad Werner, Section 9.2; Roy Williams, Sections 11.1, 12.2, 12.3 and Chapter 10. Geoffrey Fox wrote the remaining text. Appendix B describes many of the key C^{3}P contributors, with brief biographies.

C^{3}P's research depended on the support of many sponsors; central support for major projects was given by the Department of Energy and the Electronic Systems Division of the USAF. Other federal sponsors were the Joint Tactical Fusion office, NASA, NSF and the National Security Agency. C^3P's start up was only possible due to two private donations from the Parsons and System Development Foundations. Generous corporate support came from ALCOA, Digital Equipment, General Dynamics, General Motors, Hitachi, Hughes, IBM, INTEL, Lockheed, McDonnell Douglas, MOTOROLA, Nippon Steel, nCUBE, Sandia National Laboratories, and Shell.

Production of this book would have been impossible without the dedicated help of Richard Alonso, Lisa Deyo, Keri Arnold, Blaise Canzian and especially Terri Canzian.

Chapter 1

Introduction

1.1 Introduction

This book describes the activities of the Caltech Concurrent Computation Program (C^3P). This was a seven-year project (1983–1990), focussed on the question, "Can parallel computers be used effectively for large scale scientific computation?" The title of the book, "Parallel Computing Works," reveals our belief that we answered the question in the affirmative, by implementing numerous scientific applications on real parallel computers and doing computations that produced new scientific results. In the process of doing so, C^3P helped design and build several new computers, designed and implemented basic system software, developed algorithms for frequently used mathematical computations on massively parallel machines, devised performance models and measured the performance of many computers, and created a high-performance computing facility based exclusively on parallel computers. While the initial focus of C^3P was the hypercube architecture developed by C. Seitz at Caltech, many of the methods developed and lessons learned have been applied successfully on other massively parallel architectures.

Of course, C^3P was only one of many projects contributing to this field and so the contents of this book are only representative of the important activities in parallel computing during the last ten years. However, we believe that the project did address a wide range of issues and applications areas. Thus, a book focussed on C^3P has some general interest. We do, of course, cite other activities but surely not completely. Other general references which the reader will find valuable are [Almasi:89a], [Andrews:91a], [Arbib:90a], [Blelloch:90a], [Brawer:89a], [Doyle:91a], [Duncan:90a], [Fox:88a], [Golub:89a], [Hayes:89a], [Hennessy:91a], [Hillis:85a], [Hockney:81a], [Hord:90a], [Hwang:89a], [IEEE:91a], [Laksh:90a], [Lazou:87a], [Messina:87a;91d], [Schneck:87a], [Skerrett:92a], [Stone:91a], [Trew:91a], [Zima:91a].

C^3P was both a technical and social experiment. It involved a wide range of disciplines working together to understand the hardware, software, and algorithmic (applications) issues in parallel computing. Such multidisciplinary activities are generally considered of growing relevance to many new academic and research activities—including the federal high-performance computing and communication initiative. Many of the participants of C^3P are no longer at Caltech, and this has positive and negative messages. C^3P was not set up in a traditional academic fashion since its core interdisciplinary field, computational science, is not well understood or implemented either nationally or in specific universities. This is explored further in Chapter 20. C^3P has led to flourishing follow-on projects at Caltech, Syracuse University, and elsewhere. These differ from C^3P just as parallel computing has changed from an exploratory field to one that is in a transitional stage into development, production, and exploitation.

1.2   The National Vision for Parallel Computation

The technological driving force behind parallel computing is VLSI, or very large scale integration—the same technology that created the personal computer and workstation market over the last decade. In 1980, the Intel 8086 used 50,000 transistors; in 1992, the latest Digital alpha RISC chip contains 1,680,000 transistors—a factor of 30 increase. The dramatic improvement in chip density comes together with an increase in clock speed and improved design so that the alpha performs better by a factor of over one thousand on scientific problems than the 8086-8087 chip pair of the early 1980s.

The increasing density of transistors on a chip follows directly from a decreasing feature size which is now 0.75μ for the alpha. Feature size will continue to decrease and by the year 2000, chips with 50 million transistors are expected to be available. What can we do with all these transistors?

With around a million transistors on a chip, designers were able to move full mainframe functionality to about $2cm^2$ of a chip. This enabled the personal computing and workstation revolutions. The next factors of ten increase in transistor density must go into some form of parallelism by replicating several CPUs on a single chip.

By the year 2000, parallelism is thus inevitable to all computers, from your children's video game to personal computers, workstations, and supercomputers. Today we see it in the larger machines as we replicate many chips and printed circuit boards to build systems as arrays of nodes, each unit of which is some variant of the microprocessor. This is illustrated in Figure 1.1 (Color Plate), which shows an nCUBE parallel supercomputer with 64 identical nodes on each board—each node is a single-chip CPU with additional memory chips. To be useful, these nodes must be linked in some way and this is still a matter of much research and experimentation. Further, we can argue as to the most appropriate node to replicate; is it a "small" node as in the nCUBE of Figure 1.1 (Color Plate), or more powerful "fat" nodes such as those offered in CM-5 and Intel Touchstone shown in Figures 1.2 and 1.3 (Color Plates) where each node is a sophisticated multichip printed circuit board? However, these details should not obscure the basic point: Parallelism allows one to build the world's fastest and most cost-effective supercomputers.

Parallelism may only be critical today for supercomputer vendors and users. By the year 2000, all computers will have to address the hardware, algorithmic, and software issues implied by parallelism. The reward will be amazing performance and the opening up of new fields; the price will be a major rethinking and reimplementation of software, algorithms, and applications.

This vision and its consequent issues are now well understood and generally agreed. They provided the motivation in 1981 when C^3P's first roots were formed. In those days, the vision was blurred and controversial. Many believed that parallel computing would not work.

President Bush instituted, in 1992, the five-year federal High Performance Computing and Communications (HPCC) Program. This will spur the development of the technology described above and is focussed on the solution of grand challenges shown in Figure 1.4 (Color Plate). These are fundamental problems in science and engineering, with broad economic and scientific impact, whose solution could be advanced by applying high-performance computing techniques and resources.

The activities of several federal agencies have been coordinated in this program. The Advanced Research Projects Agency (ARPA) is developing the basic technologies which is applied to the grand challenges by the Department of Energy (DOE), the National Aeronautics and Space Agency

(NASA), the National Science Foundation (NSF), the National Institute of Health (NIH), the Environmental Protection Agency (EPA), and the National Oceanographic and Atmospheric Agency (NOAA). Selected activities include the mapping of the human genome in DOE, climate modelling in DOE and NOAA, coupled structural and airflow simulations of advanced powered lift and a high-speed civil transport by NASA.

More generally, it is clear that parallel computing can only realize its full potential and be commercially successful if it is accepted in the real world of industry and government applications. The clear U.S. leadership over Europe and Japan in high-performance computing offers the rest of the U.S. industry the opportunity of gaining global competitive advantage.

Some of these industrial opportunities are discussed in Chapter 19. Here we note some interesting possibilities which include

- use in the oil industry for both seismic analysis of new oil fields and the reservoir simulation of existing fields;

- environmental modelling of past and potential pollution in air and ground;

- fluid flow simulations of aircraft, and general vehicles, engines, air-conditioners, and other turbomachinery; integration of structural analysis with the computational fluid dynamics of airflow; car crash simulation;

- integrated design and manufacturing systems;

- design of new drugs for the pharmaceutical industry by modelling new compounds;

- simulation of electromagnetic and network properties of electronic systems—from new components to full printed circuit boards;

- identification of new materials with interesting properties such as superconductivity;

- simulation of electrical and gas distribution systems to optimize production and response to failures;

- production of animated films and educational and entertainment uses such as simulation of virtual worlds in theme parks and other virtual reality applications;

- support of geographic information systems including real-time analysis of data from satellite sensors in NASA's "Mission to Planet Earth."

- A relatively unexplored area is known as "command and control" in the military area and "decision support" or "information processing" in the civilian applications. These combine large databases with extensive computation. In the military, the database could be sensor information and the processing a multitrack Kalman filter. Commercially, the database could be the nation's medicaid records and the processing would aim at cost containment by identifying anomalies and inconsistencies.

- servers in multimedia networks set up by cable and telecommunication companies. These servers will provide video, information, and simulation on demand to home, education, and industrial users.

C^3P did not address such large-scale problems. Rather, we concentrated on major academic applications. This fit the experience of the Caltech faculty who led most of the C^3P teams, and further academic applications are smaller and cleaner than large-scale industrial problems. One important large-scale C^3P application was a military simulation described in Chapter 18 and produced by Caltech's Jet Propulsion Laboratory. C^3P chose the correct and only computations on which to cut its parallel computing teeth. In spite of the focus on different applications, there are many similarities between the vision and structure of C^3P and today's national effort. It may even be that today's grand challenge teams can learn from C^3P's experience.

1.3   Caltech Concurrent Computation Program

C^3P's origins dated to an early collaboration between the physics and computer science departments at Caltech in bringing up UNIX on the physics department's VAX 11/780. As an aside, we note this was motivated by the development of the Symbolic Manipulation Program (SMP) by Wolfram and collaborators; this project has now grown into the well-known system Mathematica. Carver Mead from computer science urged physics to get back to them if we had insoluble large scale computational needs. This comment was reinforced in May, 1981 when Mead gave a physics colloquium on VLSI, Very Large Scale Integration, and the opportunities it opened up. Fox, in the audience, realized that quantum chromodynamics (QCD, Section 4.3), now using up all free cycles on the VAX 11/780, was naturally parallelizable and could take advantage of the parallel machines promised by VLSI. Thus, a seemingly modest interdisciplinary interaction—a computer scientist lecturing to physicists—gave birth to a large interdisciplinary project, C^3P. Further, our interest in QCD stemmed from the installation of the VAX 11/780 to replace our previous batch computing using a remote CDC7600. This more attractive computing environment, UNIX on a VAX 11/780, encouraged theoretical physics graduate students to explore computation.

During the summer of 1981, Fox's research group, especially Eugene Brooks and Steve Otto, showed that effective concurrent algorithms could be developed, and we presented our conclusion to the Caltech computer scientists. This presentation led to the plans, described in a national context in Chapter 2, to produce the first hypercube, with Chuck Seitz and his student Erik DeBenedictis developing the hardware and Fox's group the QCD applications and systems software. The physics group did not understand what a hypercube was at that stage, but agreed with the computer scientists because the planned six-dimensional hypercube was isomorphic to a $4 \times 4 \times 4$ three-dimensional mesh, a topology whose relevance a physicist could appreciate. With the generous help of the computer scientists, we gradually came to understand the hypercube topology with its general advantage (maximum distance between nodes is $\log_2 N$) and its specific feature of including a rich variety of mesh topologies. Here N is the total number of nodes in the concurrent computer. We should emphasize that this understanding of the relevance of concurrency to QCD was not particularly novel; it followed from ideas already known from earlier concurrent machines such as the Illiac IV. We were, however, fortunate to investigate the issues at a time when microprocessor technology (in particular the Intel 8086/8087) allowed one to build large (in terms of number of nodes) cost-effective concurrent computers with interesting performance levels. The QCD problem was also important in helping ensure that the initial Cosmic Cube was built with sensible design choices; we were fortunate that in choosing parameters, such as memory size, appropriate for QCD, we also realized a machine of general capability.

While the 64-node Cosmic Cube was under construction, Fox wandered around Caltech and the associated Jet Propulsion Laboratory explaining parallel computing and, in particular, the Cosmic Cube to scientists in various disciplines who were using "large" (by the standards of 1981) scale computers. To his surprise, all the problems being tackled on conventional machines by these scientists seemed to be implementable on the Cosmic Cube. This was the origin of C^3P, which identified the Caltech-JPL applications team, whose initial participants are noted in Table 4.2. Fox, Seitz, and these scientists prepared the initial proposals which established and funded C^3P in the summer of 1983. Major support was obtained from the Department of Energy and the Parsons and System Development Foundation. Intel made key initial contributions of chips to the Cosmic Cube and follow-on machines. The Department of Energy remained the central funding support for C^3P throughout its seven years, 1983 to 1990.

The initial C^3P proposals were focussed on the question:

> *"Is the hypercube an effective computer for large-scale scientific computing?"*

Our approach was simple: Build or acquire interesting hardware and provide the intellectual and physical infrastructure to allow leading application scientists and engineers to both develop parallel algorithms and codes, and use them to address important problems. Often we liked to say that C^3P

> *"used real hardware and real software to solve real problems."*

Our project showed initial success, with the approximately ten applications of Table 4.2 developed in the first year. We both showed good performance on the hypercube and developed a performance model which is elaborated in Chapter 3. A major activity at this time was the design and development of the necessary support software, termed CrOS and later developed into the commercial software Express described in Chapter 5. Not only was the initial hardware applicable to a wide range of problems, but our software model proved surprisingly useful. CrOS was originally designed by Brooks as the "mailbox communication system" and we initially targeted the regular synchronous problems typified in Chapter 4. Only later did we realize that it supported quite efficiently the irregular and non-local communication needs of more general problems. This generalization is represented as an evolutionary track of Express in Chapter 5 and for a new communication system Zipcode in Section 16.1 developed from scratch for general asynchronous irregular problems.

Although successful, we found many challenges and intriguing questions opened up by C^3P's initial investigation into parallel computing. Further, around 1985, the DOE and later the NSF made substantial conventional supercomputer (Cray, Cyber, ETA) time available to applications scientists.

Our Cosmic Cube and the follow-on Mark II machines were very competitive with the VAX 11/780, but not with the performance offered by the CRAY X-MP. Thus, internal curiosity and external pressures moved C^3P in the direction of computer science: still developing real software but addressing new parallel algorithms and load-balancing techniques rather than a production application. This phase of C^3P is summarized in [Angus:90a], [Fox:88a;88b].

Around 1988, we returned to our original goal with a focus on parallel supercomputers. We no longer concentrated on the hypercube, but rather asked such questions as [Fox:88v],

> *"What are the cost, technology, and software trade-offs that will drive the design of future parallel supercomputers?"*

and as a crucial (and harder) question:

> *"What is the appropriate software environment for parallel machines and how should one develop it?"*

We evolved from the initial 8086/8087, 80286/80287 machines to the internal JPL Mark IIIfp and commercial nCUBE-1 and CM-2 described in Chapter 2. These were still "rough, difficult to use machines" but had performance capabilities competitive with conventional supercomputers.

This book largely describes work in the last three years of C^3P when we developed a series of large scale applications on these parallel supercomputers. Further, as described in Chapters 15, 16, and 17, we developed prototypes and ideas for higher level software environments which could accelerate and ease the production of parallel software. This period also saw an explosion of interest in the use of parallel computing outside Caltech. Much of this research used commercial hypercubes which partly motivated our initial discoveries and successes on the in-house machines at Caltech. This rapid technology transfer was in one sense gratifying, but it also put pressure on C^3P which was better placed to blaze new trails than to perform the more programmatic research which was now appropriate.

An important and unexpected discovery in C^3P was in the education and the academic support for interdisciplinary research. Many of the researchers, especially graduate students in C^3P, evolved to be "computational scientists." Not traditional physicists, chemists, or computer scientists but rather something in between. We believe that this interdisciplinary education and expertise was critical for C^{3}P's success and, as discussed in Chapter 20, it should be encouraged in more universities [Fox:91f;92d].

Further information about C^{3}P can be found in our annual reports and two reviews.
[Fox:84j;84k;85c;85e;85i;86f;87c;87d;88v;88oo;89i;89n;89cc;89dd;90o]

1.4 How Parallel Computing Works

C^{3}P's research showed that

> **PCW:** *Parallel Computers work in a large class of scientific and engineering computations.*

The book quantifies and exemplifies this assertion.

In Chapter 2, we provide the national overview of parallel computing activities during the last decade. Chapter 3 is somewhat speculative as it attempts to provide a framework to quantify the previous **PCW** statement.

We will show that, more precisely, parallel computing only works in a "scaling" fashion in a special class of problems which we call synchronous and loosely synchronous.

By scaling, we mean that the parallel implementation will efficiently extend to systems with large numbers of nodes without levelling off of the speedup obtained. These concepts are quantified in Chapter 3 with a simple performance model described in detail in [Fox:88a].

The book is organized with applications and software issues growing in complexity in later chapters. Chapter 4 describes the cleanest regular synchronous applications which included many of our initial successes. However, we already see the essential points:

> **DD:** *Domain decomposition (or data parallelism) is a universal source of scalable parallelism*
>
> **MP:** *C^{3}P's software model was a simple explicit message passing with each node of a parallel processor running conventional sequential code communicating via subroutine call with other nodes.*

CrOS and its follow-on Express, described in Chapter 5, support this software paradigm. Explicit message passing is still an important software model and in many cases, the only viable approach to high-performance parallel implementations on MIMD machines.

Chapters 6 through 9 confirm these lessons with an extension to more irregular problems. Loosely synchronous problem classes are harder to parallelize, but still use the basic principles **DD** and **MP**. Chapter 7 describes a special class, *embarrassingly parallel*, of applications where scaling parallelism is guaranteed by the independence of separate components of the problem.

Chapters 10 and 11 describe parallel computing tools developed within C^3P. DIME supports parallel mesh generation and adaptation, and its use in general finite element codes. Initially, we thought load balancing would be a major stumbling block for parallel computing because formally it is an NP-complete (intractable) optimization problem. However, effective heuristic methods were developed which avoid the exponential time complexity of NP-complete problems by searching for good but not exact minima.

In Chapter 12, we describe the most complex irregular loosely synchronous problems which include some of the hardest problems tackled in C^3P.

As described earlier, we implemented essentially all the applications described in the book using explicit user-generated message passing. In Chapter 13, we describe our initial efforts to produce a higher level data-parallel Fortran environment, which should be able to provide a more attractive software environment for the user. High Performance Fortran has been adopted as an informal industry standard for this language.

In Chapter 14, we describe the very difficult asynchronous problem class for which scaling parallel algorithms and the correct software model are less clear. Chapters 15, 16, and 17 describe four software models, Zipcode, MOOSE, Time Warp, and MOVIE which tackle asynchronous and the mixture of asynchronous and loosely synchronous problems one finds in the complex system simulations and analysis typical of many real-world problems. Applications of this class are described in Chapter 18, with the application of Section 18.3 being an event-driven simulation—an important class of difficult-to-parallelize asynchronous applications.

In Chapter 19 we look to the future and describe some possibilities for the use of parallel computers in industry. Here we note that C^3P, and much of the national enterprise, concentrated on scientific and engineering computations. The examples and "proof" that parallel computing works are focussed in this book on such problems. However, this will *not* be the dominant industrial use of parallel computers where information processing is most important. This will be used for decision support in the military and large corporations, and to supply video, information and simulation "on demand" for homes, schools, and other institutions. Such applications have recently been termed *national challenges* to distinguish them from the large scale *grand challenges*, which underpinned the initial HPCC initiative [FCCSET:94a]. The lessons C^{3}P and others have learnt from scientific computations will have general applicability across the wide range of industrial problems.

Chapter 20 includes a discussion of education in computational science—an unexpected byproduct of C^{3}P—and other retrospective remarks. The appendices list the C^{3}P reports including those not cited directly in this book. Some information is available electronically by mailing citlib@caltech.edu.

Chapter 2

Technical Backdrop

2.1   Introduction

This chapter surveys activities related to parallel computing that took place around the time that C^3P was an active project, primarily during the 1980s. The major areas that are covered are hardware, software, research projects, and production uses of parallel computers. In each case, there is no attempt to present a comprehensive list or survey of all the work that was done in that area. Rather, the attempt is to identify some of the major events during the period.

There are two major motivations for creating and using parallel computer architectures. The first is that, as surveyed in Section 1.2 parallelism is the only avenue to achieve vastly higher speeds than are possible now from a single processor. This was the primary motivation for initiating C^3P. Table 2.1 demonstrates dramatically the rather slow increase in speed of single-processor systems for one particular brand of supercomputer, CRAYs, the most popular supercomputer in the world. Figure 2.1 (Color Plate) shows a more comprehensive sample of computer performance, measured in operations per second, from the 1940s extrapolated through the year 2000.

A second motivation for the use of parallel architectures is that they should be considerably cheaper than sequential machines for systems of moderate speeds; that is, not necessarily supercomputers but instead mini-computers or mini-supercomputers would be cheaper to produce for a given performance level than the equivalent sequential system.

At the beginning of the 1980s, the goals of research in parallel computer architectures were to achieve much higher speeds than could be obtained

Table 2.1: Cycle Times

Year of Introduction	Model Name	Cycle Time in Nanoseconds
1976	CRAY 1	12.5
1982	CRAY X-MP	9.5
1985	CRAY 2	4.1*
1988	CRAY Y-MP	6.5
1992	CRAY Y-MP C-90	4.0

*Instructions could only be issued every other cycle, so the effective cycle time is 8.2 nanoseconds.

from sequential architectures and to get much better price performance through the use of parallelism than would be possible from sequential machines.

2.2 Hardware Trends

2.2.1 Parallel Scientific Computers Before 1980

There were parallel computers before 1980, but they did not have a widespread impact on scientific computing. The activities of the 1980s had a much more dramatic effect. Still, a few systems stand out as having made significant contributions that were taken advantage of in the 1980s. The first is the Illiac IV [Hockney:81b]. It did not seem like a significant advance to many people at the time, perhaps because its performance was only moderate, it was difficult to program, and had low reliability. The best performance achieved was two to six times the speed of a CDC 7600. This was obtained on various computational fluid dynamics codes. For many other programs, however, the performance was lower than that of a CDC 7600, which was the supercomputer of choice during the early and mid-1970s. The Illiac was a research project, not a commercial product, and it was reputed to be so expensive that it was not realistic for others to replicate it. While the Illiac IV did not inspire the masses to become interested in parallel computing, hundreds of people were involved in its use and in projects related to providing better software tools and better programming languages for it.

They first learned how to do parallel computing on the Illiac IV and many of them went on to make significant contributions to parallel computing in the 1980s.

The Illiac was an SIMD computer—single-instruction, multiple-data architecture. It had 32 processing elements, each of which was a processor with its own local memory; the processors were connected in a ring. High-level languages such as Glypnyr and Fortran were available for the Illiac IV. Glypnyr was reminiscent of Fortran and had extensions for parallel and array processing.

The ICL Distributed Array Processor (DAP) [DAP:79a] was a commercial product; a handful of machines were sold, mainly in England where it was designed and built. Its characteristics were that it had either 1K or 4K one-bit processors arranged in a square plane, each connected in rectangular fashion to its nearest neighbors. Like the Illiac IV, it was an SIMD system. It required an ICL mainframe as a front end. The ICL DAP was used for many university science applications. The University of Edinburgh, in particular, used it for a number of real computations in physics, chemistry, and other fields [Wallace:84a;87a]. The ICL DAP had a substantial impact on scientific computing culture, primarily in Europe. ICL did try to market it in the United States, but was never effective in doing so; the requirement for an expensive ICL mainframe as a host was a substantial negative factor.

A third important commercial parallel computer in the 1970s was the Goodyear Massively Parallel Processor (MPP) [Batcher:85a], [Karplus:87a, pp. 157–166]. Goodyear started building SIMD computers in 1969, but all except the MPP were sold to the military and to the Federal Aviation Administration for air traffic control. In the late 1970s, Goodyear produced the MPP which was installed at Goddard Space Flight Center, a NASA research center, and used for a variety of scientific applications. The MPP attracted attention because it did achieve high speeds on a few applications, speeds that, in the late 1970s and early 1980s, were remarkable—measured in the hundreds of MFLOPS in a few cases. The MPP had 16K one-bit processors, each with local memory, and was programmed in Pascal and Assembler.

In summary, the three significant scientific parallel computers of the 1970s were the Illiac IV, the ICL DAP, and the Goodyear MPP. All were SIMD computers. The DAP and the MPP were fine-grain systems based on single-bit processors, whereas the Illiac IV was a large-grain SIMD system. The other truly significant high-performance (but not parallel) computer of the 1970s was the CRAY 1, which was introduced in 1976. The CRAY 1 was a single-processor vector computer and as such it can also be classified as a special kind of SIMD computer because it had vector instructions. With a single vector instruction, one causes up to 64 data pairs to be operated on.

There were significant and seminal activities in parallel computing in the 1970s both from the standpoint of design and construction of systems and in the actual scientific use of the systems. However, the level of activity of parallel computing in the 1970s was modest compared to what followed in the 1980s.

2.2.2   Early 1980s

In contrast to the 1970s, in the early 1980s it was MIMD (multiple instruction, multiple data) computers that dominated the activity in parallel computing. The first of these was the Denelcor Heterogeneous Element Processor (HEP). The HEP attracted widespread attention despite its terrible cost performance because of its many interesting hardware features that facilitated programming. The Denelcor HEP was acquired by several institutions, including Los Alamos, Argonne National Laboratory, Ballistic Research Laboratory, and Messerschmidt in Germany. Messerschmidt was the only installation that used it for real applications. The others, however, used it extensively for research on parallel algorithms. The HEP hardware supported both fine-grain and large-grain parallelism. Any one processor had an instruction pipeline that provided parallelism at the single instruction level. Instructions from separate processes (associated with separate user programs or tasks) were put into hardware queues and scheduled for execution once the required operands had been fetched from memory into registers, again under hardware control. Instructions from up to 128 processes could share the instruction execution pipeline. The latter had eight stages; all instructions except floating-point divide took eight machine cycles to execute. Up to 16 processors could be linked to perform large-grain MIMD computations. The HEP had an extremely efficient synchronization mechanism through a full-empty bit associated with every word of memory. The bit was automatically set to indicate whether the word had been rewritten since it had last been written into and could be set to indicate that the memory location had been read. The value of the full-empty bit could be checked in one machine cycle. Fortran, C, and Assembler could be used to program the HEP. It had a UNIX environment and was front-ended by a minicomputer. Because Los Alamos and Argonne made their HEPs available for research purposes to people who were interested in learning how to program parallel machines or who were involved in parallel algorithm research, hundreds of people became familiar with parallel computing through the Denelcor HEP [Laksh:85a].

A second computer that was important in the early 1980s, primarily because it exposed a large number of computational scientists to parallelism, was the CRAY X-MP/22, which was introduced in 1982. Certainly, it had limited parallelism, namely only two processors; still, it was a parallel computer. Since it was at the very high end of performance, it exposed the hardcore scientific users to parallelism, although initially mostly in a negative way. There was not enough payoff in speed or cost to compensate for the effort that was required to parallelize a program so that it would use both processors: the maximum speedup would, of course, only be two. Typically, it was less than two and the charging algorithms of most computer centers generated higher charges for a program when it used both processors than when it used only one. In a way, though, the CRAY X-MP multiprocessor legitimized parallel processing, although restricted to very large grain, very small numbers of processors. A few years later, the IBM 3090 series had the same effect; the 3090 can have up to six vector and scalar processors in one system. Memory is shared among all processors.

Another MIMD system that was influential during the early 1980s was the New York University Ultracomputer [Gottlieb:86a] and a related system, the IBM RP3 [Brochard:92a], [Brochard:92b], [Darema:87a], [Pfister:85a]. These systems were serious attempts to design and demonstrate a shared-memory architecture that was scalable to very large numbers of processors. They featured an interconnection network between processors and memories that would avoid hot spots and congestion. The fetch-and-add instruction that was invented by Jacob Schwartz [Schwartz:80a] would avoid some of the congestion problems in omega networks. Unfortunately, these systems took a great deal of time to construct and it was the late 1980s before the IBM RP3 existed in a usable fashion. At that time, it had 64 processors but each was so slow that it attracted comparatively little attention. The architecture is certainly still considered to be an interesting one, but far fewer users were exposed to these systems than to other designs that were constructed more quickly and put in places that allowed a large number of users to have at least limited access to the systems for experimentation. Thus, the importance of the Ultracomputer and RP3 projects lay mainly in the concepts.

2.2.3   Birth of the Hypercube

Perhaps the most significant and influential parallel computer system of the early 1980s was the Caltech Cosmic Cube [Seitz:85a], developed by Charles Seitz and Geoffrey Fox. Since it was the inspiration for the C^3P project, we describe it and its immediate successors in some detail [Fox:87d;88oo], [Seitz:85a].

The hypercube work at Caltech originated in May 1981 when, as described in Chapter 1, Fox attended a seminar by Carver Mead on VLSI and its implications for concurrency. As described in more detail in Sections 4.1 and 4.3, Fox realized that he could use parallel computers for the lattice gauge computations that were central to his research at the time and that his group was running on a VAX 11/780. During the summer of 1981, he and his students worked out an algorithm that he thought would be parallel and tried it out on his VAX (simulating parallelism). The natural architecture for the problems he wanted to compute was determined to be a $4 \times 4 \times 4$ three-dimensional grid, which happens to be 64 processors (Figure 4.3).

In the fall of 1981 Fox approached Chuck Seitz about building a suitable computer. After an exchange of seminars, Seitz showed great interest in doing so and had funds to build a hypercube. Given Fox's problem, a six-dimensional hypercube (64 processors) was set as the target. Memory size of 128K was chosen after some debate; applications people (chiefly Fox) wanted at least that much. A trade-off was made between the number of processors and memory size. A smaller cube would been built if larger memory had been chosen.

From the outset a key goal was to produce an architecture with inter-processor communications that would scale well to a very large number of processors. The features that led to the choice of the hypercube topology specifically were the moderate growth in the number of channels required as the number of processors increases, and the good match between processor and memory speeds because memory is local.

The Intel 8086 was chosen because it was the only microprocessor available at the time with a floating-point co-processor, the 8087. First, a prototype 4-node system was built with wirewrap boards. It was designed, assembled, and tested during the winter of 1981–82. In the spring of 1982, message-passing software was designed and implemented on the 4-node. Eugene Brooks' proposal of simple send/receive routines was chosen and came to be known as the Crystalline Operating System (CrOS), although it was never really an operating system.

In autumn of 1982, simple lattice problems were implemented on the 4-node by Steve Otto and others. CrOS and the computational algorithm worked satisfactorily. By January 1983, Otto had the lattice gauge applications program running on the 4-node. Table 4.2 details the many projects and publications stemming from this pioneering work.

With the successful experience on the 4-node, Seitz proceeded to have printed circuit boards designed and built. The 64-node Cosmic Cube was assembled over the summer of 1983 and began operation in October 1983. It has been in use ever since, although currently it is lightly used.

The key characteristics of the Cosmic Cube are that it has 64 nodes, each with an 8086/8087, 128 Kbytes of memory, and communication channels with 2 Mbits/sec peak speed between nodes (about 0.8 Mbits/sec sustained in one direction). It is five feet long, six cubic feet in volume, and draws 700 watts.

The Cosmic Cube provided a dramatic demonstration that multicomputers could be built quickly, cheaply, and reliably. In terms of reliability, for example, there were two hard failures in the first 560,000 node hours of operation—that is, during the first year of operation. Its performance was low by today's standards, but it was still between five and ten times the performance of a DEC VAX 11/780, which was the system of choice for academic computer departments and research groups in that time period. The manufacturing cost of the system was $80,000, which at that time was about half the cost of a VAX with a modest configuration. Therefore, the price performance was on the order of 10 to 20 times better than a VAX 780. This estimate does not take into account design and software development costs; on the other hand, it was a one-of-a-kind system, so manufacturing costs were higher than for a commercial product. Furthermore, it was clearly a scalable architecture, and that is perhaps the most important feature of that particular project.

In the period from October, 1983 to April, 1984 a 2500-hour run of a QCD problem (Table 4.1) was completed, achieved 95% efficiency, and produced new scientific results. This demonstrated that hypercubes are well-suited for QCD (as are other architectures).

As described in Section 1.3, during the fall of 1982 Fox surveyed many colleagues at Caltech to determine whether they needed large-scale computation in their research and began to examine those applications for suitability to run on parallel computers. Note that this was before the 64-node Cosmic Cube was finished, but after the 4-node gave evidence that approach was sound. The Caltech Concurrent Computation Program (C^3P) was formed in Autumn of 1982. A decision was made to develop big, fast hypercubes rather than rely on Crays. By the summer of 1984, the ten applications of Table 4.2 were running on the Cosmic Cube [Fox:87d].

Two key shortcomings that were soon noticed were that too much time was spent in communications and that high-speed external I/O was not available. The first was thought to be addressable with custom communication chips.

In the summer of 1983, Fox teamed with Caltech's Jet Propulsion Laboratory (JPL) to build bigger and better hypercubes. The first was the Mark II, still based on 8086/8087 (no co-processor faster than 8087 was yet available), but with 256 KB memory, faster communications, and twice as many nodes. The first 32 nodes began operating in September, 1984. Four 32-node systems and one 128-node were built. The latter was completed in June, 1985 [Fox:88oo].

The Caltech project inspired several industrial companies to build commercial hypercubes. These included Intel, nCUBE [Karplus:87a], Ametek [Seitz:88b], and Floating Point Systems Corporation. Only two years after the 64-node Caltech Cosmic Cube was operational, there were commercial products on the market and installed at user sites.

With the next Caltech-JPL system, the Mark III, there was a switch to the Motorola family of microprocessors. On each node the Mark III had one Motorola 68020/68881 for computation and another 68020 for communications. The two processors shared the 4 Mbytes of node memory. The first 32-node Mark III was operational in April, 1986. The concept of dedicating a processor to communications has influenced commercial product design, including recently introduced systems.

In the spring of 1986, a decision was made to build a variant of the Mark III, the Mark IIIfp (originally dubbed the Mark IIIe). It was designed to compete head-on with "real" supercomputers. The Mark IIIfp has a daughter board at each node with the Weitek XL floating-point chip set running at 8 MHz, which gives a peak speed of 16 MFLOPS/node. By January 1987, an 8-node Mark IIIfp was operational. A 128-node system was built and in the spring of 1989 achieved 500 MFLOPS on two applications.

In summary, the hypercube family of computers enjoyed rapid development and was used for scientific applications from the beginning. In the period from 1982 to 1987, three generations of the family were designed, built, and put into use at Caltech. The third generation (the Mark III) even included a switch of microprocessor families. Within the same five years, four commercial vendors produced and delivered computers with hypercube architectures. By 1987, approximately 50 major applications had been completed on Caltech hypercubes. Such rapid development and adaption has few if any parallels. The remaining chapters of this book are largely devoted to lessons from these applications and their followers.

2.2.4 Mid-1980s

During this period, many new systems were launched by commercial companies, and several were quite successful in terms of sales. The two most successful were the Sequent and the Encore [Karplus:87a, pp. 111–126] products. Both were shared-memory, bus-connected multiprocessors of moderate parallelism. The maximum number of processors on the Encore product was 20; on the Sequent machine initially 16 and later 30. Both provided an extremely stable UNIX environment and were excellent for time-sharing. As such, they could be considered VAX killers since VAXes were the time-sharing system of choice in research groups in those days. The Sequent and the Encore provided perhaps a cost performance better by a factor of 10, as well as considerably higher total performance than could be obtained on a VAX at that time. These systems were particularly useful for smaller jobs, for time-sharing, and for learning to do parallel computing. Perhaps their most impressive aspect was the reliability of both hardware and software. They operated without interruption for months at a time, just as conventional mini-supercomputers did. Their UNIX operating system software was familiar to many users and, as mentioned before, very stable. Unlike most parallel computers whose system software requires years to mature, these systems had very stable and responsive system software from the beginning.

Another important system during this period was the Alliant [Karplus:87a, pp. 35–44]. The initial model featured up to eight vector processors, each of moderate performance. But when used simultaneously, they provided performance equivalent to a sizable fraction of a CRAY processor. A unique feature at the time was a Fortran compiler that was quite good at automatic vectorization and also reasonably good at parallelization. These compiler features, coupled with its shared memory, made this system relatively easy to use and to achieve reasonably good performance. The Alliant also supported the C language, although initially there was no vectorization or parallelization available in C. The operating system was UNIX-based. Because of its reasonably high floating-point performance and ease of use, the Alliant was one of the first parallel computers that was used for real applications. The Alliant was purchased by groups who wanted to do medium-sized computations and even computations they would normally

LIBRARY   3102831

do on CRAYs. This system was also used as a building block of the Cedar architecture project led by D. Kuck [Kuck:86a].

Advances in compiling technology made wide-instruction word machines an interesting and, for a few years, commercially viable architecture. The Multiflow and Cydrome systems both had compilers that effectively exploited very fine-grain parallelism and scheduling of floating-point pipelines within the processing units. Both these systems attempted to get parallelism at the instruction level from Fortran programs—the so-called dusty decks that might have convoluted logic and thus be very difficult to vectorize or parallelize in a large-grain sense. The price performance of these systems was their main attraction. On the other hand, because these systems did not scale to very high levels of performance, they were relegated to the super-minicomputer arena. An important contribution they made was to show dramatically how far compiler technology had come in certain areas.

As was mentioned earlier, hypercubes were produced by Intel, nCUBE, Ametek, and Floating Point Systems Corporation in the mid-1980s. Of these, the most significant product was the *nCUBE* with its high degree of integration and a configuration of up to 1024 nodes [Palmer:86a], [nCUBE:87a]. It was pivotal in demonstrating that massively parallel MIMD medium-grain computers are practical. The nCUBE featured a complete processor on a single chip, including all channels for connecting to the other nodes so that one chip plus six memory chips constituted an entire node. They were packaged on boards with 64 nodes so that the system was extremely compact, air-cooled, and reliable. Caltech had an early 512-node system, which was used in many C^3P calculations, and soon afterwards Sandia National Laboratories installed the 1024-node system. A great deal of scientific work was done on those two machines and they are still in use. The 1024-node Sandia machine got the world's attention by demonstrating speedups of 1000 for several applications [Gustafson:88a]. This was particularly significant because it was done during a period of active debate as to whether MIMD systems could provide speedups of more than a hundred. Amdahl's law [Amdahl:67a] was cited as a reason why it would not be possible to get speedups greater than perhaps a hundred, even if one used 1000 processors.

Towards the end of the mid-1980s, transputer-based systems [Barron:83a], [Hey:88a], both large and small, began to proliferate, especially in Europe but also in the United States. The T800 transputer was like the nCUBE processor, a single-chip system with built-in communications channels, and it had respectable floating point performance—a peak speed of nearly 2 MFLOPS and frequently achieved speeds of 1/2 to 1 MFLOPS. They provided a convenient building block for parallel systems and were quite cost-effective. Their prevalent use at the time was in boards with four or eight transputers that were attached to IBM PCs, VAXes, or other workstations.

2.2.5 Late 1980s

By the late 1980s, truly powerful parallel systems began to appear. The Meiko system at Edinburgh University, is an example; by 1989, that computer had 400 T800s [Wallace:88a]. The system was being used for a number of traditional scientific computations in physics, chemistry, engineering, and other areas [Wexler:89a]. The system software for transputer-based systems had evolved to resemble the message-passing system software available on hypercubes. Although the transputer's two-dimensional mesh connection is in principle less efficient than hypercube connections, for systems of moderate size (only a few hundred processors), the difference is not significant for most applications. Further, any parallel architecture deficiencies were counterbalanced by the transputer's excellent communication channel performance.

Three new SIMD fine-grain systems were introduced in the late 1980s: the CM-2, the MasPar, and a new version of the DAP. The *CM-2* is a version of the original Connection Machine [Hillis:85a;87a] that has been enhanced with Weitek floating-point units, one for each 32 single-bit processors, and optional large memory. In its largest configuration, such as is installed at Los Alamos National Laboratory, there are 64K single-bit processors, 2048 64-bit floating-point processors, and 8 Gbytes of memory. The CM-2 has been measured at 5.2 GFLOPS running the unlimited Linpack benchmark solving a linear system of order 26,624 and even higher performance on some applications, e.g., seismic data processing [Myczkowski:91a] and QCD [Brickner:91b], [Liu:91a]. It has attracted widespread attention both because of its extremely high performance and its relative ease of use [Boghosian:90a], [Hillis:86a;87b]. For problems that are naturally data parallel, the CM Fortran language and compiler provide a relatively easy way to implement programs and get high performance.

The MasPar and the DAP are smaller systems that are aimed more at excellent price performance than at supercomputer levels of performance. The new DAP is front-ended by Sun workstations or VAXes. This makes it much more affordable and compatible with modern computing environments than when it required an ICL front end. DAPs have been built in ruggedized versions that can be put into vehicles, flown in airplanes, and used on ships, and have found many uses in signal processing and military applications. They are also used for general scientific work. The MasPar is the newest SIMD system. Its architecture constitutes an evolutionary approach of fine-grain SIMD combined with enhanced floating-point performance coming from the use of 4-bit (Maspar MP-1) or 32-bit (Maspar MP-2) basic SIMD units. Standard 64-bit floating-point algorithms implemented on a (SIMD) machine built around an l bit CPU take time of order $(64/l)^2$ machine instructions. The DAP and CM-1,2 used $l = 1$ and here the CM-2 and later DAP models achieve floating-point performance with special extra hardware rather than by increasing l.

Two hypercubes became available just as the decade ended: the second generation nCUBE, popularly known as the nCUBE-2, and the Intel iPSC/860. The nCUBE-2 can be configured with up to 8K nodes; that configuration would have a peak speed of 27 GFLOPS. Each processor is still on a single chip along with all the communications channels, but it is about eight times faster than its predecessor—a little over 3 MFLOPS. Communication bandwidth is also a factor of eight higher. The result is a potentially very powerful system. The nCUBE-2 has a custom microprocessor that is instruction-compatible with the first-generation system. The largest system known to have been built to date is a 1024 system installed at Sandia National Laboratories. The unlimited size Linpack benchmark for this system yielded a performance of 1.91 GFLOPS solving a linear system of order 21,376.

The second hypercube introduced in 1989 (and first shipped to a customer, Oak Ridge, in January 1990), the Intel iPSC/860, has a peak speed of over 7 GFLOPS. While the communication speed between nodes is very low compared to the speed of the i860 processor, high speeds can be achieved for problems that do not require extensive communication or when the data movement is planned carefully. For example, the unlimited size Linpack benchmark on the largest configuration iPSC/860, 128 processors, ran at 1.92 GFLOPS when solving a system of order 8,600.

The iPSC/860 uses the Intel i860 microprocessor, which has a peak speed of 60 MFLOPS full precision and 80 MFLOPS with 32-bit precision. In mid-1991, a follow-on to Intel iPSC/860, the Intel Touchstone Delta System, reached a Linpack speed of 13.9 GFLOPS for a system of order 25,000. This was done on 512 i860 nodes of the Delta System. This machine has a peak speed of 32 GFLOPS and 8 Gbytes of memory and is a one-of-a-kind system built for a consortium of institutions and installed at California Institute of Technology. Although the C^{3}P project is finished at Caltech, many C^{3}P applications have very successfully used the Delta. The Delta uses a two-dimensional mesh connection scheme with mesh routing chips instead of a hypercube connection scheme. The Intel Paragon, a commercial product that is the successor to the iPSC/860 and the Touchstone Delta, became available in the fall of 1992. The Paragon has the same connection scheme as the Delta. Its maximum configuration is 4096 nodes. It uses a second generation version of the i860 microprocessor and has a peak speed of 300 GFLOPS.

The BBN TC2000 is another important system introduced in the late 1980s. It provides a shared-memory programming environment supported by hardware. It uses a multistage switch based on crossbars that connect processor memory pairs to each other [Karplus:87a, pp. 137–146], [BBN:87a]. The BBN TC2000 uses Motorola 88000 Series processors. The ratio of speeds between access to data in cache, to data respectively in the memory local to a processor, and to data in some other processor's memory, is approximately one, three and seven. Therefore, there is a noticeable but not prohibitive penalty for using another processor's memory. The architecture is scalable to over 500 processors, although none was built of that size. Each processor can have a substantial amount of memory, and the operating system environment is considered attractive. This system is one of the few commercial shared-memory MIMD computers that can scale to large numbers of nodes. It is no longer in production; the BBN Corporation terminated its parallel computer activities in 1991.

2.2.6 Parallel Systems—1992

By the late 1980s, several highly parallel systems were able to achieve high levels of performance—the Connection Machine Model CM-2, the Intel iPSC/860, the nCUBE-2, and, early in the decade of the '90s, the Intel Touchstone Delta System. The peak speeds of these systems are quite high and, at least for some applications, the speeds achieved are also high, exceeding those achieved on vector supercomputers. The fastest CRAY system until 1992 was a CRAY Y-MP with eight processors, a peak speed of 2.6 GFLOPS, and a maximum speed observed for applications of 2 GFLOPS. In contrast, the Connection Machine Model CM-2 and the Intel Delta have achieved over 5 GFLOPS for some real applications [Brickner:89b], [Messina:92a], [Mihaly:92a;92b]. There are some new Japanese vector supercomputers with a small number of processors (but a large number of instruction pipelines) that have peak speeds of over 20 GFLOPS.

Finally, the vector computers continued to become faster and to have more processors. For example, the CRAY Y-MP C-90 that was introduced in 1992 has sixteen processors and a peak speed of 16 GFLOPS.

By 1992, parallel computers were substantially faster. As was noted above, the Intel Paragon has a peak speed of 300 GFLOPS. The CM-5, an MIMD computer introduced by Thinking Machines Corporation in 1992 has a maximum configuration of 16K processors, each with a peak speed of 128 MFLOPS. The largest system at this writing is a 1024-node configuration in use at Los Alamos National Laboratory.

New introductions continue with Fall, 1992 seeing Fujitsu (Japan) and Meiko (U. K.) introducing distributed-memory parallel machines with a high-performance node featuring a vector unit using, in each case, a different VLSI implementation of the node of Fujitsu's high-end vector supercomputer. 1993 saw major Cray and Convex systems built around Digital and HP RISC microprocessor nodes.

Recently, there has been an interesting new architecture with a distributed-memory design supported by special hardware to build an appearance of shared memory to the user. The goal is to continue the cost effectiveness of distributed memory with the programmability of a shared-memory architecture. There are two major university projects: DASH at Stanford [Hennessy:93a], [Lenoski:89a] and Alewife [Agarwal:91a] at MIT. The first commercial machine, the Kendall Square KSR-1, was delivered to customers in Fall, 1991. A high-performance ring supports the apparent shared memory, which is essentially a distributed dynamic cache. The ring can be scaled up to 32 nodes that can be joined hierarchically to a full-size, 1024-node system that could have a performance of approximately 15 GFLOPS. Burton Smith, the architect of the pioneering Denelcor HEP-1, has formed Teracomputer, whose machine has a virtual shared memory and other innovative features. The direction of parallel computing research could be profoundly affected if this architecture proves successful.

In summary, the 1980s saw an incredible level of activity in parallel computing, much greater than most people would have predicted. Even those projects that in a sense failed—that is, that were not commercially successful or, in the case of research projects, failed to produce an interesting prototype in a timely fashion—were nonetheless useful in that they exposed many people to parallel computing at universities, computer vendors, and (as outlined in Chapter 19) commercial companies such as Xerox, DuPont,

General Motors, United Technologies, and aerospace and oil companies.

2.3 Software

A gross generalization of the situation in the 1980s can be made that there was good software on low- and medium-performance systems such as Alliant, Sequent, Encore, and Multiflow systems (uninteresting to those preoccupied with the highest performance levels), while there was poor quality software in the highest performance systems. In addition, there is little or no software aimed at managing the system and providing a service to a diverse user community. There is typically no software that provides information on who uses the system and how much, that is, accounting and reporting software. Batch schedulers are typically not available. Controls for limiting the amount of time interactive users can take on the system at any one time also are missing. Ways of managing the on-line disks are non-existent. In short, the system software provided with the high-performance parallel computers is at best suitable for systems used by a single person or a small tightly-knit group of people.

2.3.1 Languages and Compilers

In contrast, in the area of computer languages and compilers for those languages for parallel machines, there has been a significant amount of progress, especially in the late 1980s, for example [AMT:87a]. In February of 1984, the Argonne Workshop on Programming the Next Generation of Supercomputers was held in Albuquerque, New Mexico [Smith:84a]. It addressed topics such as:

- data versus control synchronization;

- whether minor extensions to existing languages, such as C and Fortran, are adequate or should new languages be designed and adopted;

- whether some minimal parallel oriented capabilities should be added to Fortran (even then, in early 1984, it was thought that Fortran 8X was about to be frozen into a standard).

Many people came to the workshop and showed high levels of interest, including leading computer vendors, but not very much happened in terms of real actions by compiler writers or standards-making groups. By the late

1980s, the situation had changed. Now the Parallel Computing Forum is healthy and well attended by vendor representatives. The Parallel Computing Forum was formed to develop a shared-memory multiprocessor model for parallel processing and to establish language standards for that model beginning with Fortran and C. In addition, the ANSI Standards Committee X3 formed a new technical committee, X3H5, named Parallel Processing Constructs for High Level Programming Languages. This technical committee will work on a model based upon standard practice in shared memory parallel processing. Extensions for message-passing-based parallel processing are outside the scope of the model under consideration at this time. The first meeting of X3H5 was held March 23, 1990.

Finally there are efforts under way to standardize language issues for parallel computing, at least for certain programming models. In the meantime, there has been progress in compiler technology. Compilers provided with Alliant and Multiflow machines before they went out of business, can be quite good at producing efficient code for each processor and relatively good at automatically parallelizing. On the other hand, compilers for the processors that are used on multicomputers generally produce inefficient code for the floating-point hardware. Generally, these compilers do not perform even the standard optimizations that have nothing to do with fancy instruction scheduling, nor do they do any automatic parallelization for the distributed-memory computers. While automatic parallelization for distributed-memory, as well as shared-memory systems, is a difficult task, and it is clear that it will be a few more years before good compilers exist for that task, it is a shame that so little effort is invested in producing efficient code for single processors. There are known compilation techniques that would provide a much greater percentage of the peak speed on commonly used microprocessors than is currently produced by the existing compilers.

As for languages, despite much work and interest in new languages, in most cases people still use Fortran or C with minor additions or calls to system subroutines. The language known as Connection Machine Fortran or CM-Fortran is, as discussed in Section 13.1, an important exception. It is, of course, based largely on the array extensions of Fortran 90, but is not identical to that. One might note that CM-Fortran array extensions are also remarkably similar to those defined in the Department of Energy Language Working Group Fortran effort of the early 1980s [Wetherell:82a]. Fortran 90 itself was influenced by the LWG Fortran; in the early and mid-1980s, there were regular and frequent interactions between the DOE Language Working Group and the Fortran Standards Committee. A recent variant of Fortran 90 designed for distributed-memory systems is Fortran 90D [Fox:91e], which, as described in Chapter 13, is the basis of an informal industry standard for data-parallel Fortran—High Performance Fortran (HPF) [Kennedy:93a]. HPF has attracted a great deal of attention from both users and computer vendors and it is likely to become a de facto standard in one or two years. The time for such a language must have finally come. The Fortran developments are mirrored by those in other languages, with C and, in particular, C++ receiving the most attention. Among many important projects, we select pC++ at Indiana University [Bodin:91a], which extends C++ so that it incorporates essentially the HPF parallel constructs. Further, C++ allows one to define more general data structures than the Fortran array; correspondingly pC++ supports general parallel collections.

Other languages that have seen some use include Linda [Gelertner:89a], [Ahuja:86a], and Strand [Foster:90a]. Linda has been particularly successful especially as a *coordination language* allowing one to link the many individual components of what we term *metaproblems*—a concept developed throughout this book and particularly in Chapters 3 and 18. A more recent language effort is Program Composition Notation (PCN) that is being developed at the Center for Research on Parallel Computation (an NSF Science and Technology Center) [Chandy:90a]. PCN is a parallel programming language in its own right, but additionally has the feature that one can take existing Fortran and C functions and subprograms and use them through PCN as part of a PCN parallel program. PCN is in some ways similar to Strand, which is a dataflow-oriented logic language in the flavor of Prolog. PCN has been extended to CC++ [Chandy:92a] (Compositional C++), supporting general functional parallelism. Chandy reports that users found the novel syntax in PCN uncomfortable for users familiar with existing languages. This motivated his group to embody the PCN ideas in widely used languages with CC++ for C and C++ (sequential) users, and Fortran-M for Fortran users. The combination of CC++ and data parallel pC++ is termed HPC++ and this is an attractive candidate for the software model that could support general *metaproblems*. The requirements and needs for such software models will become clear from the discussion in this book, and are summarized in Section 18.1.3.

2.3.2 Tools

Substantial efforts have been put into developing tools that facilitate parallel programming, both in shared-memory and distributed-memory systems, e.g., [Clarke:91a], [Sunderam:90a], [Whiteside:88a]. For shared-memory systems, for example, there are SCHEDULE [Hanson:90a], MONMACS, and FORCE. MONMACS and FORCE both provide higher level parallel programming constructs such as barrier synchronization and DO ALL that are useful for shared-memory environments. SCHEDULE provides a graphical interface to producing functionally decomposed programs for shared-memory systems. With SCHEDULE, one specifies a tree of calls to subroutines, and SCHEDULE facilitates and partially automates the creation of Fortran or C programs (augmented by appropriate system calls) that implement the call graphs. For distributed-memory environments, there are also several libraries or small operating systems that provide extensions to Fortran and C for programming on such architectures. A subset of MONMACS falls into that camp. More widely used systems in this area include Cosmic Environment Reactive Kernel [Seitz:88a] (see Chapter 16), Express [ParaSoft:88a] (discussed in detail in Chapter 5), and PICL [Sunderam:90a]. These systems provide message-passing routines in some cases, including those that do global operations on data such as Broadcast. They may also provide facilities for measuring performance or collecting data about message traffic, CPU utilization, and so on. Some debugging capabilities may also be provided. These are all general purpose tools and programming environments, and had been used for a wide variety of applications, chiefly scientific and engineering, but also non-numerical ones.

In addition, there are many tools that are domain-specific in some sense. Examples of these would be the Distributed Irregular Mesh Environment (DIME) by Roy Williams [Williams:88a;89b] (described in Chapter 10), and the parallel ELLPACK [Houstis:90a] partial differential equation solver and domain decomposer [Chrisochoides:91b:93a] developed by John Rice and his research group at Purdue. DIME is a programming environment for calculations with irregular meshes; it provides adaptive mesh refinement and dynamic load balancing. There are also some general purpose tools and programming systems, such as Sisal from Livermore, that provide a dataflow-oriented language capability; and Parti [Saltz:87a;91b], [Berryman:91a], which facilitates, for example, array mappings on distributed-memory machines. Load-balancing tools are described in Chapter 11 and, although they look very promising, they have yet to be packaged in a robust form for general users.

None of the general-purpose tools has emerged as a clear leader. Perhaps there is still a need for more research and experimentation with such systems.

2.4 Summary

There was remarkable progress during the 1980s in most areas related to high-performance computing in general and parallel computing in particular. There are now substantial numbers of people who use parallel computers to get real applications work done, in addition to many people who have developed and are developing new algorithms, new operating systems, new languages, and new programming paradigms and software tools for massively parallel and other high-performance computer systems. It was during this decade, especially in the last half, that there was a very quick transition towards identifying high-performance computing strongly with massively parallel computing. In the early part of the decade, only large, vector-oriented systems were used for high-performance computing. By the end of the decade, while most such work was still being done on vector systems, some of the leading-edge work was already being done on parallel systems. This includes work at universities and research laboratories, as well as in industrial applications. By the end of the decade, oil companies, brokerage companies on Wall Street, and database users were all taking advantage of parallelism in addition to the traditional scientific and engineering fields. The C^3P efforts played an important role in advancing parallel hardware, software, and applications. As this chapter indicates, many other projects contributed to this advance as well.

There is still a frustrating phenomenon of neglect of certain areas in the design of parallel computer systems, including ratios of internal computational speed versus input and output speed, and speed of communication between the processors in distributed-memory systems. Latency for both I/O and communication is still very high. Compilers are often still crude. Operating systems still lack stability and even the most fundamental system management tools. Nevertheless, much progress was made.

By the end of the 1980s, higher speeds than on any sequential computer were indeed achieved on the parallel computer systems, and this was done for a few real applications. In a few cases, the parallel systems even proved to be cheaper, that is, more cost-effective than sequential computers of equivalent power. This despite a truly dramatic increase in performance of sequential microprocessors, especially floating-point units, in the late 1980s. So, both key objectives of parallel computing—the highest achievable speed and more cost-effective performance—were achieved and demonstrated in the 1980s.

Chapter 3

A Methodology for Computation

3.1 Introduction

Computing is a controversial field. In more traditional fields, such as mathematics and physics, there is usually general agreement on the key issues—which ideas and research projects are "good," what are the critical questions for the future, and so on. There is no such agreement in computing on either the academic or industrial sides. One simple reason is that the field is young—roughly forty years old. However, another important aspect is the multidisciplinary nature of the field. Hardware, software, and applications involve practitioners from very different academic fields with different training, prejudices, and goals. Answering the question,

> *"Does and How Does Parallel Computing Work?"*

requires

> *"Solving real problems with real software on real hardware"*

and so certainly involves aspects of hardware, software, and applications. Thus, some sort of mix of disciplines seems essential in spite of the difficulties in combining several disciplines.

The Caltech Concurrent Computation program attempted to cut through some of the controversy by adopting an interdisciplinary rather than multidisciplinary methodology. We can consider the latter as separate teams of experts as shown in Figures 3.1 and 3.2, which tackle each component

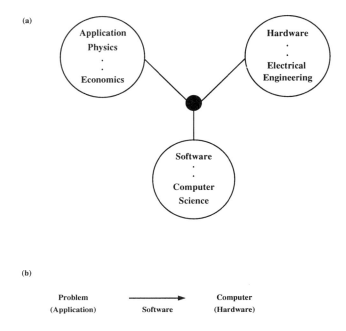

Figure 3.1: The Multi-Disciplinary (Three-Team) Approach to Computing

of the total project. In C^{3}P, we tried an integrated approach illustrated in Figure 3.3. This did not supplant the traditional fields but rather augmented them with a group of researchers with a broad range of skills that to a greater or lesser degree spanned those of the core areas underlying computing. We will return to these discipline issues in Chapter 20, but note here that this current discussion is simplistic and just designed to give context to the following analysis. The assignment of hardware to electrical engineering and software to computer science (with an underlying discipline of mathematics) is particularly idealized. Indeed, in many schools, these components are integrated. However, it is perhaps fair to say that experts in computer hardware have significantly different training and background from experts in computer software.

We believe that much of the success (and perhaps also the failures) of C^{3}P can be traced to its interdisciplinary nature. In this spirit, we will provide here a partial integration of the disparate contributions in this volume with a mathematical framework that links hardware, software, and applications. In this chapter, we will describe the principles behind this integration which will then be amplified and exemplified in the following chapters. This inte-

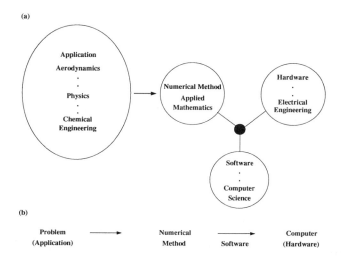

Figure 3.2: An Alternative (Four-Team) Multi-Disciplinary Approach to Computing

gration is usually contained in the first introductory section of each chapter. In Section 3.2, we define a general methodology for computation and propose that it be described as mappings between complex systems. The latter are only loosely defined but several examples are given in Section 3.3, while relevant properties of complex systems are given in Sections 3.4 through Section 3.6. Section 3.7 describes mappings between different complex systems and how this allows one to classify software approaches. Section 3.8 uses this formalism to state our results and what we mean by "parallel computing works." In particular, it offers the possibility of a quantitative approach to such questions as,

"Which parallel machine is suitable for which problems?"

and

"What software models are suitable for what problems on what machines?"

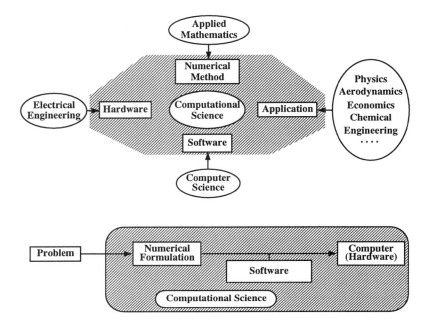

Figure 3.3: An Interdisciplinary Approach to Computing with Computational Science Shown Shaded

3.2   The Process of Computation and Complex Systems

There is no agreed-upon process behind computation, that is, behind the use of a computer to solve a particular problem. We have tried to quantify this in Figures 3.1(b), 3.2(b), and 3.3 which show a problem being first numerically formulated and then mapped by software onto a computer.

Even if we could get agreement on such an "underlying" process, the definitions of the parts of the process are not precise and correspondingly the roles of the "experts" are poorly defined. This underlies much of the controversy, and in particular, why we cannot at present or probably ever be able to define

"The best software methodology for parallel computing."

How can we agree on a solution (What is the appropriate software?) unless we can agree on the task it solves?

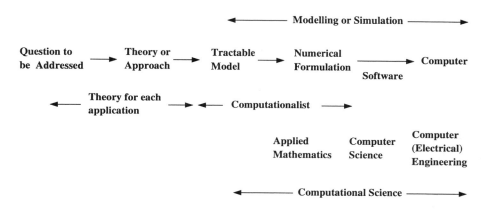

Figure 3.4: An Idealized Process of Computation

"What is computation and how can it be broken up into components?"

In other words, what is the underlying process?

In spite of our pessimism that there is any clean, precise answer to this question, progress can be made with an imperfect process defined for computation. In the earlier figures, it was stressed that software could be viewed as mapping problems onto computers. We can elaborate this as shown in Figure 3.4, with the solution to a question pictured as a sequence of idealizations or simplifications which are finally mapped onto the computer. This process is spelled out for four examples in Figures 3.5 and 3.6. In each case, we have tried to indicate possible labels for components of the process. However, this can only be approximate. We are not aware of an accepted definition for the theoretical or computational parts of the process. Again, which parts are modelling or simulation? Further, there is only an approximate division of responsibility among the various "experts"; for example, between the theoretical physicist and the computational physicist, or among aerodynamics, applied mathematics, and computer science. We have also not illustrated that, in each case, the numerical algorithm is dependent on the final computer architecture targeted; in particular, the best parallel algorithm is often different from the best conventional sequential algorithm.

We can abstract Figures 3.5 and 3.6 into a sequence of maps between complex systems S_i, $1 \leq i \leq k$.

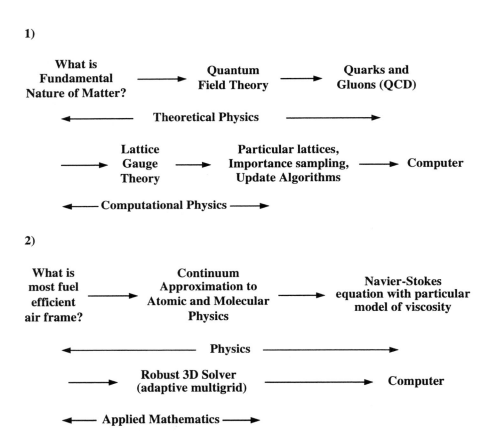

Figure 3.5: A Process for Computation in Two Examples in Basic Physics Simulations

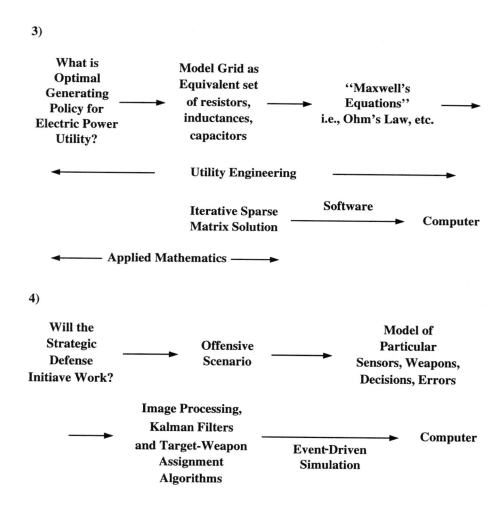

Figure 3.6: A Process for Computation in Two Examples from Large Scale System Simulations

$$
\begin{aligned}
\begin{matrix} \text{Basic} \\ \text{Question} \end{matrix} \quad \rightarrow \quad & S_1 \rightarrow S_2 \ldots \rightarrow S_{k-3} \quad \begin{matrix}\text{(numerical} \\ \text{formulation)} \end{matrix} \\[2em]
\rightarrow \quad & S_{k-2} \quad \begin{matrix}\text{(numerical formulation} \quad = S_{\text{num}} \\ \text{modified for} \\ \text{particular hardware,} \\ \text{e.g., parallelism)} \end{matrix} \\[3em]
\begin{matrix} \text{High level} \\ \xrightarrow{} \\ \text{software} \end{matrix} \quad & S_{k-1} \quad \begin{matrix}\text{(Virtual Problem or} \quad = S_{\text{HLSoft}} \\ \text{Virtual Computer)} \end{matrix} \\[3em]
\begin{matrix} \text{Low level} \\ \xrightarrow{} \\ \text{software} \end{matrix} \quad & S_{k} \quad \text{(Actual Computer)} \qquad = S_{\text{comp}}
\end{aligned}
\tag{3.1}
$$

We have anticipated (Chapter 5) and broken the software into a high level component (such as a compiler) and a lower level one (such as an assembler) which maps a "virtual computer" into the particular machine under consideration. In fact, the software could have more stages, but two is the most common case for simple (sequential) computers.

A complex system, as used here, is defined as a collection of fundamental entities whose static or dynamic properties define a connection scheme between the entities. Complex systems have a structure or architecture. For instance, a binary hypercube parallel computer of dimension d is a complex system with $N = 2^d$ members connected in a hypercube topology. We can focus in on the node of the hypercube and expand the node, viewed itself as a complex system, into a collection of memory hierarchies, caches, registers, CPU., and communication channels. Even here, we find another ill-defined point with the complex system representing the computer dependent on the resolution or granularity with which you view the system. The importance of the architecture of a computer system S_{comp} has been recognized for many years. We suggest that the architecture or structure of the problem is comparably interesting. Later, we will find that the performance of a particular problem or machine can be studied in terms of the match (similarity) between the architectures of the complex systems S_{num} and S_{comp} defined in Equation 3.1. We will find that the structure of the appropriate parallel software will depend on the broad features of the (similar) architecture of

S_{num} and S_{HLSoft}. This can be expected as software maps the two complex systems into each other.

At times, we have talked in terms of problem architecture, but this is ambiguous since it could refer to any of the complex systems $S_1 \ldots S_{k-2}$ which can and usually do have different architectures. Consider the second example of Figure 3.5 with the computational fluid dynamics study of airflow. In the language of Equation 3.1:

$$\begin{aligned}
\text{Flow around} \\
\text{the Airframe} \quad &\rightarrow S_1(\text{molecular picture}) \rightarrow S_2(\text{continuum}) \\
\rightarrow S_3(\text{multigrid}) \quad &\rightarrow S_4(\text{Virtual Problem}) \rightarrow S_5(\text{final computer})
\end{aligned} \quad (3.2)$$

S_1 is a (finite) collection of molecules interacting with long-range Van der Waals and other forces. This interaction defines a complete interconnect between all members of the complex system S_1.

S_2 is the infinite degree of freedom continuum with the fundamental entities as infinitesimal volumes of air connected locally by the partial differential operator of the Navier Stokes equation.

$S_3 = S_{\text{num}}$ could depend on the particular numerical formulation used. Multigrid, conjugate gradient, direct matrix inversion and alternating gradient would have very different structures in the direct numerical solution of the Navier Stokes equations. The more radical cellular automata approach would be quite different again.

$S_4 = S_{\text{HLSoft}}$ would depend on the final computer being used and division between high and low level in software. In the applications described in this book, S_4 would typically be a simple binary hypercube with $N = 2^d$ nodes.

$S_5 = S_{\text{comp}}$ would be S_{HLSoft} embroidered by the details of the hardware communication (circuit or packet switching, wormhole or other routing). Further, as described above, in some analyses we could look at this complex system in greater resolution and expose the details of the processor node architecture.

3.3 Examples of Complex Systems and Their Space-Time Structure

In the previous section, we showed how the process of computation could be viewed as mappings between complex systems. As the book progresses, we will quantify this by providing examples that cover a range of problem architectures. In the next three sections, we will set up the general framework and define terms which will be made clearer later on as we see the explicit problems with their different architectures. The concept of complex systems may have very general applicability to a wide range of fields but here we will focus solely on their application to computation. Thus, our discussion of their properties will only cover what we have found useful for the task at hand. These properties are surely more generally applicable, and one can expect that other ideas will be needed in a general discussion. Section 3.3 gives examples and a basic definition of a complex system and its associated space-time structure. Section 3.4 defines temporal properties and, finally, Section 3.5 spatial structures.

We wish to understand the interesting characteristics or structure of a complex system. We first introduce the concept of space-time into a general complex system. As shown in Figure 3.7, we consider a general complex system as a *space*, or data domain, that evolves deterministically or probabilistically with time. Often, the space-time associated with a given complex system is identical with physical space-time but sometimes it is not. Let us give some examples.

- For a computer considered as a complex system, the *space* is the collection of processing nodes, communication channels and peripherals as illustrated in Figures 1.1 and 1.2. *Time* is the physical time, but it is usually quantized, with for instance a unit of 0.2×10^{-7} seconds for a 50 MHz node.

- An earthquake can be considered as a physical complex system (S_1) which is first mapped, by the theoretical geophysicist who is modelling it, into displacements measured by the amplitudes of waves as a function of space and time. Here again, the complex system (S_2) *space-time* is mapped into physical space-time. One might Fourier-Transform this picture to obtain a third complex system (S_3) whose space is now labelled by wave numbers.

- One might record this earthquake on a collection of N strip recorders.

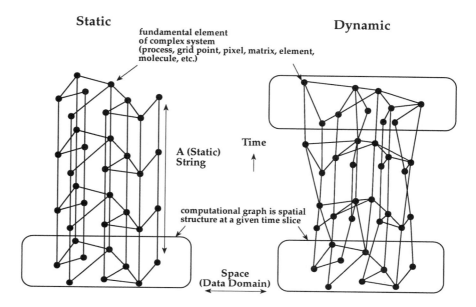

Figure 3.7: (a) Synchronous, Loosely Synchronous (Static), and (b) Asynchronous (Dynamic) Complex Systems with their Space-Time Structure

Now the resultant complex system (S_4) is a collection of N sheets of paper. The space of S_4 consists of the set of sheets and has N discrete members. The *time* associated with S_4 is the extension along the "long" (say x) direction of each sheet. This complex system is specified by the recording on the other (y) direction as a function of the *time* defined above. This example illustrates how mappings between complex systems can mix space and time. This is further illustrated by the next example, which completes the sequence of complex systems related to earthquakes.

- Suppose one writes a Fortran program to simulate such an earthquake and runs it on a conventional single processor workstation. This von Neumann model of computation has mapped the original complex system S_1 into one (S_5) with perhaps one or at best a few elements in its spatial domain corresponding to the independent functional units on the workstation. S_5 has mapped the original space-time into a totally temporal complex system. This could be viewed either as an example of the richness of mappings allowed between complex systems or as an illustration of the artificial nature of the sequential computing! Simulation of an earthquake on a parallel computer more faithfully links the space-time of the problem (S_1) with that of the simulation (S_5).

- The seismic simulation, mentioned above, could involve solution of the wave equation

$$\frac{\partial^2 P}{\partial t^2} = -k\nabla^2 P \tag{3.3}$$

Consider instead the solution of the elliptic partial differential equation

$$\nabla^2\varphi = -4\pi\rho \tag{3.4}$$

for the electrostatic potential φ in the presence of a charge density ρ. A simple, albeit usually non-optimal approach to solving Equation 3.4, is a Jacobi iteration, which in the special case of two dimensions and $\rho = 0$ involves the iterative procedure

$$\begin{aligned}
\varphi^{(n)}(x,y) &= \frac{1}{4}\Big(\varphi^{(n-1)}(x-1,y) + \varphi^{(n-1)}(x+1,y) \\
&+ \varphi^{(n-1)}(x,y-1) + \varphi^{(n-1)}(x,y+1)\Big)
\end{aligned} \tag{3.5}$$

where we assume that integer values of the indices x and y label the two-dimensional grid on which Laplace's equation is to be solved. The complex system defined by Equation 3.5 has *spatial* domain defined by the (x,y) grid and a *temporal* dimension defined by the iteration index n. Indeed, the Jacobi iteration is mathematically related to solving the parabolic partial differential equation

$$\frac{\partial\varphi}{\partial t} = -k\nabla^2\varphi \tag{3.6}$$

where one relates the discretized time t to the iteration index n. This equivalence between Equations 3.5 and 3.6 is qualitatively preserved when one compares the solution of Equations 3.3 and 3.5. As long as one views iteration as a temporal structure, Equations 3.3 and 3.4 can be formulated numerically with isomorphic complex systems S_{num}. This implies that parallelization issues, both hardware and software, are essentially identical for both equations.

The above example illustrates the most important form of parallelism—namely, *data parallelism*. This is produced by parallel execution of a computational (temporal) algorithm on each member of a *space* or *data domain*. Data parallelism is essentially synonymous with either *massive parallelism* or *massive data parallelism*. Spatial domains are usually very large, with from 10^4 to 10^8 members today; thus exploiting this data parallelism does lead to massive parallelism.

- As a final example, consider a particular simple formulation of the solution of linear equations, $A\mathbf{x} = \mathbf{b}$ with a dense (few zero elements) matrix A.

$$\sum_{j=1}^{n} A_{ij}\, x_j = b_i \qquad (3.7)$$

Parallelization of this is covered fully in [Fox:88a] and Chapter 8 of this book. Gaussian elimination (LU decomposition) for solving Equation 3.7 involves successive steps where in the simplest formulation without pivoting, at step k one "eliminates" a single variable x_{j_k} where the index $j_k = k$. At each step k, one modifies both A_{ij} and b_i

$$A_{ij}^{(0)} = A_{ij} \qquad b_i^{(0)} = b_i \qquad (3.8)$$

and $A_{ij}^{(k)}$, $b_i^{(k)}$ are formed from $A_{ij}^{(k-1)}$, $b_i^{(k-1)}$

where one ensures (if no pivoting is employed) that $A_{jk}^{(k)} = 0$ when $j > k$. Consider the above procedure as a complex system. The *spatial* domain is formed by the matrix A with a two-dimensional array of values $A_{ij}^{(k)}$. The time domain is labelled by the index k and so is a discrete space with n (number of rows or columns of A) members. The space is also discrete with n^2 members.

3.4 The Temporal Properties of Complex Systems

As shown in Equation 3.1, we will use complex systems to unify a variety of different concepts including nature and an underlying theory such as Quantum Chromodynamics; the numerical formulation of the theory; the result of expressing this with various software paradigms and the final computer used in its simulation. Different disciplines have correctly been built up around these different complex systems. Correspondingly different terminology is often used to describe related issues. This is certainly reasonable for both historical and technical reasons. However, we argue that understanding the process of computation and answering questions such as, "Which parallel computers are good for which problems?"; "What problems parallelize?"; and "What are productive parallel software paradigms?" is helped by a terminology which bridges the different complex systems. We can illustrate this with an anecdote. In a recent paper, an illustration of particles in the universe was augmented with a hierarchical set of clusters produced with the algorithm of Section 12.4. These clusters are designed to accurately represent the different length scales and physical clustering of the clouds of particles. This picture was labelled "data structure" but one computer science referee noted that this was not appropriate. Indeed, the referee was in one sense correct—we had not displayed a computer science data structure such as a Fortran array or C structure defining the linked list of particles. However, taking the point of view of the physicist, this picture was precisely showing the structure of the data and so, the caption was in one discipline (physics) correct and in another (computer science) false!

We will now define and discuss some general properties and parameters of complex systems which span the various disciplines involved.

- For completeness, we define a *complex system* as a collection of members whose extent defines the associated *space* and whose evolution defines the associated *time*. Many examples of these definitions were given in Section 3.3.

We will first discuss possible temporal structures for a complex system. Here, we draw on a computer science classification of computer architecture. In this context, aspects such as internode topology refer to the spatial structure of the computer viewed as a complex system. The control structure of the computer refers to the temporal behavior of its complex system. In our review of parallel computer hardware, we have already introduced the concepts of SIMD and MIMD, two important temporal classes which carry over to general complex systems. Returning to Figures 3.7(a) and 3.7(b), we see complex systems which are MIMD (or asynchronous as defined below) in Figure 3.7(b) and either SIMD or a restricted form of MIMD in Figure 3.7(a) (synchronous or loosely synchronous in language below). In fact, when we consider the temporal structure of problems (S_{num} in Equation 3.1), software (S_{HLSoft}), and hardware (S_{comp} in Equation 3.1), we will need to further extend this classification. Here we will briefly define concepts and give the section number where we discuss and illustrate it more fully.

- *Synchronous* complex systems are a direct generalization of SIMD parallel computers and are further described in Section 4.3. Technically, synchronous systems consist of more or less identical members which evolve synchronously with identical time evolution algorithms. We can also introduce *associative systems* as a special case of the *synchronous class*. This class includes content-addressable memories and associative processors, but we will not discuss this topic further in this book.

- *Asynchronous* complex systems contain, for the most part, disparate members which evolve dynamically in time with changing interconnect and usually different evolution algorithms for each member. This corresponds to a general distributed-memory MIMD machine with each node typically executing distinct programs and with varying and unsynchronized internode message traffic.

- *Loosely synchronous* complex systems are an important intermediate case between asynchronous and synchronous systems. They have generally disparate members evolving with possibly different temporal algorithms. However, they are synchronized "every now and then"; typically at the end of an iteration or time step in a solution. The majority of large scale scientific and engineering computations are synchronous or loosely synchronous as exemplified by the contents of this book.

  Society shows many examples of loosely synchronous behavior. Vehicles proceed more or less independently on a city street between loose synchronization points defined by traffic lights. The reader's life is loosely synchronized by such events as meals and bedtime.

When we consider computer hardware and software systems, we will need to consider other temporal classes which can be thought of as further subdivisions of the asynchronous class.

- *Static asynchronous* (or *static* MIMD) systems consist of fixed members whose interconnect—or in the application to parallel computers, message traffic—is varying. This translates into a MIMD software model of static processes interacting with a general dynamic message-passing system. We have a fixed number of processes which are spawned and then execute a particular program which remains unchanged. This leads to the important SPMD (Single Program Multiple Data) model of computation [Darema:85a;88a]. This is used in all the applications of this book except those in Chapters 14, 17 and 18. SPMD is the natural implementation of synchronous or loosely synchronous problems on MIMD distributed-memory parallel computers. In SPMD, each process runs the same program but operates on different data sets. In synchronous implementations, the different processes execute the same instructions at each computer cycle. In loosely synchronous problems, the processes are at different points of the same program at each time.

- *Dynamic asynchronous* systems generalize the above example with processes and messages able to spawn new processes dynamically. For instance, *reactive* systems are dynamic asynchronous systems that spawn services as needed in a distributed operating system. Generally, we define such systems to have both an irregular time-dependent interconnect and members which can be created and destroyed at any time.

- *Shared-memory* MIMD complex systems are defined to represent this model of parallel computer. This special case of an asynchronous complex system can only be properly described in Section 13.1, when we study software and the associated complex system S_{HLSoft} in the notation of Equation 3.1. One could include shared-memory systems as examples of *static MIMD* or *dynamic asynchronous* systems with a particular form for information to be transferred between processes or processors. In distributed-memory machines, information is transferred via the construction of messages; in shared memory by memory access instructions. Indeed, the so-called NUMA (non-uniform memory access) shared-memory machines are implemented in machines like the Kendall Square as distributed-memory hardware with (from the point of view of the user) memory access as the communication mechanism. Uniform memory access (UMA) shared memory machines, such as the Sequent, do present a rather different computational model. However, most believe that NUMA machines are the only shared-memory architectures that scale to large systems, and so in practice scalable shared-memory architectures are only distinguished

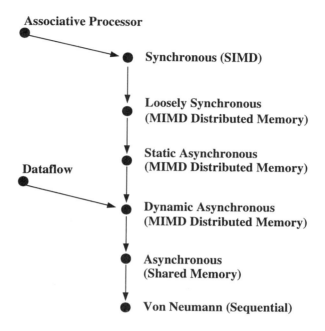

Figure 3.8: Partial Ordering of Temporal (Control) Architectures for a Complex System

from distributed-memory machines in their mechanism for information transfer.

- *Dataflow* can be considered as a special dynamic asynchronous complex system describing the dataflow hardware and/or software model of S_{comp} or S_{HLSoft} in Equation 3.1. Here, members of the complex system are dormant until all data needed for their definition is received when they "fire" and evolve according to a predetermined algorithm.

In Figure 3.8, we summarize these temporal classifications for complex systems, indicating a partial ordering with arrows pointing to more general architectures. This will become clearer in Section 3.5 when we discuss software and the relation between problem and computer. Note that although the language is drawn from the point of view of computer architecture, the classifications are important at the problem, software, and hardware level.

The hardware (computer) architecture naturally divides into SIMD (synchronous), MIMD (asynchronous), and von Neumann classes. The problem structures are synchronous, loosely synchronous, or asynchronous. One can argue that the shared-memory asynchronous architecture is naturally suggested by software (S_{HLSoft}) considerations and in particular by the goal of efficient parallel execution for sequential software models. For this reason it becomes an important computer architecture even though it is not a natural problem (S_{num}) architecture.

3.5   Spatial Properties of Complex Systems

Now we switch topics and consider the spatial properties of complex systems.

The *size* N of the complex system is obviously an important property. Note that we think of a complex system as a set of *members* with their spatial structure evolving with time. Sometimes, the time domain has a definite "size" but often one can evolve the system indefinitely in time. However, most complex systems have a natural spatial size with the spatial domain consisting of N members. In the examples of Section 3.3, the seismic example had a definite spatial extent and unlimited time domain; on the other hand, Gaussian elimination had n^2 spatial members evolving for a fixed number of n "time" steps. As usual, the value of spatial size N will depend on the granularity or detail with which one looks at the complex system. One could consider a parallel computer as a complex system constructed as a collection of transistors with a correspondingly very large value of $N \sim 10^{10}$ but here we will view the processor node as the fundamental entity and define the spatial size of a parallel computer viewed as a complex system, by the number N_{proc} of processing nodes.

Now is a natural time to define the von Neumann complex system spatial structure which is relevant, of course, for computer architecture. We will formally define this to be a system with no spatial extent, i.e. size $N_{\text{proc}} = 1$. Of course, a von Neumann node can have a sophisticated structure if we look at fine enough resolution with multiple functional units. More precisely, perhaps, we can generalize this complex system to one where N_{proc} is small and will not scale up to large values.

Consider mapping a seismic simulation with N_{num} grid points onto a parallel machine with N_{proc} processors. An important parameter is the *grain size* n of the resultant decomposition. We can introduce the problem *grain size* $n_{\text{num}} = N_{\text{num}}/N_{\text{proc}}$ and the computer *grain size* n_{mem} as the memory contained in each node of the parallel computer. Clearly we must have,

$$n_{\text{num}} < n_{\text{mem}} \tag{3.9}$$

if we measure memory size in units of seismic grid points. More interestingly, in Equation 3.10 we will relate the performance of the parallel implementation of the seismic simulation to n_{num} and other problem and computer characteristics. We find that, in many cases, the parallel performance only depends on N_{num} and N_{proc} in the combination N_{num}/N_{proc} and so *grain size* is a critical parameter in determining the effectiveness of parallel computers for a particular application.

The next set of parameters describe the topology or structure of the spatial domain associated with the complex system. The simplest parameter of this type is the geometric dimension d_{geom} of the space. As reviewed in Chapter 2, the original hardware and, in fact, software (see Chapter 5) exhibited a clear geometric structure for S_{comp} or S_{HLSoft}. The binary hypercube of dimension d had this as its geometric dimension. This was an effective architecture because it was richer than the topologies of most problems. Thus, consider mapping a problem of dimension d_{num} onto a computer of dimension d_{comp}. Suppose the software system preserves the spatial structure of the problem and that $d_{HLSoft} = d_{num}$. Then, one can show that the parallel computing overhead f has a term due to internode communication that has the form,

$$f_C \propto \frac{N_{proc}^\alpha}{n_{num}^\beta} \frac{t_{comm}}{t_{calc}} \tag{3.10}$$

with parallel speedup S given by

$$S = \frac{N_{proc}}{1 + f_C}$$
$$\text{or } f_C = \frac{N_{proc}}{S} - 1$$
$$= \left(\frac{1}{\text{efficiency } \epsilon}\right) - 1 \tag{3.11}$$

The communication overhead f_C depends on the problem *grain size* n_{num} and computer complex system N_{proc}. It also involves two parameters specifying the parallel hardware performance.

- t_{calc}: The typical time required to perform a generic calculation. For scientific problems, this can be taken as a floating-point calculation

$$a = b * c$$
$$\text{or } a = b + c$$

- t_{comm}: The typical time taken to communicate a single word between two nodes connected in the hardware topology.

The definitions of t_{comm} and t_{calc} are imprecise above. In particular, t_{calc} depends on the nature of node and can take on very different values depending on the details of the implementation; floating-point operations are much faster when the operands are taken from registers than from slower parts of the memory hierarchy. On systems built from processors like the Intel i860 chip, these effects can be large; t_{calc} could be $.02\mu$ sec from registers (50 MFLOPS) and larger by a factor of ten when the variables a, b are fetched from dynamic RAM. Again, communication speed t_{comm} depends on internode message size (a software characteristic) and the latency (startup time) and bandwidth of the computer communication subsystem.

Returning to Equation 3.10, we really only need to understand here that the term t_{comm}/t_{calc} indicates that communication overhead depends on relative performance of the internode communication system and node (floating-point) processing unit. A real study of parallel computer performance would require a deeper discussion of the exact values of t_{comm} and t_{calc}. More interesting here is the dependence $(N_{proc}^{\alpha}/n_{num}^{\beta})$ on the number of processors N_{proc} and problem *grain size* n_{num}. As described above, *grain size* $n_{num} = N_{num}/N_{proc}$ depends on both the problem and the computer. The values of α and β are given by

$$\beta = \frac{1}{d_{num}} \tag{3.12}$$

independent of computer parameters, while if

$$d_{num} < d_{comp} \quad , \quad \alpha = 0$$

$$\text{and if } d_{num} > d_{comp} \quad , \quad \alpha = \left(\frac{1}{d_{comp}} - \frac{1}{d_{num}} \right). \tag{3.13}$$

The results in Equation 3.13 quantify the penalty, in terms of a value of f_C that increases with N_{proc}, for a computer architecture that is less rich than the problem architecture. An attractive feature of the hypercube architecture is that d_{comp} is large and one is essentially always in the regime governed by the top line in Equation 3.13. Recently, there has been a trend away from rich topologies like the hypercube towards the view that the node interconnect should be considered as a routing network or switch to be implemented in the very best technology. The original MIMD machines from Intel, nCUBE, and AMETEK all used hypercube topologies, as did the SIMD Connection Machines CM-1 and CM-2. The nCUBE-2, introduced in 1990, still uses a hypercube topology but both it and the second generation Intel iPSC/2 used a hardware routing that "hides" the hypercube connectivity. The latest Intel Paragon and Touchstone Delta and Symult (ex-Ametek) 2010 use a two-dimensional mesh with wormhole routing. It is not clear how to incorporate these new node interconnects into the above picture and further research is needed. Presumably, we would need to add new complex system properties and perhaps generalize the definition of dimension d_{comp} as we will see below is in fact necessary for Equation 3.10 to be valid for problems whose structure is not geometrically based.

Returning to Equations 3.10 through 3.12, we note that we have not properly defined the correct dimension d_{num} or d_{comp} to use. We have implicitly equated this with the natural *geometric dimension* but this is not always correct. This is illustrated by the complex system S_{num} consisting of a set of particles in three dimensions interacting with a long range force such as gravity or electrostatic charge. The geometric structure is local with $d_{\text{num}}^{\text{geom}} = 3$ but the complex system structure is quite different; all particles are connected to all others. As described in Chapter 3 of [Fox:88a], this implies that $d_{\text{num}}^{\text{system}} = 1$ whatever the underlying geometric structure. We define the *system dimension* d^{system} for a general complex system to reflect the system connectivity. Consider Figure 3.9 which shows a general domain D in a complex system. We define the *volume* V_D of this domain by the information in it. Mathematically, V_D is the computational complexity needed to simulate D in isolation. In a geometric system

$$V_D \propto L^{d^{\text{geom}}} \tag{3.14}$$

where L is a geometric length scale. The domain D is not in general isolated and is connected to the rest of the complex system. Information I_D flows in D and again in a geometric system. I_D is a surface effect with

$$I_D \propto L^{d^{\text{geom}}-1} \tag{3.15}$$

If we view the complex system as a graph, V_D is related to the number of links of the graph inside D and I_D is related to the number of links cut by the surface of D. Equations 3.14 and 3.15 are altered in cases like the long-range force problem where the complex system connectivity is no longer geometric. We define the system dimension to preserve the surface versus volume interpretation of Equation 3.15 compared to Equation 3.14. Thus, generally we define

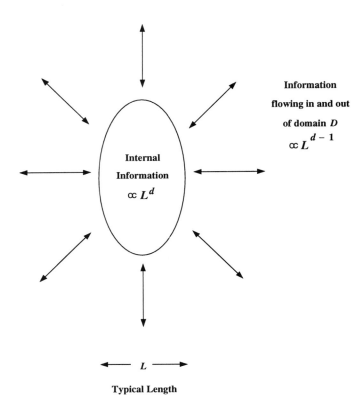

Figure 3.9: The Information Density and Flow in a General Complex System with Length Scale L

$$I_D \propto V_D^{1-1/d^{\text{system}}} \tag{3.16}$$

With this definition of *system dimension* d^{system}, we will find that Equations 3.10 through 3.12 essentially hold in general. In particular for the long range force problem, one finds $d^{\text{system}} = 1$ independent of d^{geom}.

A very important special type of spatial structure is the case $d^{\text{system}} = 0$ when we find the *embarrassingly parallel* or *spatially disconnected* complex system. Here there is no connection between the different members in the spatial domain. Applying this to parallel computing, we see that if S_{num} or S_{HLSoft} is spatially disconnected, then it can be parallelized very straightforwardly. In particular, any MIMD machine can be used whatever the temporal structure of the complex system. SIMD machines can only be used to simulate embarrassingly parallel complex systems which have spatially disconnected members with *identical* structure.

In Section 13.7, we extend the analysis of this section to cover the performance of hierarchical memory machines. We find that one needs to replace subdomains in space with those in space-time.

In Chapter 11, we describe other interesting spatial properties in terms of a particle analogy. We find system temperature and phase transitions as one heats and cools the complex system.

3.6 Compound Complex Systems

In Sections 3.4 and 3.5, we discussed basic characteristics of complex systems. In fact, many "real world examples" are a mixture of these fundamental architectures. This is illustrated by Figure 3.10, which shows a very conventional computer network with several different architectures. We cannot only regard each individual computer as a complex system but the whole network is, of course, a single complex system as we have defined it. We will term such complex systems *compound*. Note that one often puts together a network of resources to solve a "single problem" and so an analysis of the structure of compound complex systems is not an academic issue, but of practical importance.

Figure 3.10 shows a mixture of temporal, synchronous and asynchronous, and spatial, hypercube, and von Neumann architectures. We can look at both the architecture of the individual network components or, taking a higher level view, look at the network itself with member computers, such

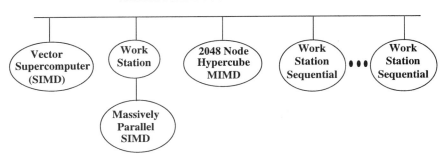

Figure 3.10: A Heterogeneous Compound Complex System S_{comp} Corresponding to a Network of Computers of Disparate Architectures

as the hypercube in Figure 3.10, viewed as "black boxes." In this example, the network is an asynchronous complex system and this seems quite a common circumstance. Figure 3.11 shows two compound problems S_{num} coming from the aerospace and battle management fields, respectively. In each case we link asynchronously problem modules which are synchronous, loosely synchronous, or asynchronous. We have found this very common. In scientific and engineering computations, the basic modules are usually synchronous or loosely synchronous. These modules have large spatial size and naturally support "massive data parallelism." Rarely do we find large asynchronous modules; this is fortunate as such complex systems are difficult to parallelize. However, in many cases the synchronous or loosely synchronous program modules are hierarchically combined with an asynchronous architecture. This is an important way in which the asynchronous problem architecture is used in large scale computations. This is explored in detail in Chapter 18. One has come to refer to systems such as those in Figure 3.10 as *metacomputers*. Correspondingly, we designate the applications in Figure 3.11 *metaproblems*.

If we combine Figures 3.10 and 3.11, we can formulate the process of computation in its most general complicated fashion.

> *"Map a compound heterogeneous problem onto a compound heterogeneous computer."*

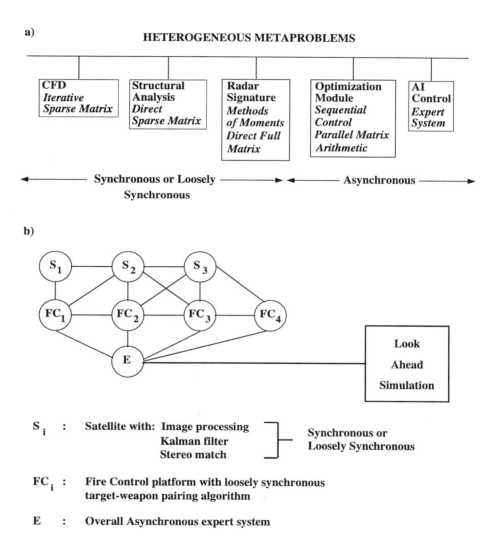

Figure 3.11: Two Heterogeneous Complex Systems S_{num} Corresponding to: a) the Integrated Design of a New Aircraft, and b) the Integrated Battle Management Problem Discussed in Chapter 18

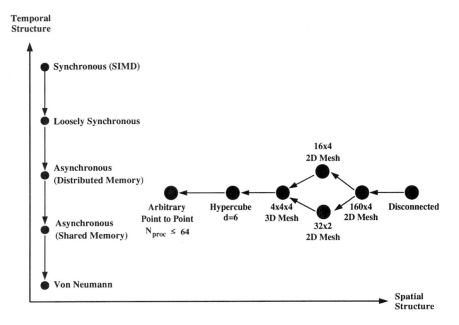

Figure 3.12: An Illustration of Problem or Computer Architecture Represented in a Two-dimensional Space. The spatial structure only gives a few examples.

3.7   Mapping Complex Systems

Equation 3.1 first stated our approach to computation as a map between different complex systems. We can quantify this by defining a partial order on complex systems written

$$A > B \text{ or } A \to B \tag{3.17}$$

Equation 3.17 states that a complex system A can be mapped to complex system B, that is, that B has a more general architecture than A. This was already seen in Figure 3.8 and is given in more detail in Figure 3.12, where we have represented complex systems in a two-dimensional space labelled by their spatial and temporal properties. In this notation, we require:

$$S_{\text{num}} \geq S_{\text{HLSoft}} \geq S_{\text{comp}}. \tag{3.18}$$

The requirement that a particular problem parallelize is that

$$S_{\text{num}} \geq S_{\text{comp}} \tag{3.19}$$

which is shown in Figure 3.13. We have drawn our space labelled by complex system properties so that the partial ordering of Figures 3.8 and 3.12 "flows" towards the origin. Roughly, complex systems get more specialized as one either moves upwards or to the right. We view the three key complex systems, S_{num}, S_{HLSoft}, and S_{comp}, as points in the space represented in Figures 3.12 and 3.13. Then Figure 3.13 shows that the computer complex system S_{comp} lies below and to the left of those representing S_{num} and S_{HLSoft}.

Let us consider an example. Suppose S_{comp} (the computer) is a hypercube of dimension $d_{comp} = 6$ with a MIMD temporal structure. Synchronous, loosely synchronous, or asynchronous problems can be mapped onto this computer as long as the problem's spatial structure is contained in the hypercube topology. Thus, we will successfully map a 160×4 two-dimensional mesh. But what about a 3×3 mesh or $742 \times 523 \times 137$ irregular lattice? The 3×3 mesh only has nine (spatial) components and insufficient parallelism to exploit the 64-node computer. The large irregular mesh can be efficiently mapped onto the hypercube as shown in Chapter 12. However, one could support this with a more general computer architecture where hardware or software routing essentially gives the general node-to-node communication shown in the bottom left corner of Figure 3.12. The hypercube work at Caltech and elsewhere always used this strategy in mapping complex spatial topologies; the *crystal-router* mechanism in CrOS or Express was a powerful and efficient software strategy. Some of the early work using transputers found difficulties with some spatial structures since the language Occam only directly supported process-to-process communication over the physical hardware channels. However, later general Occam subroutine libraries (communication "harnesses") callable from FORTRAN or C allowed the general point-to-point (process-to-process) communication model for transputer systems.

3.8 Parallel Computing Works?

The complex system classification introduced in this chapter allows a precise formulation of the lessons of current research.

The majority of large scale scientific and engineering computations have synchronous or loosely synchronous character. Detailed statistics are given in Section 14.1 but we note that our survey suggests that at most 10% of applications are asynchronous. The microscopic or macroscopic temporal synchronization in the synchronous or loosely synchronous problems ensures

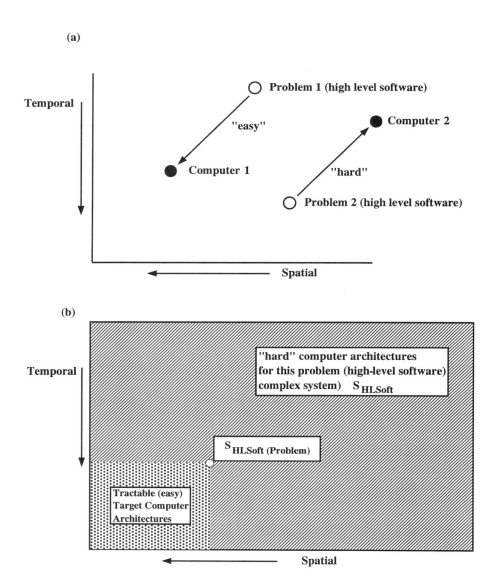

Figure 3.13: Easy and Hard Mappings of Complex Systems $S_{num} \to S_{comp}$ or $S_{HLSoft} \to S_{comp}$. We show complex systems for problems and computers in a space labelled by spatial and temporal complex system (computer architectures). Figure 3.12 illustrates possible ordering of these structures.

natural parallelism without difficult computer hardware or software synchronization. Thus, we can boldly state that

$$S_{\text{num}} \geq S_{\text{comp}} \quad \text{(MIMD)} \tag{3.20}$$

for these problems. This quantifies our statement that

"Parallel Computing Works,"

where Equation 3.20 should be interpreted in the sense shown in Figure 3.13(b).

Roughly, loosely synchronous problems are suitable for MIMD and synchronous problems for SIMD computers. We can expand Equation 3.20 and write

$$S_{\text{num}} \geq S_{\text{comp}} \text{ (SIMD)} \qquad \text{for} \sim 45\% \text{ applications}$$

$$S_{\text{comp}} \text{ (SIMD)} > S_{\text{num}}$$
$$\geq S_{\text{comp}} \text{ (MIMD)} \qquad \text{for} \sim 45\% \text{ applications.} \tag{3.21}$$

The results in Equation 3.21 are given with more details in Tables 14.1 and 14.2. The text of this book is organized so that we begin by studying the simpler synchronous applications, then give examples first of loosely synchronous and finally asynchronous and compound problems.

The bold statements in Equations 3.20 and 3.21 become less clear when one considers software and the associated software complex system S_{HLSoft}. The parallel software systems CrOS and its follow-on Express were used in nearly all our applications. These required explicit user insertion of message passing, which in many cases is tiresome and unfamiliar. One can argue that, as shown in Figure 3.14, we supported a high-level software environment that reflected the target machine and so could be effectively mapped on it. Thus, we show S_{HLSoft} (CrOS) and S_{comp} (MIMD) close together on Figure 3.14. A more familiar and attractive environment to most users would be a traditional sequential language like Fortran77. Unfortunately,

$$S_{\text{HLSoft}} \text{ (F77)} < S_{\text{comp}} \text{ (MIMD)} \tag{3.22}$$

and so, as shown in Figures 3.13(a) and 3.14, it is highly non-trivial to effectively map existing or new Fortran77 codes onto MIMD or SIMD parallel machines—at least those with distributed memory. We will touch on this

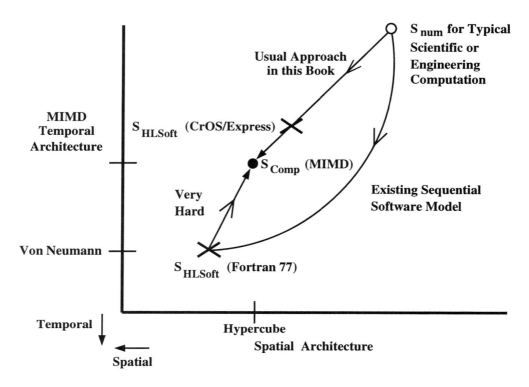

Figure 3.14: The Dusty Deck Issue in Terms of the Architectures of Problem, Software, and Computer Complex Systems

issue in this book in Sections 13.1 and 13.2, but it remains an active research area.

We also discuss *data parallel* languages, such as High Performance Fortran, in Chapter 13 [Kennedy:93a]. This is designed so that

$$S_{\text{HLSoft}} \text{ (High Performance Fortran)} > S_{\text{comp}} \text{ (MIMD)} \qquad (3.23)$$

We can show this point more graphically if we introduce a quantitative measure M of the difficulty of mapping $S_1 \to S_2$. We represent M as the difference in heights h,

$$M(S_1 \to S_2) = h(S_1) - h(S_2) \qquad (3.24)$$

where we can only perform the map if M is positive

$$
\begin{aligned}
M(S_1 \to S_2) &> 0 \text{ if} \\
S_1 &> S_2
\end{aligned}
\qquad (3.25)
$$

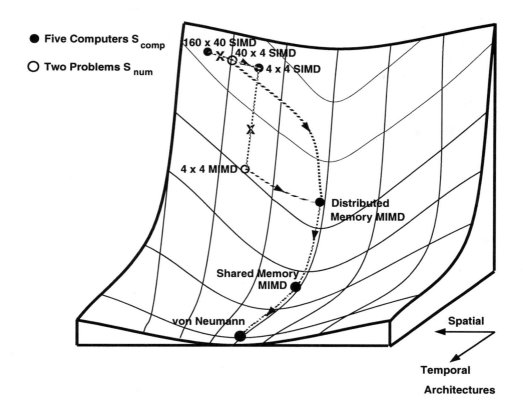

Figure 3.15: Two Problems (o) and Five Computer Architectures (•) in the Space-Time Architecture Classification of Complex Systems. An arrow represents a successful mapping and an "X" a mapping that will fail without a sophisticated compiler.

Negative values of M correspond to difficult cases such as Equation 3.22 while large positive values of M imply a possible but hard map. Figure 3.15 shows how one can now picture the process of computation as moving "downhill" in the complex system architecture space.

This formal discussion is illustrated throughout the book by numerous examples, which show that a wide variety of applications parallelize. Most of the applications chapters start with a computational analysis that refers back to the general concepts developed. This is finally summarized in Chapter 14, which exemplifies the asynchronous applications and starts with an overview of the different temporal problem classes. We build up to this by discussing synchronous problems in Chapters 4 and 6; embarrassingly parallel problems in Chapter 7; loosely synchronous problem with increasing degrees of irregularity in Chapters 8, 9, and 12. Compound problem classes—an asynchronous mixture of loosely synchronous components—are described in Chapters 17 and 18. The large missile tracking and battle management simulation built at JPL (Figure 3.11b) and described briefly in Chapter 18 was the major example of a compound problem class within C^3P. Chapters 17 and 19 indicate that we believe that this class is extremely important in many "real-world" applications that integrate many diverse functions.

Chapter 4

Synchronous Applications I

4.1   QCD and the Beginning of C³P

The Caltech Concurrent Computation Project started with QCD, or Quantum Chromodynamics, as its first application. QCD is discussed in more detail in Sections 4.2 and 4.3, but here we will put in the historical perspective. This nostalgic approach is developed in [Fox:87d], [Fox:88oo] as well as Chapters 1 and 2 of this book.

We show, in Table 4.1, fourteen QCD simulations, labelled by representative physics publications, performed within C³P using parallel machines. This activity started in 1981 with simulations, using the first four-node 8086–8087-based prototypes of the Cosmic Cube. These prototypes were quite competitive in performance with the VAX 11/780 on which we had started (in 1980) our computational physics program within high energy physics at Caltech. The 64-node Cosmic Cube was used more or less continuously from October, 1983 to mid-1984 on what was termed by Caltech, a "mammoth calculation" in the press release shown in Figure 4.2. This is the modest, $12^3 \times 16$ four-dimensional lattice calculation reported in line 3 of Table 4.1. As trumpeted in Figures 4.1 and 4.2, this was our first major use of parallel machines and a critical success on which we built our program.

Our 1983–1984 calculations totalled some 2,500 hours on the 64-node Cosmic Cube and successfully competed with 100-hour CDC Cyber 205 computations that were the state of the art at the time [Barkai:84b], [Barkai:84c], [Bowler:85a], [DeForcrand:85a]. We used a four-dimensional lattice with $12^3 \times 16$ grid points, with eight gluon field values defined on each of the 110,592 links between grid points. The resultant 884,736 degrees of freedom

Table 4.1: Quantum Chromodynamic (QCD) Calculations Within C^{3}P

Authors	Project	Hypercube	Reference
Brooks, Fox, Otto, Randeria, Athas, De Benedictis, Newton, Seitz	Glueball mass (SU(2)) $4^3 \times 8$ lattice	Cosmic Cube 4 node	[Brooks:83a]
Otto, Randeria	Glueball mass, modified action $4^3 \times 8$ lattice	Cosmic Cube 4 node	[Otto:83a]
Otto, Stack	Heavy quark potential $12^3 \times 16$ lattice	Cosmic Cube 64 node	[Otto:84a]
Otto, Stolorz	Glueball mass, enhanced statistics $12^3 \times 16$ lattice	Cosmic Cube 64 node	[Otto:85b]
Patel, Otto, Gupta	Monte Carlo renormalization group, nonperturbative β-function	Cosmic Cube 64 node	[Patel:85a]
Fucito, Soloman	Chiral symmetry breaking, mass spectrum, deconfinement transition, pseudo-fermions	Mark II 64 node	[Fucito:84a], [Fucito:85b], [Fucito:85c], [Fucito:85d] [Fucito:86a]
Flower, Otto	Field distribution $10^2 \times 12^2$ lattice	Mark II 32 node	[Flower:85a]
Flower, Otto	Heavy quark potential 20^4 lattice	Mark II 128 node	[Flower:86b]
Kolawa, Furmanski	Glueball mass (SU(2)), Hamiltonian "loop" formalism	Mark II 32 node	[Furmanski:87c]
Stolorz, Otto	Microcanonical renormalization group (SU(2))	Mark I 64 node	[Stolorz:86b]
Flower	Baryons on the lattice 20^4	Mark II 128 node	[Flower:87e]
Chiu	Random block lattice	nCUBE-1 1024 node	[Chiu:89b], [Chiu:88c], [Chiu:88e], [Chiu:88f] [Chiu:89a]
Ding, Baillie, Fox	Heavy quark potential $24^3 \times 10$, $24^3 \times 12$, $12^3 \times 24$, $16^3 \times 24$	Mark IIIfp 32 node and 64 node	[Ding:90b]
Baillie, Brickner, Gupta	QCD with dynamical Wilson fermions 16^4 lattice	TMC CM-2 16K	[Baillie:89e]

seem modest today as QCD practitioners contemplate lattices of order 100^4 simulated on machines of teraFLOP performance [Aoki:91a]. However, this lattice was comparable to those used on vector supercomputers at the time.

A hallmark of this work was the interdisciplinary team building hardware, software, and parallel application. Further, from the start we stressed large supercomputer-level simulations where parallelism would make the greatest initial impact. It was also worth noting that our use of comparatively high-level software paid off—Otto and Stack were able to code better algorithms [Parisi:83a] than the competing vector supercomputer teams. The hypercube could be programmed conveniently without use of microcode or other unproductive environments needed on some of the other high-performance machines of the time.

Our hypercube calculations used an early C plus message-passing programming approach which later evolved into the *Express* system described in the next chapter. Although not as elegant as data-parallel C and Fortran (discussed in Chapter 13), our approach was easier than hand-coded assembly, which was quite common for alternative high-performance systems of the time.

Figures 4.1 and 4.2 show extracts from Caltech and newspaper publicity of the time. We were essentially only a collection of 64 IBM PCs. Was that a good thing (as we thought) or an indication of our triviality (as a skeptical observer commenting in Figure 4.1 thought)? 1985 saw the start of a new phase as conventional supercomputers and availability increased in power and NSF and DOE allocated many tens of thousands of hours on the CRAY X-MP (2, Y-MP) and ETA-10 to QCD simulations. Our final QCD hypercube calculations in 1989 within C³P used a 64-node JPL Mark IIIfp with approximately 300 MFLOPS performance. Since this work, we switched to using the Connection Machine CM-2, which by 1990 was the commercial standard in the field. C³P helped the Los Alamos group of Brickner and Gupta (one of our early graduates!) to develop the first CM-2 QCD codes, which in 1991 performed at 6 GFLOPS on the full size 64 K CM-2 [Brickner:91a], [Liu:91a].

Caltech Scientists Develop 'Parallel' Computer Model

By LEE DEMBART
Times Science Writer

Caltech scientists have developed a working prototype for a
new super computer that can perform many tasks at once, making
possible the solution of important science and engineering
problems that have so far resisted attack.

The machine is one of the first to make extensive use of
parallel processing, which has been both the dream and the bane
of computer designers for years.

Unlike conventional computers, which perform one step at a
time while the rest of the machine lies idle, parallel computers
can do many things at the same time, holding out the prospect of
much greater computing speed than currently available--at much
less cost.

If its designers are right, their experimental device, called
the Cosmic Cube, will open the way for solving problems in
meteorology, aerodynamics, high-energy physics, seismic
analysis, astrophysics and oil exploration, to name a few.
These problems have been intractable because even the fastest of
today's computers are too slow to process the mountains of data
in a reasonable amount of time.

One of today's fastest computers is the Cray 1, which can do
20 million to 80 million operations a second. But at $5
million, they are expensive and few scientists have the
resources to tie one up for days or weeks to solve a problem.

''Science and engineering are held up by the lack of super
computers,'' says one of the Caltech inventors, Geoffrey C. Fox,
a theoretical physicist. ''They know how to solve problems that
are larger than current computers allow.''

The experimental device, 5 feet long by 8 inches high by 14
inches deep, fits on a desk top in a basement laboratory, but it
is already the most powerful computer at Caltech. It cost
$80,000 and can do three million operations a second--about
one-tenth the power of a Cray 1.

Fox and his colleague, Charles L. Seitz, a computer
scientist, say they can expand their device in coming years so
that it has 1,000 times the computing power of a Cray.

''Poor old Cray and Cyber (another super computer) don't have
much of a chance of getting any significant increase in speed,''
Fox said. ''Our ultimate machines are expected to be at least
1,000 times faster than the current fastest computers.''

''We are getting to the point where we are not going to be
talking about these things as fractions of a Cray but as
multiples of them,'' Seitz said.

But not everyone in the field is as impressed with Caltech's Cosmic Cube as its inventors are. The machine is nothing more nor less than 64 standard, off-the-shelf microprocessors wired together, not much different than the innards of 64 IBM personal computers working as a unit.

''We are using the same technology used in PCs (personal computers) and Pacmans,'' Seitz said. The technology is an 8086 microprocessor capable of doing 1/20th of a million operations a second with 1/8th of a megabyte of primary storage. Sixty-four of them together will do 3 million operations a second with 8 megabytes of storage.

Currently under development is a single chip that will replace each of the 64 8-inch-by-14-inch boards. When the chip is ready, Seitz and Fox say they will be able to string together 10,000 or even 100,000 of them.

Computer scientists have known how to make such a computer for years but have thought it too pedestrian to bother with.

''It could have been done many years ago,'' said Jack B. Dennis, a computer scientist at the Massachusetts Institute of Technology who is working on a more radical and ambitious approach to parallel processing than Seitz and Fox. He thinks his approach, called ''dataflow,'' will both speed up computers and expand their horizons, particularly in the direction of artificial intelligence.

Computer scientists dream of getting parallel processors to mimic the human brain, which can also do things concurrently.

''There's nothing particularly difficult about putting together 64 of these processors,'' he said. ''But many people don't see that sort of machine as on the path to a profitable result.''

What's more, Dennis says, organizing these machines and writing programs for them have turned out to be sticky problems that have resisted solution and divided the experts.

''There is considerable debate as to exactly how these large parallel machines should be programmed,'' Dennis said by telephone from Cambridge, Mass. ''The 64-processor machine (at Caltech) is, in terms of cost-performance, far superior to what exists in a Cray 1 or a Cyber 205 or whatever. The problem is in the programming.''

Fox responds that he has ''an existence proof'' for his machine and its programs, which is more than Dennis and his colleagues have to show for their efforts.

The Caltech device is a real, working computer, up and running and chewing on a real problem in high-energy physics. The ideas on which it was built may have been around for a while, he agreed, but the Caltech experiment demonstrates that there is something to be gained by implementing them.

For all his hopes, Dennis and his colleagues have not yet
built a machine to their specifications. Others who have built
parallel computers have done so on a more modest scale than
Caltech's 64 processors. A spokesman for IBM said that the
giant computer company had built a 16-processor machine, and is
continuing to explore parallel processing.

The key insight that made the development of the Caltech
computer possible, Fox said, was that many problems in science
are computationally difficult because they are big, not because
they are necessarily complex.

Because these problems are so large, they can profitably be
divided into 64 parts. Each of the processors in the Caltech
machine works on 1/64th of the problem.

Scientists studying the evolution of the universe have to
deal with 1 million galaxies. Scientists studying aerodynamics
get information from thousands of data points in three
dimensions.

To hunt for undersea oil, ships tow instruments through the
oceans, gathering data in three dimensions that is then analyzed
in two dimensions because of computer limitations. The Caltech
computer would permit three-dimensional analysis.

''It has to be problems with a lot of concurrency in them,''
Seitz said. That is, the problem has to be split into parts,
and all the parts have to be analyzed simultaneously.

So the applications of the Caltech computer for commercial
uses such as an airline reservation system would be limited, its
inventors agree.

Figure 4.1:   Caltech Scientists Develop "Parallel" Computer Model
[Dembart:84a]

CALTECH'S COSMIC CUBE
PERFORMING MAMMOTH CALCULATIONS

Large-scale calculations in basic physics have been successfully run on the Cosmic Cube, an experimental computer at Caltech that its developers and users see as the forerunner of supercomputers of the future. The calculations, whose results are now being published in articles in scientific journals, show that such computers can deliver useful computing power at a far lower cost than today's machines.

The first of the calculations was reported in two articles in the June 25 issue of Physical Review Letters. In addition, a second set of calculations related to the first has been submitted to Physics Letters for publication.

The June Physical Review Letters articles were:

--''Pure Gauge SU(3) Lattice Theory on an Array of Computers,'' by Eugene Brooks, Geoffrey Fox, Steve Otto, Paul Stolorz, William Athas, Erik DeBenedictis, Reese Faucette, and Charles Seitz, all of Caltech; and John Stack of the University of Illinois at Urbana-Champaign, and

--''The SU(3) Heavy Quark Potential with High Statistics,'' by Steve Otto and John Stack.

The Cosmic Cube consists of 64 computer elements, called nodes, that operate on parts of a problem concurrently. In contrast, most computers today are so-called von Neumann machines, consisting of a single processor that operates on a problem sequentially, making calculations serially.

The calculation reported in the June Physical Review Letters took 2,500 hours of the computation time on the Cosmic Cube. The calculation represents a contribution to the test of a set of theories called the Quantum Field Theories, which are mathematical attempts to explain the physical properties of subatomic particles known as hadrons, which include protons and neutrons.

These basic theories represent in a series of equations the behavior of quarks, the basic constituents of hadrons. Although theorists believe these equations to be valid, they have never been directly tested by comparing their predictions with the known properties of subatomic particles as observed in experiments with particle accelerators.

The calculations to be published in Physics Letters probe the properties, such as mass, of the glueballs that are predicted by theory.

''The calculations we are reporting are not earth-shaking,'' said Dr. Fox. ''While they are the best of their type yet done, they represent but a steppingstone to better calculations of this type.'' According to Dr. Fox, the scientists

calculated the force that exists between two quarks. This force
is carried by gluons, the particles that are theorized to carry
the strong force between quarks. The aim of the calculation was
to determine how the attractive force between quarks varies with
distance. Their results showed that the potential depends
linearly on distance.

''These results indicate that it would take an infinite
amount of energy to separate two quarks, which shows why free
quarks are not seen in nature,'' said Dr. Fox. ''These
findings represent a verification of what most people
expected.''

The Cosmic Cube has about one-tenth the power of the most
widely used supercomputer, the Cray-1, but at one hundredth the
cost, about $80,000. It has about eight times the computing
power of the widely used minicomputer, the VAX 11/780.
Physically, the machine occupies about six cubic feet, making it
fit on the average desk, and uses 700 watts of power.

Each of the 64 nodes of the Cosmic Cube has approximately the
same power as a typical microcomputer, consisting of 16-bit
Intel 8086 and 8087 processors, with 136K bytes of memory
storage. For comparison, the IBM Personal Computer uses the
same family of chips and typically possesses a similar amount of
memory. Each of the Cosmic Cube nodes executes programs
concurrently, and each can send messages to six other nodes in a
communication network based on a six-dimensional cube, or
hypercube. The chips for the Cosmic Cube were donated by Intel
Corporation, and Digital Equipment Corporation contributed
supporting computer hardware. According to Dr. Fox, a full-scale
extension of the Quantum Field Theories to yield the properties of
hadrons would require a computer 1,000 times more powerful than the
Cosmic Cube--or 100 computer projects at Caltech are developing hardware
and software for such advanced machines.

Figure 4.2: Caltech's Cosmic Cube Performing Mammoth Calculations
[Meredith:84a]

It is not surprising that our first hypercube calculations in C^{3}P did not need the full MIMD structure of the machine. This was also a characteristic of Sandia's pioneering use of the 1024-node nCUBE-1 [Gustafson:88a]. Synchronous applications like QCD are computationally important and have a simplicity that made them the natural starting point for our project.

4.2 Synchronous Applications

Table 4.2 indicates that 70 percent of our first set of applications were of the class we call synchronous. As remarked above, this could be expected in any such early work as these are the problems with the cleanest structure that are, in general, the simplest to code and, in particular, the simplest to parallelize. As already defined in Section 3.4, synchronous applications are characterized by a basic algorithm that consists of a set of operations which are applied identically in every point in a data set. The structure of the problem is typically very clear in such applications, and so the parallel implementation is easier than for the irregular loosely synchronous and asynchronous cases. Nevertheless, as we will see, there are many interesting issues in these problems and they include many very important applications. This is especially true for academic computations that address fundamental science. These are often formulated as studies of fundamental microscopic quantities such as the quark and gluon fundamental particles seen in QCD of Section 4.3. Fundamental microscopic entities naturally obey identical evolution laws and so lead to synchronous problem architectures. "Real world problems"—perhaps most extremely represented by the battle simulations of Chapter 18 in this book—typically do not involve arrays of identical objects, but rather the irregular dynamics of several different entities. Thus, we will find more loosely synchronous and asynchronous problems as we turn from fundamental science to engineering and industrial or government applications. We will now discuss the structure of QCD in more detail to illustrate some general computational features of synchronous problems.

The applications using the Cosmic Cube were well established by 1984 and Table 4.2 lists the ten projects which were completed in the first year after we started our interdisciplinary project in the summer of 1983. All but one of these projects are more or less described in this book, while the other will be found in [Fox:88a]. They covered a reasonable range of application areas and formed the base on which we first started to believe that parallel computing works! Figure 4.3 illustrates the regular lattice used in QCD

Table 4.2: The Ten Pioneer Hypercube Applications within C^3P

Field	Project Leader	Reference	Sec. No.	Problem Arch.
Lattice Gauge Theory	S. Otto	[Otto:83b], [Otto:84d]	4.3	Synchronous
Acoustic Wave Equation	R. Clayton	[Clayton:88a]	4.2	Synchronous
Coulomb Gas Monte Carlo	F. Fucito S. Solomon	[Fucito:85a] [Fucito:85f]	4.2	Synchronous
Two-Dimensional Hydrodynamics	D. Meier	[Meier:88a]	4.2	Synchronous
Chemical Reaction Dynamics	P. Hipes A. Kuppermann	[Hipes:88a], [Hipes:88b] [Wu:90a]	8.1	Synchronous
Evolution of Universe using FFT	J. Salmon	[Salmon:84a] (more advanced algorithm used in 12.4)	12.4	Synchronous
Dynamics of Sand Grains	B. Werner P. Haff	[Werner:87a] [Werner:88a]	9.2	Loosely Synchronous
Traveling Salesman Optimization by Simulated Annealing	S. Otto E. Felten S. Karlin	[Felten:85b]	11.4	Synchronous
Sorting	E. Felten S. Karlin S. Otto	[Felten:85a]	12.7	Loosely Synchronous
Melting of a Two Dimensional Solid	M. Johnson	[Johnson:86a]	14.2	Asynchronous

and its decomposition onto 64 nodes. QCD is a four-dimensional theory and all four dimensions can be decomposed. In our initial 64-node Cosmic Cube calculations, we used the three-dimensional decompositions shown in Figure 4.3 with the fourth dimension, as shown in Figure 4.4, and internal degrees of freedom stored sequentially in each node. Figure 4.3 also indicates one subtlety needed in the parallelization; namely, one needs a so-called red-black strategy with only half the lattice points updated in each of the two ("red" and "black") phases. Synchronous applications are characterized by such a regular spatial domain as shown in Figure 4.3 and an identical update algorithm for each lattice point. The update makes use of a Monte Carlo procedure described in Section 4.3 and in more detail in Chapter 12 of [Fox:88a]. This procedure is not totally synchronous since the "accept-reject" mechanism used in the Monte Carlo procedure does not always terminate at the same step. This is no problem on an MIMD machine and even makes the problem "slightly loosely synchronous." However, SIMD machines can also cope with this issue as all systems (DAP, CM-2, Maspar) have a feature that allows processors to either execute the common instruction or ignore it.

Figure 4.5 illustrates the nearest neighbor algorithm used in QCD and very many problems described by local interactions. We see that some updates require communication and some don't. In the message-passing software model used in our hypercube work described in Chapter 5, the user is responsible for organizing this communication with an explicit subroutine call. Our later QCD calculations and the *spin simulations* of Section 4.4 use the data-parallel software model on SIMD machines where a compiler can generate their messaging. Chapter 13 will mention later projects which are aimed at producing a uniform data parallel Fortran or C compiler which will generate the correct message structure for either SIMD or MIMD machines on such regular problems as QCD.

The calculations in Sections 4.3 and 4.4 used a wide variety of machines, in-house and commercial multicomputers, as well as the SIMD DAP and CM-2. The spin calculations in Section 4.4 can have very simple degrees of freedom, including that of the binary "spin" of the Ising model. These are naturally suited to the single-bit arithmetic available on the AMT DAP and CM-2. Some of the latest Monte Carlo algorithms do not use the local algorithms of Figure 4.4 but exploit the irregular domain structure seen in materials near a critical point. These new algorithms are much more efficient but very much more difficult to parallelize—especially on SIMD machines. They are discussed in Section 12.8. We also see a taste of the "embarrassingly parallel" problem structure of Chapter 7 in Section 4.4.

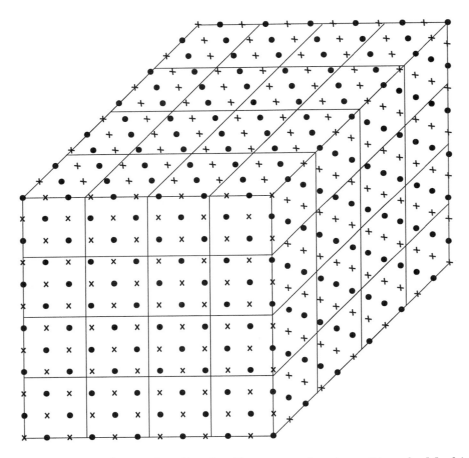

Figure 4.3: A 12^3 Problem Lattice Decomposed onto a 64-node Machine Arranged as a 4^3 Machine Lattice. Points labeled X ("red") or • ("black") can be updated at the same time.

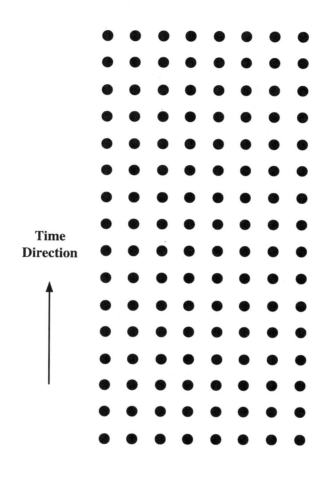

Time Direction

Gluon degrees of freedom (stored as matrix elements of 3x3 SU(3) matrix over complex numbers. This has eight independent degrees of freedom after ensuring matrix is a unitary and determinant one)

Figure 4.4: The 16 time and eight internal gluon degrees of freedom stored at each point shown in Figure 4.3

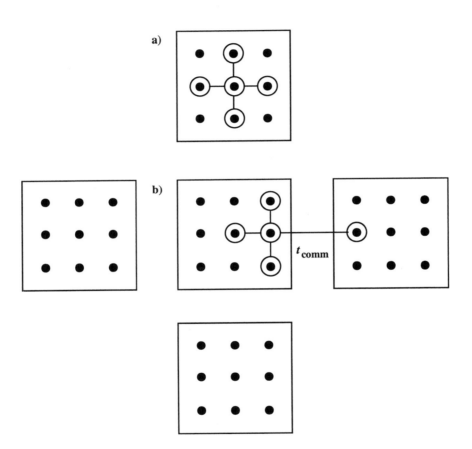

Figure 4.5: Template of a Local Update Involving No Communication in a) and the Value to be Communicated in b).

For the Potts simulation, we obtained parallelism not from the data domain (lattice of spins) but from different starting points for the evolution. This approach, described in more detail in Section 7.2, would not be practical for QCD with many degrees of freedom as one must have enough memory to store the full lattice in each node of the multicomputer.

Table 4.2 lists the early seismic simulations of the group led by Clayton, whose C³P work is reviewed in Section 18.1. These solved the elastic wave equations using finite difference methods as discussed in Section 3.5. The equations are iterated with time steps replacing the Monte Carlo iterations used above. This work is described in Chapters 5 and 7 of [Fox:88a] and represents methods that can tackle quite practical problems, for example, predicting the response of complicated geological structures such as the Los Angeles basin. The two-dimensional hydrodynamics work of Meier [Meier:88a] is computationally similar, using the regular decomposition and local update of Figures 4.3 and 4.5. These techniques are now very familiar and may seem "old-hat." However, it is worth noting that, as described in Chapter 13, we are only now in 1992 developing the compiler technology that will automate these methods developed "by-hand" by our early users. A much more sophisticated follow-on to these early seismic wave simulations is the ISIS interactive seismic imaging system described in Chapter 18.

Chapter 9 of [Fox:88a] explains the well-known synchronous implementation of long-range particle dynamics. This algorithm was not used directly in any large C³P application as we implemented the much more efficient cluster algorithms described in Sections 12.4, 12.5, and 12.8. The initial investigation of the vortex method of Section 12.5 used the $O(N^2)$ method [Harstad:87a]. We also showed a parallel database used in Kolawa's thesis on how a semi-analytic approach to QCD could be analyzed identically with the long-range force problem [Kolawa:86b;88a]. As explained in [Fox:88a], one can use the long-range force algorithm in any case where the calculation involves a set of N points with observables requiring functions of every pair of which there are N^2. In the language of Chapter 3, this problem has a system dimension of one, whatever its geometrical dimension. This is illustrated in Figures 4.6 and 4.7, which represent f_C in the form of Equations 3.10 and 3.13. We find $1/\beta = d_{num} = 2$ for the simple two-dimensional decompositions described for the Clayton and Meier applications for Table 4.2. We increase range of R "interaction" in Figure 4.7(a),(b)—defined formally by

$$\text{Calculation at } \underline{x} \text{ is a function of } (\underline{x}, \underline{y}) \text{ for all } \left|\underline{x} - \underline{y}\right| < R \qquad (4.1)$$

from small (nearest neighbor) R to $R = \infty$, the long-range force. As shown in Figure 4.7(a),(b), f_C decreases as R increases with the limiting form $\beta = d_{num} = 1$ independently of d_{geom} for $R = \infty$. Noederlinger [Lorenz:87a] and Theiler [Theiler:87a;87b] used such a "long-range" algorithm for calculating the correlation dimension of a chaotic dynamical system. This measures the essential number of degrees of freedom for a complex system which in this case was a time series becoming a plasma. The correction function involved studying histograms of $|\underline{x}(t_i) - \underline{x}(t_j)|$ over the data points $\underline{x}(t_i)$ at time t_i.

Fucito and Solomon [Fucito:85b;85f] studied a simple Coulomb gas which naturally had a long-range force. However, this was a Monte Carlo calculation that was implemented efficiently by an ingenious algorithm that cannot directly use the analysis of the particle dynamics (time-stepped) case shown in Figure 4.7. Monte Carlo is typically harder to parallelize than time evolution, where all "particles" can be evolved in time together. However, Monte Carlo updates can only proceed simultaneously if they involve disjoint particle sets. This implies the red-black ordering of Figure 4.5 and the requiring of a difficult asynchronous algorithm in the irregular melting problem of Section 14.2. Johnson's application was technically the hardest in our list of pioneers in Table 4.2.

Finally, Section 4.5 uses cellular automata ideas that lead to a synchronous architecture to grain dynamics, which, if implemented directly as in Section 9.2, would be naturally loosely synchronous. This illustrates that the problem architecture depends on the particular numerical approach.

4.3   Quantum Chromodynamics

4.3.1   Introduction

Quantum chromodynamics (QCD) is the proposed theory of the so-called strong interactions that bind quarks and gluons together to form hadrons—the constituents of nuclear matter such as the proton and neutron. It also mediates the forces between hadrons and thus controls the formation of nuclei. The fundamental properties of QCD cannot be directly tested, but a wealth of indirect evidence supports this theory. The problem is that QCD is a nonlinear theory that is not analytically solvable. For the equivalent quantum field theories of weaker forces such as electromagnetism, approximations using perturbation expansions in the interaction strength give very accurate results. However, since the QCD interaction is so strong, perturbative approximations often fail. Consequently, few precise predictions can

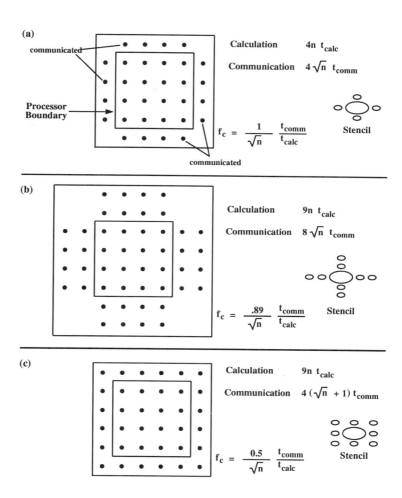

Figure 4.6: Some Examples of Communication Overhead as a Function of Increasing Range of Interaction R.

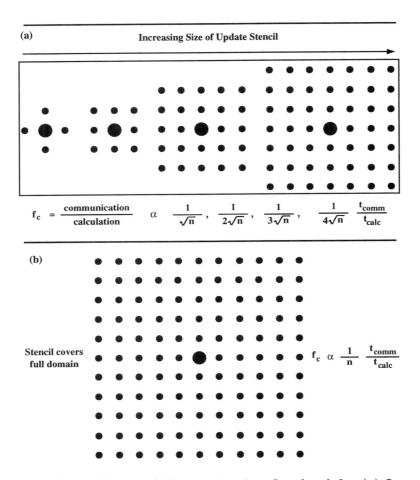

Figure 4.7: General Form of Communication Overhead for (a) Increasing and (b) Infinite Range R

be made from the theory. This led to the introduction of a non-perturbative approximation based on discretizing four-dimensional space-time onto a lattice of points, giving a theory called lattice QCD, which can be simulated on a computer.

Most of the work on lattice QCD has been directed towards deriving the masses (and other properties) of the large number of hadrons, which have been found in experiments using high energy particle accelerators. This would provide hard evidence for QCD as the theory of the strong force. Other calculations have also been performed; in particular, the properties of QCD at finite (i.e., non-zero) temperature and/or density have been determined. These calculations model the conditions of matter in the early stages of the evolution of the universe, just after the Big Bang. Lattice calculations of other quantum field theories, such as the theory of the weak nuclear force, have also been performed. For example, numerical calculations have given estimates for the mass of the Higgs boson, which is currently the Holy Grail of experimental high energy physics, and one of the motivating factors for the construction of the, now cancelled, $10 billion Superconducting Supercollider.

One of the major problems in solving lattice QCD on a computer is that the simulation of the quark interactions requires the computation of a large, highly non-local matrix determinant, which is extremely compute-intensive. We will discuss methods for calculating this determinant later. For the moment, however, we note that, physically, the determinant arises from the dynamics of the quarks. The simplest way to proceed is thus to ignore the quark dynamics and work in the so-called quenched approximation, with only gluonic degrees of freedom. This should be a reasonable approximation, at least for heavy quarks. However, even solving this approximate theory requires enormous computing power. Current state-of-the-art quenched QCD calculations are performed on lattices of size $24^3 \times 48$, which involves the numerical solution of a 21,233,664 dimensional integral. The only way of solving such an integral is by Monte Carlo methods.

4.3.2 Monte Carlo

In order to explain the computations for QCD, we use the Feynman path integral formalism [Feynman:65a]. For any field theory described by a Lagrangian density $\mathcal{L}$, the dynamics of the fields $\phi(x)$ are determined through the action functional

$$S(\phi) = \int dx \mathcal{L}(\phi). \tag{4.2}$$

In this language, the measurement of a physical observable represented by an operator $\mathcal{O}$ is given as the expectation value

$$\langle \mathcal{O}(\phi) \rangle = \frac{1}{Z} \int D\phi \mathcal{O}(\phi) e^{-S(\phi)}, \tag{4.3}$$

where the partition function Z is

$$Z = \int D\phi e^{-S(\phi)}. \tag{4.4}$$

In these expressions, the integral $D\phi$ indicates a sum over all possible configurations of the field ϕ. A typical observable would be a product of fields $\mathcal{O} = \phi(x)\phi(y)$, which says how the fluctuations in the field are correlated, and in turn, tells us something about the particles that can propagate from point x to point y. The appropriate correlation functions give us, for example, the masses of the various particles in the theory. Thus, to evaluate almost any quantity in field theories like QCD, one must simply evaluate the corresponding path integral. The catch is that the integrals range are over an infinite-dimensional space.

To put the field theory onto a computer, we begin by discretizing space and time into a lattice of points. Then the functional integral is simply defined as the product of the integrals over the fields at every site of the lattice $\phi(n)$:

$$\int D\phi \rightarrow \int \prod_n [d\phi(n)]. \tag{4.5}$$

Restricting space and time to a finite box, we end up with a finite (but very large) number of ordinary integrals, something we might imagine doing directly on a computer. However, the high dimensionality of these integrals renders conventional mesh techniques impractical. Fortunately, the presence of the exponential e^{-S} means that the integrand is sharply peaked in one region of configuration space. Hence, we resort to a statistical treatment and use Monte Carlo type algorithms to sample the important parts of the integration region [Binder:86a].

Monte Carlo algorithms typically begin with some initial configuration of fields, and then make pseudorandom changes on the fields such that the ultimate probability P of generating a particular field configuration ϕ is proportional to the Boltzmann factor,

$$P(\phi) = e^{-S(\phi)}, \tag{4.6}$$

where $S(\phi)$ is the action associated with the given configuration. There are several ways to implement such a scheme, but for many theories the simple Metropolis algorithm [Metropolis:53a] is effective. In this algorithm, a new configuration ϕ' is generated by updating a single variable in the old configuration ϕ and calculating the change in action (or energy)

$$\Delta S = S(\phi') - S(\phi). \tag{4.7}$$

If $\Delta S \leq 0$, the change is accepted; if $\Delta S > 0$, the change is accepted with probability $\exp(-\Delta S)$. In practice, this is done by generating a pseudorandom number r in the interval [0,1] with uniform probability distribution, and accepting the change if $r < \exp(-\Delta S)$. This is guaranteed to generate the correct (Boltzmann) distribution of configurations, provided "detailed balance" is satisfied. That condition means that the probability of proposing the change $\phi \rightarrow \phi'$ is the same as that of proposing the reverse process $\phi' \rightarrow \phi$. In practice, this is true if we never simultaneously update two fields which interact directly via the action. Note that this constraint has important ramifications for parallel computers as we shall see below.

Whichever method one chooses to generate field configurations, one updates the fields for some equilibration time of E steps, and then calculates the expectation value of $\mathcal{O}$ in Equation 4.3 from the next T configurations as

$$\langle \mathcal{O} \rangle = \frac{1}{T} \sum_{i=E+1}^{E+T} \mathcal{O}(\phi_i). \tag{4.8}$$

The statistical error in Monte Carlo behaves as $1/\sqrt{N}$, where N is the number of statistically independent configurations. $N = T/2\tau$, where τ is known as the autocorrelation time. This autocorrelation time can easily be large, and most of the computer time is spent in generating effectively independent configurations. The operator measurements then become a small overhead on the whole calculation.

4.3.3 QCD

QCD describes the interactions between quarks in high energy physics. Currently, we know of five types (referred to as "flavors") of quark: up, down, strange, charm, and bottom; and expect one more (top) to show up soon. In addition to having a "flavor," quarks can carry one of three possible charges known as "color" (this has nothing to do with color in the macroscopic world!); hence, quantum *chromo*dynamics. The strong color force is mediated by particles called gluons, just as photons mediate the electromagnetic force. Unlike photons, though, gluons themselves carry a color charge and, therefore, interact with one another. This makes QCD a nonlinear theory, which is impossible to solve analytically. Therefore, we turn to the computer for numerical solutions.

QCD is an example of a "gauge theory." These are quantum field theories that have a local symmetry described by a symmetry (or gauge) group. Gauge theories are ubiquitous in elementary particle physics: The electromagnetic interaction between electrons and photons is described by *quantum electrodynamics* (QED) based on the gauge group U(1); the strong force between quarks and gluons is believed to be explained by QCD based on the group SU(3); and there is a unified description of the weak and electromagnetic interactions in terms of the gauge group SU(2) × U(1). The strength of these interactions is measured by a coupling constant. This coupling constant is small for QED, so very precise analytical calculations can be performed using perturbation theory, and these agree extremely well with experiment. However, for QCD, the coupling appears to increase with distance (which is why we never see an isolated quark, since they are always bound together by the strength of the coupling between them). Perturbative calculations are therefore only possible at short distances (or large energies). In order to solve QCD at longer distances, Wilson [Wilson:74a] introduced lattice gauge theory, in which the space-time continuum is discretized and a discrete version of the gauge theory is derived which keeps the gauge symmetry intact. This discretization onto a lattice, which is typically hypercubic, gives a nonperturbative approximation to the theory that is successively improvable by increasing the lattice size and decreasing the lattice spacing, and provides a simple and natural way of regulating the divergences which plague perturbative approximations. It also makes the gauge theory amenable to numerical simulation by computer.

4.3.4 Lattice QCD

To put QCD on a computer, we proceed as follows [Wilson:74a], [Creutz:83a]. The four-dimensional space-time continuum is replaced by a four-dimensional hypercubic periodic lattice of size $N = N_s \times N_s \times N_s \times N_t$, with the quarks living on the sites and the gluons living on the links of the lattice. N_s is the spatial and N_t is the temporal extent of the lattice. The lattice has a finite spacing a. The gluons are represented by 3×3 complex SU(3) matrices associated with each link in the lattice. The 3 in SU(3) reflects the fact that there are three colors of quarks, and SU means that the matrices are unitary with unit determinant (i.e., "special unitary"). This link matrix describes how the color of a quark changes as it moves from one site to the next. For example, as a quark is transported along a link of the lattice it can change its color from, say, red to green; hence, a red quark at one end of the link can exchange colors with a green quark at the other end. The action functional for the purely gluonic part of QCD is

$$S_G = \beta \sum_P (1 - \frac{1}{3} ReTrU_P), \tag{4.9}$$

where β is a coupling constant and

$$U_P = U_{i,\mu} U_{i+\mu,\nu} U_{i+\nu,\mu}^\dagger U_{i,\nu}^\dagger \tag{4.10}$$

is the product of link matrices around an elementary square or plaquette on the lattice—see Figure 4.8. Essentially all of the time in QCD simulations of gluons is spent multiplying these SU(3) matrices together. The main component of this is the $a \times b + c$ kernel, which most supercomputers can do very efficiently. As the action involves interactions around plaquettes, in order to satisfy detailed balance we can update only half the links in any one dimension simultaneously, as shown in Figure 4.9 (in two dimensions for simplicity). The partition function for full-lattice QCD including quarks is

$$Z = \int D\psi D\bar{\psi} DU \exp(-S_G - \bar{\psi}(\not{D} + m)\psi), \tag{4.11}$$

where $\not{D} + m$ is a large sparse matrix the size of the lattice squared. Unfortunately, since the quark or fermion variables ψ are anticommuting Grassmann numbers, there is no simple representation for them on the computer. Instead, they must be integrated out, leaving a highly non-local fermion determinant:

$$Z = \int DU \det(\not{D} + m) \exp(-S_G). \tag{4.12}$$

This is the basic integral one wants to evaluate numerically.

The biggest stumbling block preventing large QCD simulations with quarks is the presence of the determinant $\det(\not{D} + m)$ in the partition function. There have been many proposals for dealing with the determinant.

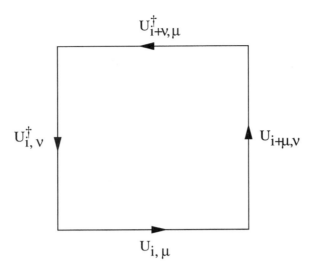

Figure 4.8: A Lattice Plaquette

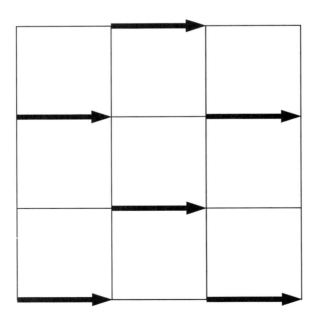

Figure 4.9: Updating the Lattice

The first algorithms tried to compute the change in the determinant when a single link variable was updated [Weingarten:81a]. This turned out to be prohibitively expensive. So instead, the approximate method of pseudofermions [Fucito:81a] was used. Today, however, the preferred approach is the so-called Hybrid Monte Carlo algorithm [Duane:87a], which is exact. The basic idea is to invent some dynamics for the variables in the system in order to evolve the whole system forward in (simulation) time, and then do a Metropolis accept/reject for the entire evolution on the basis of the total energy change. The great advantage is that the whole system is updated in one fell swoop. The disadvantage is that if the dynamics are not correct, the acceptance will be very small. Fortunately (and this is one of very few fortuitous happenings where fermions are concerned), good dynamics can be found: the Hybrid algorithm [Duane:85a]. This is a neat combination of the deterministic microcanonical method [Callaway:83a], [Polonyi:83a] and the stochastic Langevin method [Parisi:81a], [Batrouni:85a], which yields a quickly evolving, ergodic algorithm for both gauge fields and fermions. The computational kernel of this algorithm is the repeated solution of systems of equations of the form

$$(D\!\!\!/ + m)\phi = \eta, \tag{4.13}$$

where ϕ and η are vectors that live on the sites of the lattice. To solve these equations, one typically uses a conjugate gradient algorithm or one of its cousins, since the fermion matrix $(D\!\!\!/ + m)$ is sparse. For more details, see [Gupta:88a]. Such iterative matrix algorithms have as their basic component the $a \times b + c$ kernel, so again computers which do this efficiently will run QCD well.

4.3.5   Concurrent QCD Machines

Lattice QCD is truly a "grand challenge" computing problem. It has been estimated that it will take on the order of a TeraFLOP-year of dedicated computing to obtain believable results for the hadron mass spectrum in the quenched approximation, and adding dynamical fermions will involve many orders of magnitude more operations. Where is the computer power needed for QCD going to come from? Today, the biggest resources of computer time for research are the conventional supercomputers at the NSF and DOE centers. These centers are continually expanding their support for lattice gauge theory, but it may not be long before they are overtaken by several dedicated efforts involving concurrent computers. It is a revealing fact that the development of most high-performance parallel computers—the Caltech

Cosmic Cube, the Columbia Machine, IBM's GF11, APE in Rome, the Fermilab Machine and the PAX machines in Japan—was actually motivated by the desire to simulate lattice QCD [Christ:91a], [Weingarten:92a].

As described already, Caltech built the first hypercube computer, the Cosmic Cube or Mark I, in 1983. It had 64 nodes, each of which was an Intel 8086/87 microprocessor with 128 KB of memory, giving a total of about 2 MFLOPS (measured for QCD). This was quickly upgraded to the Mark II hypercube with faster chips, twice the memory per node, and twice the number of nodes in 1984. Then, QCD was run on the last internal Caltech hypercube, the 128-node Mark IIIfp (built by JPL), at 600 MFLOPS sustained [Ding:90b]. Each node of the Mark IIIfp hypercube contains two Motorola 68020 microprocessors, one for communication and the other for calculation, with the latter supplemented by one 68881 co-processor and a 32-bit Weitek floating point processor.

Norman Christ and Anthony Terrano built their first parallel computer for doing lattice QCD calculations at Columbia in 1984 [Christ:84a]. It had 16 nodes, each of which was an Intel 80286/87 microprocessor, plus a TRW 22-bit floating point processor with 1 MB of memory, giving a total peak performance of 256 MFLOPS. This was improved in 1987 using Weitek rather than TRW chips so that 64 nodes gave 1 GFLOPS peak. In 1989, the Columbia group finished building their third machine: a 256-node, 16 GFLOPS, lattice QCD computer [Christ:90a].

QCDPAX is the latest in the line of PAX (Parallel Array eXperiment) machines developed at the University of Tsukuba in Japan. The architecture is very similar to that of the Columbia machine. It is a MIMD machine configured as a two-dimensional periodic array of nodes, and each node includes a Motorola 68020 microprocessor and a 32-bit vector floating-point unit. Its peak performance is similar to that of the Columbia machine; however, it achieves only half the floating-point utilization for QCD code [Iwasaki:91a].

Don Weingarten initiated the GF11 project in 1984 at IBM. The GF11 is a SIMD machine comprising 576 Weitek floating point processors, each performing at 20 MFLOPS to give the total 11 GFLOPS peak implied by the name. Preliminary results for this project are given in [Weingarten:90a;92a].

The APE (Array Processor with Emulator) computer is basically a collection of 3081/E processors (which were developed by CERN and SLAC for use in high energy experimental physics) with Weitek floating-point processors attached. However, these floating-point processors are attached in a special way—each node has four multipliers and four adders, in order to optimize the $a \times b + c$ calculations, which form the major component of

Table 4.3: Peak and Real Performances in MFLOPS of "Homebrew" QCD Machines

Computer	Year	Nodes	Peak	Real
Caltech I	1983	64	3	2
Caltech II	1984	128	9	6
Caltech III	1989	128	2000	600
Columbia I	1984	16	256	20
Columbia II	1987	64	1000	200
Columbia III	1990	256	16000	7000
APE I	1986	4	256	20
APE II	1988	16	1000	200
APE III	1992	128	6000	5000
APE-100	1993	2048	100000	80000*
Fermilab I	1989	16	320	65
Fermilab II	1991	256	5000	1000
Fermilab III	1993	306	50000	10000*
IBM GF11	1992	512	10000	7000
QCDPAX	1992	480	14000	2500

*All real performances are measured except these predicted ones.

all lattice QCD programs. This means that each node has a peak performance of 64 MFLOPS. The first small machine—Apetto—was completed in 1986 and had four nodes yielding a peak performance of 256 MFLOPS. Currently, they have a second generation of this machine with 1 GFLOPS peak from 16 nodes. By 1993, the APE collaboration hopes to have completed the 100 GFLOPS 2048-node "Apecento," or APE-100, based on specialized VLSI chips that are software compatible with the original APE [Avico:89a], [Battista:92a]. The APE-100 is a SIMD machine with the architecture based on a three-dimensional cubic mesh of nodes. Currently, a 128-node machine is running with a peak performance of 6.4 GFLOPS.

Not to be outdone, Fermilab has also used its high energy experimental physics emulators to construct a lattice QCD machine called ACPMAPS. This is a MIMD machine, using a Weitek floating-point chip set on each node. A 16-node machine, with a peak rate of 320 MFLOPS, was finished in 1989. A 256-node machine, arranged as a 2^5 hypercube of crates, with eight nodes communicating through a crossbar in each crate, was completed in 1991 [Fischler:92a]. It has a peak rate of 5 GFLOPS, and a sustained rate of about 1 GFLOPS for QCD. An upgrade of ACPMAPS is planned, with the number of nodes being increased and the present processors being replaced with two Intel i860 chips per node, giving a peak performance of 160 MFLOPS per node. These performance figures are summarized in Table 4.3. (The "real" performances are the actual performances obtained on QCD codes.)

Major calculations have also been performed on commercial SIMD machines, first on the ICL Distributed Array Processor (DAP) at Edinburgh University during the period from 1982 to 1987 [Wallace:84a], and now on the TMC Connection Machine (CM-2); and on commercial distributed memory MIMD machines like the nCUBE hypercube and Intel Touchstone Delta machines at Caltech. Currently, the Connection Machine is the most powerful commercial QCD machine available, running full QCD at a sustained rate of approximately 5.3 GFLOPS on a 64 K CM-2 [Baillie:89e], [Brickner:91b]. However, simulations have recently been performed at a rate of 7.9 GFLOPS on the experimental Intel Touchstone Delta at Caltech. This is a MIMD machine made up of 528 Intel i860 processors connected in a two-dimensional mesh, with a peak performance of 41 GFLOPS for 32-bit arithmetic. These results compare favorably with performances on traditional (vector) supercomputers. Highly optimized QCD code runs at about 125 MFLOPS per processor on a CRAY Y-MP, or 1 GFLOPS on a fully configured eight-processor machine.

The generation of commercial parallel supercomputers, represented by the CM-5 and the Intel Paragon, have a peak performance of over 100 GFLOPS. There was a proposal for the development of a TeraFLOPS parallel supercomputer for QCD and other numerically intensive simulations [Christ:91a], [Aoki:91a]. The goal was to build a 2.6 TFLOPS machine based on the CM-5 architecture in collaboration with Thinking Machines Corporation, which would be ready by 1995 at a cost of around $40 million.

It is interesting to note that when the various groups began building their "home-brew" QCD machines, it was clear they would outperform all commercial (traditional) supercomputers; however, now that commercial parallel supercomputers have come of age [Fox:89n], the situation is not so obvious. To emphasize this, we describe QCD calculations on both the home grown Caltech hypercube and on the commercially available Connection Machine.

4.3.6 QCD on the Caltech Hypercubes

To make good use of MIMD distributed-memory machines like hypercubes, one should employ domain decomposition. That is, the domain of the problem should be divided into subdomains of equal size, one for each processor in the hypercube; and communication routines should be written to take care of data transfer across the processor boundaries. Thus, for a lattice calculation, the N sites are distributed among the $P = 2^d$ processors using a decomposition that ensures that processors assigned to adjacent subdomains are directly linked by a communication channel in the hypercube topology. Each processor then independently works through its subdomain of $n = N/P$ sites, updating each one in turn, and only communicating with neighboring processors when doing boundary sites. This communication enforces "loose synchronization," which stops any one processor from racing ahead of the others. Load balancing is achieved with equal-size domains. If the nodes contain at least two sites of the lattice, all the nodes can update in parallel, satisfying detailed balance, since loose synchronicity guarantees that all nodes will be doing black, then red sites alternately.

The characteristic timescale of the communication, t_{comm}, corresponds roughly to the time taken to transfer a single $SU(3)$ matrix from one node to its neighbor. Similarly, we can characterize the calculational part of the algorithm by a timescale, t_{calc}, which is roughly the time taken to multiply together two $SU(3)$ matrices. For all hypercubes built *without* floating-point accelerator chips, $t_{comm} << t_{calc}$ and, hence, QCD simulations are extremely "efficient," where efficiency ϵ (Equations 3.10 and 3.11) is defined by the relation

$$\epsilon = \frac{T_1}{k\,T_k}, \tag{4.14}$$

where T_k is the time taken for k processors to perform the given calculation. Typically, such calculations have efficiencies in the range $\epsilon \geq .90$, which means they are ideally suited to this type of computation since doubling the number of processors nearly halves the total computational time required for solution. However, as we shall see (for the Mark IIIfp hypercube, for example), the picture changes dramatically when fast floating-point chips are used; then $t_{comm} \simeq t_{calc}$ and one must take some care in coding to obtain maximum performance.

Rather than describe every calculation done on the Caltech hypercubes, we shall concentrate on one calculation that has been done several times as the machine evolved—the heavy quark potential calculation ("heavy" because the quenched approximation is used).

QCD provides an explanation of why quarks are confined inside hadrons, since lattice calculations reveal that the inter-quark potential rises linearly as the separation between the quarks increases. Thus, the attractive force (the derivative of the potential) is independent of the separation, unlike other forces, which usually decrease rapidly with distance. This force, called the "string tension," is carried by the gluons, which form a kind of "string" between the quarks. On the other hand, at short distances, quarks and gluons are "asymptotically free" and behave like electrons and photons, interacting via a Coulomb-like force. Thus, the quark potential V is written as

$$V(R) = -\frac{\alpha}{R} + \sigma R, \qquad (4.15)$$

where R is the separation of the quarks, α is the coefficient of the Coulombic potential and σ is the string tension. In fitting experimental charmonium data to this Coulomb plus linear potential, Eichten et al. [Eichten:80a] estimated that $\alpha = 0.52$ and $\sigma = 0.18\text{GeV}^2$. Thus, a goal of the lattice calculations is to reproduce these numbers. Enroute to this goal, it is necessary to show that the numbers from the lattice are "scaling," that is, if one calculates a physical observable on lattices with different spacings then one gets the same answer. This means that the artifacts due to the finiteness of the lattice spacing have disappeared and continuum physics can be extracted.

The first heavy quark potential calculation using a Caltech hypercube was performed on the 64-node Mark I in 1984 on a $12^3 \times 16$ lattice with β ranging from 5.8 to 7.6 [Otto:84a]. The value of α was found to be 0.25 and the string tension (converting to the dimensionless ratio) $\sqrt{\sigma}/\Lambda = 106$. The numbers are quite a bit off from the charmonium data but the string tension did appear to be scaling, albeit in the narrow window $6.0 \leq \beta \leq 6.4$.

The next time around, in 1986, the 128-node Mark II hypercube was used on a 20^4 lattice with $\beta = 6.1, 6.3, 6.5, 6.7$ [Flower:86b]. The dimensionless string tension decreased somewhat to 83, but clear violations of scaling were observed: The lattice was still too coarse to see continuum physics.

Therefore, the last (1989) calculation using the Caltech/JPL 32-node Mark IIIfp hypercube concentrated on one β value, 6.0, and investigated different lattice sizes: $24^3 \times 10$, $24^3 \times 12$, $12^3 \times 24$, $16^3 \times 24$ [Ding:90b]. Scaling was not investigated; however, the values of $\alpha = 0.58$ and $\sqrt{\sigma}/\Lambda = 77$, that is, $\sigma = 0.15\,\text{GeV}^2$, compare favorably with the charmonium data. This work is based on about 1300 CPU hours on the 32-node Mark IIIfp hypercube, which has a performance of roughly twice a CRAY X-MP processor.

The whole 128-node machine performs at 0.6 GFLOPS. As each node runs at 6 MFLOPS, this corresponds to a speedup of 100, and hence, an efficiency of 78 percent. These figures are for the most highly optimized code. The original version of the code written in C ran on the Motorola chips at 0.085 MFLOPS and on the Weitek chips at 1.4 MFLOPS. The communication time, which is roughly the same for both, is less than a 2 percent overhead for the former but nearly 30 percent for the latter. When the computationally intensive parts of the calculation are written in assembly code for the Weitek, this overhead becomes almost 50 percent. This 0.9 msec of communication, shown in lines two and three in Table 4.4, is dominated by the hardware/software message startup overhead (latency), because for the Mark IIIfp the node-to-node communication time, t_{comm}, is given by

$$t_{comm} \simeq (150 + 2 * W) \quad \mu\,\text{sec}, \tag{4.16}$$

where W is the number of words transmitted. To speed up the communication, we update all even (or odd) links (eight in our case) in each node, allowing us to transfer eight matrix products at a time, instead of just sending one in each message. This reduces the 0.9 msec by a factor of

$$\frac{8 * (150 + 18 * 2)}{150 + 8 * 18 * 2} = 3.4 \tag{4.17}$$

to 0.26 msec. On all hypercubes with fast floating-point chips—and on most hypercubes without these chips for less computationally intensive codes—such "vectorization" of communication is often important. In Figure 4.10, the speedups for many different lattice sizes are shown. For the largest lattice size, the speedup is 100 on the 128-node machine. The speedup is almost linear in number of nodes. As the total lattice volume increases, the speedup increases, because the ratio of calculation/communication increases. For more information on this performance analysis, see [Ding:90c].

4.3.7   QCD on the Connection Machine

The Connection Machine Model CM-2 is also very well suited for large scale simulations of QCD. The CM-2 is a distributed-memory, single-instruction, multiple-data (SIMD), massively parallel processor comprising up to 65536 (64 K) processors [Hillis:85a;87a]. Each processor consists of an arithmetic-logic unit (ALU), 8 Kbytes or 32 Kbytes of random-access memory (RAM), and a router interface to perform communications among the processors. There are 16 processors and a router per custom VLSI chip, with the chips

Table 4.4: Link Update Time (msec) on Mark IIIfp Node for Various Levels of Programming

Programming Level	Calc. Time	Comm. Time	Total Time	MFLOPS
1. Motorola MC68020/68881 in C	52	0.86	53	0.085
2. Weitek XL all in C	2.25	0.90	3.15	1.4
3. Weitek XL parts in Assembly	0.94	0.90	1.84	2.4
4. Weitek XL Assembly, vec. comm.	0.94	0.26	1.20	3.8
5. Weitek XL Assembly, no comm.	0.94	0.0	0.94	4.8

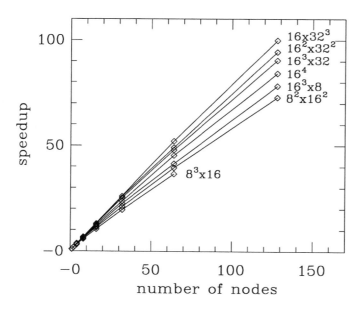

Figure 4.10: Speedups for QCD on the Mark IIIfp

interconnected as a 12-dimensional hypercube. Communications among processors within a chip work essentially like a crossbar interconnect. The router can do general communications, but only local communication is required for QCD, so we use the fast nearest-neighbor communication software called NEWS. The processors deal with one bit at a time. Therefore, the ALU can compute any two Boolean functions as output from three inputs, and all datapaths are one bit wide. In the current version of the Connection Machine (the CM-2), groups of 32 processors (two chips) share a 32-bit (or 64-bit) Weitek floating-point chip, and a transposer chip, which changes 32 bits stored bit-serially within 32 processors into 32 32-bit words for the Weitek, and vice versa.

The high-level languages on the CM, such as *Lisp and CM-Fortran, compile into an assembly language called Parallel Instruction Set (Paris). Paris regards the 64 K bit-serial processors as the fundamental units in the machine. However, floating-point computations are not very efficient in the Paris model. This is because in Paris, 32-bit floating-point numbers are stored "fieldwise"; that is, successive bits of the word are stored at successive memory locations of each processor's memory. However, 32 processors share one Weitek chip, which deals with words stored "slicewise"—that is, across the processors, one bit in each. Therefore, to do a floating-point operation, Paris loads in the fieldwise operands, transposes them slicewise for the Weitek (using the transposer chip), does the operation, and transposes the slicewise result back to fieldwise for memory storage. Moreover, every operation in Paris is an atomic process; that is, two operands are brought from memory and one result is stored back to memory, so no use is made of the Weitek registers for intermediate results. Hence, to improve the performance of the Weiteks, a new assembly language called CM Instruction Set (CMIS) has been written, which models the local architectural features much better. In fact, CMIS ignores the bit-serial processors and thinks of the machine in terms of the Weitek chips. Thus, data can be stored slicewise, eliminating all the transposing back and forth. CMIS allows effective use of the Weitek registers, creating a memory hierarchy, which, combined with the internal buses of the Weiteks, offers increased bandwidth for data motion.

When the arithmetic part of the program is rewritten in CMIS (just as on the Mark IIIfp when it was rewritten in assembly code), the communications become a bottleneck. Therefore, we need also to speed up the communication part of the code. On the CM-2, this is done using the "bi-directional multi-wire NEWS" system. As explained above, the CM chips (each containing

Table 4.5: Fermion Update Time (sec) on 64 K Connection Machine for
Various Levels of Programming

Programming Level	Calc. time Time	Comm. time Time	Total Time Time	MFLOPS
All in *Lisp	8.7	4.5	13.2	900
Inner Loop in CMIS	3.3	3.9	7.2	1600
Multi-wire CMIS	1.7	0.5	2.2	5300

16 processors) are interconnected in a 12-dimensional hypercube. However,
since there are two CM chips for each Weitek floating-point chip, the floating-
point hardware is effectively wired together as an 11-dimensional hypercube,
with two wires in each direction. This makes it feasible to do simultaneous
communications in both directions of all four space-time directions in QCD—
bidirectional multiwire NEWS—thereby reducing the communication time
by a factor of eight. Moreover, the data rearrangement necessary to make
use of this multiwire NEWS further speeds up the CMIS part of the code
by a factor of two.

In 1990–1992, the Connection Machine was the most powerful commercial QCD machine available: the "Los Alamos collaboration" ran full QCD
at a sustained rate of 5.3 GFLOPS on a 64 K CM-2 [Brickner:91a]. As was
the case for the Mark IIIfp hypercube, in order to obtain this performance,
one must resort to writing assembly code for the Weitek chips *and* for the
communication. Our original code, written entirely in the CM-2 version of
*Lisp, achieved around 1 GFLOPS [Baillie:89e]. As shown in Table 4.5, this
code spends 34 percent of its time doing communication. When we rewrote
the most computationally intensive part in the assembly language CMIS,
this rose to 54 percent. Then when we also made use of "multi-wire NEWS"
(to reduce the communication time by a factor of eight), it fell to 30 percent. The Intel Delta and Paragon, as well as Thinking Machines CM-5,
passed the CM-2 performance levels in 1993, but here optimization is not
yet complete [Gupta:93a].

4.3.8 Status and Prospects

The status of lattice QCD may be summed up as: under way. Already there have been some nice results in the context of the quenched approximation, but the lattices are still too coarse and too small to give definitive results. Results for full QCD are going to take orders of magnitude more computer time, but we now have an algorithm—Hybrid Monte Carlo—which puts real simulations within reach.

When will the computer power be sufficient? In Figure 4.11, we plot the horsepower of various QCD machines as a function of the year they started to produce physics results. The performance plotted in this case is the real sustained rate on actual QCD codes. The surprising fact is that the rate of increase is very close to exponential, yielding a factor of 10 every two years! On the same plot, we show our estimate of the computer power needed to redo correct quenched calculations on a 128^4 lattice. This estimate is also a function of time, due to algorithm improvements.

Extrapolating these trends, we see the outlook for lattice QCD is rather bright. Reasonable results for the phenomenologically interesting physical observables should be available within the quenched approximation in the mid-1990s. With the same computer power, we will be able to redo today's quenched calculations using dynamic fermions (but still on today's size of lattice). This will tell us how reliable the quenched approximation is. Finally, results for the full theory with dynamical fermions on a 128^4 lattice should follow early in the next century (!), when computers are two or three orders of magnitude more powerful.

4.4 Spin Models

4.4.1 Introduction

Spin models are simple statistical models of real systems, such as magnets, which exhibit the same behavior and hence provide an understanding of the physical mechanisms involved. Despite their apparent simplicity, most of these models are not exactly soluble by present theoretical methods. Hence, computer simulation is used. Usually, one is interested in the behavior of the system at a phase transition; the computer simulation reveals where the phase boundaries are, what the phases on either side are, and how the properties of the system change across the phase transition. There are two varieties of spins: discrete or continuous valued. In both cases, the spin

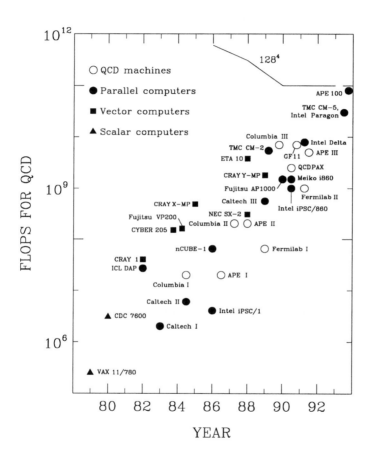

Figure 4.11: MFLOPS for QCD Calculations

variables are put on the sites of the lattice and only interact with their nearest neighbors. The partition function for a spin model is

$$Z = \int Ds \exp(S), \qquad (4.18)$$

with the action being of the form

$$S = \beta \sum_{\langle ij \rangle} (1 - s_i.s_j), \qquad (4.19)$$

where $\langle ij \rangle$ denotes nearest neighbors, s_i is the spin at site i, and β is a coupling parameter which is proportional to the interaction strength and inversely proportional to the temperature. A great deal of work has been done over the years in finding good algorithms for computer simulations of spin models; recently some new, much better, algorithms have been discovered. These so-called cluster algorithms are described in detail in Section 12.6. Here, we shall describe results obtained from using them to perform large-scale Monte Carlo simulations of several spin models—both discrete and continuous.

4.4.2 Ising Model

The Ising model is the simplest model for ferromagnetism that predicts phase transitions and critical phenomena. The spins are discrete and have only two possible states. This model, introduced by Lenz in 1920 [Lenz:20a], was solved in one dimension by Ising in 1925 [Ising:25a], and in two dimensions by Onsager in 1944 [Onsager:44a]. However, it has not been solved analytically in three dimensions, so Monte Carlo computer simulation methods have been one of the methods used to obtain numerical solutions. One of the best available techniques for this is the Monte Carlo Renormalization Group (MCRG) method [Wilson:80a], [Swendsen:79a]. The Ising model exhibits a second-order phase transition in $d = 3$ dimensions at a critical temperature T_c. As T approaches T_c, the correlation length ξ diverges as a power law with critical exponent ν:

$$\xi = \xi_0 (T/T_c - 1)^{-\nu} \qquad (4.20)$$

and the pair correlation function $G(r)$ at $T = T_c$ falls off to zero with distance r as a power law defining the critical exponent η:

$$G(r) = G_0 r^{-(d-2+\eta)}. \qquad (4.21)$$

T_c, ν and η determine the critical behavior of the 3-D Ising model and it is their values we wish to determine using MCRG.

In 1984, this was done by Pawley, Swendsen, Wallace and Wilson [Pawley:84a] in Edinburgh on the ICL DAP computer with high statistics. They ran on four lattice sizes—8^3, 16^3, 32^3 and 64^3—measuring seven even and six odd spin operators. We are essentially repeating their calculation on the new AMT DAP computer. Why should we do this? First, to investigate finite size effects—we have run on the biggest lattice used by Edinburgh, 64^3, and on a bigger one, 128^3. Second, to investigate truncation effects— qualitatively the more operators we measure for MCRG, the better, so we have included 53 even and 46 odd operators. Third, we are making use of the new cluster-updating algorithm due to Swendsen and Wang [Swendsen:87a], implemented according to Wolff [Wolff:89b]. Fourth, we would like to try to measure another critical exponent more accurately—the correction-to-scaling exponent ω, which plays an important role in the analysis.

The idea behind MCRG is that the correlation length diverges at the critical point, so that certain quantities should be invariant under "renormalization", which here means a transformation of the length scale. On the lattice, we can double the lattice size by, for example, "blocking" the spin values on a square plaquette into a single spin value on a lattice with 1/4 the number of sites. For the Ising model, the blocked spin value is given the value taken by the majority of the 4 plaquette spins, with a random tie-breaker for the case where there are 2 spins in either state. Since quantities are only invariant under this MCRG procedure at the critical point, this provides a method for finding the critical point.

In order to calculate the quantities of interest using MCRG, one must evaluate the spin operators S_α. In [Pawley:84a], the calculation was restricted to seven even spin operators and six odd; we evaluated 53 and 46, respectively [Baillie:91d]. Specifically, we decided to evaluate the most important operators in a $3 \times 3 \times 3$ cube [Baillie:88h]. To determine the critical coupling (or inverse temperature), K_c, one performs independent Monte Carlo simulations on a large lattice L of size M^3 and on smaller lattices S of size $(M/2^m)^3$, $m = 1, 2, \ldots$, and compares the operators measured on the large lattice blocked m times more than the smaller lattices. $K = K_c$ when they are the same. Since the effective lattice sizes are the same, unknown finite size effects should cancel. The critical exponents, y_a, are obtained directly from the eigenvalues, λ_a, of the stability matrix, $T_{\alpha\beta}$, which measures changes between different blocking levels, according to $\lambda_a = 2^{y_a}$. In particular, the leading eigenvalue y_t of $T_{\alpha\beta}$ for the even S_α gives ν from $y_5 = 1/\nu$, and, similarly, $y_h = (d + 2 - \eta)/2$ from the odd eigenvalue y_h of $T_{\alpha\beta}$.

The Distributed Array Processor (DAP) is a SIMD computer consisting of $D \times D$ bit-serial processing elements (PEs) configured as a cyclic two-dimensional grid with nearest-neighbor connectivity. The Ising model computer simulation is well suited to such a machine since the spins can be represented as single-bit (logical) variables. In three-dimensions, the system of spins is configured as an $M \times M \times M$ simple cubic lattice, which is "crinkle mapped" onto the $D \times D$ DAP by storing $N \times N$ pieces of each of M planes in each PE: $M \times M \times M = M \times (N \times D) \times (N \times D)$, with $N = M/D$. Our Monte Carlo simulation uses a hybrid algorithm in which each sweep consists of 10 standard Metropolis [Metropolis:53a] spin updates followed by one cluster update using Wolff's single-cluster variant of the Swendsen and Wang algorithm. On the 128^3 lattice, the autocorrelation time of the magnetization reduces from 73 ± 2 sets of 100 sweeps for Metropolis alone to 5.0 ± 0.2 sets of 10 Metropolis plus one cluster update for the hybrid algorithm. In order to measure the spin operators, S_α, the DAP code simply histograms the spin configurations so that an analysis program can later pick out each particular spin operator using a look-up table. Currently, the code requires the same time to do one histogram measurement, one Wolff single-cluster update or 100 Metropolis updates. Therefore, our hybrid of 10 Metropolis plus one cluster update takes about the same time as a measurement. On a DAP 510, this hybrid update takes on average 127 secs (13.5 secs) for the 128^3 (64^3) lattices. We have performed simulations on 64^3 and 128^3 lattices at two values of the coupling: $K_{nn} = 0.221654$ (Edinburgh's best estimate of the critical coupling) and $K_{nn} = 0.221644$. We accumulated 140 K measurements for each of the 128^3 simulations and 100 K for the 64^3 so that the total time used for this calculation is roughly 11,000 hours. For error analysis, this is divided into bins of 10 K measurements.

In analyzing our results, the first thing we have to decide is the order in which to arrange our 53 even and 46 odd spin operators. Naively, they can be arranged in order of increasing total distance between the spins [Baillie:88h] (as was done in [Pawley:84a]). However, the ranking of a spin operator is determined physically by how much it contributes to the energy of the system. Thus, we did our analysis initially with the operators in the naive order to calculate their energies, then subsequently we used the "physical" order dictated by these energies. This physical order of the first 20 even operators is shown in Figure 4.12 with 6 of Edinburgh's operators indicated; the 7th Edinburgh operator (E-6) is our 21st. This order is important in assessing the systematic effects of truncation, as we are going to analyze

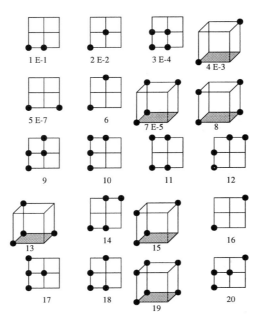

Figure 4.12: Our Order for Even Spin Operators

our data as a function of the number of operators included. Specifically, we successively diagonalize the 1×1, 2×2, ... , (53×53 for even, 46×46 for odd) stability matrix $T_{\alpha\beta}$ to obtain its eigenvalues and, thus, the critical exponents.

We present our results in terms of the eigenvalues of the even and odd parts of $T_{\alpha\beta}$. The leading even eigenvalue on the first four blocking levels starting from the 64^3 lattice is plotted against the number of operators included in the analysis in Figure 4.13, and on the first five blocking levels starting from the 128^3 lattice in Figure 4.14. Similarly, the leading odd eigenvalues for 64^3 and 128^3 lattices are shown in Figures 4.15 and 4.16, respectively. First of all, note that there are significant truncation effects—the value of the eigenvalues do not settle down until at least 30 and perhaps 40 operators are included. We note also that our value agrees with Edinburgh's when around 7 operators are included—this is a significant verification that the two calculations are consistent. With most or all of the operators included, our values on the two different lattice sizes agree, and the agreement improves with increasing blocking levels. Thus, we feel that we have overcome the finite size effects so that a 64^3 lattice is just large enough. However,

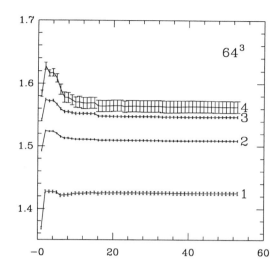

Figure 4.13: Leading Even Eigenvalue on 64^3 Lattice

the advantage in going to 128^3 is obvious in Figures 4.14 and 4.16: There, we can perform one more blocking, which reveals that the results on the fourth and fifth blocking levels are consistent. This means that we have eliminated most of the transient effects near the fixed point in the MCRG procedure. We also see that the main limitation of our calculation is statistics—the error bars are still rather large for the highest blocking level.

Now in order to obtain values for ν and η, we must extrapolate our results from a finite number of blocking levels to an infinite number. This is done by fitting the corresponding eigenvalues λ_t and λ_h according to

$$\lambda(n) = \lambda^* + a2^{-\omega n} \tag{4.22}$$

where λ^* is the extrapolated value and ω is the correction-to-scaling exponent. Therefore, we first need to calculate ω, which comes directly from the second leading even eigenvalue: $\omega = -y_{t,2}$. Our best estimate is in the interval $\omega = 0.80$–0.85, and we use the value 0.85 for the purpose of extrapolation, since it gives the best fits. The final results are $\nu = 0.624 \pm 0.001 \pm 0.002$, $\eta = 0.0262 \pm 0.0002 \pm 0.0030$, where the first errors are statistical and the second errors are estimates of the systematic error coming from the uncertainty in ω.

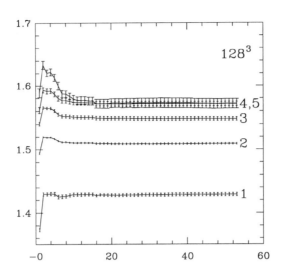

Figure 4.14: Leading Even Eigenvalue on 128^3 Lattice

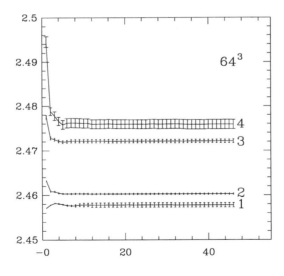

Figure 4.15: Leading Odd Eigenvalue on 64^3 Lattice

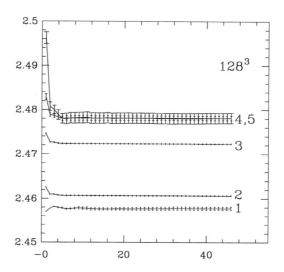

Figure 4.16: Leading Odd Eigenvalue on 128^3 Lattice

Finally, perhaps the most important number, because it can be determined the most accurately, is K_{nn}^c. By comparing the fifth blocking level on the 128^3 lattice to the fourth on the 64^3 lattice for both coupling values and taking a weighted mean, we obtain $K_{nn}^c = 0.221652 \pm 0.000003 \pm 0.000001$, where again the first error is statistical and the second is systematic.

Thus, MCRG calculations give us very accurate values for the three critical parameters K_{nn}^c, η, and ν, and give a reasonable estimate for ω. Each parameter is obtained independently and directly from the data. We have shown that truncation and finite-size errors at all but the highest blocking level have been reduced to below the statistical errors. Future high statistics simulations on 256^3 lattices will significantly reduce the remaining errors and allow us to determine the exponents very accurately.

4.4.3 Potts Model

The q-state Potts model [Potts:52a] consists of a lattice of spins σ_i, which can take q different values, and whose Hamiltonian is

$$H = K \sum_{\langle i, j \rangle} \delta_{\sigma_i \sigma_j}. \tag{4.23}$$

For $q = 2$, this is equivalent to the Ising model. The Potts model is thus a simple extension of the Ising model; however, it has a much richer phase structure, which makes it an important testing ground for new theories and algorithms in the study of critical phenomena [Wu:82a].

Monte Carlo simulations of Potts models have traditionally used local algorithms such as that of Metropolis, et al. [Metropolis:53a], however, these algorithms have the major drawback that near a phase transition, the autocorrelation time (the number of sweeps needed to generate a statistically independent configuration) increases approximately as L^2, where L is the linear size of the lattice. New algorithms have recently been developed that dramatically reduce this "critical slowing down" by updating clusters of spins at a time (these algorithms are described in Section 12.6). The original cluster algorithm of Swendsen and Wang (SW) was implemented for the Potts model [Swendsen:87a], and there is a lot of interest in how well cluster algorithms perform for this model. At present, there are very few theoretical results known about cluster algorithms, and theoretical advances are most likely to come from first studying the simplest possible models.

We have made a high statistics study of the SW algorithm and the single cluster Wolff algorithm [Wolff:89b], as well as a number of variants of these algorithms, for the $q = 2$ and $q = 3$ Potts models in two dimensions [Baillie:90n]. We measured the autocorrelation time τ in the energy (a local operator) and the magnetization (a global one) on lattice sizes from 8^2 to 512^2. About 10 million sweeps were required for each lattice size in order to measure autocorrelation times to within about 1 percent. From these values, we can extract the dynamic critical exponent z, given by $\tau(L) \sim L^z$, where $\tau(L)$ is measured at the infinite volume critical point (which is known exactly for the two-dimensional Potts model).

The simulations were performed on a number of different parallel computers. For lattice sizes of 128^2 or less, it is possible to run independent simulations on each processor of a parallel machine, enabling us to obtain 100 percent efficiency by running 10 or 20 runs for each lattice size in parallel, using different random number streams. These calculations were done using a 32-processor Meiko Computing Surface, a 20-processor Sequent Symmetry, a 20-processor Encore Multimax, and a 96-processor BBN GP1000 Butterfly, as well as a network of SUN workstations. The calculations ook approximately 15,000 processor-hours. For the largest lattice sizes, 256^2 and 512^2, a parallel cluster algorithm was required, due to the large amount of calculation (and memory) required. We have used the self-labelling algorithm described in Section 12.6, which gives fairly good efficiencies of about

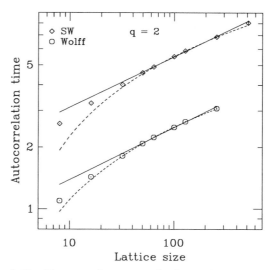

Figure 4.17: Energy Autocorrelation Times, $q = 2$

70 percent on the machines we have used (an nCUBE-1 and a Symult S2010), by doing multiple runs of 32 nodes each for the 256^2 lattice, and 64 nodes for 512^2. Since this problem does not vectorize, using all 512 nodes of the nCUBE gives a performance approximately five times that of a single processor CRAY X-MP, while all 192 nodes of the Symult is equivalent to about six CRAYs. The calculations on these machines have so far taken about 1000 hours.

Results for the autocorrelation times of the energy for the Wolff and SW algorithms are shown in Figure 4.17 for $q = 2$ and Figure 4.18 for $q = 3$. As can be seen, the Wolff algorithm has smaller autocorrelation times than SW. However, the dynamical critical exponents for the two algorithms appear to be identical, being approximately 0.25(1) and 0.57(1) for $q = 2$ and $q = 3$ respectively (shown as straight lines in Figures 4.17 and 4.18), compared to values of approximately 2 for the standard Metropolis algorithm.

Burkitt and Heermann [Heermann:90a] have suggested that the increase in the autocorrelation time is a logarithmic one, rather than a power law for the $q = 2$ case (the Ising model), that is, $z = 0$. Fits to this are shown as dotted lines in Figure 4.17. These have smaller χ^2 values than the power law fits, favoring logarithmic behavior. However, it is very difficult to dis-

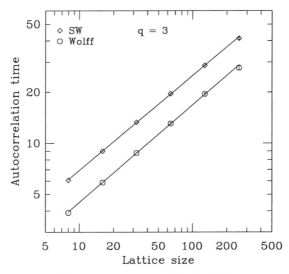

Figure 4.18: Energy Autocorrelation Times, $q = 3$

tinguish between a logarithm and a small power even on lattices as large as 512^2. In any case, the performance of the cluster algorithms for the Potts model is quite extraordinary, with autocorrelation times for the 256^2 lattice hundreds of times smaller than for the Metropolis algorithm. In the future, we hope to use the cluster algorithms to perform greatly improved Monte Carlo simulations of various Potts models, to study their critical behavior.

There is little theoretical understanding of why cluster algorithms work so well, and in particular there is no theory which predicts the dynamic critical exponents for a given model. These values can currently only be obtained from measurements using Monte Carlo simulation. Our results, which are the best currently available, are shown in Table 4.6. We would like to know why, for example, critical slowing down is virtually eliminated for the two-dimensional 2-state Potts model, but z is nearly one for the 4-state model; and why the dynamic critical exponents for the SW and Wolff algorithms are approximately the same in two dimensions, but very different in higher dimensions.

The only rigorous analytic result so far obtained for cluster algorithms was derived by Li and Sokal [Li:89a]. They showed that the autocorrelation time for the energy using the SW algorithm is bounded (as a function of the

Table 4.6: Measured Dynamic Critical Exponents for Potts Model Cluster Algorithms.

Dimension	q	z_Ei SW	z_E Wolff
2	2	0.25(1)*	0.25(1)*
3	2	0.54(2)	0.33(1)*
4	2	0.86(2)	0.25(1)*
2	3	0.55(1)	0.57(1)
2	4	0.87(1)	0.94(2)

*Asterisks indicate that the data is also consistent with a logarithmic divergence ($z_E = 0$).

lattice size) by the specific heat C_H, that is, $\tau_E \geq$ constant $\times C_H$, which implies that the corresponding dynamic critical exponent is bounded by $z_E \geq \alpha/\nu$, where α and ν are critical exponents measuring the divergence at the critical point of the specific heat and the correlation length, respectively. A similar bound has also been derived for the Metropolis algorithm, but with the susceptibility exponent substituted for the specific heat exponent.

No such result is known for the Wolff algorithm, so we have attempted to check this result empirically using simulation [Coddington:92a]. We found that for the Ising model in two, three, and four dimensions, the above bound appears to be satisfied (at least to a very good approximation); that is, there are constants a and b such that $\tau_E^W = a + b \times C_H$, and thus $z_E^W = \alpha/\nu$, for the Wolff algorithm.

This led us to investigate similar empirical relations between dynamic and static quantities for the SW algorithm. The power of cluster update algorithms comes from the fact that they flip large clusters of spins at a time. The average size of the largest SW cluster (scaled by the lattice volume), m, is an estimator of the magnetization for the Potts model, and the exponent β/ν characterizing the divergence of the magnetization has values which are similar to our measured values for the dynamic exponents of the SW algorithm. We therefore scaled the SW autocorrelations by m, and found that within the errors of the simulations, this gave either a constant (in three and four dimensions) or a logarithm (in two dimensions). This implies that the SW autocorrelations scale in the same way (up to logarithmic corrections) as the magnetization, that is, $z_{int,E}^{SW} = \beta/\nu$.

These simple empirical relations are very surprising, and if true, would be the first analytic results equating dynamic quantities, which are dependent on the Monte Carlo algorithm used, to static quantities, which depend only on the physical model. These relations could perhaps stem from the fact that the dynamics of cluster algorithms are closely linked to the physical properties of the system, since the Swendsen-Wang clusters are just the Coniglio-Klein-Fisher droplets which have been used to describe the critical behavior of these systems [Fisher:67a] [Coniglio:80a].

We are currently doing further simulations to check whether these relations hold up with larger lattices and better statistics, or whether they are just good approximations. We are also trying to determine whether similar results hold for the general q-state Potts model. However, we have thus far only been able to find simple relations for the $q = 2$ (Ising) model. This work is being done using both parallel machines (the nCUBE-1, nCUBE-2, and Symult S2010) and networks of DEC, IBM, and Hewlett-Packard workstations. These high-performance RISC workstations were especially useful in obtaining good results for the Wolff algorithm, which does not vectorize or parallelize, apart from the trivial parallelism we used in running independent simulations on different processors.

4.4.4   XY Model

The XY (or O(2)) model consists of a set of continuous valued spins regularly arranged on a two-dimensional square lattice. Fifteen years ago, Kosterlitz and Thouless (KT) predicted that this system would undergo a phase transition as one changed from a low-temperature spin wave phase to a high-temperature phase with unbound vortices. KT predicted an approximate transition temperature, T_c, and the following unusual exponential singularity in the correlation length and magnetic susceptibility:

$$\xi = a_\xi e^{b_\xi t^{-\nu}}, \qquad \chi = a_\chi e^{b_\chi t^{-\nu}}, \tag{4.24}$$

with

$$\nu = \frac{1}{2}, \qquad \eta = \frac{1}{4}, \tag{4.25}$$

where $t = (T - T_c)/T_c$ and the correlation function exponent η is defined by the relation $\chi = c\xi^{2-\eta}$.

Our simulation [Gupta:88a] was done on the 128-node FPS (Floating Point Systems) T-Series hypercube at Los Alamos. FPS software allowed the use of C with a software model similar (communication implemented

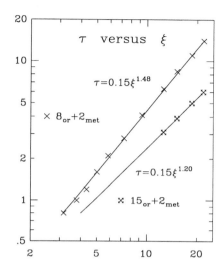

Figure 4.19: Autocorrelation Times for the XY Model

by subroutine call) to that used on the hypercubes at Caltech. Each FPS node is built around Weitek floating-point units, and we achieved 2 MFLOPS per node in this application. The total machine ran at $1/4$ GFLOPS, or at about twice the performance of one processor of a CRAY X-MP for this application. We use a $1 - D$ torus topology for communications, with each node processing a fraction of the rows. Each row is divided into red/black alternating sites of spins and the vector loop is over a given color. This gives a natural data structure of $(n \times 128)$ words for lattices of size $(n \times 256)$. The internode communications, in both lattice update and measurement of observables, can be done asynchronously and are a negligible overhead.

Previous numerical work was unable to confirm the KT theory, due to limited statistics and small lattices. Our high-statistics simulations are done on 64^2, 128^2, 256^2, and 512^2 lattices using a combination of over-relaxed and Metropolis algorithms which decorrelates as $\tau \approx 0.15\xi^{1.2}$. (For comparison, a Metropolis algorithm decorrelates as $\tau \approx 5\xi^2$.) Each configuration represents N_{or} over-relaxed sweeps through the lattice followed by N_{met} Metropolis sweeps. Measurement of observables is made on every configuration. The over-relaxed algorithm consists of reflecting the spin at a given site about Σ,

Table 4.7: Results of the XY Model Fits: (a) χ in T, and (b) ξ in T Assuming the KT Form. The fits KT1–3 are pseudominima while KT4 is the true minimum. All data points are included in the fits and we give the $\chi^2/_{dof}$ for each fit and an estimate of the exponent η.

	KT1	KT2	KT3	KT4
a_χ	2.155	0.270	0.784	0.2727(3)
b_χ	1.088	2.809	1.844	2.7734(5)
T_c	0.701	0.911	0.867	0.8987(1)
ν	1.460	0.472	0.701	0.4995(11)
$\chi^2/_{dof}$	73.0	13.2	1.82	1.70
a_ξ	0.708	0.228	0.441	0.2280(3)
b_ξ	0.740	1.693	1.100	1.6725(8)
T_c	0.689	0.910	0.867	0.8967(2)
ν	1.412	0.471	0.700	0.5007(3)
$\chi^2/_{dof}$	7.94	2.62	0.89	0.37
η	0.53	0.34	0.324	0.34

where Σ is the sum of the nearest-neighbor spins, that is,

$$s_{new} = \Sigma \, s_{old}^{\dagger} \, \Sigma. \tag{4.26}$$

This implementation [Creutz:87a], [Brown:87a] of the over-relaxed algorithm is microcanonical, and it reduces critical slowing down even though it is a local algorithm. The "hit" elements for the Metropolis algorithm are generated as $e^{i\theta}$, where θ is a uniform random number in the interval $[-\delta, \delta]$, and δ is adjusted to give an acceptance rate of 50 to 60 percent. The Metropolis hits make the algorithm ergodic, but their effectiveness is limited to local changes in the energy. In Figure 4.19, we show the autocorrelation time τ vs. the correlation length ξ; for $N_{or} = 8$, $N_{met} = 2$ we extract $\tau = 0.15\xi^{1.48}$, and for $N_{or} = 15$, $N_{met} = 2$ we get $\tau = 0.15\xi^{1.20}$.

We ran at 14 temperatures near the phase transition and made unconstrained fits to all 14 data points (four parameter fits according to Equation 4.24), for both the correlation length (Figure 4.20) and susceptibility (Figure 4.21). The key to the interpretation of the data is the fits. We find that fitting programs (e.g., MINUIT, SLAC) move incredibly slowly towards

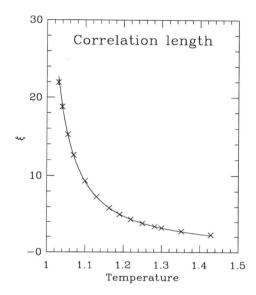

Figure 4.20: Correlation Length for the XY Model

the true minimum from certain points (which we label spurious minima), which, unfortunately, are the attractors for most starting points. We found three such spurious minima (KT1-3) and the true minimum KT4, as listed in Table 4.7.

Thus, our data was found to be in excellent agreement with the KT theory and, in fact, this study provides the first direct measurement of ν from both χ and ξ data that is consistent with the KT predictions.

4.4.5 O(3) Model

The XY model is the simplest O(N) model, having $N = 2$, the O(N) model being a set of rotors (N-component continuous valued spins) on an N-sphere. For $N \geq 3$, this model is asymptotically free [Polyakov:75a], and for $N = 3$, there exist so called instanton solutions. Some of these properties are analogous to those of gauge theories in four dimensions; hence, these models are interesting. In particular, the O(3) model in two dimensions should shed some light on the asymptotic freedom of QCD (SU(3)) in four dimensions. The predictions of the renormalization group for the susceptibility χ and in-

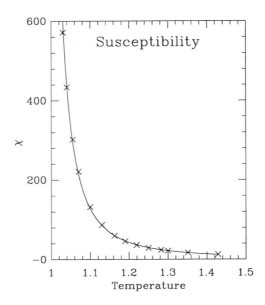

Figure 4.21: Susceptibility for the XY Model

verse correlation length (i.e., mass gap) m in the O(3) model are [Brezin:76a]

$$\chi = C\beta^{-4} \exp\left(4\pi\beta\right)\left(1 + O(1/\beta)\right) \qquad (4.27)$$

and

$$m = \frac{1}{\xi} = C'\beta \exp\left(-2\pi\beta\right)\left(1 + O(1/\beta)\right), \qquad (4.28)$$

respectively. If m and χ vary according to these equations, without the correction of order $1/\beta$, they are said to follow asymptotic scaling. Previous work was able to confirm that this picture is qualitatively correct, but was not able to probe deep enough in the area of large correlation lengths to obtain good agreement.

The combination of the over-relaxed algorithm and the computational power of the FPS T-Series allowed us to simulate lattices of sizes up to 1024^2. We were thus able to simulate at coupling constants that correspond to correlation lengths up to 300, on lattices where finite-size effects are negligible. We were also able to gather large statistics and thus obtain small statistical errors. Our simulation is in good agreement with similar cluster calculations [Wolff:89b;90a]. Thus, we have validated and extended these

Table 4.8: Coupling Constant, Lattice Size, Autocorrelation Time, Number of Overrelaxed Sweeps, Susceptibility, and Correlation Length for the O(3) Model

Beta	L,T	τ	N_{or}	χ		ξ
1.50	256	1.3	12	176.4 $\pm$	0.2	11.1
1.60	256	2.5	12	448.4 $\pm$	0.7	19.0
1.70	256	7.0	12	1263 $\pm$	3	34.4
	512	1.8	35	1264 $\pm$	3	34.4
1.75	768	1.8	50	2197 $\pm$	15	47.2
1.80	512	3.5	40	3850 $\pm$	10	64.7
	768	3.0	45	3820 $\pm$	20	64.5
1.85	768	2.3	80	6730 $\pm$	25	88.7
1.90	1024, 512	2.0	150	11600 $\pm$	60	121.5
	1024	1.5	200	11870 $\pm$	60	122.7
1.95	1024	1.7	200	20640 $\pm$	310	164.8
2.00	1024	1.7	250	35100 $\pm$	400	224.3
2.05	1024	1.7	300	56220 $\pm$	550	295.6

results in a regime where our algorithm is the only known alternative to clustering.

We have made extensive runs at 10 values of the coupling constant. At the lowest β, several hundred thousand sweeps were collected, while for the largest values of β, between 50,000 and 100,000 sweeps were made. Each sweep consists of between 10 iterations through the lattice at the former end and 150 iterations at the latter. The statistics we have gathered are equivalent to about 200 days, use of the full 128-node FPS machine.

Our results for the correlation length and susceptibility for each coupling β and lattice size are shown in Table 4.8. The autocorrelation times are also shown. The quantities measured on different-sized lattices at the same β agree, showing that the infinite volume limit has been reached.

To compare the behavior of the correlation length and susceptibility with the asymptotic scaling predictions, we use the "correlation length defect" δ_ξ and "susceptibility defect" δ_χ, which are defined as follows: $\delta_\xi = \beta(e^{-2\pi\beta})\xi$, $\delta_\chi = \beta^4(e^{-4\pi\beta})\chi$, so that asymptotic scaling is seen if δ_ξ, δ_χ go to constants as $\beta \to \infty$. These defects are shown in Figures 4.22 and 4.23, respectively.

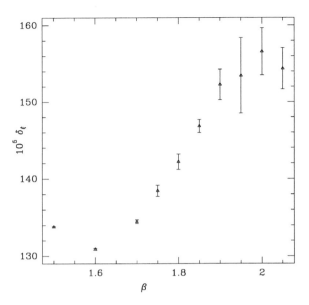

Figure 4.22: Correlation Length Defect Versus the Coupling Constant for the O(3) Model

It is clear that asymptotic scaling does not set in for $\beta < 2$, but it is not possible to draw a clear conclusion for $\beta > 2$—though the trends of the last two or three points may be toward constant behavior.

We gauged the speed of the algorithm in producing statistically independent configurations by measuring the autocorrelation time τ. We used this to estimate the dynamical critical exponent z, which is defined by $\tau = c \cdot \xi^z$. For constant $N_{or} = 12$, our fits give $z = 1.33(1)$. However, we discovered that by increasing N_{or} in rough proportion to ξ, we can improve the performance of the algorithm significantly. To compare the speed of decorrelation between runs with different N_{or}, we define a new quantity, which we call "effort," $e = N_{or} \times \tau$. This measures the computational effort expended to obtain a decorrelated configuration. We define a new exponent z' from $e \sim \xi^{z'}$, where N_{or} is chosen to keep τ constant. We also found that the behavior of the decorrelation time can be approximated over a good range by

$$\tau = C'' \cdot \xi^z \cdot N_{or}^{-z/z'}. \tag{4.29}$$

A fit to the set of points $(N_{or}, \xi, \tau > 1.0)$ gives $z = 1.301 \pm 0.012$, $z' = 1.079 \pm 0.010$. Thus, z' is significantly lower than z. Figure 4.24 shows τ

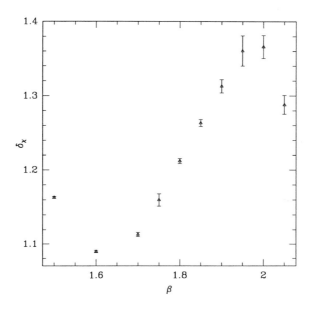

Figure 4.23: Susceptibility Defect Versus the Coupling Constant for the O(3) Model

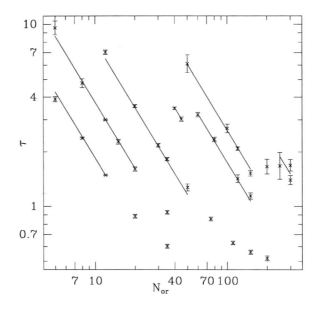

Figure 4.24: Decorrelation Time τ Versus Number of Over-relations Sweeps N_{or} for Different Values of β

versus N_{or}, with the fits shown as solid lines.

4.5   An Automata Model of Granular Materials

4.5.1   Introduction

Physical systems comprised of discrete, macroscopic particles or grains which are not bonded to one another are important in civil, chemical, and agricultural engineering, as well as in natural geological and planetary environments. Granular systems are observed in rock slides, sand dunes, clastic sediments, snow avalanches, and planetary rings. In engineering and industry they are found in connection with the processing of cereal grains, coal, gravel, oil shale, and powders, and are well known to pose important problems associated with the movement of sediments by streams, rivers, waves, and the wind.

The standard approach to the theoretical modelling of multiparticle systems in physics has been to treat the system as a continuum and to formulate the model in terms of differential equations. As an example, the science of soil mechanics has traditionally focussed mainly on quasi-static granular systems, a prime objective being to define and predict the conditions under which failure of the granular soil system will occur. Soil mechanics is a macroscopic continuum model requiring an explicit constitutive law relating, for example, stress and strain. While very successful for the low-strain quasi-static applications for which it is intended, it is not clear how it can be generalized to deal with the high-strain, explicitly time-dependent phenomena which characterize a great many other granular systems of interest. Attempts at obtaining a generalized theory of granular systems using a differential equation formalism [Johnson:87a] have met with limited success.

An alternate approach to formulating physical theories can be found in the concept of cellular automata, which was first proposed by Von Neumann in 1948. In this approach, the space of a physical problem would be divided up into many small, identical cells each of which would be in one of a finite number of states. The state of a cell would evolve according to a rule that is both local (involves only the cell itself and nearby cells) and universal (all cells are updated simultaneously using the same rule).

The Lattice Grain Model [Gutt:89a] (LGrM) we discuss here is a microscopic, explicitly time-dependent, cellular automata model, and can be applied naturally to high-strain events. LGrM carries some attributes of both particle dynamics models [Cundall:79a], [Haff:87a;87b], [Walton:84a],

[Werner:87a] (PDM), which are based explicitly on Newton's second law, and lattice gas models [Frisch:86a], [Margolis:86a] (LGM), in that its fundamental element is a discrete particle, but differs from these substantially in detail. Here we describe the essential features of LGrM, compare the model with both PDM and LGM, and finally discuss some applications.

4.5.2　Comparison to Particle Dynamics Models

The purpose of the lattice grain model is to predict the behavior of large numbers of grains (10,000 to 1,000,000) on scales much larger than a grain diameter. In this respect, it goes beyond the particle dynamics calculations of Section 9.2, which are limited to no more than $\sim 10,000$ grains by currently available computing resources [Cundall:79a], [Haff:87a;87b], [Walton:84a], [Werner:87a]. The particle dynamics models follow the motion of each individual grain exactly, and may be formulated in one of two ways depending upon the model adopted for particle-particle interactions.

In one formulation, the interparticle contact times are assumed to be of finite duration, and each particle may be in simultaneous contact with several others [Cundall:79a], [Haff:87a], [Walton:84a], [Werner:87a]. Each particle obeys Newton's law, $F = ma$, and a detailed integration of the equations of motion of each particle is performed. In this form, while useful for applications involving a much smaller number of particles than LGrM allows, PDM cannot compete with LGrM for systems involving large numbers of grains because of the complexity of PDM "automata."

In the second, simpler formulation, the interparticle contact times are assumed to be of infinitesimal duration, and particles undergo only binary collisions (the hard-sphere collisional models) [Haff:87b]. Hard-sphere models usually rely upon a collision-list ordering of collision events to avoid the necessity of checking all pairs of particles for overlaps at each time step. In regions of high particle number density, collisions are very frequent; and thus in problems where such high-density zones appear, hard-sphere models spend most of their time moving particles through very small distances using very small time steps. In granular flow, zones of stagnation where particles are very nearly in contact much of the time, are common, and the hard-sphere model is therefore unsuitable, at least in its simplest form, as a model of these systems. LGrM avoids these difficulties because its time-stepping is controlled, not by a collision list but by a scan frequency, which in turn is a function of the speed of the fastest particle and is independent of number density. Furthermore, although fundamentally a collisional model, LGrM can also mimic the behavior of consolidated or stagnated zones of granular material in a manner which will be described.

4.5.3   Comparison to Lattice Gas Models

LGrM closely resembles LGM [Frisch:86a], [Margolis:86a] in some respects. First, for two-dimensional applications, the region of space in which the particles are to move is discretized into a triangular lattice-work, upon each node of which can reside a particle. The particles are capable of moving to neighboring cells at each tick of the clock, subject to certain simple rules. Finally, two particles arriving at the same cell (LGM) or adjacent cells (LGrM) at the same time, may undergo a "collision" in which their outgoing velocities are determined according to specified rules chosen to conserve momentum.

Each of the particles in LGM has the same magnitude of velocity and is allowed to move in one of six directions along the lattice, so that each particle travels exactly one lattice spacing in each time step. The single-velocity magnitude means that all collisions between particles are perfectly elastic and that energy conservation is maintained simply through particle number conservation. It also means that the temperature of the gas is uniform throughout time and space, thus limiting the application of LGM to problems of low Mach number. An exclusion principle is maintained in which no two particles of the same velocity may occupy one lattice point. Thus, each lattice point may have no more than six particles, and the state of a lattice point can be recorded using only six bits.

LGrM differs from LGM in that it has many possible velocity states, not just six. In particular, in LGrM not only the direction but the magnitude of the velocity can change in each collision. This is a necessary condition because the collision of two macroscopic particles is always inelastic, so that mechanical energy is not conserved. The LGrM particles satisfy a somewhat different exclusion principle: No more than one particle at a time may occupy a single site. This exclusion principle allows LGrM to capture some of the volume-filling properties of granular material—in particular, to be able to approximate the behavior of static granular masses.

The determination of the time step is more critical in LGrM than in LGM. If the time step is long enough that some particles travel several lattice spacings in one clock tick, the problem of finding the intersection of particle trajectories arises. This involves much computation and defeats the purpose of an automata approach. A very short time step would imply that most particles would not move even a single lattice spacing. Here we choose a time step such that the fastest particle will move exactly one lattice spacing. A "position offset" is stored for each of the slower particles, which are moved accordingly when the offset exceeds one-half lattice spacing. These extra requirements for LGrM automata imply a slower computation speed than expected in LGM simulations; but, as a dividend, we can compute inelastic grain flows of potential engineering and geophysical interest.

4.5.4 The Rules for the Lattice Grain Model

In order to keep the particle-particle interaction rules as simple as possible, all interparticle contacts, whether enduring contacts or true collisions, will be modelled as collisions. Collisions that model enduring contacts will transmit, in each time step, an impulse equal to the force of the enduring contact multiplied by the time step. The fact that collisions take place between particles on adjacent lattice nodes means that some particles may undergo up to six collisions in a time step. For simplicity, these collisions will be resolved as a series of binary collisions. The order in which these collisions are calculated at each lattice node, as well as the order in which the lattice nodes are scanned, is now an important consideration.

The rules of the Lattice Grain Model may be summarized as follows:

1. The particles reside on the nodes of a two-dimensional triangular lattice, obeying the exclusion principle that no node may have more than one particle.

2. Each particle has two components of velocity, which may take on any value. At the beginning of each time step, each particle's velocity is incremented due to the acceleration of gravity.

3. The size of each time step is set so that the fastest particle will travel one lattice spacing in that time step.

4. Two components of a "position offset" are maintained for each particle. This offset is incremented after the velocities in each time step according to gravitational acceleration and the particle's velocity:

$$\Delta q_i = v_i \Delta t + \frac{1}{2} g_i \Delta t^2 \qquad (4.30)$$

where:

$$
\begin{aligned}
i &= 1,2; \\
\Delta q_i &= ith \text{ component of increment in position offset;} \\
v_i &= ith \text{ component of particle velocity;} \\
g_i &= ith \text{ component of gravitational acceleration;} \\
\Delta t &= \text{current time step.}
\end{aligned}
$$

Once the offset exceeds half the distance to the nearest lattice node, and that node is empty, the particle is moved to that node, and its offset is decremented appropriately. Also, in a collision, the component of the offset along the line connecting the centers of the colliding particles is set to zero.

5. The order in which the lattice is scanned is chosen so as not to create a coupling between the scan pattern and the particle motions. Thus, the particle position updates are done on every third lattice point of every third row, with this pattern being repeated nine times to cover all lattice sites.

6. Particle collisions are calculated assuming that they are smooth hard disks with a given coefficient of restitution. Particles on adjacent nodes are assumed to collide if their relative velocity is bringing them to- gether. The following order has been adopted for evaluating possible collisions on odd time steps: 3b, 3c, 3f, 2f, 2c, 2b, 4b, 4c, 4f, 1f, 1c, 1b; and for even time steps: 1b, 1c, 1f, 4f, 4c, 4b, 2b, 2c, 2f, 3f, 3c, 3b (where the lattice numbers and collision directions are defined in Figure 4.25).

7. In order to incorporate a container, wall, or other barrier within these rules, a second type of particle is introduced—the wall particle. This particle is similar to the movable particles, and interacts with them through binary collisions (with a separately defined inelasticity), but is regarded as having infinite mass. To allow for the introduction of shearing motion from a wall (as in a Couette flow problem), the parti- cles making up the wall are given a common constant velocity, which is used in the usual fashion for calculating the results of collisions. However, the position of the wall particles in the lattice remains fixed throughout the simulation.

8. Though a single particle does not accurately predict the trajectory of a single grain, we still regard each particle as representing one grain

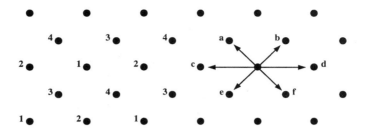

Figure 4.25: Definition of Lattice Numbers and Collision Directions

when we are extracting information from the simulation regarding the behavior of groups of grains. Thus, the size of one particle, as well as the spacing between lattice points, is taken to be one grain-diameter.

The transmission of "static" contact forces within a mass of grains (as in grains at rest in a gravitational field) is handled naturally within the above framework. Though a particle in a static mass of grains may be nominally at rest, its velocity may be nonzero (due to gravitational or pressure forces); and it will transmit the appropriate force (in the form of an impulse) to the particles under it by means of collisions. When these impulses are averaged over several time steps, the proper weights and pressures will emerge.

4.5.5 Implementation on a Parallel Computer

When implementing this algorithm on a computer, what is stored in the computer's memory is information concerning each point in the lattice, regardless of whether or not there is a particle at that lattice point. This allows for very efficient checking of the space around each particle for the presence of other particles (i.e., information concerning the six adjacent points in a triangular lattice will be found at certain known locations in memory). The need to keep information on empty lattice points in memory does not entail as great a penalty as might be thought; many lattice grain model problems involve a high density of particles, typically one for every one to four lattice points, and the memory cost per lattice point is not large. The memory requirements for the implementation of LGrM as described here are five variables per lattice site: two components of position, two of velocity, and one status variable, which denotes an empty site, an occupied site, or a bounding "wall" particle. If each variable is stored using four bytes of memory, then each lattice point requires 20 bytes.

The standard configuration for a simulation consists of a lattice with a specified number of rows and columns bounded at the top and bottom by two rows of wall particles (thus forming the top and bottom walls of the problem space), and with left and right edges connected together to form periodic boundary conditions. Thus, the boundaries of the lattice are handled naturally within the normal position updating and collision rules, with very little additional programming. (Note: Since the gravitational acceleration can point in an arbitrary direction, the top and bottom walls can become side walls for chute flow. Also, the periodic boundary conditions can be broken by the placement of an additional wall, if so desired.)

Because of the nearest-neighbor type interactions involved in the model, the computational scheme was well suited to an nCUBE parallel processor. For the purpose of dividing up the problem, the hypercube architecture is unfolded into a two-dimensional array, and each processor is given a roughly equal-area section of the lattice. The only interaction between sections will be along their common boundaries; thus, each processor will only need to exchange information with its eight immediate neighbors. The program itself was written in C under the Cubix/CrOS III operating system.

4.5.6   Simulations

The LGrM simulations performed so far have involved from $\sim 10^4$ to 10^6 automata. Trial application runs included two-dimensional, vertical, time-dependent flows in several geometries, of which two examples are given here: Couette flow and flow out of an hourglass-shaped hopper.

The standard Couette flow configuration consists of a fluid confined between two flat parallel plates of infinite extent, without any gravitational accelerations. The plates move in opposite directions with velocities that are equal and parallel to their surfaces, which results in the establishment of a velocity gradient and a shear stress in the fluid. For fluids that obey the Navier-Stokes equation, an analytical solution is possible in which the velocity gradient and shear stress are constant across the channel. If, however, we replace the fluid by a system of inelastic grains, the velocity gradient will no longer necessarily be constant across the channel. Typically, stagnation zones or plugs form in the center of the channel with thin shear-bands near the walls. Shear-band formation in flowing granular materials was analyzed earlier by Haff and others [Haff:83a], [Hui:84a] based on kinetic theory models.

The simulation was carried out with 5760 grains, located in a channel 60

(a)

(b)

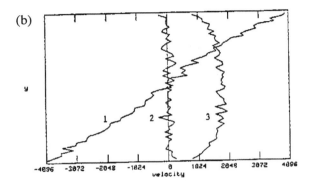

Figure 4.26: (a) Elastic Particle Couette Flow; (b) x-component (1), y-component (2), and Second Moment (3) of Velocity

lattice points wide by 192 long. Due to the periodic boundary conditions at the left and right ends, the problem is effectively infinite in length. The first simulation is intended to reproduce the standard Couette flow for a fluid; consequently, the particle-particle collisions were given a coefficient of restitution of 1.0 (i.e., perfectly elastic collisions) and the particle-wall collisions were given a .75 coefficient of restitution. The inelasticity of the particle-wall collisions is needed to simulate the conduction of heat (which is being generated within the fluid) from the fluid to the walls. The simulation was run until an equilibrium was established in the channel (Figure 4.26(a)). The average x- and y-components of velocity and the second moment of velocity, as functions of distance across the channel, are plotted in Figure 4.26(b).

The second simulation used a coefficient of restitution of .75 for both the particle-particle and particle-wall collisions. The equilibrium results are shown in Figure 4.27(a) and (b). As can be seen from the plots, the flow consists of a central region of particles compacted into a plug, with each

(a)
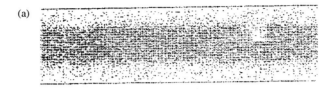

(b)
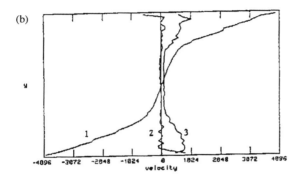

Figure 4.27: (a) Inelastic Particle Couette Flow; (b) x-component (1), y-component (2), and Second Moment (3) of Velocity.

particle having almost no velocity. Near each of the moving walls, a region of much lower density has formed in which most of the shearing motion occurs. Note the increase in value of the second moment of velocity (the granular "thermal velocity") near the walls, indicating that grains in this area are being "heated" by the high rate of shear. It is interesting to note that these flows are turbulent in the sense that shear stress is a quadratic, not a linear, function of shear rate.

In the second problem, the flow of grains through a hopper or an hourglass with an opening only a few grain diameters wide, was studied; the driving force was gravity. This is an example of a granular system which contains a wide range of densities, from groups of grains in static contact with one another to groups of highly agitated grains undergoing true binary collisions. Here, the number of particles used was 8310, and the lattice was

240 points long by 122 wide. Additional walls were added to form the sloped sides of the bin and to close off the bottom of the lattice to prevent the periodic boundary conditions from reintroducing the falling particles back into the bin (Figure 4.28(a)). This is a typical feature of automata modelling. It is often easier to configure the simulation to resemble a real experiment—in this case by explicitly "catching" spent grains—than by reprogramming the basic code to erase such particles.

The hourglass flow in Figure 4.28(b) showed internal shear zones, regions of stagnation, free-surface evolution toward an angle of repose, and an exit flow rate approximately independent of pressure head, as observed experimentally [Tuzun:82a]. It is hard to imagine that one could solve a partial differential equation describing such a complex, multiple-domain, time-dependent problem, even if the right equation were known (which is not the case).

4.5.7 Conclusion

These exploratory numerical experiments show that an automata approach to granular dynamics problems can be implemented on parallel computing machines. Further work remains to be done to assess more quantitatively how well such calculations reflect the real world, but the prospects are intriguing.

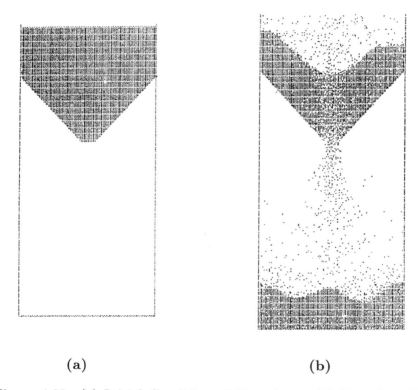

(a)   (b)

Figure 4.28: (a) Initial Condition of Hourglass; (b) Hourglass Flow after
2048 Time Steps

Chapter 5

Express and CrOS — Loosely Synchronous Message Passing

5.1 Multicomputer Operating Systems

As already noted in Chapter 2, the initial software used by C^3P was called CrOS, although its modest functionality hardly justified CrOS being called an operating system. Actually, this is an interesting issue. In our original model, the "real" operating system (UNIX in our case) ran on the "host" that directly or indirectly (via a network) connected to the hypercube. The nodes of the parallel machine need only provide the minimal services necessary to support user programs. This is the natural mode for all SIMD systems and is still offered by several important MIMD multicomputers. However, systems such as the IBM SP-1, Intel's Paragon series, and Meiko's CS-1 and 2 offer a full UNIX (or equivalent, such as MACH) on each node. This has many advantages, including the ability of the system to be arbitrarily configured—in particular we can consider a multicomputer with N nodes as "just" N "real" computers connected by a high-performance network. This would lead to particularly good performance on remote disk I/O, such as that needed for the Network File System (NFS). The design of an operating system for the node is partly based on the programming usage paradigm, and partly on the hardware. The original multicomputers all had small node memories (128 Kbytes on the Cosmic Cube) and could not possibly hold UNIX on a node. Current multicomputers such as the CM-5, Paragon, and Meiko CS-2 would consider 32 Mbytes a normal minimum node memory. This is easily sufficient to hold a full UNIX implementation with the extra functionality needed to support parallel programming. There are some, such as IBM Owego (Execube), Seitz at Caltech (MOSAIC) [Seitz:90a;92a], and Dally at MIT (J Machine) [Dally:90a;92a], who are developing very interesting families of highly parallel "small node" multicomputers for which a full UNIX on each node may be inappropriate.

Essentially, all the applications described in this book are not sensitive to these issues, which would only affect the convenience of program development and operating environment. C^3P's applications were all developed using a simple message-passing system involving C (and less often Fortran) node programs that sent messages to each other via subroutine call. The key function of CrOS and Express, described in Section 5.2, was to provide this subroutine library.

There are some important capabilities that a parallel computing environment needs in addition to message passing and UNIX services. These include:

- scheduling of multiple users—at its simplest, this is provided by space sharing with distinct sets of nodes assigned to individual users. More sophisticated time sharing is also becoming available.

- performance visualization or profiling—the C^3P tool is described in Section 5.4.

- load balancing—this is still not well understood at the operating system level, although at the data (user) level the situation is much clearer. C^3P research is summarized in Chapter 11 and Section 15.2.

- parallel input/output—this topic needs a more elaborate discussion given below.

We did not perform any major computations in C^3P that required high-speed input/output capabilities. This reflects both our applications mix and the poor I/O performance of the early hypercubes. The applications described in Chapter 18 needed significant but not high bandwidth input/output during computation, as did our analysis of radio astronomy data. However, the other applications used input/output for checkpointing, interchange of parameters between user and program, and in greatest volume, checkpoint and restart. This input/output was typically performed between the host and (node 0 of) the parallel ensemble. Section 5.2.7 and in greater detail [Fox:88a] describe the Cubix system, which we developed to make this input/output more convenient. This system was overwhelmingly preferred by the C^3P community as compared to the conventional host-node programming style. Curiously, Cubix seems to have made no impact on the "real world." We are not aware of any other group that has adopted it.

5.2   A "Packet" History of Message-passing Systems

The evolution of the various message-passing paradigms used on the Caltech/JPL machines involved three generations of hypercubes and many different software concepts, which ultimately led to the development of *Express*, a general, asynchronous buffered communication system for heterogeneous multiprocessors.

Originally designed, developed, and used by scientists with applications-oriented research goals, the Caltech/JPL system software was written to generate near-term needed capability. Neither hindered nor helped by any preconceptions about the type of software that should be used for parallel processing, we simply built useful software and added it to the system library.

Hence, the software evolved from primitive hardware-dependent implementations into a sophisticated runtime library, which embodied the concepts of "loose synchronization," domain decomposition, and machine independence. By the time the commercial machines started to replace our homemade hypercubes, we had evolved a programming model that allowed us to develop and debug code effectively, port it between different parallel computers, and run with minimal overheads. This system has stood the test of time and, although there are many other implementations, the functionality of CrOS and Express appears essentially correct. Many of the ideas described in this chapter, and the later *Zipcode* System of Section 16.1, are embodied in the current message-passing standards activity, MPI [Walker:94a]. A detailed description of CrOS and Express will be found in [Fox:88a] and [Angus:90a], and is not repeated here.

How did this happen?

5.2.1 Prehistory

The original hypercubes described in Chapter 20, the Cosmic Cube
[Seitz:85a], and Mark II [Tuazon:85a] machines, had been designed and built
as exploratory devices. We expected to be able to do useful physics and, in
particular, were interested in high-energy physics. At that time, we were
merely trying to extract exciting physics from an untried technology. These
first machines came equipped with "64-bit FIFOs," meaning that at a software level, two basic communication routines were available:

```
rdELT(packet, chan)
wtELT(packet, chan).
```

The latter pushed a 64-bit "packet" into the indicated hypercube channel,
which was then extracted with the rdELT function. If the read happened
before the write, the program in the reading node stopped and waited for
the data to show up. If the writing node sent its data before the reading
node was ready, it similarly waited for the reader.

To make contact with the world outside the hypercube cabinet, a node
had to be able to communicate with a "host" computer. Again, the FIFOs
came into play with two additional calls:

```
rdIH(packet)
wtIH(packet),
```

which allowed node 0 to communicate with the host.

This rigidly defined behavior, executed on a hypercubic lattice of nodes,
resembled a crystal, so we called it the *Crystalline Operating System* (CrOS).
Obviously, an operating system with only four system calls is quite far removed from most people's concept of the breed. Nevertheless, they were the
only system calls available and the name stuck.

5.2.2 Application-driven Development

We began to build algorithms and methods to exploit the power of parallel computers. With little difficulty, we were able to develop algorithms
for solving partial differential equations [Brooks:82b], FFTs [Newton:82a],
[Salmon:86b], and high-energy physics problems described in the last chapter [Brooks:83a].

As each person wrote applications, however, we learned a little more
about the way problems were mapped onto the machines. Gradually, additional functions were added to the list to download and upload data sets

from the outside world and to combine the operations of the rdELT and wtELT functions into something that exchanged data across a channel.

In each case, these functions were adopted, not because they seemed necessary to complete our operating system, but because they fulfilled a real need. At that time, debugging capabilities were nonexistent; a mistake in the program running on the nodes merely caused the machine to stop running. Thus, it was beneficial to build up a library of routines that performed common communication functions, which made reinventing tools unnecessary.

5.2.3   Collective Communication

Up to this point, our primary concern was with communication between neighboring processors. Applications, however, tended to show two fundamental types of communication: local exchange of boundary condition data, and global operations connected with control or extraction of physical observables.

As seen from the examples in this book, these two types of communication are generally believed to be fundamental to all scientific problems—the modelled application usually has some structure that can be mapped onto the nodes of the parallel computer and its structure induces some regular communication pattern. A major breakthrough, therefore, was the development of what have since been called the "collective" communication routines, which perform some action across all the nodes of the machine.

The simplest example is that of "broadcast"—a function that enabled node 0 to communicate one or more packets to all the other nodes in the machine. The routine "concat" enabled each node to accumulate data from every other node, and "combine" let us perform actions, such as addition, on distributed data sets. The routine combine is often called a *reduction* operator.

The development of these functions, and the natural way in which they could be mapped to the hypercube topology of the machines, led to great increases in both productivity on the part of the programmers and efficiency in the execution of the algorithms. CrOS quickly grew to a dozen or more routines.

5.2.4 Automated Decomposition—whoami

By 1985, the Mark II machine was in constant use and we were beginning to examine software issues that had previously been of little concern. Algorithms, such as the standard FFT, had obvious implementations on a hypercube [Salmon:86b], [Fox:88a]—the "bit-twiddling" done by the FFT algorithm could be mapped onto a hypercube by "twiddling" the bits in a slightly revised manner. More problematic was the issue of two- or three-dimensional problem solving. A two- or three-dimensional problem could easily be mapped into a small number of nodes. However, one cannot so easily perform the mapping of grids onto 128 nodes connected as a seven-dimensional hypercube.

Another issue that quickly became apparent was that C^3P users did not have a good feel for the "chan" argument used by the primitive communication functions. Users wanted to think of a collection of processors each labelled by a number, with data exchanged between them, but unfortunately the software was driven instead by the hypercube architecture of the machine. Tolerance of the explanation of "Well, you XOR the processor number with one shifted left by the ..." was rapidly exceeded in all but the most stubborn users.

Both problems were effectively removed by the development of whoami [Salmon:84b]. We used the well-known techniques of binary grey codes to automate the process of mapping two, three, or higher dimensional problems to the hypercube. The whoami function took the dimensionality of the physical system being modelled and returned all the necessary "chan" values to make everything else work out properly. No longer did the new user have to spend time learning about channel numbers, XORing, and the "mapping problem"—everything was done by the call to whoami. Even on current hardware, where long-range communication is an accepted fact, the techniques embodied by whoami result in programs that can run up to an order of magnitude faster than those using less convenient mapping techniques (see Figure 5.1).

5.2.5 "Melting"—a Non-crystalline Problem

Up to this point, we had concentrated on the most obvious scientific problems: FFTs, ordinary and partial differential equations, matrices, and so on, which were all characterized by their amenability to the lock step, short-range communication primitives available. Note that some of these, such as

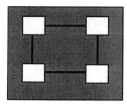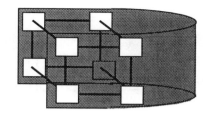

Figure 5.1: Mapping a Two-dimensional World

the FFT and matrix algorithms, are not strictly "nearest neighbor" in the sense of the communication primitives discussed earlier, since they require data to be distributed to nodes further than one step away. These problems, however, are amenable to the "collective communication" strategies.

Based on our success with these problems, we began to investigate areas that were not so easily cast into the crystalline methodology. A long-term goal was the support of event-driven simulations, database machines, and transaction-processing systems, which did not appear to be crystalline.

In the shorter term, we wanted to study the physical process of "melting" [Johnson:86a] described in Section 14.2. The melting process is different from the applications described thus far, in that it inherently involves some indeterminacies—the transition from an ordered solid to a random liquid involves complex and time-varying interactions. In the past, we had solved such an irregular problem—that of N-body gravity [Salmon:86b] by the use of what has since been called the "long-range-force" algorithm [Fox:88a]. This is a particularly powerful technique and leads to highly efficient programs that can be implemented with crystalline commands.

The melting process differs from the long-range force algorithm in that the interactions between particles do not extend to infinity, but are localized to some domain whose size depends upon the particular state of the solid/fluid. As such, it is very wasteful to use the long-range force technique, but the randomness of the interactions makes a mapping to a crystalline algorithm difficult (see Figure 5.2).

To address these issues effectively, it seemed important to build a communication system that allowed messages to travel between nodes that were not necessarily connected by "channels," yet didn't need to involve all nodes collectively.

At this point, an enormous number of issues came up—routing, buffering, queueing, interrupts, and so on. The first cut at solving these problems was

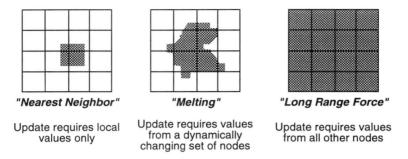

Figure 5.2: Interprocessor Communication Requirements

a system that never acquired a real name, but was known by the name of
its central function, "rdsort" [Johnson:85a]. The basic concept was that a
message could be sent from any node to any other node, at any time, and
the receiving node would have its program *interrupted* whenever a message
arrived. At this point, the user provided a routine called "rdsort" which,
as its name implies, needed to read, sort and process the data.

While simple enough in principle, this programming model was not initially adopted (although it produced an effective solution to the melting
problem). To users who came from a number-crunching physics background,
the concept of "interrupts" was quite alien. Furthermore, the issues of sorting, buffering, mutual exclusion, and so on, raised by the asynchronous nature of the resulting programs, proved hard to code. Without debugging
tools, it was extremely hard to develop programs using these techniques.
Some of these ideas were taken further by the Reactive Kernel [Seitz:88b]
(see Section 16.2), which do not, however, implement "reaction" with an
interrupt level handler. The recent development of active messages on the
CM-5 has shown the power of the rdsort concepts [Eiken:92a].

5.2.6   The Mark III

The advent of the Mark III machine [Peterson:85a] generated a rapid development in applications software. In the previous five years, the crystalline
system had shown itself to be a powerful tool for extracting maximum performance from the machines, but the new Mark III encouraged us to look
at some of the "programmability" issues, which had previously been of secondary importance.

The first and most natural development was the generalization of the

CrOS system for the new hardware [Johnson:86c], [Kolawa:86d]. Christened "CrOS III," it allowed us the flexibility of arbitrary message lengths (rather than multiples of the FIFO size), hardware-supported collective communication—the Mark III allowed hardware support of simultaneous communication down multiple channels, which allowed fast cube and sub-cube broadcast [Fox:88a]. All of these enhancements, however, maintained the original concept of nearest-neighbor (in a hypercube) communication supported by collective communication routines that operated throughout (or on a subset of) the machine. In retrospect, the hypercube's specific nature of CrOS should *not* have been preserved in the major redesign of CrOS III.

5.2.7 Host Programs

At this point, the programming model for the machines remained pretty much as it had been in 1982. A program running on the host computer loaded an application into the hypercube nodes, and then passed data back and forth with routines similar in nature to the `rdIH` and `wtIH` calls described earlier. This remained the only method through which the nodes could communicate with the outside world.

During the Mark II period, it had quickly become apparent that most users were writing host programs that, while differing in detail, were identical in outline and function. An early effort to remove from the user the burden of writing yet another host program was a system called C3PO [Meier:84b], which had a generic host program providing a shell in which subroutines could be executed in the nodes. Essentially, this model freed the user from writing an explicit host program, but still kept the locus of control in the host.

Cubix [Salmon:87a] reversed this. The basic idea was that the parallel computer, being more powerful than its host, should play the dominant role. Programs running in the nodes should decide for themselves what actions to take and merely instruct the host machine to intercede on their behalf. If, for example, the node program wished to read from a file, it should be able to tell the host program to perform the appropriate actions to open the file and read data, package it up into messages, and transmit it back to the appropriate node. This was a sharp contrast to the older method in which the user was effectively responsible for each of these actions.

The basic outcome was that the user's host programs were replaced with a standard "file-server" program called `cubix`. A set of library routines were then created with a single protocol for transactions between the node programs and `cubix`, which related to such common activities as opening, reading and writing files, interfacing with the user, and so on.

This change produced dramatic results. Now, the node programs could contain calls to such useful functions as `printf`, `scanf`, and `fopen`, which had previously been forbidden. Debugging was much easier, albeit in the old-fashioned way of "let's print everything and look at it." Furthermore, programs no longer needed to be broken down into "host" and "node" pieces and, as a result, parallel programs began to look almost like the original sequential programs.

Once file I/O was possible from the individual nodes of the machine, graphics soon followed through Plotix [Flower:86c], resulting in the development system shown in the heart of the family tree (5.3). The ideas embodied in this set of tools—CrOS III, Cubix, and Plotix—form the basis of the vast majority of C^{3}P parallel programs.

5.2.8   A Ray Tracer—and an "Operating System"

While the radical change that led to Cubix was happening, the non-crystalline users were still developing alternative communication strategies. As mentioned earlier, `rdsort` never became popular due to the burden of bookkeeping that was placed on the user and the unfamiliarity of the interrupt concept.

The "9 routines" [Johnson:86a] attempted to alleviate the most burdensome issues by removing the interrupt nature of the system and performing buffering and queueing internally. The resultant system was a simple generalization of the `wtELT` concept, which replaced the "channel" argument with a processor number. As a result, messages could be sent to non-neighboring nodes. An additional level of sophistication was provided by associating a "type" with each message. The recipient of the messages could then sort incoming data into functional categories based on this type.

The benefit to the user was a simplified programming model. The only remaining problem was how to handle this new found freedom of sending messages to arbitrary destinations.

We had originally planned to build a ray tracer from the tools developed while studying melting. There is, however, a fundamental difference between the melting process and the distributed database searching that goes on in a ray tracer. Ray tracing is relatively simple if the whole model can be stored in each processor, but we were considering the case of a geometric database

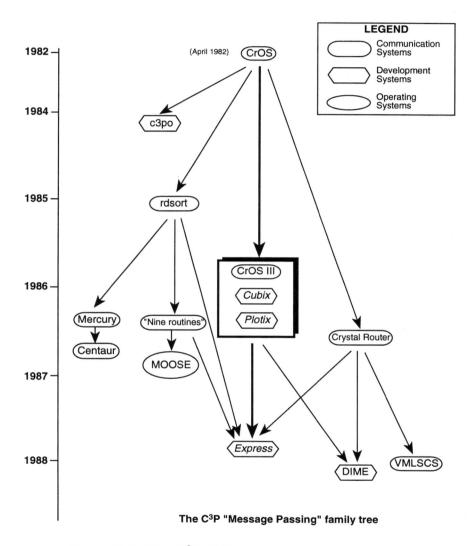

Figure 5.3: The C^{3}P "Message-passing" Family Tree

larger than this.

Melting posed problems because the exact nature of the interaction was known only statistically—we might need to communicate with all processors up to two hops away from our node, or three hops, or some indeterminate number. Other than this, however, the problem was quite homogeneous, and every node could perform the same tasks as the others.

The database search is inherently non-deterministic and badly load-balanced because it is impossible to map objects into the nodes where they will be used. As a result, database queries need to be directed through a tree structure until they find the necessary information and return it to the calling node.

A suitable methodology for performing this kind of exercise seemed to be a real multitasking system where "processes" could be created and destroyed on nodes in a dynamic fashion which would then map naturally onto the complex database search patterns. We decided to create an operating system.

The crystalline system had been described, at least in the written word, as an operating system. The concept of writing a real operating system with file systems, terminals, multitasking, and so on, was clearly impossible while communication was restricted to single hops across hypercube channels. The new system, however, promised much more. The result was the "Multitasking, Object-Oriented, Operating System" (MOOOS, commonly known as MOOSE) [Salmon:86a]. The follow-up MOOS II is described in Section 15.2.

The basic idea was to allow for multitasking—running more than one process per node, with remote task creation, scheduling, semaphores, signals—to include everything that a real operating system would have. The implementation of this system proved quite troublesome and strained the capabilities of our compilers and hardware beyond their breaking points, but was nothing by comparison with the problems encountered by the users.

The basic programming model was of simple, "light weight" processes communicating through message box/pipe constructs. The overall structure was vaguely reminiscent of the standard UNIX multiprocessing system; **fork/exec** and pipes (Figure 5.4). Unfortunately, this was by now completely alien to our programmers, who were all more familiar with the crystalline methods previously employed. In particular, problems were encountered with naming. While a process that created a child would automatically know its child's "ID," it was much more difficult for siblings to identify each other, and hence, to communicate. As a natural result, it was reasonably

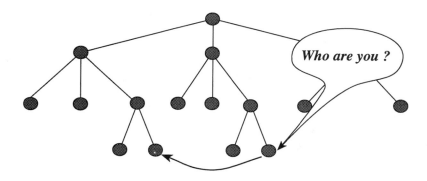

A "MOOSE" process tree
(Only processes connected by lines automatically know about each other)

Figure 5.4: A "MOOSE" Process Tree

easy to build tree structures but difficult to perform domain decompositions. Despite these problems, useful programs were developed including the parallel ray tracer with a distributed database that had originally motivated the design [Goldsmith:86a;87a].

An important problem was that architectures offered no memory protection between the lightweight processes running on a node. One had to guess how much memory to allocate to each process, which complicated debugging when the user guessed wrong. Later, the Intel iPSC implemented the hardware memory protection, which made life simpler ([Koller:88b] and Section 15.2).

In using MOOSE, we wanted to explore dynamic load-balancing issues. A problem with standard domain decompositions is that irregularities in the work loads assigned to processors lead to inefficiencies since the entire simulation, proceeding in lock step, executes at the speed of the slowest node. The *Crystal Router*, developed at the same time as MOOSE, offered a simpler strategy.

5.2.9   The Crystal Router

By 1986, we began to classify our algorithms in order to generalize the performance models and identify applications that could be expected to perform well using the existing technology. This led to the idea of "loosely synchronous" programming.

The central concept is one in which the nodes compute for a while, then synchronize and communicate, continually alternating between these two types of activities. This computation model was very well-suited to our crystalline communication system, which enforced synchronization automatically. In looking at some of the problems we were trying to address with our asynchronous communication systems (The "9 routines" and MOOSE), we found that although the applications were not naturally loosely synchronous at the level of the individual messages, they followed the basic pattern at some higher level of abstraction.

In particular, we were able to identify problems in which it seemed that messages would be generated at a fairly uniform rate, but in which the moment when the data had to be physically delivered to the receiving nodes was synchronized. A load balancer, for example, might use some type of simulated-annealing [Flower:87a] or neural-network [Fox:88e] approach, as seen in Chapter 11, to identify work elements that should be relocated to a different processor. As each decision is made, a message can be generated to tell the receiving node of its new data. It would be inefficient, however, to physically send these messages one at a time as the load-balancing algorithm progresses, especially since the results need only be acted upon once the load-balancing cycle has completed.

We developed the Crystal Router to address this problem [Fox:88a;88h]. The idea was that messages would be buffered on their node of origin until a synchronization point was reached when a single system call sent every message to its destination in one pass. The results of this technology were basically twofold.

- Since the messages were accumulated locally and then sent en masse, much longer communication streams were generated than would be the case if each message were sent individually. As a result, the effects of latency were minimized.

- The act of sending the messages involved all the nodes of the machine at once, so that messages could be routed to nodes other than those to which direct connections existed.

The resultant system had some of the attractive features of the "9 routines," in that messages could be sent between arbitrary nodes. But it maintained the high efficiency of the crystalline system by performing all its internode communications synchronously. A glossary of terms used is in Figure 5.5.

Message Passing Glossary

Asynchronous Communication

The style of communication in which a node is free to send messages to any other node at any time and regardless of hardware interconnectivity.

Blocking and Non-Blocking Communication

In the blocking style, receive operations suspend the calling program until a suitable message has arrived. In the non-blocking style, a read returns immediately with (typically) a status code indicating whether or not a suitable message has arrived. Message send operations usually return as soon as the data is safely "in transit," whether or not it has been received.

Collective Communication

High-level communication calls that carry out send/receive operations on groups of nodes, e.g., broadcast or multicast. These routines free the user from determining the optimal method to carry out such communications and if efficiently implemented result in large performance gains.

Crystalline Communication

The style in which a node reading or writing a message is blocked until the matching operation is performed in target node. Messages can only be sent/received to processors connected by hardware links.

Domain Decomposition (Data Parallelism)

The programming style in which parallelism is achieved by dividing among the processors the data upon which the algorithm operates.

Interrupt Driven Communication

A system in which messages arriving at a node cause an interruption in the flow of the program executing there. The user program is typically forced to handle the incoming message before returning to the place where the interruption occurred.

Loosely Synchronous Programming

The model in which an application alternately computes and communicates. Each communication cycle is "synchronized" in that all processors participate in it together, typically using the "collective communication" strategies.

Figure 5.5: Glossary

The crystal router was an effective system on early Caltech, JPL, and commercial multicomputers. It minimized latency, interrupt overhead and used optimal routing. It has not survived as a generally important concept as it is not needed in this form on modern machines with different topologies and automatic hardware routing.

5.2.10 Portability

In all of the software development cycles, one of our primary concerns was portability. We wanted our programs to be portable not only between various types of parallel computers, but also between parallel and sequential computers. It was in this sense that Cubix was such a breakthrough, since it allowed us to leave all the standard runtime system calls in our programs. In most cases, Cubix programs will run either on a supported parallel computer or on a simple sequential machine through the provision of a small number of dummy routines for the sequential machine. Using these tools, we were able to implement our codes on all of the commercially and locally built hypercubes.

The next question to arise, however, concerned possible extensions to alternative architectures, such as shared-memory or mesh-based structures. The crystal router offered a solution. By design, messages in the crystal router can be sent to any other node. This step merely involves construction of a set of appropriate queues. When the interprocessor communication is actually invoked, the system is responsible for routing messages between processors—a step in which potential differences in the underlying hardware architecture can be concealed. As a result, applications using the crystal router can conceivably operate on any type of parallel or sequential hardware.

5.2.11 Express

At the end of 1987, ParaSoft Corporation was founded by a group from C^3P with the goal of providing a uniform software base—a set of portable programming tools—for all types of parallel processors (Figure 5.6).

The resultant system, Express [ParaSoft:88a], is a merger of the C^3P message passing tools, developed into a unified system that can be supported on all types of parallel computers. The basic components are:

- a "long-range" message-passing system similar in concept to the "9 routines";

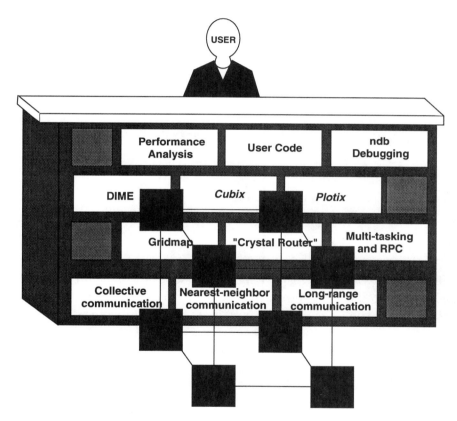

Express system components and the user's view of the hardware

Figure 5.6: Express System Components

- extensions to the collective communication routines to support nonhypercube architectures;

- implementation of the grid-map decomposition tools for non-hypercube topologies;

- enhanced versions of the Cubix and Plotix subsystems to deal with a broader range of problem styles;

- an implementation of the crystal router for nonhypercube topologies; and

- an implementation of the crystalline communication system tailored to nonhypercube topologies.

Additionally, ParaSoft added:

- a message-based multitasking and remote task creation system;

- support for non-homogeneous architectures in which the nodes of the parallel machine may be of different types, and which are potentially located at different physical sites.

ParaSoft extended the parallel debugger originally developed for the nCUBE hypercube [Flower:87c] and created a set of powerful performance analysis tools [Parasoft:88f] to help users analyze and optimize their parallel programs. This toolset, incorporating all of the concepts of the original C^3P work and available on a wide range of parallel computers, has been widely accepted and is now the most commonly used system at Caltech. It is interesting to note that the most successful parallel programs are still built around the crystalline style of internode communication originally developed for the Mark II hypercube in 1982. While other systems occasionally seem to offer easier routes to working algorithms, we usually find that a crystalline implementation offers significantly better performance.

At the current stage of development, we also believe that parallel processing is reasonably straightforward. The availability of sophisticated debugging tools, and I/O systems has resulted in several orders of magnitude reduction in debugging time. Similarly, the performance evaluation system has proved itself very powerful in analyzing areas where potential improvements can be made in algorithms.

ParaSoft also supports a range of other parallel computing tools, some of which are described later in this chapter.

5.2.12   Other Message-passing Systems

It is interesting to compare the work of other organizations with that performed at Caltech. In particular, our problem-solving approach to the art of parallel computing has, in some cases, led us down paths which we have since abandoned but which are still actively pursued by other groups. Yet, a completely fresh look at parallel programming methods may produce a more consistent paradigm than our evolutionary approach. In any case, the choice of a parallel programming system depends on whether the user is more interested in machine performance or ease of programming.

These are several systems that offer some or all of the features of Express, based on long-range communication by message passing. Many are more general operating environments with the features of "real" operating systems missing in Express and especially CrOS. We summarize some examples in the following:

1. Mercury/Centaur

   JPL developed this message-passing system [Lee:86a] at the same time as we developed the 9 routines at Caltech. *Mercury* is similar to the 9 routines in that messages can be transmitted between any pair of nodes, irrespective of whether a channel connects them. Messages also have "types" and can be sorted and buffered by the system as in the 9 routines or Express. A special type of message allows one node to broadcast to all others.

   Centaur is a simulation of CrOS III built on Mercury. This system was designed to allow programmers with crystalline applications the ability to operate either at the level of the hardware with high performance (with the CrOS III library) or within the asynchronous Mercury programming model, which had substantially higher (about a factor of three) message startup latency. When operating in Centaur mode, CrOS III programs may use advanced tools, such as the debugger, which require asynchronous access to the communication hardware.

2. VERTEX

   VERTEX is the native operating system of the nCUBE. It shares with Express, Mercury, and the 9 routines the ability to send messages, with types, between arbitrary pairs of processors. Only two basic functions are supported to send and receive messages. I/O is not supported in the earliest versions of VERTEX, although this capability has been added in support of the second generation nCUBE hypercube.

3. The Reactive Kernel

    The *Reactive Kernel* [Seitz:88b] is a message-passing system based on the idea that nodes will normally be sending messages in response to messages coming from other nodes. Like all the previously mentioned systems, the Reactive Kernel can send messages between any pair of nodes with a simple send/receive interface. However, the system call that receives messages does not distinguish between incoming messages. All sorting and buffering must be done by the user. As described in Chapter 16, Zipcode has been built on top of the Reactive Kernel to provide similar capabilities to Express.

4. "NX"

    The *NX* system provided for the Intel iPSC series of multicomputers is also similar in functionality to the previously described long-range communication systems. It supports message types and provides sorting and buffering capabilities similar to those found in Express. No support is provided for nearest-neighbor communication in the crystalline style, although some of the collective communication primitives are supported.

5. MACH

    The *MACH* operating system [Tevanian:89a] is a full implementation of UNIX for a shared-memory parallel computer. It supports all of the normally expected operating system facilities, such as multiuser access, disks, terminals, printers, and so on, in a manner compatible with the conventional Berkeley UNIX. MACH is also built with an elegant small (micro) kernel and a careful architecture of the system and user level functionality.

    While this provides a strong basis for multiuser processing, it offers only simple parallel processing paradigms, largely based on the conventional UNIX interprocess communication protocols, such as "pipes" and "sockets." As mentioned earlier in connection with MOOSE, these types of tools are not the easiest to use in tightly coupled parallel codes. The Open Software Foundation (OSF) has extended and commercialized MACH. They also have an AD (Advanced Development) prototype version for distributed memory machines. The latest Intel

Paragon multicomputer offers OSF's new AD version of MACH on every node, but the operating system has been augmented with NX to provide high-performance message passing.

6. Helios

Helios [DSL:89a] is a distributed-memory operating system designed for transputer networks—distributed-memory machines. It offers typical UNIX-like utilities, such as compilers, editors, and printers, which are all accessible from the nodes of the transputer system, although fewer than the number supported by MACH. In common with MACH, however, the level of parallel processing support is quite limited. Users are generally encouraged to use pipes for interprocessor communication—no collective or crystalline communication support is provided.

7. Linda

The basic concept used in *Linda* [Ahuja:86a] is the idea of a tuple-space (database) for objects of various kinds. Nodes communicate by dropping objects into the database, which other nodes can then extract. This concept has a very elegant implementation, which is extremely simple to learn, but which can suffer from quite severe performance problems. This is especially so on distributed-memory architectures, where the database searching necessary to find an "object" can require intensive internode communication within the operating system.

More recent versions of Linda [Gelertner:89a] have extended the original concept by adding additional tuple-spaces and allowing the user to specify to which space an object should be sent and from which it should be retrieved. This new style is reminiscent of a mailbox approach, and is thus, quite similar to the programming paradigm used in CrOS III or Express.

8. PVM

PVM is a very popular elegant system that is available freely from Oak Ridge [Sunderam:90a], [Geist:92a]. This parallel virtual machine is notable for its support of a heterogeneous computing environment with, for instance, a collection of disparate architecture computers networked together.

There are several other message-passing systems, including active messages [Eiken:92a] discussed earlier, P4 [Boyle:87a], PICL [Geist:90b], EUI on the IBM SP-1, CSTools from Meiko, Parmacs [Hempel:91a], and CMMD on the CM-5 from Thinking Machines. PICL's key feature is the inclusion of primitives to support the gathering of data to support performance visualization (Section 5.4). This could be an important feature in such low-level systems.

Most of the ideas in Express, PVM, and the other basic message-passing systems are incorporated in a new Message-Passing Interface (MPI) standard [Walker:94a]. This important development tackles basic point to point, and collective communication. MPI does not address issues such as "active messages" or distributed computing and wide-area networks (e.g., what are correct protocols for video-on-demand and multimedia with real time constraints). Operating systems issues, outside the communication layer, are also not considered in MPI.

5.2.13   What Did We Learn?

- The loosely synchronous programming model leads to programs that are easily developed, debugged, and modelled, and perform extremely well on parallel machines.

- Using high-level and collective communication routines simplifies coding for the user and allows implementors the flexibility to generate high performance on arbitrary architectures.

- A good parallel model of I/O and graphics leads to programs that are portable, efficient, and easily understood. They also adapt well to special-purpose hardware.

- You don't need a "real operating system" to get high performance from parallel computers. This is not surprising; a critical "reality" for generally useable systems is the "ease of use" and flexibility of "real" operating systems. They are not designed just for performance, and, indeed, sacrifice it for the other design features.

- Portability, programmability, and performance are the most important message-passing system qualities, and are not mutually exclusive.

5.2.14   Conclusions

The history of our message-passing system work at Caltech is interesting in that its motivation departs significantly from that of most other institutions.

Since our original goals were problem-oriented rather than motivated by the desire to do parallel processing research, we tended to build utilities that matched our hardware and software goals rather than for our aesthetic sense. If our original machine had had multiplexed DMA channels and specialized routing hardware, we might have started off in a totally different direction. Indeed, this can be seen as motivation for developing some of the alternative systems described in the previous section.

In retrospect, we may have been lucky to have such limited hardware available, since it forced us to develop tools for the user rather than rely on an all-purpose communication system. The resultant decomposition and collective communication routines still provide the basis for most of our successful work—even with the development of Express, we still find that we return again and again to the nearest-neighbor, crystalline communication style, albeit using the portable Express implementation rather than the old `rdELT` and `wtELT` calls. Even as we attempt to develop automated mechanisms for constructing parallel code, we rely on this type of technology.

The advent of parallel UNIX variants has not solved the problems of message passing—indeed these systems are among the weakest in terms of providing user-level support for interprocessor communication. We continually find that the best performance, both from our parallel programs and the scientists who develop them, is obtained when working in a loosely synchronous programming environment such as Express, even when this means implementing such a system on top of a native, "parallel UNIX."

We believe that the work done by C^3P is still quite unique, at least in its approach to problem solving. It is amusing to recall the comment of one new visitor to Caltech who, coming from an institution building sophisticated "parallel UNIXs," was surprised to see the low level at which CrOS III operated. From our point of view, however, it gets the job done in an efficient and timely manner, which is of paramount importance.

5.3 Parallel Debugging

5.3.1 Introduction and History

Relatively little attention was paid in the early days of parallel computers to debugging the resulting parallel programs. We developed our approaches by trial and error during our various experiments in C^3P, and debugging was never a major research project in C^3P.

In this section, we shall consider some of the history and current technology of parallel debugging, as developed by C^3P.

Method 1. Source Scrutiny

The way one worked on the early C^3P machines was to compile the target code, download it to the nodes, and wait. If everything worked perfectly, results might come back. Under *any* other circumstances, nothing would come out. The only real way to debug was to stare at the source code.

The basic problem was that while the communication routines discussed in the previous chapter were adequate (and in some sense ideal) for the task of algorithm development, they lacked a lot in terms of debugging support. In order to "see" the value of a variable inside the nodes, one had to package it up into a message and then send it to the host machine. Similarly, the host code had to be modified to receive this message at the right time and format it for the user's inspection. Even then only node 0 could perform this task directly, and all the other nodes had to somehow get their data to node 0 before it could be displayed.

Given the complexity of this task it is hardly surprising that users typically stared at their source code rather than attempt it. Ironically this procedure actually tended to introduce new bugs in the process of detecting the old ones because incorrect synchronization of the messages in nodes and host would lead to the machine hanging, probably somewhere in the new debugging code rather than the location that one was trying to debug. After several hours of fooling around, one would make the painful discovery that the debugging code itself was wrong and would have to start once more.

Method 2. Serial Channels

In building the first C^3P hypercubes, each node had been given a serial RS-232 channel. No one quite knew why this had been done, but it was pointed out that by attaching some kind of terminal, or even a PC, it might be possible to send "print" statements out of the back of one or more nodes.

This was quickly achieved but proved less than the dramatic improvement one would have hoped. The interface was really slow and only capable of printing simple integer values. Furthermore, one had to use it while sitting in the machine room and it was necessary to attach the serial cable from the debugging terminal to the node to be debugged—an extremely hazardous process that could cause other cables to become loose.

A modification of the process that should probably have pointed us in the right direction immediately was when the MS-DOS program `DEBUG` was modified for this interface. Finally, we could actually insert breakpoints in the target node code and examine memory!

Unfortunately, this too failed to become popular because of the extremely low level at which it operated. Memory locations had to be specified in hexadecimal and code could only be viewed as assembly language instructions.

A final blow to this method was that our machines still operated in "single-user" mode—that is, only a single user could be using the system at any one time. As a result, it was intolerable for a single individual to "have" the machine for a couple of hours while struggling with the `DEBUG` program while others were waiting.

Method 3. Cubix

As has been described in the previous section on communication systems, the advent of the Cubix programming style brought a significant improvement to the life of the parallel code developer. For the first time, any node could print out its data values, not using some obscure and arcane functions but with normal `printf` and `WRITE` statements. To this extent, debugging parallel programs really did become as simple as debugging sequential ones.

Using this method took us out of the stone age: Each user would generate huge data files containing the values of all the important data and then go to work with a pocket calculator to see what went wrong.

Method 4. Help from the Manufacturer

The most significant advance in debugging technology, however, came with the first nCUBE machine. This system embodied two important advances:

- a "space-sharing" system on the nodes which allowed multiple users to run jobs concurrently, and

- a "real" kernel on each processor which supported breakpoint debugging.

The first item finally made breakpoint debugging a feasible concept since, while one user was slowly debugging, others could still use the machine for other purposes.

The "real" kernel was a mixed blessing. As has been pointed out previously, we didn't really need most of its resources and resented the fact that the kernel imposed a message latency almost ten times that of the basic hardware. On the other hand, it supported real debugging capabilities.

Unfortunately, the system software supplied with the nCUBE hadn't made much more progress in this direction than we had with our "DEBUG" program. The debugger expected to see addresses in hex and displayed code as assembly instructions. Single stepping was only possible at the level of a single machine instruction.

Method 5. The Node Debugger: ndb

Our initial attempt to get something useful out of the nCUBE's debugging potential was something called "bdb" that communicated with nCUBE's own debugger through a pipe and attempted to provide a slightly more friendly user interface. In particular, it allowed stack frames to be unrolled and also showed the names of functions rather than the absolute addresses. It was extremely popular.

As a result of this experience, we decided to build a full-blown, user-friendly, *parallel programming debugger*, finally resulting in the C^3P and now ParaSoft tool known as "ndb," the "node debugger."

5.3.2   Designing a Parallel Debugger

The basics of the design were straightforward, but tedious to code. Much work had to be done building symbol tables from executables, figuring out how line numbers mapped to memory addresses, and so on, but the most important discoveries lay in that a parallel *program debugger* had to work in a rather different way than normal sequential versions.

Lesson 1. Avoiding Deadlock

The first important discovery was that a parallel program debugger couldn't operate in the "on" or "off" modes of conventional debuggers. In sdb or dbx, for example, either the debugger is in control or the user program is running. There are no other states. Once you have issued a "continue" command, the user program continues to run until it either terminates or reaches another breakpoint, at which time you may once again issue debugger commands.

To see how this fails for a parallel program, consider the code outline

	Node 0			**Node 1**
1:	a = 3;		1:	a = 3;
2:	send_message;	$\longrightarrow$	2:	get_message;
3:	b = 4;		3:	b = 4;
4:	get_message;	$\longleftarrow$	4:	send_message;
5:	c = 5;		5:	c = 5;

Figure 5.7: Single-Stepping Through Message-Passing Code

shown in Figure 5.7. Assume that we have two nodes, both stopped at breakpoints at line one. At this point, we can do all of the normal debugger activities including examination of variables, listing of the program, and so on. Now assume that we single-step *only node 0*. Since line one is a simple assignment we have no problem and we move to line two.

Repeating this process is a problem, however, since we now try to send a message to node 1 which is not ready to receive it—node 1 is still sitting in its breakpoint at line one in its node. If we adopted the sequential debugger standard in which the user program takes control whenever a command is given to step or continue the program, we would now have a deadlock, because node 0 will never return from its single-step command until node 1 does something. On the other hand node 1 cannot do anything until it is given a debugger command.

In principle, we can get around this problem by redefining the action of the **send_message** function used in node 0. In the normal definition of our system at that time, this call should block until the receiving node is ready. By relaxing this constraint, we can allow the **send_message** function to return as soon as the data to be transmitted is safely reusable, without waiting for the receive.

This does not save the debugger. We now expect the single step from line two to line three to return, as will the trivial step to line four. But the single step to line five involves receiving a message from node 1 and no possible relaxing of the communication specification can deal with the fact that node 1 hasn't sent anything.

Deadlock is unavoidable.

The solution to this problem is to simply make debugging a completely autonomous process which operates independently of the user program. Essentially, this means that any debugger command immediately returns and gives the user a new prompt. The single-step command, for example, doesn't wait for anything important to happen but allows the user to carry on giving debugger commands even though the user process may be "hung" as a consequence of the single step as shown in Figure 5.7.

Lesson 1a. Who Gets the Input?

As an immediate consequence of the decision to leave the debugger in control of the keyboard at all times, we run into the problem of how to pass input to the program being debugged.

Again, sequential debuggers don't have this problem because the moment you continue or run the program it takes control of the keyboard and you enter data in the normal manner. In **ndb**, life is not so simple because if you start up your code and it prints on the screen

```
Enter two integers:   [I,J]
```

or some such, you can't actually type the values because they would be interpreted as debugger commands! One way around this is to have multiple windows on your workstation; in one you type debugger commands; in the other, input to your program. Another solution is to have a debugger command that explicitly switches control to the user program in just the same way that a sequential debugger would: **ndb** supports both mechanisms.

Lesson 2. Show State

Because the debugger operates in the manner just described, it becomes very important to give the user a quick way of seeing when something has really happened. Normal sequential debuggers give you this feedback by simply returning a prompt whenever the user program has encountered a breakpoint or terminated. In our case, we provide a simple command, "**show state**," to allow the user to monitor the progress of the node program.

As an example, the output when executed on node 0 at line two might be something like

```
Node 0:   Breakpoint, PC=[foo.c,2]
```

which shows that the node is stopped at a breakpoint at the indicated line of a source file named "`foo.c`". If we step again, the debugger gives us back a prompt and a very quick "`show state`" command might now show

```
Node 0:   Running, PC=[send.c, 244]
```

showing that the node is now running code somewhere inside a source file called "`send.c`". Another similar command would probably show something like

```
Node 0:   Breakpoint, PC=[foo.c, 3]
```

indicating that the node had now reached the breakpoint on the next line. If the delay between the first two "`show state`" commands were too long, you might never see the "Running" state at all because the node will have performed its "send" operation and reached line three.

If you continued with this process of single stepping and probing with the "`show state`" command, you would eventually get to a state where the node would show as "Running" in the receive function from which it would never return until node 1 got around to sending its message.

Lesson 3. Sets of Nodes

The simplest applications of a sequential debugger for parallel programs would be similar to those already seen. Each command issued by the user to the debugger is executed on a particular node. Up to now, for example, we have considered only actions on node 0. Obviously, we can't make much progress in the example code shown in Figure 5.7 until node 1 moves from its initial breakpoint at line one.

We might extend the syntax by adding a "`pick`" command that lets us, for example,

```
pick node 1
```

and then execute commands there instead of on node 0. This would clearly allow us to make progress in the example we have been studying. On the other hand, it is very tedious to debug this way. Even on as few as four nodes, the sequence

```
pick 0
show state
pick 1
show state
pick 2
show state
pick 3
show state
```

is used frequently and is very painful to type. Running on 512 nodes in this manner is out of the question. The solution adopted for **ndb** is to use "node sets." In this case, the above effect would be achieved with the command

```
on all show state
```

or alternatively

```
pick all
show state
```

The basic idea is that debugger commands can be applied to more than a single processor at once. In this way, you can obtain global information about your program without spending hours typing commands.

In addition to the simple concepts of a single node and "all" nodes, **ndb** supports other groups such as contiguous ranges of nodes, discontinuous ranges of nodes, "even" and "odd" parity groups, the "neighbors" of a particular node, and user-defined sets of nodes to facilitate the debugging process. For example, the command

```
on 0, 1, nof 1, even show state
```

executes the "show state" command on nodes 0, 1, the neighbors of node 1, and all "even parity" nodes.

Lesson 4. Smart stepping

Once node sets are available to execute commands on multiple processors, another tricky issue comes up concerning single stepping. Going back to the example shown in Figure 5.7, consider the effect of executing the sequence of commands

```
pick 0, 1
next
next
next
next
```

starting from the initial state in which both nodes are at a breakpoint at line one. The intent is fairly obvious—the user wants to single-step over the intermediate lines of code from line one, eventually ending up at line five.

In principle, the objections that gave rise to the independence of debugger and user program should no longer hold, because when we step from line two, both nodes are participating and thus the send/receive combination should be satisfied properly.

The problem, however, is merely passed down to the internal logic of the debugger. While it is true that the user has asked both nodes to step over their respective communication calls, the debugger is hardly likely to be able to deduce that. If the debugger expands (internally) the single-step command to something like

```
pick 0
step
pick 1
step
```

then all might be well, since node 0 will step over its "send" before node 1 steps over its receive—a happy result. If, however, the debugger chooses to expand this sequence as

```
pick 1
step
pick 0
step
```

it will hang just as badly as the original user interaction.

Even though the "obvious" expansion is the one that works in this case, this is not generally true—in fact, it fails when stepping from line four to line five in the example.

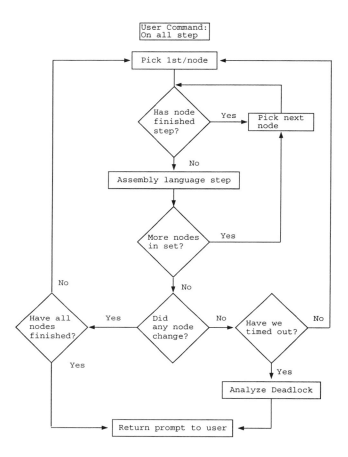

Figure 5.8: Logic for Single Stepping on Multiple Nodes

In general, there is no way for the debugger to know how to expand such command sequences reliably, and as a result a much "smarter" method of single stepping must be used, such as that shown schematically in Figure 5.8.

The basic idea is to loop over each of the nodes in the set being stepped trying to make "some" progress towards reaching the next stopping point. If no nodes can make progress, we check to see if some time-out has expired and if not, continue. This allows us to step over system calls that may take a significant time to complete when measured in machine instructions.

Finally, if no more progress can be made, we attempt to analyze the reason for the deadlock and return to the user anyway.

This process is not foolproof in the sense that we will sometimes "give up" on single steps that are actually going to complete, albeit slowly. But it has the great virtue that even when the user program "deadlocks", the debugger comes back to the user, often with a correct analysis of the reason for the deadlock.

Lesson 5. Show queue

Another interesting question about the debugger concerns the extensions and/or modifications that one might make to a sequential debugger.

One might be tempted to say that the parallel debugger is so different from its sequential counterparts that a totally new syntax and method of operation is justified. One then takes the chance that no one will invest the time needed to learn the new tool and it will never be useful.

For **ndb**, we decided to adopt the syntax of the well-known UNIX **dbx** debugger that was available on the workstations that we used for development. This meant that the basic command syntax was familiar to everyone using the system.

Of course we have already introduced several commands that don't exist in **dbx**, simply because sequential debuggers don't have need for them. The "**show state**" command is never required in sequential debuggers because the program is either running or it's stopped at a point that the debugger can tell you about. Similarly, one never has to give commands to multiple processors.

Another command that we learned early on was very important was "**show q**", which monitored the messages in transit between processors. Because our parallel programs were really just sequential programs with additional message passing, the "bugs" that we were trying to find were not normally algorithmic errors but message-passing ones.

A typical scenario would be that the nodes would compute (correctly) and then reach some synchronization or communication point at which point the logic relating to message transfer would be wrong and everything would hang. At this point, it proved to be immensely useful to be able to go in with the debugger and look at which nodes had actually sent messages to other nodes.

Often one would see something like

```
Node 0:
        Node 1, type 12, len 32
```

```
                (12 4a 44 82 3e 00 ...)
        Node 2, type 12, len 32
                (33 4a 5f ff 00 00 ...)
Node 1:   No messages
Node 2:   No messages
```

indicating that node 0 has received two messages of type 12 and length 32 bytes from node 1 and node 2 but that neither node 1 nor node 2 has any.

Armed with this type of information, it is usually extremely easy to detect the commonest type of parallel processing problem.

Lesson 5a. Message Passing Is Easy

An interesting corollary to the debugging style just described is that we learned that debugging message-passing programs was *much* easier than other types of parallel programming.

The important advantage that a user-friendly debugger brings to the user is the ability to slow down the execution of the program to the point where the user can "see" the things that go wrong. This fits well with the "message-passing" methodology since bugs in message passing usually result in the machine hanging. In this state, you have plenty of time to examine what's happening and deduce the error. Furthermore, the problem is normally completely repeatable since it usually relates to a logic error in the code.

In contrast, shared-memory or multiprocessing paradigms are much harder because the bugs tend to depend on the relative timing of various events within the code. As a result, the very act of using the debugger can cause the problem to show up in a different place or even to go away all together. This is akin to that most frustrating of problems when you are tracking down a bug with print statements, only to find that just as you insert the climactic final statement which will isolate your problem, it goes away altogether!

Lesson 6. How Many Windows?

The debugger **ndb** was originally designed to be driven from a terminal by users typing commands, but with the advent of graphical workstations with windowing systems it was inevitable that someone would want a "windowing" version of the debugger.

It is interesting to note that many users' original conception was that it would now be correct to port a sequential debugger and have multiple instances of it, each debugging one node.

This illusion is quickly removed, however, when we are debugging a program on many nodes with many invocations of a sequential debugger. Not only is it time-consuming setting up all of the windows, but activities such as single stepping become extremely frustrating since one has to go to each window in turn and type the "continue" command. Even providing a "button" that can be clicked to achieve this doesn't help much because you still have to be able to see the button in the overlapping windows, and however fast you are with the mouse it gets harder and harder to achieve this effect as the number of nodes on which your program is running grows.

Our attempt at solving this problem is to have two different window types: an **ndb** console and a node window. The console is basically a window-oriented version of the standard debugger. The lower panel allows the user to type any of the normal debugger commands and have them behave in the expected fashion. The buttons at the top of the display allow "shortcuts" for the often issued commands, and the center panel allows a shortcut for the most popular command of all:

```
on all show state
```

This button doesn't actually generate the output from this command in the normal mode since, brief as its output is, it can still be tedious watching 512 copies of

```
Node XXX: Breakpoint, [foo.c, 13]
```

scroll past. Instead, it presents the node state as a colored bar chart in which the various node states each have different colors. In this way, for example, you can "poll" until all the nodes hit a breakpoint by continually hitting the "Update" button until the status panel shows a uniform color and the message shows that all nodes have reached a breakpoint.

In addition to this usage, the color coding also vividly shows problems such as a node dividing by zero. In this case, the bar chart would show uniform colors except for the node that has died, which might show up in some contrasting shade.

The second important use of the "Update" button is to synchronize the views presented by the second type of window, the "node windows."

Each of these presents a view of a "group" of nodes represented by a particular choice. Thus, for example, you might choose to make a node window for the nodes 0–3, represented by node 0. In this case, the upper panel of the node window would show the source code being executed by node 0 while the lower panel would automatically direct commands to all four nodes in the group. The small status bar in the center shows a "smiley" face if all nodes in the group appear to be at the same source line number and a "sad" face if one or more nodes are at different places.

This method allows the user to control large groups of nodes and simultaneously see their source code while also monitoring differences in behavior. A common use of the system, for example, is to start with a single node window reflecting "all nodes" and to continue in this way until the happy face becomes sad, at which point additional node windows can be created to monitor those nodes which have departed from the main thread of execution.

The importance of the "Update" button in this regard is that the node windows have a tendency to get out of sync with the actual execution of the program. In particular, it would be prohibitively expensive to have each node window constantly tracking the program location of the nodes it was showing, since this would bombard the node program with status requests and also cause constant scrolling of the displayed windows. Instead, ndb chooses its own suitable points to update the displayed windows and can be forced to update them at other times with the "Update" button.

5.3.3 Conclusions

This section has emphasized the differences between ndb and sequential debuggers since those are the interesting features from the implementation standpoint. On the other hand, from the user's view, the most striking success of the tool is that it has made the debugging process so little different from that used on sequential codes. This can be traced to the loosely synchronous structure of most (C^3P) parallel codes. Debugging fully asynchronous parallel codes can be much more challenging than the sequential case.

In practice, users have to be shown only once how to start up the debugging process, and be given a short list of the new commands that they might want to use. For users who are unfamiliar with the command syntax, the simplest route is to have them play with dbx on a workstation for a few minutes.

After this, the process tends to be very straightforward, mostly because of the programming styles that we tend to use. As mentioned in an earlier section, debugging totally asynchronous programs that generate multiple threads synchronizing with semaphores in a time-dependent manner is not ndb's forte. On the other hand, debugging loosely synchronous message-passing programs has been reduced to something of a triviality.

In some sense, we can hardly be said to have introduced anything new. The basis on which ndb operates is very conventional, although some of the implications for the implementation are non-trivial. On the other hand, it provides an important and often critical service to the user. The next section will describe some of the more revolutionary steps that were taken to simplify the development process in the areas of performance analysis and visualization.

5.4 Parallel Profiling

From the earliest days of parallel computing, the fundamental goal was to accelerate the performance of algorithms that ran too slowly on sequential machines. As has been described in many other places in this book, the effort to do basic research in computer science was always secondary to the need for algorithms that solved practical problems more quickly than was possible on other machines.

One might think that an important prerequisite for this would be advanced profiling technology. In fact, about the most advanced piece of equipment then in use was a wristwatch! Most algorithms were timed on one node, then on two, then on four, and so on. The results of this analysis were then compared with the theoretically derived models for the applications. If all was well, one proceeded to number-crunch; if not, one inserted print statements and timed the gaps between them to see what pieces of code were behaving in ways not predicted by the models.

Even the breakthrough of having a function that a program could call to get at timing information was a long time coming, and even then proved somewhat unpopular, since it had different names on different machines and didn't even exist on the sequential machines. As a result, people tended to just not bother with it rather than mess up their codes with many different timing routines.

5.4.1   Missing a Point

Of course, this was all totally adequate for the first few applications that were parallelized, since their behavior was so simple to model. A program solving Laplace's equation on a square grid, for example, has a very simple model that one would actually have to work quite hard not to find in a parallel code. As time passed, however, more complex problems were attempted which weren't so easy to model and tools had to be invented.

Of course, this discussion has missed a rather important point which we also tended to overlook in the early days.

When comparing performance of the problems on one, two, four, eight, and so on nodes, one is really only assessing the efficiency of the parallel version of the code. However, an algorithm that achieves 100 percent efficiency on a parallel computer may still be worthless if its absolute performance is lower than that of a sequential code running on another machine.

Again, this was not so important in the earliest days, since the big battle over architectures had not yet arisen. Nowadays, however, when there is a multitude of sequential and parallel supercomputers, it is extremely important to be able to know that a parallel version of a code is going to outperform a sequential version running on another architecture. It is becoming increasingly important to be able to understand what complex algorithms are doing and why, so that the performance of the software and hardware can both be tuned to achieve best results.

This section attempts to discuss some of the issues surrounding algorithm visualization, parallelization and performance optimization, and the tools which C^3P developed to help in this area. A major recent general tool, PABLO [Reed:91a] has been developed at Illinois by Reed's group, but here we only describe the C^3P activity. One of the earliest tools was Seecube [Couch:88a;88b].

5.4.2   Visualization

The first question that must be asked of any algorithm when a parallel version is being considered is, "What does it do?" Surprisingly, this question is often quite hard to answer. Vague responses such as "some sort of linear algebra" are quite common and even if the name of the algorithm is actually known, it is quite surprising how often codes are ported without anyone actually having a good impression of what the code does.

One attempt to shed light on these issues by providing a data visualiza-

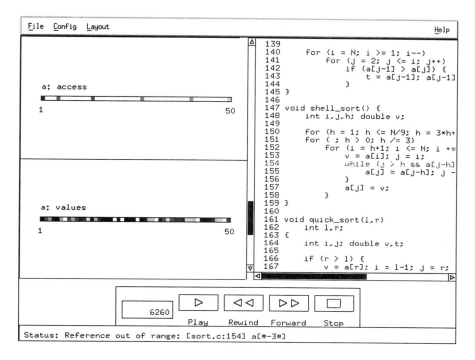

Figure 5.9: Analysis of a Sorting Algorithm Using `vtool`

tion service is `vtool`. One takes the original (sequential) source code and runs it through a preprocessor that instruments various types of data access. The program is then compiled with a special run time library and run in the normal manner. The result is a database describing the ways in which the algorithm or application makes use of its data.

Once this has been collected, `vtool` provides a service analogous to a home VCR which allows the application to be "played back" to show the memory accesses being made. Sample output is shown in Figure 5.9.

The basic idea is to show "pictures" of arrays together with a "hot spot" that shows where accesses and updates are being made. As the hot spot moves, it leaves behind a trail of continuingly fading colors that dramatically show the evolution of the algorithm. As this proceeds, the corresponding source code can be shown and the whole simulation can be stopped at any time so that a particularly interesting sequence can be replayed in slow motion or even one step at a time, both forward and backward.

In addition to showing simple access patterns, the display can also show the values being stored into arrays, providing a powerful way of debugging applications.

In the parallel processing arena, this tool is normally used to understand how an algorithm works at the level of its memory references. Since most parallel programs are based on the ideas of data distribution, it is important to know how the values at a particular grid point or location in space depend on those of neighbors. This is fundamental to the selection of a parallelization method. It is also central to the understanding of how the parallel and sequential versions of the code will differ which becomes important when the optimization process begins.

It should be mentioned in passing that we have been surprised in using this tool how often people's conceptions of the way that numerical algorithms work are either slightly or completely revised after seeing the visualization system at work.

5.4.3   Goals in Performance Analysis

Hopefully, the visualization system goes some way towards the development of a parallel algorithm. One must then code and debug the application which, as has been described previously, can be a reasonably time-consuming process. Finally, one comes to the "crisis" point of actually running the parallel code and seeing how fast it goes.

One of our major concerns in developing performance analysis tools was to make them easy to use. The standard UNIX method of taking the completed program, deleting all its object files, and then recompiling them with special switches seemed to be asking too much for parallel programs because the process is so iterative. On a sequential machine, the profiler may be run once or twice, usually just to check that the authors' impressions of performance are correct. On a parallel computer, we feel that the optimization phase should more correctly be included in the development cycle than as an afterthought, because we believe that few parallel applications perform at their best immediately after debugging is complete. We wanted, therefore, to have a system that could give important information about an algorithm without any undue effort.

The system to be described works with the simple addition of either a runtime switch or the definition of an "environment" variable, and makes available about 90% of the capabilities of the entire package. To use some of the most exotic features, one must recompile code.

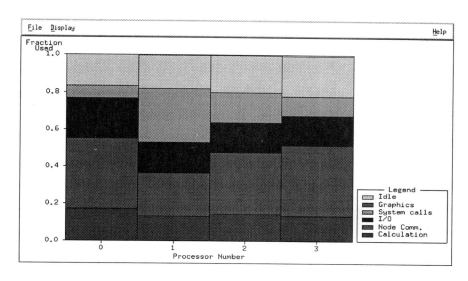

Figure 5.10: Overhead Summary from `ctool`

5.4.4 Overhead Analysis

As an example of the "free" profiling information that is available consider the display from the `ctool` utility shown in Figure 5.10. This provides a summary of the gross "overheads" incurred in the execution of a parallel application divided into categories such as "calculation," "I/O," "internode communication," "graphics," and so on. This is the first type of information that is needed in assessing a parallel program and is obtained by simply adding a command line argument to an existing program.

At the next level of detail after this, the individual overhead categories can be broken down into the functions responsible for them. Within the "internode communication" category, for example, one can ask to be shown the times for each of the high-level communication functions, the number of times each was called and the distribution of message lengths used by each. This output is normally presented graphically, but can also be generated in tabular form (Figure 5.11) for accurate timing measurements. Again, this information can be obtained more or less "for free" by giving a command line argument.

File Display   Help

```
 Idle                          :  7320.00 milliseconds
```

Routine	calls	time	errs	0	1	2	4	8	16	32	64	128	256+
exbroadcast	3	0.00	0	0	0	0	0	0	0	0	0	0	3
excombine	3	459.99	0	0	0	0	0	3	0	0	0	0	0
exconcat	20	1909.92	0	0	0	0	0	0	0	5	10	5	0
exchange	40	1659.94	0	26	0	0	0	0	0	0	8	3	3
exread	63	7729.90	0	0	0	0	63	0	0	0	0	0	0
exwrite	63	5200.07	0	0	0	0	0	3	0	0	0	1	59
write	60	3959.91	0	0	0	0	0	0	60	0	0	0	0
time	21	1899.95	0	0	0	0	0	0	0	0	0	0	21
lseek	19	859.96	0	0	0	0	0	0	0	0	0	0	19
isatty	1	150.00	0	0	1	0	0	0	0	0	0	0	0
mwrite	20	5859.89	0	20	0	0	0	0	0	0	0	0	0

```
Node      1
===========
   Elapsed time              :  44630.00 milliseconds
   Calculation               :   5920.33 milliseconds
   Node Comm.                :  10469.85 milliseconds
   I/O                       :   7319.93 milliseconds
   System calls              :  13029.89 milliseconds
   Graphics                  :      0.00 milliseconds
   Idle                      :   7890.00 milliseconds
```

Routine	calls	time	errs	0	1	2	4	8	16	32	64	128	256+
exbroadcast	3	2050.00	0	0	0	0	0	0	0	0	0	0	3
excombine	3	159.99	0	0	0	0	0	3	0	0	0	0	0
exconcat	20	1309.91	0	0	0	0	0	0	0	5	10	5	0
exchange	40	1939.94	0	22	0	0	0	0	0	0	11	4	3

Figure 5.11: Tabular Overhead Summary

5.4.5   Event Tracing

The overhead summaries just described offer replies to the important question, "What are the costs of executing this algorithm in parallel?" Once this information is known, one typically proceeds to the question, "Why do they cost this much?"

To answer this question we use `etool`, the event-tracing profiler.

The purpose of this tool is probably most apparent from its sample output, Figure 5.12. The idea is that we present timelines for each processor on which the most important "events" are indicated by either numbered boxes or thin bars. The former indicate atomic events such as "calling subroutine `foo`" or "beginning of loop at line 12," while the bars are used to indicate the beginning and end of extended events such as a read operation on a file or a global internode communication operation.

The basic idea of this tool is to help understand why the various overheads observed in the previous analysis exist. In particular, one looks for behavior that doesn't fit with that expected of the algorithm.

One common situation, for example, is to look for places where a "loosely synchronous" operation is held up by the late arrival of one or more processors at the synchronization point. This is quite simple in `etool`; an "optimal" loosely synchronous event would have bars in each processor that aligned perfectly in the vertical direction. The impact of a late processor

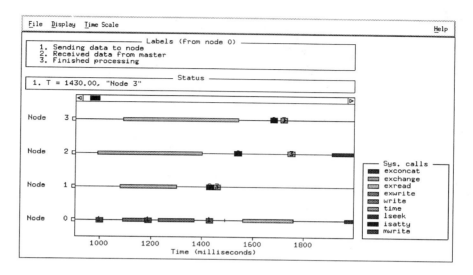

Figure 5.12: Simple Event Traces

shows up quite vividly, as shown in Figure 5.13.

This normally occurs either because of a poorly constructed algorithm or because of poor load balancing due to data dependencies.

An alternative pattern that shows up remarkably well is the sequential behavior of "master-slave" or "client-server" algorithms in which one particular node is responsible for assigning work to a number of other processors. These algorithms tend to show patterns similar to that of Figure 5.12, in which the serialization of the loop that distributed work is quite evident.

Another way that the event-profiling system can be used is to collect statistics regarding the usage of particular code segments. Placing calls to the routine `eprof_toggle` around a particular piece of code causes information to be gathered describing how many times that block was executed, and the mean and variance of the time spent there. This is analogous to the "block profiling" supported by some compilers.

5.4.6   Data Distribution Analysis

The system first described, `vtool`, had as its goal the visualization of sequential programs prior to their parallelization. The distribution profiler `dtool` serves a similar purpose for parallel programs which rely on data distribution for their parallelism. The basic idea is that one can "watch" the distribution of a particular data object change as an algorithm progresses.

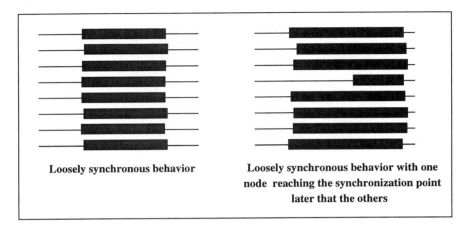

Figure 5.13: Sample Application Behavior as Seen by `etool`

Sample output is shown in Figure 5.14.

At the bottom of the display is a timeline which looks similar to that used in the event profiler, `etool`. In this case, however, the events shown are the redistribution operations on a particular data object. Clicking on any event with the mouse causes a picture of the data distribution among the nodes to be shown in the upper half of the display. Other options allow for fast and slow replays of a particular sequence of data transformations.

The basic idea of this tool is to look at the data distributions that are used with a view to either optimizing their use or looking for places in which redundant transformations are being made that incur high communication costs. Possible restructuring of the code may eliminate these transformations, thus improving performance. This is particularly useful in conjunction with automatic parallelization tools, which have a tendency to insert redundant communication in an effort to ensure program correctness.

5.4.7   CPU Usage Analysis

As mentioned earlier, the most often neglected question with parallel applications is how fast they are in absolute terms. It is possible that this is a throwback to sequential computers, where profiling tools, although available, are rarely used. In most cases, if a program doesn't run fast enough when all the compiler's optimization capabilities are exhausted, one merely moves to a higher performance machine. Of course, this method doesn't scale well and doesn't apply at all in the supercomputer arena. Even more

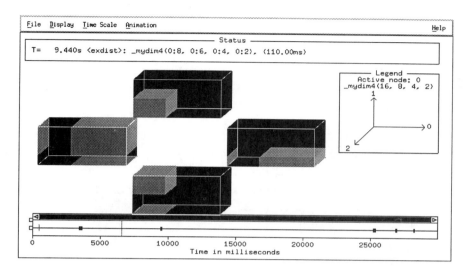

Figure 5.14: Data Distribution Analysis

importantly, as processor technology becomes more and more complex, the performance gap between the peak speed of a system and that attained by compiled code gets ever wider.

The typical solution for sequential computers is the use of profiling tools like **prof** or **gprof** that provide a tabular listing of the routines in a program and the amount of time spent in each. This avoids the use of the wristwatch but only goes so far. You can certainly see which routines are the most expensive but no further.

The profiler **xtool** was designed to serve this purpose for parallel computers and in addition to proceed to lower levels of resolution: source code and even machine instructions. Sample displays are shown in Figure 5.15. At the top is a graphical representation of the time spent executing each of the most expensive routines. The center shows a single routine at the level of its source code and the bottom panel shows individual machine instructions.

The basic goal of this presentation is to allow the user to see where CPU time is being spent at any required level of detail. At the top level, one can use this information to develop or restructure algorithms, while at the lowest level one can see how the processor instructions operate and use this data to rework pieces of code in optimized assembly language.

Note that while the other profiling tools are directed specifically towards understanding the parallel processing issues of an application, this tool is

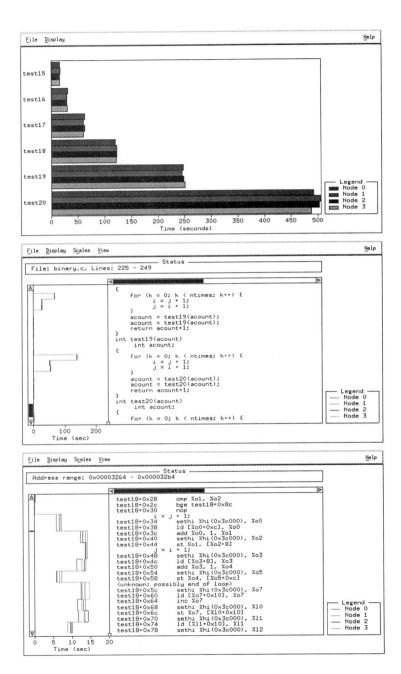

Figure 5.15: Output from the CPU Usage Profiler

aimed mostly at a thorough understanding of sequential behavior.

5.4.8 Why So Many Separate Tools?

One of the most often asked questions about this profiling system is why there are so many separate tools rather than an all-encompassing system that tells you everything you wish to know about the application.

Our fundamental reason for choosing this method was to attempt to minimize the "self-profiling" problem that tends to show up in many systems in which the profiling activity actually spends most of its time profiling the analysis system itself. Users of the UNIX profiling tools, for example, have become adept at ignoring entries for routines such as `mcount`, which correspond to time spent within the profiling system itself.

Unfortunately, this is not so simple in a parallel program. In sequential applications, the effect of the profiling system is merely to slow down other types of operation, an effect which can be compensated for by merely subtracting the known overheads of the profiling operations. On a parallel computer, things are much more complicated, since slowing down one processor may affect another which in turn affects another, and so on until the whole system is completely distorted by the profiling tools.

Our approach to this problem is to package up the profiling subsystems in subsets which have more or less predictable effects, and then to let the user decide which systems to use in which cases. For example, the communication profiler, `ctool`, incurs very small overheads—typically a fraction of 1%—while the event profiler costs more and the CPU usage profiler, `xtool`, most of all. In common use, therefore, we tend to use the communication profiler first, and then enable the event traces. If these two trials yield consistent results, we move on to the execution and distribution profilers. We have yet to encounter an application in which this approach has failed, although the fact that we are rarely interested in microsecond accuracy helps in this regard.

Interestingly, we have found problems due to "clock-skewing" to have negligible impact on our results. It is true that clock skewing occurs in most parallel systems, but we find that our profiling results are accurate enough to be helpful without taking any special precautions in this regard. Again, this is mostly due to the fact that, for the kinds of performance analysis and optimization in which we are interested, resolution of tens or even hundreds of microseconds is usually quite acceptable.

5.4.9   Conclusions

Our assumption that parallel algorithms are complex entities seems to be borne out by the fact that nearly everyone who has invested the (minimal) time to use the profiling tools on their application has come away understanding something better than before. In some cases, the revelations have been so profound that significant performance enhancements have been made possible.

In general, the system has been found easy to use, given a basic understanding of the parallel algorithm being profiled, and most users have no difficulty recognizing their applications from the various displays. On the other hand, the integration between the different profiling aspects is not yet as tight as one might wish and we are currently working on this aspect.

Another interesting issue that comes up with great regularity is the request on behalf of the users for a button marked "Why?", which would automatically analyze the profile data being presented and then point out a block of source code and a suggestion for how to improve its performance. In general, this is clearly too difficult, but it is interesting to note that certain types of runtime system are more amenable to this type of analysis than others. The "distribution profiler," for instance, possesses enough information to perform quite complex communication and I/O optimizations on an algorithm and we are currently exploring ways of implementing these strategies. It is possible that this line of thought may eventually lead us to a more complete programming model than is in use now—one which will be more amenable to the automation of parallel processing that has long been our goal.

Chapter 6

Synchronous Applications II

6.1 Computational Issues in Synchronous Problems

Synchronous problems have been defined in Section 3.4 as having the simplest temporal or computational structure. The problems are typically defined by a regular grid, as illustrated in Figure 4.3, and are parallelized by a simple domain decomposition. A synchronous temporal structure corresponds to each point in the data domain being evolved with an identical computational algorithm, and we summarize this in the caricature shown in Figure 6.1. We find several important synchronous problems in the academic applications, which formed the core of C³P's work. We expect—as shown in Chapter 19—that the "real world" (industry and government) will show fewer problems of the synchronous class. One hopes that a fundamental theory will describe phenomena in terms of simple elegant and uniform laws; these are likely to lead to a synchronous or computational (temporal) structure. On the other hand, real-world problems typically involve macroscopic phenomenological models as opposed to fundamental theories of the microscopic world. Correspondingly, we find in the real world more loosely synchronous problems that only exhibit macroscopic temporal synchronization.

There is no black-and-white definition of synchronous since, practically, we allow some violations of the rigorous microscopic synchronization. This is already seen in Section 4.2's discussion of the irregularity of Monte Carlo "accept-reject" algorithms. A deeper example is irregular geometry problems, such as the partial differential equations of Chapters 9 and 12 with

SYNCHRONOUS PROBLEMS

For example:

Microscopic Description of Fundamental Interactions
In Particular, QCD

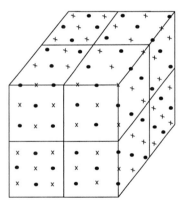

- Computational structure (almost) identical for all elements in the data domain
- Parallelize by regular partition of data domain
- Run well on SIMD machines
- Message Passing or High Performance Fortran implementation on MIMD machines

Figure 6.1: The Synchronous Problem Class

an irregular mesh. The simplest of these can be implemented well on SIMD machines as long as each node can access different addresses. In the High Performance Fortran analysis of Chapter 13, there is a class of problems lacking the regular grid of Figure 4.3. They cannot be expressed in terms of Fortran 90 with arrays of values. However, the simpler irregular meshes are topologically rectangular—they can be expressed in Fortran 90 with an array of pointers. The SIMD Maspar MP-1,2 supports this node-dependent addressing and has termed this an "autonomous SIMD" feature. We believe that just as SIMD is not a precise computer architecture, the synchronous problem class will also inevitably be somewhat vague, with some problems having architectures in a grey area between synchronous and loosely synchronous.

The applications described in Chapter 4 were all run on MIMD machines using the message-passing model of Chapter 5. Excellent speedups were obtained. Interestingly, even when C^3P acquired a SIMD CM-2, which also supported this problem class well, we found it hard to move onto this machine because of the different software model—the data parallel languages of Chapter 13—offered by SIMD machines. The development of High Performance Fortran, reviewed in Section 13.1, now offers the same data-parallel programming model on SIMD and MIMD machines for synchronous problems. Currently, nobody has efficiently ported the message-passing model to SIMD machines—even with the understanding that it would only be effective for synchronous problems. It may be that with the last obvious restriction, the message-passing model could be implemented on SIMD machines.

This chapter includes a set of neural network applications. This is an important class of naturally parallel problems, and represents one approach to answering the question:

> *"How can one apply massively parallel machines to artificial intelligence (AI)?"*

We were asked this many times at the start of C^3P, since AI was one of the foremost fields in computer science at the time. Today, the initial excitement behind the Japanese fifth-generation project has abated and AI has transitioned to a routine production technology which is perhaps more limited than originally believed. Interestingly, the neural network approach leads to synchronous structure, whereas the complementary actor or expert system approaches have a very different asynchronous structure.

The high temperature superconductivity calculations in Section 6.3 made a major impact on the condensed matter community. Quoting from *Nature* [Maddox:90a]

> ''Yet some progress seems to have been made. Thus
> Hong-Qiang Ding and Miloje S. Makivić, from California
> Institute of Technology, now describe an exceedingly
> powerful Monte Carlo calculation of an antiferromagnetic
> lattice designed to allow for the simulation
> of $La_2 Cu O_4$ (*Phys. Rev. Lett.* **64**, 1,449; 1990). In this
> context, a Monte Carlo simulation entails starting with an
> arbitrary arrangement of spins on the lattice, and then
> changing them in pairs according to rules that allow all
> spin states to be reached without violating the overall
> constraints. The authors rightly boast of their access to
> Caltech's parallel computer system, but they have also devised
> a new and efficient algorithm for tracing out the evolution
> of their system. As is the custom in this part of the trade,
> they have worked with square patches of two-dimensional lattice
> with as many as 128 lattice spacings to each side.
>
> The outcome is a relationship between correlation
> length--the distance over which order, on the average,
> persists--and temperature; briefly, the logarithm of the
> correlation length is inversely proportional to the
> temperature. That, apparently, contradicts other models
> of the ordering process. In lanthanum copper oxide, the
> correlation length agrees well with that measured by
> neutron diffraction below $500\,K$ (where there is a phase
> transition), provided the interaction energy is chosen
> appropriately. For what it is worth, that energy is not
> very different from estimates derived from Raman-scattering
> experiments, which provide a direct measurement of the energy
> of interaction by the change of frequency of the scattered light.''

The hypercube allowed much larger high-T_c calculations than the previous state of the art, with conventional machines. Curiously, with QCD simulations (described in Section 4.3), we were only able at best to match the size of the Cray calculations of other groups. This probably reflects different cultures and computational expectations of the QCD and condensed matter communities. C^3P had the advantage of dedicated facilities and could devote them to the most interesting applications.

Section 6.2 describes an early calculation, which was a continuation of our collaboration with Sandia on nCUBE applications. They, of course, followed this with a major internal activity, including their impressive performance analysis of 1024-node applications [Gustafson:88a]. There were several other synchronous applications in C^3P that we will not describe in this book. Wasson solved the single-particle Schrödinger equation in a regular grid to study the ground state of nuclear matter as a function of temperature and pressure. His approach used the time-dependent Hartree-Fock method, but was never taken past the stage of preliminary calculations on the early Mark II machines [Wasson:87a]. There were also two interesting signal-processing algorithms. Pollara implemented the Viterbi algorithm for convolutional decoding of data sent on noisy communication channels [Pollara:85a], [Pollara:86a]. This has similarities with the Cooley-Tukey binary FFT parallelization described in [Fox:88a]. We also looked at alternatives to this binary FFT in a collaboration with Aloisio from the Italian Space Agency. The prime number (nonbinary) discrete Fourier transform produces a more irregular communication pattern than the binary FFT and, further, the node calculations are less easy to pipeline than the conventional FFT. Thus, it is hard to achieve the theoretical advantage of the nonbinary FFT. This often has less floating-point operations needed for a given analysis whose natural problem size may not be the power of two demanded by the binary FFT [Aloisio:88a;89b;90b;91a;91b]. This parallel discrete FFT was designed for synthetic aperture radar applications for the analysis of satellite data [Aloisio:90c;90d].

The applications in Sections 6.7.3, 6.5, and 6.6 use the important multiscale approach to a variety of vision or image processing problems. Essentially, all physical problems are usefully considered at several different length scales, and we will come back to this in Chapters 9 and 12 when we study partial differential equations (multigrid) and practice dynamics (fast multipole).

6.2 Convectively-Dominated Flows and the Flux-Corrected Transport Technique

This work implemented a code on the nCUBE-1 hypercube for studying the evolution of two-dimensional, convectively-dominated fluid flows. An explicit finite difference scheme was used that incorporates the flux-corrected transport (FCT) technique developed by Boris and Book [Boris:73a]. When this work was performed in 1986–1987, it was expected that explicit finite difference schemes for solving partial differential equations would run efficiently on MIMD distributed-memory computers, but this had only been demonstrated in practice for "toy" problems on small hypercubes of up to 64 processors. The motivation behind this work was to confirm that a bona fide scientific application could also attain high efficiencies on a large commercial hypercube. The work also allowed the capabilities and shortcomings of the newly-acquired nCUBE-1 hypercube to be assessed.

6.2.1   An Overview of the FCT Technique

Although first-order finite difference methods are monotonic and stable, they are also strongly dissipative, causing the solution to become smeared out. Second-order techniques are less dissipative, but are susceptible to nonlinear, numerical instabilities that cause nonphysical oscillations in regions of large gradient. The usual way to deal with these types of oscillation is to incorporate artificial diffusion into the numerical scheme. However, if this is applied uniformly over the problem domain, and enough is added to dampen spurious oscillations in regions of large gradient, then the solution is smeared out elsewhere. This difficulty is also touched upon in Section 12.3.1. The FCT technique is a scheme for applying artificial diffusion to the numerical solution of a convectively-dominated flow problem in a spatially nonuniform way. More artificial diffusion is applied in regions of large gradient, and less in smooth regions. The solution is propagated forward in time using a second-order scheme in which artificial diffusion is then added. In regions where the solution is smooth, some or all of this diffusion is subsequently removed, so the solution there is basically second order. Where the gradient is large, little or none of the diffusion is removed, so the solution in such regions is first order. In regions of intermediate gradient, the order of the solution depends on how much of the artificial diffusion is removed. In this way, the FCT technique prevents nonphysical extrema from being introduced into the solution.

6.2.2   Mathematics and the FCT Algorithm

The governing equations are similar to those in Section 12.3.1, namely, the two-dimensional Euler equations,

$$\frac{\partial \mathbf{U}}{\partial t} + \frac{\partial \mathbf{F}_x}{\partial x} + \frac{\partial \mathbf{F}_y}{\partial y} = \mathbf{S}(x, y) \tag{6.1}$$

where,

$$
\mathbf{U} = \begin{bmatrix} \rho \\ \rho u \\ \rho v \\ \rho E \end{bmatrix}, \quad
\mathbf{F}_x = \begin{bmatrix} \rho u \\ \rho u^2 + p \\ \rho uv \\ \rho u(E + p/\rho) \end{bmatrix}, \quad
\mathbf{F}_y = \begin{bmatrix} \rho v \\ \rho uv \\ \rho v^2 + p \\ \rho v(E + p/\rho) \end{bmatrix},
$$

$$
\mathbf{S}(x, y) = \begin{bmatrix} 0 \\ b_x \\ b_y \\ b_x u + b_y v \end{bmatrix}
$$

Here ρ is the fluid mass density, E is the specific energy, u and v are the fluid velocities in the x and y directions, b_x and b_y are body force components, and the pressure, p, is given by,

$$
p = \rho(\gamma - 1)\left(E - \frac{u^2}{2} - \frac{v^2}{2}\right) \tag{6.2}
$$

where γ is the constant adiabatic index. The motion of the fluid is tracked by introducing massless marker particles and allowing them to be advected with the flow. Thus, the number density of the marker particles, ρ_α, satisfies,

$$
\frac{\partial \rho_\alpha}{\partial t} + \frac{\partial}{\partial x}(u\rho_\alpha) + \frac{\partial}{\partial y}(v\rho_\alpha) = 0 \tag{6.3}
$$

The equations are solved on a rectilinear two-dimensional grid. Second-order accuracy in time is maintained by first advancing the velocities by a half time step, and then using these velocities to update all values for the full time step. The size of the time step is governed by the Courant condition.

The basic procedure in each time step is to first apply a five-point difference operator at each grid point to convectively transport the field values. These field values are then diffused in each of the positive and negative x and y directions. The behavior of the resulting fields in the vicinity of each grid point is then examined to determine how much diffusion to remove at that point. In regions where a field value is locally monotonic, nearly all the diffusion previously applied is removed for that field. However, in regions close to extrema, the amount of diffusion removed is less.

6.2.3 Parallel Issues

The code used in this study parallelizes well for a number of reasons. The discretization is static and regular, and the same operations are applied at each grid point, even though the evolution of the system is nonlinear. Thus, the problem can be statically load balanced at the start of the code by ensuring that each processor's rectangular subdomain contains the same number of grid points. In addition, the physics, and hence the algorithm, is local so the finite difference algorithm only requires communication between nearest neighbors in the hypercube topology. The extreme regularity of the FCT technique means that it can also be efficiently used to study convective transport on SIMD concurrent computers, such as the Connection Machine, as has been done by Oran, et al. [Oran:90a].

No major changes were introduced into the sequential code in parallelizing it for the hypercube architecture. Additional subroutines were inserted to decompose the problem domain into rectangular subdomains, and to perform interprocessor communication. Communication is necessary in applying the Courant condition to determine the size of the next time step, and in transferring field values at grid points lying along the edge of a processor's subdomain. Single rows and columns of field values were communicated as the algorithm required. Some inefficiency, due to communication latency, could have been avoided if several rows and/or columns were communicated at the same time, but in order to avoid wasting memory on larger communication buffers, this was not done. This choice was dictated by the small amount of memory (about 476 Kbytes) available on each nCUBE-1 processor.

6.2.4   Example Problem

As a sample problem, the onset and growth of the Kelvin-Helmholtz instability was studied. This instability arises when the interface between two fluids in shear motion is perturbed, and for this problem the body forces, b_x and b_y, are zero. In Figure 6.2 (Color Plate), we show the development of the Kelvin-Helmholtz instability at the interface of two fluids in shear motion. In these figures, the density of the massless marker particles normalized by the fluid density is plotted on a color map, with red corresponding to a density of one through green, blue, and white to a density of zero. Initially, all the marker particles are in the upper half of the domain, and the fluids in the lower- and upper-half domains have a relative shear velocity in the horizontal direction. An 80×80 finite difference grid was used. Vortices form along the interface and interact before being lost to numerical diffusion. By processing the output from the nCUBE-1, a videotape of the evolution of the instability was produced. This sample problem demonstrates that the

Table 6.1: Timing Results in Seconds for a 512-processor and a 1-processor nCUBE-1. The values n_x and n_y represent the numbers of grid points per processor in the x and y directions. The concurrent efficiency, overhead, and speedup are denoted by ϵ, f, and S.

n_x	n_y	n	T_{512}	T_1	$\epsilon\,(\%)$	f	S
6	6	36	0.68	156.67	44.8	1.232	230
12	12	144	1.78	626.69	68.6	0.457	352
18	18	324	3.57	1410.05	77.2	0.296	395
24	24	576	6.07	2506.75	80.7	0.239	413
28	28	784	8.11	3411.97	80.7	0.239	421
30	30	900	9.26	3916.80	82.6	0.210	423
32	32	1024	10.47	4456.45	83.1	0.203	426
36	36	1296	13.14	5640.19	83.8	0.193	429

FCT technique is able to track the physical instability without introducing numerical instability.

6.2.5 Performance and Results

The code was timed for the Kelvin-Helmholtz problem for hypercubes with dimension ranging from zero to nine. The results for the 512-processor case are presented in Table 6.1, and show a speedup of 429 for the largest problem size considered. Subsequently, a group at Sandia National Laboratories, using a modified version of the code, attained a speedup of 1009 on a 1024-processor nCUBE-1 for a similar type of problem [Gustafson:88a]. The definitions of concurrent speedup, overhead, and efficiency are given in Section 3.5.

An analytic model of the performance of the concurrent algorithm was developed, and ignoring communication latency, the concurrent overhead was found to be proportional to $1/\sqrt{n}$, where n is the number of grid points per processor. This is in approximate agreement with the results plotted in Figure 6.3, that shows the concurrent overhead for a number of different hypercubes dimensions and grain sizes.

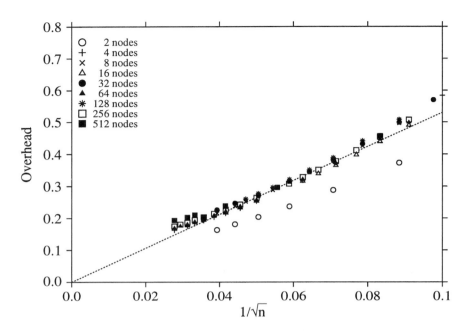

Figure 6.3: Overhead, f, as a Function of $1/\sqrt{n}$, Where n Is the Number of Grid Points per Processor. Results are shown for nCUBE-1 hypercubes of dimension one to nine. The overhead for the 2-processor case (open circles) lies below that for the higher dimensional hypercubes. This is because the processors only communicate in one direction in the 2-processor case, whereas for hypercubes of dimension greater than one, communication is necessary in both the x and y directions.

6.2.6   Summary

The FCT code was ported to the nCUBE-1 by David W. Walker [Walker:88b]. Gary Montry of Sandia National Laboratories supplied the original code, and made several helpful suggestions. A videotape of the evolution of the Kelvin-Helmholtz instability was produced by Jeff Goldsmith at the Image Processing Laboratory of the Jet Propulsion Laboratory.

6.3 Magnetism in the High-Temperature Superconductor Materials

6.3.1 Introduction

Following the discovery of high-temperature superconductivity, two-dimensional quantum antiferromagnetic spin systems have received enormous attention from physicists worldwide. It is generally believed that high-temperature superconductivity occurs in the CuO planes, which is shown in Figure 6.4. Many features can be explained [Anderson:87a] in the Hubbard theory of the strongly coupled electron, which at half-filling is reduced to spin-1/2 antiferromagnetic Heisenberg model:

$$H = J \sum_{\langle ij \rangle} (S_i^x S_j^x + S_i^y S_j^y + S_i^z S_j^z) \qquad (6.4)$$

where S^a are quantum spin operators. Furthermore, the neutron scattering experiments on the parent compound, $La_2 CuO_4$, reveal a rich magnetic structure which is also modelled by this theory.

Physics in two dimensions (as compared to three dimensions) is characterized by the large fluctuations. Many analytical methods work well in three dimensions, but fail in two dimensions. For the quantum systems, this means additional difficulties in finding solutions to the problem.

New analytical methods have been developed to understand the low-T behavior of these two-dimensional systems, and progress had been made. These methods are essentially based on a $1/S$ expansion. Unfortunately, the extreme quantum case $S = 1/2$ lies in the least reliable region of these methods. On the other hand, given sufficient computer power, Quantum Monte Carlo simulation [Ding:90g] can provide accurate numerical solutions of the model theory and quantitative comparison with the experiment (see Figure 6.5). Thus, simulations become a crucial tool in studying these problems. The work described here has made a significant contribution to the understanding of high-T_c materials, and has been well received by the science community [Maddox:90a].

6.3.2 The Computational Algorithm

Using the Suzuki-Trotter transformation, the two-dimensional quantum problem is converted into three-dimensional classical Ising spins with complicated interactions. The partition function becomes a product of transfer

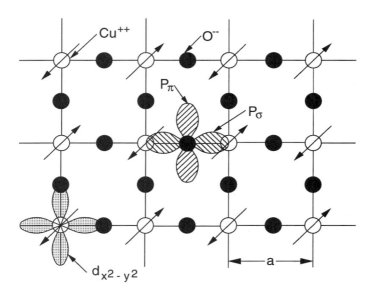

Figure 6.4: The Copper-Oxygen Plane, Where the Superconductivity Is Generally Believed to Occur. The arrows denote the quantum spins. P_π, P_σ, $d_{x^2-y^2}$ denote the wave functions which lead to the interactions among them.

matrices for each four-spin interaction

$$
W = \begin{vmatrix}
e^K & 0 & 0 & 0 \\
0 & e^{-K}ch(2K) & e^{-K}sh(2K) & 0 \\
0 & e^{-K}sh(2K) & e^{-K}ch(2K) & 0 \\
0 & 0 & 0 & e^K
\end{vmatrix}
$$

with $K = \beta/4m$. These four-spin squares go in the time direction on the three-dimensional lattice. This transfer matrix serves as the probability basis for a Monte Carlo simulation. The zero matrix elements are the consequence of the quantum conservation law. To avoid generating trial configurations with zero probability, thus wasting the CPU time since these trials will never be accepted, one should have the conservation law built into the updating scheme. Two types of local moves may locally change the spin configurations, as shown in Figure 6.6. A global move in the time direction flips all the spins along this time line. This update changes the magnetization. Another global move in spatial directions changes the winding numbers.

This classical spin system in three dimensions is simulated using the Metropolis Monte Carlo algorithm. Starting with a given initial configuration,

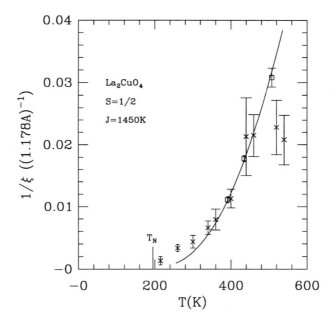

Figure 6.5: Inverse Correlation Length of La_2CuO_4 Measured in Neutron Scattering Experiment, Denoted by Cross; and Those Measured in our Simulation, Denoted by Squares (Units in $(1.178\text{Å})^{-1}$). $J = 1450\,\text{K}$. At $T \approx 500\,\text{K}$, La_2CuO_4 undergoes a structural transition. The curve is the fit shown in Figure 6.11.

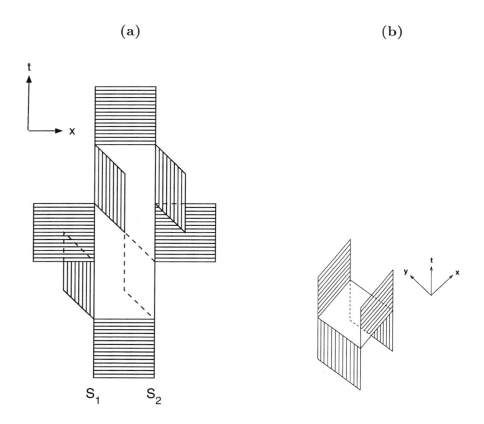

Figure 6.6: (a) A "Time-Flip." The white 3×1 plaquette is a non-interacting one. The eight plaquettes surrounding it are interacting ones. (b) A "Space-Flip." The white 1×1 plaquette is a non-interacting one lying in spatial dimensions. The four plaquettes going in time direction are interacting ones.

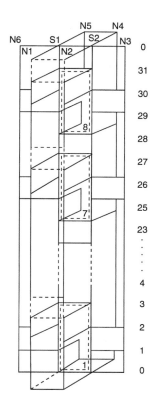

Figure 6.7: A Vectorization of Eight "Time-Flips." Spins along the t-direction are packed into computer words. The two 32-bit words, S1 and S2, contain eight "time plaquettes," indicated by the dashed lines.

we locate a closed loop C of L spins, in one of the four moves. After checking that they satisfy the conservation law, we compute P_i, the probability before all L spins are flipped, which is a product of the diagonal elements of the transfer matrix; and P_f, the probability after the spins are flipped, which is a product of the off-diagonal elements of the transfer matrix along the loop C. The Metropolis procedure is to accept the flip according to the probability $P = P_f/P_i$.

We implemented a simple and efficient multispin coding method which facilitates vectorization and saves index calculation and memory space. This is possible because each spin only has two states, up (1) or down (0), which is represented by a single bit in a 32-bit integer. Spins along the t-direction are packed into 32-bit words, so that the boundary communication along the x or

y direction can be handled more easily. All the necessary checks and updates can be handled by the bitwise logical operations OR, AND, NOT, and XOR. Note that this is a natural vectorization, since AND operations for the 32 spins are carried out in the single AND operation by the CPU. The index calculations to address these individual spins are also minimized, because one only computes the index once for the 32 spins. The same principles are applied for both local and global moves. Figure 6.7 shows the case for time-loop coding.

6.3.3   Parallel Implementation and Performance

The fairly large three-dimensional lattices (usually $128 \times 128 \times 192$) are partitioned into a ring of M processors with x-dimension which is uniformly distributed among the M processors. The local updates are easily parallelized since the connection is, at most, next-nearest neighbor (for the time-loop update). The needed spin-word arrays from its neighbor are copied into the local storage by the *shift* routine in the CrOS communication system [Fox:88a] before doing the update. One of the global updates, the time line, can also be done in the same fashion. The communication is very efficient in the sense that a single communication shift, $Ny \times Nt$, spins instead of Nt spins in the case where the lattice is partitioned into a two-dimensional grid. The overhead/latency associated with the communication is thus significantly reduced.

The winding-line global update along the x-direction is difficult to do in this fashion, because it involves spins on all the M nodes. In addition, we need to compute the correlation functions which have the same difficulty. However, since these operations are not used very often, we devised a fairly elegant way to parallelize these global operations. A set of *gather-scatter* routines, based on the *cread* and *cwrite* in CrOS, is written. In *gather*, the subspaces on each node are gathered into complete spaces on each node, preserving the original geometric connection. Parallelism is achieved now since the global operations are done on each node just as in the sequential computer, with each node only doing the part it originally covers. In *scatter*, the updated (changed) lattice configuration on a particular node (number zero) is scattered (distributed) back to all the nodes in the ring, exactly according to the original partition. Note that this scheme differs from the earlier decomposition scheme [Fox:84a] for the gravitation problem, where memory size constraint is the main concern.

The hypercube nodes were divided into several *independent* rings, each

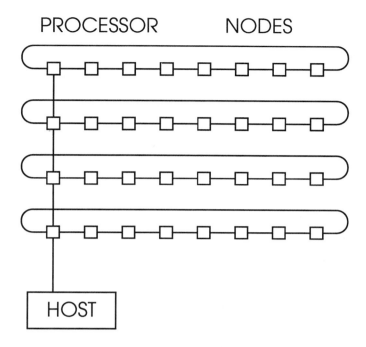

Figure 6.8: The Configuration of the Hypercube Nodes. In the example, 32 nodes are configured as four independent rings, each consisting of 8 nodes. Each ring does an independent simulation.

ring holding an independent simulation, as shown in Figure 6.8. At higher temperatures, a spin system of 32×32 is enough, so that we can simulate several independent systems at the same time. At low temperatures, one needs larger systems, such as 128×128—all the nodes will then be dedicated to a single large system. This simple parallelism makes the simulation very flexible and efficient. In the simulation, we used a parallel version of the Fibonacci additive random numbers generator [Ding:88d], which has a period larger that 2^{127}.

We have made a systematic performance analysis by running the code on different sizes and different numbers of nodes. The timing results for a realistic situation (20 sweeps of update, one measurement) are measured [Ding:90k]. The speedup, t_1/t_M, where t_1 (t_M) is the time for the same size spins system to run same number operations on one (M) node, is plotted in Figure 6.9. One can see that speedup is quite close to the ideal case, denoted by the dashed line. For the 128×128 quantum spin system, the

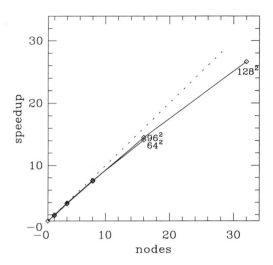

Figure 6.9: Speedup of the Parallel Algorithm for Lattice Systems 64×64, 96×96 and 128×128. The dashed line is the ideal case.

32-node hypercube speeds up the computation by a factor of 26.6, which is a very good result. However, running the same spin system on a 16-node is more efficient, because we can run two independent systems on the 32-node hypercube with a total speedup of $2 \times 14.5 = 29$ (each speedup a factor 14.5). This is better described by *efficiency*, defined as speedup/nodes, which is plotted in Figure 6.10. Clearly, the efficiency of the implementation is very high, generally over 90%.

Comparison with other supercomputers is interesting. For this program, the one-head CRAY X-MP speed is approximately that of a 2-node Mark II-Ifp. This indicates that our 32-node Mark IIIfp performs better than the CRAY X-MP by about a factor of $(32/2) \times 90\% = 14$! We note that our code is written in C and the vectorization is limited to the 32-bit inside the words. Rewriting the code in Fortran (Fortran compilers on the CRAY are more efficient) and fully vectorizing the code, one may gain a factor of about three on the CRAY. Nevertheless, this quantum Monte Carlo code is clearly a good example, in that parallel computers easily (i.e., at same programming level) outperform the conventional supercomputers.

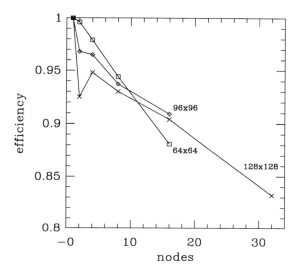

Figure 6.10: Efficiency of the Parallel Algorithm

6.3.4 Physics Results

We obtained many good results which were previously unknown. Among them, the correlation functions are perhaps the most important. First, the results can be directly compared with experiments, thus providing new understanding of the magnetic structure of the high-temperature superconducting materials. Second, and no less important, is the behavior of the correlation function we obtained which gives a crucial test of the assessment of various approximate methods.

In the large spin-S (classical) system, the correlation length goes as

$$\xi = A \cdot \exp(2\pi S^2 J/T) \tag{6.5}$$

at low temperatures. This predicts a too-large correlation length, compared with experimental results. As $S \to 1/2$, the quantum fluctuations in the system become significant. Several approximate methods [Chakravarty:88a], [Auerbach:88a] predict a similar low-T behavior. $\xi = (A/T^p) \times \exp(2\pi\rho_s/T)$, $\rho_s = Z_\xi^S S(S+1)J$, and $p = 0$ or 1. $Z_\xi^S \leq 1$ is a quantum renormalization constant.

Our extensive quantum Monte Carlo simulations were performed [Ding:90g] on the spin-1/2 system as large as 128×128 at low tempera-

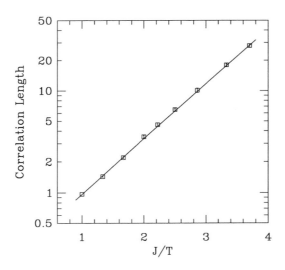

Figure 6.11: Correlation Length Measured at Various Temperatures. The straight line is the fit.

ture range $T/J = 0.27$–1.0. The correlation length, as a function of $1/T$, is plotted in Figure 6.11. The data points fall onto a straight line, surprisingly well, throughout the whole temperature range, leading naturally to the pure exponential form:

$$\xi(T)/a = 0.276 e^{1.25 J/T}, \tag{6.6}$$

where a is the lattice constant. This provides a crucial support to the above-mentioned theories. Quantitatively,

$$Z_\xi^{1/2} = 0.265(2) \tag{6.7}$$

or

$$\rho_s = Z_\xi^S S(S+1) J = 0.199(2) J. \tag{6.8}$$

Direct comparison with experiments will not only test the validity of the Heisenberg model, but also determine the important parameter, the exchange coupling J. The spacing between Cu atoms in CuO plane is $a = 3.79\,\text{Å}$. Setting $J = 1450\,\text{K}$, the Monte Carlo data is compared with those from neutron scattering experiments [Endoh:88a] in Figure 6.5. The agreement is very good. This provides strong evidence that the essential magnetic behavior is captured by the Heisenberg model. The quantum Monte Carlo result is an accurate first principle calculation; no adjustable parameter is involved. Comparing directly with the experiment, the only adjustable parameter is J. This gives an independent determination of the *effective* exchange coupling:

$$J = 1450 \pm 30 \, \mathrm{K}. \qquad (6.9)$$

Note that near $T_N \simeq 200 \, \mathrm{K}$, the experimentally measured correlation is systematically smaller than the theoretical curve, shown in Equation 6.4. This is a combined result of small effects: frustration, anisotropies, interlayer coupling, and so on.

Various moments of the Raman spectrum are calculated using series expansions and comparing with experiments [Singh:89a]. This gives an estimate, $J = 1030 \pm 50 \mathrm{cm}^{-1}$ ($1480 \pm 70 \, \mathrm{K}$), which is quite close to the above value determined from correlation functions. Raman scattering probes the short wavelength region, whereas neutron scattering measures the long-range correlations. The agreement of J's obtained from these two rather different experiments is another significant indication that the magnetic interactions are dominated by the Heisenberg model.

Equation 6.4 is valid for all the quantum AFM spins. The classic two-dimensional antiferromagnetic system discovered twenty years ago [Birgeneau:71a], K_2NiF_4, is a spin-one system with $J = 104 \, \mathrm{K}$. Very recently, Birgeneau [Birgeneau:90a] fitted the measured correlation lengths to

$$\frac{\xi(T)}{a} = \frac{0.123 e^{5.31J/T}}{(1 + T/5.31J)} \qquad (6.10)$$

The fit is very good, as shown in Figure 6.12. The factor $(1 + T/5.31J)$ comes from integration of the two-loop β-function without taking the $T \to 0$ limit, and could be neglected if T is very close to 0. For the spin-5/2 AFM $Rb_2 Mn_x Cr_{1-x} Cl_4$, Equation 6.4 also describes the data quite well [Higgins:88a].

A common feature from Figures 6.11 and 6.12 is that the scaling equation Equation 6.4, which is derived near $T_c = 0$, is valid for a wide range of T, up to $T \sim 2J$. This differs drastically from the range of criticality in three-dimensional systems, where the width $t \equiv (T - T_c)/T_c$ is usually about 0.2 or less. This is a consequence of the crossover temperature T_{cr} [Chakravarty:88a], where the Josephson length scale becomes compatible with the thermal wave length, being relatively high, $T_{cr} \sim J$. This property

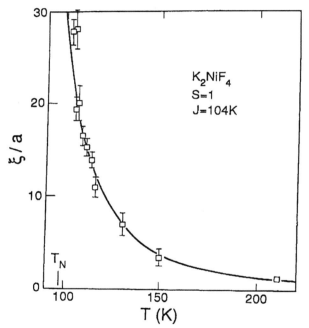

Figure 6.12: Correlation Length of $K_2 Ni F_4$ Measured in Neutron Scattering Experiment with the Fit.

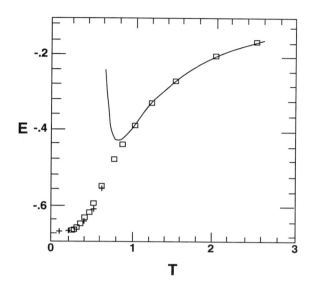

Figure 6.13: Energy Measured as a Function of Temperature. Squares are from our work. The curve is the 10th order high-T expansion.

is a general character in the low critical dimensions. In the quantum XY model, a Kosterlitz-Thouless transition occurs [Ding:90b] at $kT_c/J = 0.350$ and the critical behavior remains valid up to $kT/J = 0.7$.

As emphasized by Birgeneau, the spin-wave value

$$2\pi\rho_s = 2\pi JS^2(1 + 0.158/2S)^2(1 - 0.552/2S), \qquad (6.11)$$

$S = 1$, $2\pi\rho_s = 5.30$, fits the experiment quite well, whereas for $S = 1/2$, spin-wave value $2\pi\rho_s = 0.944$ differs significantly from the correct value 1.25 as in Equation 6.4. This indicates that the large quantum fluctuations in the spin-1/2 system are not adequately accounted for in the spin-wave theory, whereas for the spin-one system, they are.

Figure 6.13 shows the energy density at various temperatures. At higher T, the high-temperature series expansion accurately reproduces our data. At low T, E approaches a finite ground state energy. Another useful thermodynamical quantity is uniform susceptibility, which is shown in Figure 6.14. Again, at high-T, series expansion coincides with our data. The maximum point occurs at $kT/J = 0.93$ with $\chi_{max}J/N_0g^2\mu_B = 2.825(2)$. This is useful in determining J and N_0 for the material.

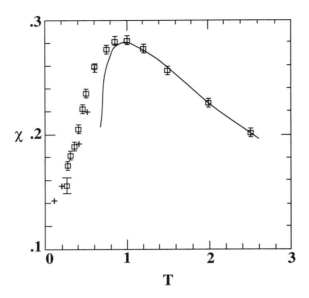

Figure 6.14: Uniform Susceptibility Measured as a Function of Temperature. Symbols are similar to Figure 6.13.

6.3.5   Conclusions

In conclusion, the quantum AFM Heisenberg spins are now well understood theoretically. The data from neutron scattering experiments for both $S = 1/2$, $La_2 CuO_4$ and $S = 1$, $K_2 Ni F_4$ compare quite well. For $La_2 CuO_4$, this leads to a direct determination $J = 1450 \pm 30K$.

Quantum spins are well suited for the hypercube computer. Its spatial decomposition is straightforward; the short-range nature (excluding the occasional long-range one) of interaction makes the extension to large numbers of processors simple. Hypercube connections made the use of the node computer efficient and flexible. High speedup can be achieved with reasonable ease, provided one improves the algorithm to minimize the communications.

The work described here is the result of the collaboration between H. Q. Ding and M. S. Makivic.

6.4 Phase Transitions in Two-dimensional Quantum Spin Systems

In this section, we discuss two further important developments based on the previous section (Section 6.3) on the isotropic Heisenberg quantum spins. These extensions are important in treating the observed phase transitions in the two-dimensional magnetic systems. Theoretically, two-dimensional isotropic Heisenberg quantum spins remain in paramagnetic state at all temperatures [Mermin:66a]. However, all crystals found in nature with strong two-dimensional magnetic characters go through phase transitions into ordered states [Birgeneau:71a], [DeJongh:74a]. These include the recently discovered high-T_c materials, $La_2\,CuO_4$ and $Y\,Ba_2\,Cu_3\,O_6$, despite the presence of large quantum fluctuations in the spin-1/2 antiferromagnets.

We consider the cases where the magnetic spins interact through

$$H = \sum_{[ij]} JS_i \cdot S_j + hS_i^z S_j^z \tag{6.12}$$

In the case $h \ll J$, the system goes through an Ising-like antiferromagnetic transition, very similar to those that occur in the high-T_c materials. In the case $h = -J$, that is, the XY model, the system exhibits a Kosterlitz-Thouless type of transition. In both cases, our simulation provides convincing and complete results for the first time.

Through the Matsubara-Matsuda transformation between spin-1/2 operator S_i and bosonic creation/destruction operations $\psi_i : \psi_i^+ \rightarrow S_i^x + S_i^y$ and $\psi_i^+ \psi_i \rightarrow S_i^z + 1/2$, a general quantum system can be mapped into quantum spin system. Therefore, the phase transitions described here apply to general two-dimensional quantum systems. These results have broad implications in two-dimensional physical systems in particular, and the statistical systems in general.

6.4.1 The case of h ≪ J: Antiferromagnetic Transitions

The popular explanation for the antiferromagnetic ordering transitions in these high-T_c materials emphasizes the very small coupling, J', between the two-dimensional layers, J'/J, and is estimated to be about 10^{-5}. However, all these systems exhibit some kind of in-plane anisotropies, which is of order 10^{-3}. An interesting case is the spin-one crystal, $K_2\,Ni\,F_4$, discovered twenty years ago [Birgeneau:71a]. The magnetic behavior of $K_2\,Ni\,F_4$ exhibits very strong two-dimensional characters with an exchange coupling $J = 104\,\mathrm{K}$.

It has a Néel ordering transition at $T_N = 97K$, induced by an Ising-like anisotropy, $h^A \approx 0.002$.

Our simulation provides clear evidence to support the picture that the in-plane anisotropy is also quite important in bringing about the observed antiferromagnetic transition at the most interesting spin-1/2 case. Adding an anisotropy energy as small as $h^A = 0.0025$ will induce an ordering transition at $T_c/kJ = 0.295$. This striking effect and related results agree well with a wide class of experiments, and provide some insights into these types of materials.

Origin of the Interaction

In the antiferromagnetic spin system, superexchange leads to the dominant isotropic coupling. One of the high-order effects, due to crystal field, is written as $-DS_z^2$, which is a constant for these spin-1/2 high-T_c materials. Another second-order effect is the spin-orbital coupling. This effect will pick up a preferred direction and lead to an $S_i^z S_j^z$ term, which also arises due to the lattice distortion in $La_2 Cu O_4$. More complicated terms, like the antisymmetric exchange, can also be generated. For simplicity and clarity, we focus the study on the antiferromagnetic Heisenberg model with an Ising-like anisotropy as in Equation 6.12. The anisotropy parameter h relates to the usual reduced anisotropy energy h^A through $h^A = h/4J$. In the past, the anisotropy field model, $\Sigma \epsilon_i H_A S_i^z$, has also been included. However, its origin is less clear and, furthermore, the Ising symmetry is explicitly broken.

Simulation Results

For the large anisotropy system, $h = 1$, the specific heat C_V are shown for several spin systems in Figure 6.15(a). The peak becomes sharper and higher as the system size increases, indicating a divergent peak in an infinite system, similar to the two-dimensional Ising model. Defining the transition temperature $T_c(L)$ at the peak of C_V for the finite $L \times L$ system, the finite-size scaling theory [Landau:76a] predicts that $T_c(L)$ relates to T_c through the scaling law

$$T_c(L) - T_c \propto L^{-\nu}. \tag{6.13}$$

Setting $\nu = 1$, the Ising exponent, a good fit with $T_c = 1.063 \pm 0.003$, is shown in Figure 6.15(b). A different scaling with the same exponent for the correlation length,

$$\xi \propto (T - T_c)^{-\nu}, \tag{6.14}$$

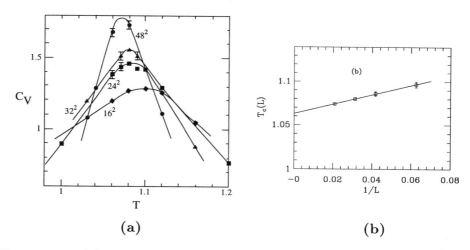

(a)   **(b)**

Figure 6.15: (a) The Specific Heat for Different Size Systems of $h = 1$. (b) Finite Size Scaling for $T_c(L) - T_c \propto L^{-1}$.

is also satisfied quite well, resulting in $T_c = 1.05 \pm 0.01$. The staggered magnetization drops down near T_c, although the behaviors are rounded off on these finite-size systems. All the evidence clearly indicates that an Ising-like antiferromagnetic transition occurs at $T_c = 1.06$, with a divergent specific heat. In the smaller anisotropy case, $h = 0.1$, similar behaviors are found. The scaling for the correlation length is shown in Figure 6.16, indicating a transition at $T_c = 0.44$. However, the specific heat remains finite at all temperatures.

The most interesting case is $h = 0.01$ (or $h^A = 0.0025$, very close to those in K_2NiF_4 [Birgeneau:71a]). Figure 6.17 shows the staggered correlation function at $T = 0.3$ compared with those on the isotropic model [Ding:90g]. The inverse correlation length measured, together with those for the isotropic model ($h = 0$), are shown in Figure 6.16. Below $\xi^{-1} \approx 0.1$, the Ising behavior of a straight line becomes clear. Clearly, the system becomes antiferromagnetically ordered around $T = 0.3$. The best estimate is

$$T_c = 0.295, \quad h = 0.01. \tag{6.15}$$

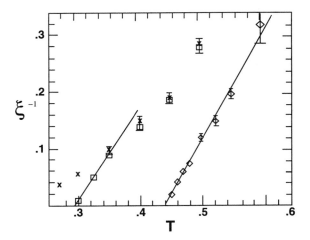

Figure 6.16: The Inverse Correlation Lengths for $h = 0.1$ System ($\diamond$), $h = 0.01$ System ($\sqcap$), and $h = 0$ System ($\times$) for the Purpose of Comparison. The straight lines are the scaling relation: $\xi^{-1} \propto T - T_c$. From it we can pin down T_c.

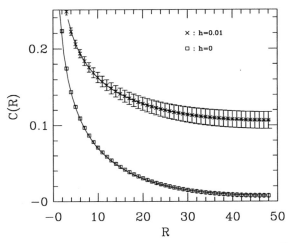

Figure 6.17: The Correlation Function on the 96×96 System at $T = 0.3$ for $h = 0.01$ system. It decays with correlation length $\xi \approx 120$. Also shown is the isotropic case $h = 0$, which has $\xi = 17.5$.

Theoretical Interpretation

It may seem a little surprising that a very small anisotropy can lead to a substantially high T_c. This may be explained by the following argument. At low T, the spins are highly correlated in the isotropic case. Since no direction is preferred, the correlated spins fluctuate in all directions, resulting in zero net magnetization. Adding a very small anisotropy into the system introduces a preferred direction, so that the already highly correlated spins will fluctuate around this direction, leading to a global magnetization.

More quantitatively, the crossover from the isotropic Heisenberg behavior to the Ising behavior occurs at T_{cr}, where the correlation length is of order of some power of the inverse anisotropy. From the scaling arguments [Riedel:69a], $\xi \sim h^{-\nu/\phi} \approx h^{-1/2}$ where ϕ is the crossover exponent. In the two-dimensional model, both ν and ϕ are infinite, but the ratio is approximately $1/2$. For $h = 0.01$, this relation indicates that the Ising behavior is valid for $\xi^{-1} \leq 0.1$, which is clearly observed in Figure 6.16. Similar crossover around $\xi^{-1} \approx 0.3$ for $h = 0.1$ is also observed in Figure 6.16. At low T, for the isotropic quantum model, the correlation length behaves as [Ding:90g] $\xi \sim e^{2\pi\rho/T}$ where $\rho = Z_\xi^{(S)} \times S(S+1)$. Therefore, we expect

$$T_c \approx \frac{Z^{(S)}S(S+1)}{\log(h^{-1})}, \tag{6.16}$$

where $Z^{(S)}$ is spin-S dependent constant of order one. Therefore, even a very small anisotropy (h) will induce a phase transition at a substantially high temperature ($T_c \gg h$). This crude picture, suggested a long time ago to explain the observed phase transitions, is now confirmed by the extensive quantum Monte Carlo simulations for the first time. Note that this problem is an extreme case both because it is an antiferromagnet (more difficult to become ordered than the ferromagnet), and because it has the largest quantum fluctuations (spin-1/2). Since $\log(h^{-1})$ varies slowly with h, we can estimate $Z^{(S)}$ at $h = 0.01$:

$$Z^{(1/2)} \simeq 1.9. \tag{6.17}$$

Comparison with Experiments

This simple result correctly predicts T_c for a wide class of crystals found in nature, assuming the same level of anisotropy, that is, $h^A \sim 0.002$. The high-T_c superconductor $Y Ba_2 Cu_3 O_{6.1}$ exhibits a Néel transition at $T_N = 435\,\text{K}$.

With $J \approx 1400\,\mathrm{K}$, our results give quite a close estimate: $T_c = 420\,\mathrm{K}$. Similar close predictions hold for other $S = 1/2$ systems, such as superconductor $Er\,Ba_2\,Cu_3\,O_7$ and insulator $K_2\,Co\,F_4$. For the high-T_c material $La_2\,Cu\,O_4$, $J = 1450\,\mathrm{K}$ [Ding:90g]. This material undergoes a Néel transition at $T_N \simeq$ 220 K. Our prediction of $T_c = 428\,\mathrm{K}$ is in the same range of T_N, and much better than the naive expectation that $T_c \sim h \sim 10\,\mathrm{K}$. In this crystal, there is some degree of frustration (see below), so the actual transition is pushed down. These examples clearly indicate that the in-plane anisotropy could be quite important to bring the system to the Néel order for these high-T_c materials. For the $S = 1$ system, $K_2\,Ni\,F_4$, our results predict a $T_c = 81\,\mathrm{K}$, quite close to the observed $T_N = 97\,\mathrm{K}$.

These results have direct consequences regarding the critical exponents. The onset of transition is entirely due to the Ising-like anisotropy. Once the system becomes Néel-ordered, different layers in the three-dimensional crystals will order at the same time. Spin fluctuations, in different layers, are incoherent so that the critical exponents such as β, γ, and ν will be the two, rather than three-dimensional Ising exponents. $Er\,Ba_2\,Cu_3\,O_7$ and $K_2\,Co\,F_4$ show such behaviors clearly. However, the interlayer coupling, although very small (much smaller than the in-plane anisotropy), could induce coherent correlations between the layers, so that the critical exponents will be somewhere between the two and three-dimensional Ising exponents. $La_2\,Cu\,O_4$ and $Y\,Ba_2\,Cu_3\,O_6$ seem to belong to this category.

Whether the ground state of the spin-1/2 antiferromagnet spins has the long-range Néel order, is a longstanding problem [Anderson:87a]. The existence of the Néel order is vigorously proved for $h \geq 0.78$. In the most interesting case ($h = 0$), numerical calculations on small lattices suggested the existence of the long-range order. Our simulation establishes the long-range order for $h \geq 0.01$.

The fact that near T_c, the spin system is quite sensitive to the tiny anisotropy could have a number of important consequences. For example, the correlation lengths measured in $La_2\,Cu\,O_4$ are systematically smaller than the theoretical prediction [Ding:90g] near T_c. The weaker correlations probably indicate that the frustrations, due to the next to nearest neighbor interaction, come into play. This is consistent with the fact that T_N is below the T_c suggested by our results.

6.4.2 The Case of h = −J: Quantum XY Model and the Topological Transition

It is well known now that the two-dimensional (2D) classical (planar) XY model undergoes Kosterlitz-Thouless (KT) [Kosterlitz:73a] transition at $kT_c/J = 0.898$ [Gupta:88a], characterized by exponentially divergent correlation length and in-plane susceptibility. The transition, due to the unbinding of vortex-antivortex pairs, is weak; the specific heat has a finite peak above T_c.

Does the two-dimensional quantum XY model go through a phase transition? If so, what type of transition? This is a longstanding problem in statistical physics. The answers are relevant to a wide class of two-dimensional problems such as magnetic insulators, superfluidity, melting, and possibly to the recently discovered high-T_c superconducting transition. Physics in two dimensions is characterized by large fluctuations. Changing from the classical model to the quantum model, additional quantum fluctuations (which are particularly strong in the case of spin-1/2) may alter the physics significantly. A direct consequence is that the already weak KT transition could be washed out completely.

A Brief History

The quantum XY model was first proposed [Matsubara:56a] in 1956 to study the lattice quantum fluids. Later, high-temperature series studies raised the possibility of a divergent susceptibility for the two-dimensional model. For the classical planar model, the remarkable theory of Kosterlitz and Thouless [Kosterlitz:73a] provided a clear physical picture and correctly predicted a number of important properties. However, much less is known about the quantum model. In fact, it has been controversial. Using a large-order high-temperature expansion, Rogiers, et al. [Rogiers:79a] suggested a second-order transition at $kT_c/J = 0.39$ for spin-1/2. Later, real-space renormalization group analysis was applied to the model with contradictory and inconclusive results. DeRaedt, et al. [DeRaedt:84a] then presented an exact solution and Monte Carlo simulation, both based on the Suzuki-Trotter transformation with small Trotter number m. Their results, both analytical and numerical, supported an Ising-like (second-order) transition at the Ising point $kT_c/J = 1/2\log(1 + \sqrt{2}) = 0.567$, with a logarithmically divergent specific heat. Loh, et al. [Loh:85a] simulated the system with an improved technique. They found that specific peak remains finite and argued that a phase transition occurs at $T_c = 0.4$–0.5 by measuring the change of the "twist energy" from the 4×4 lattice to the 8×8 lattice. The dispute between DeRaedt, et al., and Loh, et al., centered on the importance of using a large Trotter number m and the global updates in small-size systems, which move the system from one subspace to another. Recent attempts to solve this problem still add fuel to the controversy.

Evidence for the Transition

The key to pinning down the existence and type of transition is a study of correlation length and in-plane susceptibility, because their divergences constitute the most direct evidence of a phase transition. These quantities are much more difficult to measure, and large lattices are required in order to avoid finite size effects. These key points are lacking in the previous works, and are the focus of our study. By extensive use of the Mark IIIfp Hypercube, we are able to measure spin correlations and thermodynamic quantities accurately on very large lattices (96×96). Our work [Ding:90h;92a] provides convincing evidence that a phase transition does occur at a finite temperature in the extreme quantum case, spin-1/2. At transition point, $kT_c/J = 0.350 \pm 0.004$, the correlation length and susceptibility diverge exactly according to the form of Kosterlitz-Thouless (Equation 6.18).

We plot the correlation length, ξ, and the susceptibility, χ, in Figures 6.18 and 6.19. They show a tendency of divergence at some finite T_c. Indeed, we fit them to the form predicted by Kosterlitz and Thouless for the classical model

$$\xi(T) = A e^{B/(T-T_c)^{\nu}}, \quad \nu = \frac{1}{2}. \tag{6.18}$$

The fit is indeed very good (χ^2 per degree of freedom is 0.81), as shown in Figure 6.18. The fit for correlation length gives

$$A_{\xi} = 0.27(3), \quad B_{\xi} = 1.18(6), \quad T_c = 0.350(4). \tag{6.19}$$

A similar fit for susceptibility, χ is also very good ($\chi^2/\text{DOF} = 1.06$):

$$A_{\chi} = 0.060(5), \quad B_{\chi} = 2.08(6), \quad T_c = 0.343(3), \tag{6.20}$$

as shown in Figure 6.19. The good quality of both fits and the closeness of T_c's obtained are the main results of this work. The fact that these fits also reproduce the expected scaling behavior $\chi \propto \xi^{2-\eta}$ with

$$\eta = 2 - B_{\chi}/B_{\xi} = 0.24 \pm 0.10 \tag{6.21}$$

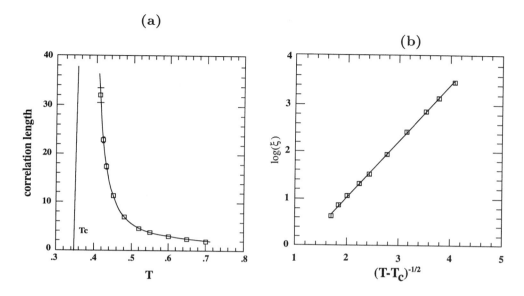

Figure 6.18: Correlation Length and Fit. (a) ξ versus T. The vertical line indicates ξ diverges at T_c; (b) $\log(\xi)$ versus $(T - T_c)^{-1/2}$. The straight line indicates $\nu = 1/2$.

is a further consistency check. These results strongly indicate that the spin-1/2 XY model undergoes a Kosterlitz-Thouless phase transition at $T_c = 0.350 \pm 0.004$. We note that this T_c is consistent with the trend of the "twist energy" [Loh:85a] and that the rapid increase of vortex density near $T = 0.35 - 0.40$ is due to the unbinding of vortex pairs. Figures 6.18 and 6.19 also indicate that the critical region ΔT is quite wide ($\sim T_c$), which is very similar to the spin-1/2 Heisenberg model, where the $T \rightarrow 0$ behavior holds up to $T \sim 2J$. These two-dimensional phenomena are in sharp contrast to the usual second-order transitions in three dimensions.

The algebraic exponent η is consistent with the Ornstein-Zernike exponent $(d - 1)/2 = 1/2$ at higher T. As $T \rightarrow T_c$, η shifts down slightly and shows signs of approaching $1/4$, the value at T_c for the classical model. This is consistent with Equation 6.21.

We measured energy and specific heat, C_V (for $T \leq 0.41$ we used a 32×32 lattice). The specific heat is shown in Figure 6.20. We found that C_V has a peak above T_c, at around $T = 0.45$. The peak clearly shifts away from $T = 0.52$ on the much smaller 8×8 lattice. DeRaedt, et al. [DeRaedt:84a] suggested a logarithmic divergent C_V in their simulation, which is likely an

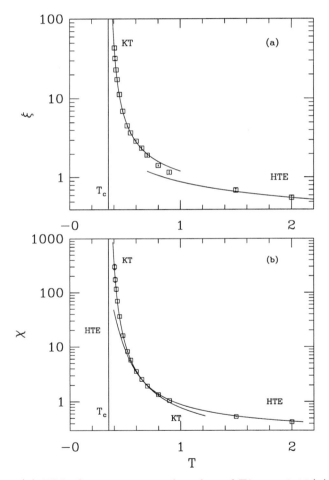

Figure 6.19: (a) This figure repeats the plot of Figure 6.18(a) showing on a coarser scale both the high temperature expansion (HTE) and the Kosterlitz-Thouless fit (KT). (b) Susceptibility χ and Fit

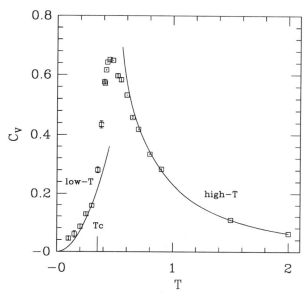

Figure 6.20: Specific Heat C_V. For $T < 0.41$, the lattice size is 32×32.

artifact of their small m values. One striking feature in Figure 6.20 is a very steep increase of C_V at $T \approx T_c$. The shape of the curve is asymmetric near the peak. These features of the C_V curve differ from that in the classical XY model [Gupta:88a].

Implications

Quantum fluctuations are capable of pushing the transition point from $T_c = 0.898$ in the classical model, down to $T_c = 0.35$ in the quantum spin-1/2 case, although they are not strong enough to push it down to 0. They also reduced the constant B_ξ from 1.67 in the classical case to 1.18 in the spin-1/2 case.

The critical behavior in the quantum case is of the KT-type, as in the classical case. This is a little surprising, considering the differences regarding the spin space. In the classical case, the spins are confined to the X-Y plane (thus the model is conventionally called a "planar rotator" model). This is important for the topological order in KT theory. The quantum spins are not restricted to the X-Y plane, due to the presence of S^z for the commutator relation. The KT behavior found in the quantum case indicates that the extra dimension in the spin space (which does not appear in the Hamiltonian) is actually unimportant. These correlations are very weak and short-ranged. The out-of-plane susceptibility remains a small quantity in the whole temperature range.

These results for the XY model, together with those on the quantum Heisenberg model, strongly suggest that although quantum fluctuations at finite T can change the quantitative behavior of these nonfrustrated spin systems with *continuous* symmetries, the qualitative picture of the classical system persists. This could be understood following universality arguments that, near the critical point, the dominant behavior of the system is determined by long wavelength fluctuations which are characterized by symmetries and dimensionality. The quantum effects only change the short-range fluctuations which, after integrated out, only enter as renormalization of the physical parameters, such as B_ξ.

Our data also show that, for the XY model, the critical exponents are spin-S independent, in agreement with universality. More specifically, ν in Equation 6.18 could, in principle, differ from its classical value 1/2. Our data are sufficient to detect any systematic deviation from this value. For this purpose, we plotted ξ in Figure 6.18(b), using $\log(\xi)$ versus $(T - T_c)^{-1/2}$. As expected, data points all fall well on a straight line (except the point at $T = 0.7$ where the critical region presumably ends). A systematic deviation from $\nu = 1/2$ would lead to a slightly curved line instead of a straight line. In addition, the exponent, η at T_c, seems to be consistent with the value for the classical system.

Our simulations reveal a rich structure, as shown in the phase diagram (Figure 6.21) for these $S = 1/2$ quantum spins. The antiferromagnetic ordered region and the topological ordered region are especially relevant to the high-T_c materials.

Finally, we point out the connection between the quantum XY system and the general two-dimensional quantum system with continuous symmetry. Through the above-mentioned Matsubara-Matsuda transformations, our result implies the existence of the Kosterlitz-Thouless condensation in two-dimensional quantum systems. The symmetry in the XY model now becomes $\psi_i \rightarrow \psi_i\, e^{i\alpha}$, a continuous phase symmetry. This quantum KT condensation may have important implications on the mechanism of the recently discovered high-temperature superconducting transitions.

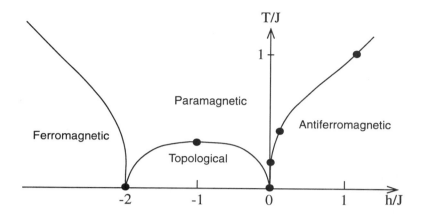

Figure 6.21: Phase Diagram for the Spin-1/2 Quantum System Shown in Equation 6.12. The solid points are from quantum Monte Carlo simulations. For large $|h|$, the system is practically an Ising system. Near $h = 0$ or $h = -2$, the logarithmic relation, Equation 6.16 holds.

6.5   A Hierarchical Scheme for Surface Reconstruction and Discontinuity Detection

Vision (both biological and computer-based) is a complex process that can be characterized by multiple stages where the original iconic information is progressively distilled and refined. The first researchers to approach the problem underestimated the difficulty of the task—after all, it does not require a lot of effort for a human to open the eyes, form a model of the environment, recognize objects, move, and so on. But in the last years a scientific basis has been given to the first stages of the process (*low- and intermediate-level vision*) and a large set of special-purpose algorithms are available for *high-level* vision.

It is already possible to execute low-level operations (like filtering, edge detection, intensity normalization) in real time (30 frames/sec) using special-purpose digital hardware (like digital signal processors). On the contrary, higher level visual tasks tend to be specialized to the different applications, and require general-purpose hardware and software facilities.

Parallelism and multiresolution processing are two effective strategies to reduce the computational requirements of higher visual tasks (see, for example, [Battiti:91a;91b], [Furmanski:88c], [Marr:76a]). We describe a general software environment for implementing medium-level computer vision on large-grain-size MIMD computers. The purpose has been to implement a multiresolution strategy based on iconic data structures (two-dimensional arrays that can be indexed with the pixels' coordinates) distributed to the computing nodes using *domain decomposition.*

In particular, the environment has been applied successfully to the *visible surface reconstruction* and *discontinuity detection* problems. Initial constraints are transformed into a robust and explicit representation of the space around the viewer. In the *shape from shading* problem, the constraints are on the orientation of surface patches, while in the *shape from motion problem* (for example), the constraints are on the depth values.

We will describe a way to compute the motion (*optical flow*) from the intensity arrays of images taken at different times in Section 6.7.

Discontinuities are necessary both to avoid mixing constraints pertaining to different physical objects during the reconstruction, and to provide a primitive perceptual organization of the visual input into different elements related to the human notion of objects.

6.5.1   Multigrid Method with Discontinuities

The purpose of early vision is to undo the image formation process, recovering the properties of visible three-dimensional surfaces from the two-dimensional array of image intensities.

Computationally, this amounts to solving a very large system of equations. In general, the solution is not unique or does not exist (and therefore, one must settle for a suitable approximation).

The class of admissible solutions can be restricted by introducing a priori knowledge: the desired "typical" properties are enforced, transforming the inversion problem into the *minimization of a functional.* This is known as the *regularization method* [Poggio:85a]. Applying the calculus of variations, the *stationary* points are found by solving the Euler-Lagrange partial differential equations.

In standard methods for solving PDEs, the problem is first discretized on a finite-dimensional approximation space. The very large algebraic system obtained is then solved using, for example, "relaxation" algorithms which are local and iterative. The local structure is essential for the efficient use of parallel computation.

By the local nature of the relaxation process, solution errors on the scale of the solution grid step are corrected in a few iterations; however, larger

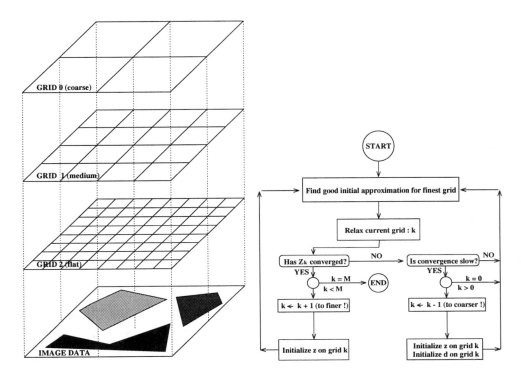

Figure 6.22: Pyramidal Structure for Multigrid Algorithms and General Flow of Control

scale errors are corrected very slowly. Intuitively, in order to correct them, information must be spread over a large scale by the "sluggish" neighbor-neighbor influence. If we want a *larger spread of influence* per iteration, we need large scale connections for the processing units, that is, we need to solve a simplified problem on a coarser grid.

The pyramidal structure of the multigrid solution grids is illustrated in Figure 6.22.

This simple idea and its realization in the *multigrid algorithm* not only leads to asymptotically optimal solution times (i.e., convergence in $O(n)$ operations), but also dramatically decreases solution times for a variety of practical problems, as shown in [Brandt:77a].

The multigrid "recipe" is very simple. First use *relaxation* to obtain an approximation with smooth error on a fine grid. Then, given the smoothness of the error, calculate corrections to this approximation on a coarser grid, and to do this first relax, then correct *recursively* on still coarser grids. Optionally, you can also use *nested iteration* (that coarser grids provide a good starting point for finer grids) to speed up the initial part of the computation.

Historically, these ideas were developed starting from the 1960s by Bakhvalov, Fedorenko, and others (see Stüben, et al. [Stuben:82a]). The sequential multigrid algorithm has been used for solving PDEs associated with different early vision problems in [Terzopoulos:86a].

It is shown in [Brandt:77a] that, with a few modifications in the basic algorithms, *the actual solution* (not the error) can be stored in each layer (*full approximation storage algorithm*). This method is particularly useful for visual reconstruction where we are interested not only in the finest scale result, but also in the multiscale representation developed as a byproduct of the solution process.

6.5.2 Interacting Line Processes

Line processes [Marroquin:84a] are binary variables arranged in a two-dimensional array. An active line process (LP = 1) between two neighboring pixels indicates that there is a physical discontinuity between them. Activation is, therefore, based on a measure of the difference in pixel properties but must also take into account the presence of other LPs. The idea is that continuous nonintersecting chains of LPs are preferred to discontinuous and intersecting ones, as it is shown in Figure 6.23.

We propose to combine the surface reconstruction and discontinuity detection phases *in time and scale space*. To do this, we introduce line processes at different scales, "connect" them to neighboring *depth processes* (henceforth DPs) at the same scale and to neighboring LPs on the finer and coarser scale. The reconstruction assigns equal priority to the two process types.

This scheme not only greatly improves convergence speed (the typical multigrid effect) but also produces a more consistent reconstruction of the piecewise smooth surface at the different scales.

6.5.3 Generic Look-up Table and Specific Parametrization

Creation of discontinuities must be favored either by the presence of a "large" difference in the z values of the nearby DPs, or by the presence of a partial discontinuity structure that can be improved.

Figure 6.23: The Multiscale Interaction Favors the Formation of Continuous Chains of Line Processes. The figure on the left sketches the multiscale interaction of LPs that, together with the local interaction at the same scale, favors the formation of continuous chains of Line Processes (LP caused by "noise" are filtered out at the coarse scales, the LPs caused by real discontinuities remain and act on the finer scales, see Figure 6.24). On the right, we show a favored (top) and a penalized (bottom) configuration. On the left, we see coarsest scale with increasing resolution in two lower outlines of hand.

To measure the two effects in a quantitative way, it is useful to introduce two functions: *cost* and *benefit*. The benefit function for a vertical LP is $(\partial z/\partial x)^2 \approx (z_{i+1,j} - z_{i,j})^2/h_k^2$, and analogously for a horizontal one. The idea is that the activation of one LP is beneficial when this quantity is large.

Cost is a function of *neighborhood* configuration. A given LP updates its value in a manner depending on the values of nearby LPs. These LPs constitute the neighborhood, and we will to refer to its members as the LPs *connected* to the original one. The neighborhood is shown in Figure 6.24.

The updating rule for the LPs derived from the above requirements is:

$$LP \leftarrow 1 \quad \text{iff} \quad \text{cost} < \text{benefit}$$

Because *Cost* is a function of a limited number of binary variables, we used a *look-up table* approach to increase simulation speed and to provide a convenient way for simulating different heuristical proposals.

A specific parametrization for the values in the table is suggested in [Battiti:90a].

6.5.4   Pyramid on a Two-Dimensional Mesh of Processors

The multigrid algorithm described in the previous section can be executed in many different ways on a parallel computer. One essential distinction that has to be made is related to the number of processors available and the "size" of a single processor.

The drawback of implementations on fine grain-size SIMD computers (where we assign one processor to each grid point) is that when iteration is on a coarse scale, all the nodes in the other scales (i.e., the majority of nodes) are idle, and the efficiency of computation is seriously compromised.

Furthermore, if the implementation is on a hypercube parallel computer and the mapping is such that all the communications paths in the pyramid are mapped into communication paths in the hypercube with length bounded by two [Chan:86b], a fraction of the nodes is never used because the total number of grid points is not equal to a power of two. This fraction is one third for two-dimensional problems encountered in vision.

Fortunately, if we use a MIMD computer with powerful processors, sufficient distributed memory, and two-dimensional internode connections (the hypercube contains a two-dimensional mesh), the above problems do not exist.

In this case, a two-dimensional domain decomposition can be used efficiently: A slice of the image with its associated pyramidal structure is

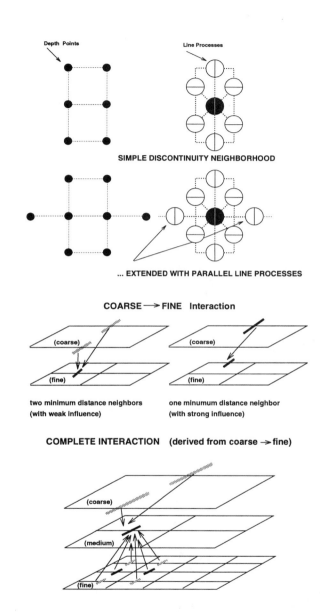

Figure 6.24: "Connections" Between Neighboring Line Processes, at the Same Scale and Between Different Scales

assigned to each processor. All nodes are working all the time, switching between different levels of the pyramid as illustrated in Figure 6.25.

No modification of the sequential algorithm is needed for points in the image belonging to the interior of the assigned domain. Conversely, points *on* the boundary need to know values of points assigned to a nearby processor. With this purpose, the assigned domain is extended to contain points assigned to nearby processors, and a communication step before each iteration on a given layer is responsible for updating this strip so that it contains the correct (most recent) values. Two exchanges are sufficient.

The recursive multiscale call `mg(lay)` is based on an alternation of relaxation steps and discontinuity detection steps as follows (software is written in C language):

```
int mg(lay) int lay;
{
 int i;
 if(lay==coarsest)step(lay);
 else{
 i=na;while(i--)step(lay);
 i=nb;if(i!=0)
 {up(lay);while(i--)mg(lay-1);down(lay-1);}
 i=nc;while(i--)step(lay);
 }
}


int step(lay) int lay;
{
 exchange_border_strip(lay);
 update_line_processes(lay); relax_depth_processes(lay);
}
```

Each step is preceded by an exchange of data on the border of the assigned domains.

Because the communication overhead is proportional to the linear dimension of the assigned image portion, the efficiency is high as soon as the number of pixels in this portion is large. Detailed results are in [Battiti:91a].

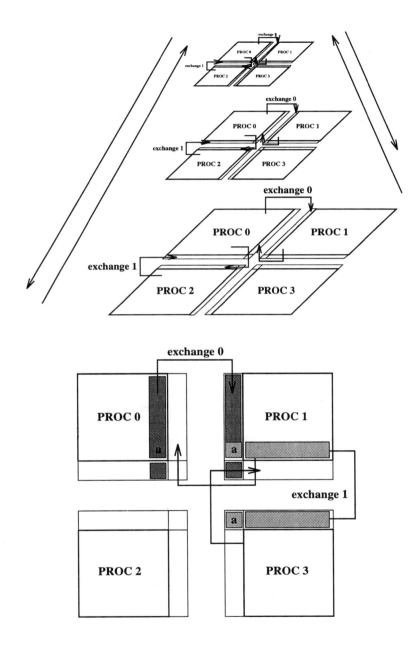

Figure 6.25: Domain Decomposition for Multigrid Computation. Processor communication is on a two-dimensional grid; each processor operates at all levels of the pyramid.

6.5.5   Results for Orientation Constraints

An iterative scheme for solving the shape from shading problem has been proposed in [Horn:85a]. A preliminary phase recovers information about orientation of the planes tangent to the surface at each point by minimizing a functional containing the image irradiance equation and an *integrability constraint*, as follows:

$$E(p, q) = \int_{Image} (I(x, y) - R(p, q))^2 + \lambda(p_y - q_x)^2 \, dx \, dy,$$

where $p = \partial z/\partial x$, $q = \partial z/\partial y$, I = measured intensity, and R = theoretical reflectance function.

After the tangent planes are available, the surface z is reconstructed, minimizing the following functional:

$$E(z) = \int_{Image} (z_x - p)^2 + (z_y - q)^2 \, dx \, dy.$$

Euler-Lagrange differential equations and discretization are left as an exercise to the reader.

Figure 6.26 shows the reconstruction of the shape of a hemispherical surface starting from a ray-traced image [1]. Left is the result of standard relaxation after 100 sweeps, right the "minimal multigrid" result (with computation time equivalent to 3 to 4 sweeps at the finest resolution).

This case is particularly hard for a standard relaxation approach. The image can be interpreted "legally" in two possible ways, as either a *concave* or *convex* hemisphere. Starting from random initial values, after some relaxations, some image patches typically "vote" for one or the other interpretation and try to extend the local interpretation to a global one. This is slow (given the local nature of the updating rule) and encounters an endless struggle in the regions that mark the border between different interpretations. The multigrid approach solves this "democratic impasse" on the coarsest grids (much faster because information spreads over large distances) and propagates this decision to the finer grids, that will now concentrate their efforts on refining the initial approximation.

In Figure 6.27, we show the reconstruction of the Mona Lisa face painted by Leonardo da Vinci.

---

[1]A simple Lambertian reflection model is used.

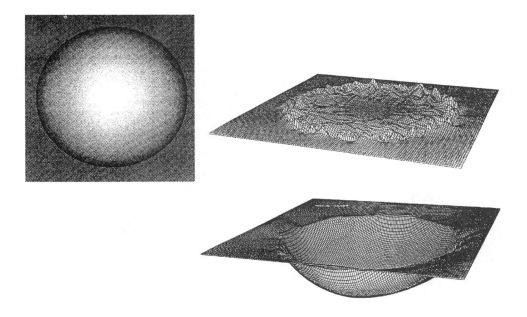

Figure 6.26: Reconstruction of Shape From Shading: Standard Relaxation (top right) Versus Multigrid (bottom right). The original image is shown on left.

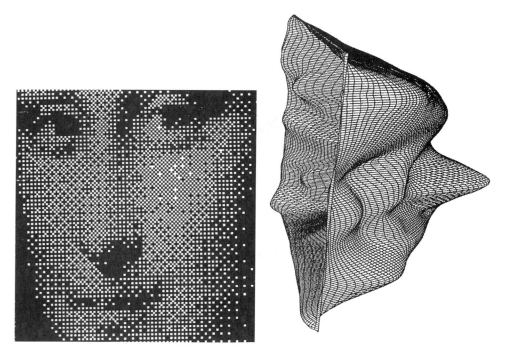

Figure 6.27: Mona Lisa in Three Dimensions. The right figure shows the multigrid reconstruction.

6.5.6 Results for Depth Constraints

For the surface reconstruction problem (see [Terzopoulos:86a]) the energy functional is:

$$E(z(x,y)) = \int_{Image} (z(x,y) - d(x,y))^2 + \lambda(z_x^2 + z_y^2)\, dx\, dy$$

A physical analogy is that of fitting the depth constraints $d(x,y)$ with a membrane pulled by springs connected to them. The effect of active discontinuities ($DN = 1$) is that of "cutting the membrane" in the proper places.

Figure 6.28 to 6.30 show the simulation environment on the SUN workstation, and the reconstruction of a "Randomville" image (random quadrangular blocks placed in the image plane). The original surface, the surface corrupted by noise (25%), are shown in Figure 6.29 while reconstruction on different scales is shown in Figure 6.30.

For 129×129 "images" and 25% noise, a faithful reconstruction of the surface (within a few percent of the original one) is obtained after a single multiscale sweep (with V cycles) on four layers. The total computational time corresponds approximately to the time required by three relaxations on the finest grid. Because of the optimality of multiscale methods, time increases linearly with the number of image pixels.

6.5.7 Conclusions

The parallel simulation environment was written by Roberto Battiti [Battiti:90a]. Geoffrey Fox, Christof Koch, and Wojtek Furmanski contributed with many ideas and suggestions [Furmanski:88c].

A JPL group [Synnott:90a] also used the Mark III hypercube to find three-dimensional properties of planetary objects from the two-dimensional images returned from NASA's planetary missions, and from the Hubble Space Telescope. The hypercube was used in a simple parallel mode with each node assigned calculations for a subset of the image pixels, with no internodal communication required. The estimation uses an iterative linear least-squares approach where the data are the pixel brightness values in the images; and partials of theoretical models of these brightness values are computed for use in a square root formulation of the normal equations. The underlying three-dimensional model of the object consists of a triaxial ellipsoid overlaid with a spherical harmonic expansion to describe low- to mid-spatial frequency topographic or surface composition variations. The initial results were not followed through into production use for JPL missions, but this is

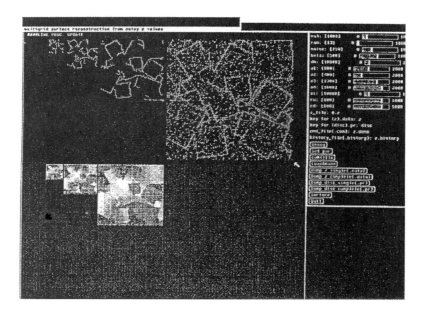

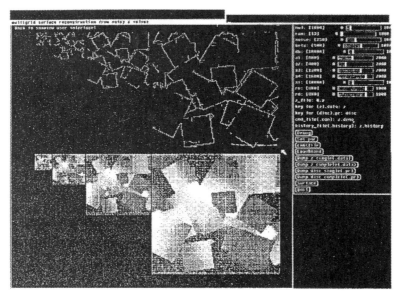

Figure 6.28: Simulation Environment for Multigrid Surface Reconstruction from a Noisy Image. The top screen shows an intermediate, and the bottom final results. For each screen, the upper part displays the activated discontinuities; the lower part, the gray-encoded z values of the surface.

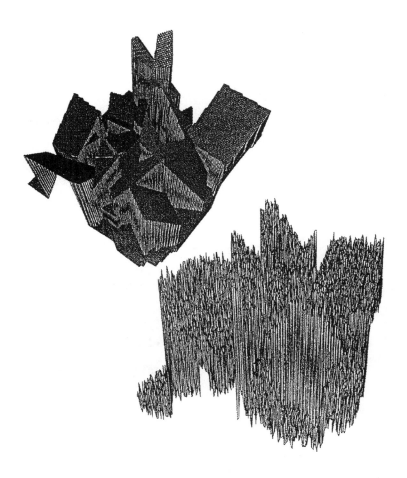

Figure 6.29: The Original Surface (top) and Surface Corrupted by 25% Noise (bottom)

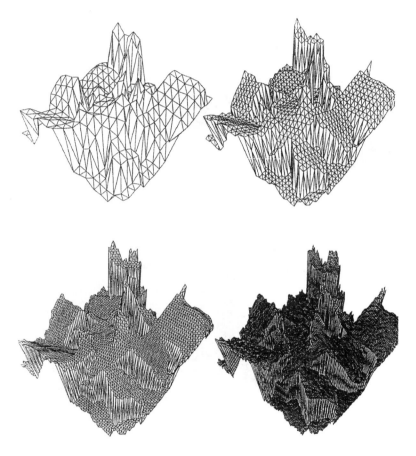

Figure 6.30: The Reconstruction of a "Randomville" Scenery using Multigrid Method. Each figure shows a different resolution.

likely to become an important application of parallel computing to image processing from planetary missions.

6.6 Character Recognition by Neural Nets

Much of the current interest in neural networks can be traced to the introduction a few years ago of effective learning algorithms for these systems ([Denker:86a], [Parker:82a], [Rumelhart:86a]). In [Rumelhart:86a] Chapter 8, it was shown that for some problems using multi-layer perceptrons (MLP), back-propagation was capable of finding a solution very reliably and quickly. Back-propagation has been applied to a number of realistic and complex problems [Sejnowski:87a], [Denker:87a]. The work of this section is described in [Felten:90a].

Real-world problems are inherently structured, so methods incorporating this structure will be more effective than techniques applicable to the general case. In practice, it is very important to use whatever knowledge one has about the form of possible solutions in order to restrict the search space. For multilayer perceptrons, this translates into constraining the weights or modifying the learning algorithm so as to embody the topology, geometry, and symmetries of the problem.

Here, we are interested in determining how automatic learning can be improved by following the above suggestion of restricting the search space of the weights. To avoid high-level cognition requirements, we consider the problem of classifying hand-printed upper-case Roman characters. This is a specific pattern-recognition problem, and has been addressed by methods other than neural networks. Generally the recognition is separated into two tasks: the first one is a pre-processing of the image using translation, dilation, rotations, and so on, to bring it to a standardized form; in the second, this preprocessed image is compared to a set of templates and a probability is assigned to each character or each category of the classification. If all but one of the probabilities are close to zero, one has a high confidence level in the identification. This second task is the more difficult one, and the performance achieved depends on the quality of the matching algorithm. Our focus is to study how well an MLP can learn a satisfactory matching to templates, a task one believes the network should be good at.

In regard to the task of preprocessing, MLPs have been shown capable [Rumelhart:86a] Chapter 8 of performing translations at least in part, but it is simpler to implement this first step using standard methods. This

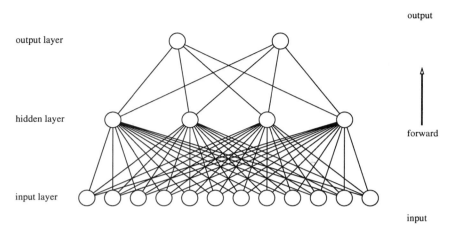

Figure 6.31: A Multi-Layer Perceptron

combination of traditional methods and neural network matching can give us the best of both worlds. In what follows, we suggest and test a learning procedure which preserves the geometry of the two-dimensional image from one length scale transformation to the next, and embodies the difference between coarse and fine scale features.

6.6.1   MLP in General

There are many architectures for neural networks; we shall work with Multi-Layer Perceptrons. These are feed-forward networks, and the network to be used in our problem is schematically shown in Figure 6.31. There are two processing layers: output and hidden. Each one has a number of identical units (or "neurons"), connected in a feed-forward fashion by wires, often called weights because each one is assigned a real number w_i. The input to any given unit is $\sum w_i x_i$, where i labels incoming wires and x_i is the input (or current) to that wire. For the hidden layer, x_i is the value of a bit of the input image; for the output layer, it is the output from a unit of the hidden layer.

Generally, the output of a unit is a nonlinear, monotonic-increasing function of the input. We make the usual choice and take

$$g(x) = \frac{1}{1 + e^{-x + \theta}}$$

to be our neuron input/output function. θ is the threshold and can be different for each neuron. The weights and thresholds are usually the only quantities which change during the learning period. We wish to have a network perform a mapping M from the input space to the output space. Introducing the actual output $A(I)$ for an input I, one first chooses a metric for the output space, and then seeks to minimize $d(A(I), M(I))$, where d is a measure of the distance between the two points. This quantity is also called the error function, the energy, or (the negative of) the harmony function. Naturally, $A(I)$ depends on the w_i's. One can then apply standard minimization searches like simulated annealing [Kirkpatrick:83a] to attempt to change the w_i's so as to reduce the error. The most commonly used method is gradient descent, which for MLP is called back-propagation because the calculation of the gradients is performed in a feed-backwards fashion. Improved descent methods may be found in [Dahl:87a], [Parker:87a] and in Section 9.9 of this book.

The minimization often runs into difficulties because one is searching in a very high-dimensional space, and the minima may be narrow. In addition, the straightforward implementation of back-propagation will often fail because of the many minima in the energy landscape. This process of minimization is referred to as learning or memorization as the network tries to match the mapping M. In many problems, though, the input space is so huge that it is neither conceivable nor desirable to present all possible inputs to the network for it to memorize. Given part of the mapping M, the network is expected to guess the rest: This is called generalization. As shown clearly in [Denker:87a] for the case of a discrete input space, generalization is often an ill-posed problem: Many generalizations of M are possible. To achieve the kind of generalization humans want, it is necessary to tell the network about the mapping one has in mind. This is most simply done by constraining the weights to have certain symmetries as in [Denker:87a]. Our approach will be similar, except that the "outside" information will play an even more central role during the learning process.

6.6.2 Character Recognition using MLP

To do character recognition using an MLP, we assume the input layer of the network to be a set of image pixels, which can take on analogue (or grey scale) values between 0 and 1. The two-dimensional set of pixels is mapped onto the set of input neurons in a fairly arbitrary way: For an $N \times N$ image, the top row of N pixels is associated with the first N neurons, the next row of N pixels is associated with the next N neurons, and so forth. At the start of the training process, the network has no knowledge of the underlying two-dimensional structure of the problem (that is, if a pixel is on, nearby pixels in the two-dimensional space are also likely to be on). The network discovers the two-dimensional nature of the problem during the learning process.

We taught our networks the alphabet of 26 upper-case Roman characters. To encourage generalization, we show the net many different hand-drawn versions of each character. The 320-image training set is shown in Figure 6.32. These images were hand-drawn using a mouse attached to a SUN workstation. The output is encoded in a very sparse way. There are only 26 outputs we want the net to give, so we use 26 output neurons and map the output pattern: first neuron on, rest off, to the character "A;" second neuron on, rest off, to "B;" and so on. Such an encoding scheme works well here, but is clearly unworkable for mappings with large output sets such as Chinese characters or Kanji. In such cases, one would prefer a more compact output encoding, with possibly an additional layer of hidden units to produce the more complex outputs.

As mentioned earlier, we do not feed images directly into the network. Instead, simple, automatic preprocessing is done which dilates the image to a standard size and then translates it to the center of the pixel space. This greatly enhances the performance of the system—it means that one can draw a character in the upper left-hand corner of the pixel space and the system easily recognizes it. If we did not have the preprocessing, the network would be forced to solve the much larger problem of character recognition of all possible sizes and locations in the pixel space. Two other worthwhile preprocessors are rotations (rotate to a standard orientation) and intensity normalization (set linewidths to some standard value). We do not have these in our current implementation.

The MLP is used only for the part of the algorithm where one matches to templates. Given any fixed set of exemplars, a neural network will usually learn this set perfectly, but the performance under generalization can be very poor. In fact, the more weights there are, the faster the learning (in the sense of number of iterations, not of CPU time), and the worse the ability to generalize. This was in part realized in [Gullichsen:87a], where the input grid was 16×16. If one has a very fine mesh at the input level, so that a great amount of detail can be seen in the image, one runs the risk of having terrible generalization properties because the network will tend to focus upon tiny features of the image, ones which humans would consider irrelevant.

We will show one approach to overcoming this problem. We desire the

Figure 6.32: The Training Set of 320 Handwritten Characters, Digitized on a 32×32 Grid

potential power of the large, high-resolution net, but with the stable generalization properties of small, coarse nets. Though not so important for upper-case Roman characters, where a rather coarse grid does well enough (as we will see), a fine mesh is necessary for other problems such as recognition of Kanji characters or handwriting. A possible "fix," similar to what was done for the problem of clump counting [Denker:87a], is to hard wire the first layer of weights to be local in space, with a neighborhood growing with the mesh fineness. This reduces the number of weights, thus postponing the deterioration of the generalization. However, for an MLP with a single hidden layer, this approach will prevent the detection of many nonlocal correlations in the images, and in effect this fix is like removing the first layer of weights.

6.6.3   The Multiscale Technique

We would like to train large, high-resolution nets. If one tries to do this directly, by simply starting with a very large network and training by the usual back-propagation methods, not only is the training slow (because of the large size of the network), but the generalization properties of such nets are poor. As described above, a large net with many weights from the input layer to the hidden layer tends to "grandmother" the problem, leading to poor generalization.

The hidden units of an MLP form a set of feature extractors. Considering a complex pattern such as a Chinese character, it seems clear that some of the relevant features which distinguish it are large, long-range objects requiring little detail while other features are fine scale and require high resolution. Some sort of multiscale decomposition of the problem therefore suggests itself. The method we will present below builds in long-range feature extractors by training on small networks and then uses these as an intelligent starting point on larger, higher resolution networks. The method is somewhat analogous to the multigrid technique for solving partial differential equations.

Let us now present our multiscale training algorithm. We begin with the training set, such as the one shown in Figure 6.32, defined at the high resolution (in this case, 32×32). Each exemplar is coarsened by a factor of two in each direction using a simple grey scale averaging procedure. 2×2 blocks of pixels in which all four pixels were "on" map to an "on" pixel, those in which three of the four were "on" map to a "3/4 on" pixel, and so on. The result is that each 32×32 exemplar is mapped to a 16×16

exemplar in such a way as to preserve the large scale features of the pattern. The procedure is then repeated until a suitably coarse representation of the exemplars is reached. In our case, we stopped after coarsening to 8×8.

At this point, an MLP is trained to solve the coarse mapping problem by one's favorite method (back-propagation, simulated annealing, and so on). In our case, we set up an MLP of 64 inputs (corresponding to 8×8), 32 hidden units, and 26 output units. This was then trained on the set of 320 coarsened exemplars using the simple back propagation method with a momentum term [Rumelhart:86a], Chapter 8. Satisfactory convergence was achieved after approximately 50 cycles through the training set.

We now wish to boost back to a high-resolution MLP, using the results of the coarse net. We use a simple interpolating procedure which works well. We leave the number of hidden units unchanged. Each weight from the input layer to the hidden layer is split or "un-averaged" into four weights (each now attached to its own pixel), with each 1/4 the size of the original. The thresholds are left untouched during this boosting phase. This procedure gives a higher resolution MLP with an intelligent starting point for additional training at the finer scale. In fact, before any training at all is done with the 16×16 MLP (boosted from 8×8), it recalls the 16×16 exemplars quite well. This is a measure of how much information was lost when coarsening from 16×16 to 8×8. The boost and train process is repeated to get to the desired 32×32 MLP. The entire multiscale training process is illustrated in Figure 6.33.

6.6.4 Results

Here we give some details of our results and compare with the standard approach. As mentioned in the previous section, a 32×32 MLP (1024 inputs, 32 hidden units, 26 output units) was trained on the set of Figure 6.32 using the multiscale method. Outputs are never exactly 0 or 1, so we defined a "successful" recognition to occur when the output value of the desired letter was greater than 0.9, and all other outputs were less than 0.1. The training on the 8×8 grid used back-propagation with a momentum term and went through the exemplars sequentially. The weights are changed to reduce the error function for the current character. The result is that the system does not reach an absolute minimum. Rather, at long times the weight values oscillate with a period equal to the time of one sweep through all the exemplars. This is not a serious problem as the oscillations are very small in practice. Figure 6.34 shows the training curve for this problem. The first

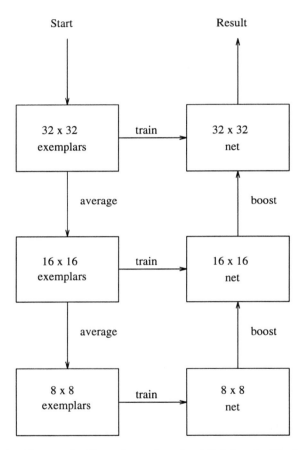

Figure 6.33: An Example Flowchart for the Multiscale Training Procedure. This was the procedure used in this text, but the averaging and boosting can be continued through an indefinite number of stages.

part of the curve is the training of the 8×8 network; even though the grid is a bit coarse, almost all of the characters can be memorized. Proceeding to the next grid by scaling the mesh size by a factor of two and using the 16×16 exemplars, we obtained the second part of the learning curve in Figure 6.34. The 8×8 net got 315/320 correct. After 12 additional sweeps on the 16×16 net, a perfect score of 320/320 is achieved. The third part of Figure 6.34 shows the result of the final boost to 32×32. In just two cycles on the 32×32 net, a perfect score of 320/320 was achieved and the training was stopped. It is useful to compare these results with a direct use of backpropagation on the 32×32 mesh without using the multiscale procedure. Figure 6.35 shows the corresponding learning curve, with the result from Figure 6.34 drawn in for comparison. Learning via the multiscale method takes much less computer time. In addition, the internal structure of the resultant network is much different and we will now turn to this question.

How do these two networks compare for the real task of recognizing exemplars not belonging to the training set? We used as a generalization test set 156 more handwritten characters. Though there are no ambiguities for humans in this test set, the networks did make mistakes. The network from the direct method made errors 14% of the time, and the multiscale network made errors 9% of the time. We feel the improved performance of the multiscale net is due to the difference in quality of the feature extractors in the two cases. In a two-layer MLP, we can think of each hidden-layer neuron as a feature extractor which looks for a certain characteristic shape in the input; the function of the output layer is then to perform the higher level operation of classifying the input based on which features it contains. By looking at the weights connecting a hidden-layer neuron to the inputs, we can determine what feature that neuron is looking for.

For example, Figure 6.36 shows the input weights of two neurons in the 8×8 net. The neuron of (a) seems to be looking for a stroke extending downward and to the right from the center of the input field. This is a feature common to letters like A, K, R, and X. The feature extractor of (b) seems to be a "NOT S" recognizer and, among other things, discriminates between "S" and "Z".

Even at the coarsest scale, the feature extractors usually look for blobs rather than correlating a scattered pattern of pixels. This is encouraging since it matches the behavior we would expect from a "good" character recognizer. The multiscale process accentuates this locality, since a single pixel grows to a local clump of four pixels at each rescaling. This effect can be seen in Figure 6.37, which shows the feature extractor of Figure 6.36(b)

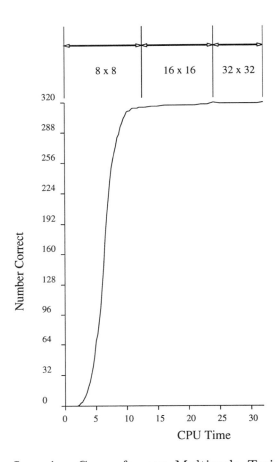

Figure 6.34: The Learning Curve for our Multiscale Training Procedure Applied to 320 Handwritten Characters. The first part of the curve is the training on the 8×8 net, the second on the 16×16 net, and the last on the full, 32×32 net. The curve is plotted as a function of CPU time and not sweeps through the presentation set, in order to exhibit the speed of training on the smaller networks.

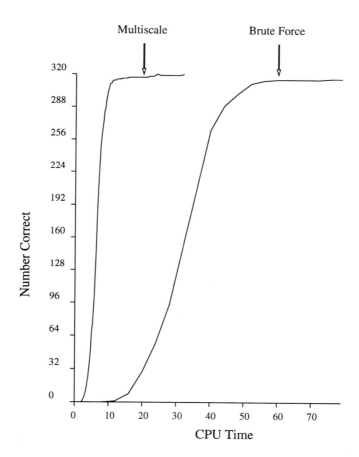

Figure 6.35: A Comparison of Multiscale Training with the Usual, Direct Back-propagation Procedure. The curve labelled "Multiscale" is the same as Figure 6.34, only rescaled by a factor of two. The curve labelled "Brute Force" is from directly training a 32 × 32 network, from a random start, on the learning set. The direct approach does not quite learn all of the exemplars, and takes much more CPU time.

(a)

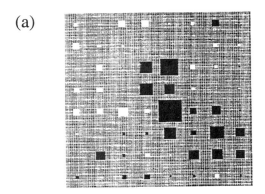

(b)

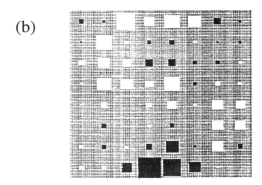

Figure 6.36: Two Feature Extractors for the Trained 8×8 net. This figure shows the connection weights between one hidden-layer, and all the input-layer neurons. Black boxes depict positive weights, while white depict negative weights; the size of the box shows the magnitude. The position of each weight in the 8×8 grid corresponds to the position of the input pixel. We can view these pictures as maps of the features which each hidden-layer neuron is looking for. In (a), the neuron is looking for a stroke extending down and to the right from the center of the input field; this neuron fires upon input of the letter "A," for example. In (b), the neuron is looking for something in the lower center of the picture, but it also has a strong "NOT S" component. Among other things, this neuron discriminates between an "S" and a "Z". The outputs of several such feature extractors are combined by the output layer to classify the original input.

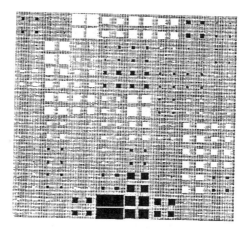

Figure 6.37: The Same Feature Extractor as in Figure 6.36(b), after the Boost to 16 × 16. There is an obvious correspondence between each connection in Figure 6.36(b) and 2 × 2 clumps of connections here. This is due to the multiscale procedure, and leads to spatially smooth feature extractors.

after scaling to 16 × 16 and further training. Four-pixel clumps are quite obvious in the 16 × 16 network. The feature extractors obtained by direct training on large nets are much more scattered (less smooth) in nature.

6.6.5   Comments and Variants on the Method

Before closing, we would like to make some additional comments on the multiscale method and suggest some possible extensions.

In a pattern-recognition problem such as character recognition, the two-dimensional spatial structure of the problem is important. The multiscale method preserves this structure so that "reasonable" feature extractors are produced. An obvious extension to the present work is to increase the number of hidden units as one boosts the MLP to higher resolution. This corresponds to adding completely new feature extractors. We did not do this in the present case since 32 hidden units were sufficient—the problem of recognizing upper-case Roman characters is too easy. For a more challenging problem such as Chinese characters, adding hidden units will probably be necessary. We should mention that incrementally adding hidden units is easy to do and works well—we have used it to achieve perfect convergence of a back-propagation network for the problem of tic-tac-toe.

When boosting, the weights are scaled down by a factor of four and so it is important to also scale down the learning rate (in the back-propagation algorithm) by a factor of four.

We defined our "blocking," or coarsening, procedure to be a simple, grey scale averaging of 2×2 blocks. There are many other possibilities, well known in the field of real-space renormalization in physics. Other interesting blocking procedures include: using a scale factor, λ, different from two; using majority rule averaging; simple decimation; and so on.

Multiscale methods work well in cases where spatial locality or smoothness is relevant (otherwise, the interpolation approximation is bad). Another way of thinking about this is that we are decomposing the problem onto a set of spatially local basis functions such as gaussians. In other problems, a different set of basis functions may be more appropriate and hence give better performance.

The multiscale method uses results from a small net to help in the training of a large network. The different-sized networks are related by the rescaling or dilation operator. A variant of this general approach would be to use the translation operator to produce a pattern matcher for the game of Go. The idea is that at least *some* of the complexity of Go is concerned with local strategies. Instead of training an MLP to learn this on the full 19×19 board of Go, do the training on a "mini-Go" board of 5×5 or 7×7. The appropriate way to relate these networks to the full-sized one is not through dilations, but via the translations: The same local strategies are valid everywhere on the board.

Steve Otto had the original idea for the MultiScale training technique. Otto and Ed Felten and Olivier Martin developed the method. Jim Hutchinson contributed by supplying the original back-propagation program.

6.7   An Adaptive Multiscale Scheme for Real-Time Motion Field Estimation

When moving objects in a scene are projected onto an image plane (for example, onto our retina), the real velocity field is transformed into a two-dimensional field, known as the motion field.

By taking more images at different times and calculating the motion field, we can extract useful parameters like the time to collision, useful for obstacle avoidance. If we know the motion of a camera (or our ego motion), we can reconstruct the entire three-dimensional structure of the environment (if the camera translates, near objects will have a larger motion field with respect to distant ones). The depth measurements can be used as starting constraints for a surface reconstruction algorithm like the one described in Section 9.9.

In particular situations, the apparent motion of the brightness pattern, known as the optical flow, provides a sufficiently accurate estimate of the motion field. Although the adaptive scheme that we propose is applicable to different methods, the discussion will be based on the scheme proposed by Horn and Schunck [Horn:81a]. They use the assumptions that the image brightness of a given point remains constant over time, and that the optical flow varies smoothly almost everywhere. Satisfaction of these two constraints is formulated as the problem of minimizing a quadratic energy functional (see also [Poggio:85a]). The appropriate Euler-Lagrange equations are then discretized on a single or multiple grid and solved using, for example, the Gauss-Seidel relaxation method [Horn:81a], [Terzopoulos:86a]). The resulting system of equations (two for every pixel in the image) is:

$$\left(I_x\, u_{i,j} + I_y\, v_{i,j} + I_t\right) I_x = \frac{\alpha^2}{\Delta x^2}\left(\bar{u}_{i,j} - u_{i,j}\right)$$

$$\left(I_x\, u_{i,j} + I_y\, v_{i,j} + I_t\right) I_y = \frac{\alpha^2}{\Delta x^2}\left(\bar{v}_{i,j} - v_{i,j}\right)$$

where $u_{i,j} = dx/dt$ and $v_{i,j} = dy/dt$ are the optical flow variables to be determined, I_x, I_y, I_t are the partial derivatives of the image brightness with respect to space and time, $\bar{u}$ and $\bar{v}$ are local averages, Δx is the spatial discretization step, and α controls the smoothness of the estimated optical flow.

6.7.1 Errors in Computing the Motion Field

Now, we need to estimate the partial derivatives in the above equations with *discretized formulas* starting from brightness values that are *quantized* (say integers from 0 to n) and noisy. Given these derivative estimation problems, the optimal step for the discretization grid depends on local properties of the image. Use of a single discretization step produces large errors on some images. Use of a *homogeneous* multiscale approach, where a set of grids at different resolutions is used, may in some cases produce a good estimation on

an intermediate grid and a bad one on the final and finest grid. Enkelmann
and Glazer [Enkelmann:88a], [Glazer:84a] encountered similar problems.

These difficulties can be illustrated with the following one-dimensional
example. Let's suppose that the intensity pattern observed is a superposition
of two sinusoids of different wavelengths:

$$I(x,t) \propto \left(1 + R + \sin\left(\frac{2\pi}{6}(x - 2t)\right) + R\sin\left(\frac{2\pi}{3}(x - 2t)\right)\right)$$

where R is the ratio of short to long wavelength components.   Using
the *brightness constancy* assumption $(dI/dt = 0$ or $vI_x + I_t = 0$, see
[Horn:81a]) the measured velocity $\tilde{v}$ is given by:

$$\tilde{v} = -\tilde{I}_t/\tilde{I}_x$$

where $\tilde{I}_x$ and $\tilde{I}_t$ are the three-point approximations of the spatial and temporal brightness derivatives.[2]

Now, if we calculate the estimated velocity on two different grids, with
spatial step Δx equal to one and two, as a function of the parameter, R, we
obtain the result illustrated in Figure 6.38.

While on the coarser grid, the correct velocity is obtained (in this case);
on the finer one, the measured velocity depends on the value of R.   In
particular, if R is greater than 0.5, we obtain a velocity in the opposite
direction!

We propose a method for "tuning" the discretization grid to a measure
of the reliability of the optical flow derived at a given scale. This measure is
based on a *local estimate of the errors* due to noise and discretization, and
is described in [Battiti:89g;91b].

6.7.2   Adaptive Multiscale Scheme on a Multicomputer

First, a Gaussian pyramid [Burt:84a] is computed from the given images.
This consists of a hierarchy of images obtained filtering the original ones
with Gaussian filters of progressively larger size.

Then, the optical flow field is computed at the coarsest scale using relaxation, and the estimated error is calculated for every pixel. If this quantity is
less than a given threshold T_{err}, the current value of the flow is interpolated
to the finer resolutions without further processing. This is done by setting
an *inhibition flag* contained in the grid points of the pyramidal structure,

---

[2]That is $\tilde{I}_x = 1/(2\Delta x)(I(x + \Delta x) - I(x - \Delta x))$ and analogously for $\tilde{I}_t$.

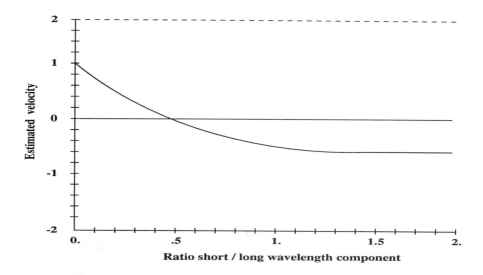

Figure 6.38: Measured velocity for superposition of sinusoidal patterns as a function of the ratio of short to long wavelength components. Dashed line: $\Delta x = 2$, continuous line: $\Delta x = 1$.

so that these points do not participate in the relaxation process. On the contrary, if the error is larger than T_{err}, the approximation is relaxed on a finer scale and the entire process is repeated until the finest scale is reached.

In this way, we obtain a *local inhomogeneous* approach where areas of the images, characterized by different spatial frequencies or by different motion amplitudes, are processed at the appropriate resolutions, avoiding corruption of good estimates by inconsistent information from a different scale (the effect shown in the previous example). The optimal grid structure for a given image is translated into a pattern of active and *inhibited* grid points in the pyramid, as illustrated in Figure 6.39.

The motivation for *freezing* the motion field as soon as the error is below threshold, is that the estimation of the error may *itself* become incorrect at finer scales and, therefore, useless in the decision process. It is important to point out that single-scale or homogeneous approaches cannot adequately solve the above problem. Intuitively, what happens in the adaptive multiscale approach is that the velocity is *frozen* as soon as the spatial and temporal differences at a given scale are big enough to avoid quantization errors, but small enough to avoid errors in the use of discretized formulas. The only assumption made in this scheme is that the largest motion in the

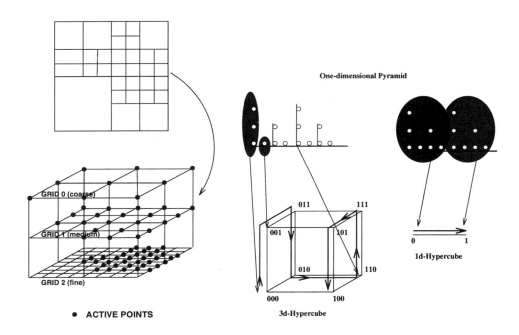

Figure 6.39: Adaptive Grid (shown on left) in the Multiresolution Pyramid; (middle) Gray Code Mapping Strategy; (right) Domain Decomposition Mapping Strategy. In the middle and right pictures, the activity pattern for three resolutions is shown at the top, for a simple one-dimensional case.

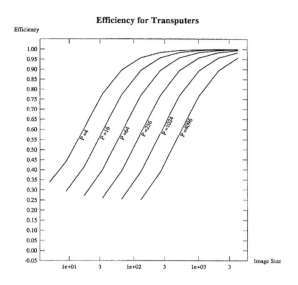

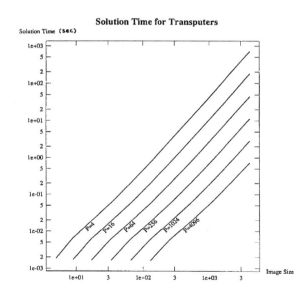

Figure 6.40: Efficiency and Solution Times

scene can be reliably computed at one of the used resolutions. If the images contain motion discontinuities, *line processes* (indicating the presence of these discontinuities) are necessary to prevent smoothing where it is not desired (see [Battiti:90a] and the contained references).

Large grain-size multicomputers, with a mapping based on domain decomposition and limited coarsening, have been used to implement the adaptive algorithm, as described in Section 6.5. The efficiency and solution times for an implementation with *transputers* (details in [Battiti:91a]) are shown in Figure 6.40.

Real-time computation with high efficiency is within the reach of available digital technology!

On a board with four transputers, and using the Express communication routines from ParaSoft, the solution time for 129×129 images is on the order of one second.

The software implementation is based on the multiscale vision environment developed by Roberto Battiti and described in Section 9.9. Christof Koch and Edoardo Amaldi collaborated on the project.

6.7.3   Conclusions

Results of the algorithm show that the adaptive method is capable of effectively reducing the solution error. In the last Figures 6.41 to 6.43, we show two test images (showing a "plaid" pattern and a natural scene), with the obtained optical flow.

For the "plaid" image, we show the r.m.s. error obtained with the adaptive (lower-line) and homogeneous (upper-line) scheme and the resulting fields.

For the natural image, we show in Figure 6.42, the average computed velocity (in a region centered on the pine cone) as a function of the correct velocity for different number of layers. Increasing the number of resolution grids increases the range of velocities that are detected correctly by the algorithm. The pine cone is moving upward at the rate of 1.6 pixels per frame. The multiscale algorithm is always better than single-level algorithm, especially at larger velocity v_y.

6.8   Collective Stereopsis

The collective stereopsis algorithm described in [Marr:76a] was historically one of the first "cooperative" algorithms based on relaxation proposed for

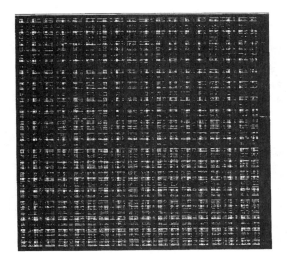

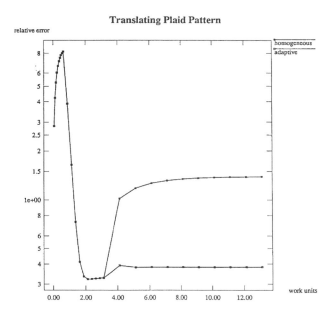

Figure 6.41: Plaid Image (top); The Error in Calculation of Optical Flow for both Homogeneous (Upper-line) and Adaptive (Lower-line) Algorithms. The error is plotted as a function of computation time.

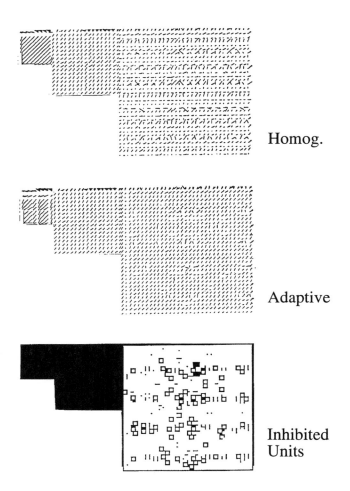

Figure 6.42: Reconstructed Optical Flow for Translating "Plaid" Pattern of Figure 6.41. Homogeneous Multiscale Strategy (top), Adaptive Multiscale Strategy (middle), and Active (black) and Inhibited (white) Points

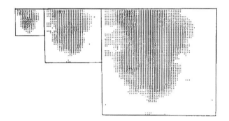

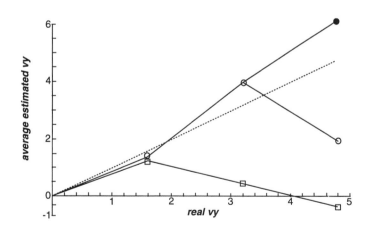

Figure 6.43: Test Images and Motion Fields for a Natural (pine-cone) Image at Three Resolutions (top). Estimated versus Actual Velocity Plotted for Three Choices of Resolution (bottom). The dotted line indicates a "perfect" prediction.

early vision.

The goal in stereopsis is to measure the difference in retinal position (*disparity*) of features of a scene observed with two eyes (or video cameras). This is achieved by placing a fiber of "neurons" (one for each disparity value) at each pixel position. Each neuron inhibits neurons of different disparities at the same location (because the disparity is unique) and excites neurons of the same disparity at near location (because disparity tends to vary smoothly). After, convergence the activation pattern corresponds to the disparity field defined above.

The parallel implementation is based on a straightforward domain decomposition and the results are illustrated in Figure 6.44. They show the initial state of disparity computation and the evolution in time of the different layers of disparity neurons. Details are described in [Battiti:88a].

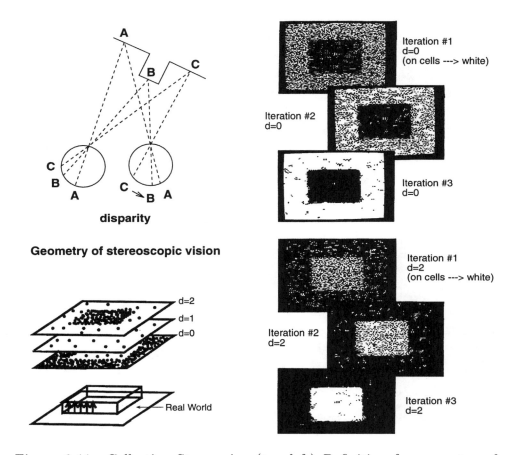

Figure 6.44: Collective Stereopsis: (top left) Definition for geometry of stereoscopic vision. (bottom left) Neural Network Activity (top three layers disparity $d = 0, 1, 2$) corresponding to real world structure illustrated. (right) Results of iterations for $d = 0$ and $d = 2$ layers of neurons. d measures disparity value for pixels.

Chapter 7

Independent Parallelism

7.1 Embarrassingly Parallel Problem Structure

In Chapters 4 and 6, we studied the *synchronous* problem class where the uniformity of the computation, that is, of the *temporal* structure, made the parallel implementation relatively straightforward. This chapter contains examples of the other major problem class, where the simple *spatial* structure leads to clear parallelization. We define the *embarrassingly parallel* class of problems for which the computational graph is disconnected. This spatial structure allows a simple parallelization as no (temporal) synchronization is involved. In Chapters 4 and 6, on the other hand, there was often substantial synchronization and associated communication; however, the uniformity of the synchronization allowed a clear parallelization strategy. One important feature of embarrassingly parallel problems is the modest node-to-node communication requirements—the definition of no spatial connection implies in fact no internode communication, but a practical problem would involve some amount of communication, if only to set up the problem and accumulate results. The low communication requirements of embarrassingly parallel problems make them particularly suitable for a distributed computing implementation on a network of workstations; even the low bandwidth of an Ethernet is often sufficient. Indeed, we used such a network of Sun workstations to support some of the simulations described in Section 7.2.

The caricature of this problem class, shown in Figure 7.1, uses a database problem as an example. This is illustrated in practice by the DOWQUEST program where a CM-2 supports searching of financial data contained in articles that are partitioned equally over the nodes of this SIMD machine

Essentially Independent Parallel Processes

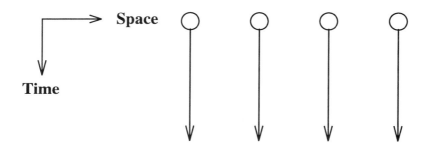

Example: Divide large database among processors and independently
search each portion of database to answer query.

Figure 7.1: Embarrassingly Parallel Problem Class

[Waltz:87a;88a,90a].

This problem class can have either a synchronous or asynchronous temporal structure. We have illustrated the former above and analysis of a large (high energy) physics data set exhibits asynchronous temporal structure. Such experiments can record 10^5–10^8 separate events, which can be analyzed independently. However, each event is usually quite different and would require both distinct instruction streams and very different execution times. This was realized early in the high energy physics community and so-called farms—initially of special-purpose machines and now of commercial workstations—have been used extensively for production data analysis [Gaines:87a], [Hey:88a], [Kunz:81a].

The applications in Sections 7.2 and 7.6 obtain their embarrassingly parallel structure from running several full simulations—each with independent data. Each simulation could in fact also be decomposed spatially and in fact this spatial parallelization has since been pursued and is described for the neural network simulator in Section 7.6. Some of Chiu's random block lattice calculations also used an embarrassingly parallel approach with 1024 separate 40^4 lattices being calculated on the 1024 nCUBE-1 at Sandia [Chiu:90a], [Fox:89i;89n]. This would not, of course, be possible for the QCD of Section 4.3, where each node would not be available to hold an interesting size lattice. The spatial parallelism in the examples of Sections 7.2 and 7.6 is nontrivial to implement as the irregularities makes these problems loosely synchronous. This relatively difficult domain parallelism made it attractive to first explore the independent structure gotten by exploiting the parallelism coming from simulations with different parameters.

It is interesting that Sections 6.3 and 7.3 both address simulations of spin systems relevant to high T_c—depending on the algorithm used, one can get very different problem architectures (either synchronous or embarrassingly parallel in this case) for a given application.

The embarrassingly parallel gravitational lens application of Section 7.4 was frustrating for the developers as it needed software support not available at the time on the Mark III. Suitable software (MOOSE in Section 15.2) had been developed on the Mark II to support graphics ray tracing as briefly discussed in Section 14.1. Thus, the calculation is embarrassingly parallel, but a distributed database is essentially needed to support the calculation of each ray. This was not available in CrOS III at the time of the calculations described in Section 7.4.

7.2 Dynamically Triangulated Random Surfaces

7.2.1 Introduction

In this section, we describe some large scale parallel simulations of dynamically triangulated random surfaces [Baillie:90c], [Baillie:90d], [Baillie:90e], [Baillie:90j], [Baillie:91c], [Bowick:93a]. Dynamically triangulated random surfaces have been suggested as a possible discretization for string theory in high energy physics and fluid surfaces or membranes in biology [Lipowski:91a]. As physicists, we shall focus on the former.

String theories describe the interaction of one-dimensional string-like objects in a fashion analogous to the way particle theories describe the interaction of zero-dimensional point-like particles. String theory has its genesis in the dual models that were put forward in the 1960s to describe the behavior of the hadronic spectrum then being observed. The dual model amplitudes could be derived from the quantum theory of a stringlike object [Nambu:70a], [Nielsen:70a], [Susskind:70a]. It was later discovered that these so-called bosonic strings could apparently only live in 26 dimensions [Lovelace:68a] if they were to be consistent quantum-mechanically. They also had tachyonic (negative mass-squared) ground states, which is normally the sign of an instability. Later, fermionic degrees of freedom were added to the theory, yielding the supersymmetric Neveu-Schwarz-Ramond

[Neveu:71a] (NSR) string. This has a critical dimension of 10, rather than 26, but still suffers from the tachyonic ground state. Around 1973, it became clear that QCD provided a plausible candidate for a model of the hadronic spectrum, and the interest in string models of hadronic interactions waned. However, about this time it was also postulated by numerous groups that strings [Scherk:74a] might provide a model for gravity because of the prescence of higher spin excitations in a natural manner. A further piece of the puzzle fell into place in 1977 when [Gliozzi:77a] found a way to remove the tachyon from the NSR string. The present explosion of work on string theory began with the work of Green and Schwarz [Green:84a], who found that only a small number of string theories could be made tachyon free in 10 dimensions, and predicted the occurrence of one such that had not yet been constructed. This appeared soon after in the form of the heterotic string [Gross:85a], which is a sort of composite of the bosonic and supersymmetric models.

After these discoveries, the physics community leaped on string models as a way of constructing a unified theory of gravity [Schwarz:85a]. Means were found to compactify the unwanted extra dimensions and produce four-dimensional theories that were plausible grand unified models, that is, models which include both the standard model and gravity. Unfortunately, it now seems that much of the predictive power that came from the constraints on the 10-dimensional theories is lost in the compactification, so interest in string models for constructing grand unified theories has begun to fade. However, considered as purely mathematical entities, they have led and are leading to great advances in complex geometry and conformal field theory. Many of the techniques that have been used in string theory can also be directly translated to the field of real surfaces and membranes, and it is from this viewpoint that we want to discuss the subject.

7.2.2   Discretized Strings

As a point particle in space moves through time, it traces out a line, called the *worldline*; similarly, as the string which looks like a line in space moves through time, it sweeps out a two-dimensional surface called the *worldsheet*. Thus, there are two ways in which to discretize the string: either the worldsheet is discretized or the (d-dimensional) space-time in which the string is embedded is discretized. We shall consider the former, which is referred to as the *intrinsic* approach; the latter is reviewed in [Ambjorn:89a]. Such discretized surface models fall into three categories: regular, fixed random, and dynamical random surfaces. In the first, the surface is composed of plaquettes in a d-dimensional regular hypercubic lattice; in the second, the surface is randomly triangulated once at the beginning of the simulation; and in the third, the random triangulation becomes dynamical (i.e., is changed during the simulation). It is these dynamically triangulated random surfaces we wish to simulate. Such a simulation is, in effect, that of a fluid surface. This is because the varying triangulation means that there is no fixed reference frame, which is precisely what one would expect of a fluid where the molecules at two different points could interchange and still leave the surface intact. In string theory, this is called reparametrization invariance. If, instead, one used a regular surface, one would be simulating a tethered or crystalline surface on which there is considerable literature (see [Ambjorn:89b] for a survey of the work in the field). In this case, the molecules of the surface are frozen in a fixed array. There have also been simulations of fixed random surfaces; see, for example, [Baig:89a]. One other reason for studying random surface models is to understand integration over geometrical objects and discover whether the nonperturbative discretization procedures, which work so well for local field theories like QCD, can be applied successfully.

The partition function describing the quantum mechanics of a surface was first formulated by Polyakov [Polyakov:81a]. For a bosonic string embedded in d-dimensions, it is written as

$$Z = \int DX \, Dg \, \exp\left(-T \int d^2 x \sqrt{g} \, g^{ab} \, \partial_a X^\mu \, \partial_b X_\mu\right), \tag{7.1}$$

where $\mu = 1, 2, \ldots, d$ labels the dimensions of the embedding space, $a, b = 1, 2$ are the coordinates on the worldsheet, and T is the string tension. The integration is over both the fields X_μ and the metric on the worldsheet g^{ab}. X_μ gives the embedding of the two-dimensional worldsheet swept out by the string in the d-dimensional space in which it lives. If we integrate over the metric, we obtain an area action for the worldsheet,

$$Z \simeq \exp\left(-T \int d^2 x \sqrt{|h|}\right), \quad h_{ab} = \partial_z X^\mu \, \partial_b X_\mu, \tag{7.2}$$

which is a direct generalization of the length action for a particle, i.e.,

$$Z \simeq \exp\left(-\text{length of worldline}\right). \tag{7.3}$$

We can thus see that the action in Equation 7.1 is the natural area action that one might expect for a surface whose dynamics were determined by the surface tension.

The first discretized model of this partition function was suggested independently by three groups: [Ambjorn:85a], [David:85a], and [Kazakov:85a].

$$Z = \sum_{t \,\epsilon\, T} \rho\,(t) \int \prod_i^N DX_i \exp\left(-\frac{1}{2}\sum_{\langle ij\rangle}(X_i - X_j)^2\right), \qquad (7.4)$$

where the outer sum runs over some set T of allowed triangulations of the surface, weighted by their importance factors $\rho\,(t)$, and is supposed to represent the effect of the metric integration in the path integral. The inner sum in the exponential is over the edges $\langle ij\rangle$ of the triangulation, or mesh, and working with a fixed number of nodes N corresponds to working in a microcanonical ensemble of fixed intrinsic area. The model is that of a dynamically triangulated surface because one is instructed to perform the sum over different triangulations, so both the fields, X_μ on the mesh and the mesh itself, are dynamical objects.

A considerable amount of effort has been devoted to simulating this pure area action, both in microcanonical form with a fixed number of nodes [Billoire:86a], [Boulatov:86a], [Jurkiewicz:86a] and in grand canonical form, where the number of nodes is allowed to change in a manner which satisfies detailed balance [Ambjorn:87b], [David:87a], [Jurkiewicz:86b]. (This allows measurements to be made of how the partition function varies with the number of nodes N, which determines an exponent called the *string susceptibility*.) The results are rather disappointing, in that the surfaces appear to be in a very crumpled state, as can be seen from measuring the gyration radius $X2$, which gives a figure for the "mean size" of the surface. Its discretized form is

$$X2 = \frac{1}{9N(N-1)}\left\langle \sum_{ij}^N (X_i - X_j)^2 \right\rangle, \qquad (7.5)$$

where the sum now runs over all pairs of nodes ij. $X2$ is observed to grow only logarithmically with N. This means that the Hausdorff dimension, d_H, which measures how the surface grows upon the addition of intrinsic area and is defined by

$$X2 \simeq N^{\frac{2}{d_H}}, \qquad (7.6)$$

is infinite. Analytical work [Durhuus:84a] shows that the string tension fails to scale in the continuum limit so that, heuristically speaking, it becomes so strong that it collapses the surface into something like a branched polymer.

Thus, the pure area action does not provide a good continuum limit. It was observed in [Ambjorn:85a] and [Espriu:87a] that another way to understand the pathological behavior of the simulations, was to note that spikelike configurations in the surface were not suppressed by the area action, allowing it to degenerate into a spiky, crumpled object. An example of such a configuration is shown in Figure 7.2(a).

To overcome this difficulty, one uses the fact that adding to the pure area action a term in the extrinsic curvature squared (as originally suggested by Polyakov [Polyakov:86a] and Kleinert [Kleinert:86a] for string models of hadron interactions) smooths out the surface. In three dimensions, the extrinsic curvature of a two-dimensional surface is given by

$$K(x) = \frac{1}{r_1(x)} + \frac{1}{r_2(x)}, \tag{7.7}$$

where the rs are the principle radii of curvature at a point x on the surface. Two discretized forms of this extrinsic curvature term are possible, namely

$$K^2 = 3 \sum_i \frac{1}{\Omega_i} \left(\sum_{j(i)} (X_i - X_j) \right)^2, \tag{7.8}$$

where the inner sum is over the neighbors j of a node i and Ω_i is the sum of the areas of the surrounding triangles as shown in Figure 7.3; and

$$K^2 = \sum_{\langle ij \rangle} (1 - \hat{n}_i^\mu \, \hat{n}_{j\mu}), \tag{7.9}$$

where one takes the dot product of the unit normals $\hat{n}_i^\mu$ of triangles which share a common edge $\langle ij \rangle$. For sufficiently large values of the K^2 coupling, the worldsheet is smooth, as shown in Figure 7.2(b). Analytical work [Ambjorn:87a;89b] strongly suggests, however, that a continuum limit will only be found in the limit of infinite extrinsic curvature coupling.

It came as something of a surprise, therefore, when a simulation by Catterall [Catterall:89a] revealed that the discretization (Equation 7.8) seems to give a third-order phase transition to the smooth phase and the discretization (Equation 7.9) a *second*-order phase transition, the latter offering the possibility of defining a continuum limit at a *finite* value of the extrinsic curvature coupling (because of the divergence of correlation length at a second-order transition). Further work by Baillie, Johnston, and Williams [Baillie:90j] confirmed the existence of this "crumpling transition." Typical results, for a

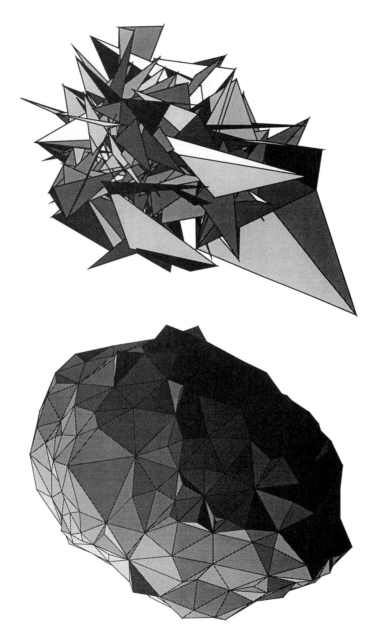

Figure 7.2: (a) Crumpled Phase (b) Smooth Phase

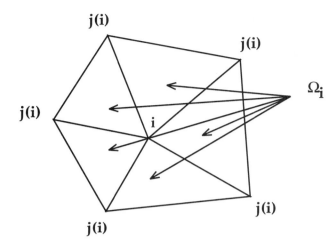

Figure 7.3: Illustration of First Form of Extrinsic Curvature (Equation 7.8)

surface consisting of 288 nodes, are shown in the series of Figure 7.4 (Color Plate), for the discretization of Equation 7.8. The extrinsic curvature coupling, λ, is increased from 0 (the crumpled phase) to 1.5 (the smooth phase). We estimate that the crumpling transition is around $\lambda = 0.75$.

Further studies of the crumpling transition using the "edge action" discretization (Equation 7.9) have recently been performed [Ambjorn:92a], [Bowick:93a] on larger lattices in order to see whether this is a genuine phase transition, or just a finite size effect due to the small mesh sizes which had been simulated.

To summarize, a dynamically triangulated random surface with a pure area action does not offer a good discretization of a bosonic string or of a fluid surface. The addition of an extrinsic curvature term appears to give a crumpling transition between a smooth and crumpled phase, but the nature of this transition is unclear. In order for the continuum limit to give a string theory, it is necessary that there be a second-order phase transition, so that the correlation length diverges and the details of the lattice discretization are irrelevant, as in lattice QCD (see Section 4.3).

7.2.3   Computational Aspects

In order to give the reader a feel for how one actually simulates a dynamically triangulated random surface, we briefly explain our computer program, *string*, which does this—more details can be found in [Baillie:90e]. As we explained previously, in order to incorporate the metric fluctuations, we randomly triangulate the worldsheet of the string or random surface to obtain a mesh and make it dynamical by allowing flips in the mesh that do not change the topology. The incorporation of the flips into the simulation makes vectorization difficult, so running on traditional supercomputers like the Cray is not efficient. Similarly, the irregular nature of the dynamically triangulated random surface inhibits efficient implementation on SIMD computers like the Distributed Array Processor and the Connection Machine. Thus, in order to get a large amount of CPU power behind our random surface simulations, we are forced to run on *MIMD parallel* computers. Here, we have a choice of two main architectures: distributed-memory hypercubes or shared-memory computers. We initially made use of the former, as several machines of this type were available to us—all running the *same* software environment, namely, ParaSoft's Express System [ParaSoft:88a]. Having the same software on different parallel computers makes porting the code from one to another very easy. In fact, we ran our strings simulation program on the nCUBE hypercube (for a total of 1800 hours on 512 processors), the Symult Series 2010 (900 hours on 64 processors), and the Meiko Computing Surface (200 hours on 32 processors). Since this simulation fits easily into the memory of a single node of any of these hypercubes, we ran multiple simulations in parallel—giving, of course, linear speedup. Each node was loaded with a separate simulation (using a different random number generator seed), starting from a single mesh that has been equilibrated elsewhere, say on a Sun workstation. After allowing a suitable length of time for the meshes to decorrelate, data can be collected from each node, treating them as separate experiments. More recently, we have also run *string* on the GP1000 Butterfly (1000 hours on 14 processors) and TC2000 Butterfly II (500 hours on 14 processors) shared-memory computers—again with each processor performing a unique simulation. Parallelism is thereby obtained by "decomposing" the space of Monte Carlo configurations.

The reason that we run multiple independent Monte Carlo simulations, rather than distribute the mesh over the processors of the parallel computer, is that this domain decomposition would be difficult for such an irregular problem. This is because, with a distributed mesh, each processor wanting to change its part of the mesh would have to first check that the affected pieces were not simultaneously being changed by another processor. If they were, detailed balance would be violated and the Metropolis algorithm would no longer work. For a regular lattice this is not a problem, since we can do a simple red/black decomposition (Section 4.3); however this is not the case for an irregular lattice. Similar parallelization difficulties arise in other irregular Monte Carlo problems, such as gas and liquid systems (Section 14.2). For the random surfaces application, the size of the system which can be simulated using independent parallelism is limited not by memory requirements, but by the time needed to decorrelate the different meshes on each processor, which grows rapidly with the number of nodes in the mesh.

The mesh is set up as a linked list in the programming language C, using software developed at Caltech for doing computational fluid dynamics on unstructured triangular meshes, called DIME (Distributed Irregular Mesh Environment) [Williams:88a;90b] (Sections 10.1 and 10.2). The logical structure is that of a set of triangular elements corresponding to the faces of the triangulation of the worldsheet, connected via nodes corresponding to the nodes of the triangulation of the worldsheet. The data required in the simulation (of random surfaces or computational fluid dynamics) is then stored in either the nodes or the elements. We simulate a worldsheet with a fixed number of nodes, N, which corresponds to the partition function of Equation 7.1 evaluated at a fixed area. We also fix the topology of the mesh to be spherical. (The results for other topologies, such as a torus, are similar). The Monte Carlo procedure sweeps through the mesh moving the Xs which live at the nodes, and doing a Metropolis accept/reject. It then sweeps through the mesh a second time doing the flips, and again performs a Metropolis accept/reject at each attempt. Figure 7.5 illustrates the local change to the mesh called a *flip*. For any edge, there is a triangle on each side, forming the quadrilateral ABCD, and the flip consists of changing the diagonal AC to BD. Both types of Monte Carlo updates to the mesh can be implemented by identifying which elements and nodes would be affected by the change, then

1. saving the data from these affected elements and nodes;

2. making the proposed change;

3. recalculating the element data;

4. recalculating the node data;

5. calculating the change in the action δS as the difference of the sums of the new and the old action contributions from the affected nodes;

6. given δS, deciding whether to accept or reject the change using the standard Metropolis algorithm—if the change is rejected, we replace

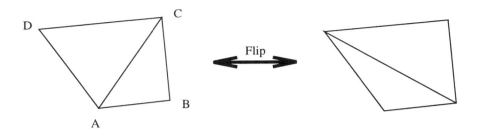

Figure 7.5: Flip Move

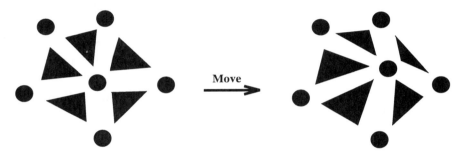

Figure 7.6: Nodes and Elements Affected by X Move

the element and node data with the saved values; if accepted, we need do nothing since the change has already been made.

For the X move, the affected elements are the neighbors of node i, and the affected nodes are the node i itself and its node neighbors, as shown in Figure 7.6. For the flip, the affected elements are the two sharing the edge, and the affected nodes are the four neighbor nodes of these elements, as shown in Figure 7.7.

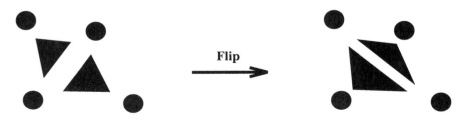

Figure 7.7: Nodes and Elements Affected by Flip Move

7.2.4   Performance of String Program

Due to its irregular nature, string is an extremely good benchmark of the *scalar* performance of a computer. Hence, we timed it on several machines we had access to, yielding the numbers in Table 7.1. Note that we timed *one* processor of the parallel machines. We see immediately that the Sun 4/60, known as the SPARCstation 1, had the highest performance of the Suns we tested. Moreover, this machine (running with TI 8847 floating-point processor at clock rate of 20 MHz) is as fast as the Motorola 88000 processor (at 16 MHz) which is used in the TC2000 Butterfly. Turning to the hypercubes, we see that the nCUBE-2 is faster than the Meiko, which is twice as fast as the (scalar) Symult, which in turn is twice as fast as the nCUBE-1, per processor, for the string program. We have also run on the Weitek vector processors of the Mark III and Symult. The vector processors are faster than the scalar processors, but since string is entirely scalar, it does not run very efficiently on the vector processors and, hence, is still slower than on the Sun 4/60. The Mark III is as fast as the Symult, despite having one-third the clock rate, because it has a high-performance cache between its vector processor and memory. We have also timed the code on the new IBM and Hewlett-Packard workstations, and Cimarron Boozer of Sky Computers has optimized the code for the Intel i860. As a final comparison, the modern RISC workstations run the string code as fast as the CRAY X-MP.

We should emphasize that these performances are for *scalar* codes. A completely different picture emerges for codes which vectorize well, like QCD. QCD, with dynamical fermions, runs on the CRAY X-MP at around 100 MFLOPS and pure-gauge QCD runs on one processor of the Mark III at 6 MFLOPS. In contrast, the Sun 4/60 only achieves about 1 MFLOPS for pure-gauge QCD. This ratio of QCD performance (which we may claim as the "realistic peak" performance of the machines) 100:6:1 compares with 5:0.7:1 for strings. Thus, these two calculations from one area of physics illustrate clearly that the preferred computer architecture depends on the problem.

7.2.5   Conclusion

Large scale numerical simulations are becoming increasingly important in many areas of science. Lattice QCD calculations have been commonplace in high energy physics for many years. More recently, this technique has been applied to string theories formulated as dynamically triangulated random

Table 7.1: Time Taken to Execute the String Program

Computer	Floating-Point Processor	Clock Rate (M Hz)	"string" (seconds)
Sun 3/50	68881	15	148
Sun 3/60	68881	20	94
Sun 3/160	FPA	16.7	73
Sun 386i	80387	20	23
Sun 4/280	W 1164/65	16	15
Sun 4/60	SPARC FP	20	12
Sun 4/60	TI 8847	20	11
DEC 5000/125	MIPS R3010	25	4.8
IBM RS-6000	320	20	2.6
IBM RS-6000	340	33	1.9
IBM RS-6000	550	41	1.5
HP 9000	720	50	2.6
HP 9000	750	66	1.9
Intel	i860	40	4.0
Intel (optimized)	i860	40	2.1
GP 1000	68882	16	40
TC 2000	88000	16	11
nCUBE-1	Custom	6.7	90
nCUBE-2	Custom	25	16
Symult	68882	25	47
Symult	Weitek 13364	25	15
Meiko	T800	20	23
Mark III	68882	16	63
Mark III	Weitek 3164	8	15
CRAY	X-MP	105	1.8

surfaces. As we have pointed out, such computer simulations of strings are difficult to implement efficiently on all but MIMD computers, due to the inherent irregular nature of random surfaces. Moreover, on most MIMD machines, it is possible to get 100% speedup by doing multiple independent Monte Carlos, since an entire simulation easily fits within each processor.

7.3 Numerical Study of High-T$_c$ Spin Systems

Although the mechanism of high-temperature superconductivity is not yet established, an enormous amount of experimental work has been completed on these materials and, as a result, a "magnetic" explanation has probably gained the largest number of adherents. In this picture, high-temperature superconductivity results from the effects of dynamical holes on the magnetic properties of CuO_2 planes, perhaps through the formation of bound hole pairs. In the undoped materials ("precursor insulators"), these CuO_2 planes are magnetic insulators and appear to be well described by the two-dimensional spin-1/2 Heisenberg antiferromagnet,

$$H = \sum_{\langle ij \rangle} \vec{S}_i \cdot \vec{S}_j , \tag{7.10}$$

where each spin represents a d-electron on a CuO_2 site. Since many aspects of the two-dimensional Heisenberg antiferromagnet were obscure before the discovery of high-T$_c$, this model has been the subject of intense numerical study, and comparisons with experiments on the precursor insulators have generally been successful. (A review of this subject including recent references has been prepared for the C^{3}P group [Barnes:91a].) If the proposed "magnetic" origin of high-temperature superconductivity is correct, one may only need to incorporate dynamical holes in the Heisenberg antiferromagnet to construct a model that exhibits high-temperature superconductivity. Unfortunately, such models (for example, the "t-J" model) are dynamical many-fermion systems and exhibit the "minus sign problem" which makes them very difficult to simulate on large lattices using Monte Carlo techniques. The lack of appropriate algorithms for many-fermion systems accounts in large part for the uncertainty in the predictions of these models.

In our work, we carried out numerical simulations of the low-lying states of one- and two-dimensional Heisenberg antiferromagnets; the problems we studied on the hypercube which relate to high-T$_c$ systems were the determination of low-lying energies and ground state matrix elements of the two-dimensional spin-1/2 Heisenberg antiferromagnet, and in particular the response of the ground state to anisotropic couplings in the generalized model

$$H = \sum_{\langle ij \rangle} S_{zi}S_{zj} + g(S_{xi}S_{xj} + S_{yi}S_{yj}) . \qquad (7.11)$$

Until recently, the possible existence of infinite-range spin antialignment "staggered magnetization" in the ground state of the two-dimensional Heisenberg antiferromagnet, which would imply spontaneous breaking of rotational symmetry, was considered an open question. Since the precursor insulators such as La_2CuO_4 are observed to have a nonzero staggered magnetization, one might hope to observe it in the Heisenberg model as well. (It has actually been proven to be zero in the isotropic model above zero temperature, so this is a very delicate kind of long-range order.) Assuming that such order exists, one might expect to see various kinds of singular behavior in response to anisotropies, which would choose a preferred direction for symmetry breaking in the ground state. In our numerical simulations we measured the ground state energy per spin e_0, the energy gap to the first spin excitation E_{gap}, and the $\hat{z}$ component of the staggered magnetization N_z, as a function of the anisotropy parameter g on L×L square lattices, extrapolated to the bulk limit. We did indeed find evidence of singular behavior at the isotropic point $g = 1$, specifically that $de_0(g)/dg$ is probably discontinuous there (Figure 7.8), $E_{gap}(g)$ decreases to zero at $g = 1$ (Figure 7.9) and remains zero for $g > 1$, and $N_z(g)$ decreases to a nonzero limit as g approaches one, is zero for $g > 1$, and is undefined at $g = 1$ ([Barnes:89a;89c]). Finite lattice results which led to this conclusion are shown in Figure 7.10. (Perturbative and spin-wave predictions also appear in these figures; details are discussed in the publications we have cited.) These results are consistent with a "spin flop" transition, in which the long-range spin order is oriented along the energetically most favorable direction, which changes discontinuously from $\hat{z}$ to planar as g passes through the isotropic point. The qualitative behavior of the energy gap can be understood as a consequence of Goldstone's theorem, given these types of spontaneous symmetry breaking. Our results also provided interesting tests of spin-wave theory, which has been applied to the study of many antiferromagnetic systems including the two-dimensional Heisenberg model, but is of questionable accuracy for small spin. In this spin-1/2 case, we found that finite-size and anisotropic effects were qualitatively described surprisingly well by spin-wave theory, but that actual numerical values were sometimes rather inaccurate; for example, the energy gap due to a small easy-axis anisotropy was in error by about a factor

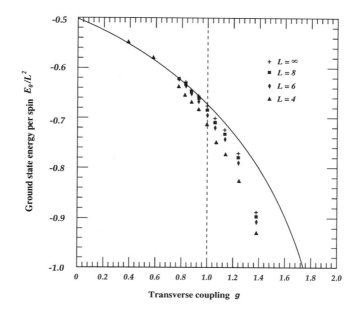

Figure 7.8: Ground State Energy per Spin

of two.

In related work, we developed hypercube programs to study static holes in the Heisenberg model, as a first step towards more general Monte Carlo investigations of the behavior of holes in antiferromagnets. Preliminary static-hole results have been published [Barnes:90b], and our collaboration is now continuing to study high-T$_c$ models on an Intel iPSC/860 hypercube at Oak Ridge National Laboratory.

For our studies on the Caltech machine, we used the DGRW (discrete guided random-walk) Monte Carlo algorithm [Barnes:88c], and incorporated algorithm improvements which lowered the statistical errors [Barnes:89b]. This algorithm solves the Euclidean time Schrödinger equation stochastically by running random walks in the configuration space of the system and accumulating a weight factor, which implicitly contains energies and matrix elements. Since the algorithm only requires a single configuration, our memory requirements were very small, and we simply placed a copy of the program on each node; no internode communication was necessary. A previously developed DGRW spin system Fortran program written by T. Barnes was rewritten in C and adapted to the hypercube by D. Kotchan,

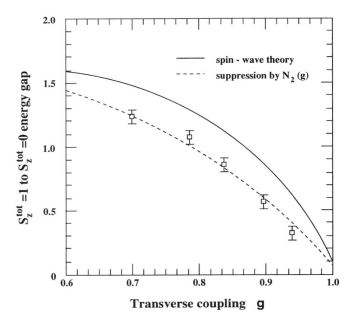

Figure 7.9: Spin Excitation Energy Gap

and an independent DGRW code was written by E. S. Swanson for debugging purposes. Our collaboration for this work eventually grew to include K. J. Cappon (who also wrote a DGRW Monte Carlo code) and E. Dagotto (UCSB/ITP) and A. Moreo (UCSB), who wrote Lanczos programs to give essentially exact results on the 4×4 lattice. This provided an independent check of the accuracy of our Monte Carlo results.

In addition to providing resources that led to these physics results, access to the hypercube and the support of the C^3P group were very helpful in the PhD programs of D. Kotchan and E. S. Swanson, and their experience has encouraged several other graduate-level theorists at the University of Toronto to pursue studies in computational physics, in the areas of high-temperature superconductivity (K. J. Cappon and W. MacReady) and Monte Carlo studies of quark model physics (G. Grondin).

7.4 Statistical Gravitational Lensing

This project of Apostolakis and Kochanek used the Caltech/JPL Mark III to simulate gravitational lenses. These are galaxies which bend the light

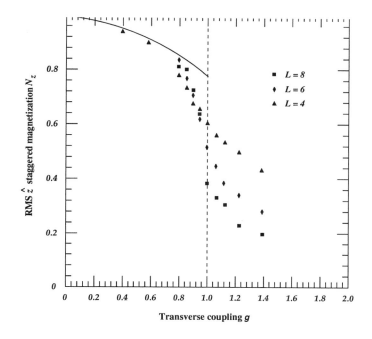

Figure 7.10: Ground State Staggered Magnetization N_z

of a background quasar to produce multiple images of it. Astronomers are very interested in these objects, and have discovered more than 10 of them to date. Several exhibit symptoms of lensing by more than one galaxy. This spurred us to simulate models of this class of lens. Our model systems were composed of two galaxy-like lensing potentials in different positions and redshifts. We studied about 100 cases at a resolution of 1536^2, taking about three weeks of running time on a 32-node Mark III. The algorithm we used is based on ray tracing. The problem is very irregular; this led us to use a scattered block decomposition. We achieved the performance needed for our purposes, but did not gain large speedups. The feature of the machine that was essential for our calculation was its large memory, because of the need for high resolution. Two of the cases we studied are illustrated in Figures 7.11 and 7.12: Areas on the source plane that produce one, three, five, or seven images, and the respective image regions on the image plane can be seen. An interesting example of an extended source is also shown in each case. A detailed exposition of our results and a description of our algorithm for a concurrent machine are contained in [Kochanek:88a] and [Apostolakis:88d].

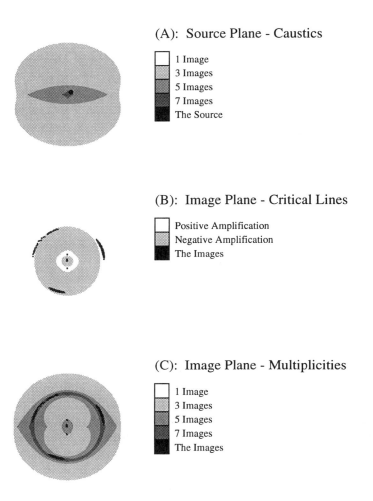

Figure 7.11: Part A shows the areas of the source plane that produce different numbers of images. Part B is a map of the areas of the image plane with negative amplification, i.e., flipped images, and positive amplification. Part C is a similar plot of the image plane, separating the areas by the total number of images of the same source. An example extended source is shown in A, whose images can be seen in Part B and Part C.

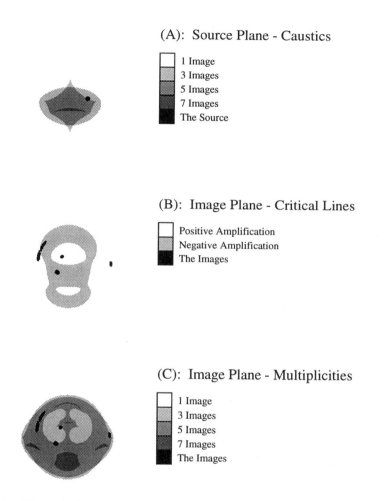

(A): Source Plane - Caustics

☐	1 Image
	3 Images
	5 Images
	7 Images
■	The Source

(B): Image Plane - Critical Lines

☐	Positive Amplification
	Negative Amplification
■	The Images

(C): Image Plane - Multiplicities

☐	1 Image
	3 Images
	5 Images
	7 Images
■	The Images

Figure 7.12: Part A shows the areas of the source plane that produce different numbers of images. Part B is a map of the areas of the image plane with negative amplification, that is, flipped images, and positive amplification. Part C is a similar plot of the image plane, separating the areas by the total number of images of the same source. An example of an extended source is shown in A, whose images can be seen in Parts B and C.

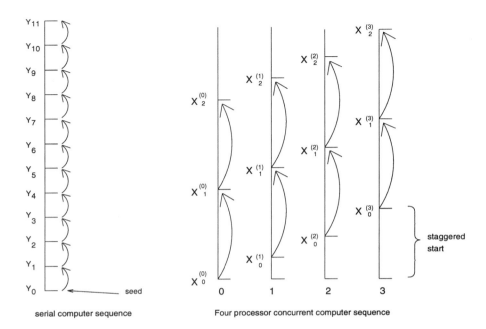

serial computer sequence　　　　　　Four processor concurrent computer sequence

Figure 7.13: A Comparison of the Sequential and Concurrent Generation of Random Numbers

7.5　Parallel Random Number Generators

Many important algorithms in science and engineering are of the Monte Carlo type. This means that they employ pseudorandom number generators to simulate physical systems which are inherently probabilistic or statistical in nature. At other times, Monte Carlo is used to getting a fast approximation to what is actually a large, deterministic computation. Examples of this are Lattice Gauge computations (Section 4.3) and Simulated Annealing methods (Sections 11.1.4 and 11.4).

Even for a sequential algorithm, the question of correlations between members of the pseudorandom number sequence is nontrivial. In the parallel case, at least for the popular linear congruential algorithm, it is easy for the parallel algorithm to exactly mimic what a sequential algorithm would do. This means that the parallel case can be reduced to the well-understood sequential case.

The fundamental idea is that the processors of an N processor concurrent computer each compute only the Nth number of the sequential random number sequence. The parallel sequences are staggered and interleaved so that the parallel computer exactly reproduces the sequential sequence. Figure 7.13 illustrates what happens in the parallel case versus the sequential case for a four-processor concurrent computer.

Chapter 12 of [Fox:88a] has an extensive discussion of the parallel algorithm. This reference also has a discussion of what to do to achieve exact matching between parallel and sequential computations in more complex applications. We extend this work from the linear congruential method of [Fox:88a] to the so-called shift register sequences, which have longer periods and less correlations than the congruential method [Chiu:88b], [Ding:88d]. As an illustration, we use Ding's Fibonacci additive random number generator developed for the QCD calculations on the Mark IIIfp, as previously described in Section 4.3. This uses the sequence

$$x_n = (x_{n-63} + x_{n-127}) \bmod \left(2^{31}\right). \tag{7.12}$$

This has a period longer than 2^{127}. The assembly language code for Equation 7.12 on the Mark IIIfp took $4\,\mu$s to generate a floating-point random number normalized to the range [0,1).

7.6 Parallel Computing in Neurobiology: The GENESIS Project

7.6.1 What Is Computational Neurobiology?

Neurobiology is the study of the nervous system. Until recently, most neurobiology research centered around exposing different neural tissue preparations to a wide range of environmental stimuli and seeing how they responded. More recently, the growing field of computational neurobiology has involved constructing models of how we think the nervous system works [Segev:89a], [Wehmeier:89a], [Yamada:89a]. These models are then exposed to a wide range of experimental conditions and their responses compared to the real neural systems. Those models that are demonstrated to accurately and reliably mimic the behavior of real neural systems are then used to predict the neural system's response to new and untried experimental situations, and to make firm predictions about how the neural system should respond if our theory of neural functioning is correct. Simplified models are also used to determine which features of a real neural system are critical to its underlying behavior and function. In doing so, they also indicate which features of the real system have no effect on desired system performance.

Computer modelling of neural structures from the level of single cells to that of large networks has, until recently, been rather isolated from mainstream experimental neurophysiology [Koch:92a]. Largely, this has been due to limitations of computer power which have necessitated reducing the models to such a basic level that their biological relevance becomes questionable. More powerful computer platforms, such as the parallel computers which have been used at Caltech, allow the construction of simulations of sufficient detail for their results to be compared directly with experimental results. Furthermore, the inherent flexibility of the modelling approach allows the neurophysiologist to observe the effect of experimental manipulations which are presently difficult or impossible to carry out on a biological basis. In this way, neural modelling can make firm predictions that can be confirmed by later experimentation [Bhalla:93a].

7.6.2   Parallel Computers?

The neural modelling community at Caltech has been fortunate in gaining access to several parallel computers. One of these, the experimental supercomputer produced by Intel called the Intel Touchstone Delta and described in Chapter 2, held the record as the World's fastest computer while much of this work was being carried out. Unlike a traditional (serial) computer, a parallel computer is more analogous to our own biological computer (the nervous system) where tasks such as vision and hearing can continue to function independently of one another. The parallel style of computer would therefore seem to lend itself very well to neural modelling applications where many neural compartments (whether individual ion channels or whole cells) are active simultaneously [Nelson:89a;90b].

7.6.3   Problems with Most Present Day Parallel Computers

Having listed the suitability of the newer style of parallel computers for neural modelling tasks, it is important to examine why they are not in wider use. Traditionally, parallel computers have been much harder to program than traditional computers and the typical neurobiologist was expected to understand a lot about advanced computer science issues before he or she could adequately construct neural models on such a machine. As this is not considered a reasonable expectation in neural modelling circles, most modellers have continued to use traditional (serial) computers and have had to sacrifice model detail in order to get acceptable performance figures. Such cut-down models may still require more than 12 hours to complete on a traditional high-performance computer [Bhalla:92a]. Parallel computers hold the promise of allowing more detailed models to be run in an acceptable period of simulation time. In order to make this power available to a range of neural modellers, it was decided to produce a version of a widely used neural simulation system [Wilson:89a] which could take advantage of such a parallel computer with only minimal manipulation by the neural modeller.

7.6.4 What is GENESIS?

GENESIS is a package designed to allow the construction of a wide variety of neural simulations. It was originally designed by Matt Wilson at Caltech to assist in his doctoral modelling work on the Piriform Cortex [Wilson:89b]. One of the design objectives was to allow the easy construction and alteration of a wide variety of neural models from detailed single cells all the way up to complex multilayered neural network structures. In order to make the simulator as flexible as possible, it was decided to adopt an object-oriented approach to the underlying simulator and to allow the user to include precompiled libraries of elements appropriate to their particular scale of modelling (e.g., detailed single cells or network-scale models). The structure of individual models was described via neural description script language files, which were interpreted as execution of the model proceeded. This combination of interpreted script files and precompiled element libraries has proved to be a very powerful approach to the problems of neural modelling at a variety of levels of detail from detailed single cell models all the way up to large network-scale simulations composed of thousands of neural elements.

GENESIS is an object-oriented neural simulator. All communication between the elements composing the simulation is via well-defined messages. As such, it was expected to fit well into the distributed computing environment of modern parallel computers.

It is designed in an object-oriented manner where each GENESIS element has private internal data that other elements cannot access directly. They can only access this information via predefined messages that request the internal state information from an element.

The GENESIS neural simulation system has now been running successfully on two of the Intel parallel computers at Caltech since 1991 and has already produced biologically interesting and previously unobtainable results.

Much of the use of the simulator to date has been in the construction of a
highly detailed model of the Cerebellar Purkinje Cell (work produced by Dr.
Erik de Schutter at Caltech using the parallel GENESIS system provided by
ourselves) [Schutter:91a;93a]. This is thought to be one of the most detailed
and biologically realistic single-cell models developed to date. By utilizing
the special capabilities of the Parallel GENESIS system, it has been possible
to carry out simulated experiments which are presently very difficult to carry
out experimentally. The initial results have been very promising and have
shown several previously unsuspected properties of the Purkinje Cell, which
arise as a result of the anatomical and physiological properties of the cell's
dendritic tree. The ability to run up to 512 different Purkinje Cell models
simultaneously has allowed the construction of statistically significant pro-
files of Purkinje Cell response patterns. This research has previously been
impossible to conduct for detailed cell models because of the excessive computational power required. Until now, the only statistical behavior that has
been described is for population dynamics of very simplified neural elements.

Currently, these machines are being used in two distinct ways (the task
farming approach and the distributed model via the postmaster element)
[Speight:92a;92b].

7.6.5   Task Farming

In the *task farming approach*, each node runs its own copy of a neural simulation (generally a detailed single-cell model). Each node and, therefore,
each simulation runs totally independently of all other nodes. This method
is particularly suited to examining large parameter spaces. In many of
our applications, there are a wide variety of free parameters (i.e., those
not defined experimentally). By using the task farming approach on these
supercomputer-class machines, we can range widely across this huge parameter space looking for combinations which give biologically realistic results
[Bhalla:93a] (i.e., similar to those measured experimentally). This allows us
to make predictions for the future experimental measurement of these free
parameters. It is also possible to run the same model many times in order
to build up statistically significant summaries of the overall model behavior. The task farming approach is inherently parallel (zero communication
between nodes and, therefore, linear scaling of computation with number
of nodes available) and as such it is one of the most efficient programming
styles available on any parallel machine (i.e., it allows the full utilization of
the available computational power of the machine). This approach allows

modelling in a single overnight run what would otherwise take a full year of nonstop computation on previously available computing platforms.

7.6.6 Distributed Modelling via the Postmaster Element

The *postmaster element* is a self-contained object within the GENESIS neural simulator. Like the objects in a true object-oriented language it is an entity composed of public (externally available) data, private (internal) data, and functions to operate on the object. Like other GENESIS elements, it is a black box that can be used to construct a neural simulation. For the present, modellers wishing to produce large distributed simulations that are able to take full advantage of the power inherent in our current parallel computers must specify how to distribute the different parts of their simulation over the available hardware computing nodes. While this may be an annoying necessity to certain neural modellers, it must be remembered that this technique allows the construction of simulations of such a size and computational complexity that they can be modelled on no other existing computer platforms (e.g., traditional serial supercomputers). Bearing this in mind, the requirement of explicitly stating how to distribute the model is a small price to pay for the power gained. This explicit method also brings with it certain advantages. Firstly, because the modeller is familiar with the computational demands of the different parts of his model, he is able to accurately balance the computational load over the available parallel hardware. This makes for far more efficient load balancing and scaling behavior than would be possible with an automatic decomposition scheme that has to balance the very different needs of both single-cell modellers and network-scale modellers. It is also less efficient to carry out automatic decomposition because the various GENESIS elements comprising a complete neural simulation have widely varying computational demands. As with other GENESIS elements, the postmaster acts as a self-contained black box which usually communicates information about its changing state via messages to other elements. It can both send messages to, and receive messages from, other GENESIS elements which may exist either on this particular hardware node or on others in the network. As a result of this, it is an element that ties together and coordinates the disparate parts of a model running on separate hardware nodes of the parallel computer. The actual messages transferred depend on the type of element with which it communicates. The postmaster element neither knows nor cares whether the quantity it is communicating is a membrane potential, a channel conductance (simple current flow), or the concentration of any substance from ions to complex neurotransmitters. The postmaster is a two-faced element. Its first face is that of a normal GENESIS element which it presents to the rest of the simulation. This first aspect of the postmaster is able to pass GENESIS messages between elements and allows use of the GENESIS Script Language to query its state. The second aspect of the postmaster is aware of the parallel nature of the underlying hardware and can use the operating system primitives for communicating information between separate physical nodes. In summary, the postmaster element is a conduit along which information can flow between nodes. It allows the modeller to tie together the disparate aspects of the simulation into a coherent whole.

To show how this mechanism works in practice, performance measurements are presented in Figure 7.14, which are taken on the Intel Touchstone Delta parallel supercomputer based at Caltech. These figures show both scaling of performance, where more nodes allow the model to complete in a shorter timescale, and the construction of models so large that it has been impossible to model them before now.

The previous record for the most complex GENESIS model produced on a traditional serial computer is approximately 80,000 elements, the Purkinje Cell model produced at Caltech by Dr. de Schutter [Schutter:91a;93a]. Using the postmaster element on a parallel supercomputer (the 512-node Intel Touchstone Delta), this limit has now been pushed to over two million GENESIS elements (actually $2 \times 1024 \times 1024$). As can be seen, this now allows for the construction of far more complex and realistic models than was previously possible. The present price to be paid for this freedom is the decision to make the modeller explicitly distribute his simulation over the available hardware. This was a design decision that has allowed far greater efficiency of load balancing than would be possible using an automatic distribution technique as the illustrated scaling graphs confirm. This technique also has the advantage of leaving the basic GENESIS script interface unaltered and is applicable to a wide variety of parallel hardware. As a result of the requirement to retain compatibility with the existing serial GENESIS implementation, another benefit has become obvious. By changing only the network layer of the postmaster element, it is possible to produce a version of the postmaster that can use traditional serial machines distributed across the Internet to produce a distributed model, which ties together existing supercomputers based anywhere on the network. The potential size of model that can be constructed in this manner is staggering, although the reality of network communication delays will limit its area of application to

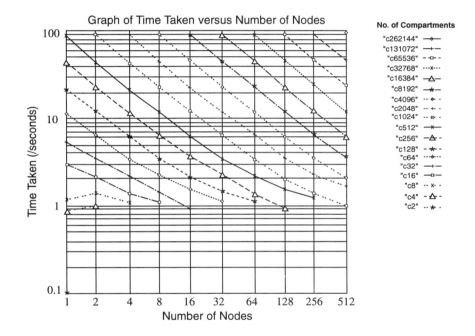

Figure 7.14: Results from Running a GENESIS Simulation of a Passive Cable Model Composed of Varying Numbers of Compartments Distributed Across Varying Numbers of Nodes on the Intel Touchstone Delta Parallel Supercomputer

compute-limited tasks (cf. communication-bound simulations).

The assessment of the usefulness of a parallel neural modelling platform can be demonstrated by two extremes of neural modelling applications:

1. Detailed single-cell models

   The individual subcompartments which make up a neuron's dendritic tree are active simultaneously, and each of these compartments may be studded with several independently functioning ionic membrane channels. This is illustrated in Figure 7.15.

2. Large network simulations

   A detailed network simulation may be composed of many thousands of individual nerve cells from a smaller number of biological cell types.

What does a parallel computer have to offer the single-cell modeller?

Most of the work on the parallel GENESIS at Caltech to date has been in the field of single-cell modelling. Several distinct ways of using the system have been developed allowing a variety of approaches by the single-cell modeller.

- Examining large parameter spaces

  Each individual node on the parallel computer runs a separate, complete, single-cell model (task farming). This facility can be used to examine the sensitivity of the cell's performance to a wide range of physiological states including testing the effect of parameters which are at present difficult to measure experimentally [Bhalla:93a]. A selection of these appear below:

  - Channel Blocker Experiments.
    Like the experimentalist, the neural modeller can block or poison different ion channel subsets, with the added advantage that it is possible to block both channels where no chemical blocking agent currently exists and also to have 100% channel-blocking specificity (e.g., work conducted by D. Jaeger, Caltech [Jaeger:93a]).

  - Effect of stimulation in different parts of the dendritic arbor
    An experiment at present difficult or impossible to perform in any physiological setup can easily be tested on the computer model system. For example, the independence of stimulation site on Purkinje Cell response (Work performed by E. de Schutter, Caltech [Schutter:91a;93a]).

— Prediction of ionic channel distribution

The prediction of ionic channel distribution over different parts of a cell's dendritic arbor by observing the effect of changed distribution on the model cell's electrophysiological properties, and relating this to the experimentally measured behavior of the real neuron [Bhalla:93a]. Experimental confirmation of channel distribution predicted by the manipulation of such computer models seems likely to appear in the near future due to advances in monoclonal antibody techniques for different channel subsets.

— Effect of changing membrane properties

Predicting the effect of changing membrane properties which are impossible to measure experimentally—for example, in the distal dendritic arbor or in "spines" (e.g., E. de Schutter, Caltech [Bhalla:93a], [Schutter:91a]).

The first example above is of modelling following and confirming physiology experiments. The latter examples are uses of neural modelling to predict future experimental findings. Although rarely used to date (because of computer limits on the model's level of biological realism), this synergistic use of neural modelling in predicting experimental results and suggesting new experiments appears to offer substantial benefits to the neurobiology community at large. Neural modelling on parallel computers, such as the Intel Touchstone Delta, is allowing modelling to adopt these new closer links to experimental work, thereby closing the dichotomy between experimenters and modellers. In the past, this dichotomy has caused several experimentalists to question the relevance of funding modelling work. Hopefully, this attitude will change as more results of synergy between modelling experiments and physiology experiments become widely known.

• Construction of large and detailed cell models

The system allows the construction of larger and more detailed cell models than is possible on a traditional serial computer. The level of detail included in models to date has been limited either by the memory size constraints of the computer used, or by the computational time requirements of the model [Bhalla:92a]. A distributed model of a single cell on a parallel computer alleviates both of these constraints simultaneously. This allows the construction of larger cell models than have been previously possible but which nevertheless run in acceptable time frames.

What does a parallel computer have to offer the neural network modeller?

Much of the work to date has been on task farming (as described above), whereby each node runs its own copy of a cell. This is less useful to the network modeller but still allows detailed statistical information to be built up about network and population behavior. A more interesting way of using the parallel machine for network modelling is the distributed model scheme mentioned above. This allows networks to be both larger and to run more quickly than their counterparts on equivalent serial machines. A promising project in this category, although still in its very early stages, is the construction by Upinder Bhalla at Caltech of a detailed model of the rat olfactory bulb [Bhalla:93a]. This incorporates detailed cellular elements, which are rare in network class models. Such a network model makes far greater communication demands of the internode communications mechanism on the parallel computer than a distributed single-cell model. Initially an expanded version of the postmaster element [Speight:92a;92b] which was used for distributed single-cell models will be employed, but this may change as the different demands of a large network model become apparent.

All of the work on the Parallel GENESIS project was carried out in the laboratory of Professor James Bower at the California Institute of Technology.

Chapter 8

Full Matrix Algorithms and Their Applications

8.1 Full and Banded Matrix Algorithms

Concurrent matrix algorithms were among the first to be studied on the hypercubes at Caltech [Fox:82a], and they have also been intensively studied at other institutions, notably Yale [Ipsen:87b], [Johnsson:87b;89a], [Saad:85a], and Oak Ridge National Laboratory [Geist:86a;89a], [Romine:87a;90a]. The motivation for this interest is the fact that matrix algorithms play a prominent role in many scientific and engineering computations. In this chapter, we study the so called-*full* or *dense* (and closely related *banded*) matrix algorithms where essentially all elements of the matrix are nonzero. In Chapters 9 and 12, we will treat the more common case of problems, which, if formulated as matrix equations, are represented by *sparse* matrices. Here, most of the elements of the matrix are zero; one can apply full matrix algorithms to such sparse cases, but there are much better algorithms that exploit the sparseness to reduce the computational complexity. Within C^3P, we found two classes of important problems that needed full matrix algorithms. In Sections 8.2 and 8.3, we cover two chemical scattering problems, which involve relatively small full matrices—where the matrix rows and columns are labelled by the different reaction channels. The currently most important real-world use of full matrix algorithms is computational electromagnetic simulations [Edelman:92a]. These are used by the defense industry to design aircraft and other military vehicles with low radar cross sections. Solutions of large sets of linear equations come from the method of moments approach to electromagnetic equations [Wang:91b]. We investigated this method successfully at JPL [Simoni:89a] but in this book, we only describe (in Section 9.4) the alternative approaches, finite elements, to electromagnetic simulations. Such sparse matrix formulation will be more efficient for large electromagnetic problems, but the moment method and associated full matrix is probably the most common and numerically reliable approach.

Early work at Caltech on full matrices (1983 to 1987) focused on specific algorithms, such as matrix multiplication, matrix-vector products, and LU decomposition. A major issue in determining the optimal algorithm for these problems is choosing a decomposition which has good load balance and low communication overhead. Many matrix algorithms proceed in a series of steps in which rows and/or columns are successively made inactive. The scattered decomposition described in Section 8.1.2 is usually used to balance the load in such cases. The block decomposition, also described in Section 8.1.2, generally minimizes the amount of data communicated, but results in sending several short messages rather than a few longer messages. Thus, a block decomposition is optimal for a multiprocessor with low message latency, or startup cost, such as the Caltech/JPL Mark II hypercube. For machines with high message latency, such as the Intel iPSC/1, a row decomposition may be preferable. The best decomposition, therefore, depends crucially on the characteristics of the concurrent hardware.

In recent years (1988–1990), interest has centered on the development of libraries of concurrent linear algebra routines. As discussed in Section 8.1.7, two approaches have been followed at Caltech. One approach by Fox, et al. has led to a library of routines that are optimal for low latency, homogeneous hypercubes, such as the Caltech/JPL Mark II hypercubes. In contrast, Van de Velde has developed a library of routines that are generally suboptimal, but which may be ported to a wider range of multiprocessor architectures, and are suitable for incorporation into programs with dynamically changing data distributions.

8.1.1 Matrix Decomposition

The data decomposition (or distribution) is a major factor in determining the efficiency of a concurrent matrix algorithm, so before detailing the research into concurrent linear algebra done at Caltech, we shall first introduce some basic decomposition strategies.

The processors of a concurrent computer can be uniquely labelled by

$0, 1, \ldots, N_{\text{proc}} - 1$, where N_{proc} is the number of processors. A vector of length M may be decomposed over the processors by assigning the vector entry with global index m (where $0 \leq m < M$) to processor p, where it is stored as the ith entry in a local array. Thus, the decomposition of a vector can be regarded as a mapping of the global index, m, to an index pair, (p, i), specifying the processor number and local index.

For matrix problems, the processors are usually arranged as a $P \times Q$ grid. Thus, the grid consists of P rows of processors and Q columns of processors, and $N_{\text{proc}} = PQ$. Each processor can be uniquely identified by its position, (p, q), on the processor grid. The decomposition of an $M \times N$ matrix can be regarded as the Cartesian product of two vector decompositions, μ and ν. The mapping μ decomposes the M rows of the matrix over the P processor rows, and ν decomposes the N columns of the matrix over the Q processor columns. Thus, if $\mu(m) = (p, i)$ and $\nu(n) = (q, j)$, then the matrix entry with global index (m, n) is assigned to the processor at position (p, q) on the processor grid, where it is stored in a local array with index (i, j).

Two common decompositions are the *linear* and *scattered* decompositions. The linear decomposition, λ, assigns contiguous entries in the global vector to the processors in blocks,

$$\lambda(m) = (\, p, \; m - pL - \min(p, R) \,), \tag{8.1}$$

where

$$p = \max \left(\left\lfloor \frac{m}{L+1} \right\rfloor, \left\lfloor \frac{m - R}{L} \right\rfloor \right) \tag{8.2}$$

and $L = \lfloor M/P \rfloor$ and $R = M \bmod P$. The scattered decomposition, σ, assigns consecutive entries in the global vector to different processors,

$$\sigma(m) = (\, m \bmod P, \lfloor m/P \rfloor \,) \tag{8.3}$$

Figure 8.1 shows examples of these two types of decomposition for a 10×10 matrix.

The mapping of processors onto the processor grid is determined by the programming methodology, which in turn depends closely on the concurrent hardware. For machines such as the nCUBE-1 hypercube, it is advantageous to exploit any locality properties in the algorithm in order to reduce communication costs. In such cases, processors may be mapped onto the processor grid by a binary Gray code scheme [Fox:88a], [Saad:88a], which ensures that adjacent processors on the processor grid are directly connected by a communication channel. For machines such as the Symult 2010, for which the

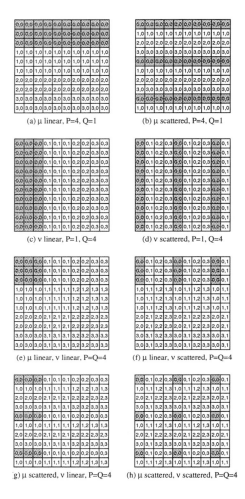

Figure 8.1: These Eight Figures Show Different Ways of Decomposing a 10×10 Matrix. Each cell represents a matrix entry, and is labelled by the position, (p, q), in the processor grid of the processor to which it is assigned. To emphasize the pattern of decomposition, the matrix entries assigned to the processor in the first row and column of the processor grid are shown shaded. Figures (a) and (b) show linear and scattered row-oriented decompositions, respectively, for four processors arranged as a 4×1 grid ($P = 4$, $Q = 1$). In Figures (c) and (d), the corresponding column-oriented decompositions are shown ($P = 1$, $Q = 4$). Figures (e) through (h) show linear and scattered block-oriented decompositions for 16 processors arranged as a 4×4 grid ($P = Q = 4$).

time to send a message between any two processors is almost independent of their separation in the hardware topology, locality of communication is not an issue, and the processors can be mapped arbitrarily onto the processor grid.

8.1.2 Basic Matrix Arithmetic

One of the first linear algebra algorithms implemented on the Caltech/JPL Mark II hypercube was the multiplication of two dense matrices, **A** and **B**, to form the product, **C** = **AB** [Fox:85b]. The algorithm uses a block-oriented, linear decomposition, which is optimal for machines with low message latency when the subblocks are (as nearly as possible) square. Let us denote by $A_{(p,q)}$ the subblock of **A** in the processor at position (p, q) of the processor grid, with a similar designation applying to the subblocks of **B** and **C**. Then, if the processor grid is square, that is, $P = Q = \sqrt{N_{\text{proc}}}$, the matrix multiplication algorithm in block form is,

$$C_{(p,q)} = \sum_{r=0}^{P-1} A_{(p,r)} B_{(r,q)} \quad \text{for } p, q = 0, 1, \ldots, P - 1 \tag{8.4}$$

The case in which $P \neq Q$ involves some extra bookkeeping, but does not change the concurrent algorithm in any essential way.

On the Mark II hypercube, communication cost increases with processor separation, so processors are mapped onto the processor grid using a binary Gray code scheme. Two types of communication are required at each stage of the algorithm, and both exploit the hypercube topology to minimize communication costs. Matrix subblocks are communicated to the processor above in the processor grid, and subblocks are broadcast along processor rows by a communication pipeline (Figure 8.2).

The matrix multiplication algorithm has been modified for use on the Caltech/JPL Mark IIIfp hypercube [Hipes:89b]. The Mark II hypercube is a homogeneous machine in the sense that there is only one level in the memory hierarchy, that is, the local memory of each processor. However, each processor of the Mark IIIfp hypercube has a Weitek floating-point processor with a 64 Kbyte data cache. To take full advantage of the high processing speed of the Weitek, data transfer between local memory and the Weitek data cache must be minimized. Since there are two levels in the memory hierarchy of each processor (local memory and cache), the Mark IIIfp is an inhomogeneous hypercube. The main computational task in each stage of

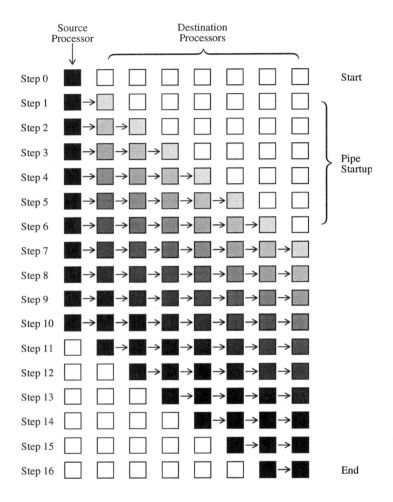

Figure 8.2: A Schematic Representation of a Pipeline Broadcast for an Eight-Processor Computer. White squares represent processors not involved in communication, and such processors are available to perform calculations. Shaded squares represent processors involved in communication, with the degree of shading indicating how much of the data have arrived at any given step. In the first six steps, those processor not yet involved in the broadcast can continue to perform calculations. Similarly, in steps 11 through 16, processors that are no longer involved in communicating can perform useful work since they now have all the data necessary to perform the next stage of the algorithm.

the concurrent algorithm is to multiply the subblocks in each processor, and for large problems not all of the data will fit into the cache. The multiplication is, therefore, done in inner product form on the Weitek by further subdividing the subblocks in each processor. This intraprocessor subblocking allows the multiplication in each processor to be done in a number of stages, during each of which only the data needed for that stage are explicitly loaded into the cache.

Independently, Cherkassky, et al. in [Cherkassky:88a], Berntsen in [Berntsen:89a], and Aboelaze [Aboelaze:89a] improved Fox's algorithm for dense $N \times N$ matrix multiplication, reducing the time complexity from

$$T = \frac{2N^3}{N_{\text{proc}}} \tau + \frac{2N^2}{\sqrt{N_{\text{proc}}}} t_{transf} + \sqrt{N_{\text{proc}}} \left(\sqrt{N_{\text{proc}}} - 1 \right) t_{start}$$

to

$$T = \frac{2N^3}{N_{\text{proc}}} \tau + \frac{2N^2}{\sqrt{N_{\text{proc}}}} t_{transf} + \left(\sqrt{N_{\text{proc}}} - 1 \right) t_{start}$$

where N_{proc} is the number of processors, τ is the time for one addition or one multiplication, and t_{transf}, t_{start} are machine-dependent communication parameters defining bandwidth and latency [Chrisochoides:92a]. In fact, the communication cost of transferring w words is $wt_{transf} + t_{start}$

A concurrent algorithm to perform the matrix-vector product $\mathbf{y} = \mathbf{A}\mathbf{x}$ has also been implemented on the Caltech/JPL Mark II hypercube [Fox:88a]. Again, a block-oriented, linear decomposition is used for the matrix $\mathbf{A}$. The vector $\mathbf{x}$ is decomposed linearly over the processors' columns, so that all the processors in the same processor column contain the same portion of $\mathbf{x}$. Similarly, at the end of the algorithm, the vector $\mathbf{y}$ is decomposed over the processor rows, so that all the processors in the same processor row contain the same portion of $\mathbf{y}$. In block form the matrix-vector product is,

$$\mathbf{y}_{(p)} = \sum_{q=0}^{Q-1} A_{(p,q)} \mathbf{x}_{(q)} \quad \text{for } p = 0, 1, \ldots, P - 1 \tag{8.5}$$

As in the matrix multiplication algorithm, the concurrent matrix-vector product algorithm is optimal for low latency, homogeneous hypercubes if the subblocks of $\mathbf{A}$ are square.

8.1.3   Matrix Multiplication for Banded Matrices

Banded Matrix-Vector Multiplication

First, we consider the parallelization of the operation $\mathbf{c} = \beta\mathbf{c} + \alpha\mathbf{A}\mathbf{b}$ on a linear array of N_{proc} processors when $\mathbf{A}$ is a banded $N \times N$ matrix with w_1, w_2 upper and lower bandwidths, and we assume that matrices are stored using a sparse scheme [Rice:85a]. For simplicity, we describe the case $N = N_{\text{proc}}$. The proposed implementation is based on a decomposition of matrix $\mathbf{A}$ into an upper $\mathbf{U}$ (including the diagonal of $\mathbf{A}$) and lower $\mathbf{L}$ triangular matrices, such as $\mathbf{A} = \mathbf{L} + \mathbf{U}$. Furthermore, we assume that row $\{a_{i,j}\}_{j=1}^{N}$ and b_i are stored in processor i. Without loss of generality, we can assume $\alpha = 1$ and $\beta = 1$. The vector $\mathbf{c}$ can then be expressed as $\mathbf{c} = \mathbf{c} + (\mathbf{L}\mathbf{b} + \mathbf{U}\mathbf{b})$. The products $\mathbf{U}\mathbf{b}$ and $\mathbf{L}\mathbf{b}$ are computed within $w_1 + 1$ and w_2 iterations, respectively. The computation involved is described in Figure 8.3. In order to compute the complexity of the above algorithm, we assume without any loss of generality, that $\mathbf{A}$ has K non-zero elements, and $N \gg w_1 + w_2 + 1$. Then it can be shown that the time complexity is

$$T_P = \frac{K}{N_{\text{proc}}}\tau + (w_1 + w_2 + 1)\left\{t_{start} + t_{transf}\frac{N}{N_{\text{proc}}}\right\} \qquad (8.6)$$

and the memory space required for each subdomain is $O\left(\frac{K}{N_{\text{proc}}} + 3\frac{N}{N_{\text{proc}}}\right)$.

Banded Matrix—Matrix Multiplication

Second, we consider the implementation of $\mathbf{C} = \beta\mathbf{C} + \alpha\mathbf{A}\mathbf{B}$, on a ring of N_{proc} processors when $\mathbf{A}$, $\mathbf{B}$ are banded $N \times N$ matrices with u_1, u_2 upper, and l_1, l_2 lower bandwidths, respectively. Again, we describe the realization for $N = N_{\text{proc}}$. The case $N \gg N_{\text{proc}}$ is straightforward generalization. The processor i computes column C_i of matrix $\mathbf{C}$ and holds one row of matrix $\mathbf{A}$ (denoted by A_i) and a column of matrix $\mathbf{B}$ (denoted by B_i).

The algorithm consists of two phases as in banded-matrix vector multiplication. Without loss of generality, we can assume $\alpha = 1$, and $\beta = 1$. In the first phase, each node starts by calculating $c_{ii} = c_{ii} + A_i \times B_i$, then each node i passes B_i to node $i - 1$, this phase is repeated $\min(u_1, u_2) + 1$ times. In the second phase, each node restores B_i and passes it to node $i + 1$. This phase is repeated $\min(l_1, l_2)$ times. The implementation proposed for this operation is described in Figure 8.4.

Without loss of generality, we assume that K_1, K_2 are the number of non-zero elements for the matrices $\mathbf{A}$, $\mathbf{B}$ respectively, and denote by $w_1 =$

Phase 1: Multiply the Upper Triangular U by b

```
temp := d
For each node i do in parallel
  For j := 0 to w2
    if (i + j =< Nproc) then
       begin
        if ( i = 1) then do nothing
         else Send d to node i-1
         c := c + a(i, j+1) * d
         if ( i = Nproc) then do nothing
         else Receive d from node i+1
       end
     endif
  end
end
```

Phase 2: Multiply the Lower Triangular L by b

```
For each node i do in parallel
  begin
  d := temp
    For j := 1 to w2
      if (i < j) then
        begin
          if ( i = Nproc) then do nothing
          else (Send d to node i + 1
          if ( i = 1 ) then do nothing
          else Receive d from node i - 1
          c := c + a(i, i-j) * d
        end
      endif
    end
end
```

Figure 8.3: The Pseudo Code for Banded Matrix-Vector Multiplication

Phase 1

```
temp := b
For each node i do in parallel
/* each node contains a = A_i, b = B_i */
  For j := 0 to min(u1 , u2)
    if (i + j =< N) then
        begin
          if (i = 1) do nothing
          else Send b to node i-1
          c(i,i+j) := c(i,I+1) + a * b
          if (i = N_proc) then do nothing
          else Receive b from node i+1
      endif
    endfor
endfor
```

Phase 2

```
b := temp
For Each node i in parallel do
  For j := 1 to min(l1 , l2) do
    if (i > j) then
        begin
          if(i = N_proc) then do nothing
          else send b to node i+1
          if( i = 1) then do nothing
          else receive b from node i-1
          c(i, i-j) := c(I,i-j) + a * b
      endif
    endfor
endfor
```

Figure 8.4: The Pseudo Code for Banded Matrix-Matrix Multiplication

Table 8.1: Measured maximum total elapsed time (in seconds) for multiplication of a block tridiagonal matrices with a vector.

Matrix Size Per Node	4 nodes	8 nodes	16 nodes	32 nodes	64 nodes
8×24	0.0634	0.0644	0.0644	0.0644	0.0645
16×48	0.0221	0.0222	0.0222	0.0222	0.0222
32×96	0.0847	0.0848	0.0848	0.0849	0,0849
64×192	0.3345	0.3346	0.3346	0.3347	0.3347

Each block is of size $n \times n$, where $n = 8, 16, 32, 64$, respectively, in each table row.

$u_1 + l_1 + 1$ and $w_2 = u_2 + l_2 + 1$. Then we can show that the parallel execution time T_P is given by

$$T_P = \frac{\min(K_1 w_2, K_2 w_1)}{N_{\text{proc}}} \tau$$
$$+ \left\{ t_{start} + t_{transf} \frac{N}{N_{\text{proc}}} \min(w_1, w_2) \right\} \min(w_1, w_2) \quad (8.7)$$

The above realization has been implemented on the nCUBE-1 [Chrisochoides:90a]. Tables 8.1 and 8.2 indicate the performance of BLAS 2 computation for a block tridiagonal matrix where each block is dense. In these experiments, each processor has the same computation to perform. The results indicate very satisfactory performance for these type of data.

8.1.4 Systems of Linear Equations

Factorization of Full Matrices

LU factorization of dense matrices, and the closely related Gaussian elimination algorithm, are widely used in the solution of linear systems of equations of the form $A\mathbf{x} = \mathbf{b}$. LU factorization expresses the coefficient matrix, A, as the product of a lower triangular matrix, L, and an upper triangular matrix, U. After factorization, the original system of equations can be written as a pair of triangular systems,

$$L\mathbf{y} = \mathbf{b} \quad \text{and} \quad U\mathbf{x} = \mathbf{y} \quad (8.8)$$

Table 8.2: Measured maximum elapsed time (in seconds) for multiplication of a block tridiagonal matrix by a block tridiagonal matrix.

Matrix Size Per Node	4 nodes	8 nodes	16 nodes	32 nodes	64 nodes
8×24	0.275	0.281	0.281	0.281	0.281
16×48	4.029	4.030	4.030	4.030	4.030

Each block is of size $n \times n$, where $n = 8, 16$, respectively, in each table row.

The first of the systems can be solved by forward reduction, and then back substitution can be used to solve the second system to give $\mathbf{x}$. If A is an $M \times M$ matrix, LU factorization proceeds in $M - 1$ steps, in the kth of which column k of L and row k of U are found,

$$
\begin{aligned}
\ell_{k,k} &= 1 \\
\ell_{k+i,k} &= a_{k+i,k}/a_{k,k} \quad \text{for } 1 \le i < M \\
u_{k,k+j} &= a_{k,k+j} \quad\quad\;\; \text{for } 0 \le j < M
\end{aligned}
$$

and the entries of A in a "window" extending from column $k + 1$ to $M - 1$ and row $k + 1$ to $M - 1$ are updated,

$$
a_{k+i,k+j} = a_{k+i,k+j} - \ell_{k+i,k}\, u_{k,k+j} \quad \text{for } 1 \le i, j < M \tag{8.9}
$$

Partial pivoting is usually performed to improve numerical stability. This involves reordering the rows or columns of A.

In the absence of pivoting, the row- and column-oriented decompositions involve almost the same amounts of communication and computation. However, the row-oriented approach is generally preferred as it is more convenient for the back substitution phase [Chu:87a], [Geist:86a], although column-based algorithms have been proposed [Li:87a], [Moler:86a]. A block-oriented decomposition minimizes the amount of data communicated, and is the best approach on hypercubes with low message latency. However, since the block decomposition generally involves sending shorter messages, it is not suitable for machines with high message latency. In all cases, pipelining is the most efficient way of broadcasting rows and columns of the matrix since it minimizes the idle time that a processor must wait when participating in a broadcast, and effectively overlaps communication and calculation.

0,0	0,0	0,0	0,1	0,1	0,1	0,2	0,2	0,3	0,3
0,0	0,0	0,0	0,1	0,1	0,1	0,2	0,2	0,3	0,3
0,0	0,0	0,0	0,1	0,1	0,1	0,2	0,2	0,3	0,3
1,0	1,0	1,0	1,1	1,1	1,1	1,2	1,2	1,3	1,3
1,0	1,0	1,0	1,1	1,1	1,1	1,2	1,2	1,3	1,3
1,0	1,0	1,0	1,1	1,1	1,1	1,2	1,2	1,3	1,3
2,0	2,0	2,0	2,1	2,1	2,1	2,2	2,2	2,3	2,3
2,0	2,0	2,0	2,1	2,1	2,1	2,2	2,2	2,3	2,3
3,0	3,0	3,0	3,1	3,1	3,1	3,2	3,2	3,3	3,3
3,0	3,0	3,0	3,1	3,1	3,1	3,2	3,2	3,3	3,3

(a) Linear block decomposition

0,0	0,1	0,2	0,3	0,0	0,1	0,2	0,3	0,0	0,1
1,0	1,1	1,2	1,3	1,0	1,1	1,2	1,3	1,0	1,1
2,0	2,1	2,2	2,3	2,0	2,1	2,2	2,3	2,0	2,1
3,0	3,1	3,2	3,3	3,0	3,1	3,2	3,3	3,0	3,1
0,0	0,1	0,2	0,3	0,0	0,1	0,2	0,3	0,0	0,1
1,0	1,1	1,2	1,3	1,0	1,1	1,2	1,3	1,0	1,1
2,0	2,1	2,2	2,3	2,0	2,1	2,2	2,3	2,0	2,1
3,0	3,1	3,2	3,3	3,0	3,1	3,2	3,3	3,0	3,1
0,0	0,1	0,2	0,3	0,0	0,1	0,2	0,3	0,0	0,1
1,0	1,1	1,2	1,3	1,0	1,1	1,2	1,3	1,0	1,1

(b) Scattered block decomposition

Figure 8.5: The Shaded Area in These Two Figures Shows the Computational Window at the Start of Step Three of the LU Factorization Algorithm. In (a) we see that by this stage the processors in the first row and column of the processor grid have become idle if a linear block decomposition is used. In contrast, in (b) we see that all processors continue to be involved in the computation if a scattered block decomposition is used.

Load balance is an important issue in LU factorization. If a linear decomposition is used, the computation will be imbalanced and processors will become idle once they no longer contain matrix entries in the computational window. A scattered decomposition is much more effective in keeping all the processors busy, as shown in Figure 8.5. The load imbalance is least when a scattered block-oriented decomposition is used.

At Caltech, Van de Velde has investigated LU factorization of full matrices for a number of different pivoting strategies, and for various types of matrix decomposition on the Intel iPSC/2 hypercube and the Symult 2010 [Velde:90a]. One observation based on this work was that if a linear decomposition is used, then in many cases pivoting results in a faster algorithm than with no pivoting, since the exchange of rows effectively randomizes the decomposition, resulting in better load balance. Van de Velde also introduces a clever enhancement to the standard concurrent partial pivoting procedure. To illustrate this, consider partial pivoting over rows. Usually, only the processors in a single-processor column are involved in the search for the pivot candidate, and the other processors are idle at this time. In Van de Velde's multirow pivoting scheme, in each processor column a search for a pivot is conducted concurrently within a randomly selected column of the matrix. This incurs no extra cost compared with the standard pivot-

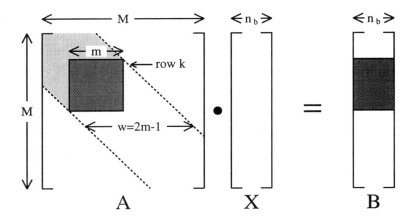

Figure 8.6: Schematic Representation of Step k of LU Factorization for an $M \times M$ Matrix, A, with Bandwidth w. The $m \times m$ computational window is shown as a dark-shaded square, and matrix entries in this region are updated at step k. The light-shaded part of the band above and to the left of the window has already been factorized, and in an in-place algorithm contains the appropriate columns and rows of L and U. The unshaded part of the band below and to the right of the window has not yet been modified. The shaded region of the matrix B represents the $m \times n_b$ window updated in step k of forward reduction, and in step $M - k - 1$ of back substitution.

ing procedure, but improves the numerical stability. A similar multicolumn pivoting scheme can be used when pivoting over columns. Van de Velde concludes from his extensive experimentation with LU factorization schemes that a scattered decomposition generally results in a more efficient algorithm on the iPSC/2 and Symult 2010, and his work illustrates the importance of decomposition and pivoting strategy in determining load balance, and hence concurrent efficiency.

LU Factorization of Banded Matrices

Aldcroft, et al. [Aldcroft:88a] have investigated the solution of linear systems of equations by LU factorization, followed by forward elimination and back substitution, when the coefficient matrix, A, is an $M \times M$ matrix of bandwidth $w = 2m - 1$. The case of multiple right-hand sides was considered, so the system may be written as $AX = B$, where X and B are $M \times n_b$ matrices. The LU factorization algorithm for banded matrices is essentially the same as that for full matrices, except that the computational window containing the entries of A updated in each step is different. If no pivoting is performed, the window is of size $m \times m$ and lies along the diagonal, as shown in Figure 8.6. If partial pivoting over rows is performed, then fill-in will occur, and the window may attain a maximum size of $m \times (2m - 1)$. In the work of Aldcroft, et al. the size of the window was allowed to vary dynamically. This involved some additional bookkeeping, but is more efficient than working with a fixed window of the maximum size. Additional complications arise from only storing the entries of A within the band in order to reduce memory usage.

As in the full matrix case, good load balance is ensured by using a scattered block decomposition for the matrices. As noted previously, this choice of decomposition also minimizes communication cost on low latency multiprocessors, such as the Caltech/JPL Mark II hypercube used in this work, but may not be optimal for machines in which the message startup cost is substantial.

A comparison between an analytic performance model and results on the Caltech/JPL Mark II hypercube shows that the concurrent overhead for the LU factorization algorithm falls to zero as $1/\hat{m}$, where $\hat{m} = \lfloor m/\sqrt{N_p} \rfloor$. This is true in both the pivoting and non-pivoting cases. Thus, the LU factorization algorithm scales well to larger machines.

8.1.5 The Gauss-Jordan Method

As described for his chemistry application in Section 8.2, Hipes has studied the use of the Gauss-Jordan (GJ) algorithm as a means of solving systems of linear equations [Hipes:89b]. On a sequential computer, LU factorization followed by forward reduction and back substitution is preferable over GJ for solving linear systems since the former has a lower operation count. Another apparent drawback of GJ is that it has generally been believed that the right hand sides must be available a priori, which in applications requiring the solution for multiple right-hand sides is a handicap. Hipes' work has shown that this is not the case, and that a well-written, parallel GJ solver is significantly more efficient than using LU factorization with triangular solvers on hypercubes.

As noted by Gerasoulis, et al. [Gerasoulis:88a], GJ does not require the solution of triangular systems. The solution of such systems by LU factorization features an outer loop of fixed length and two inner loops of decreasing length, whereas GJ has two outer fixed-length loops and only one inner loop of decreasing length. GJ is, therefore, intrinsically more parallel than the LU solver, and its better load balance compensates for its higher operation count. Hipes has pointed out that the multipliers generated in the GJ algorithm can be saved where zeros are produced in the coefficient matrix. The entries in the coefficient matrix are, therefore, overwritten by the GJ multipliers, and we shall call this the GJ factorization (although we are not actually expressing the original matrix A as the product of two matrices). It is now apparent that the right-hand side matrix does *not* have to be known in advance, since a solution can be obtained using the previously computed multipliers. Another factor, noted by Hipes, favoring the use of the GJ solver on a multiprocessor, is the larger grain size maintained throughout the GJ factorization and solution phases, and the lower communication cost in the GJ solution phase.

Hipes has implemented his GJ solver on the Caltech/JPL Mark III and nCUBE-1 hypercubes, and compared the performance with the usual LU solver [Hipes:89d]. In the GJ factorization, a scattered column decomposition is used, similar to that shown in Figure 8.1(d). This ensures good load balance as columns become eliminated in the course of the algorithm. In the LU factorization, both rows and columns are eliminated so a scattered block decomposition is used. On both machines, it was found that the GJ approach is faster for sufficiently many right-hand sides.

8.1.6   Other Matrix Algorithms

Hipes has also compared the Gaussian-Jordan (GJ) and Gaussian Elimination (GE) algorithms for finding the inverse of a matrix [Hipes:88a]. This work was motivated by an application program that integrates a special system of ordinary differential equations that arise in chemical dynamics simulations [Hipes:87a], [Kuppermann:86a]. The sequential GJ and GE algorithms have the same operation count for matrix inversion. However, Hipes found the parallel GJ inversion has a more homogeneous load distribution, and requires fewer communication calls than GE inversion, and so should result in a more efficient parallel algorithm. Hipes has compared the two methods on the Caltech/JPL Mark II hypercube, and as expected found that GJ inversion algorithm to be the fastest.

Fox and Furmanski have also investigated matrix algorithms at Caltech [Furmanski:88b]. Among the parallel algorithms they discuss is the power method for finding the largest eigenvalue, and corresponding eigenvector, and a matrix A. This starts with an initial guess, $\mathbf{x}_0$, at the eigenvector, and then generates subsequent estimates using

$$\mathbf{y}_k = A\mathbf{x}_k, \quad \text{and} \quad \mathbf{x}_{k+1} = \frac{\mathbf{y}_k}{|\mathbf{y}_k|} \quad \text{for} \quad k = 0, 1, \ldots \quad (8.10)$$

As k becomes large, $|\mathbf{y}_k|$ tends to the eigenvalue with the largest absolute value (except for a possible sign change), and $\mathbf{x}_k$ tends to the corresponding eigenvector. Since the main component of the algorithm is matrix-vector multiplication, it can be done as discussed in Section 8.1.2.

A more challenging algorithm to parallelize is the tridiagonalization of a symmetric matrix by Householder's method, which involves the application of a series of rotations to the original matrix. Although the basic operations involved in each rotation are straightforward (matrix-vector multiplication, scalar products, and so on), special care must be taken to balance the load. This is particularly difficult since the symmetry of the matrix A means that the basic structure being processed is triangular, and this is decomposed into a set of local triangular matrices in the individual processors. Load balance is optimized by scattering the rows over the processors, and the algorithm requires vectors to be broadcast and transposed.

8.1.7 Concurrent Linear Algebra Libraries

Since matrix algorithms play such an important role in scientific computing, it is desirable to develop a library of linear algebra routines for concurrent multiprocessors. Ideally, these routines should be optimal and general-purpose, that is, portable to a wide variety of multiprocessors. Unfortunately, these two objectives are antagonistic, and an algorithm that is optimal on one machine will often not be optimal on another machine. Even among hypercubes it is apparent that the optimal decomposition, and hence the optimal algorithm, depends on the message latency, with a block decomposition being best for low latency machines, and a row decomposition often being best for machines with high latency. Another factor to be considered is that often a matrix algorithm is only part of a larger application code. Thus, the data decomposition before and after the matrix computation may not be optimal for the matrix algorithm itself. We are faced with the choice of either transforming the decomposition before and after the matrix computation so that the optimal matrix algorithm can be used, or leaving the decomposition as it is and using a suboptimal matrix algorithm. To summarize, the main issues that must be addressed are:

- optimal or general-purpose routines, and

- optimal algorithms with data transformation, or suboptimal algorithms with no data transformation.

Two approaches to designing linear algebra libraries have been followed at Caltech. Fox, Furmanski, and Walker choose optimality as the most important concern in developing a set of linear algebra routines for low latency, homogeneous hypercubes, such as the Caltech/JPL Mark II hypercube. These routines feature the use of the scattered decomposition to ensure load balance, and to minimize communication costs. Transformations between decompositions are performed using the *comutil* library of global communication routines [Angus:90a], [Fox:88h], [Furmanski:88b]. This approach was mainly dictated by historical factors, rather than being a considered design decision—the hypercubes used most at Caltech up to 1987 were homogeneous and had low latency.

A different, and probably more useful approach, has been taken at Caltech by Van de Velde [Velde:89b] who opted for general-purpose library routines. The decomposition currently in use is passed to a routine through its argument list, so in general the decomposition is not changed and a suboptimal algorithm is used. The main advantage of this approach is that it is decomposition-independent and allows portability of code among a wide variety of multiprocessors. Also, the suboptimality of a routine must be weighed against the possibly large cost of transforming the data decomposition, so suboptimality does not necessarily result in a slower algorithm if the time to change the decomposition is taken into account.

Occasionally, it may be advantageous to change the decomposition, and most changes of this type are what Van de Velde calls *orthogonal*. In an orthogonal redistribution of the data, each pair of processors exchanges the same amount of data. Van de Velde has shown [Velde:90c] that any orthogonal redistribution can be performed by the following sequence of operations:

Local permutation – Global transposition – Local permutation

A local permutation merely involves reindexing the local data within individual processors. If we have P processors and P data items in each processor, then the global transposition, τ, takes the item with local index i in processor p and sends it to processor i, where it is stored with local index p. Thus,

$$\tau((p, i)) = (i, p) \tag{8.11}$$

Van de Velde's *transpose* routine is actually a generalization of the hypercube-specific *index* routine in the comutil library.

Van de Velde has implemented his linear algebra library on the Intel iPSC/2 and the Symult 2010, and has used it in investigations of concurrent LU and QR factorization algorithms [Velde:89b], [Velde:90a], and in studies of invariant manifolds of dynamical systems [Lorenz:89a], [Velde:90b].

A group centered at Oak Ridge National Laboratory and the University of Tennessee is leading the development of a major new portable parallel full matrix library called ScaLAPACK [Choi:92a], [Choi:92b]. This is built around an elegant formulation of matrix problems in terms of the so-called level three BLAS, which are a set of submatrix operations introduced to support the basic LAPACK library [Anderson:90c], [Dongarra:90a]. This full matrix system embodies earlier ideas from LINPACK and EISPACK and is designed to ensure data locality and get good performance on shared-memory and vector supercomputers. The multicomputer ScaLAPACK is built around the scattered block decomposition described earlier.

8.1.8 Problem Structure

The basic matrix algorithms appear to fall in the synchronous class in the language of Section 3.4. Correspondingly, one would expect to get good performance on SIMD machines. This is indeed true for matrix multiplication, but it is hard to get good SIMD performance on LU factorization and the more complicated matrix algorithms. Here the algorithm is not fully synchronous. In particular, there are several operations involving row or column operations. These lead to two problems. Firstly, the parallelism is reduced from $O(M^2)$ (for an $M \times M$ matrix) to $O(M)$—this is typically a serious problem on SIMD machines, such as the CM-2 or Maspar MP-1,2 which are fine grain and require "massive parallelism." Secondly, the use of pivoting clearly introduces irregularity into the algorithm, which complicates the SIMD implementation. For these reasons, most research on matrix algorithms has concentrated on MIMD multicomputers, such as the hypercube.

8.1.9 Conclusions

Work on the concurrent Gauss-Jordan algorithm was mostly done by Paul Hipes. Eric Van de Velde developed the linear algebra library discussed in Section 8.1.7, and collaborated with Jens Lorenz in their work on invariant manifolds. Many of the other current algorithms were devised by Geoffrey Fox. Wojtek Furmanski and David Walker worked on routines

for transforming decompositions. The implementation of the banded LU
solver on the Caltech/JPL Mark II hypercube was done by Tom Aldcroft,
Arturo Cisneros, and David Walker.

8.2 Quantum Mechanical Reactive Scattering Using a High-Performance Parallel Computer

8.2.1 Introduction

There is considerable current interest in performing accurate quantum mechanical, three-dimensional, reactive scattering cross section calculations.
Accurate solutions have, until recently, proved to be difficult and computationally expensive to obtain, in large part due to the lack of sufficiently powerful computers. Prior to the advent of supercomputers, one
could only solve the equations of motion for model systems or for sufficiently light atom-diatom systems at low energy [Schatz:75a;76a;76b]. As
a result of the current development of efficient methodologies and increased access to supercomputers, there has been a remarkable surge of
activity in this field. The use of symmetrized hyperspherical coordinates
[Kuppermann:75a] and of the local hyperspherical surface function formalism [Hipes:87a], [Kuppermann:86a], [Ling:75a], has proven to be a successful approach to solving the three-dimensional Schrödinger equation [Cuc-
caro:89a;89b], [Hipes:87a], [Kuppermann:86a]. However, even for modest
reactive scattering calculations, the memory and CPU demands are so great
that even CRAY-type supercomputers will soon be insufficient to sustain
progress.

In this section, we show how quantum mechanical reactive scattering calculations can be structured so as to use MIMD-type parallel computer architectures efficiently. We present a concurrent algorithm for calculating local hyperspherical surface functions (LHSF) and use a parallelized version [Hipes:88b] of Johnson's logarithmic derivative method
[Johnson:73a;77a;79a], modified to include the improvements suggested by
Manolopoulos [Manolopoulos:86a], for integrating the resulting coupled
channel reactive scattering equations. We compare the results of scattering calculations on the Caltech/JPL Mark IIIfp 64-processor hypercube
for the $H + H_2$ system $J = 0, 1, 2$ partial waves on the LSTH [Liu:73a],
[Siegbahn:78a], [Truhlar:78a;79a], potential energy surface, with those of cal-

culations done on a CRAY X-MP/48 and a CRAY-2. Both accuracy and performance are discussed, and speed estimates are made for the Mark IIIfp 128-processor hypercube soon to become available and compared with those of the San Diego Supercomputer Center CRAY Y-MP/864 machine which has recently been put into operation.

8.2.2   Methodology

The detailed formulation of reactive scattering based on hyperspherical coordinates and local variational hyperspherical surface functions (LHSF) is discussed elsewhere [Kuppermann:86a], [Hipes:87a], [Cuccaro:89a]. We present a very brief review to facilitate the explanation of the parallel algorithms.

For a triatomic system, we label the three atoms A_α, A_β and A_γ. Let (λ, ν, κ) be any cyclic permutation of the indices (α, β, γ). We define the λ coordinates, the mass-scaled [Delves:59a;62a] internuclear vector $\mathbf{r}_\lambda$ from A_ν to A_κ, and the mass-scaled position vector $\mathbf{R}_\lambda$ of A_λ with respect to the center of mass of $A_\nu A_\kappa$ diatom. The symmetrized hyperspherical coordinates [Kuppermann:75a] are the hyper-radius $\rho = (R_\lambda^2 + r_\lambda^2)^{1/2}$, and a set of five angles ω_λ, γ_λ, θ_λ, ϕ_λ and ψ_λ, denoted collectively as ζ_λ. The first two of these are in the range 0 to π and are, respectively, $2\arctan\frac{r_\lambda}{R_\lambda}$ and the angle between $\mathbf{R}_\lambda$ and $\mathbf{r}_\lambda$. The angles θ_λ, ϕ_λ are the polar angles of $\mathbf{R}_\lambda$ in a space-fixed frame and ψ_λ is the tumbling angle of the $\mathbf{R}_\lambda$, $\mathbf{r}_\lambda$ half-plane around its edge $\mathbf{R}_\lambda$. The Hamiltonian $\hat{H}_\lambda$ is the sum of a radial kinetic energy operator term in ρ, and the surface Hamiltonian $\hat{h}_\lambda$, which contains all differential operators in ζ_λ and the electronically adiabatic potential $V(\rho, \omega_\lambda, \gamma_\lambda)$. The surface Hamiltonian $\hat{h}_\lambda$ depends on ρ parametrically and is therefore the "frozen" hyperradius part of $\hat{H}_\lambda$.

The scattering wave function $\Psi^{JM\Pi\Gamma}$ is labelled by the total angular momentum J, its projection M on the laboratory-fixed Z axis, the inversion parity Π with respect to the center of mass of the system, and the irreducible representation Γ of the permutation group of the system (P_3 for $H + H_2$) to which the electronuclear wave function, excluding the nuclear spin part, belongs [Lepetit:90a;90b]. It can be expanded in terms of the LHSF $\Phi^{JM\Pi\Gamma}$, defined below, and calculated at the values $\bar{\rho}_q$ of ρ:

$$\Psi_i^{JM\Pi\Gamma}(\rho, \zeta_\lambda) = \sum_n b_{ni}^{J\Pi\Gamma}(\rho; \bar{\rho}_q) \, \Phi_n^{JM\Pi\Gamma}(\zeta_\lambda; \bar{\rho}_q) \qquad (8.12)$$

The index i is introduced to permit consideration of a set of many linearly independent solutions of the Schrödinger equation corresponding to distinct initial conditions which are needed to obtain the appropriate scattering matrices.

The LHSF $\Phi_n^{JM\,\Pi\Gamma}(\zeta_\lambda; \bar{\rho}_q)$ and associated energies $\epsilon_n^{J\,\Pi\Gamma}(\bar{\rho}_q)$ are, respectively, the eigenfunctions and eigenvalues of the surface Hamiltonian $\hat{h}_\lambda$. They are obtained using a variational approach [Cuccaro:89a]. The variational basis set consists of products of Wigner rotation matrices $D_{M\Omega}^J(\phi_\lambda, \theta_\lambda, \psi_\lambda)$, associated Legendre functions of γ_λ and functions of ω_λ which depend parametically on $\bar{\rho}_q$ and are obtained from the numerical solution of one-dimensional eigenvalue-eigenfunction differential equations in ω_λ, involving a potential related to $V(\bar{\rho}, \omega_\lambda, \gamma_\lambda)$.

The variational method leads to an eigenvalue problem with coefficient and overlap matrices $h^{J\,\Pi\Gamma}(\bar{\rho}_q)$ and $s^{J\,\Pi\Gamma}(\bar{\rho}_q)$ and whose elements are five-dimensional integrals involving the variational basis functions.

The coefficients $b_{ni}^{J\,\Pi\Gamma}(\rho; \bar{\rho}_q)$ defined by Equation 8.12 satisfy a coupled set of second-order differential equations involving an interaction matrix $\mathcal{I}^{J\,\Pi\Gamma}(\rho; \bar{\rho}_q)$ whose elements are defined by

$$[\mathcal{I}^{J\,\Pi\Gamma}(\rho; \bar{\rho}_q)]_n^{n'} = \left\langle \Phi_n^{JM\,\Pi\Gamma}(\zeta_\lambda; \bar{\rho}_q) \middle| V(\rho, \omega_\lambda, \gamma_\lambda) \right.$$
$$\left. - (\bar{\rho}_q/\rho)^2 V(\bar{\rho}_q, \omega_\lambda, \gamma_\lambda) \middle| \Phi_{n'}^{JM\,\Pi\Gamma}(\zeta_\lambda; \bar{\rho}_q) \right\rangle \quad (8.13)$$

The configuration space ρ, ζ_λ is divided into a set of Q hyperspherical shells $\rho_q \leq \rho \leq \rho_{q+1}\,(q = 1, 2, \ldots, Q)$ within each of which we choose a value $\bar{\rho}_q$ used in expansion 8.12.

When changing from the LHSF set at $\bar{\rho}_q$ to the one at $\bar{\rho}_{q+1}$, neither $\Psi_i^{JM\,\Pi\Gamma}$ nor its derivative with respect to ρ should change. This imposes continuity conditions on the $b_{ni}^{J\,\Pi\Gamma}$ and their ρ-derivatives at $\rho = \rho_{q+1}$, involving the overlap matrix $\mathcal{O}^{J\,\Pi\Gamma}(\bar{\rho}_{q+1}, \bar{\rho}_q)$ between the LHSF evaluated at $\bar{\rho}_q$ and $\bar{\rho}_{q+1}$

$$[\mathcal{O}^{J\,\Pi\Gamma}(\bar{\rho}_{q+1}, \bar{\rho}_q)]_n^{n'} = \left\langle \Phi_n^{JM\,\Pi\Gamma}(\zeta_\lambda; \bar{\rho}_{q+1}) \middle| \Phi_{n'}^{JM\,\Pi\Gamma}(\zeta_\lambda; \bar{\rho}_q) \right\rangle \quad (8.14)$$

The five-dimensional integrals required to evaluate the elements of $h^{J\,\Pi\Gamma}$, $s^{J\,\Pi\Gamma}$, $\mathcal{I}^{J\,\Pi\Gamma}$, and $\mathcal{O}^{J\,\Pi\Gamma}$ are performed analytically over ϕ_λ, θ_λ, and ψ_λ and by two-dimensional numerical quadratures over γ_λ and ω_λ. These quadratures account for 90% of the total time needed to calculate the LHSF $\Phi_n^{JM\,\Pi\Gamma}$ and the matrices $\mathcal{I}^{J\,\Pi\Gamma}$ and $\mathcal{O}^{J\,\Pi\Gamma}$.

The system of second-order ordinary differential equations in the $b_{ni}^{J\,\Pi\Gamma}$ is integrated as an initial value problem from small values of ρ to large values using Manolopoulos' logarithmic derivative propagator [Manolopoulos:86a]. Matrix inversions account for more than 90% of the time used by this propagator. All aspects of the physics can be extracted from the solutions at large ρ by a constant ρ projection [Hipes:87a], [Hood:86a], [Kuppermann:86a].

8.2.3   Parallel Algorithm

The computer used for this work is a 64-processor Mark IIIfp hypercube. The Crystalline Operating System (CrOS)-channel-addressed synchronous communication provides the library routines to handle communications between nodes [Fox:85d;85h;88a]. The programs are written in C programming language except for the time-consuming two-dimensional quadratures and matrix inversions, which are optimized in assembly language.

The hypercube was configured as a two-dimensional array of processors. The mapping is done using binary Gray codes [Gilbert:58a], [Fox:88a], [Salmon:84b], which gives the Cartesian coordinates in processor space and communication channel tags for a processor's nearest neighbors.

We mapped the matrices into processor space by local decomposition. Let N_r and N_c be the number of processors in the rows and columns of the hypercube configuration, respectively. Element $A(i,j)$ of an $M \times M$ matrix is placed in processor row $P_r = int \left(\frac{i \times N_r}{M} \right)$ and column $P_c = int \left(\frac{j \times N_c}{M} \right)$, where $int\ x$ means the integer part of x.

The parallel code implemented on the hypercube consists of five major steps. Step one constructs, for each value of $\bar{\rho}_q$, a primitive basis set composed of the product of Wigner rotation matrices, associated Legendre functions, and the numerical one-dimensional functions in ω_λ mentioned in Section 8.2.2 and obtained by solving the corresponding one-dimensional eigenvalue-eigenvector differential equation using a finite difference method. This requires that a subset of the eigenvalues and eigenvectors of a tridiagonal matrix be found.

A bisection method [Fox:84g], [Ipsen:87a;87c], which accomplishes the eigenvalue computation using the TRIDIB routine from EISPACK [Smith:76a], was ported to the Mark IIIfp. This implementation of the bisection method allows computation of any number of consecutive eigenvalues specified by their indices. Eigenvectors are obtained using the EISPACK inverse iteration routine TINVIT with modified Gram-Schmidt orthogonalization. Each processor solves independent tridiagonal eigenproblems since the number of eigenvalues desired from each tridiagonal system is small, but there are a large number of distinct tridiagonal systems. To achieve load balancing, we distributed subsets of the primitive functions among the processors in such a way that no processor computes greater than one eigenvalue and eigenvector more than any other. These large grain tasks are most easily implemented on MIMD machines; SIMD (Single Instruction Multiple Data) machines would require more extensive modifications and would be less efficient because of the sequential nature of effective eigenvalue iteration procedures. The one-dimensional bases obtained are then broadcast to all the other nodes.

In step two, a large number of two-dimensional quadratures involving the primitive basis functions which are needed for the variational procedure are evaluated. These quadratures are highly parallel procedures requiring no communication overhead once each processor has the necessary subset of functions. Each processor calculates a subset of integrals independently.

Step three assembles these integrals into the real symmetric dense matrices $s^{J\,\Pi\,\Gamma}(\bar{\rho}_q)$ and $h^{J\,\Pi\,\Gamma}(\bar{\rho}_q)$ which are distributed over processor space. The entire spectrum of eigenvalues and eigenvectors for the associated variational problem is sought. With the parallel implementation of the Householder method [Fox:84h], [Patterson:86a], this generalized eigensystem is tridiagonalized and the resulting single tridiagonal matrix is solved completely in each processor with the QR algorithm [Wilkinson:71a]. The QR implementation is purely sequential since each processor obtains the entire solution to the eigensystem. However, only different subsets of the solution are kept in different processors for the evaluation of the interaction and overlap matrices in step four. This part of the algorithm is not time consuming and the straightforward sequential approach was chosen. It has the further effect that the resulting solutions are fully distributed, so no communication is required.

Step four evaluates the two-dimensional quadratures needed for the interaction $\mathcal{I}^{J\,\Pi\,\Gamma}(\rho;\bar{\rho}_q)$ and overlap $\mathcal{O}^{J\,\Pi\,\Gamma}(\bar{\rho}_{q+1};\bar{\rho}_q)$ matrices. The same type of algorithms are used as in step two. By far, the most expensive part of the sequential version of the surface function calculation is the calculation of the large number of two-dimensional numerical integrals required by steps two and four. These steps are, however, highly parallel and well suited for the hypercube.

Step five uses Manolopoulos' [Manolopoulos:86a] algorithm to integrate the coupled linear ordinary differential equations. The parallel implementation of this algorithm is discussed elsewhere [Hipes:88b]. The algorithm is dominated by parallel Gauss-Jordan matrix inversion and is I/O intensive, requiring the input of one interaction matrix per integration step. To reduce the I/O overhead, a second source of parallelism is exploited. The entire interaction matrix (at all ρ) and overlap matrix (at all $\bar{\rho}_q$) data sets are loaded across the processors, and many collision energies are calculated simultaneously. This strategy works because the same set of data is used for each collision energy, and because enough main memory is available. Calculation of scattering matrices from the final logarithmic derivative matrices is not computationally intensive, and is done sequentially.

The program steps were all run on the Weitek coprocessor, which only supports 32-bit arithmetic. Experimentation has shown that this precision is sufficient for the work reported below. The 64-bit arithmetic hardware needed for larger calculations was installed after the present calculations were completed.

8.2.4 Results and Discussion

Accuracy

Calculations were performed for the $H + H_2$ system on the LSTH surface [Liu:73a], [Siegbahn:78a], [Truhlar:78a;79a] for partial waves with total angular momentum $J = 0, 1, 2$ and energies up to 1.6 eV. Flux is conserved to better than 1% for $J = 0$, 2.3% for $J = 1$, and 3.6% for $J = 2$ for all open channels over the entire energy range considered.

To illustrate the accuracy of the 32-bit arithmetic calculations, the scattering results from the Mark IIIfp with 64 processors are shown in Figure 8.7 for $J = 0$, in which some transition probabilities as a function of the total collision energy, E, are plotted. The differences between these results, and those obtained using a CRAY X-MP/48 and a CRAY-2, do not exceed 0.004 in absolute value over the energy range investigated.

Timing and Parallel Efficiency

In Tables 8.3 and 8.4, we present the timing data on the 64-processor Mark IIIfp, a CRAY X-MP/48 and a CRAY 2, for both the surface function code (including calculation of the overlap $\mathcal{O}^{J\,\Pi\,\Gamma}$ and interaction $\mathcal{I}^{J\,\Pi\,\Gamma}$ matrices) and the logarithmic derivative propagation code. For the surface function code, the speeds on the first two machines are about the same. The CRAY 2 is 1.43 times faster than the Mark IIIfp and 1.51 times faster than the CRAY X-MP/48 for this code. The reason is that this program is dominated by matrix-vector multiplications which are done in optimized assembly code in all three machines. For this particular operation, the CRAY 2 is 2.03

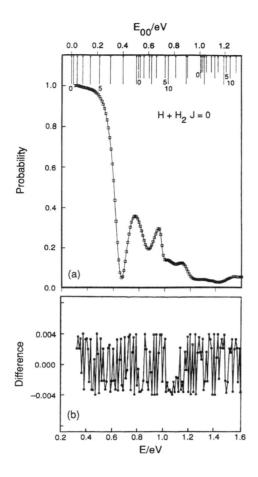

Figure 8.7: Probabilities as a Function of Total Energy E (Lower Abscissa) and Initial Relative Translational Energy E_{00} (Upper Abscissa) for the $J = 0(0,0,0) \rightarrow (0,0,0)$ A_1 Symmetry Transition in $H + H_2$ Collisions on the LSTH Potential Energy Surface. The symbol (v, j, Ω) labels an asymptotic state of the $H + H_2$ system in which v, j, and Ω are the quantum numbers of the initial or final H_2 states. The vertical arrows on the upper abscissa denote the energies at which the corresponding $H_2(v, j)$ states open up. The length of those arrows decreases as v spans the values 0, 1, and 2, and the numbers 0, 5, and 10 associated with the arrows define a labelling for the value of j. The number of LHSF used was 36 and the number of primitives used to calculate these surface functions was 80.

Table 8.3: Performance of the surface function code.*

J	Mark IIIfp 64 processors		CRAY X-MP/48		CRAY 2	
	Time (hr)	Speed (MFLOPS)	Time (hr)	Speed (MFLOPS)	Time (hr)	Speed (MFLOPS)
0	0.71	100	0.74	96	0.49	145
1	2.88	112	3.04	106	2.01	160
2	5.60	124	5.94	117	3.96	176

*Note: This code calculates the surface functions at the 51 values of $\bar{\rho}$ from 2.0 bohr to 12.0 bohr in steps of 0.2 bohr, the corresponding overlap matrices between consecutive values of $\bar{\rho}$ and the propagation matrices in ρ steps of 0.1 bohr. The number of primitives used for each J and described in the remaining figure captions, permits us to generate enough LHSF to achieve the accuracy described in the text.

times faster than the CRAY X-MP/48 whereas, for more memory-intensive operations, the CRAY 2 is slower than the CRAY X-MP/48 [Pfeiffer:90a]. A slightly larger primitive basis set is required on the Mark IIIfp in order to obtain surface function energies of an accuracy equivalent to that obtained with the CRAY machines. This is due to the lower accuracy of the 32-bit arithmetic of the former with respect to the 64-bit arithmetic of the latter.

The efficiency (ε) of the parallel LHSF code was determined using the definition $\varepsilon = \frac{T_1}{(N \times T_N)}$, where T_1 and T_N are, respectively, the implementation times using a single-processor and N processors. The single processor times are obtained from runs performed after removing the overhead of the parallel code, that is, after removing the communication calls and some logical statements. Perfect efficiency ($\varepsilon = 1.0$) implies that the N-processor hypercube is N times faster than a single processor. In Figure 8.8, efficiencies for the surface function code (including the calculation of the overlap and interaction matrices) as a function of the size of the primitive basis set are plotted for 2, 4, 8, 16, 32 and 64 processor configurations of the hypercube. The global dimensions of the matrices used are chosen to be integer multiples of the number of processor rows and columns in order to insure load balancing among the processors. Because of the limited size of a single-processor memory, the efficiency determination is limited to 32 primitives. As shown in Figure 8.8, the efficiencies increase monotonically and approach

Table 8.4: Performance of the logarithmic derivative code. Based on a calculation using 245 surface functions and 131 energies, and a logarithmic derivative integration step of 0.01 bohr.

	Mark IIIfp		CRAY X-MP/48	CRAY 2
	64-Processor Global Configuration	8 Clusters of 8 Processors		
Total time (hrs)	4.8	3.4	1.5	2.9
Total for 1 energy (min)	2.2	1.6	0.7	1.3
Efficiency	0.52	0.81	. . .	. . .
Speed (MFLOPS)	34.4	48.5	110	55.4

unity asymptotically as the size of the calculation increases. Converged results require large enough primitive basis sets so that the efficiency of the surface function code is estimated to be about 0.95 or greater.

The data for the logarithmic derivative code given in Table 8.4 for a 245-channel (i.e., LHSF) example show that the Mark IIIfp has a speed about 62% of that of the CRAY 2, but only about 31% of that of the CRAY X-MP/48. This code is dominated by matrix inversions, which are done in optimized assembly code in all three machines. The reason for the slowness of the hypercube with respect to the CRAYs is that the efficiency of the parallel logarithmic derivative code is 0.52. This relatively low value is due to the fact that matrix inversions require a significant amount of interprocessor communication. Figure 8.9 displays efficiencies of the logarithmic derivative code as a function of the number of channels propagated for different processor configurations, as done previously for the Mark III [Hipes:88b], [Messina:90a] hypercubes. The data can be described well by an operations count formula developed previously for the matrix inversion part of the code [Hipes:88a]; this formula can be used to extrapolate the data to larger numbers of processors or channels. It can be seen that for an 8-processor configuration, the code runs with an efficiency of 0.81. This observation suggested that we divide the Mark IIIfp into eight clusters of eight processors each, and perform calculations for different energies in different clusters. The corresponding timing information is also given in Table 8.4. As can be seen from the last row of this table, the speed of the logarithmic

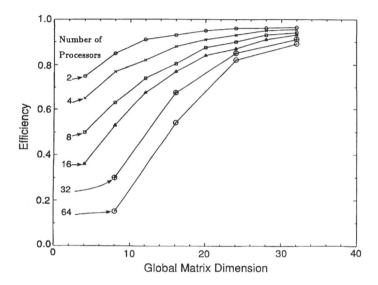

Figure 8.8: Efficiency of the Surface Function Code (Including the Calculation of the Overlap and Interaction Matrices) as a Function of the Global Matrix Dimension (i.e., the Size of the Primitive Basis Set) for 2, 4, 8, 16, 32, and 64 Processors. The solid curves are straight line segments connecting the data points for a fixed number of processors and are provided as an aid to examine the trends.

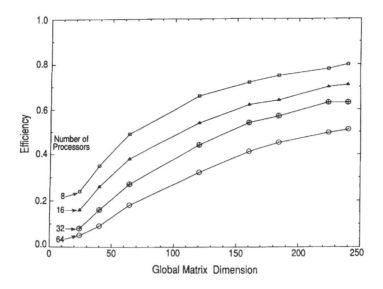

Figure 8.9: Efficiency of Logarithmic Derivative Code as a Function of the Global Matrix Dimension (i.e., the Number of Channels or LHSF) for 8, 16, 32, and 64 Processors. The solid curves are straight-line segments connecting the data points for a fixed number of processors, and are provided as an aid to examine the trends.

derivative code using this configuration of the 64-processor Mark IIIfp is 48.5 MFLOPS, which is about 44% of that of the CRAY X-MP/48 and 88% of that of the CRAY 2. As the number of channels increases, the number of processors per cluster may be made larger in order to increase the amount of memory available in each cluster. The corresponding efficiency should continue to be adequate due to the larger matrix dimensions involved.

Planned upgrades of the Mark IIIfp include increasing the number of processors to 128, and replacement of the I/O system will be high-performance CIO (concurrent I/O) hardware. Further new Weitek co-processors, installed since the present calculations were done, perform 64-bit floating-point arithmetic at about the same nominal peak speed as the 32-bit boards. From the data in the present paper, it is possible to predict with good reliability the performance of this upgraded version of the Mark IIIfp

Table 8.5: Overall speed of reactive scattering codes on several machines.

	Mark IIIfp		CRAY X-MP/48	CRAY 2	CRAY Y-MP/864
	64 Proc.	128 Proc.			
Surface function code for $J = 2$ (MFLOPS)	124	240	117	176	232
Logarithmic derivative code (MFLOPS)	48.5	127	110	55.4	187
Total main memory of computer (64 bit Mwords)	32	64	8	256	64

(the CIO upgrade was never performed). A CRAY Y-MP/864 was installed at the San Diego Supercomputer Center and measurements show that it is about two times faster than the CRAY X-MP/48 for the surface function code and 1.7 times faster for the logarithmic derivative code. In Table 8.5, we summarize the available or predicted speed information for the present codes for the current 64-processor and the planned 128-processor Mark IIIfp, as well as the CRAY X-MP/48, CRAY 2, and CRAY Y-MP/864 supercomputers. It can be seen that Mark IIIfp machines are competitive with all of the currently available CRAYs (operating as single-processor machines). The results described in this paper demonstrate the feasibility of performing reactive scattering calculations with high efficiency in parallel fashion. As the number of processors continues to increase, such parallel calculations in systems of greater complexity will become practical in the not-too-distant future.

8.3   Studies of Electron-Molecule Collisions on Distributed-Memory Parallel Computers

8.3.1   Introduction

Collisions of low-energy electrons with atoms and molecules have been of both fundamental and practical interest since the early days of the quantum theory. Indeed, one of the first successes of quantum mechanics was an explanation of the curious transparency of certain gases to very slow electrons [Mott:87a]. Today, we have an excellent understanding of the physical principles involved in low-energy electron collisions in gases, and with it an ability to calculate the cross section, or probability, for various electron-*atom* collision processes to high accuracy [Bartschat:89a]. The case of electron collisions in *molecular* gases is, however, quite different. Although the same principles are involved, complications arising from the nonspherical shapes of molecules and their numerous internal degrees of freedom (vibrations and rotations) make calculating reliable cross sections for low-energy electron-molecule collisions a significant computational challenge.

At the same time, electron-molecule collision data is of growing practical importance. Plasma-based processing of materials [Manos:89a], [JTIS:88a] relies on collisions between "hot" electrons, with kinetic energies on the order of tens of electron-volts ($1\,\text{eV} = 12,000°\,\text{K}$), and gas molecules at temperatures of hundreds of $°\,\text{K}$ to generate reactive fragments—atoms, radicals, and ions—that could otherwise be obtained only at temperatures high enough to damage or destroy the surface being treated. Such low-temperature plasma processing is a key technology in the manufacture of semiconductors [Manos:89a], and has applications in many other areas as well [JTIS:88a], ranging from the hardening of metals to the deposition of polymer coatings.

The properties of materials-processing plasmas are sensitive to operating conditions, which are generally optimized by trial and error. However, efforts at direct numerical modelling of plasmas are being made [Kushner:91a], which hold the potential to greatly increase the efficiency of plasma-based processing. Since electron-molecule collisions are responsible for the generation of reactive species, clearly, an essential ingredient in plasma modelling is knowledge of the electron-molecule collision cross sections.

We have been engaged in studies of electron-molecule collisions for a number of years, using a theoretical approach, the Schwinger Multichannel (SMC) method, specifically formulated to handle the complexities of electron-molecule interactions [Lima:90a], [Takatsuka:81a;84a]. Implementations of the SMC method run in production mode both on small platforms (e.g., Sun SPARCstations) and on CRAY machines, and cross sections for several diatomic and small polyatomic molecules have been reported [Brescansin:89a], [Huo:87a;87b], [Lima:89a], [Pritchard:89a], [Winstead:90a]. Recently, however, the computational demands of detailed studies, combined with the high cost of cycles on CRAY-type machines, have led us to implement the SMC method on distributed-memory parallel computers, beginning with the JPL/Caltech Mark IIIfp and currently including Intel's iPSC/860 and Touchstone Delta machines. In the following, we will describe the SMC method, our strategy and experiences in porting it to parallel architectures, and its performance on different machines. We conclude with selected results produced by the parallel SMC code and some speculation on future prospects.

8.3.2 The SMC Method and Its Implementation

The collision of an electron with a molecule A may be illustrated schematically as

$$e^-(E_i, \vec{k}_i) + A \rightarrow e^-(E_f, \vec{k}_f) + A^*,$$

where E_i is the electron's initial kinetic energy and the momentum vector $\vec{k}_i$ points in its initial direction of travel; after the collision, the electron travels along $\vec{k}_f$ with kinetic energy E_f. If E_f differs from E_i, the collision is said to be inelastic, and energy is transferred to the target, leaving it in an excited state, denoted A^*. The quantity we seek is the probability of occurrence or cross section for this process, as a function of the energies E_i and E_f and of the angle between the directions $\hat{k}_i$ and $\hat{k}_f$. (Since a gas is a very large ensemble of randomly oriented molecules, orientational dependence of these quantities for an asymmetric target A is averaged over in calculations.)

The SMC procedure [Lima:90a], [Takatsuka:81a;84a], a multichannel extension of Schwinger's variational principle [Schwinger:47a], is a method for obtaining cross sections for low-energy electron-molecule collision processes, including elastic scattering and vibrational or electronic excitation. As such, it is capable of accurately treating effects arising from electron indistinguishability and from polarization of the target by the charge of the incident electron, both of which can be important at low collision velocities. Moreover, it is formulated to be applicable to and efficient for molecules of arbitrary geometry.

The scattering amplitude $f(\vec{k}_i, \vec{k}_f)$, a complex quantity whose square modulus is proportional to the cross section, is approximated in the SMC method as

$$f(\vec{k}_i, \vec{k}_f) = -\frac{1}{2\pi} \sum_{j,k} \langle S_i(\vec{k}_i)|V|\chi_j \rangle (\mathbf{A^{-1}})_{jk} \langle \chi_k|V|S_f(\vec{k}_f) \rangle,$$

where $S_i(\vec{k}_i)$ is an $(N+1)$-electron interaction-free wave function of the form

$$S_i(\vec{k}_i) = \Phi_{\text{target}}^{(i)}(1, 2, \ldots, N) e^{i\vec{k}_i \cdot \vec{r}_{N+1}},$$

V is the interaction potential between the scattering electron and the target, and the $(N+1)$-electron functions χ_j are spin-adapted Slater determinants which form a linear variational basis set for approximating the exact scattering wave functions $\Psi_f^{(+)}(\vec{k}_f)$ and $\Psi_i^{(-)}(\vec{k}_i)$. The $(\mathbf{A^{-1}})_{jk}$ are elements of the inverse of the matrix representation in the basis χ_j of the operator

$$A^{(+)} = \frac{1}{2}(PV + VP) - VG_P^{(+)}V - \frac{1}{N+1}\left\{\hat{H} - \frac{N+1}{2}(\hat{H}P + P\hat{H})\right\}.$$

Here P is the projector onto open (energetically accessible) electronic states,

$$P = \sum_{\ell \in open} |\Phi_\ell(1, 2, \ldots, N)\rangle \langle \Phi_\ell(1, 2, \ldots, N)|,$$

$G_P^{(+)}$ is the $(N+1)$-electron Green's function projected onto open channels, and $\hat{H} = (E - H)$, where E is the total energy of the system and H is the full Hamiltonian.

In our implementation, the $(N + 1)$-electron functions χ_j are formed from antisymmetrized products of one-electron molecular orbitals which are themselves combinations of Cartesian Gaussian orbitals

$$N_{\ell mn}(x - A_x)^\ell (y - A_y)^m (z - A_z)^n \exp(-\alpha|\vec{r} - \vec{A}|^2),$$

commonly used in molecular electronic-structure studies. Expansion of the trial scattering wave function in such a basis of exponentially decaying functions is possible since the trial function of the SMC method need not satisfy scattering boundary conditions asymptotically [Lima:90a], [Takatsuka:81a;84a]. All matrix elements needed in the evaluation of $f(\vec{k}_i, \vec{k}_f)$ can then be obtained analytically, except those of $VG_P^{(+)}V$. These terms are evaluated numerically via a momentum-space quadrature procedure [Lima:90a],

[Takatsuka:81a,84a]. Once all matrix elements are calculated, the final step in the calculation is solution of a system of linear equations to obtain the scattering amplitude $f(\vec{k}_i, \vec{k}_f)$ in the form given above.

The computationally intensive step in the above formulation is the evaluation of large numbers of so-called "primitive" two-electron integrals

$$\langle \alpha\,\beta\,|V|\,\gamma\,\vec{k}\rangle = \int\!\!\int d^3\vec{r}_1\,d^3\vec{r}_2\,\alpha(\vec{r}_1)\,\beta(\vec{r}_1)\,\frac{1}{r_{12}}\,\gamma(\vec{r}_2)e^{i\vec{k}\cdot\vec{r}_2}$$

for all unique combinations of Cartesian Gaussians α, β, and γ, and for a wide range of $\vec{k}$ in both magnitude and direction. These integrals are evaluated analytically by a set of subroutines comprising approximately two thousand lines of FORTRAN. Typical calculations might require 10^9 to 10^{10} calls to this integral-evaluation suite, consuming roughly 80% of the total computation time. Once calculated, the primitive integrals are assembled in appropriate combinations to yield the matrix elements appearing in the variational expression for $f(\vec{k}_i, \vec{k}_f)$. The original CRAY code performs this procedure in two steps: first, a repeated linear transformation to integrals involving molecular orbitals, then a transformation from the molecular-orbital integrals to physical matrix elements. The latter step is equivalent to an extremely sparse linear transformation, whose coefficients are determined in an elaborate subroutine with a complicated logical flow.

8.3.3   Parallel Implementation

The necessity of evaluating large numbers of primitive two-electron integrals makes the SMC procedure a natural candidate for parallelization on a coarse-grain MIMD machine. With a large memory per processor, it is feasible to load the integral evaluator on each node and to distribute the evaluation of the primitive integrals among all the processors. Provided issues of load balance and subsequent data reduction can be addressed successfully, high parallel efficiency may be anticipated, since the stage of the calculation which typically consumes the bulk of the computation time is thereby made perfectly parallel.

In planning the decomposition of the set of integrals onto the nodes, two principal issues must be considered. First, there are too many integrals to store in memory simultaneously, and certain indices must therefore be processed sequentially. Second, the transformation from primitive integrals to physical matrix elements, which necessarily involves interprocessor communication, should be as efficient and transparent as possible. With these considerations in mind, the approach chosen was to configure the nodes logically as a two-torus, on which is mapped an array of integrals whose columns are labeled by Gaussian pairs (α, β), and whose rows are labeled by directions $\hat{k}$; the indices $|\vec{k}|$ and γ are processed sequentially. With this decomposition, the transformation steps and associated interprocessor communication can be localized and "hidden" in parallel matrix multiplications. This approach is both simple and efficient, and results in a program that is easily ported to new machines.

Care was needed in designing the parallel transformation procedure. Direct emulation of the sequential code—that is, transformation first to molecular-orbital integrals and then to physical matrix elements—is undesirable, because the latter step would entail a parallel routine of great complexity governing the flow of a relatively limited amount of data between processors. Instead, the two transformations are combined into a single step by using the logical outline of the original molecular-orbital–to–physical–matrix-element routine in a perfectly parallel routine which builds a distributed transformation matrix. The combined transformations are then accomplished by a single series of large, almost-full complex–arithmetic-matrix multiplications on the primitive-integral data set.

The remainder of the parallel implementation involves relatively straightforward modifications of the sequential CRAY code, with the exception of a series of integrations over angles $\hat{k}$ arising in the evaluation of the $VG_P^{(+)}V$ matrix elements, and of the solution of a system of linear equations in the final phase of the calculation. The angular integration, done by Gauss-Legendre quadrature, is compactly and efficiently coded as a distributed matrix multiplication of the form $\mathbf{A}\mathrm{diag}(\omega_i)\mathbf{A}^\dagger$. The solution of the linear system is performed by a distributed LU solver [Hipes:89b] modified for complex arithmetic.

The implementation described above has proven quite successful [Hipes:90a], [Winstead:91d] on the Mark IIIfp architecture for which it was originally designed, and has since been ported with modest effort to the Intel iPSC/860 and subsequently to the 528-processor Intel Touchstone Delta. No algorithmic modifications were necessary in porting to the Intel machines; modifications to improve efficiency will be described below. Complications did arise from the somewhat different communication model embodied in Intel's NX system, as compared to the more rigidly structured, loosely synchronous CrOS III operating system of the Mark IIIfp described in Chapter 5. These problems were overcome by careful typing of all interprocessor messages—essentially, assigning of sequence numbers and source labels. In porting to the Delta, the major difficulty was the absence of a host processor. Our original parallel version of the SMC code left certain initialization and end-stage routines, which were computationally trivial but logically complicated, as sequential routines to be executed on the host. In porting to the Delta, we chose to parallelize these routines as well rather than allocate an extra node to serve as host. There is thus only one program to maintain and to port to subsequent machines, and a rectangular array of nodes, suitable for a matrix-oriented computation, is preserved.

8.3.4 Performance

Mark IIIfp

Performance assessment on the Mark IIIfp has been published in [Hipes:90a]. In brief, a small but otherwise typical case was run both on the Mark IIIfp and on one processor of a CRAY Y-MP. Performance on 32 nodes of the Mark IIIfp surpassed that of the sequential code on the Y-MP; on 64 nodes, the performance was approximately three times higher than on the CRAY. Considering the small size of the test case, a reasonable parallel efficiency (60% on 64 nodes) was observed.

Intel Machines

Performance of the original port of the parallel code from the Mark IIIfp to a 64-processor iPSC/860 hypercube, while adequate, was below expectations based on the 4:1 ratio of 64-bit floating-point peak speeds. Moreover, initial runs on up to 512 nodes of the Delta indicated very poor speedups. Timings at the subroutine level revealed that an excessive amount of time was being spent both in matrix multiplication and in construction of the distributed transformation matrix. Optimization is still in progress, and performance is still a small fraction of the machine's peak speed, but some improvements have been made.

Several steps were taken to improve the matrix multiplication. Blocking sends and receives were replaced with asynchronous NX routines, overlapping communication with computation; the absolute number of communications was reduced by grouping together small data blocks and by computing rather than communicating block sizes; one of the matrices was transposed in order to maximize the length of the innermost loop; and finally, the inner loop was replaced with a level-one BLAS call. Presently the floating-point

Table 8.6: SMC Performance on the Delta (MFLOPS)

Nodes	Small Gaussian Basis				Large Basis
	64	128	256	512	512
Integrals	158	304	580	1059	1070*
Transformation Matrix	253	445	784	1146	1040
Multiply	251	410	632	617	1012
Overall	176	319	530	611	1000*

*Estimated

work proceeds at 7 to 8.5 MFLOPS/node, including loop overhead, depending on problem size. On the iPSC/860, throughput for the subroutine as a whole is generally limited by communication bandwidth to approximately 2 MFLOPS/node. We expect to increase this by better matching the sizes of the two matrices being multiplied, which will require minor modifications in the top-level routine. Higher throughput, approximately 4 MFLOPS/node, is obtained on the Delta. Further improvement is certainly possible, but communication overhead on the Delta is already below 10% for the application as a whole, and matrix multiplication time is no longer a major limitation.

Reducing the time spent in constructing the transformation matrix proved to be a matter of removing index computations in the innermost loops. In the original implementation, integer modulo arithmetic was used on each call to determine the local components of the transformation matrix. This form of parallel overhead proved surprisingly costly. It was essentially eliminated by precomputing and storing three lists of pointers to the data elements needed locally. These pointers are used for indirect indexing of elements needed in a vector-vector outer product, which now runs at approximately 3.5 MFLOPS/node. (Preceding the outer product with an explicit gather using the same pointers was tested, but proved counterproductive.) A BLAS call (daxpy), timed at 13.1 to 16.6 MFLOPS/node for typical cases, was inserted elsewhere. Construction of the transformation matrices is now typically 1% of the total time, with throughput, including all logic and integer arithmetic as overhead, around 4 MFLOPS/node.

In the present state of the program, the perfectly parallel integral-calculation step is the dominant element in most of our calculations, as

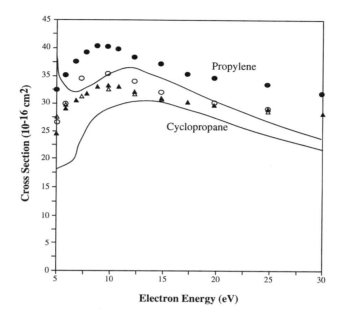

Figure 8.10: Calculated Integral Elastic Cross Sections for Electron Scattering by the C_3H_6 Isomers Cyclopropane and Propylene. For comparison, experimental total cross sections of Refs. [Floeder:85a] (open symbols) and [Nishimura:91a] (filled symbols) are shown; triangles are cyclopropane and circles propylene data.

desired and expected based on the amount of floating-point work. It is also the most complex step, however, with little linear algebra but with many math library calls (sin, cos, exp, sqrt), floating-point divides, and branches. Not surprisingly, therefore, it is comparatively slow. We have timed the CRAY version at 13.3 MFLOPS on a single-processor Y-MP, reflecting the routine's intrinsically scalar character. Present performance on the i860 is about 2.3 MFLOPS/node. Some additional optimization is planned, but substantial improvement may have to await more mature versions of the compiler and libraries.

With the program components as described above, the present code should run on 512 nodes of the Delta at a sustained rate of approximately 1.4 GFLOPS. In practice, lower performance is obtained, due to synchronization delays, load imbalance, file I/O, etc. Actual timings taken from 64- to 512-node production runs are given in Table 8.6. The limited data available for the integral-evaluation package reflects the difficulty of obtaining an accurate operation count; for the case shown, a count was obtained using flow-tracing utilities on a CRAY. For the "large" case shown in the table, we estimate overall performance at 1.0 GFLOPS, inclusive of all I/O and overhead, on 512 nodes of the Delta; this estimate is based on an approximate operation count for the integral package and actual counts for the remaining routines.

8.3.5 Selected Results

The distributed-memory SMC program has been applied to a number of elastic and inelastic electron-molecule scattering problems, emphasizing polyatomic gases of interest in low-temperature plasma applications [JTIS:88a], [Manos:89a]. Initial applications [Hipes:90a], [Winstead:91d] on the Mark II-Ifp were to elastic scattering by ethylene (C_2H_4), ethane (C_2H_6), propane (C_3H_8), disilane (Si_2H_6), germane (GeH_4), and tetrafluorosilane (SiF_4). We have since studied elastic scattering by other systems, including phosphine (PH_3), propylene (C_3H_6) and its isomer cyclopropane, n-butane (C_4H_{10}), and 1,2-*trans*-difluoroethylene, both on the Mark IIIfp and on the Intel machines. We have also examined inelastic collisions with ethylene [Sun:92a], formaldehyde (CH_2O), methane (CH_4), and silane (SiH_4). Below we present selected results of these calculations, where possible comparing to experimental data.

Figure 8.10 shows integral elastic cross sections—that is, cross sections summed over all angles of scattering, plotted as a function of the electron's kinetic energy—for the two C_3H_6 isomers, cyclopropane and propylene. Scattering from propylene requires some special consideration, because of its small dipole moment [Winstead:92a]. These calculations were performed in the static-exchange approximation, neglecting polarization and excitation effects, on 256-node partitions of the Delta. The results in Figure 8.10 should be considered preliminary, since studies to test convergence of the cross section with respect to basis set are in progress, but we do not expect major changes at the energies shown. Corresponding experimental values have not been reported, but the total scattering cross section, of which elastic scattering is the dominant component, has been measured [Floeder:85a], [Nishimura:91a], and these data are included in Figure 8.10. Both the calculation and the measurements show a clear isomer effect in the vicinity of the broad maximum, which gradually lessens at higher energies. At the level of approximation (static-exchange) used in these calculations, the maxima

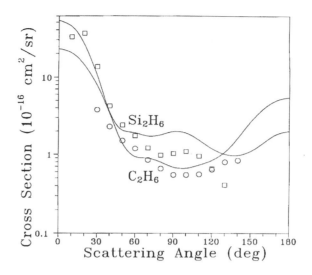

Figure 8.11: Differential Cross Sections for Elastic Scattering of 15 eV Electrons by Disilane and Ethane. Experimental points for ethane (circles) are from Ref. [Tanaka:88a]; disilane data (squares) are from Ref. [Tanaka:89a].

in the cross sections are expected to appear shifted to higher energies and somewhat broadened and lowered in intensity. Thus, for propylene, where some discrepancy is seen between the two measurements, our calculation appears to support the larger values of [Nishimura:91a].

Figure 8.11 shows the plotting of the calculated differential cross section, that is, the cross section as a function of scattering angle, for elastic scattering of 15 eV electrons from ethane and its analogue disilane. These results were obtained on the Mark IIIfp within the static-approximation. Agreement with experiment [Tanaka:88a;89a], is quite good; although there are quantitative differences where the magnitude of the cross section is small, the qualitative features are well reproduced for both molecules.

Calculations of electronic excitation cross sections are shown in Figures 8.12 and 8.13. In Figure 8.12, we present the integral cross section for excitation of the $\tilde{a}^3 B_{1u}$ state of ethylene [Sun:92a], obtained on the Mark II-Ifp in a two-channel approximation. This $\pi \rightarrow \pi^*$ excitation weakens the C–C bond, and its cross section is relevant to the dissociation of ethylene by low-energy electron impact. As seen in the figure, the cross section increases rapidly from threshold (experimental value 4.6 eV) and reaches a fairly high

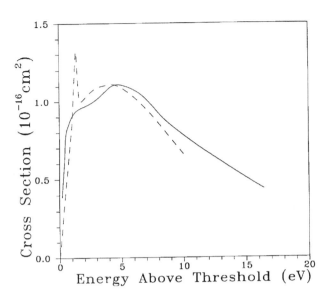

Figure 8.12: Integral Cross Section for Electron-Impact Excitation of the $\tilde{a}^3\,B_{1u}$ State of Ethylene. Solid line: present two-channel result; dashed line: relative measurement of Ref. [Veen:76a], normalized to the calculated value at the broad maximum.

peak value before beginning a gradual decline. The threshold rise is largely due to a d-wave ($\ell = 2$) contribution, seen as a shoulder around 1.4 eV above threshold, which may arise from a core-excited shape resonance. Relative measurements of this cross section [Veen:76a], which we have placed on an absolute scale by normalizing to our calculated value at the broad maximum, show a much sharper structure near threshold, but are otherwise in good agreement.

Figure 8.13 shows the cross section for electron-impact excitation of the $\tilde{a}^3\,B_{1u}$ and $\tilde{A}^1A_2$ states of formaldehyde, obtained from a three-channel calculation. Portions of this calculation were done on the Mark IIIfp, the iPSC/860, and the Delta. Experimental data for these excitations are not available, but an independent calculation at a similar level of theory has been reported [Rescigno:90a], and is shown in the figure. Since the complex-Kohn calculation of [Rescigno:90a] included only partial waves up to $\ell = 4$, we show both the full SMC result, obtained from $f(\vec{k}_i, \vec{k}_f)$, and a restricted SMC result, obtained with f projected onto a spherical-harmonic

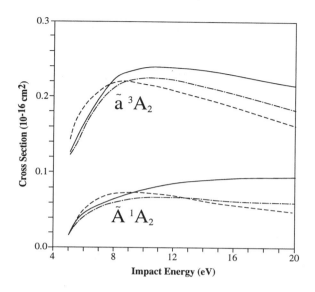

Figure 8.13: Calculated Integral Cross Sections for Electron-Impact Excitation of the $\tilde{a}^3 B_{1u}$ and $\tilde{A}^1 A_2$ States of Formaldehyde, Obtained from Three-Channel Calculations. Solid lines: present SMC results; short-dashed lines: SMC results, limited to $\ell \leq 4$; long-dashed lines: complex-Kohn calculations of Ref. [Rescigno:90a].

basis $Y_\ell^m(\hat{k})$, $\ell \leq 4$. The agreement between the restricted SMC result and that of [Rescigno:90a] is in general excellent; however, comparison to the full SMC result indicates that such a restriction introduces some errors at higher energies.

8.3.6 Conclusion

The concurrent implementation of a large sequential code which is in production on CRAY-type machines is a type of project which is likely to become increasingly common as commercial parallel machines proliferate and "mainstream" computer users are attracted by their potential. Several lessons which emerge from the port of the SMC code may prove useful to those contemplating similar projects. One is the value of focusing on the concurrent implementation and, so far as possible, avoiding or deferring minor improvements. If the original code is a reasonably effective production tool, such tinkering is unlikely to be of great enough benefit to justify the distraction from the primary goal of achieving a working concurrent version. On the other hand, major issues of structure and organization which bear directly on the parallel conversion deserve very careful attention, and should ideally be thought through before the actual conversion has begun. In the SMC case, the principal such issue was how to implement efficiently the transformation from primitive integrals to physical matrix elements. The solution arrived at not only suggested that a significant departure from the sequential code was warranted but also determined the data decomposition. A further point worth mentioning is that the conversion was greatly facilitated by the C^3P environment which fostered collaboration between workers familiar with the original code and its application, and workers adept at parallel programming practice, and in which there was ready access both to smaller machines for debugging runs and to larger production machines. Finally, we believe that the emphasis on achieving a simple communication strategy has justified itself in practice, not only in efficiency but in the portability and reliability of the program.

At present the parallel SMC code is essentially in production mode, all capabilities of the original sequential code having been implemented and some optimization performed. Further optimization of the primitive-integral package is in progress, but the major focus in the near future is likely to be applications on the one hand and extending the capabilities of the parallel code on the other. We are particularly interested in modifying the program to allow the study of electron scattering from open-shell systems (i.e., those with unpaired electrons), with a view to obtaining cross sections for some of the more important polyatomic species found in materials-processing plasmas. With continued progress in parallel hardware, we are very optimistic about the prospects for theory to make a substantial contribution to our knowledge of electron-polyatomic collisions.

Chapter 9

Loosely Synchronous Problems

9.1 Problem Structure

The significance of loosely synchronous problems and their natural parallelism was an important realization that emerged gradually (perhaps in 1987 as a clear concept) as we accumulated results from C^3P research. As described in Figure 9.1, fundamental theories often describe phenomena in terms of a set of similar entities obeying a single law. However, one does not usually describe practical problems in terms of their fundamental description in a theory such as QCD in Section 4.3. Rather, we use macroscopic concepts. Looking at society, a particle physicist might view it as a bunch of quarks and gluons; a nuclear physicist as a collection of protons and neutrons; a chemist as a collection of molecules; a biochemist as a set of proteins; a biologist as myriad cells; and a social scientist as a collection of people. Each description is appropriate to answer certain questions, and it is usually clear which description should be used. If we consider a simulation of society, or a part there of, only the QCD description is naturally synchronous. The other fields view society as a set of macroscopic constructs, which are no longer identical and typically have an irregular interconnect. This is caricatured in Figure 9.1 as an irregular network. The simulation is still data-parallel and, further, there is a critical macroscopic synchronization—in a time-stepped simulation at every time step t_0, $t_0 + \delta t$, $t_0 + 2\delta t$. This is an algorithmic synchronization that ensures natural scaling parallelism, that is, that the

Loosely Synchronous Problems

For example: Macroscopic description of physical system in terms of interactions between irregular inhomogeneous objects evolved as a time synchronized simulation. In particular - biological neural network

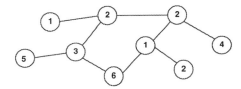

Parallelize by irregular partition of data domain

Hardware:
In general will not run well on SIMD machine.

Software:
Initial version of High Performance Fortran cannot describe.

Message passing or extensions of High Performance Fortran on MIMD machines will describe.

Figure 9.1: The Loosely Synchronous Problem Class

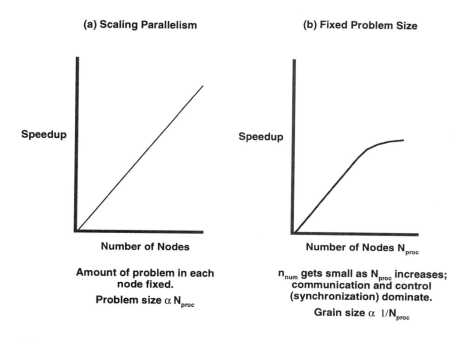

Figure 9.2: Speedup as a Function of Number of Processors N_{proc}

efficiency of Equations 3.10 and 3.11 is given by

$$\varepsilon = \frac{1}{(1 + f_C)} \tag{9.1}$$

and

$$f_C \propto \frac{1}{n_{\text{num}}^{\beta}} \frac{t_{\text{comm}}}{t_{\text{calc}}}, \tag{9.2}$$

with the parameter α of Equation 3.10 equal to zero. β is given by Equation 3.10 in terms of the system dimension. The efficiency only depends on the problem grain size and not explicitly on the number of processing nodes. As emphasized in [Gustafson:88a], these problems scale so that if one doubles both the machine and problem size, the speedup will also double with constant efficiency. This situation is summarized in Figure 9.2.

Why is there no synchronization overhead in this problem class? Picturesquely, we can say that the processors "know" that they are synchronized at the end of each algorithmic time step. We use time in the generalized complex system language of Section 3.3 and so it would represent, for instance, iteration number in a matrix problem. Operationally, we can describe

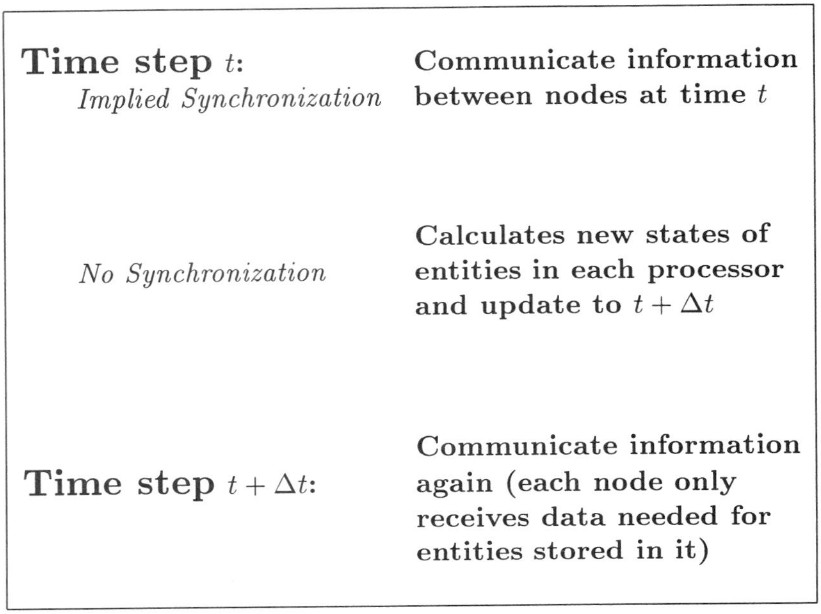

Time step t: *Implied Synchronization*	**Communicate information between nodes at time** t
No Synchronization	**Calculates new states of entities in each processor and update to** $t + \Delta t$
Time step $t + \Delta t$:	**Communicate information again (each node only receives data needed for entities stored in it)**

Figure 9.3: Communication-Calculation Phases in a Loosely Synchronous Problem

the loosely synchronous class on a MIMD machine by the communication-calculation sequence in Figure 9.3. The update (calculate) phase can involve very different algorithms and computations for the points stored in different processors. Thus, a MIMD architecture is needed in the general case. Synchronization is provided, as in Figure 9.3 by the internode communication phases at each time step. As described in Chapters 5 and 16, this does not need, but certainly can use, the full asynchronous message-passing capability of a MIMD machine.

We have split the loosely synchronous problems into two chapters, with those in Chapter 12 showing more irregularities and greater need for MIMD architectures than the applications described in this chapter. There has been no definitive study of which loosely synchronous problems can run well on SIMD machines. Some certainly can, but not all. We have discussed some of these issues in Section 6.1. If, as many expect, SIMD will remain a cost-effective architecture offered commercially, it will be important to better clarify the class of irregular problems that definitely need the full MIMD architecture.

As mentioned above, the applications in this chapter are "modestly" loosely synchronous. They include particle simulations (Sections 9.2 and 9.3), solutions of partial differential equation (Sections 9.3, 9.4, 9.5, 9.7), and circuit simulation (Sections 9.5 and 9.6). In Section 9.8, we describe an optimal assignment algorithm that can be used for multiple target Kalman filters and was developed for the large scale battle management simulation of Sections 18.3 and 18.4. Section 9.9 covers the parallelization of learning ("back-propagation") neural nets with improved learning methods. An interesting C^3P application not covered in detail in this book was the calculation of an exchange energy in solid He^3 at temperatures below $0.001°$ K [Callahan:88a;88b]. This was our first major use of the nCUBE-1 in production mode and Callahan suffered all the difficulties of a pioneer with the, at the time, decidely unreliable hardware and software. He used 250 hours on our 512-node nCUBE-1, which was equivalent to 1000 hours of a *non-vectorized* CRAY X-MP implementation. In discussing SIMD versus MIMD, one usually concentrates on the synchronization aspects. However, Callahan's application illustrates another point; namely, commercial SIMD machines typically have many more processors than a comparable MIMD computer. For example, Thinking Machines introduced the 32-node MIMD CM-5 as roughly equivalent (in price) to an 8 K SIMD CM-2. The SIMD architecture has 256 times as many nodes. Of course, the SIMD nodes are much simpler, but this still implies that one needs a large enough problem to exploit this extra number of nodes. There are some coarse-grain SIMD machines—especially special-purpose QCD machines [Battista:92a], [Christ:86a], [Fox:93a], [Marinari:93a]—but it is more natural to build fine-grain machines. If the node is large, one might as well add MIMD capability! Full matrix algorithms, such as LU decomposition, (see Chapter 8), are often synchronous, but do not perform very well on SIMD machines due to insufficient parallelism [Fox:92j]. Many of the operations only involve single rows and columns and have severe load imbalance on fine-grain machines. Callahan's He^3 application did not exhibit "massive" parallelism, and so "had" to use a MIMD machine irrespective of his problem's temporal structure. He used 512 nodes on the nCUBE-1 by combining three forms of parallelism: Two came from the problem formulation with spatial and temporal parallelism, the other from running four different parameter values concurrently.

A polymer simulation [Ding:88a;88b] [Ding:88a] [Ding:88b] by Ding and Goddard, using the reptation method, exhibited a similar effect. There is a chain of N chemical units and the algorithm involves special treatment of the two units at the beginning and end of the linear polymer. The MIMD program ran successfully on the Mark III and FPS T-Series, but the problem is too "small" (parallelism of $O(N)$) for this algorithm to run on a SIMD machine even though most of the basic operations can be run synchronously.

This issue of available parallelism also complicates the implementation of multigrid algorithms on SIMD machines [Frederickson:88a;88b;89a;89b].

9.2 Geomorphology by Micromechanical Simulations

Geomorphology is the study of the small-scale surface evolution of the earth under the forces resulting from such agents as wind, water, gravity, and ice. Understanding and prediction in geomorphology are critically dependent upon the ability to model the processes that shape the landscape. Because these processes in general are too complicated on large scales to describe in detail, it is necessary to adopt a system of hierarchical models in which the behavior of small systems is summarized by a set of rules governing the next larger system; in essence, these rules constitute a simplified algorithm for the physical processes in the smaller system that cannot be treated fully at larger scales. A significant fraction of the processes in geomorphology involve entrainment, transport and deposition of particulate matter. Where the intergrain forces become comparable to or greater than the forces arising from the transporting agents, consideration of the properties of a granular material, a system of grains which collide with the slide against neighboring grains, is warranted. A micromechanical description of granular materials has proved difficult, except in energetic flow regimes [Haff:83a], [Jenkins:83a]. Thus, researchers have turned to dynamical and computer simulations at the level of individual grains in order to elucidate some of the basic mechanical properties of granular materials ([Cundall:79a], [Walton:83a] pioneered this simulation technique). In this section, we discuss the role that hypercube concurrent processing has played and is expected to play both in grain-level dynamical simulations and in relating these simulations to modelling the formation and evolution of landforms.

As an example of this approach to geomorphology, we shall consider efforts to model transport of sand by the wind based upon the grain-to-grain dynamics. Sand is transported by the wind primarily in saltation and in reptation [Bagnold:41a]. Saltating grains are propelled along the surface in short hops by the wind. Each collision between a saltating sand grain and the surface results in a loss of energy which is compensated, on the average, by energy acquired from the wind. Reptating grains are ejected from the sand surface by saltating grain-sand bed impacts; they generally come to rest shortly after returning to the sand surface.

Computer simulations of saltating grain impacts upon a loose grain bed were performed on an early version of the hypercube [Werner:88a;88b]. Collisions between a single impacting grain and a box of 384 circular grains were simulated. The grains interact through stiff, inelastic compressional contact forces plus a Coulomb friction force. The equations of motion for the particles are integrated forward in time using a predictor-corrector technique. At each step in time, the program checks for contacts between particles and, where contacts exist, computes the contact forces. Dynamical simulations of granular materials are computationally intensive, because the time scale of the interaction between grains (tens of microseconds) is much smaller than the time scale of the simulation (order one second).

The simulation was decomposed on a Caltech hypercube by assigning the processors to regions of space lying on a rectangular grid. The computation time is a combination of calculation time in each processor due to contact searches and to force computations, and of communication time in sending information concerning grain positions and velocities to neighboring processors for interparticle force calculations on processor boundaries. Because the force computation is complicated, the communication time was found to be a negligible fraction of the total computation time for granular materials in which enduring intergrain contacts are dominant. The boundaries between processors are changed incrementally throughout the calculation in order to balance the computational load among the processors. The optimal decomposition has enough particles per processor to diminish the relative importance of statistical fluctuations in the load, and a system of boundaries which conforms as much as possible to the geometry of the problem. For grain-bed impacts, efficiencies between 0.89 and 0.97 were achieved [Werner:88a].

Irregularities of the geometry are important in determining which sand grains interact with each other. Thus, it is not possible to find an efficient synchronous algorithm for this and many other particle interaction problems. The very irregular inhomogeneous astrophysical calculations described in Section 12.4 illustrate this point clearly. One also finds the same issue in molecular dynamics codes, such as CHARMM which are extensively used in chemistry. This problem is, however, loosely synchronous as we can naturally macroscopically synchronize the calculation after each time step—thus a MIMD implementation where each processor processes its own irregular collection of grains is very natural and efficient. The sand grain problem, unlike that of Section 12.4, has purely local forces as the grains must be in physical contact to affect each other. Thus, only very localized communication is necessary. Note that Section 4.5 describes a synchronous formulation of this problem.

The results of the grain-bed impact simulations have facilitated treatment of two larger scale problems. A simulation of steady-state saltation in which calculation of saltating grain trajectories and modifications to the wind velocity profile, due to acceleration of saltating grains, were combined with a grain-bed impact distribution function derived from experiments and simulations. This simulation yielded such characteristics of saltation as flux and erosive potential [Werner:90a]. A simulation of the rearrangement of surface grains in reptation led to the formation of self-organized small-scale bedforms, which resemble wind ripples in both size and shape [Landry:93a], [Werner:91a;93a]. Larger, more complicated ripple formation simulations and a simulation of sand dune formation, using a similar approach which is under development, are problems that will require a combination of processing power and memory not available on present supercomputers. Ripple and dune simulations are expected to run efficiently with a spatial decomposition on a hypercube.

Water is an important agent for the transport of sediment. Unlike wind-blown sand transport, underwater sand transport requires simultaneous simulation of the grains and the fluid because water and sand are similar in density. We are developing a grain/fluid mixture simulation code for a hypercube in which the fluid is modelled by a gas composed of elastic hard circles (spheres in three dimensions). The simulation steps the gas forward at discrete time intervals, allowing the gas particles to collide (with another gas particle or a macroscopic grain) only once per step. The fluid velocity and the fluid force on each grain are computed by averaging. Since a typical void between macroscopic grains will be occupied by up to 1000 gas particles, the requisite computational speed and memory capacity can be found only in the hypercube architecture. Communication is expected to be minimal and load balancing can be accomplished for a sufficiently large system. It is expected that larger scale simulations of erosion and deposition by water [Ahnert:87a] will benefit from the findings of the fluid/grain mixture simulations. Also, these large-scale landscape evolution simulations are suitable themselves for a MIMD parallel machine.

Computer simulation is assuming an increasing role in geomorphology. We suggest that the development and availability of high-performance

MIMD concurrent processors will have considerable influence upon the future of computing in geomorphology.

9.3 Plasma Particle-in-Cell Simulation of an Electron Beam Plasma Instability

9.3.1 Introduction

Plasmas—gases of electrically charged particles—are one of the most complex fluids encountered in nature. Because of the long-range nature of the electric and magnetic interactions between plasma electrons and the ions composing them, plasmas exhibit a wide variety of collective forms of motions, for example, coherent motions of large number of electrons, ions, or both. This leads to an extremely rich physics of plasmas. Plasma particle-in-cell (PIC) simulation codes have proven to be a powerful tool for the study of complex nonlinear plasma problems in many areas of plasma physics research such as space and astrophysical plasmas, magnetic and inertial confinement, free electron lasers, electron and ion beam propagation and particle accelerators. In PIC codes, the orbits of thousands to millions of interacting plasma electrons and ions are followed in time as the particles move in electromagnetic fields calculated self-consistently from the charge and current densities created by these same plasma particles.

We developed an algorithm, called the *general concurrent particle-in-cell algorithm* (GCPIC) for implementing PIC codes efficiently on MIMD parallel computers [Liewer:89c]. This algorithm was first used to implement a well-benchmarked [Decyk:88a] one-dimensional electrostatic PIC code. The benchmark problem, used to benchmark the Mark IIIfp, was a simulation of an electron beam plasma instability ([Decyk:88a], [Liewer:89c]). Dynamic load balancing has been implemented in a one-dimensional electromagnetic GCPIC code [Liewer:90a]; this code was used to study electron dynamics in magnetosonic shock waves in space plasmas [Liewer:91a]. A two-dimensional electrostatic PIC code has also been implemented using the GCPIC algorithm with and without dynamic load balancing [Ferraro:90b;93a]. More recently, the two-dimensional electrostatic GCPIC code was extended to an electromagnetic code [Krucken:91a] and used to study parametric instabilities of large amplitude Alfvén waves in space plasmas [Liewer:92a].

9.3.2   GCPIC Algorithm

In plasma PIC codes, the orbits of the many interacting plasma electrons and ions are followed as an initial value problem as the particles move in self-consistently calculated electromagnetic fields. The fields are found by solving Maxwell's equations, or a subset, with the plasma currents and charge density as source terms; the electromagnetic fields determine the forces on the particles. In a PIC code, the particles can be anywhere in the simulation domain, but the field equations are solved on a discrete grid. At each time step in a PIC code, there are two stages to the computation. In the first stage, the position and velocities of the particles are updated by calculating the forces on the particles from interpolation of the field values at the grid points; the new charge and current densities at the grid points are then calculated by interpolation from the new positions and velocities of the particles. In the second stage, the updated fields are found by solving the field equations on the grid using the new charge and current densities. Generally, the first stage accounts for most of the computation time because there are many more particles than grid points.

The GCPIC algorithm [Liewer:89c] is designed to make the most computationally intensive portion of a PIC code, which updates the particles and the resulting charge and current densities, run efficiently on a parallel processor. The time used to make these updates is generally on the order of 90% of the total time for a sequential code, with the remaining time divided between the electromagnetic field solution and the diagnostic computations.

To implement a PIC code in parallel using the GCPIC algorithm, the physical domain of the particle simulation is partitioned into subdomains, equal in number to the number of processors, such that all subdomains have roughly equal numbers of particles. For problems with nonuniform particle densities, these subdomains will be of unequal physical size. Each processor is assigned a subdomain and is responsible for storing the particles and the electromagnetic field quantities for its subdomain and for performing the particle computations for its particles. For a one-dimensional code on a hypercube, nearest-neighbor subdomains are assigned to nearest-neighbor processors. When particles move to new subdomains, they are passed to the appropriate processor. As long as the number of particles per subdomain is approximately equal, the processors' computational loads will be balanced. Dynamic load balancing is accomplished by repartitioning the simulations domain into subdomains with roughly equal particle numbers when the processor loads become sufficiently unbalanced. The computation of the new partitions, done in a simple way using a crude approximation to the plasma density profile, adds very little overhead to the parallel code.

The decomposition used for dividing the particles is termed the *primary decomposition*. Because the primary decomposition is not generally the optimum one for the field solution on the grid, a *secondary decomposition* is used to divide the field computation. The secondary decomposition remains fixed. At each time step, grid data must be transferred between the two decompositions [Ferraro:90b;93a], [Liewer:89c].

The GCPIC algorithm has led to a very efficient parallel implementation of the benchmarked one-dimensional electrostatic PIC code [Liewer:89c]. In this electrostatic code, only forces from self-consistent (and external) electric fields are included; neither an external nor a plasma-generated magnetic field is included.

9.3.3 Electron Beam Plasma Instability

The problem used to benchmark the one-dimensional electrostatic GCPIC code on the Mark IIIfp was a simulation of an instability in a plasma due to the presence of an electron beam. The six color pictures in Figure 9.4 (Color Plate) show results from this simulation from the Mark IIIfp. Plotted is electron phase space—position versus velocity of the electrons—at six times during the simulation. The horizontal axis is the velocity and the vertical axis is the position of the electrons. Initially, the background plasma electrons (magenta dots) have a Gaussian distribution of velocities about zero. The width of the distribution in velocity is a measure of the temperature of the electrons. The beam electrons (yellow dots) stream through the background plasma at five times the thermal velocity. The beam density was 10% of the density of the background electrons. Initially, these have a Gaussian distribution about the beam velocity. Both beam and background electrons are distributed uniformly in x. This initial configuration is unstable to an electrostatic plasma wave which grows by tapping the free energy of the electron beam. At early times, the unstable waves grow exponentially. The influence of this electrostatic wave on the electron phase space is shown in the subsequent plots. The beam electrons lose energy to the wave. The wave acts to try to "thermalize" the electron's velocity distribution in the way collisions would act in a classical fluid. At some point, the amplitude of the wave's electrostatic potential is enough to "trap" some of the beam and background electrons, leading the visible swirls in the phase space plots. This trapping causes the wave to stop growing. In the end, the beam and

Table 9.1: Hypercube Push Efficiency for Increasing Problem Size

Processors	Particles	Mark III Push Time μ secs	Mark III Push Eff.	Mark IIIfp Push Time μ secs	Mark IIIfp Push Eff.
1	11,264	241.5	...	49.0	...
2	22,528	121.2	100%	24.7	99%
4	45,056	60.6	100%	12.3	99%
8	90,112	30.5	100%	6.3	99%
16	180,224	15.6	97%	3.1	98%
32	360,448	7.8	97%	1.6	98%

background electrons are mixed and the final distribution is "hotter" kinetic energy from the electron beam which has gone into heating both the background and beam electrons.

9.3.4   Performance Results for One-Dimensional Electrostatic Code

Timing results for the benchmark problem, using the one-dimensional code without dynamic load balancing, are given in the tables. In Table 9.1, results for the *push time* are given for various hypercube dimensions for the Mark III and Mark IIIfp hypercubes. Here, we define the push time as the time per particle per time step to update the particle positions and velocities (including the interpolation to find the forces at the particle positions) and to *deposit* (interpolate) the particles' contributions to the charge and/or current densities onto the grid. Table 9.1 shows the efficiency of the push for runs in which the number of particles *increased linearly* with the number of processors used, so that the number of particles per processor was constant (*fixed grain size*). The *efficiency* is defined to be $\epsilon = \frac{t(1)}{Nt(N)}$, where $t(N)$ is the run time on N processors. In the ideal situation, a code's run time on N will be $1/N$ of its run time on one processor, and the efficiency is 100%. In practice, communication between nodes and unequal processor loads leads to a decrease in the efficiency.

The Mark III Hypercube consists of up to 64 independent processors, each with four megabytes of dynamic random access memory and 128 kilobytes of static RAM. Each processor consists of two Motorola MC68020 CPUs with a MC68882 Co-processor. The newer Mark IIIfp Hypercubes have, in addition, a Weitek floating-point processor on each node. In Table 9.1, push times are given for both the Mark III processor (Motorola MC68882) and the Mark IIIfp processor (Weitek). For the Weitek runs, the entire parallel code was downloaded into the Weitek processors. The push time for the one-dimensional electrostatic code has been benchmarked on many computers [Decyk:88a]. Some of the times are given in Table 9.2; times for other computers can be found in [Decyk:88a]. For the Mark III and Mark IIIfp runs, 720,896 particles were used (11,264 per processor); for the other runs in Table 9.2, 11,264 particles were used. In all cases, the push time is the time per particle per time step to make the particle updates. It can be seen that for the push portion of the code, the 64-processor Mark III-Ifp is nearly twice the speed of a one-processor CRAY X-MP and 2.6 times the speed of a CRAY 2.

We have also compared the total run time for the benchmark code for a case with 720,896 particles and 1024 grid points run for 1000 time steps. The total run time on the 64-node Mark IIIfp was 1062 secs; on a one-processor CRAY 2, 1714 secs. For this case, the 64-node Mark IIIfp was 1.6 times faster than the CRAY 2 for the entire code. For the Mark IIIfp run, about 10% of the total run time was spent in the initialization of the particles, which is done sequentially.

Benchmark times for the two-dimensional GCPIC code can be found in [Ferraro:90b].

9.3.5 One-Dimensional Electromagnetic Code

The parallel one-dimensional electrostatic code was modified to include the effects of external and self-consistent magnetic fields. This one-dimensional electromagnetic code, with kinetic electrons and ions, has been used to study electron dynamics in oblique collisionless shock waves such as in the earth's bow shock. Forces on the particles are found from the fields at the grid points by interpolation. For this code, with variation in the x direction only, the orbit equations for the ith particle are

$$\frac{d\,x_i}{dt} = v_{x,i}$$
$$\frac{d\,\mathbf{v_i}}{dt} = \frac{q_i}{m_i}\left(\mathbf{E} + \frac{\mathbf{v}_i \times \mathbf{B}}{c}\right). \tag{9.3}$$

Table 9.2: Comparison of Push Times on Various Computers

Computer	Push Time $\mu\, secs$
Mark IIIfp hypercube (64 processor)	0.8
CRAY X-MP/48 (1 processor)	
Vectorized	1.5
Scalar	4.1
CRAY 2 (1 processor)	
Vectorized	2.1
Scalar	10.1
IBM 3090 VF	
Vectorized	2.9
Scalar	6.0
Mark III hypercube (64 processor)	3.9
Alliant FX/8	12.6
VAX 11/750, F.P.A.	200.9

Motion is followed in the x direction only, but all three velocity components must be calculated in order to calculate the $\mathbf{v} \times \mathbf{b}$ force. The longitudinal (along x) electric field is found by solving Poisson's equation

$$\nabla \cdot \mathbf{E} = 4\pi \rho_q\,(x,\, t). \tag{9.4}$$

The transverse (to x) electromagnetic fields, E_y, E_z, B_y, and B_z, are found by solving

$$\frac{\partial \mathbf{B}}{\partial t} = -\frac{1}{c}\nabla \times \mathbf{E}$$
$$\frac{\partial \mathbf{E}}{\partial t} = c\,\nabla \times \mathbf{B} - 4\pi \mathbf{j}. \tag{9.5}$$

The plasma current density $\mathbf{j}(x, t)$ and charge density $\rho_q(x, t)$ are found at the grid points by interpolation from the particle positions. Only the transverse (y and z) components of the plasma current are needed. These coupled particle and field equations are solved in time as an initial value problem. As in the electrostatic code, the fields are solved by Fourier-transforming the charge and current densities and solving the equation in k space, and advancing the Fourier components in time. External fields and currents can also be included. At each time step, the fields are transformed back to configuration space to calculate the forces needed to advance the particles to the next time step. The hypercube FFT routine described in Section 12.4 was used in the one-dimensional codes. Extending the existing parallel electrostatic code to include the electromagnetic effects required no change in the parallel decomposition of the code.

9.3.6 Dynamic Load Balancing

In the GCPIC electrostatic code, the partitioning of the grid was static. The grid was partitioned so that the computational load of the processors was initially balanced. As simulations progress and particles move among processors, the spatial distribution of the particles can change, leading to load imbalance. This can severely degrade the parallel efficiency of the push stage of the computation. To avoid this, dynamic load balancing has been implemented in a one-dimensional electromagnetic code [Liewer:90a] and a two-dimensional electrostatic code [Ferraro:93a].

To implement dynamic load balancing, the grid is repartitioned into new subdomains with roughly equal numbers of particles as the simulation progresses. The repartitioning is not done at every time step. The load imbalance is monitored at a user-specified interval. When the imbalance becomes sufficiently large, the grid is repartitioned and the particles moved to the appropriate processors, as necessary. The load was judged sufficiently imbalanced to warrant load balancing when the number of particles per processor deviated from the ideal value n_{ideal} (= number of particles/number of processors) by $2\sqrt{n_{ideal}}$, for example, twice the statistical fluctuation level.

The dynamic load balancing is performed during the push stage of the computation. Specifically, the new grid partitions are computed after the particle positions have been updated, but before the particles are moved to new processors to avoid an unnecessary moving of particles. If the loads are sufficiently balanced, the subroutine computing the new grid partitions is not called. The subroutine, which moves the particles to appropriate processors, is called in either case.

To accurately represent the physics, a particle cannot move more than one grid cell per time step. As a result, in the static one-dimensional code, the routine which moves particles to new processors only had to move particles to nearest-neighbor processors. To implement dynamic load balancing, this subroutine had to be modified to allow particles to be moved to processors any number of steps away. Moving the particles to new processors after grid repartitioning can add significant overhead; however, this is incurred only at time steps when load balancing occurs.

The new grid partitions are computed by a very simple method which adds very little overhead to the parallel code. Each processor constructs an approximation to the plasma density profile, $\bar{n}(x)$, and uses this to compute the grid partitioning to load balance. To construct the approximate density profile, each processor sends the locations of its current subdomain boundaries and its current number of particles to all other processors. From this information, each processor can compute the average plasma density in each processor and from this can create the approximate-to-density profile (with as many points as processors). This approximate profile is used to compute the grid partitioning which approximately divides the particles equally among the processors. This is done by determining the set of subdomain boundaries x_{left} and x_{right} such that

$$n_{ideal} \approx \int_{x_{left}}^{x_{right}} \bar{n}(x)\, dx. \tag{9.6}$$

Linear interpolation of the approximate profile is used in the numerical integration. The actual plasma density profile could also be used in the integration to determine the partitions. No additional computation would be necessary to obtain the local (within a processor) $n(x_{grid})$ because it is already computed for the field solution stage. However, it would require more communication to make the density profile global. Other methods of calculating new subdomain boundaries, such as sorting particles, require a much larger amount of communication and computational overhead.

9.3.7 Summary

The GCPIC algorithm was developed and implemented by Paulett C. Liewer, Jet Propulsion Laboratory, Caltech, and Viktor K. Decyk, Physics Department, University of California, Los Angeles. R. D. Ferraro, Jet Propulsion

Laboratory, Caltech, implemented the two-dimensional electrostatic PIC code using the GCPIC algorithm with dynamic load balancing.

9.4 Computational Electromagnetics

A group at JPL, led by Jean Patterson, developed several hypercube codes for the solution of large-scale electromagnetic scattering and radiation problems. Two codes were parallel implementations of standard production-level EM analysis codes and the remaining are largely or entirely new. Included in the parallel implementations of existing codes is the widely used *numerical electromagnetics code* (NEC-2) developed at Lawrence Livermore National Laboratory. Other codes include an integral equation formulation Patch code, a time-domain finite-difference code, a three-dimensional finite-elements code, and infinite and finite frequency selective surfaces codes. Currently, we are developing an anisotropic material modeling capability for the three-dimensional Finite Elements code and a three-dimensional coupled approach code. In the Coupled Approach, one uses finite elements to represent the interior of a scattering object, and the boundary integrals for the exterior. Along with the analysis tools, we are developing an Electromagnetic Interactive Analysis Workstation (EIAW) as an integrated environment to aid in design and analysis. The workstation provides a general user interface for specification of an object to be analyzed and graphical representations of the results. The EIAW environment is implemented on an Apollo DN4500 Color Graphics Workstation, and a Sun Sparc2. This environment provides a uniform user interface for accessing the available parallel processor resources (e.g., the JPL/Caltech Mark IIIfp and the Intel iPSC/860 hypercubes.) [Calalo:89b].

One of the areas of current emphasis is the development of the anisotropic three-dimensional finite element analysis tool. We briefly describe this effort here. The finite element method is being used to compute solutions to open region electromagnetic scattering problems where the domain may be irregularly shaped and contain differing material properties. Such a scattering object may be composed of dielectric and conducting materials, possibly with anisotropic and inhomogeneous dielectric properties. The domain is discretized by a mesh of polygonal (two-dimensional) and polyhedral (three-dimensional) elements with nodal points at the corners. The finite element solution that determines the field quantities at these nodal points is stated using the Helmholtz equation. It is derived from Maxwell's equations describing the incident and scattered field for a particular wave number, k. The two-dimensional equation for the out-of-plane magnetic field, H_z, is given by

$$\nabla \left(\frac{1}{\epsilon} \nabla H_z \right) + k^2 \mu H_z = 0 \tag{9.7}$$

where ϵ is the relative permittivity and μ is the relative magnetic permeability. The equation for the electric field is similarly stated, interchanging ϵ and μ.

The open region problem is solved in a finite domain by imposing an artificial boundary condition for a circular boundary. For the two-dimensional case, we are applying the approach of Bayliss and Turkel [Bayliss:80a]. The cylindrical artificial boundary condition on scattered field, H_z^s (where $H_z^s = H_z - H_{\mathrm{inc}}$), is given by

$$\frac{\partial H_z^s}{\partial \rho} = A(\rho) H_z^s + B(\rho) \frac{\partial^2 H_z^s}{\partial \varphi^2} \tag{9.8}$$

where ρ is the radius of artificial boundary, φ is the angular coordinate, and A and B are operators that are dependent on ρ.

The differential Equation 9.7 can be converted to an integral equation by multiplying by a test function which has certain continuity properties. If the total field is expressed in terms of the incident and scattered fields, then we may substitute Equation 9.8 to arrive at our weak form equation

$$\iint_\Gamma \left(\frac{1}{\epsilon} \nabla T \cdot \nabla H_z^s - k^2 \mu T H_z^s \right) dx dy -$$
$$\oint_{\partial \Gamma} \frac{1}{\epsilon} T \left(A H_z^s + B \frac{\partial^2 H_z^s}{\partial \varphi^2} \right) dl = F \tag{9.9}$$

where F is the excitation, which depends on the incident field.

$$F = \iint_\Gamma \left(T \nabla (\frac{1}{\epsilon} \nabla H_z^{\mathrm{inc}}) + k^2 \mu T H_z^{\mathrm{inc}} \right) dx dy \tag{9.10}$$

Substituting the field and test function representations in terms of nodal basis functions into Equation 9.9 forms a set of linear equations for the coefficients of the basis functions. The matrix which results from this finite-element approximation is sparse with nonzero elements clustered about the diagonal.

The solution technique for the finite-element problem is based on a domain decomposition. This decomposition technique divides the physical problem space among the processors of the hypercube. While elements are

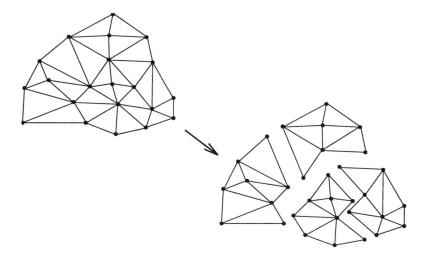

Figure 9.5: Domain Decomposition of the Finite Element Mesh into Subdomains, Each of Which are Assigned to Different Hypercube Processors.

the exclusive responsibility of hypercube processors, the nodal points on the boundaries of the subdomains are shared. Because shared nodal points require that there be communication between hypercube processors, it is important for processing efficiency to minimize the number of these shared nodal points.

The tedious process of specifying the finite-element model to describe the geometry of the scattering object is greatly simplified by invoking the graphical editor, PATRAN-Plus, within the Hypercube Electromagnetics Interactive Analysis Workstation. The graphical input is used to generate the finite-element mesh. Currently, we have implemented isoparametric three-node triangular, six-node triangular, and nine-node quadrilateral elements for the two-dimensional case, and linear four-node tetrahedral elements for the three-dimensional case.

Once the finite-element mesh has been generated, the elements are allocated to hypercube processors with the aid of a partitioning tool which we have developed. In order to achieve good load balance, each of the hypercube processors should receive approximately the same number of elements (which reflects the computation load) and the same number of subdomain edges (which reflects the communication requirement). The *recursive inertial partitioning* (RIP) algorithm chooses the best bisection axis of the mesh based on calculated moments of inertia. Figure 9.6 illustrates one possible

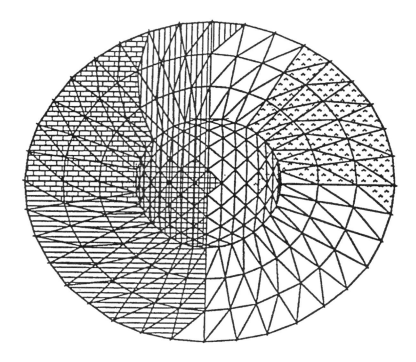

Figure 9.6: Finite Element Mesh for a Dielectric Cylinder Partitioned Among Eight Hypercube Processors

partitioning for a dielectric cylinder.

The finite-element problem can be solved using several different strategies: iterative solution, direct solution, or a hybrid of the two. We employ all of these techniques in our finite elements testbed. We use a preconditioned biconjugate gradients approach for iterative solutions and a Crout solver for the direct solution [Peterson:85d;86a]. We also have developed a hybrid solver which uses first Gaussian elimination locally within hypercube processors, and then biconjugate gradients to resolve the remaining degrees of freedom [Nour-Omid:87b].

The output from the finite elements code is displayed graphically at the Electromagnetics Interactive Analysis Workstation. In Figure 9.7 (Color Plate) are plotted the real (on the left) and the imaginary (on the right) components of the total scalar field for a conducting cylinder of $ka = 50$. The absorbing boundary is placed at $kr = 62$. Figure 9.8 (Color Plate) shows

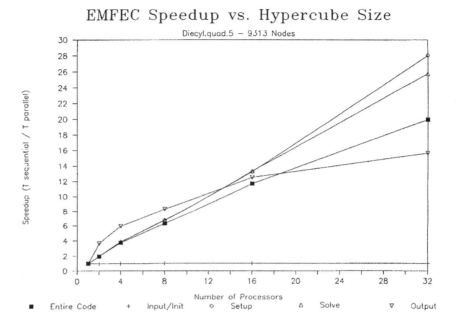

Figure 9.10: Finite-Element Execution Speedup Versus Hypercube Size

the plane wave propagation indicated by vectors in a rectangular box (no scatterer). The box is modeled using linear tetrahedral elements. Figure 9.9 (Color Plate) shows the plane wave propagation (no scatterer) in a spherical domain, again using tetrahedral linear elements. The half slices show the internal fields. In the upper left is the x-component of the field, the lower left is the z-component, and on the right is the y-component with the fields shown as contours on the surface.

The speedups over the problem running on one processor are plotted for hypercube configurations ranging from 1 to 32 processors in Figure 9.10. The problem for this set of runs is a two-dimensional dielectric cylinder model consisting of 9313 nodes.

The setup and solve portions of the total execution time demonstrate 87% and 81% efficiencies, respectively. The output portion where the results obtained by each processor are sent back to the workstation run at about 50% efficiency. The input routine exhibits no speedup and greatly reduces the overall efficiency, 63% of the code. Clearly, this is an area on which we now must focus. We have recently implemented the partitioning code on parallel. We are also now reducing the size of the input file by compressing the contents of the mesh data file and removing formatted reads and writes. We are also developing a parallel mesh partitioner which iteratively refines a coarse mesh which was generated by the graphics software.

We are currently exploring a number of accuracy issues with regards to the finite elements and coupled approach solutions. Such issues include gridding density, element types, placement of artificial boundaries, and specification of basis functions. We are investigating outgoing wave boundary conditions; currently, we are using a modified Sommerfield radiation condition in three dimensions. In addition, we are exploring a number of higher order element types for three dimensions. Central to our investigations is the objective of developing analysis techniques for massive three-dimensional problems.

We have demonstrated that the parallel processing environments offered by the current coarse-grain MIMD architectures are very well suited to the solution of large-scale electromagnetic scattering and radiation problems. We have developed a number of parallel EM analysis codes that currently run in production mode. These codes are being embedded in a Hypercube Electromagnetic Interactive Analysis Workstation. The workstation environment simplifies the user specification of the model geometry and material properties, and the input of run parameters. The workstation also provides an ideal environment for graphically viewing the resulting currents and near- and far-fields. We are continuing to explore a number of issues to fully exploit the capabilities of this large-memory, high-performance computing environment. We are also investigating improved matrix solvers for both dense and sparse matrices, and have implemented out-of-core solving techniques, which will prevent us from becoming memory-limited. By establishing testbeds, such as the finite-element one described here, we will continue to explore issues that will maintain computational accuracy, while reducing the overall computation time for EM scattering and radiation analysis problems.

9.5   LU Factorization of Sparse, Unsymmetric Jacobian Matrices

Efficient sparse linear algebra *cannot* be achieved as a straightforward extension of the dense case described in Chapter 8, even for concurrent imple-

mentations. This paper details a new, general-purpose unsymmetric sparse
LU factorization code built on the philosophy of Harwell's MA28, with variations. We apply this code in the framework of Jacobian-matrix factorizations, arising from Newton iterations in the solution of nonlinear systems
of equations. Serious attention has been paid to the data-structure requirements, complexity issues, and communication features of the algorithm.
Key results include reduced communication pivoting for both the "analyze"
A-mode and repeated B-mode factorizations, and effective general-purpose
data distributions useful incrementally to trade-off process-column load balance in factorization against triangular solve performance. Future planned
efforts are cited in conclusion.

9.5.1 Introduction

The topic of this section is the implementation and concurrent performance
of sparse, unsymmetric LU factorization for medium-grain multicomputers. Our target hardware is distributed-memory, message-passing concurrent
computers such as the Symult s2010 and Intel iPSC/2 systems. For both of
these systems, efficient cut-through *wormhole* routing technology provides
pairwise communication performance essentially independent of the spatial
location of the computers in the ensemble [Athas:88a]. The Symult s2010
is a two-dimensional, mesh-connected concurrent computer; all examples in
this paper were run on this variety of hardware. Message-passing performance, portability, and related issues relevant to this work are detailed in
[Skjellum:90a].

Questions of linear-algebra performance are pervasive throughout scientific and engineering computation. The need for high-quality, high-
performance linear algebra algorithms (and libraries) for multicomputer systems therefore requires no attempt at justification. The motivation for
the work described here has a specific origin, however. Our main higher
level research goal is the concurrent dynamic simulation of systems modelled by ordinary differential and algebraic equations; specifically, dynamic
flowsheet simulation of chemical plants (e.g., coupled distillation columns)
[Skjellum:90c]. Efficient sequential integration algorithms solve staticized
nonlinear equations at each time point via modified Newton iteration (cf.,
[Brenan:89a], Chapter 5). Consequently, a sequence of structurally identical
linear systems must be solved; the matrices are finite-difference approximations to Jacobians of the staticized system of ordinary differential-algebraic
equations. These Jacobians are large, sparse, and unsymmetric for our ap-

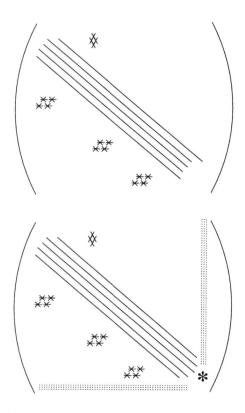

Figure 9.11: An Example of Jacobian Matrix Structures. In chemical-engineering process flowsheets, Jacobians with main-band structure, lower-triangular structure (feedforwards), upper-triangular structure (feedbacks), and borders (global or artificially restructured feedforwards and/or feedbacks) are common.

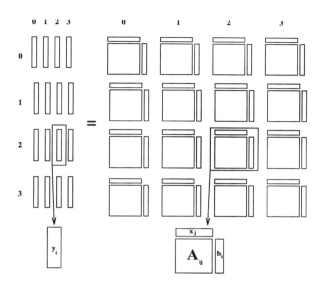

Figure 9.12: Process-Grid Data Distribution of $Ax = b$. Representation of a concurrent matrix, and distributed-replicated concurrent vectors on a 4×4 logical process grid. The solution of $Ax = b$ first appears in x, a column-distributed vector, and then is normally "transposed" via a global *combine* to the row-distributed vector y.

plication area. In general, they possess both band and significant off-band structure. Generic structures are depicted in Figure 9.11. This work should also bear relevance to electric power network/grid dynamic simulation where sparse, unsymmetric Jacobians arise, and elsewhere.

9.5.2   Design Overview

We solve the problem $Ax = b$ where A is large, and includes many zero entries. We assume that A is unsymmetric both in sparsity pattern and in numerical values. In general, the matrix A will be computed in a distributed fashion, so we will inherit a distribution of the coefficients of A (cf., Figures 9.12 and 9.13). Following the style of Harwell's MA28 code for unsymmetric sparse matrices, we use a two-phase approach to this solution. There is a first LU factorization called A-mode or "analyze," which builds data structures dynamically, and employs a user-defined pivoting function. The repeated B-mode factorization uses the existing data structures statically to factor a new, similarly structured matrix, with the previous pivoting

$$
\begin{pmatrix}
A^{0,0} & A^{0,1} & A^{0,2} & A^{0,3} \\
A^{1,0} & A^{1,1} & A^{1,2} & A^{1,3} \\
A^{2,0} & A^{2,1} & A^{2,2} & A^{2,3} \\
A^{3,0} & A^{3,1} & A^{3,2} & A^{3,3}
\end{pmatrix}_{\mathcal{G}} =
$$

$$
\left(
\begin{array}{cc|cc|cc|cc}
a_{0,1} & a_{0,5} & a_{0,2} & a_{0,6} & a_{0,3} & a_{0,7} & a_{0,0} & a_{0,4} & a_{0,8} \\
a_{1,1} & a_{1,5} & a_{1,2} & a_{1,6} & a_{1,3} & a_{1,7} & a_{1,0} & a_{1,4} & a_{1,8} \\ \hline
a_{2,1} & a_{2,5} & a_{2,2} & a_{2,6} & a_{2,3} & a_{2,7} & a_{2,0} & a_{2,4} & a_{2,8} \\
a_{3,1} & a_{3,5} & a_{3,2} & a_{3,6} & a_{3,3} & a_{3,7} & a_{3,0} & a_{3,4} & a_{3,8} \\ \hline
a_{4,1} & a_{4,5} & a_{4,2} & a_{4,6} & a_{4,3} & a_{4,7} & a_{4,0} & a_{4,4} & a_{4,8} \\
a_{5,1} & a_{5,5} & a_{5,2} & a_{5,6} & a_{5,3} & a_{5,7} & a_{5,0} & a_{5,4} & a_{5,8} \\
a_{6,1} & a_{6,5} & a_{6,2} & a_{6,6} & a_{6,3} & a_{6,7} & a_{6,0} & a_{6,4} & a_{6,8} \\
a_{7,1} & a_{7,5} & a_{7,2} & a_{7,6} & a_{7,3} & a_{7,7} & a_{7,0} & a_{7,4} & a_{7,8} \\ \hline
a_{8,1} & a_{8,5} & a_{8,2} & a_{8,6} & a_{8,3} & a_{8,7} & a_{8,0} & a_{8,4} & a_{8,8} \\
a_{9,1} & a_{9,5} & a_{9,2} & a_{9,6} & a_{9,3} & a_{9,7} & a_{9,0} & a_{9,4} & a_{9,8} \\
a_{10,1} & a_{10,5} & a_{10,2} & a_{10,6} & a_{10,3} & a_{10,7} & a_{10,0} & a_{10,4} & a_{10,8}
\end{array}
\right)
$$

Figure 9.13: Example of Process-Grid Data Distribution. An 11×9 array with block-linear rows $(B = 2)$ and scattered columns on a 4×4 logical process grid. Local arrays are denoted at left by $A^{p,q}$ where (p,q) is the grid position of the process on $\mathcal{G} \equiv \left(\{ (\lambda_2, \lambda_2^{-1}, \lambda_2^{\sharp}); P = 4, M = 11 \}, \{ (\sigma_1, \sigma_1^{-1}, \sigma_1^{\sharp}); Q = 4, N = 9 \} \right)$. Subscripts (i.e., $a_{I,J}$) are the global (I,J) indices.

pattern. B-mode monitors stability with a simple growth factor estimate. In practice, A-mode is repeated whenever instability is detected. The two key contributions of this sparse concurrent solver are reduced communication pivoting, and new data distributions for better overall performance.

Following Van de Velde [Velde:90a], we consider the LU factorization of a real matrix A, $A \in \Re^{N \times N}$. It is well known (e.g., [Golub:89a], pp. 117-118), that for any such matrix A, an LU factorization of the form

$$
\mathsf{P}_R A \mathsf{P}_C^T = \hat{L} \hat{U}
$$

exists, where $\mathsf{P}_R, \mathsf{P}_C$ are square, (orthogonal) permutation matrices, and $\hat{L}, \hat{U}$ are the unit lower- and upper-triangular factors, respectively. Whereas the pivot sequence is stored (two N-length integer vectors), the permutation matrices are not stored or computed with explicitly. Rearranging, based on the orthogonality of the permutation matrices, $A = \mathsf{P}_R^T \hat{L} \hat{U} \mathsf{P}_C$. We factor A with implicit pivoting (no rows or columns are exchanged explicitly as a result of pivoting). Therefore, we do not store $\hat{L}, \hat{U}$ directly, but instead: $L = \mathsf{P}_R^T \hat{L} \mathsf{P}_C$, $U = \mathsf{P}_R^T \hat{U} \mathsf{P}_C$. Consequently, $\hat{L} \mathsf{P}_R L \mathsf{P}_C^T$, $\hat{U} = \mathsf{P}_R U \mathsf{P}_C^T$, and $A = L(\mathsf{P}_C^T \mathsf{P}_R) U$. The "unravelling" of the permutation matrices is accomplished readily (without implication of additional interprocess communication) during the triangular solves.

For the sparse case, performance is more difficult to quantify than for the dense case, but, for example, banded matrices with bandwidth β can be factored with $O(\beta^2 N)$ work; we expect subcubic complexity in N for reasonably sparse matrices, and strive for subquadratic complexity, for very sparse matrices. The triangular solves can be accomplished in work proportional to the number of entries in the respective triangular matrix L or U. The pivoting strategy is treated as a parameter of the algorithm and is not predetermined. We can consequently treat the pivoting function as an application-dependent function, and sometimes tailor it to special problem structures (cf., Section 7 of [Velde:88a]) for higher performance. As for all sparse solvers, we also seek subquadratic memory requirements in N, attained by storing matrix entries in linked-list fashion, as illustrated in Figure 9.14.

For further discussion of LU factorizations and sparse matrices, see [Golub:89a], [Duff:86a].

9.5.3 Reduced-Communication Pivoting

At each stage of the concurrent LU factorization, the pivot element is chosen by the user-defined pivot function. Then, the pivot row (new row of U) must be broadcast, and pivot column (new column of L) must be computed and broadcast on the logical process grid (cf., Figure 9.12), vertically and horizontally, respectively. Note that these are interchangeable operations. We use this degree of freedom to reduce the communication complexity of particular pivoting strategies, while impacting the effort of the LU factorization itself negligibly.

We define two "correctness modes" of pivoting functions. In the first correctness mode, "first row fanout," the exit conditions for the pivot function are: All processes must know $\hat{p}$ (the pivot process row); the pivot process row must know $\hat{q}$ (the pivot process column) as well as $\hat{\imath}$, the $\hat{p}$-local matrix row of the pivot; and the pivot process must know in addition the pivot value and $\hat{q}$-local matrix column $\hat{\jmath}$ of the pivot. Partial column pivoting and preset

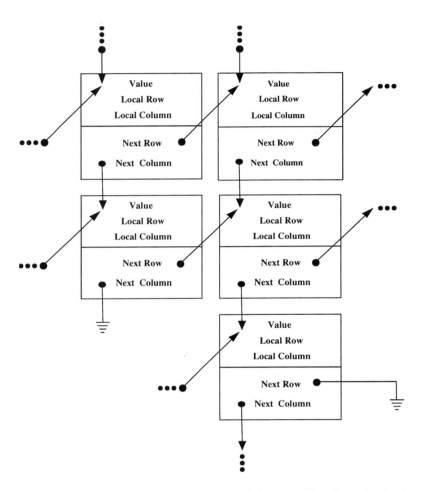

Figure 9.14: Linked-list Entry Structure of Sparse Matrix. A single entry consists of a double-precision value (8 bytes), the local row (i) and column (j) index (2 bytes each), a "Next Column Pointer" indicating the next current column entry (fixed j), and a "Next Row Pointer" indicating the next current row entry (fixed i), at 4 bytes each. Total: 24 bytes per entry.

pivoting can be set up to satisfy these correctness conditions as follows. For partial column pivoting, the kth row is eliminated at the kth step of the factorization. From this fact, each process can derive the process row $\hat{p}$ and $\hat{p}$-local matrix row $\hat{\imath}$ using the row data distribution function. Having identified themselves, the pivot-row processes can look for the largest element in local matrix row $\hat{\imath}$ and choose the pivot element globally among themselves via a combine. At completion, this places $\hat{q}$, $\hat{\jmath}$, and the pivot value in the entire pivot process row. This completes the requirements for the "first row fanout" correctness mode. For preset pivoting, the kth elimination row and column are both stored as $\hat{p}, \hat{\imath}, \hat{q}, \hat{\jmath}$, and each process knows these values *without communication*.[1] Furthermore, the pivot process looks up the pivot value. Hence, preset pivoting satisfies the requirements of this correctness mode also.

For "first row fanout," the universal knowledge of $\hat{p}$ and knowledge of the pivot matrix row $\hat{\imath}$ by the pivot process row, allow the vertical broadcast of this row (new row of U). In addition, we broadcast $\hat{q}$, $\hat{\jmath}$, and the pivot value simultaneously. This extends the correct value of $\hat{q}$ to all processes, as well as $\hat{\jmath}$ and the pivot value to the pivot process column. Hence, the multiplier (L) column may be correctly computed and broadcast. Along with the multiplier column broadcast, we include the pivot value. After this broadcast, all processes have the correct indices $\hat{p}, \hat{\imath}, \hat{q}, \hat{\jmath}$ and the pivot value. This provides all that's required to complete the current elimination step.

For the second correctness mode "first column fanout," the exit conditions for the pivot function are: All processes must know $\hat{q}$ and the entire pivot process column must know $\hat{\jmath}$, the pivot value, and $\hat{p}$. The pivot process in addition knows $\hat{\imath}$. Partial row pivoting can be set up to satisfy these correctness conditions. The arguments are analogous to partial column pivoting and are given in [Skjellum:90c].

For "first column fanout," the entire pivot process column knows the pivot value, and local column of the pivot. Hence, the multiplier column may be computed by dividing the pivot matrix column by the pivot value. This column of L can then be broadcast horizontally, including the pivot value, $\hat{p}$, and $\hat{\imath}$ as additional information. After this step, the entire ensemble has the correct pivot value, and $\hat{p}$; in addition, the pivot process row has the correct $\hat{\imath}$. Hence, the pivot matrix row may be identified and broadcast. This second broadcast completes the needed information in each process for effecting the kth elimination step.

---

[1]Memory unscalabilities can be removed very cheaply; see [Skjellum:90c].

Table 9.3: Evaluation Times for Three Data Distributions

Distribution:	$\mu(I, P, M)$	$\mu^{-1}(p, i, P, M)$
One-Parameter (ζ)	$5.5554 \times 10^1 \pm 5 \times 10^{-3}$	$4.0024 \times 10^1 \pm 7 \times 10^{-3}$
Two-Parameter (ξ)	$6.1710 \times 10^1 \pm 1 \times 10^{-2}$	$4.2370 \times 10^1 \pm 8 \times 10^{-3}$
Block-Linear (λ)	$5.4254 \times 10^1 \pm 7 \times 10^{-3}$	$3.5404 \times 10^1 \pm 5 \times 10^{-3}$

Note: For the data distributions and inverses described here, evaluation time in μs is quoted for the Symult s2010 multicomputer. Cardinality function calls are inexpensive, and fall within lower order work anyway—their timing is hence omitted. The cheapest distribution function (scatter) costs $\approx 15\mu$s by way of comparison.

Thus, when using partial row or partial column pivoting, only local combines of the pivot process column (respectively row) are needed. The other processes don't participate in the combine, as they must without this methodology. Preset pivoting implies no pivoting communication, except very occasionally (e.g., 1 in 5000 times), as noted in [Skjellum:90c], to remove memory unscalabilities. This pivoting approach is a direct savings, gained at a negligible additional broadcast overhead. See also [Skjellum:90c].

9.5.4 New Data Distributions

We introduce new closed-form $O(1)$-time, $O(1)$-memory data distributions useful for sparse matrix factorizations and the problems that generate such matrices. We quantify evaluation costs in Table 9.3.

Every concurrent data structure is associated with a logical process grid at creation (cf., Figure 9.12 and [Skjellum:90a;90c]). Vectors are either row- or column-distributed within a two-dimensional process grid. Row-distributed vectors are *replicated* in each process column, and distributed in the process rows. Conversely, column-distributed vectors are replicated in each process row, and distributed in the process columns. Matrices are distributed both in rows and columns, so that a single process owns a subset of matrix rows and columns. This partitioning follows the ideas proposed by Fox et al. [Fox:88a] and others. Within the process grid, coefficients of vectors and matrices are distributed according to one of several data distributions. Data distributions are chosen to compromise between load-balancing

requirements and constraints on where information can be calculated in the
ensemble.

Definition 1 (Data-Distribution Function)

*A data-distribution function μ maps three integers $\mu(I, P, M) \mapsto (p, i)$ where
I, $0 \leq I < M$, is the global name of a coefficient, P is the number of
processes among which all coefficients are to be partitioned, and M is the
total number of coefficients. The pair (p, i) represents the process p ($0 \leq p <
P$) and local (process-p) name i of the coefficient ($0 \leq i < \mu^{\sharp}(p, P, M)$). The
inverse distribution function $\mu^{-1}(p, i, P, M) \mapsto I$ transforms the local name
i back to the global coefficient name I.*

*The formal requirements for a data-distribution function are as follows.
Let $\mathcal{I}^p$ be the set of global coefficient names associated with process p, $0 \leq
p < P$, defined implicitly by a data distribution function $\mu(\bullet, P, M)$. The
following set properties must hold:*

$$
\mathcal{I}^{p_1} \cap \mathcal{I}^{p_2} = \emptyset, \ \forall \ p_1 \neq p_2, \quad 0 \leq p_1, p_2 < P
$$

$$
\bigcup_{p=0}^{P-1} \mathcal{I}^p = \{0, \ldots, M - 1\} \equiv \mathcal{I}_M
$$

The cardinality of the set $\mathcal{I}^p$, is given by $\mu^{\sharp}(p, P, M)$.

The linear and scatter data-distribution functions are most often defined.
We generalize these functions (by blocking and scattering parameters) to incorporate practically important degrees of freedom. These generalized distribution functions yield optimal static load balance as do the unmodified
functions described in [Velde:90a] for unit block size, but they differ in coefficient placement. This distinction is technical, but necessary for efficient
implementations.

Definition 2 (Generalized Block-Linear)

*The definitions for the generalized block-linear distribution function, inverse,
and cardinality function are:*

$$
\lambda_B(I, P, M) \mapsto (p, i),
$$

$$
p \equiv P - 1 - \\
\max\left(\left\lfloor \frac{I_B^{\text{rev}}}{l + 1} \right\rfloor, \left\lfloor \frac{I_B^{\text{rev}} - r}{l} \right\rfloor \right),
$$

$$i \;\equiv\; I - B\left(pl + \Theta^1\left(p - (P - r)\right)\right),$$

while

$$\lambda_B^{-1}(p, i, P, M) \;\equiv\; i + B\left((pl + \Theta^1\left(p - (P - r)\right)\right),$$

$$\lambda_B^{\sharp}(p, P, M) \;\equiv\; B\left(\left\lfloor \frac{b+p}{P} \right\rfloor - \theta\right) +$$
$$(M \bmod B)\theta,$$

where B denotes the coefficient block size,

$$b \;=\; \begin{cases} \dfrac{M}{B} & \text{if } M \bmod B = 0 \\[2ex] \left\lfloor \dfrac{M}{B} \right\rfloor + 1 & \text{otherwise,} \end{cases}$$

$$I_B \;=\; \left\lfloor \frac{I}{B} \right\rfloor, \quad I_B^{\text{rev}} \;=\; b - 1 - I_B,$$

$$l \;=\; \left\lfloor \frac{b}{P} \right\rfloor, \quad r = b \bmod P,$$

$$\Theta^k(t) \;\equiv\; \begin{cases} 0 & t \le 0 \\ t^k & t > 0, \; k > 0 \\ 1 & t > 0, \; k = 0 \end{cases},$$

$$\theta \;=\; \left\lfloor \frac{p+1}{P} \right\rfloor \Theta^0(M \bmod B)$$

and where $b \ge P$.

   For $B = 1$, a load-balance-equivalent variant of the common linear data-distribution function is recovered. The general block-linear distribution function divides coefficients among the P processes $p = 0, \ldots, P - 1$ so that each $\mathcal{I}^p$ is a set of coefficients with contiguous global names, while optimally load-balancing the b blocks among the P sets. Coefficient boundaries between processes are on multiples of B. The maximum possible coefficient imbalance between processes is B. If $B \bmod P \ne 0$, the last block in process $P - 1$ will be foreshortened.

Definition 3 (Parametric Functions)

To allow greater freedom in the distribution of coefficients among processes, we define a new, two-parameter distribution function family, ξ. The B blocking parameter (just introduced in the block-linear function) is mainly suited *to the clustering of coefficients that must not be separated by an interprocess boundary (again, see [Skjellum:90c] for a definition of general block-scatter, σ). Increasing B worsens the static load balance. Adding a second scaling parameter S (of no impact on the static load balance) allows the distribution to scatter coefficients to a greater or lesser degree, directly as a function of this one parameter. The two-parameter distribution function, inverse and cardinality function are defined below. The one-parameter distribution function family, ζ, occurs as the special case B = 1, also as noted below:*

$$\xi_{B,S}(I, P, M) \;\mapsto\; (p, i) \;\equiv\; \begin{cases} (p_0, i_0) & \Lambda_0 \geq l_S \\ (p_1, i_1) & \Lambda_0 < l_S \end{cases}$$

where

$$l_S \;\equiv\; \left\lfloor \frac{l}{S} \right\rfloor, \quad \Lambda_0 \;\equiv\; \left\lfloor \frac{i_0}{BS} \right\rfloor,$$

$$(p_0, i_0) \;\leftarrow\; \lambda_B(I, P, M),$$

$$I_{BS} \;=\; p_0 l_S + \Lambda_0,$$

$$p_1 \;\equiv\; I_{BS} \bmod P \;,$$

$$i_1 \;\equiv\; BS \left\lfloor \frac{I_{BS}}{P} \right\rfloor + (i_0 \bmod BS),$$

with

$$\zeta_S(I, P, M) \;\equiv\; \xi_{1,S}(I, P, M),$$
$$\xi^{\sharp}_{B,S}(p, P, M) \;\equiv\; \lambda^{\sharp}_B(p, P, M),$$
$$\zeta^{\sharp}_S(p, P, M) \;\equiv\; \lambda^{\sharp}_1(p, P, M),$$

and where r, b, etc. are as defined above. The inverse distribution function ξ^{-1} *is defined as follows:*

$$\xi^{-1}_{B,S}(p, i, P, M) \;\mapsto\; I \;=\; \lambda^{-1}_B(p^*, i^*, P, M),$$

$$(p^*, i^*) \;\equiv\; \begin{cases} (p, i) & \Lambda \geq l_S \\ (p_2, i_2) & \Lambda < l_S \;, \end{cases}$$

$$\Lambda \;\equiv\; \left\lfloor \frac{i}{BS} \right\rfloor, \quad I^*_{BS} \;=\; p + \Lambda P \;,$$

$$p_2 \;\equiv\; \left\lfloor \frac{I^*_{BS}}{l_S} \right\rfloor,$$

$$i_2 \;\equiv\; BS \left(I^*_{BS} \bmod l_S \right) + (i \bmod BS),$$

with

$$\zeta_S^{-1}(p, i, P, M) \equiv \xi_{1,S}^{-1}(p, i, P, M).$$

For $S = 1$, a block-scatter distribution results, while for $S \geq S_{crit} \equiv \lfloor l/2 \rfloor + 1$, the generalized block-linear distribution function is recovered. See also [Skjellum:90c].

Definition 4 (Data Distributions)

Given a data-distribution function family $(\mu, \mu^{-1}, \mu^{\sharp})$ $((\nu, \nu^{-1}, \nu^{\sharp}))$, a process list of P (Q), M (N) as the number of coefficients, and a row (respectively, column) orientation, a row (column) data distribution $\mathcal{G}^{row}$ $(\mathcal{G}^{col})$ is defined as:

$$\mathcal{G}^{row} \equiv \left\{ (\mu, \mu^{-1}, \mu^{\sharp}); P, M \right\},$$

respectively,

$$\mathcal{G}^{col} \equiv \left\{ (\nu, \nu^{-1}, \nu^{\sharp}); Q, N \right\}.$$

A two-dimensional data distribution may be identified as consisting of a row and column distribution defined over a two-dimensional process grid of $P \times Q$ processes, as $\mathcal{G} \equiv (\mathcal{G}^{row}, \mathcal{G}^{col})$.

Further discussion and detailed comparisons on data-distribution functions are offered in [Skjellum:90c]. Figure 9.13 illustrates the effects of linear and scatter data-distribution functions on a small rectangular array of coefficients.

9.5.5   Performance Versus Scattering

Consider a fixed logical process grid of R processes, with $P \times Q = R$. For the sake of argument, assume partial row pivoting during LU factorization for the retention of numerical stability. Then, for the LU factorization, it is well known that a scatter distribution is "good" for the matrix rows, and optimal if no off-diagonal pivots were chosen. Furthermore, the optimal column distribution is also scatter, because columns are chosen in order for partial row pivoting. Compatibly, a scatter distribution of matrix rows is also "good" for the triangular solves. However, for triangular solves, the best column distribution is linear, because this implies less intercolumn communication, as we detail below. In short, the optimal configurations conflict, and because explicit redistribution is expensive, a static compromise must be chosen. We address this need to compromise through the one-parameter distribution function, ζ, described in the previous section, offering a variable degree of scattering via the S-parameter. To first order, changing S does not affect the cost of computing the Jacobian (assuming columnwise finite-difference computation), because each process column works independently.

It's important to note that triangular solves derive no benefit from $Q > 1$. The standard column-oriented solve keeps one process column active at any given time. For any column distribution, the updated right-hand-side vectors are retransmitted W times (process column-to-process column) during the triangular solve—whenever the active process column changes. There are at least $W_{min} \equiv Q - 1$ such transmissions (linear distribution), and at most $W_{max} \equiv N - 1$ transmissions (scatter distribution). The complexity of this retransmission is $O(WN/P)$, representing quadratic work in N for $W \sim N$.

Calculation complexity for a sparse triangular solve is proportional to the number of elements in the triangular matrix, with a low leading coefficient. Often, there are $O(N^{1.x})$ with $x < 1$ elements in the triangular matrices, including fill. This operation is then $O(N^{1.x}/P)$, which is less than quadratic in N. Consequently, for large W, the retransmission step is likely of greater cost than the original calculation. This retransmission effect constrains the amount of scattering and size of Q in order to have any chance of concurrent speedup in the triangular solves.

Using the one-parameter distribution with $S \geq 1$ implies that $W \approx N/S$, so that the retransmission complexity is $O(N^2/SP)$. Consequently, we can bound the amount of retransmission work by making S sufficiently large. Clearly, $S = S_{crit}$ is a hard upper bound, because we reach the linear distribution limit at that value of the parameter. We suggest picking $S \approx 10$ as a first guess, and $S \sim \sqrt{N}$, more optimistically. The former choice basically reduces retransmission effort by an order of magnitude. Both examples in the following section illustrate the effectiveness of choosing S by these heuristics.

The two-parameter ξ distribution can be used on the matrix rows to trade off load balance in the factorizations and triangular solves against the amount of (communication) effort needed to compute the Jacobian. In particular, a greater degree of scattering can dramatically increase the time required for a Jacobian computation (depending heavily on the underlying equation structure and problem), but significantly reduce load imbalance during the linear algebra steps. The communication overhead caused by multiple process rows suggests shifting toward smaller P and larger Q (a squatter grid), in which case greater concurrency is attained in the Jacobian computation, and the additional communication previously induced is then somewhat mitigated. The one-parameter distribution used on the matrix columns then proves effective in controlling the cost of the triangular solves by choosing the minimally allowable amount of column scattering.

Let's specify make explicit the performance objectives we consider when tuning S, and, more generally, when tuning the grid shape $P \times Q = R$. In the modified Newton iteration, for instance, a Jacobian factorization is reused until convergence slows unacceptably. An "LU Factorization + Backsolve" step is followed by η "Forward + Backsolves," with $\eta \sim O(1)$ typically (and varying dynamically throughout the calculation). Assuming an averaged η, say η^* (perhaps as large as five [Brenan:89a]), then our first-level performance goal is a heuristic minimization of

$$T_{LU} + (\eta^* + 1)T_{Back} + \eta^* T_{Forward}$$

over S for fixed P, Q. $\eta^* > 1$ more heavily weights the reduction of triangular solve costs versus B-mode factorization than we might at first have assumed, placing a greater potential gain on the one-parameter distribution for higher overall performance. We generally want heuristically to optimize

$$T_{Jac} + T_{LU} + (\eta^* + 1)T_{Back} + \eta^* T_{Forward}$$

over S, P, Q, R. Then, the possibility of fine-tuning row and column distributions is important, as is the use of non-power-of-two grid shapes.

9.5.6   Performance

Order 13040 Example

We consider an order 13040 banded matrix with a bandwidth of 326 under partial row pivoting. For this example, we have compiled timing results for a 16×12 process grid with random matrices (entries have range 0–10,000), using different values of S on the column distribution (Table 9.4). We indicate timing for A-mode, B-mode, Backsolves and Forward- and Backsolves together ("Solve" heading). For this example, $S = 30$ saves 76% of the triangular solve cost compared to $S = 1$, or approximately 186 seconds, roughly 6 seconds above the linear optimal. Simultaneously, we incur about 17 seconds additional cost in B-mode, while saving about 93 seconds in the Backsolve. Assuming $\eta^* = 1$ ($\eta^* = 0$), in the first above-mentioned objective function, we save about 262 (respectively, 76) seconds. Based on this example, and other experiences, we conclude that this is a successful practical technique for improving overall sparse linear algebra performance. The following example further bolsters this conclusion.

Table 9.4: Order 13040 Band Matrix Performance

Distribution:		(time in seconds)			
Row	Column	A-Mode	B-Mode	Backsolve	Solve
Scatter	S=1	1.140×10^3	1.603×10^2	1.196×10^2	2.426×10^2
	S=10	1.148×10^3	1.696×10^2	3.294×10^1	6.912×10^1
	S=25	1.091×10^3	1.670×10^2	2.713×10^1	5.752×10^1
	S=30	1.095×10^3	1.769×10^2	2.653×10^1	5.631×10^1
	S=40	1.116×10^3	2.157×10^2	2.573×10^1	5.472×10^1
	S=50	1.127×10^3	2.157×10^2	2.764×10^1	5.743×10^1
	S=100	1.279×10^3	4.764×10^2	2.520×10^1	5.367×10^1
	Linear	2.247×10^3	1.161×10^3	2.333×10^1	4.993×10^1

Note: The above timing data, for the 16×12 grid configuration with scattered rows, indicates the importance of the one-parameter distribution with $S > 1$ for balancing factorization cost versus triangular-solve cost. The random matrices, of order 13040, have an upper bandwidth of 164 and a lower bandwidth of 162. "Best" performance occurs in the range $S \approx 25 \ldots 40$.

Order 2500 Example

Now, we turn to a timing example of an order 2500 sparse, random matrix. The matrix has a random diagonal, plus 2 percent random fill of the off-diagonals; entries have a dynamic range of 0–10,000. Normally, data is averaged over random matrices for each grid shape (as noted), and over four repetitive runs for each random matrix. Partial row pivoting was used exclusively. Table 9.5 compiles timings for various grid shapes of row-scatter/column-scatter, and row-scatter/column-$(S = 10)$ distributions, for as few as nine nodes and as many as 128. Memory limitations set the lower bound on the number of nodes.

This example demonstrates that speedups are possible for this reasonably small sparse example with this general-purpose solver, and that the one-parameter distribution is critical to achieving overall better performance even for this random, essentially unstructured example. Without the one-parameter distribution, triangular-solve performance is poor, except in grid configurations where the factorization is itself degraded (e.g., 2×16). Furthermore, the choice of $S = 10$ is universally reasonable for the $Q > 1$

Table 9.5: Order 2500 Matrix Performance. Performance is a function of grid shape and size, and S-parameter. "Best" performance is for the 16×6 grid with $S = 10$.

Shape	Column Dist.*	A-Mode	B-Mode	Backsolve	Solve	Avgs
			(time in seconds)			
6×1	Scatter	4.859×10^2	2.145×10^2	3.025×10^0	6.696×10^0	3
3×3	Scatter	3.567×10^2	1.783×10^2	1.997×10^1	4.115×10^1	1
3×4	Scatter	3.101×10^2	1.303×10^2	2.149×10^1	4.452×10^1	1
4×3	Scatter	2.778×10^2	1.526×10^2	1.728×10^1	3.537×10^1	1
2×16	Scatter	4.500×10^2	3.350×10^2	3.175×10^0	1.101×10^1	1
12×1	Scatter	2.636×10^2	1.206×10^2	4.0188×10^0	8.340×10^0	3
16×1	Scatter	2.085×10^2	1.000×10^2	4.856×10^0	9.8744×10^0	3
8×2	Scatter	2.013×10^2	9.41×10^1	1.127×10^1	2.295×10^1	3
	$S = 10$	1.997×10^2	9.63×10^1	4.508×10^0	9.399×10^0	3
4×4	Scatter	2.371×10^2	1.056×10^2	1.225×10^1	3.549×10^1	3
	$S = 10$	2.329×10^2	1.104×10^2	4.192×10^0	9.406×10^0	3
4×6	Scatter	1.456×10^2	7.72×10^1	1.723×10^1	3.528×10^1	3
	$S = 10$	1.684×10^2	8.85×10^1	4.206×10^0	9.303×10^0	3
12×2	Scatter	1.490×10^2	6.95×10^1	9.08×10^0	1.851×10^1	3
	$S = 10$	1.425×10^2	6.54×10^1	4.557×10^0	9.439×10^0	3
12×3	Scatter	1.0429×10^2	5.39×10^1	9.34×10^0	1.898×10^1	3
	$S = 10$	1.0382×10^2	5.42×10^1	4.539×10^0	9.390×10^0	3
8×8	Scatter	1.154×10^2	6.16×10^1	1.1082×10^1	2.2906×10^1	3
	$S = 10$	1.145×10^2	6.64×10^1	4.4600×10^0	9.651×10^0	3
12×6	Scatter	6.470×10^1	3.527×10^1	9.410×10^0	1.9141×10^1	3
	$S = 10$	6.265×10^1	3.417×10^1	4.555×10^0	9.495×10^0	3
16×6	Scatter	5.014×10^1	2.744×10^1	9.085×10^0	1.8327×10^1	3
	$S = 10$	4.984×10^1	2.905×10^1	5.2811×10^0	1.0740×10^1	3
16×8	Scatter	7.046×10^1	3.879×10^1	8.9535×10^0	1.8243×10^1	3
	$S = 10$	6.70×10^1	3.854×10^1	5.239×10^0	1.0816×10^1	3

*Row distribution always scattered.

grid shapes illustrated here, so the distribution proves easy to tune for this type of matrix. We are able to maintain an almost constant speed for the triangular solves while increasing speed for both the A-mode and B-mode factorizations. We presume, based on experience, that triangular-solve times are comparable to the sequential solution times—further study is needed in this area to see if and how performance can be improved. The consistent A-mode to B-mode ratio of approximately two is attributed primarily to reduced communication costs in B-mode, realized through the elimination of essentially all combine operations in B-mode.

While triangular-solve performance exemplifies sequentialism in the algorithm, it should be noted that we do achieve significant overall performance improvements between 6 nodes and 96 (16 × 6 grid) nodes, and that the repeatedly used B-mode factorization remains dominant compared to the triangular solves even for 128 nodes. Consequently, efforts aimed at increasing performance of the B-mode factorization (at the expense of additional A-mode work) are interesting to consider. For the factorizations, we also expect that we are achieving nontrivial speedups relative to one node, but we are unable to quantify this at present because of the memory limitations alluded to above.

9.5.7 Conclusions

There are several classes of future work to be considered. First, we need to take the A-mode "analyze" phase to its logical completion, by including pivot-order sorting of the L/U pointer structures to improve performance for systems that should demonstrate subquadratic sequential complexity. This will require minor modifications to B-mode (that already takes advantage of column-traversing elimination), to reduce testing for inactive rows as the elimination progresses. We already realize optimal computation work in the triangular solves, and we mitigate the effect of $Q > 1$ quadratic communication work using the one-parameter distribution.

Second, we need to exploit "timelike" concurrency in linear algebra—multiple pivots. This has been addressed by Alaghband for shared-memory implementations of MA28 with $O(N)$-complexity heuristics [Alaghband:89a]. These efforts must be reconsidered in the multicomputer setting and effective variations must be devised. This approach should prove an important source of additional speedup for many chemical engineering applications, because of the tendency towards extreme sparsity, with mainly band and/or block-diagonal structure.

Third, we could exploit new communication strategies and data redistribution. Within a process grid, we could incrementally redistribute L/U by utilizing the inherent broadcasts of L columns and U rows to improve load balance in the triangular solves at the expense of slightly more factorization computational overhead and significantly more memory overhead (a factor of nearly two). Memory overhead could be reduced at the expense of further communication if explicit pivoting were used concomitantly.

Fourth, we can develop adaptive broadcast algorithms that track the known load imbalance in the B-mode factorization, and shift greater communication emphasis to nodes with less computational work remaining. For example, the pivot column is naturally a "hot spot" because the multiplier column (L column) must be computed before broadcast to the awaiting process columns. Allowing the non-pivot columns to handle the majority of the communication could be beneficial, even though this implies additional overall communication. Similarly, we might likewise apply this to the pivot row broadcast, and especially for the pivot process, because it must participate in two broadcast operations.

We could utilize two process grids. When rows (columns) of $U(L)$ are broadcast, extra broadcasts to a secondary process grid could reasonably be included. The secondary process grid could work on redistributing L/U to an efficient process grid shape and size for triangular solves while the factorization continues on the primary grid. This overlapping of communication and computation could also be used to reduce the cost of transposing the solution vector from column-distributed to row-distributed, which normally follows the triangular solves.

The sparse solver supports arbitrary user-defined pivoting strategies. We have considered but not fully explored issues of fill-reduction versus minimum time; in particular we have implemented a Markowitz-count fill-reduction strategy [Duff:86a]. Study of the usefulness of partial column pivoting and other strategies is also needed. We will report on this in the future.

Reduced-communication pivoting and parametric distributions can be applied immediately to concurrent dense solvers with definite improvements in performance. While triangular solves remain lower-order work in the dense case, and may sensibly admit less tuning in S, the reduction of pivot communication is certain to improve performance. A new dense solver exploiting these ideas is under construction at present.

In closing, we suggest that the algorithms generating the sequences of sparse matrices must themselves be reconsidered in the concurrent setting. Changes that introduce multiple right-hand sides could help to amortize linear algebra cost over multiple timelike steps of the higher level algorithm. Because of inevitable load imbalance, idle processor time is essentially free— algorithms that find ways to use this time by asking for more speculative (partial) solutions appear useful in working towards higher performance.

This work was performed by Anthony Skjellum and Alvin Leung while the latter held a Caltech Summer Undergraduate Research Fellowship. A helpful contribution was the dense concurrent linear algebra library provided by Eric Van de Velde, as well as his prototype sparse concurrent linear algebra library.

9.6 Concurrent DASSL Applied to Dynamic Distillation Column Simulation

The accurate, high-speed solution of systems of ordinary differential-algebraic equations (DAEs) of low index is of great importance in chemical, electrical, and other engineering disciplines. Petzold's Fortran-based DASSL is the most widely used sequential code for solving DAEs. We have devised and implemented a completely new C code, Concurrent DASSL, specifically for multicomputers and patterned on DASSL [Skjellum:89a;90c]. In this work, we address the issues of data distribution and the performance of the overall algorithm, rather than just that of individual steps. Concurrent DASSL is designed as an open, application-independent environment below which linear algebra algorithms may be added in addition to standard support for dense and sparse algorithms. The user may furthermore attach explicit data interconversions between the main computational steps, or choose compromise distributions. A "problem formulator" (simulation layer) must be constructed above Concurrent DASSL, for any specific problem domain. We indicate performance for a particular chemical engineering application, a sequence of coupled distillation columns. Future efforts are cited in conclusion.

9.6.1 Introduction

We discuss the design of a general-purpose integration system for ordinary differential-algebraic equations of low index, following up on our more preliminary discussion in [Skjellum:89a]. The new solver, Concurrent DASSL, is a parallel, C-language implementation of the algorithm codified in Petzold's DASSL, a widely used Fortran-based solver for DAE's [Petzold:83a], [Brenan:89a], and is based on a loosely synchronous model of communicating sequential processes [Hoare:78a]. Concurrent DASSL retains the same numerical properties as the sequential algorithm, but introduces important new degrees of freedom compared to it. We identify the main computational steps in the integration process; for each of these steps, we specify algorithms that have correctness independent of data distribution.

We cover the computational aspects of the major computational steps, and their data distribution preferences for highest performance. We indicate the properties of the concurrent sparse linear algebra as it relates to the rest of the calculation. We describe the proto-Cdyn simulation layer, a distillation-simulation-oriented Concurrent DASSL driver which, despite specificity, exposes important requirements for concurrent solution of ordinary DAE's; the ideas behind a template formulation for simulation are, for example, expressed.

We indicate formulation issues and specific features of the chemical engineering problem—dynamic distillation simulation. We indicate results for an example in this area, which demonstrates not only the feasibility of this method, but also the need for additional future work. This is needed both on the sparse linear algebra, and on modifying the DASSL algorithm to reveal more concurrency, thereby amortizing the cost of linear algebra over more time steps in the algorithm.

9.6.2   Mathematical Formulation

We address the following initial-value problem consisting of combinations of N linear and nonlinear coupled, ordinary differential-algebraic equations over the interval $t \in [T_0, T_1]$:

$$\mathbf{IVP}(\mathbf{F}, \mathbf{u}, \mathbf{Z}_0, [T_0, T_1]; N, P):$$

$$\mathbf{F}(\mathbf{Z}, \dot{\mathbf{Z}}, \mathbf{u}; t) = \mathbf{0}, \qquad t \in [T_0, T_1],$$
$$\mathbf{Z}(t = T_0) \equiv \mathbf{Z}_0, \quad \dot{\mathbf{Z}}(t = T_0) \equiv \dot{\mathbf{Z}}_0, \qquad (9.11)$$

with unknown state vector $\mathbf{Z}(t) \in \Re^N$, known external inputs $\mathbf{u}(t) \in \Re^P$, where $\mathbf{F}(\bullet; t) \mapsto \Re^N$ and $\mathbf{Z}_0, \dot{\mathbf{Z}}_0 \in \Re^N$ are the given initial-value, derivative vectors, respectively. We will refer to Equation 9.11's deviation from $\mathbf{0}$ as the residuals or residual vector. Evaluating the residuals means computing $\mathbf{F}(\mathbf{Z}, \dot{\mathbf{Z}}, \mathbf{u}; t)$ ("model evaluation") for specified arguments $\mathbf{Z}, \dot{\mathbf{Z}}, \mathbf{u}$ and t.

DASSL's integration algorithm can be used to solve systems fully implicit in $\mathbf{Z}$ and $\dot{\mathbf{Z}}$ and of index zero or one, and specially structured forms of index two (and higher) [Brenan:89a, Chapter 5], where the index is the minimum number of times that part or all of Equation 9.11 must be differentiated with respect to t in order to express $\dot{\mathbf{Z}}$ as a continuous function of $\mathbf{Z}$ and t [Brenan:89a, page 17].

By substituting a finite-difference approximation $\mathcal{D}_i \mathbf{Z}$ for $\dot{\mathbf{Z}}$, we obtain:

$$\mathbf{F}_{\mathcal{D}}(\mathbf{Z}_i; \tau_i) \equiv \mathbf{F}(\mathbf{Z}_i, \mathcal{D}_i \mathbf{Z}, \mathbf{u}_i; t = \tau_i) = \mathbf{0}, \qquad (9.12)$$

a set of (in general) nonlinear *staticized* equations. A sequence of Equation 9.12's will have to be solved, one at each discrete time $t = \tau_i$, $i =$

$1, 2, \ldots, M^2$, in the numerical approximation scheme; neither M nor the τ_i's need be predetermined. In DASSL, the variable step-size integration algorithm picks the τ_i's as the integration progresses, based on its assessment of the local error. The discretization operator for $\dot{\mathbf{Z}}$, $\mathcal{D}$, varies during the numerical integration process and hence is subscripted as $\mathcal{D}_i$.

The usual way to solve an instance of the staticized equations, Equation 9.12, is via the familiar Newton-Raphson iterative method (yielding $\mathbf{Z}_i \equiv \mathbf{Z}_i^\infty$):

$$\mathbf{Z}_i^{k+1} = \mathbf{Z}_i^k - c \left\{ \nabla_{\mathbf{Z}} \mathbf{F}_{\mathcal{D}} \left(\mathbf{Z}_i^{m_k}; \tau_i \right) \right\}^{-1} \mathbf{F}_{\mathcal{D}} \left(\mathbf{Z}_i^k; \tau_i \right), \quad k = 0, 1, \ldots \quad (9.13)$$

given an initial, sufficiently good approximation $\mathbf{Z}_i^0$. The classical method is recovered for $m_k = k$ and $c = 1$, whereas a modified (damped) Newton-Raphson method results for $m_k < k$ (respectively, $c < 1$). In the original DASSL algorithm and in Concurrent DASSL, the Jacobian $\nabla_{\mathbf{Z}} \mathbf{F}_{\mathcal{D}}(\mathbf{Z})$ is computed by finite differences rather than analytically; this departure leads in another sense to a modified Newton-Raphson method even though $m_k = k$ and $c = 1$ might always be satisfied. For termination, a limit $k \leq k^*$ is imposed; a further stopping criterion of the form $\|\mathbf{Z}_i^{k+1} - \mathbf{Z}_i^k\| < \epsilon$ is also incorporated (see Brenan et al. [Brenan:89a, pages 121–124]).

Following Brenan et al., the approximation $\mathcal{D}_i \mathbf{Z}$ is replaced by a BDF-generated linear approximation, $\alpha \mathbf{Z} + \beta$, and the Jacobian

$$\nabla_{\mathbf{Z}} \mathbf{F}(\mathbf{Z}, \alpha \mathbf{Z} + \beta, \mathbf{u}; t) = \frac{\partial \mathbf{F}}{\partial \mathbf{Z}} + \alpha \frac{\partial \mathbf{F}}{\partial \dot{\mathbf{Z}}}. \quad (9.14)$$

From this approximation, we define $\mathbf{F}_{\alpha,\beta}(\mathbf{Z}; \tau_i)$ in the intuitive way. We then consider Taylor's Theorem with remainder, from which we can easily express a forward finite-difference approximation for each Jacobian column (assuming sufficient smoothness of $\mathbf{F}_{\alpha,\beta}$) with a scaled difference of two residual vectors:

$$\mathbf{F}_{\alpha,\beta} \left(\mathbf{Z} + \delta_j; \tau_i \right) - \mathbf{F}_{\alpha,\beta} \left(\mathbf{Z}; \tau_i \right) = \left\{ \nabla_{\mathbf{Z}} \mathbf{F}_{\alpha,\beta} \left(\mathbf{Z}; \tau_i \right) \right\} \delta_j + O \left(\|\delta_j\|_2^2 \right) \quad (9.15)$$

By picking δ_j proportional to $\mathbf{e}_j$, the jth unit vector in the natural basis for $\Re^N$, namely $\delta_j = d_j \, \mathbf{e}_j$, Equation 9.15 yields a first-order-accurate approximation in d_j of the jth column of the Jacobian matrix:

$$\frac{\mathbf{F}_{\alpha,\beta}(\mathbf{Z} + \delta_j; \tau_i) - \mathbf{F}_{\alpha,\beta}(\mathbf{Z}; \tau_i)}{d_j} = \left\{ \nabla_{\mathbf{Z}} \mathbf{F}_{\alpha,\beta}(\mathbf{Z}; \tau_i) \right\} \mathbf{e}_j + O(d_j),$$
$$j = 1, \ldots, N \quad (9.16)$$

---

[2]And more at trial timepoints which are discarded by the integration algorithm.

Each of these N Jacobian-column computations is independent and trivially parallelizable. It's well known, however, that for special structures such as banded and block n-diagonal matrices, and even for general sparse matrices, a single residual can be used to generate multiple Jacobian columns [Brenan:89a], [Duff:86a]. We discuss these issues as part of the concurrent formulation section below.

The solution of the Jacobian linear system of equations is required for each k-iteration, either through a direct (e.g., LU-factorization) or iterative (e.g., preconditioned-conjugate-gradient) method. The most advantageous solution approach depends on N as well as special mathematical properties and/or structure of the Jacobian matrix $\nabla_{\mathbf{Z}} \mathbf{F}_{\mathcal{D}}$. Together, the inner (linear equation solution) and outer (Newton-Raphson iteration) loops solve a single time point; the overall algorithm generates a sequence of solution points $\mathbf{Z}_i$, $i = 0, 1, \ldots, M$.

In the present work, we restrict our attention to direct, sparse linear algebra as described in [Skjellum:90d], although future versions of Concurrent DASSL will support the iterative linear algebra approaches by Ashby, Lee, Brown, Hindmarsh et al. [Ashby:90a], [Brown:91a]. For the sparse LU factorization, the factors are stored and reused in the modified Newton scenario. Then, repeated use of the old Jacobian implies just a forward- and back-solve step using the triangular factors L and U. Practically, we can use the Jacobian for up to about five steps [Brenan:89a]. The useful lifetime of a single Jacobian evidently depends somewhat strongly on details of the integration procedure [Brenan:89a].

9.6.3   proto-Cdyn – Simulation Layer

To use the Concurrent DASSL system on other than toy problems, a simulation layer must be constructed above it. The purpose of this layer is to accept a problem specification from within a specific problem domain, and formulate that specification for concurrent solution as a set of differential-algebraic equations, including any needed data. On one hand, such a layer could explicitly construct the subset of equations needed for each processor, generate the appropriate code representing the residual functions, and create a set of node programs for effecting the simulation. This is the most flexible approach, allowing the user to specify arbitrary nonlinear DAEs. It has the disadvantage of requiring a lot of compiling and linking for each run in which the problem is changed in any significant respect (including but not limited to data distribution), although with sophisticated tactics, parametric variations within equations could be permitted without recompiling from scratch, and incremental linking could be supported.

We utilize a template-based approach here, as we do in the Waveform-Relaxation paradigm for concurrent dynamic simulation [Skjellum:88a]. This is akin to the *ASCEND II* methodology utilized by Kuru and many others [Kuru:81a]. It is a compromise approach from the perspective of flexibility; interesting physical prototype subsystems are encapsulated into compiled code as templates. A template is a conceptual building block with states, nonstates, parameters, inputs, and outputs (see below). A general network made from instantiations of templates can be constructed at run time without changing any executable code. User input specifies the number and type of each template, their interconnection pattern, and the initial value of systemic states and extraneous (nonstate) variables, plus the value of adjustable parameters and more elaborate data, such as physical properties. The addition of templates requires new subroutines for the evaluation of the residuals of their associated DAEs, and for interfacing to the remainder of the system (e.g., parsing of user input, interconnectivity issues). With suitable automated tools, this addition process can be made straightforward to the user.

Importantly, the use of a template-based methodology does not imply a degradation in the numerical quality of the model equations or solution method used. We are not obliged to tear equations based on templates or groups of templates as is done in sequential-modular simulators [Westerberg:79a], [Cook:80a], where "sequential" refers in this sense to the stepwise updating of equation subsets, without connection to the number of computers assigned to the problem solution.

Ideally, the simulation layer could be made universal. That is, a generic layer of high flexibility and structural elegance would be created once and for all (and without predilection for a specific computational engine). Thereafter, appropriate templates would be added to articulate the simulator for a given problem domain. This is certainly possible with high-quality simulators such as ASCEND II and Chemsim (a recent Fortran-based simulator driving DASSL and MA28 [Andersen:88a], [Duff:77a], [Petzold:83a]). Even so, we have chosen to restrict our efforts to a more modest simulation layer, called proto-Cdyn, which can create arbitrary networks of coupled distillation columns. This restricted effort has required significant effort, and already allows us to explore many of the important issues of concurrent dynamic simulation. General-purpose simulators are for future consideration. They must address significant questions of user-interface in addition to concurrency-formulation issues.

In the next paragraphs, we describe the important features of proto-Cdyn. In doing so, we indicate important issues for any Concurrent DASSL driver.

Template Structure

A template is a prototype for a sequence of DAEs which can be used repeatedly in different instantiations. Normally, but not always, the template corresponds to some subsystem of a physical-model description of a system, like a tank or distillation tray. The key characteristics of a template are: the number of integration states it incorporates (typically fixed), the number of nonstate variables it incorporates (typically fixed), its input and output connections to other templates, and external sources (forcing functions) and sinks. State variables participate in the overall DASSL integration process. Nonstates are defined as variables which, given the states of a template alone, may be computed uniquely. They are essentially local tear variables. It is up to the template designer whether or not to use such local tear variables: They impact the numerical quality of the solution, in principle. Alternative formulations, where all variables of a template are treated as states, can be posed and comparisons made. Because of the superlinear growth of linear algebra complexity, the introduction of extra integration states must be justified on the basis of numerical accuracy. Otherwise, they artificially slow down the problem solution, perhaps significantly. Nonstates are extremely convenient and practically useful; they appear in all the dynamic simulators we have come across.

The template state and nonstate structure imply a two-phase residual computation. First, given a state $\mathbf{Z}$, the non-states of each template are updated on a template-by-template basis. Then, given its states and nonstates, inputs from other templates and external inputs, each template's residuals may be computed. In the sequential implementation, this poses no particular nuisances, other than having two evaluation loops over all templates. However, in concurrent evaluation, a communication phase intervenes between nonstate and residual updates. This communication phase transmits all states and nonstates appearing as outputs of templates to their corresponding inputs at other templates. This transmission mechanism is considered below under concurrent formulation.

Problem Preformulation

In general, the "optimal" ordering for the equations of a dynamic simulation will in general be too difficult to establish[3], because of the NP-hard issues involved in structure selection. However, many important heuristics can be applied, such as those that precedence-order the nonlinear equations, and those that permute the Jacobian structure to a more nearly triangular or banded form [Duff:86a]. For the proto-Cdyn simulator, we skirt these issues entirely, because it proves easy to arrange a network of columns to produce a "good structure"—a main block tridiagonal Jacobian structure with off-block-diagonal structure for the intercolumn connections, simply by taking the distillation columns with their states in tray-by-tray, top-down (or bottom-up) order.

Given a set of DAEs, and an ordering for the equations and states (i.e., rows and columns of the Jacobian, respectively), we need to partition these equations between the multicomputer nodes, according to a two-dimensional process grid of shape $P \times Q = R$. The partitioning of the equations forms, in main part, the so-called concurrent database. This grid structure is illustrated in [Skjellum:90d, Figure 2.]. In proto-Cdyn, we utilize a single process grid for the entire Concurrent DASSL calculation. That is, we do not currently exploit the Concurrent DASSL feature which allows explicit transformations between the main calculational phases (see below). In each process column, the entire set of equations is to be reproduced, so that any process column can compute not only the entire residual vector for a prediction calculation, but also, any column of the Jacobian matrix.

A mapping between the global and local equations must be created. In the general case, it will be difficult to generate a closed-form expression for either the global-to-local mapping or its inverse (that also require $< O(N)$ storage). At most, we will have on a hand a partial (or weak) inverse in each process, so that the corresponding global index of each local index will be available. Furthermore, in each node, a partial global-to-local list of indices associated with the given node will be stored in global sort order. Then, by binary search, a weak global-to-local mapping will be possible in each process. That is, each process will be able to identify if a global index resides within it, and the corresponding local index. A strong mapping for row (column) indices will require communication between all the processes

---

[3]Optimality per se hinges on what our objective is. If, for instance, we want minimum time for LU factorization, the objective of minimum fill-in still does not guarantee minimum time in a concurrent setting.

in a process row (respectively, column). In the foregoing, we make the tacit assumption that it is an unreasonable practice to use storage proportional to the entire problem size N in each node, except if this unscalability can be removed cheaply when necessary for large problems.

The proto-Cdyn simulator works with templates of specific structure—each template is a form of a distillation tray and generates the same number of integration states. It therefore skirts the need for weak distributions. Consequently, the entire row-mapping procedure can be accomplished using the closed-form general two-parameter distribution function family ξ described in [Skjellum:90d], where the block size B is chosen as the number of integration states per template. The column-mapping procedure is accomplished with the one-parameter distribution function family ζ also described in [Skjellum:90d]. The effects of row and column degree-of-scattering are described in [Skjellum:90d] with attention to linear algebra performance.

9.6.4 Concurrent Formulation

Overview

Next, we turn to Equation 9.11's (that is, **IVP**'s) concurrent numerical solution via the DASSL algorithm. We cover the major computational steps in abstract, and we also describe the generic aspects of proto-Cdyn in this connection. In the subsequent section, we discuss issues peculiar to the distillation simulation.

Broadly, the concurrent solution of **IVP** consists of three block operations: startup, dynamic simulation, and a cleanup phase. Significant concurrency is apparent only in the dynamic simulation phase. We will assume that the simulation interval requested generates enough work so that the startup and cleanup phases prove insignificant by comparison and consequently pose no serious Amdahl's-law bottleneck. Given this assumption, we can restrict our attention to a single step of **IVP** as illustrated schematically in Figure 9.15.

In the startup phase, a sequential host program interprets the user specification for the simulation. From this it generates the concurrent database: the templates and their mutual interconnections, data needed by particular templates, and a distribution of this information among the processes that are to participate. The processes are themselves spawned and fed their respective databases. Once they receive their input information, the processes rebuild the data structures for interfacing with Concurrent DASSL, and

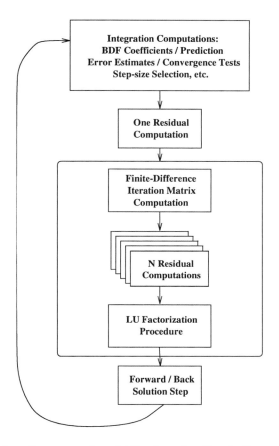

Figure 9.15: Major Computational Blocks of a Single Integration Step. A single step in the integration begins with a number of BDF-related computations, including the solution "prediction" step. Then, "correction" is achieved through Newton iteration steps, each involving a Jacobian computation, and linear-system solution (LU factorization plus forward- and back-solves). The computation of the Jacobian in turn relies upon multiple independent residual calculations, as shown. The three items enclosed in the rounded rectangle (Jacobian computation—through at most N Residual computations—and LU factorization) are, in practice, computed less often than the others—the old Jacobian matrix is used in the iteration loop until convergence slows intolerably.

for generating the residuals. Tolerances and initial derivatives must be computed and/or estimated. Furthermore, in each process column, the processes must rendezvous to finalize their communication labelling for the transmission of states and nonstates to be performed during the residual calculation. This provides the basis for a reactive, deadlock-free update procedure described below.

The cleanup phase basically retrieves appropriate state values and returns them to the host for propagation to the user. Cleanup may be interspersed intermittently with the actual dynamic simulation. It provides a simple record of the results of simulation and terminates the concurrent processes at the simulation's conclusion.

The dynamic simulation phase consists of repetitive prediction and correction steps, and marches in time. Each successful time step requires the solution of one or more instances of Equation 9.12—additional time steps that converge but fail to satisfy error tolerances, or fail to converge quickly enough, are necessarily discarded. In the next section, we cover aspects of these operations in more detail, for a single step.

Single Integration Step

The Integration Computations These computations of DASSL are a fixed-leading-coefficient, variable-stepsize and -order, backward-differentiation-formula (BDF) implicit integration scheme, described clearly in [Brenan:89a, Chapter 5] and outlined in [Petzold:83a]. Concurrent DASSL faithfully implements this numerical method, with no significant differences. Test problems run with the DASSL Fortran code and the new C code (on one and multiple computers) certify this degree of compatibility.

The sequential time complexity of the integration computations is $O(N)$, if considered separately from the residual calculation called in turn, which is also normally $O(N)$ (see below). We pose these operations on a $P \times Q = R$ grid, where we assume that each process column can compute complete residual vectors. Each process column repeats the entire prediction operations: There is no speedup associated with $Q > 1$, and we replicate all DASSL BDF and predictor vectors in each process column. Taller, narrower grids are likely to provide the overall greatest speedup, though the residual calculation may saturate (and slow down again) because of excessive vertical communication requirements. It's definitely not true that the $R \times 1$ shape is optimal in all cases.

The distribution of coefficients in the rows has no impact on the integration operations, and is dictated largely by the requirements of the residual calculation itself. In practical problems, the concurrent database cannot be reproduced in each process (cf., [Lorenz:92a]), so a given process will only be able to compute some of the residuals. Furthermore, we may not have complete freedom in scattering these equations, because there will often be a trade-off between the degree of scattering and the amount of communication needed to form the entire residual vector.

The amount of $O(N)$ integration-computation work is not terribly large—there is consequently a nontrivial but not tremendous effort involved in the integration computations. (Residual computations dominate in many if not most circumstances.) Integration operations consist mainly of vector-vector operations not requiring any interprocess communication and, in addition, fixed startup costs. Operations include prediction of the solution at the time point, initiation and control of the Newton iteration that "corrects" the solution, convergence and error-tolerance checking, and so forth. For example, the approximation $\mathcal{D}_i$ is chosen within this block using the BDF formulas. For these operations, each process column currently operates independently, and repetitively forms the results. Alternatively, each process column could stride with step Q, and row-combines could be used to propagate information across the columns [Skjellum:90a]. This alternative would increase speed for sufficiently large problems, and can easily be implemented. However, because of load imbalance in other stages of the calculation, we are convinced that including this type of synchronization could be an overall negative rather than positive to performance. This alternative will nevertheless be a future user-selectable option.

Included in these operations are a handful of norm operations, which constitute the main interprocess communication required by the integration computations step; norms are implemented concurrently via recursive doubling (combine) [Stone:87a], [Skjellum:90a]. Actually, the weighted norm used by DASSL requires two recursive doubling operations, each of which combines a scalar. The first operation obtains the vector coefficient of maximum absolute value, the second sums the weighted norm itself. Each can be implemented as Q independent column combines, each producing the same repetitive result, or a single Q-striding norm that takes advantage of the repetition of information, but utilizes two combines over the entire process grid. Both are supported in Concurrent DASSL, although the former is the default norm. As with the original DASSL, the norm function can be replaced, if desired.

Single Residuals   These are computed in prediction and as needed during correction. Multiple residuals are computed when forming the finite-difference Jacobian. Single residuals are computed repetitively in each process column, whereas the multiple residuals of a Jacobian computation are computed uniquely in the process columns.

Here, we consider the single residual computation required by the integration computations just described. Given a state vector $\mathbf{Z}$, and approximation for $\dot{\mathbf{Z}}$, we need to evaluate $\mathbf{F}(\mathbf{Z}, \dot{\mathbf{Z}}, \tau_i) \equiv \mathbf{F}_{\mathcal{D}}(\mathbf{Z}, \tau_i)$. The exploitable concurrency available in this step is strictly a function of the model equations. As defined, there are N equations in this system, so we expect to use at best N computers for this step. Practically, there will be interprocess communication between the process rows, corresponding to the connectivity among the equations. This will place an upper limit on $P \leq K$ (the number of row processes) that can be used before the speed will again decrease: We can expect efficient speedup for this step provided that the cost of the interprocess communication is insignificant compared to the single-equation grain size. As estimated in [Skjellum:90a], the granularity T_{comm}/T_{calc} for the Symult s2010 multicomputer is about fifty, so this implies about 450 floating-point operations per communication in order to achieve 90% concurrent efficiency in this phase.

Jacobian Computation   There is evidently much more available concurrency in this computational step than for the single residual and integration operations, since, for finite differencing, N independent residual computations are apparently required, each of which is a single-state perturbation of $\mathbf{Z}$. Based on our overview of the residual computation, we might naively expect to use $K \times N$ processes effectively; however, the simple perturbations can actually require much less model evaluation effort because of latency [Duff:86a], [Kuru:81a], which is directly a function of the sparsity structure of the model equations as seen in, Equation 9.11. In short, we can attain the same performance with much less than $K \times N$ processors.

In general, we'd like to consider the Jacobian computation on a rectangular grid. For this, we can consider using $P \times Q = R$ to accomplish the calculation. With a general grid shape, we exploit some concurrency in *both* the column evaluations and the residual computations, with $T_{Jac,P \times Q=R}$ the time for this step, $S_{Jac,P \times Q=R}$ the corresponding speedup, $T_{res,P}$ the residual evaluation time with P row processes, and $S_{res,P}$ the apparent speedup compared to one row process:

$$T_{Jac,P \times Q=R} \approx \lceil N/Q \rceil \times T_{res,P}$$
$$S_{Jac,P \times Q=R} \approx \frac{N}{\lceil N/Q \rceil} \times S_{res,P}$$

assuming no shortcuts are available as a result of latency. This timing is exemplified in the example below, which does not take advantage of latency.

There is additional work whenever the Jacobian structure is rebuilt for better numerical stability in the subsequent LU factorization (A-mode). Then, $O(N^2/PQ)$ work is involved in each process in the filling of the initial Jacobian. In the normal case, work proportional to the number of local nonzeroes plus fill elements is incurred in each process for refilling the sparse Jacobian structure.

Exploitation of Latency This approach has been considered in the Concurrent DASSL framework. We currently have experimental versions of two mechanisms, both of which are designed to work with the sparse-matrix structures associated with direct, sparse LU factorization ([Skjellum:90d]). The first is called "bandlike" Jacobian evaluation. For a banded Jacobian matrix of bandwidth b, only b residuals are needed to evaluate the Jacobian. This feature is incorporated into the original DASSL, along with a LINPACK banded solver. In Concurrent DASSL, collections of Jacobian columns are placed in each process column, according to the column data distribution, which thus far is picked solely to balance LU factorization and triangular-solve performance [Skjellum:90d]. In each process column, there will be "compatible" columns that can be evaluated using a single, composite perturbation. Identification of these compatible columns is accomplished by checks on the bandwidth overlap condition. Columns that possess off-band structure are stricken from the list and evaluated separately. Presumably, a heuristic algorithm could be employed further to increase the size of the compatible sets, but this is yet to be implemented. The same "greedy" algorithm of Curtis et al. used for the sequential reduction of Jacobian computation effort would be applied independently to each process column (see comments by [Duff:86a, Section 12.3]). Then, clearly, the column distribution affects the performance of the Jacobian computation, and the linear-algebra performance can no longer be viewed so readily in isolation.

We have also devised a "blocklike" format, which will be applied to block n-diagonal matrices that include some off-block entries as well. Optimally, fewer residual computations will be needed than for the banded case. The same column-by-column compatible sets will be created, and the Curtis algorithm can also be applied. Hopefully, because of the less restrictive compatibility requirement, the blocklike case will produce higher concurrent speedups than those attained using the conservative bandlike assumption for Jacobians possessing blocklike structure. Comparative results will be presented in a future paper.

The LU Factorization   Following the philosophy of Harwell's MA28, we have interfaced a new concurrent sparse solver to Concurrent DASSL, the details of which are quoted elsewhere in this proceedings [Skjellum:90d]. In short, there is a two-step factorization procedure: A-mode, which chooses stable pivots according to a user-specified function, and builds the sparse data structures dynamically; and B-mode, which reuses the data structures and pivot sequence on a similar matrix, but monitors stability with a growth-factor test. A-mode is repeated whenever necessary to avoid instability. We expect subcubic time complexity and subquadratic space complexity in N for the sparse solver. We attain acceptable factorization speedups for systems that are not narrow banded, and of sufficient size. We intend to incorporate multiple pivoting heuristic strategies, following [Alaghband:89a], to further improve performance of future versions of the solver. This may also contribute to better performance of the triangular solves.

Forward- and Back-solving Steps   These take the factored form $\mathsf{P}_R A \mathsf{P}_C^T = \hat{L}\hat{U}$, with $\hat{L}$ unit lower-triangular, $\hat{U}$ upper-triangular, and permutation matrices P_R, P_C, and solve $Ax = b$, using the implicit pivoting approach described in [Skjellum:90d]. Sequentially, the triangular solves each require work proportional to the number of entries in the respective triangular factor, including fill-in. We have yet to find an example of sufficient size for which we actually attain speedup for these operations, at least for the sparse case. At most, we try to prevent these operations from becoming competitive in cost to the B-mode factorization; we detail these efforts in [Skjellum:90d]. In brief, the optimum grid shape for the triangular solves has $Q = 1$, and P somewhat reduced from what we can use in all the other steps. As stated, P small seems better thus far, although for many examples increasing the overhead as a function of increasing P is not unacceptable (see [Skjellum:90d] and the example below).

Residual Communication This is an important aspect of the proto-Cdyn layer. As indicated in the startup-phase discussion, the members of a process column initially share information about the groups of states and nonstates they will exchange during a residual computation. For residual communication, a reactive transmission mechanism is employed to avoid deadlocks. Each process transmits its next group of states to the appropriate process and then looks for any receipt of state information. Along with the state values are indices that directly drive the destinations for these values. This index information is shared during the startup phase and allows the messages to drive the operation. Through nonblocking receives, this procedure avoids problems of transmission ordering. Regardless of the template structure, at most one send and receive is needed between any pair of column processes.

9.6.5 Chemical Engineering Example

The algorithms and formalism needed to run this example amount to about 70,000 lines of C code including the simulation layer, Concurrent DASSL, the linear algebra packages, and support functions [Skjellum:90a;90c;90d].

In this simulation, we consider seven distillation columns arranged in a tree sequence [Skjellum:90c], working on the distillation of eight alcohols: methanol, ethanol, propan-1-ol, propan-2-ol, butan-1-ol, 2-methyl propan-1-ol, butan-2-ol, and 2-methyl propan-2-ol. Each column has 143 trays. Each tray is initialized to a nonsteady condition, and the system is relaxed to the steady state governed by a single-feed stream to the first column in the sequence. This setup generates suitable dynamic activity for illustrating the cost of a single "transient" integration step.

We note the performance in Table 9.6. Because we have not exploited latency in the Jacobian computation, this calculation is quite expensive, as seen for the sequential times on a Sun 3/260 depicted there. (The timing for the Sun 3/260 is quite comparable to a single Symult s2010 node and was lightly loaded during this test run.) As expected, Jacobian calculations speed up efficiently, and we are able to get an approximate speedup of 100 for this step using 128 nodes. The A-mode linear algebra also speeds up significantly. The B-mode factorization speeds up negligibly and quickly slows down again for more than 16 nodes. Likewise, the triangular solves are significantly slower than the sequential time. It should be noted that B-mode reflects two orders of magnitude speed improvement over A-mode. This reflects the fact that we are seeing almost linear time complexity in B-mode, since this

Table 9.6: Order 9009 Dynamic Simulation Data

Grid Shape	Jacobian	(time in seconds)			
		A-mode	B-mode	Back-Solve	Solve
1x1	64672.2	5089.96	61.82	2.5	4.7
8x1	6870.82	1024.41	47.827	15.619	30.825
16x1	3505.13	547.625	52.402	19.937	39.491
32x1	1829.93	316.544	56.713	24.383	47.692
64x1	1060.40	219.148	77.302	39.942	59.553
32x4	491.526	181.082	71.482	57.049	101.994
64x2	520.029	161.052	82.696	46.013	86.935
128x1	608.946	170.022	90.905	37.498	67.982

Note: Key single-step calculation times with the 1×1 case run an unloaded
Sun 3/260 (similar performance-wise to a single Symult s2010 node) for
comparison. The Jacobian rows were distributed in block-linear form, with
$B = 9$, reflecting the distillation-tray structure. The Jacobian columns were
scattered. This is a seven-column simulation of eight alcohols, with a total
of 1,001 trays. See [Skjellum:90d] for more on data distributions.

example has a narrow block tridiagonal Jacobian with too little off-diagonal
coupling to generate much fill-in. It seems hard to imagine speeding up
B-mode for such an example, unless we can exploit multiple pivots. We
expect multiple-pivot heuristics to do reasonably well for this case, because
of its narrow structure, and nearly block tridiagonal structure. We have
used Wilson Equation Vapor-Liquid Equilibrium with the Antoine Vapor
equation. We have found that the thermodynamic calculations were much
less demanding than we expected, with bubble-point computations requiring
"$1 + \epsilon$" iterations to converge. Consequently, there was not the greater
weight of Jacobian calculations we expected beforehand. Our model assumes
constant pressure, and no enthalpy balances. We include no flow dynamics
and include liquid and vapor flows as states, because of the possibility of
feedbacks.

If we utilize latency in the Jacobian calculation, we could reduce the sequential time by a factor of about 100. This improvement would also carry
through to the concurrent times for Jacobian solution. At that ratio, Jacobian computation to B-mode factorization has a sequential ratio of about

10:1. As is, we achieve legitimate speedups of about five. We expect to improve these results using the ideas quoted elsewhere in this book and in [Skjellum:90d].

From a modelling point-of-view, two things are important to note. First, the introduction of more nonideal thermodynamics would improve speedup, because these calculations fall within the Jacobian computation phase and single-residual computation. Furthermore, the introduction of a more realistic model will likewise bear on concurrency, and likely improve it. For example, introducing flow dynamics, enthalpy balances, and vapor holdups makes the model more difficult to solve numerically (higher index). It also increases the chance for a wide range of stepsizes, and the possible need for additional A-mode factorizations to maintain stability in the integration process. Such operations are more costly, but also have a higher speedup. Furthermore, the more complex models will be less likely to have near diagonal dominance; consequently more pivoting is to be expected, again increasing the chance for overall speedup compared to the sequential case. Mainly, we plan to consider the waveform-relaxation approach more heavily, and also to consider new classes of dynamic distillation simulations with Concurrent DASSL [Skjellum:90c].

9.6.6   Conclusions

We have developed a high-quality concurrent code, Concurrent DASSL, for the solution of ordinary differential-algebraic equations of low index. This code, together with appropriate linear algebra and simulation layers, allows us to explore the achievable concurrent performance of nontrivial problems. In chemical engineering, we have applied it thus far to a reasonably large, simple model of coupled distillation columns. We are able to solve this large problem, which is quite demanding on even a large mainframe because of huge memory requirements and nontrivial computational requirements; the speedups achieved thus far are legitimately at least five, when compared to an efficient sequential implementation. This illustrates the need for improvements to the linear algebra code, which are feasible because sparse matrices will admit multiple pivots heuristically. It also illustrates the need to consider hidden sources of additional timelike concurrency in Concurrent DASSL, perhaps allowing multiple right-hand sides to be attacked simultaneously by the linear algebra codes, and amortizing their cost more efficiently. Furthermore, the performance points up the need for detailed research into novel numerical techniques, such as waveform relaxation, which we have begun to do as well [Skjellum:88a].

9.7   Adaptive Multigrid

9.7.1   Introduction

Simple relaxation methods reduce the high-frequency components of the solution error by an order of magnitude in a few iterations. This observation is used to derive the multigrid method; see Brandt [Brandt:77a], Hackbusch [Hackbusch:85a]; Hackbusch and Trottenberg [Hackbusch:82a]. In the multigrid method, a smoothed problem is projected to a coarser grid. This coarse-grid problem is then solved recursively by smoothing and coarse-grid correction. The recursion terminates on the coarsest grid, where an exact solver is used. In the full multigrid method, a coarser grid is also used to compute an initial guess for the multigrid iteration on a finer grid. With this method, it is possible to solve the problem with an operation count proportional to the number of unknowns.

Multigrid methods are best understood for elliptic problems, that is, the Poisson equation, stationary reaction-diffusion equations, implicit time-steps in parabolic problems, and so on. However, the multigrid approach is also successful for many other applications, from fluid flow to computer vision. Parallelization issues are independent of particular applications, and elliptic problems are a good test bed for the study of concurrent multigrid. We chose two- and three-dimensional stationary nonlinear reaction-diffusion equations in a rectangular domain Ω as our model problem, that is,

$$-\Delta u + g(\vec{x}, u) = 0,$$

with suitable boundary conditions.

To parallelize multigrid, we proceed as follows (see also [Velde:87a], [Velde:87b]). First, a sequential multigrid procedure is developed. Here, the basic numerical problems are addressed: which smoothing, restriction, and prolongation operators to use, the resolution required (size of the finest grid), the number of levels (size of the coarsest grid), and the coarsest-grid solver. Second, this sequential multigrid code is generalized to include local grid refinement (in the neighborhood of singularities, for example). Three basic problems are addressed in this second stage: the algorithmic aspect of local grid refinement, the numerical treatment of interior boundaries, and the relaxation of partially overlapping grid patches. In the third and last step, the multigrid code is parallelized. This can now be done without introducing new numerical issues. Each concurrent process starts a sequential multigrid procedure, each one locally refining to a particular subdomain. To achieve this, a communication operation for the exchange of interior boundary values is needed. Depending on the size of the coarsest grid, it might be required to develop, independently, a concurrent coarsest grid solver.

This parallelization strategy has the advantage that all numerical problems can be addressed in the sequential stages. Although our implementation is for regular grids, the same strategy is also valid for irregular grids.

9.7.2 The Basic Algorithm

To simplify the switch to adaptive grids later, we use a multigrid variant known as the *full approximation scheme*. Thus, on every level, we compute an approximation to the solution of the original equation, not of an error equation. This multigrid procedure is defined by the following basic building blocks: a coarsest-grid solver, a solution restriction operator, a right-hand-side restriction operator, a prolongation operator, and a smoothing operator.

Two feasible coarsest-grid solvers are relaxation until convergence and a direct solver (embedded in a Newton iteration if the problem is nonlinear). The cost of solving a problem on the coarsest grid is, of course, related to the size of the coarsest grid. If the coarsest grid is very coarse, the cost is negligible. However, numerical reasons often dictate a minimum resolution for the coarsest grid. Moreover, elaborate computations may take place on the coarsest grid; see [Bolstadt:86a], [Chan:82a], [Dinar:85a] for examples of multigrid continuation. In some instances, the performance of the computations on the coarsest grids cannot be neglected.

Many alternatives exist for smoothing. Parallelization will be easiest with point relaxations. Jacobi underrelaxation and red-black Gauss-Seidel relaxation are particularly suited for concurrent implementations and for adaptive grids. Hence, we shall restrict our attention to point relaxation methods.

The intergrid transfers are usually simple: linear interpolation as the prolongation operator, injection or full-weight restriction as the restriction operator.

The main data structure of the sequential nonadaptive algorithm is a doubly linked list of grids, where a grid structure provides memory for the solution and right-hand-side vectors, and each grid is connected to one finer and one coarser grid. The sequential multigrid code has the following struc-

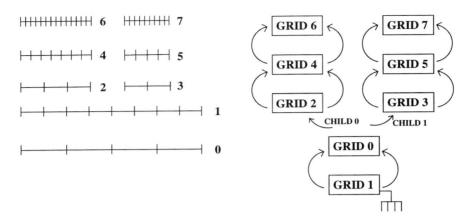

Figure 9.16: One-Dimensional Adaptive Multigrid Structure

ture: a library of operations on grid functions, a code related to the construction of a doubly linked list of grids, and the main multigrid algorithm. We maintain this basic structure for the concurrent and adaptive algorithms. Although the doubly linked list of grids will be replaced by a more complex structure, the basic multigrid algorithm will not be altered. While the library of grid function operations will be expanded, the fundamental operations will remain the same. This is important, because the basic library for a general multigrid package with several options for each operator is large.

9.7.3   The Adaptive Algorithm

Here, we focus on the use of adaptive grids for sequential computations. We shall apply these ideas in the next section to achieve concurrency. Figure 9.16 illustrates the grid structure of a one-dimensional adaptive multigrid procedure. Fine grids are introduced only where necessary, in the neighborhood of a singularity, for example. In two and three dimensions the topology is more complicated, and it makes sense to refine in several subdomains that partially overlap.

We focus first on the intergrid transfers. Although these operators are straightforward, they are the source of some implementation difficulties for the concurrent algorithm, because load-balanced data distributions of fine and coarse grids are not compatible. The structure introduced here avoids these difficulties. Before introducing a fine grid on a subdomain, we construct an artificial coarse grid on the same subdomain. This artificial coarse grid, called a *child grid*, differs from a normal grid data structure only because its data vectors (the solution and right-hand side) are subvectors of the parent-grid data vectors. Thus, child grids do not use extra memory for data (except for some negligible amount for bookkeeping). In Figure 9.16, grid 1 is a parent-grid with two children, grids 2 and 3. With child grids, the intergrid transfers of the nonadaptive procedure can be reused. The restriction, for example, takes place between a fine grid (defined over a subdomain) and a coarse child grid (in Figure 9.16, between grids 4 and 2 and between grids 5 and 3, respectively). Because data memory of child and parent grid are shared, the appropriate subvectors of the coarse grid data are updated automatically. Similarly, prolongation occurs between the child grid and the fine grid.

The basic data structure of the nonadaptive procedure, the doubly linked list of grids, is transformed radically as a result of child grids and their refinements. The data structure is now a tree of doubly linked lists; see Figure 9.16. As mentioned before, the intergrid transfers are not affected by this complicated structure. For relaxation, the only significant difference is that more than one grid may have to be relaxed on each level. When the boundary of one grid intersects the interior of another grid on the same level, the boundary values must be interpolated (Figure 9.17). This does not affect the relaxation operators, as long as the relaxation step is preceded by a boundary-interpolation step.

9.7.4   The Concurrent Algorithm

The same structure that made the multigrid code adaptive allows us to parallelize it. For now, assume that every process starts out with a copy of the coarsest grid, defined on the whole domain. Each process is assigned a subdomain in which to compute the solution to maximum accuracy. The collection of subdomains assigned to all processes covers the computational domain. Within each process, an adaptive grid structure is constructed so that the finest level at which the solution is needed envelops the assigned subdomain; see Figure 9.18. The set of all grids (in whatever process they reside) forms a tree structure like the one described in the previous section. The same algorithm can be applied to it. Only one addition must be made to the program: overlapping grids on the same level but residing in different processes must communicate in order to interpolate boundary values. This is an operation to be added to the basic library.

The coarsest grid can often be ignored as far as machine efficiency is

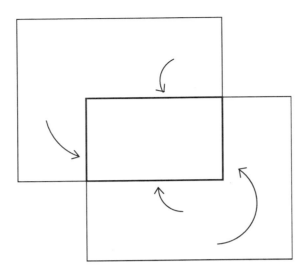

Figure 9.17: Boundary Interpolation

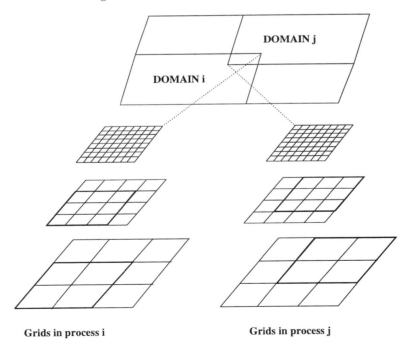

Figure 9.18: Use of Adaptive Multigrid for Concurrency

concerned. As mentioned in Section 9.7.2, the computations on the coarsest grid are sometimes substantial. In such cases, it is crucial to parallelize the coarsest-grid computations. With relaxation until convergence as the coarsest-grid solver, one could simply divide up the coarsest grid over all concurrent processes. It is more likely, however, that the coarsest-grid computations involve a direct solution method. In this case, the duplicated coarsest grid is well suited as an interface to a concurrent direct solver, because it simplifies the initialization of the coefficient matrix. We refer to Section 8.1 and [Velde:90a] for details on some direct solvers.

The total algorithm, adaptive multigrid and concurrent coarsest grid solver, is heterogeneous: its communication structure is irregular and varies significantly from one part of the program to the next, making the data distribution for optimal load balance difficult to predict. On the coarsest level, we achieve load balance by exploiting the data distribution independence of our linear algebra code; see [Lorenz:92a]. On the finer levels, load balance is obtained by allocating an approximately equal number of finest-grid points to each process.

9.7.5 Summary

The concurrent multigrid program was developed by Eric F. Van de Velde. Associated C³P references are [Lorenz:89a], [Lorenz:92a], [Velde:87a], [Velde:87b], [Velde:89b], [Velde:90a].

9.8 Munkres Algorithm for Assignment

9.8.1 Introduction

The so-called *assignment problem* is of considerable importance in a variety of applications, and can be stated as follows. Let

$$\mathcal{A} \equiv \{a_1, a_2, \ldots, a_{N_A}\} \tag{9.17}$$

and

$$\mathcal{B} \equiv \{b_1, b_2, \ldots, b_{N_B}\} \tag{9.18}$$

be two sets of items, and let

$$d_{ij} \equiv d[a_i, b_j] \geq 0, \; a_i \in \mathcal{A}, \; b_j \in \mathcal{B} \tag{9.19}$$

be a measure of the distance (dissimilarity) between individual items from the two lists. Taking $N_A \leq N_B$, the objective of the assignment problem is to find the particular mapping

$$i \mapsto \Pi(i),\ 1 \leq i \leq N_A,\ 1 \leq \Pi(i) \leq N_B \tag{9.20}$$

$$i \neq j \Rightarrow \Pi(i) \neq \Pi(j)$$

such that the total association score

$$S_{TOT} \equiv \sum_{i=1}^{N_A} d[i, \Pi(i)] \tag{9.21}$$

is minimized over all permutations Π.

For $N_A \leq N_B$, the naive (exhaustive search) complexity of the assignment problem is $O[N_B!/(N_B - N_A)!]$. There are, however, a variety of exact solutions to the assignment problem with reduced complexity $O[N_A^2 N_B]$ ([Blackman:86a], [Burgeios:71a], [Kuhn:55a]). Section 9.8.2 briefly describes one such method, Munkres algorithm [Kuhn:55a], and presents a particular sequential implementation. Performance of the algorithm is examined for the particularly nasty problem of associating lists of random points within the unit square. In Section 9.8.3, the algorithm is generalized for concurrent execution, and performance results for runs on the Mark III hypercube are presented.

9.8.2   The Sequential Algorithm

The input to the assignment problem is the matrix $D \equiv \{d_{ij}\}$ of dissimilarities from Equation 9.19. The first point to note is that the particular assignment which minimizes Equation 9.21 is not altered if a *fixed* value is added to or subtracted from all entries in any row or column of the cost matrix D. Exploiting this fact, Munkres' solution to the assignment problem can be divided into two parts

M1: Modifications of the distance matrix D by row/column subtractions, creating a (large) number of zero entries.

M2: With $\{R_Z(i)\}$ denoting the row indices of all zeros in column i, construction of a so-called *minimal representative set*, meaning a distinct selection $R_Z(i)$ for each i, such that $i \neq j \Rightarrow R_Z(i) \neq R_Z(j)$.

The steps of Munkres algorithm generally follow those in the constructive proof of P. Hall's theorem on minimal representative sets.

The preceding paragraph provides a hopelessly incomplete hint as to the number theoretic basis for Munkres algorithm. The particular implementation of Munkres algorithm used in this work is as described in Chapter 14 of [Blackman:86a]. To be definite, take $N_A \leq N_B$ and let the columns of the distance matrix be associated with items from list $\mathcal{A}$. The first step is to subtract the smallest item in each column from all entries in the column. The rest of the algorithm can be viewed as a search for *special* zero entries (starred zeros Z^*), and proceeds as follows:

Munkres Algorithm

Step 1: Setup

1. Find a zero Z in the distance matrix.

2. If there is no starred zero already in its row or column, star this zero.

3. Repeat steps 1.1, 1.2 until all zeros have been considered.

Step 2: Z^* Count, Solution Assessment

1. Cover every column containing a Z^*.

2. Terminate the algorithm if all columns are covered. In this case, the locations of the Z^* entries in the matrix provide the solution to the assignment problem.

Step 3: Main Zero Search

1. Find an uncovered Z in the distance matrix and prime it, $Z \mapsto Z'$. If no such zero exists, go to Step 5

2. If No Z^* exists in the row of the Z', go to Step 4.

3. If a Z^* exists, cover this row and uncover the column of the Z^*. Return to Step 3.1 to find a new Z.

Step 4: Increment Set of Starred Zeros

1. Construct the "alternating sequence" of primed and starred zeros:

   Z_0: Unpaired Z' from Step 3.2

   Z_1: The Z^* in the column of Z_0

Z_{2N}:   The Z' in the row of Z_{2N-1}, *if* such a zero exists

Z_{2N+1}:   The Z^* in the column of Z_{2N}

The sequence eventually terminates with an unpaired $Z' = Z_{2N}$ for some N.

2. Unstar each starred zero of the sequence.

3. Star each primed zero of the sequence, thus increasing the number of starred zeros by one.

4. Erase all primes, uncover all columns and rows, and return to Step 2.

Step 5:   New Zero Manufactures

1. Let h be the smallest uncovered entry in the (modified) distance matrix.

2. Add h to all covered rows.

3. Subtract h from all uncovered columns

4. Return to Step 3, without altering stars, primes, or covers.

A (very) schematic flowchart for the algorithm is shown in Figure 9.19. Note that Steps 1,5 of the algorithm overwrite the original distance matrix.

The preceding algorithm involves flags (starred or primed) associated with zero entries in the distance matrix, as well as "covered" tags associated with individual rows and columns. The implementation of the zero tagging is done by first noting that there is *at most* one Z^* or Z' in any row or column. The covers and zero tags of the algorithm are accordingly implemented using five simple arrays:

CC(k):   Covered column tags, $1 \leq k \leq N_{COLS}$.

CR(j):   Covered row tags, $1 \leq j \leq N_{ROWS}$

ZS(k): Z^* locators for columns of the matrix. If positive, $ZS(k)$ is the row index of the Z^* in the kth column of the matrix.

ZR(j): Z^* locators for rows of the matrix. If positive, $ZR(j)$ is the column of the Z^* in the jth row of the matrix.

ZP(j): Z' locators for rows of the matrix. If positive, $ZP(j)$ is the column of the Z' in the jth row of the matrix.

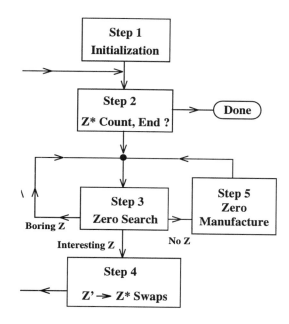

Figure 9.19: Flowchart for Munkres Algorithm

Entries in the cover arrays CC and CR are one if the row or column is covered zero otherwise. Entries in the zero-locator arrays ZS, ZR, and ZP are zero if no zero of the appropriate type exists in the indexed row or column.

With the star-prime-cover scheme of the preceding paragraph, a sequential implementation of Munkres algorithm is completely straightforward. At the beginning of Step 1, all cover and locator flags are set to zero, and the initial zero search provides an initial set of nonzero entries in ZS(). Step 2 sets appropriate entries in CC() to one and simply counts the covered columns. Steps 3 and 5 are trivially implemented in terms of the cover/zero arrays and the "alternating sequence" for Step 4 is readily constructed from the contents of ZS(), ZR() and ZP().

As an initial exploration of Munkres algorithm, consider the task of associating two lists of random points within a 2D unit square, assuming the cost function in Equation 9.19 is the usual Cartesian distance. Figure 9.20 plots total CPU times for execution of Munkres algorithm for equal size lists versus list size. The vertical axis gives CPU times in seconds for one node of the Mark III hypercube. The circles and crosses show the time spent in Steps 5 and 3, respectively. These two steps (zero search and zero manufac-

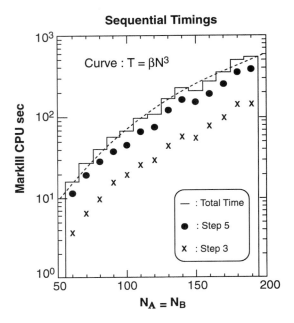

Figure 9.20: Timing Results for the Sequential Algorithm Versus Problem Size

ture) account for essentially *all* of the CPU time. For the 190×190 case, the total CPU time spent in Step 2 was about 0.9 CPU sec, and that spent in Step 4 was too small to be reliably measured. The large amounts of time spent in Steps 3 and 5 arise from the very large numbers of times these parts of the algorithm are executed. The 190×190 case involves 6109 entries into Step 3 and 593 entries into Step 5.

Since the zero searching in Step 3 of the algorithm is required so often, the implementation of this step is done with some care. The search for zeros is done column-by-column, and the code maintains pointers to both the last column searched and the most recently uncovered column (Step 3.3) in order to reduce the time spent on subsequent re-entries to the Step 3 box of Figure 9.19.

The dashed line of Figure 9.20 indicates the nominal $\Delta T \propto N^3$ scaling predicted for Munkres algorithm. By and large, the timing results in Figure 9.20 are consistent with this expected behavior. It should be noted, however, that both the nature of this scaling and the coefficient of N^3 are very dependent on the nature of the data sets. Consider, for example, two

CPU Time Per Step [sec]

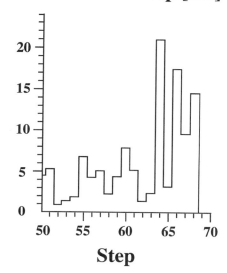

Figure 9.21: Times Per Loop (i.e., $N[Z^*]$ increment) for the Last Several Loops in the Solution of the 150×150 Problem

identical trivial lists

$$a_i \equiv b_i \equiv i,\ 1 \leq i \leq N \qquad (9.22)$$

with the distance between items given by the absolute value function. For the data sets in Equation 9.22, the preliminaries and Step 1 of Munkres algorithm completely solve the association in a time which scales as N^2. In contrast, the random-point association problem is a much greater challenge for the algorithm, as nominal pairings indicated by the initial nearest-neighbor searches of the preliminary step are tediously undone in the creation of the staircaselike sequence of zeros needed for Step 4. As a brief, instructive illustration of the nature of this processing, Figure 9.21 plots the CPU time *per step* for the last passes through the outer loop of Figure 9.19 for the 150×150 assignment problem (recall that each pass through the outer loop increases the Z^* count by one). The processing load per step is seen to be highly nonuniform.

9.8.3   The Concurrent Algorithm

The timing results from Figure 9.20 clearly dictate the manner in which the calculations in Munkres algorithm should be distributed among the nodes of a hypercube for concurrent execution. The zero and minimum element searches for Steps 3 and 5 are the most time consuming and should be done concurrently. In contrast, the essentially bookkeeping tasks associated with Steps 2 and 4 require insignificant CPU time and are most naturally done in lockstep (i.e., all nodes of the hypercube perform the same calculations on the same data at the same time). The details of the concurrent algorithm are as follows.

Data Decomposition

The distance matrix $\{d_{ij}\}$ is distributed across the nodes of the hypercube, with entire columns assigned to individual nodes. (This assumes, effectively, that $N_{COLS} \gg N_{NODES}$, which is always the case for assignment problems which are big enough to be "interesting.") The cover and zero locator lists defined in Section 9.8.2 are duplicated on all nodes.

Task Decomposition

The concurrent implementation of Step 5 is particularly trivial. Each node first finds its own minimum uncovered value, setting this value to some "infinite" token if all columns assigned to the node are covered. A simple loop on communication channels determines the global minimum among the node-by-node minimum values, and each node then modifies the contents of its local portion of the distance matrix according to Steps 5.2 and 5.3.

The concurrent implementation of Step 3 is just slightly more awkward. On entry to Step 3, each node searches for zeros according to the rules of Section 9.8.2, and fills a three-element status list:

$$L[j] \equiv L[\text{Node}_j] \equiv \{S, k_{ROW}, k_{COL}\} \tag{9.23}$$

where S is a zero-search status flag,

$$S \equiv \begin{cases} -1 & \text{No } Z \text{ was found} \\ 0 & Z \text{ with } Z^* \text{ in row (Boring)} \\ 1 & Z \text{ without } Z^* \text{ (Interesting)} \end{cases} \tag{9.24}$$

If the status is nonnegative, the last two entries in the status list specify the location of the found zero. A simple channel loop is used to collect the individual status lists of each node into all nodes, and the action taken next by the program is as follows:

- If all nodes give negative status (no Z found), all nodes proceed to Step 5.

- If any node gives status one, all nodes proceed to Step 4 for lockstep updates of the zero location lists, using the row-column indices of the node which gave status one as the starting point for Step 4.1. If more than one node returns status one (highly unlikely, in practice), only the first such node (lower node number) is used.

- If all zeros uncovered are "Boring," the cover switching in Step 3.3 of the algorithm is performed. This is done in lockstep, processing the Zs returned by the nodes in order of increasing node number. Note that the cover rearrangements performed for one node may well cover a Z returned by a node with a higher node number. In such cases, the nominal Z returned by the later node is simply ignored.

It is worth emphasizing that only the actual *searches* for zero and minimum entries in Steps 3 and 5 are done concurrently. The updates of the cover and zero locator lists are done in unison.

The concurrent algorithm has been implemented on the Mark III hypercube, and has been tested against random point association tasks for a variety of list sizes. Before examining results of these tests, however, it is worth noting that the concurrent implementation is not particularly dependent on the hypercube topology. The only communication-dependent parts of the algorithm are

1. Determination of the ensemble-wide minimum value for Step 5;

2. Collection of the local Step 3 status lists (Equation 9.24),

either of which could be easily done for almost any MIMD architecture.

Table 9.7 presents performance results for the association of random lists of 200 points on the Mark III hypercube for various cube dimensions. (For consistency, of course, the same input lists are used for all runs.) Time values are given in CPU seconds for the total execution time, as well as the time spent in Steps 3 and 5. Also given are the standard concurrent execution efficiencies,

$$\epsilon_N \equiv \frac{T[\ 1\ \text{Node}\ ]}{N \times T[\ N\ \text{Nodes}\ ]}, \tag{9.25}$$

as well as the number of times the Step 3 box of Figure 9.19 is entered during execution of the algorithm. The numbers of entries into the other boxes of Figure 9.19 are independent of the hypercube dimension.

Table 9.7: Concurrent Performance for 200×200 Random Points. T is time, ϵ efficiency, and N[Step 3] the number of times Step 3 is executed.

N[Nodes]	1	2	4	8
T[Total]	654.83	372.70	205.48	119.25
T[Step 3]	183.80	128.04	81.59	56.66
T[Step 5]	462.06	237.54	117.39	57.94
ϵTotal	. . .	0.878	0.800	0.686
ϵStep 3	. . .	0.718	0.563	0.405
ϵStep 5	. . .	0.973	0.984	0.997
N[Step 3]	7075	4837	3483	2778

There is an aspect of the timing results in Table 9.7 which should be noted. Namely, essentially *all* inefficiencies of the concurrent algorithm are associated with Step 3 for two nodes compared to Step 3 for one node. The times spent in Step 5 are approximately halved for each increase in the dimension of the hypercube. However, the efficiencies associated with the zero searching in Step 3 are rather poorer, particularly for larger numbers of nodes.

At a simple, qualitative level, the inefficiencies associated with Step 3 are readily understood. Consider the task of finding a single zero located somewhere inside an $N \times N$ matrix. The mean sequential search time is

$$\langle T_{\text{Search}}[1 \text{ Node}]\rangle \propto \frac{N \times N}{2} \qquad (9.26)$$

since, on average, half of the entries of the matrix will be examined before the zero is found. Now consider the same zero search on two nodes. The node which has the half of the matrix containing the zero will find it in about half the time of Equation 9.26. *However*, the other node will *always* search through all of its $N \times N/2$ items before returning a null status for Equation 9.24. Since the node which found the zero must wait for the other node before the (lockstep) modifications of zero locators and cover tags, the node without the zero determines the actual time spent in Step 3, so that

$$\langle T_{\text{Search}}[\, 2 \text{ Nodes }]\rangle \approx \langle T_{\text{Search}}[\, 1 \text{ Node }]\rangle. \qquad (9.27)$$

Table 9.8: Concurrent Performance for 100×100 Random Points

N[Nodes]	1	2	4	8
T[Total]	68.08	38.79	23.11	16.40
T[Step 3]	19.63	13.09	9.69	8.00
T[Step 5]	44.99	22.99	11.79	6.16
ϵTotal	...	0.878	0.736	0.519
ϵStep 3	...	0.750	0.506	0.307
ϵStep 5	...	0.978	0.954	0.913
N[Step 3]	2029	1430	1134	991

In the full program, the concurrent bottleneck is not as bad as Equation 9.27 would imply. As noted above, the concurrent algorithm can process multiple "Boring" Zs in a single pass through Step 3. The frequency of such multiple Zs per step can be estimated by noting the decreasing number of times Step 3 is entered with increasing hypercube dimension, as indicated in Table 9.7. Moreover, each node maintains a counter of the last column searched during Step 3. On subsequent re-entries, columns prior to this marked column are searched for zeros only if they have had their cover tag changed during the prior Step 3 processing. While each of these algorithm elements does diminish the problems associated with Equation 9.27, the fact remains that the search for zero entries in the distributed distance matrix is the least efficient step in concurrent implementations of Munkres algorithm.

The results presented in Table 9.7 demonstrate that an efficient implementation of Munkres algorithm is certainly feasible. Next, we examine how these efficiencies change as the problem size is varied.

The results shown in Tables 9.8 and 9.9 demonstrate an improvement of concurrent efficiencies with increasing problem size—the expected result. For the 100×100 problem on eight nodes, the efficiency is only about 50%. This problem is too small for eight nodes, with only 12 or 13 columns of the distance matrix assigned to individual nodes.

While the performance results in Tables 9.7 through 9.9 are certainly acceptable, it is nonetheless interesting to investigate possible improvements of efficiency for the zero searches in Step 3. The obvious candidate for an algorithm modification is some sort of checkpointing: At intermediate times

Table 9.9: Concurrent Performance for 300×300 Random Points

N[Nodes]	1	2	4	8
T[Total]	2046.91	1154.27	622.53	353.30
T[Step 3]	585.61	399.41	235.49	154.57
T[Step 5]	1442.22	742.90	377.89	188.59
ϵTotal	. . .	0.887	0.822	0.728
ϵStep 3	. . .	0.733	0.621	0.473
ϵStep 5	. . .	0.971	0.954	0.956
N[Step 3]	13250	8583	5785	4365

during the zero search, the nodes exchange a "Zero Found Yet?" status flag, with all nodes breaking out of the zero search loop if any node returns a positive result.

For message-passing machines such as the Mark III, the checkpointing scheme is of little value, as the time spent in individual entries to Step 3 is not enormous compared to the node-to-node communication time. For example, for the two-node solution of the 300×300 problem, the mean time for a single entry to Step 3 is only about 46 msec, compared to a typical node-to-node communications time which can be a significant fraction of a millisecond. The time required to perform a single Step 3 calculation is not large compared to node-to-node communications. As a (not unexpected) consequence, all attempts to improve the Step 3 efficiencies through various "Found Anything?" schemes were completely unsuccessful.

The checkpointing difficulties for a message-passing machine could disappear, of course, on a shared-memory machine. If the zero-search status flags for the various nodes could be kept in memory locations readily (i.e., rapidly) accessible to all nodes, the problems of the preceding paragraph might be eliminated. It would be interesting to determine whether significant improvements on the (already good) efficiencies of the concurrent Munkres algorithm could be achieved on a shared-memory machine.

9.9 Optimization Methods for Neural Nets: Automatic Parameter Tuning and Faster Convergence

Computers and standard programming languages can be used efficiently for high-level, clearly formulated problems such as computing balance sheets and income statements, solving partial differential equations, or managing operations in a car factory. It is much more difficult to write efficient and fault-tolerant programs for "simple" primitive tasks like hearing, seeing, touching, manipulating parts, recognizing faces, avoiding obstacles, and so on. Usually, the existing artificial systems for the above tasks are within a narrowly limited domain of application, very sensitive to hardware and software failures, and difficult to modify and adapt to new environments.

Neural nets represent a new approach to bridging the gap between cheap computational power and solutions for some of the above-cited tasks. We as human beings like to consider ourselves good examples of the power of the neuronal approach to problem solving.

To avoid naive optimism and over inflated expectations about "self-programming" computers, it is safer to see this development as the creation of another level of tools insulating generic users looking for fast solutions from the details of sophisticated learning mechanisms. Today, generic users do not care about writing operating systems; in the near future *some* users will not care about programming and debugging. They will have to choose appropriate off-the-shelf subsystems (both hardware and software) and an appropriate set of examples and high-level specifications; neural nets will do the rest. Neural networks have already been useful in areas like pattern classification, robotics, system modeling, and forecasting over time ([Borsellino:61a], [Broomhead:88a], [Gorman:88a], [Sejnowski:87a], [Rumelhart:86b], [Lapedes:87a]).

The focus of this work is on "supervised learning", that is, learning an association between input and output patterns from a set of examples. The mapping is executed by a feed-forward network with different layers of units, such as the one shown in Figure 9.22.

Each unit that is not in the input layer receives an input given by a weighted sum of the outputs of the previous layer and produces an output using a "sigmoidal" transfer function, with a linear range and saturation for large positive and negative inputs. This particular architecture has been considered because it has been used extensively in neural network research,

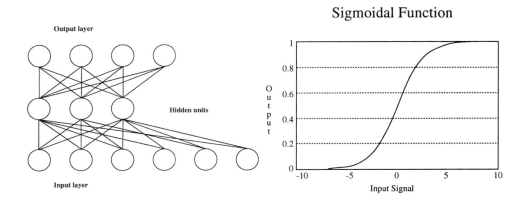

Figure 9.22: Multilayer Perceptron and Transfer Function

but the learning method presented can be used for different network designs ([Broomhead:88a]).

9.9.1 Deficiencies of Steepest Descent

The multilayer perceptron, initialized with random weights, presents random output patterns. We would like to execute a learning stage, progressively modifying the values of the connection strengths in order to make the outputs nearer to the prescribed ones.

It is straightforward to transform the learning task into an optimization problem (i.e., a search for the minimum of a specified function, henceforth called *energy*). If the *energy* is defined as the sum of the squared errors between *obtained* and *desired* output pattern over the set of examples, minimizing it will accomplish the task.

A large fraction of the theoretical and applied research in supervised learning is based on the *steepest descent* method for minimization. The negative gradient of the energy with respect to the weights is calculated during each iteration, and a step is taken in that direction (if the step is small enough, energy reduction is assured). In this way, one obtains a sequence of weight vectors, $\mathbf{w}_n$, that converges to a local minimum of the energy function:

$$\mathbf{w}_{n+1} = \mathbf{w}_n - \epsilon \ \mathbf{grad} \ E(\mathbf{w}_n).$$

Now, given that we are interested in converging to the local minimum in the shortest time (this is not always the case: to combat noise some slowness may be desired), there is no good reason to restrict ourselves to steepest descent, and there are at least a couple of reasons in favor of other methods. First, the *learning speed*, ϵ, is a free parameter that has to be chosen carefully for each problem (if it is too small, progress is slow; if too large, oscillations may be created). Second, even in the optimal case of a step along the steepest descent direction bringing the system to the absolute minimum (*along this direction*), it can be proved that steepest descent can be arbitrarily slow, particularly when "the search space contains long ravines that are characterized by sharp curvature across the ravine and a gently sloping floor" [Rumelhart:86b]. In other words, if we are unlucky with the choice of units along the different dimensions (and this is a frequent event when the number of weights is 1000 or 10,000), it may be the case that during each iteration, the previous error is reduced by 0.000000001%!

The problem is essentially caused by the fact that the gradient does not necessarily point in the direction of the minimum, as it is shown in Figure 9.23.

If the energy is quadratic, a large ratio of the maximum to minimum eigenvalues causes the "zigzagging" motion illustrated. In the next sections, we will illustrate two suggestions for tuning parameters in an adaptive way and selecting better descent directions.

9.9.2 The "Bold Driver" Network

There are *no general prescriptions* for selecting an appropriate learning rate ϵ in back-propagation, in order to avoid oscillations and converge to a good local minimum of the energy in a short time. In many applications, some kind of "black magic," or trial-and-error process, is employed. In addition, usually no *fixed* learning rate is appropriate for the entire learning session.

Both problems can be solved by *adapting* the learning rate to the local structure of the energy surface.

We start with a given learning rate (the value does not matter) and monitor the energy after each weight update. If the energy decreases, the learning rate for the next iteration is increased by a factor ρ. Conversely, if the energy increases (an "accident" during learning), this is taken as an indication that the step made was too long, the learning rate is decreased by a factor σ, the last change is cancelled, and a new trial is done. The process of reduction is repeated until a step that decreases the energy value is found (this will inevitably happen because the search direction is that of the negative gradient). An example of the size of the learning rate as a

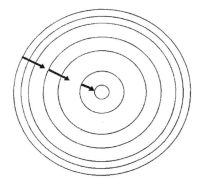

Gradient points in the direction of the minimum

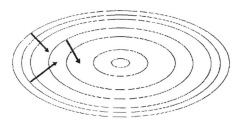

Gradient does not point in the direction of the minimum

Figure 9.23: Gradient Direction for Different Choice of Units

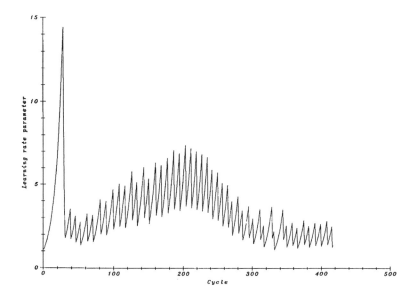

Figure 9.24: Learning Rate Magnitude as a Function of the Iteration Number for a Test Problem

function of the iteration number is shown in Figure 9.24.

The name "Bold Driver" was selected for the analogy with the learning process of young and inexperienced car drivers.

By using this "brutally heuristic" method, learning converges in a time that is comparable to, and usually better than that of standard (batch) back-propagation with an optimal and fixed learning rate. The important difference is that the time-consuming *meta-optimization* phase for choosing ϵ is avoided. The values for ρ and σ can be fixed once and for all (e.g., $\rho = 1.1$, $\sigma = 0.5$) and performance does not depend critically on their choice.

9.9.3 The Broyden-Fletcher-Goldfarb-Shanno One-Step Memoryless Quasi-Newton Method

Steepest descent suffers from a bad reputation with researchers in optimization. From the literature (e.g., [Gill:81a]), we found a wide selection of more appropriate optimization techniques. Following the "decision tree" and considering the characteristics of large supervised learning problems (large memory requirements and time-consuming calculations of the energy and the gradient), the Broyden-Fletcher-Goldfarb-Shanno one-step memoryless quasi-Newton method (all adjectives are necessary to define it) is a good candidate in the competition and performed very efficiently on different problems.

Let's define the following vectors: $\mathbf{g}_n = \mathbf{grad}\ E(\mathbf{w}_n)$, $\mathbf{p}_n = \mathbf{w}_n - \mathbf{w}_{n-1}$ and $\mathbf{y}_n = \mathbf{g}_n - \mathbf{g}_{n-1}$. The one-dimensional search direction for the nth iteration is a modification of the gradient $\mathbf{g}_n$, as follows:

$$\mathbf{d}_n = -\mathbf{g}_n + A_n\mathbf{p}_n + B_n\mathbf{y}_n$$

Every N steps (N being the number of weights in the network), the search is restarted in the direction of the negative gradient.

The coefficients A_n and B_n are combinations of scalar products:

$$A_n = -\left(1 + \frac{\mathbf{y}_n \cdot \mathbf{y}_n}{\mathbf{p}_n \cdot \mathbf{y}_n}\right)\frac{\mathbf{p}_n \cdot \mathbf{g}_n}{\mathbf{p}_n \cdot \mathbf{y}_n} + \frac{\mathbf{y}_n \cdot \mathbf{g}_n}{\mathbf{p}_n \cdot \mathbf{y}_n}\ ;\quad B_n = \frac{\mathbf{p}_n \cdot \mathbf{g}_n}{\mathbf{p}_n \cdot \mathbf{y}_n}$$

The one-dimensional minimization used in this work is based on quadratic interpolation and tuned to back-propagation where, in a single step, both the energy value and the negative gradient can be efficiently obtained. Details on this step are contained in [Williams:87b].

The computation during each step requires $O(N)$ operations (the same behavior as standard batch back-propagation), while the CPU time for each step increases by an average factor of three for the problems considered. Because the total number of steps for convergence is much smaller, we measured a large net benefit in computing time.

Last but not least, this method can be efficiently implemented on MIMD parallel computers.

9.9.4   Parallel Optimization

Neural nets are "by definition" parallel computing systems of many densely interconnected units. Parallel computation is the basic method used by our brain to achieve response times of hundreds of milliseconds, using sloppy biological hardware with computing times of a few milliseconds per basic operation.

Our implementation of the learning algorithm is based on the use of MIMD machines with large grain size. An efficient mapping strategy consists of assigning a subset of the examples (input-output pairs) and the *entire* network structure to each processor. To obtain proper generalization, the

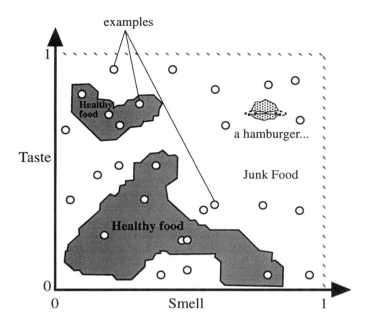

Figure 9.25: "Healthy Food" Has to Be Distinguished from "Junk Food" Using Taste and Smell Information.

number of example patterns has to be much larger (say, $\geq 10\,X$) than the number of parameters defining the architecture (i.e., the number of connection weights). For this reason, the amount of memory used for storing the weights is not too large for significant problems.

Function and gradient evaluation is executed in parallel. Each processor calculates the contribution of the assigned patterns (with no communication), and a global combining-distributing step (see the *ADDVEC* routine in [Fox:88a]) calculates the total energy and gradient (let's remember that the energy is a *sum* of the patterns' contributions) and communicates the result to all processors.

Then the one-dimensional minimization along the search direction is completed and the weights are updated.

This simple parallelization approach is promising: It can be easily adapted to different network representations and learning strategies, and it is going to be a fierce competitor with analog implementations of neural networks, when these are available for significant applications (let's remember that airplanes do not flap their wings . . .).

9.9.5   Experiment: the Dichotomy Problem

This problem consists of classifying a set of randomly generated patterns (with real values) in two classes. An example in two dimensions is given by the "healthy food" learning problem. Inputs are given by points in the "smell" and "taste" plane, corresponding to the different foods. The learning task consists of producing the correct classification as "healthy food" or "junk food" (Figure 9.25).

On this problem we obtained a speedup of 20–120 (going from 6 to 100 patterns in two dimensions).

9.9.6   Experiment: Time Series Prediction

In this case, the task is to predict the next value in the sequence (ergodic and chaotic) generated by the logistic map [Lapedes:87a], according to the recurrence relation:

$$x_{n+1} = 4 \, x_n \, (1 - x_n).$$

We tried different architecture and obtained a speedup of 400–500, and slightly better generalization properties for the BFGS optimization method presented.

In general, we obtained a larger speedup for problems with high-precision requirements (using real values for inputs or outputs). See also [Battiti:89a].

9.9.7   Summary

The distributed optimization [Battiti:89a;89e] software was developed by Roberto Battiti, modifying a back-propagation program written by Steve Otto. Fox and Williams inspired our first investigations into the optimization literature (Shanno's conjugate gradient [Shanno:78a] is used in [Williams:87b]).

Chapter 10

DIME Programming Environment

10.1   DIME: Portable Software for Irregular Meshes for Parallel or Sequential Computers

In the next two chapters, we describe software tools developed to aid the user in the parallelization of some of the harder algorithms. Here we describe DIME, which is designed to generate both statically and adaptively irregular meshes. DIME was already used in the application of Section 7.2; however, it is more typically used for partial differential equations describing problems with nonuniform and varying density.

A large fraction of the problems that we wish to solve with a computer are continuum simulations of physical systems, where the interesting variable is not a finite collection of numbers but a function on a domain. For the purposes of the computation such a continuous spatial domain is given a structure, or mesh, to which field values may be attached and neighboring values compared to calculate derivatives of the field.

If the domain of interest has a simple shape, such as a cylinder or cuboid, there may be a natural choice of mesh whose structure is very regular like that of a crystal, but when we come to more complex geometries such as the space surrounding an aircraft or inside turbomachinery, there are no regular structures that can adequately represent the domain. The only way to mesh such complex domains is with an unstructured mesh, such as that shown in

Figure 10.1: Mesh and Solution of Laplace Equation

Figure 10.1. At the right is a plot of a solution to Laplace's equation on the domain.

Notice that the mesh is especially fine at the sharp corners of the boundary where the solution changes rapidly: A desirable feature for a mesh is its ability to adapt, so that when the solution begins to emerge, the mesh may be made finer where necessary.

Naturally, we would like to run our time-consuming physical simulation with the most cost-effective general-purpose computer, which we believe to be the MIMD architecture. In view of the difficulty of programming an irregular structure such as one of these meshes, and the special difficulty of doing so with an MIMD machine, I decided to write not just a program for a specialized application, but a *programming environment* for unstructured triangular meshes.

The resulting software (DIME: Distributed Irregular Mesh Environment, [Williams:90b]) is responsible for the mesh structure, and a separate application code runs a particular type of simulation on the mesh. DIME keeps track of the mesh structure, allowing mesh creation, reading and writing meshes to disk, and graphics; also adaptive refinement and certain topological changes to the mesh. It hides the parallelism from the application code, and splits the mesh among the processors in an efficient way.

The application code is responsible for attaching data to the elements and nodes of the mesh, manipulating and computing with these data and the data from its mesh neighborhood. DIME is designed not only to be portable between different MIMD parallel machines, but it also runs on any Unix machine, treating this as a parallel machine with just one processor. This ability to run on a sequential machine is due to DIME's use of the Cubix server (Section 5.2).

10.1.1 Applications and Extensions

The most efficient speed for aircraft flight is just below the speed of sound: the transonic regime. Simulations of flight at these speeds consume large quantities of computer time, and are a natural candidate for a DIME application. In addition to the complex geometries of airfoils and turbines for which these simulations are required, the flow tends to develop singular regions or shocks in places that cannot be predicted in advance; the adaptive refinement capability of a DIME mesh allows the mesh to be fine and detail resolved near shocks while keeping the regions of smooth flow coarsely meshed for economy (Section 12.3).

The version of DIME developed within C^3P was only able to mesh two-dimensional manifolds. More recent developments are described in Section 10.1.7. The manifold may, however, be embedded in a higher-dimensional space. In collaboration with the Biology division at Caltech, we have simulated the electrosensory system of the weakly electric fish *Apteronotus leptorhynchus*. The simulation involves creating a mesh covering the skin of the fish, and using the *boundary element method* to calculate field strengths in the three-dimensional space surrounding the fish (Section 12.2).

In the same vein of embedding the mesh in higher dimensions, we have simulated a bosonic string of high-energy physics, embedding the mesh in up to 26 spatial dimensions. The problem here is to integrate over not only all positions of the mesh nodes, but also over all *triangulations* of the mesh (Section 7.2).

The information available to a DIME application is certain data stored in the elements and nodes of the mesh. When doing finite-element calculations, one would like a somewhat higher level of abstraction, which is to refer to functions defined on a domain, with certain smoothness constraints and boundary conditions. We have made a further software layer on top of DIME to facilitate this: DIMEFEM. With this we may add, multiply, differentiate and integrate functions defined in terms of the Lagrangian finite-element family, and define linear, bilinear, and nonlinear operators acting on these

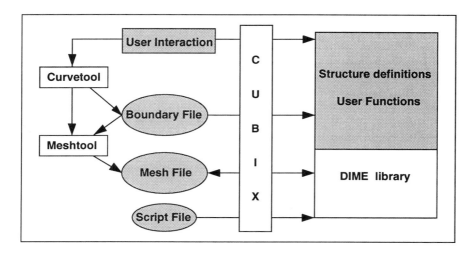

Figure 10.2: Major Components of DIME

functions. When a bilinear operator is defined, a variational principle may be solved by conjugate-gradient methods. The preconditioner for the CG method may in itself involve solving a variational principle. The DIMEFEM package has been applied to a sophisticated incompressible flow algorithm (Section 10.2).

10.1.2   The Components of DIME

Figure 10.2 shows the structure of a DIME application. The shaded parts represent the contribution from the user, being a definition of a domain which is to be meshed, a definition of the data to be maintained at each element, node, and boundary edge of the mesh, and a set of functions that manipulate this data. The user may also supply or create a script file for running the code in batch mode.

The first input is the definition of a domain to be meshed. A file may be made using the elementary CAD program `curvetool`, which allows straight lines, arcs, and cubic splines to be manipulated interactively to define a domain.

Before sending a domain to a DIME application, it must be predigested to some extent, with the help of a human. The user must produce a coarse mesh that defines the topology of the domain to the machine. This is done with the program `meshtool`, which allows the user to create nodes and connect them to form a triangulation.

The user writes a program for the mesh, and this program is loaded into each processor of the parallel machine. When the DIME function `readmesh()` is called, (or "Readmesh" clicked on the menu), the mesh created by `meshtool` is read into a single processor, and then the function `balance_orb()` may be called (or "Balance" clicked on the menu) to split the mesh into domains, one domain for each processor.

The user may also call the function `writemesh()` (or click "Writemesh" in the menu), which causes the parallel mesh to be written to disk. If that mesh is subsequently read in, it is read in its domain-decomposed form, with different pieces assigned to different processors.

In Figure 10.2, the Cubix server is not mandatory, but only needed if the DIME application is to run in parallel. The application *also runs on a sequential machine*, which is considered to be a one-processor parallel machine.

10.1.3 Domain Definition

Figure 10.3 shows an example of a DIME boundary structure. The filled blobs are *points*, with *curves* connecting the points. Each curve may consist of a set of curve segments, shown in the figure separated by open circles. The curve segments may be straight lines, arcs of circles, or Bezier cubic sections. The program `curvetool` is for the interactive production of boundary files. When the domain is satisfactory, it should be meshed using `meshtool`.

The program `meshtool` is used for defining boundaries and creating a triangulation of certain regions of a grid. Meshtool adds nodes to an existing triangulation using the Delaunay triangulation [Bowyer:81a]. A new node may be added anywhere except at the position of an existing node. Figure 10.4 illustrates how the Delaunay triangulation (thick gray lines) is derived from the Voronoi tesselation (thin black lines).

Each node (shown by a blob in the figure) has a "territory," or Voronoi polygon, which is the part of the plane closer to the node than to any other node. The divisions between these territories are shown as thin lines in the figure, and are the perpendicular bisectors of the lines between the nodes. This procedure tesselates the plane into a set of disjoint polygons and is called the Voronoi tesselation. Joining nodes whose Voronoi polygons have a common border creates a triangulation of the nodes known as the Delaunay triangulation. This triangulation has some desirable properties, such as the diagonal dominance of a finite-element stiffness matrix derived from the mesh [Young:71a].

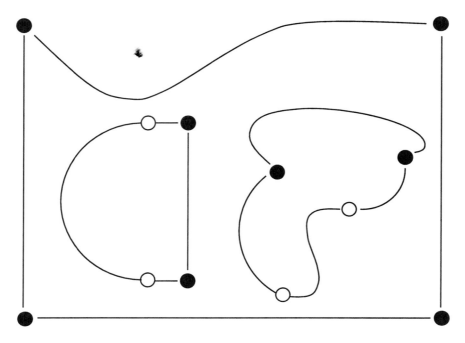

Figure 10.3: Boundary Structure

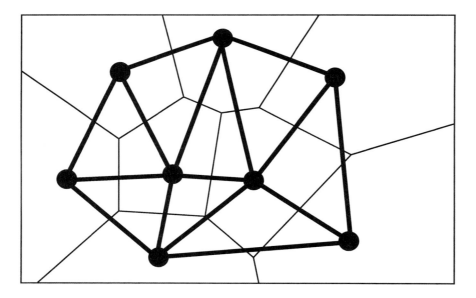

Figure 10.4: Voronoi Tesselation and Resulting Delaunay Triangulation

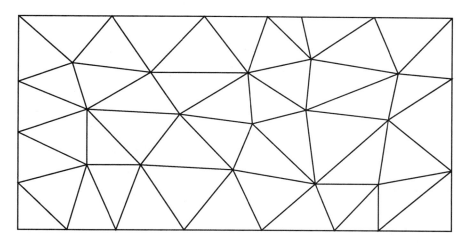

Figure 10.5: A Mesh Covering a Rectangle

10.1.4 Mesh Structure

Figure 10.5 shows a triangular mesh covering a rectangle, and Figure 10.6 the logical structure of that mesh split among four processors. The logical mesh shows the elements as shaded triangles and nodes as blobs. Each element is connected to exactly three nodes, and each node is connected to one or more elements. If a node is at a boundary, it has a boundary structure attached, together with a pointer to the next node clockwise around the boundary.

Each node, element and boundary structure has user data attached to it, which is automatically transferred to another processor if load-balancing causes the node or element to be moved to another processor. DIME knows only the size of the user data structures. Thus, these structures may not contain pointers, since when those data are moved to another processor the pointers will be meaningless.

The shaded ovals in Figure 10.5 are *physical nodes*, each of which consists of one or more *logical nodes*. Each logical node has a set of aliases, which are the other logical nodes belonging to the same physical node. The physical node is a conceptual object, and is unaffected by parallelism; the logical node is a copy of the data in the physical node, so that each processor which owns a part of that physical node may access the data as if it had the whole node.

DIME is meant to make distributed processing of an unstructured mesh almost as easy as sequential programming. However, there is a remaining "kernel of parallelism" that the user must bear in mind. Suppose each node

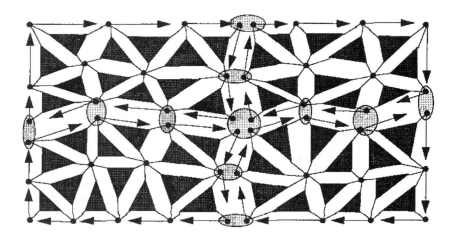

Figure 10.6: The Logical Structure of the Mesh Split Among Four Processors

of the mesh gathers data from its local environment (i.e., the neighboring elements); if that node is split among several processors, it will only gather the data from those elements which lie in the same processor and consequently each node will only have part of the result. We need to combine the partial results from the logical nodes and return the combined result to each. This facility is provided by a macro in DIME called `NODE_COMBINE`, which is called each time the node data is changed according to its local environment.

10.1.5   Refinement

The Delaunay triangulation used by `meshtool` would be an ideal way to refine the working mesh, as well as making a coarse mesh for initial download. Unfortunately, adding a new node to an existing Delaunay triangulation may have global consequences; it is not possible to predict in advance how much of the current mesh should be replaced to accommodate the new node. Doing this in parallel requires an enormous amount of communication to make sure that the processors do not tread on each others' toes [Williams:89c].

DIME uses the algorithm of Rivara [Rivara:84a;89a] for refinement of the mesh, which is well suited to loosely synchronous parallel operation, but results in a triangulation which is not a Delaunay triangulation, and thus lacks some desirable properties. The process of topological relaxation changes the connectivity of the mesh to make it a Delaunay triangulation.

It is usually desirable to avoid triangles in the mesh which have particularly acute angles, and topological relaxation will reduce this tendency. Another method of doing this is by moving the nodes toward the average position of their neighboring nodes; a physical analogy would be to think of the edges of the mesh as damped springs and allowing the nodes to move under the action of the springs.

10.1.6   Load Balancing

When DIME operates in parallel, the mesh should be distributed among the processors of the machine so that each processor has about the same amount of mesh to deal with, and the communication time is as small as possible. There are several ways to do this, such as with a computational neural net, by simulated annealing, or even interactively.

DIME uses a strategy known as *recursive bisection* [Fox:88mm], which has the advantages of being robust, simple, and deterministic, though sometimes the resulting communication pattern may be less than optimal. The method is illustrated in Figure 10.7: each blob represents the center of an element, and the vertical and horizontal lines represent processor divisions. First, a median vertical line is found which splits the set of elements into two sets of approximately equal numbers, then (with two-way parallelism) two horizontal medians which split the halves into four approximately equal quarters, then (with four-way parallelism) four vertical medians, and so on. Chapter 11 describes more general and powerful load-balancing methods.

Figure 10.8 (Color Plate) and Figure 10.9 (Color Plate) are from a calculation of transonic flow over an airfoil (see Section 12.3). Figure 10.9 shows the parallel structure of the DIME mesh used to calculate the flow. The redundant copies of shared nodes have been separated to show the data connections between them in yellow and blue.

In the pressure plot, there is a vertical shock about two-thirds of the way downstream from the leading edge of the airfoil. This can also be seen in the mesh plot since the same region has especially small triangles and high mesh density. Since each processor has about the same number of triangles, the processor regions are also small in the neighborhood of the shock.

10.1.7   Summary

The DIME software was written by Roy Williams, and the C^3P work is published in [Baillie:90e], [Williams:87a;87b;88a;88d;89c;90b].

DIME has evolved recently into something rather more general: instead

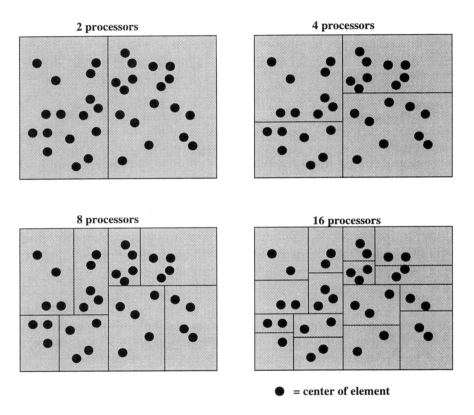

Figure 10.7: Recursive Bisection

of a set of explicitly triangular elements which have access to the three nodes around them, the new language DIME++ has the idea of a set of objects that have an index to another set of objects. Just as DIME is able to refine its mesh dynamically, and load-balance the mesh, so in DIME++ the indices may be created and modified dynamically and the sets load-balanced [Williams:91a;91c;92a;93b].

This more general formulation of the interface frees the system from explicitly triangular meshes, and greatly expands and generalizes the range of problems that can be addressed: higher dimensions, different kinds of elements, multigrid, graph problems, and multiblock. Instead of linked lists, DIME++ stores data in long vectors for maximum efficiency; it is written as a C++ class library for extensibility and polymorphism.

10.2 DIMEFEM: High-level Portable Irregular-Mesh Finite-Element Solver

DIMEFEM [Williams:89a] is a software layer which enables finite-element calculations to be done with the irregular mesh maintained by DIME. The data objects dealt with by DIMEFEM are finite-element functions (FEFs), which may be scalar or have several components (vector fields), as well as linear, multilinear and nonlinear operators which map these FEFs to numbers. The guiding principle is that interesting physical problems may be expressed in variational terms involving FEFs and operators on them [Bristeau:87a], [Glowinski:84a]. We shall use as an example a Poisson solver.

Poisson's equation is $\nabla^2 u = f$, which may also be expressed variationally as: Find u such that for all v

$$a(u,v) \equiv \int \nabla u \cdot \nabla v \, d\Omega = \int fv \, d\Omega \equiv L(v), \tag{10.1}$$

where the unknown u and the dummy variable v are taken to have the correct boundary conditions. To implement this with DIMEFEM, we first allocate space in each element for the FEFs u and f, then explicitly set f to the desired function. We now define the linear operator L and bilinear operator a as above, and call the linear solver to evaluate u.

10.2.1 Memory Allocation

When DIME creates a new element by refinement, it comes equipped with a pointer to a block of memory of user-specified size which DIMEFEM uses to store the data representing FEFs and corresponding linear operators. A template is kept of this element memory containing information about which one is already allocated and which one is free. When an FEF is to be created, the memory allocator is called, which decides how much memory is needed per element and returns an offset from the start of the element-data-space for storing the new FEF. Thus, a function in DIMEFEM typically consists of allocating a stack of work space, doing calculations, then freeing the work space.

An FEF thus consists of a specification of an element type, a number of fields (one for scalar, two or more for vector), and an offset into the element data for the nodal values.

10.2.2 Operations and Elements

Finite-element approximations to functions form a finite-dimensional vector space, and as such may be multiplied by a scalar and added. Functions are provided to do these operations. If the function is expressed as Lagrangian elements it may also be differentiated, which changes the order of representation: For example, differentiating a quadratic element produces a linear element.

At present, DIMEFEM provides two kinds of elements, Lagrangian and Gaussian, although strictly speaking the latter is not a finite element because it possesses no interpolation functions. The Gaussian element is simply a collection of function values at points within each triangle and a set of weights, so that integrals may be done by summing the function values multiplied by the weights. As with one-dimensional Gaussian integration, integrals are exact to some polynomial order. We cannot differentiate Gaussian FEFs, but can apply pointwise operators such as multiplication and function evaluation that cannot be done in the Lagrangian representation.

Consider the nonlinear operator L defined by

$$L(u) = \int \exp[du/dx]d\Omega. \tag{10.2}$$

The most accurate way to evaluate this is to start with u in Lagrangian form, differentiate, convert to Gaussian representation, exponentiate, then multiply by the weights and sum. This can be done explicitly with DIMEFEM, but in the future we hope to create an environment which "knows" about representations, linearity, and so on, and can parse an expression such as the above and evaluate it correctly.

The computational kernel of any finite-element software is the linear solver. We have implemented this with preconditioned conjugate gradient, so that the user supplies a linear operator L, an elliptic bilinear operator a, a scalar product S (a strongly elliptic symmetric bilinear operator which satisfies the triangle inequality), and an initial guess for the solution. The conjugate-gradient solver replaces the guess by the solution u of the standard variational equation

$$a(u, v) = L(v) \qquad \forall v \tag{10.3}$$

using the preconditioner S.

10.2.3 Navier-Stokes Solver

We have implemented a sophisticated incompressible flow solver using DIME and DIMEFEM. The algorithm is described more completely in [Bristeau:87a]. The evolution equation for an incompressible Newtonian fluid of viscosity n is

$$du/dt + \nu\nabla^2 u + (u \cdot \nabla)u + \nabla p = f\nabla \cdot u = 0. \tag{10.4}$$

We use a three-stage operator-split scheme whereby for each time step of length dt, the equation is integrated

- from t to $t + \vartheta dt$ with incompressibility and no convection, then

- from $t + \vartheta dt$ to $t + (1 - \vartheta)dt$ with convection and no incompressibility condition, then

- to $t + dt$ as in stage one with incompressibility and no convection.

The parameter ϑ is $1 - 1/\sqrt{2} \approx 0.29$.

Each of these three implicit steps involves the solution of either a Stokes problem:

$$\alpha u - \nu\nabla^2 u + \nabla p = f\nabla \cdot u = 0, \tag{10.5}$$

or the nonlinear problem:

$$\alpha u - \nu\nabla^2 u + (u \cdot \nabla)u = f, \tag{10.6}$$

where α is a parameter inversely proportional to the time step. We solve the Navier-Stokes equation, and consequently also these subsidiary problems, with given velocity at the boundary (Dirichlet boundary conditions).

10.2.4   Results

With velocity approximated by quadratic, and pressure by linear Lagrangian elements, we found that both the Stokes and nonlinear solvers converged in three to five iterations. We ran the square cavity problem as a benchmark.

To reach a steady-state solution, we adopted the following strategy: With a coarse mesh, keep advancing simulation time until the velocity field no longer changes, then refine the mesh, iterate until the velocity stabilizes, refine, and so on. The refinement strategy was as follows. The velocity is approximated with quadratic elements with discontinuous derivatives, so we can calculate the maximum of this derivative discontinuity for each element, then refine those elements above the 70th percentile of this quantity.

Figure 10.10 shows the results. At top left is the mesh after four cycles of this refinement and convergence, at Reynolds number 1000. We note heavy refinement at the top left and top right, where the boundary conditions force a discontinuity in velocity, and also along the right side where the near discontinuous vorticity field is being transported around the primary vortex. Bottom left shows the logical structure, split among four transputers. The top right and bottom right show streamlines and vorticity, respectively. The results accord well with the benchmark of [Schreiber:83a].

10.2.5   Summary

The DIMEFEM software was written by Roy Williams, and the flow algorithm developed by R. Glowinski of the University of Houston [Williams:89a;90b].

Figure 10.10: Results for Square Cavity Problem with Reynolds Number 1000

Chapter 11

Load Balancing and Optimization

11.1   Load Balancing as an Optimization Problem

We have seen many times that parallel computing involves breaking problems into parts which execute concurrently. In the simple regular problems seen in the early chapters, especially Chapters 4 and 6, it was usually reasonably obvious how to perform this breakup to optimize performance of the program on a parallel machine. However, in Chapter 9 and even more so in Chapter 12, we will find that the nature of the parallelism is as clear as before, but that it is nontrivial to implement efficiently.

Irregular loosely synchronous problems consist of a collection of heterogeneous tasks communicating with each other at the macrosynchronization points characteristic of this problem class. Both the execution time per task and amount and pattern of communication can differ from task to task. In this section, we describe and compare several approaches to this problem. We note that formally this is a very hard—so-called NP-complete—optimization problem. With N_{task} tasks running on N_{proc} processors we cannot afford to examine every one of the $N_{\text{task}} C_{N_{\text{proc}}}$ assignments of tasks to processors. Experience has shown that this problem is easier than one would have thought—partly at least because one does not require the exactly optimal assignment. Rather, a solution whose execution time is, say, within 10% of the optimal value is quite acceptable. Remember, one has probably chosen to "throw away" a larger fraction than this of the possible MPP performance by using a high-level language such as Fortran or C on the node (independent of any parallelism issues). The physical optimization methods described in Section 11.3 and more problem-specific heuristics have shown themselves very suitable for this class of approximate optimization [Fox:91j;92i]. In 1985, at a DOE contract renewal review at Caltech, we thought that this load balancing issue would be a major and perhaps the key stumbling block for parallel computing. However, this is not the case—it is a hard and important problem, but for loosely synchronous problems it can be solved straightforwardly [Barnard:93a], [Fox:92c;92h;92i], [Fox:92h] [Mansour:92d]. Our approach to this uses physical analogies and stems in fact from dinner conversations between Fox and David Jefferson, a collaborator from UCLA, at this meeting [Fox:85k;86a;88e;88mm]. An interesting computer science challenge is to understand why the NP-complete load-balancing problem appears "easier in practice" than the Travelling Salesman Problem, which is the generic NP-complete optimization problem. We will return to this briefly in Section 11.3, but note that the "shape of the objection function" (in physics language, the "energy landscape") illustrated in Figure 11.1 appears critical. Load-balancing problems appear to fall into the "easy class" of NP-complete optimization problems with the landscape of Figure 11.1(a). The methods discussed in the following are only a sample of the many effective approaches developed recently: [Barhen:88a], [Berger:87a], [Chen:88a], [Chrisochoides:91a], [Ercal:88a], [Ercal:88b], [Farhat:88a;89b], [Fox:88nn], [Hammond:92b], [Houstis:90a], [Livingston:88a], [Miller:92a], [Nolting:91a], [Teng:91a], [Walker:90b]. The work of Simon [Barnard:93a], [Pothen:90a], [Simon:91b], [Venkatakrishnan:92a] on recursive spectral bisection—a method with similarities to the *eigenvector recursive bisection* (ERB) method mentioned later—has been particularly successful.

A few general remarks are necessary; we use the phrases "load balancing" and "data decomposition" interchangeably. One needs both *ab initio* and dynamic distribution and redistribution of data on the parallel machine. We also can examine load balancing at the level of data or of tasks that encapsulate the data and algorithm. In elegant (but currently inefficient) software models with one datum per task, these formulations are equivalent. Our examples will do load balancing at the level of data values, but the task and data distribution problems are essentially equivalent.

Our methods are applicable to general loosely synchronous problems and indeed can be applied to arbitrary problem classes. However, we will choose a particular finite-element problem to illustrate the issues where one needs to distribute a mesh, such as that illustrated in Figure 11.2. Each triangle or element represents a task which communicates with its neighboring three

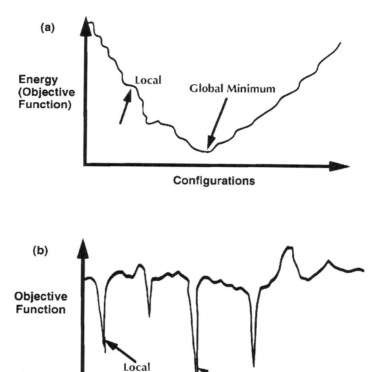

Figure 11.1: Two Possible "Energy Landscapes" for an Optimization Problem

triangles. In doing, for example, a simulation of fluid flow on the mesh, each element of the mesh communicates regularly with its neighbors, and this pattern may be repeated thousands of times.

We may classify load-balancing strategies into four broad types, depending on when the optimization is made and whether the cost of the optimization is included in the optimization itself:

- **By Inspection:** The load-balancing strategy may be determined by inspection, such as with a rectangular lattice of grid points split into smaller rectangles, so that the load-balancing problem is solved before the program is written. This is illustrated by the QCD decomposition of Figure 4.3.

- **Static:** The optimization is nontrivial, but may be done by a sequential machine before starting the parallel program, so that the load-balancing problem is solved before the parallel program begins.

- **Quasi-Dynamic:** The circumstances determining the optimal balance change during program execution, but discretely and infrequently. Because the change is discrete, the load-balance problem, and hence its solution, remain the same until the next change. If these changes are infrequent enough, any savings made in the subsequent computation make up for the time spent solving the load-balancing problem. The difference between this and the static case is that the load balancing must be carried out in parallel to prevent a sequential bottleneck.

  Koller calls these problems *adiabatic* [Fox:90nn], using a physical analogy where the load balancer can be viewed as a heatbath keeping the problem in equilibrium. In adiabatic systems, changes are sufficiently slow that the heatbath can "keep up" and the system evolves from equilibrium state to equilibrium state.

- **Dynamic:** The circumstances determining the optimal balance change frequently or continuously during execution, so that the cost of the load balancing calculation after each change should be minimized in addition to optimizing the splitting of the actual calculation. This means that there must be a decision made every so often to decide if load balancing is necessary, and how much time to spend on it. The chess program in Section 14.3 shows very irregular dynamic behavior so that statistical load-balancing methods similar to the *scattered* decomposition of Section 11.2 must be used.

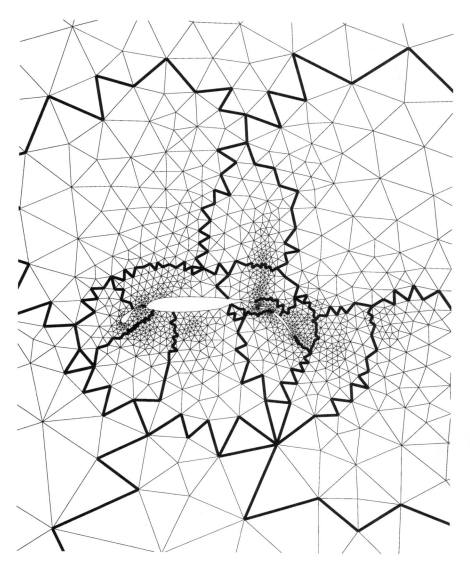

Figure 11.2: An Unstructured Triangular Mesh Surrounding a Four-Element Airfoil. The mesh is distributed among 16 processors, with divisions shown by heavy lines.

If the mesh is solution-adaptive, that is, if the mesh, and hence the load-balancing problem, change discretely during execution of the code, then it is most efficient to decide the optimal mesh distribution in parallel. In this section, three parallel algorithms, *orthogonal recursive bisection* (ORB), *eigenvector recursive bisection* (ERB) and a simple parallelization of *simulated annealing* (SA) are discussed for load-balancing a dynamic unstructured triangular mesh on 16 processors of an nCUBE machine.

The test problem is a solution-adaptive Laplace solver, with an initial mesh of 280 elements, refined in seven stages to 5772 elements. We present execution times for the solver resulting from the mesh distributions using the three algorithms, as well as results on imbalance, communication traffic, and element migration.

In this section, we shall consider the quasi-dynamic case with observations on the time taken to do the load balancing that bear on the dynamic case. The testbed is an unstructured-mesh finite-element code, where the elements are the atoms of the problem, which are to be assigned to processors. The mesh is solution-adaptive, meaning that it becomes finer in places where the solution of the problem dictates refinement.

We shall show that a class of finite-element applications share common load-balancing requirements, and formulate load balancing as a graph-coloring problem. We shall discuss three methods for solving this graph-coloring problem: one based on statistical physics, one derived from a computational neural net, and one cheap and simple method.

We present results from running these three load-balancing methods, both in terms of the quality of the graph-coloring solution (machine-independent results), and in terms of the particular machine (16 processors of an nCUBE) on which the test was run.

11.1.1   Load Balancing a Finite-Element Mesh

An important class of problems are those which model a continuum system by discretizing continuous space with a mesh. Figure 11.2 shows an unstructured triangular mesh surrounding a cross-section of a four-element airfoil from an Airbus A-310. The variations in mesh density are caused by the nature of the calculation for which the mesh has been used; the airfoil is flying at Mach 0.8 to the left, so that a vertical shock extends upward at the trailing edge of the main airfoil, which is reflected in the increased mesh density.

The mesh has been split among 16 processors of a distributed machine, with the divisions between processors shown by heavy lines. Although the areas of the processor domains are different, the numbers of triangles or elements assigned to the processors are essentially the same. Since the work done by a processor in this case is the same for each triangle, the workloads for the processors are the same. In addition, the elements have been assigned to processors so that the number of adjacent elements which are in different processors is minimized.

In order to analyze the optimal distribution of elements among the processors, we must consider the way the processors need to exchange data during a calculation. In order to design a general load balancer for such calculations, we would like to specify this behavior with the fewest possible parameters, which do not depend on the particular mesh being distributed. The following remarks apply to several application codes, written to run with the DIME software (Section 10.1), which use two-dimensional unstructured meshes, as follows:

- **Laplace:** A scalar Laplace solver with linear finite elements, using Jacobi relaxation;

- **Wing:** A finite-volume transonic Euler solver, with harmonic and biharmonic artificial dissipation [Williams:89b];

- **Convect:** A simple finite-volume solver which convects a scalar field with uniform velocity, with no dissipation;

- **Stress:** A plane-strain elasticity solver with linear finite elements using conjugate gradient to solve the stiffness matrix;

- **Fluid:** An incompressible flow solver with quadratic elements for velocity and linear elements for pressure, using conjugate gradient to solve the Stokes problem and a nonlinear least-squares technique for the convection [Williams:89a].

As far as load balancing is concerned, all of these codes are rather similar. This is because the algorithms used are local: Each element or node of the mesh gets data from its neighboring elements or nodes. In addition, a small amount of global data is needed; for example, when solving iteratively, each processor calculates the norm of the residual over its part of the mesh, and all the processors need the minimum value of this to decide if the solve has converged.

We can analyze the performance of code using an approach similar to that in Section 3.5. In this case, the computational kernel of each of these applications is iterative, and each iteration may be characterized by three numbers:

- the number of floating-point operations during the iteration, which is proportional to the number of elements (or nodes or mesh points) owned by the processor;

- the number of global combining operations during the iteration;

- the number and size of local communication events, in which the elements at the boundary of the processor region communicate data loosely synchronously [Fox:88a] with their neighboring elements in other processors, which is proportional to the number of elements at the boundary of the processor domain.

These numbers are listed in the following table for the five applications listed above:

Application	Algorithm	Flops per element	Global combines	Local communications per boundary element	c
Laplace	Jacobi relaxation	12	1	1	12
Wing	Finite volume	742		40	19
Convect	Finite volume	100		5	20
Stress	Conjugate gradient	85	2	2	42
Fluid	Quadratic CG	330	2	4	83

The two finite-volume applications do not have iterative matrix solves, so they have no convergence checking and thus have no need for any global data exchange. The ratio c in the last column is the ratio of the third to the fifth columns and may be construed as follows. Suppose a processor has E elements, of which B are at the processor boundary. Then the amount of communication the processor must do compared to the amount of calculation is given by the general form of Equation 3.10, which here becomes

$$\frac{\text{floats communicated}}{\text{floats multipled or added}} = \frac{B}{cE}. \tag{11.1}$$

It follows that a large value of c corresponds to an eminently parallelizable operation, since the communication rate is low compared to calculation. The "Stress" example has a high value of c because the solution being sought is a two-dimensional strain field; while the communication is doubled, the calculation is quadrupled, because the elements of the scalar stiffness matrix are replaced by 2×2 block matrices, and each block requires four multiplies instead of one. For the "Fluid" example, with quadratic elements, there are the two components of velocity being communicated at both nodes and edges, which is a factor of four for communication, but the local stiffness matrix is now 6×6 because of the quadratic elements. Thus, we conclude that the more interacting fields, and the higher the element order, the more efficiently the application runs in parallel.

11.1.2   The Optimization Problem and Physical Analogy

We wish to distribute the elements among the processors of the machine to minimize both load imbalance (one processor having more elements than another) and communication between elements.

Our approach here is to write down a cost function which is minimized when the total running time of the code is minimized and is reasonably simple and independent of the details of the code. We then minimize this cost function and distribute the elements accordingly.

The load-balancing problem [Fox:88a;88mm], may be stated as a graph-coloring problem: Given an undirected graph of N nodes (finite elements), color these nodes with P colors (processors) to minimize a cost function H which is related to the time taken to execute the program for a given coloring. For DIME applications, it is the finite elements which are to be distributed among the processors, so the graph to be colored is actually the dual graph to the mesh, where each graph node corresponds to an element of the mesh and has (if it is not at a boundary) three neighbors.

We may construct the cost function as the sum of a part that minimizes load imbalance and one that minimizes communication:

$$H = H_{calc} + \mu H_{comm}, \tag{11.2}$$

where H_{calc} is the part of the cost function which is minimized when each processor has equal work, H_{comm} is minimal when communication time is minimized, and μ is a parameter expressing the balance between the two, with μ related to the number c discussed above. If H_{calc} and H_{comm} were proportional to the times taken for calculation and communication, then μ

should be inversely proportional to c. For programs with a great deal of calculation compared to communication, μ should be small, and vice versa.

As μ is increased, the number of processors in use will decrease until eventually the communication is so costly that the entire calculation must be done on a single processor.

Let e, f, ... label the nodes of the graph, and $p(e)$ be the color (or processor assignment) of graph node e. Then the number of graph nodes of color q is:

$$N_q = \sum_e \delta_{q,p(e)}, \qquad (11.3)$$

and H_{calc} is proportional to the maximum value of N_q, because the whole calculation runs at the speed of the slowest processor, and the slowest processor is the one with the most graph nodes. This ignores node and link (node-to-node communication) contention, which contribute to idle time.

The formulation as a maximum of N_q is, however, not satisfactory when a perturbation is added to the cost function, such as that from the communication cost function. If, for example, we were to add a linear forcing term proportional to N_0, the cost function would be:

$$H_{calc}^{perturbed} = \max N_q + \varepsilon N_0 \qquad (11.4)$$

and the minimum of this perturbed cost function is either $N_0 = N_1 = \ldots = N/P$ if ε is less than $1/(P-1)$, or $N_0 = 0$, $N_1 = N_2 = N/(P-1)$ if ε is larger than this. This discontinuous behavior as a result of perturbations is undesirable, so we use a sum of squares instead, whose minima change smoothly with the magnitude of a perturbation:

$$H_{calc} = \zeta \sum_q N_q^2, \qquad (11.5)$$

where ζ is a scaling constant to be determined.

We now consider the communication part of the cost function. Let us define the matrix

$$B_{qr} = \sum_{e \leftrightarrow f} 1 - \delta_{q,p(e)}\, \delta_{r,p(f)}, \qquad (11.6)$$

which is the amount of communication between processors q and r, and the notation $e \leftrightarrow f$ means that the graph nodes e and f are connected by an edge of the graph.

The cost of communication from processors q to r depends on the machine architecture; for some parallel machines it may be possible to write down this metric explicitly. For example, with the early hypercubes, the cost is the number of bits which are different in the binary representations of the processor numbers q and r. The metric may also depend on the message-passing software, or even on the activities of other users for a shared machine. A truly portable load balancer would have no option but to send sample messages around and measure the machine metric, then distribute the graph appropriately. In this book, however, we shall avoid the question of the machine metric by simply assuming that all pairs of processors are equally far apart, except of course a processor may communicate with itself at no cost.

The cost of sending the quantity B_{qr} of data also depends on the programming: the cost will be much less if it is possible for the B_{qr} messages to be bundled together and sent as one, rather than separately. The major problem is latency: The cost to send a message in any distributed system is the sum of an initial fixed price and one proportional to the size of the message. This is also the case for the pricing of telephone calls, freight shipping, mail service, and many other examples from the everyday world. If the message is large enough, we may ignore latency: For the nCUBE used in Section 11.1.7 of this book, latency may be ignored if the message is longer than a hundred bytes or so. In the tests of Section 11.1.7, most of the messages are indeed long enough to neglect latency, though there is certainly further work needed on load balancing in the presence of this important effect. We also ignore blocking (idling) due to needed resources being unavailable due to contention.

The result of this discussion is that we shall assume that the cost of communicating the quantity B_{qr} of data is proportional to B_{qr}, unless $q = r$, in which case the cost is zero. This is a good assumption on many new machines, such as the Intel Touchstone series.

We shall now make the assumption that the total communication cost is the sum of the individual communications between processors:

$$H_{comm} = \varepsilon \sum_{q \neq r} B_{qr}, \qquad (11.7)$$

where ε is a constant to be determined. Notice that any overlap between calculation and communication is ignored. Here, we have ignored "global" contributions to H_{comm}, such as collective communication (global sums or reductions) mentioned in Section 11.1.1.

Substituting the expression for B_{qr}, the expression for the load balance cost function simplifies to

$$H = \zeta \sum_q N_q^2 + \mu\varepsilon \sum_{e \leftrightarrow f} 1 - \delta_{p(e),p(f)} \qquad (11.8)$$

The assumptions made to derive this cost function are significant. The most serious deviation from reality is neglecting the parallelism of communication, so that a minimum of this cost function may have grossly unbalanced communication loads. This turns out not to be the case, however, because when the mesh is equally balanced, there is a lower limit to the amount of boundary, analogous to a bubble having minimal surface area for fixed volume; if we then minimize the sum of surface areas for a set of bubbles of equal volumes, each surface must be minimized and equal.

We may now choose the scaling constants ζ and ε. A convenient choice is such that the optimal H_{calc} and H_{comm} have contributions of about unit size from each processor; the form of the scaling constant ε is because the surface area of a compact shape in d dimensions varies as the $d-1$ power of the size, while volume varies as the d power. The final form for H is

$$H = \frac{P^2}{N^2} \sum_q N_q^2 + \mu \left(\frac{P}{N}\right)^{\frac{d-1}{d}} \sum_{e \leftrightarrow f} 1 - \delta_{p(e),p(f)} \qquad (11.9)$$

where d is the dimensionality of the mesh from which the graph came.

The formalism of this section has a simple physical interpretation [Fox:86a;88kk;88mm;88tt;88uu], which we introduce here and discuss further in Section 11.2. The data points (tasks) to be distributed can be thought of as particles moving around in the discrete space formed by the processors. This physical system is controlled by the Hamiltonian (energy function) given in Equation 11.9. The two terms in the Hamiltonian have simple physical meanings illustrated in Figure 11.3. The first term in Equation 11.9 ensures equal work per node and is a short-range repulsive force trying to push particles away if they land in the same node. The second term in Equation 11.9 is a long-range attractive force which links "particles" (data points) which communicate with each other. This force tries to pull particles together (into the same node) with a strength proportional to the information needed to be communicated between them. In general, this communication force depends on the architecture of the interconnect of the parallel machine, although Equation 11.9 has assumed a simple form for this. The analogy is preserved in general with the MPP interconnect architecture translating into a topology for the discrete space formed by the processors in the analogy. This topology implies a distance dependence force for the communication term in H. We can also extend the discussion to include the cost of moving data between processors to rebalance a dynamically changing problem. This migration cost becomes a third force attracting each particle to the processor in which it currently resides. Figure 11.3 illustrates these three forces.

Note that the load-balancing problem becomes that of finding the equilibrium state of a system of particles with a "conflict" between short-range repulsive (hardcore) and long-range attractive forces. This scenario is qualitatively similar to classical atomic physics problems and leads one to expect that the physically based optimization methods could be effective. This physical analogy is extended in Section 11.2 where we show that the physical system exhibits effects that can be associated with temperature and phase transitions. We also indicate how it needs to be extended for problems with microscopic structure in their temporal properties.

11.1.3 Algorithms for Load Balancing

This book presents performance evaluation of three load-balancing algorithms, all of which run in parallel. With a massively parallel machine, it would not be possible to load-balance the mesh sequentially. This is because (1) there would be a serious sequential bottleneck, (2) there would not be enough memory in a host machine to store the entire distributed mesh, and (3) the large cost incurred in communicating the entire mesh.

The three methods are:

- **SA**—Simulated annealing: We directly minimize the above cost function by a process analogous to slow physical cooling.

- **ORB**—Orthogonal recursive bisection: A simple method which cuts the graph into two by a vertical cut, then cuts each half into two by a horizontal cut, then cuts each quarter vertically, and so on. These cuts are usually motivated by the natural geometrical or physical structure of the problem [Baden:87a], [Fox:88mm]. However, they can also be generated in more abstract fashion directly from a graph [Fox:88nn].

- **ERB**—Eigenvector recursive bisection: This method also cuts the graph in two then each half into two, and so on, but the cutting is done using an eigenvector of a matrix with the same sparsity structure as the adjacency matrix of the graph. The method is an approximation to a computational neural net [Fox:88e], [Williams:91a].

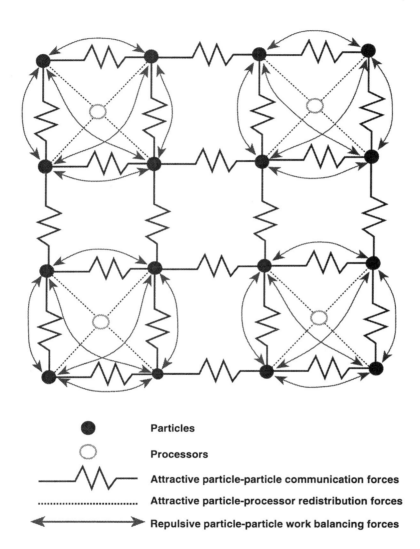

Figure 11.3: Sixteen Data Points Distributed Optimally on Four Processors, Illustrating the Physical Analogy of Section 11.3. We take a simple two-dimensional mesh connection for the particles.

11.1.4   Simulated Annealing

Simulated annealing [Fox:88mm], [Hajek:88a], [Kirkpatrick:83a], [Otten:89a] is a very general optimization method which stochastically simulates the slow cooling of a physical system. The idea is that there is a cost function H (in physical terms, a Hamiltonian) which associates a cost with a state of the system, a "temperature" T, and various ways to change the state of the system. The algorithm works by iteratively proposing changes and either accepting or rejecting each change. Having proposed a change we may evaluate the change δH in H. The proposed change may be accepted or rejected by the *Metropolis* criterion; if the cost function decreases ($\delta H < 0$) the change is accepted unconditionally; otherwise it is accepted but only with probability $\exp(-\delta H/T)$. A crucial requirement for the proposed changes is *reachability* or *ergodicity*—that there be a sufficient variety of possible changes that one can always find a sequence of changes so that any system state may be reached from any other.

When the temperature is zero, changes are accepted only if H decreases, an algorithm also known as *hill-climbing*, or more generally, the *greedy algorithm* [Aho:83a]. The system soon reaches a state in which none of the proposed changes can decrease the cost function, but this is usually a poor optimum. In real life, we might be trying to achieve the highest point of a mountain range by simply walking upwards; we soon arrive at the peak of a small foothill and can go no further.

On the contrary, if the temperature is very large, all changes are accepted, and we simply move at random ignoring the cost function. Because of the reachability property of the set of changes, we explore all states of the system, including the global optimum.

Simulated annealing consists of running the accept/reject algorithm between the temperature extremes. We propose many changes, starting at a high temperature and exploring the state space, and gradually decreasing the temperature to zero while hopefully settling on the global optimum. It can be shown that if the temperature decreases sufficiently slowly (the inverse of the logarithm of the time), then the probability of being in a global optimum tends to certainty [Hajek:88a].

Figure 11.4 shows simulated annealing applied to the load-balancing cost function in one dimension. The graph to be colored is a periodically connected linear array of 200 nodes, to be colored with four colors. The initial configuration, at the bottom of the figure, is the left 100 nodes colored white, two domains of 50 each in mid grays, and with no nodes colored in the dark-

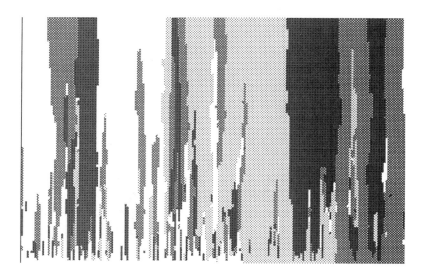

Figure 11.4: Simulated Annealing of a Ring Graph of Size 200, with the Four Graph Colors Shown by Gray Shades. The time history of the annealing runs vertically, with the maximum temperature and the starting configuration at the bottom, and zero temperature and the final optimum at the top. The basic move is to change the color of a graph node to a random color.

est gray. We know that the global optimum is 50 nodes of each color, with all the nodes of the same color consecutive. Iterations run up the figure with the final configurations at the top.

At each iteration of the annealing, a random node is chosen, and its color changed to a random color. This proposed move is accepted if the Metropolis criterion is accepted. At the end of the annealing, a good balance is achieved at the top of the figure, with each color having equal numbers of nodes; but there are 14 places where the color changes (communication cost = 14), rather than the minimum four.

Heuristics

In choosing the change to be made to the state of the system, there may be intuitive or heuristic reasons to choose a change which tends to reduce the cost function. For our example of load balancing, we know that the optimal coloring of the graph has equal-sized compact "globules"; if we were to restrict the new color of a node to the color of one of its two neighbors, then the boundaries between colors move without creating new domains.

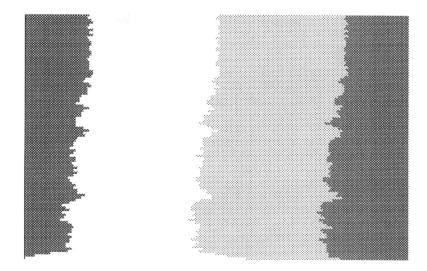

Figure 11.5: Same as Figure 11.4, Except the Basic Move Is to Change the Color of a Graph Node to the Color of One of the Neighbors.

The effect of this algorithm is shown in Figure 11.5, with the same number of iterations as Figure 11.4. The imbalance of 100 white nodes is quickly removed, but there are only three colors of 67 nodes each in the (periodically connected) final configuration. The problem is that the changes do not satisfy reachability; if a color is not present in graph coloring, then it can never come back.

Even if reachability is satisfied, a heuristic may degrade the quality of the final optimum, because a heuristic is coercing the state toward local minima in much the same way that a low temperature would. This may reduce the ability of the annealing algorithm to explore the state space, and cause it to drop into a local minimum and stay there, resulting in poor performance overall.

Figure 11.6 shows a solution to this problem. There is a high probability the new color is one of the neighbors, but also a small probability of a "seed" color, which is a randomly chosen color. Now we see a much better final configuration, close to the global optimum. The balance is perfect and there are five separate domains instead of the optimal four.

Collisional Simulated Annealing

As presented so far, simulated annealing is a sequential algorithm, since whenever a move is made an acceptance decision must be made before an-

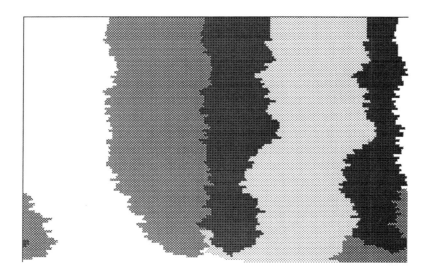

Figure 11.6: Same as Figure 11.4, Except the Basic Move Is to Change the Color of a Graph Node to the Color of One of the Neighbors with Large Probability, and to a Random Color with Small Probability.

other move may be evaluated. A parallel variant, which we shall call *collisional* simulated annealing, would be to propose several changes to the state of the system, evaluate the Metropolis criterion on each simultaneously, then make those changes which are accepted. Figure 11.7 shows the results of the same set of changes as Figure 11.6, but doing 16 changes simultaneously instead of sequentially. Now there are eight domains in the final configuration rather than five. The essential difference from the sequential algorithm is that δH resulting from several simultaneous changes is not the sum of the δH values if the changes are made in sequence. We tend to get *parallel collisions*, where there may be two changes, each of which is beneficial, but which together are detrimental. For example, a married couple might need to buy a lawnmower; if either buys it, the result is beneficial to the couple, but if both simultaneously buy lawn mowers, the result is detrimental because they only need one.

Figure 11.8 shows how parallel collisions can adversely affect the load-balancing process. At left, two processors share a small mesh, shown by the two colors, with a sawtooth division between them. There are seven edges with different colors on each side. In the middle are shown each processor's separate views of the situation, and each processor discovers that by changing

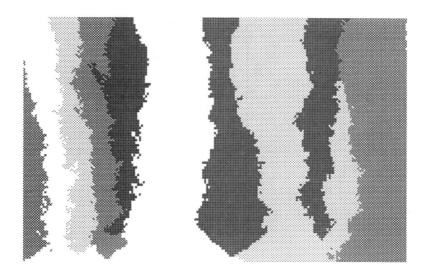

Figure 11.7: Same as Figure 11.6, Except the Optimization Is Being Carried Out in Parallel by 16 Processors. Note the fuzzy edges of the domains caused by parallel collisions.

the color of the teeth of the sawtooth it can reduce the boundary from 7 to 4. On the right is shown the result of these simultaneous changes; the boundary has increased to 15, instead of the 4 that would result if only one processor went ahead.

The problem with this parallel variant is, of course, that we are no longer doing the correct algorithm, since each processor is making changes without consulting the others. As noted in [Baiardi:89a], [Barajas:87a], [Braschi:90a], [Williams:86b], we have an algorithm which is highly parallel, but not particularly efficient. We should note that when the temperature is close to zero, the success rate of changes (ratio of accepted to proposed changes) falls to zero: Since a parallel collision depends on two successful changes, the parallel collision rate is proportional to the square of the low success rate, so that the effects of parallel collisions must be negligible at low temperatures.

One approach [Fox:88a] [Johnson:86a] to the parallel collision problem is *rollback*. We make the changes in parallel, as above, then check to see if any parallel collisions have occurred, and if so, undo enough of the changes so that there are no collisions. While rollback ensures that the algorithm is carried out correctly, there may be a great deal of overhead, especially in a tightly coupled system at high temperature, where each change may collide

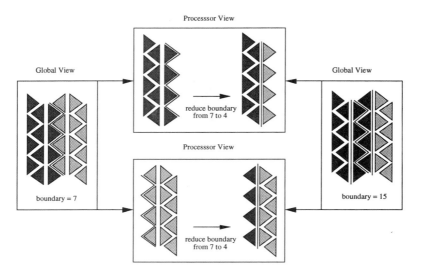

Figure 11.8: Illustration of a Parallel Collision During Load Balance. Each processor may take changes which decrease the boundary length, but the combined changes increase the boundary.

with many others, and where most changes will be accepted. In addition, of course, rollback involves a large software and memory overhead since each change must be recorded in such a way that it can be rescinded, and a decision must be reached about which changes are to be undone.

For some cost functions and sets of changes, it may be possible to divide the possible changes into classes such that parallel changes within a class do not collide. An important model in statistical physics is the *Potts model* [Wu:82a], whose cost function is the same as the communication part of the load-balance cost function. If the underlying graph is a square lattice, the graph nodes may be divided into "red" and "black" classes, so called because the arrangement is like the red and black squares of a checkerboard. Then we may change all the red nodes or all the black nodes in parallel with no collisions.

Some highly efficient parallel simulated annealing algorithms have been implemented [Coddington:90a] for the Potts model using clustering. These methods are based on the locality of the Potts cost function: the change in cost function from a change in the color of a graph node depends only on the colors of the neighboring nodes of the graph. Unfortunately, the balance part of the cost function interferes with this locality in that widely separated (in terms of the Hamming distance) changes may collide, so these methods are not suitable for load balancing.

In this book, we shall use the simple collisional simulated annealing algorithm, making changes without checking for parallel collisions. Further work is required to invent and test more sophisticated parallel algorithms for simulated annealing, which may be able to avoid the degradation of performance caused by parallel collisions without unacceptable inefficiency from the parallelism [Baiardi:89a].

Clustering

Since the basic change made in the graph-coloring problem is to change the color of one node, a boundary can move at most one node per iteration. The boundaries between processors are diffusing toward their optimal configurations. A better change is to take a connected set of nodes which are the same color, and change the color of the entire set at once [Coddington:90a]. This is shown in Figure 11.9 where the cluster is chosen first by picking a random node; we then add nodes probabilistically to the cluster; in this case, the neighbor is added with probability 0.8 if it has the same color, and never if it has a different color. Once a neighbor has failed to be added, the cluster generation finishes. The coloring of the graph becomes optimal extremely quickly compared to the single color change method of Figure 11.6.

Figure 11.10 shows the clustered simulated annealing running in parallel, where 16 clusters are chosen simultaneously. The performance is degraded, but still better than Figure 11.7, which is parallel but with single color changes.

Summary of the Algorithm

The annealing algorithm as presented so far requires that several parameters be chosen for tuning, which are in *italic font* in the description below.

First, we pick the initial coloring of the graph so that each graph node takes a color corresponding to the processor in which it currently resides. We form a population table, of which each processor has a copy of N_q, the number of nodes which have color q. We pick a value for μ, the *importance of communication*.

We pick a *maximum temperature* and the *number of stages* during which the temperature is to be reduced to zero. Each stage consists of a number of changes to the graph coloring which may be accepted or rejected, with no communication between the processors. At the end of the stage, each processor has a different idea of the population table, and the colors

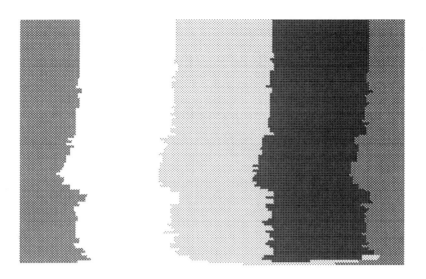

Figure 11.9: Same as Figure 11.6, Except the Basic Move Is to Change the Color of a Connected Cluster of Nodes.

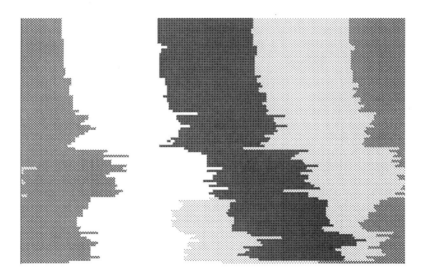

Figure 11.10: Same as Figure 11.7, Except That the Cluster Method Is Being Carried Out in Parallel by 16 Processors.

of neighboring graph nodes which are in different processors, because each processor has made changes without knowledge of the others. At the end of the stage, the processors communicate to update the population tables and local neighbor information so that each processor has up-to-date information. Each stage consists of either having a given *number of accepted changes*, or a *given number of rejected changes*, whichever comes first, followed by a loosely synchronous communication between processors.

Each trial move within a stage consists of looking for a cluster of uniform color, choosing a new color for the cluster, evaluating the change in cost function, and using the Metropolis criterion to decide whether to accept it. The cluster is chosen by first picking a random graph node as a seed, and probabilistically forming a cluster. Neighboring nodes are added to the cluster with a given *cluster probability* if they are the same color as the seed and reside in the same processor.

The proposed new color for the cluster is chosen to be either random with given *seed probability*, or a random color chosen from the set of neighbors of the cluster. The Metropolis criterion is then used to decide if the color change is to be accepted, and if so, the local copy of the population table is updated.

11.1.5 Recursive Bisection

Rather than coloring the graph by direct minimization of the load-balance cost function, we may do better to reduce the problem to a number of smaller problems. The idea of recursive bisection is that it is easier to color a graph with two colors than many colors. We first split the graph into two halves, minimizing the communication between the halves. We can then color each half with two colors, and so on, recursively bisecting each subgraph.

There are two advantages to recursive bisection; first, each subproblem (coloring a graph with two colors) is easier than the general problem; second, there is natural parallelism. While the first stage is splitting a single graph in two, and is thus a sequential problem, there is two-way parallelism at the second stage, when the two halves are being split, and four-way parallelism when the four quarters are being split. Thus, coloring a graph with P colors is achieved in a number of stages which is logarithmic in P.

Both of the recursive bisection methods we shall discuss split a graph into two by associating a scalar quantity, s_e, with each graph node, e, which we may call a *separator* field. By evaluating the median S of the s_e, we can color the graph according to whether s_e is greater or less than S. The

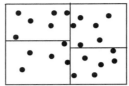

Figure 11.11: Load Balancing by ORB for Four Processors. The elements (left) are reduced to points at their centers of mass (middle), then split into two vertically, then each half split into two horizontally. The result (right) shows the assignment of elements to processors.

median is chosen as the division so that the number of nodes in each half is automatically equal; the problem is now reduced to that of choosing the field, s_e, so that the communication is minimized.

Orthogonal Recursive Bisection

A simple and cheap choice [Fox:88mm] for the separator field is based on the position of the finite elements in the mesh. We might let the value of s_e be the x-coordinate of the center of mass of the element, so that the mesh is split in two by a median line parallel to the y-axis. At the next stage, we split the submesh by a median line parallel to the x-axis, alternating between x and y stage by stage, as shown in Figure 11.11. Another example is shown in Figure 12.13.

11.1.6   Eigenvalue Recursive Bisection

Better but more expensive methods for splitting a graph are based on finding a particular eigenvector of a sparse matrix which has the structure of the adjacency matrix of the graph, and using this eigenvector as a separator field [Barnes:82a], [Boppana:87a], [Pothen:89a].

Neural Net Model

For our discussion of eigenvector bisection, we use the concept of a computational neural net, based on the model of Hopfield and Tank [Fox:88tt], [Hopfield:85b]. When the graph is to be colored with two colors, these may be conveniently represented by the two states of a neuron, which we conventionally represent by the numbers -1 and $+1$. The Hopfield-Tank neural net finds the minimum of a "computational energy," which is a negative-definite quadratic form over a space of variables which may take these values -1

and +1, and consequently is ideally suited to the two-processor load-balance problem. Rewriting the load balance cost function,

$$H \propto \sum_{e \leftrightarrow f} \frac{1}{2}(V_e - V_f)^2 + \mu^{-1}\left(\sum_e V_e\right)^2 - \xi \sum_e (V_e^2 - 1) \qquad (11.10)$$

where the V_e are "neural firing rates," which are continuous variables during the computation and tend to 1 as the computation progresses. The first term of this expression is the communication part of the cost function, the second term ensures equal numbers of the two colors if μ is small enough, and the third term is zero when the V_e are 1, but pushes the V_e away from zero during the computation. The latter is to ensure that H is negative-definite, and the large but arbitrary constant ξ plays no part in the final computation. The firing rate or output V_e of a neuron is related to its *activity* u_e by a sigmoid function which we may take to be $V_e = \tanh \beta u_e$. The constant β adjusts the "gain" of the neuron as an amplifier. The evolution equations to be solved are then:

$$\frac{d}{dt} u_e = -\frac{u_e}{\tau} - d_e V_e + \sum_{e \leftrightarrow f} V_f + \xi V_e - \mu^{-1} \sum_e V_e \qquad (11.11)$$

where τ is a time constant for the system and d_e is the degree (number of neighbors) of the graph node e. If the gain is sufficiently low, the stable solution of this set of equations is that all the u_e are zero, and as the gain becomes large, the u_e grow and the V_e tend to either -1 or $+1$. The neural approach to load balancing thus consists of slowly increasing the gain from zero while solving this set of coupled nonlinear differential equations.

Let us now linearize this set of equations for small values of u_e, meaning that we neglect the hyperbolic tangent, because for small x, $\tanh x \approx x$. This linear set of equations may be written in terms of the vector $\mathbf{u}$ of all the u_e values and the adjacency matrix $\mathbf{A}$ of the graph, whose element A_{ef} is 1 if and only if the distinct graph nodes e and f are connected by an edge of the graph. We may write

$$\frac{d\mathbf{u}}{dt} + \frac{\mathbf{u}}{\tau} = \beta(-\mathbf{D} + \mathbf{A} + \xi\mathbf{I} - \mu^{-1}\mathbf{E})\mathbf{u} = \beta\mathbf{N}\mathbf{u}, \qquad (11.12)$$

where $\mathbf{D}$ is a diagonal matrix whose elements are the degrees of the graph nodes, $\mathbf{I}$ is the identity matrix, and $\mathbf{E}$ is the matrix with 1 in each entry. This linear set of equations may be solved exactly from a knowledge of the eigenvalues and eigenvectors of the symmetric matrix $\mathbf{N}$. If ξ is sufficiently large, all eigenvalues of $\mathbf{N}$ are positive, and when β is greater than a critical value, the eigenvector of $\mathbf{N}$ corresponding to its largest eigenvalue grows exponentially. Of course, when the neuron activities are no longer close to zero, the growth is no longer exponential, but this initial growth determines the form of the emerging solution.

If μ is sufficiently small, so that balance is strongly enforced, then the eigenspectrum of $\mathbf{N}$ is dominated by that of $\mathbf{E}$. The highest eigenvalue of $\mathbf{N}$ must be chosen from the space of the lowest eigenvalue of $\mathbf{E}$. The lowest eigenvalue of $\mathbf{E}$ is zero, with eigenspace given by those vectors with $\mathbf{E}\mathbf{x} = 0$, which is just the balance condition. We observe that multiples of the identity matrix make no difference to the eigenvectors, and conclude that the dominant eigenvector $\mathbf{s}$ satisfies $(-\mathbf{D} + \mathbf{A})\mathbf{s} = \lambda\mathbf{s}$ and $\mathbf{E}\mathbf{s} = 0$, where λ is maximal. The matrix $\mathbf{D} - \mathbf{A}$ is the *Laplacian* matrix of the graph [Pothen:89a], and is positive semi-definite. The lowest eigenvector of the Laplacian has eigenvalue zero, and is explicitly excluded by the condition $\mathbf{E}\mathbf{s} = 0$. Thus, it is the second eigenvector which we use for load balancing.

In summary, we have set up the load balance problem for two processors as a neural computation problem, producing a set of nonlinear differential equations to be solved. Rather than solve these, we have assumed that the behavior of the final solution is governed by the eigenstate which first emerges at a critical value of the gain. This eigenstate is the second eigenvector of the Laplacian matrix of the graph.

If we split a connected graph in two equal pieces while minimizing the boundary, we expect each half to be a connected subgraph of the original graph. This is not true in all geometries, but is in "reasonable cases." This intuition is supported by a theorem of Fiedler [Fiedler:75a;75b] that when we do the splitting by the second eigenvector of the Laplacian matrix, at least one-half is always connected.

To calculate this second eigenstate, we use the Lanczos method [Golub:83a], [Parlett:80a], [Pothen:89a]. We can explicitly exclude the eigenvector of value zero, because the form of this eigenvector is equal entries for each element of the vector. The accuracy of the Lanczos method increases quickly with the number of *Lanczos vectors* used. We find that 30 Lanczos vectors are sufficient for splitting a graph of 4000 nodes.

A closely related eigenvector method [Barnes:82a], [Boppana:87a] is based on the second highest eigenvector of the adjacency matrix of the graph, rather than the second lowest eigenvector of the Laplacian matrix. The advantage of the Laplacian method is in the implementation: The first

Figure 11.13: Solution of the Laplace Equation Used to Test Load-Balancing Methods. The outer boundary has voltage increasing linearly from −1.2 to 1.2 in the vertical direction, the light shade is voltage 1, and the dark shade voltage −1.

eigenvector is known exactly (the vector of all equal elements), so that it can be explicitly deflated in the Lanczos method.

Figure 11.12 (Color Plate) shows eigenvector recursive bisection in action. A triangular mesh surrounding a four-element airfoil has already been split into eight pieces, with the pieces separated by gray lines. Each of these pieces is being split into two, and the plot shows the value of the eigenvector used to make the next split, shown by black lines. The eigenvector values range from large and positive in red through dark and light blue, green, yellow, and back to red. The eight eigenvector calculations are independent and are, of course, done in parallel.

The splitting is constructed by finding a median value for the eigenvector so that half the triangles have values greater than the median and half lower. The black line is the division between these.

Figure 11.14: Initial and Final Meshes for the Load-Balancing Test. The initial mesh with 280 elements is essentially a uniform meshing of the square, and the final mesh of 5772 elements is dominated by the highly refined S-shaped region in the center.

11.1.7   Testing Procedure

The applications described in Section 11.1.1 have been implemented with DIME (Distributed Irregular Mesh Environment), described in Section 10.1.

We have tested these three load-balancing methods using the application code "Laplace" described in Section 11.1.1. The problem is to solve Laplace's equation with Dirichlet boundary conditions, in the domain shown in Figure 11.13. The square outer boundary has voltage linearly increasing vertically from -1.2 to $+1.2$, the lightly shaded S-shaped internal boundary has voltage $+1$, and the dark shaded hook-shaped internal boundary has voltage -1. Contour lines of the solution are also shown in the figure, with contour interval 0.08.

The test begins with a relatively coarse mesh of 280 elements, all residing in a single processor, with the others having none. The Laplace equation is solved by Jacobi iteration, the mesh is refined based on the solution obtained so far, then is balanced by the method under test. This sequence—solve, refine, balance—is repeated seven times until the final mesh has 5772 elements. The starting and ending meshes are shown in Figure 11.14.

The refinement is solution-adaptive, so that the set of elements to be refined is based on the solution that has been computed so far. The refinement criterion is the magnitude of the gradient of the solution, so that the most heavily refined part of the domain is that between the S-shaped and hook-shaped boundaries where the contour lines are closest together. At each refinement, the criterion is calculated for each element of the mesh, and a value is found such that a given proportion of the elements are to be refined, and those with higher values than this are refined loosely synchronously. For this test of load balancing, we refined 40% of the elements of the mesh at each stage.

This choice of refinement criterion is not particularly to improve the accuracy of the solution, but to test the load-balancing methods as the mesh distribution changes. The initial mesh is essentially a square covered in mesh of roughly uniform density, and the final mesh is dominated by the long, thin S-shaped region between the internal boundaries, so the mesh changes character from two-dimensional to almost one-dimensional.

We ran this test sequence on 16 nodes of an nCUBE/10 parallel machine, using ORB and ERB and two runs with SA, the difference being a factor of ten in cooling rate, and different starting temperatures.

The eigenvalue recursive bisection used the deflated Lanczos method for diagonalization, with three iterations of 30 Lanczos vectors each to find the second eigenvector. These numbers were chosen so that more iterations and Lanczos vectors produced no significant improvement, and fewer degraded the performance of the algorithm.

The parameters used for the collisional annealing were as follows:

- The starting temperature for the run labelled SA1 was 0.2, and for SA2, 1.0. In the former case, movement of the boundaries is allowed, but a significant memory of the initial coloring is retained. In the latter case, large fluctuations are allowed, the system is heated to randomness, and all memory of the initial configuration is erased.

- The interface (boundary) importance, μ, was set at 0.1, which is large enough to make communication important in the cost function, but small enough that all processors will get their share of elements.

- The curves labelled SA1 correspond to cooling to zero temperature in 500 stages, those labelled SA2 to cooling in 5000 stages.

- Each stage consisted of finding either one successful change (per processor) or 200 unsuccessful changes before communicating, and thus getting the correct global picture.

- The cluster probability was set to 0.58, giving an average cluster size of about 22. This is a somewhat arbitrary choice and further work is required to optimize this.

In Figure 11.15, we show the divisions between processor domains for the three methods at the fifth stage of the refinement, with 2393 elements in the mesh. The figure also shows the divisions for the ORB method at the fourth stage: Note the unfortunate processor division to the left of the S-shaped boundary which is absent at the fifth stage.

11.1.8   Test Results

We made several measurements of the running code, which can be divided into three categories:

Machine-independent Measurements

These are measurements of the quality of the solution to the graph-partitioning problem which are independent of the particular machine on which the code is run.

Let us define *load imbalance* to be the difference between the maximum and minimum numbers of elements per processor compared to the average number of elements per processor. More precisely, we should use equations (i.e., work) per processor as, for instance, with Dirichlet boundary conditions, the finite element boundary nodes are inactive and generate no equations [Chrisochoides:93a].

The two criteria for measuring communication overhead are the *total traffic size*, which is the sum over processors of the number of floating-point numbers sent to other processors per iteration of the Laplace solver, and the *number of messages*, which is the sum over processors of the number of messages used to accomplish this communication.

These results are shown in Figure 11.16. The load imbalance is significantly poorer for both the SA runs, because the method does not have the exact balance built in as do the RB methods, but instead exchanges load imbalance for reducing the communication part of the cost function. The imbalance for the RB methods comes about from splitting an odd number of elements, which of course cannot be exactly split in two.

There is a sudden reduction in total traffic size for the ORB method between the fourth and fifth stages of refinement. This is caused by the geometry of the mesh as shown at the top of Figure 11.15; at the fourth stage the first vertical bisection is just to the left of the light S-shaped region

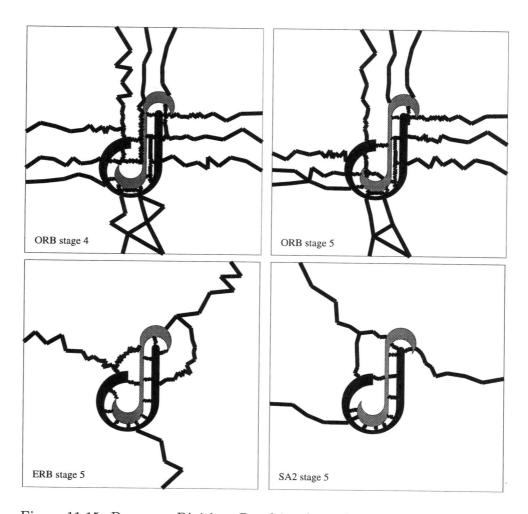

Figure 11.15: Processor Divisions Resulting from the Load-Balancing Algorithms. Top, ORB at the fourth and fifth stages; lower left, ERB at the fifth stage; lower right, SA2 at the fifth stage.

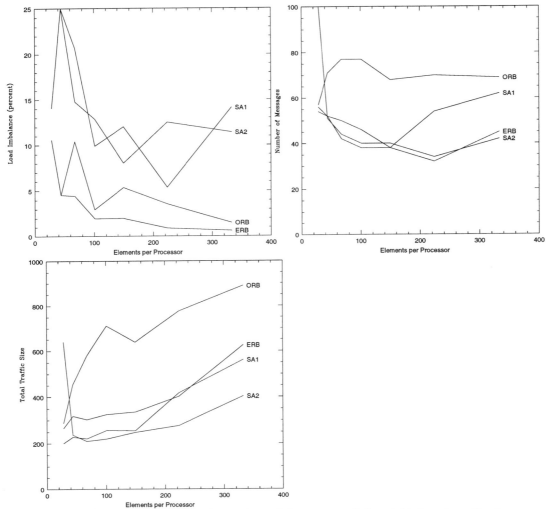

Figure 11.16: Machine-independent Measures of Load-Balancing Performance. Left, percentage load imbalance; lower left, total amount of communication; right, total number of messages.

creating a large amount of unnecessary communication, and for the fifth and subsequent stages the cut fortuitously misses the highly refined part of the mesh.

Machine-dependent Measurements

These are measurements which depend on the particular hardware and message-passing software on which the code is run. The primary measurement is, of course, the time it takes the code to run to completion; this is the sum of startup time, load-balancing time, and the product of the number of iterations of the inner loop times the time per iteration. For quasi-static load balancing, we are assuming that the time spent on the basic problem computation is much longer than the load-balance time, so parallel computation time is our primary measurement of load-balancing performance. Rather than use an arbitrary time unit such as seconds for this measurement, we have counted this time per iteration as an equivalent number of floating-point operations (flops). For the nCUBE, this time unit is 15 μs for a 64-bit multiply. Thus, we measure *flops per iteration* of the Jacobi solver.

The secondary measurement is the *communication time* per iteration, also measured in flops. This is just the local communication in the graph, and does not include the time for the global combine which is necessary to decide if the Laplace solver has reached convergence.

Figure 11.17 shows the timings measured from running the test sequence on the 16-processor nCUBE. For the largest mesh, the difference in running time is about 18% between the cheapest load-balancing method (ORB) and the most expensive (SA2). The ORB method spends up to twice as much time communicating as the others, which is not surprising, since ORB pays little attention to the structure of the graph it is splitting, concentrating only on getting exactly half of the elements on each side of an arbitrary line.

The curves on the right of Figure 11.17 show the time spent in local communication at each stage of the test run. It is encouraging to note the similarity with the lower left panel of Figure 11.16, showing that the time spent communicating is roughly proportional to the total traffic size, confirming this assumption made in Section 11.1.2.

Measurements for Dynamic Load Balancing

After refinement of the mesh, one of the load-balancing algorithms is run and decisions are reached as to which of a processor's elements are to be sent away, and to which processor they are to be sent. As discussed in Section 10.1, a significant fraction of the time taken by the load balancer is

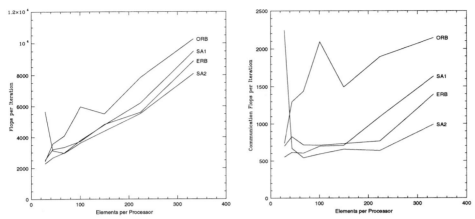

Figure 11.17: Machine-dependent Measures of Load-Balancing Performance. Left, running time per Jacobi iteration in units of the time for a floating-point operation (flop); right, time spent doing local communication in flops.

taken in this migration of elements, since not only must the element and its data be communicated, but space must be allocated in the new processor and other processors must be informed of the new address of the element, and so on. Thus, an important measure of the performance of an algorithm for dynamic (in contrast to quasi-dynamic) load balancing is the number of *elements migrated*, as a proportion of the total number of elements.

Figure 11.18 shows the percentage of the elements which migrated at each stage of the test run. The one which does best here is ORB, because refinement causes only slight movement of the vertical and horizontal median lines. The SA runs are different because of the different starting temperatures: SA1 started at a temperature low enough that the edges of the domains were just "warmed up," in contrast to SA2 which started at a temperature high enough to completely forget the initial configuration and, thus, essentially all the elements are moved. The ERB method causes the largest amount of element migration, which is because of two reasons. The first is because some elements are migrated several times because the load balancing is done in $\log_2 P$ stages for P processors; this is not a fundamental problem, and arises from the particular implementation of the method used here. The second reason is that a small change in mesh refinement may lead to a large change in the second eigenvector; perhaps a modification of the method could use the distribution of the mesh before refinement to create an inertial term so that the change in eigenvector as the mesh is refined could

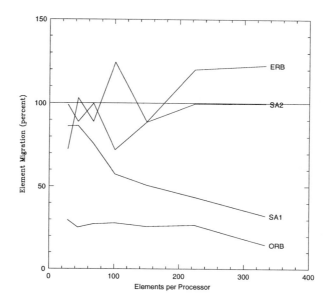

Figure 11.18: Percentage of Elements Migrated During Each Load-Balancing Stage. The percentage may be greater than 100 because the recursive bisection methods may cause the same element to be migrated several times.

be controlled.

The migration time is only part of the time taken to do the load balancing, the other part being that taken to make the decisions about which element goes where. The total times for load balancing during the seven stages of the test run (solving the coloring problem plus the migration time) are shown in the table below:

Method	Time (minutes)
ORB	5
ERB	11
SA1	25
SA2	230

For the test run, the time per iteration was measured in fractions of a second, and it took few iterations to obtain full convergence of the Laplace equation, so that a high-quality load balance is obviously irrelevant for this simple case. The point is that the more sophisticated the algorithm for which the mesh is being used, the greater the time taken in using the distributed mesh compared to the time taken for the load balance. For a sufficiently complex application—for example, unsteady reactive flow simulation—the calculations associated with each element of the mesh may be enough that a few minutes spent load balancing is completely negligible, so that the quasi-dynamic assumption is justified.

11.1.9   Conclusions

The Laplace solver that we used for the test run embodies the typical operation that is done with finite-element meshes. This operation is matrix-vector multiply. Thus, we are not testing load-balancing strategies just for a Laplace solver but for a general class of applications, namely, those which use matrix-vector multiply as the heart of a scheme which iterates to convergence on a fixed mesh, then refines the mesh and repeats the convergence.

The case of the Laplace solver has a high ratio of communication to calculation, as may be seen from the discussion of Section 11.1.1, and thus brings out differences in load-balancing algorithms particularly well.

Each load-balancing algorithm may be measured by three criteria:

- the quality of the solution it produces, measured by the time per iteration in the solver;

- the time it takes to do the load balancing, measured by the time it takes to solve the graph-coloring problem and by the number of elements which must then be migrated; and

- the portability of the method for different kinds of applications with different kinds of meshes, and the number of parameters that must be set to obtain optimal performance from the method.

Orthogonal recursive bisection is certainly cheap, both in terms of the time it takes to solve the graph-coloring problem and the number of elements which must be migrated. It is also portable to different applications, the only required information being the dimensionality of the mesh. And it is easy to program. Our tests indicate, however, that more expensive methods can improve performance by over 20%. Because ORB pays no attention to the connectivity of the element graph, one suspects that as the geometry of the underlying domain and solution becomes more complex, this gap will widen.

Simulated annealing is actually a family of methods for solving optimization problems. Even when run sequentially, care must be taken in choosing the correct set of changes that may be made to the state space, and in choosing a temperature schedule to ensure a good optimum. We have tried a "brute force" parallelization of simulated annealing, essentially ignoring the parallelism. For sufficiently slow cooling, this method produces the best solution to the load-balancing problem when measured either against the load-balance cost function, or by timings on a real parallel computer. Unfortunately, it takes a long time to produce this high-quality solution, perhaps because some of the numerous input parameters are not set optimally. A more sensitive treatment is probably required to reduce or eliminate parallel collisions [Baiardi:89a]. Clearly, further work is required to make SA a portable and efficient parallel load balancer for parallel finite-element meshes. True portability may be difficult to achieve for SA, because the problem being solved is graph coloring, and graphs are extremely diverse; perhaps something approaching an expert system may be required to decide the optimal annealing strategy for a particular graph.

Eigenvalue recursive bisection seems to be a good compromise between the other methods, providing a solution of quality near that of SA at a price little more than that of ORB. There are few parameters to be set, which are concerned with the Lanczos algorithm for finding the second eigenvector. Mathematical analysis of the ERB method takes place in the familiar territory of linear algebra, in contrast to analysis of SA in the jungles of nonequilibrium thermodynamics. A major point in favor of ERB for balancing finite-element meshes is that the software for load balancing with ERB is shared to a large extent with the body of finite-element software: The heart of the eigenvector calculation is a matrix-vector multiply, which has already been efficiently coded elsewhere in the finite-element library. Recursive spectral bisection [Barnard:93a] has been developed as a production load balancer and very successfully applied to a variety of finite-element problems.

The C^3P research described in this section has been continued by Mansour in Fox's new group at Syracuse [Mansour:91a;92a–e]. He has considered simulating annealing, genetic algorithms, neural networks, and spectral bisection producing in each parallel implementation. Further, he introduced a multiscale or graph contraction approach where large problems to be decomposed are not directly tackled but are first "clumped" or contracted to a smaller problem [Mansour:93b], [Ponnusamy:93a]. The latter can be decomposed using the basic techniques discussed above and this solution of the small problem used to initialize a fast refinement algorithm for the original large problem. This strategy has an identical philosophy to the multigrid approach (Section 9.7) for partial differential equations. We are currently collaborating with Saltz in integrating these data decomposers into the high-level data-parallel languages reviewed in Section 13.1.

11.2   Applications and Extensions of the Physical Analogy

In [Fox:86a;92c;92h;93a], we point out some interesting features of the physical analogy and energy function introduced in Section 11.1.4.

Suppose that we are using the simulating annealing method of Section 11.1.4 on a dynamically varying system. Assume that this annealing algorithm is running in parallel in the same machine on which the problem executes. Suppose that we use a (reasonably) optimal annealing strategy. Even in this case, the "heatbath" formed by load balancer and operating system can only "cool" the problem to a minimum temperature T_s. At this temperature, any further gains from improved decomposition by lowering the temperature will be outweighed by time taken to perform the annealing. This *temperature T_s* is independent of performance of computer; it is a property of the system being simulated. Thus, we can consider this temperature T_s as a new property of a dynamical complex system. High values of T_s imply that the system is rapidly varying; low values that it is slowly varying.

Now we want to show that decompositions can lead to phase transitions between different states of the physical system defined by analogy of Section 11.1.2. In the language of Chapter 3, we can say that the complex system representing this problem exhibits a phase transition. We illustrate this with a trivial particle dynamics problem shown in Figure 11.19. Typically, we use on such problems the domain decomposition of Figure 11.19(a), where each node of the parallel machine contains a single connected region (compare Section 12.4). Alternatively, we can use the scattered decomposition—described for matrices in Section 8.1 and illustrated in Figure 11.19(b). One assigns to each processor several small regions of the space scattered uniformly throughout the domain. Each processor gets "a piece of the action" and shares those parts of the domain where the particle density and hence computational work is either large or small. This was explored for partial differential equations in [Morison:86a]. The scattered decomposition is a local minimum—there is an optimal size for the scattered blocks of space assigned to each processor. Both in this example and generally, the scattered decomposition is not as good as domain decomposition. This is shown

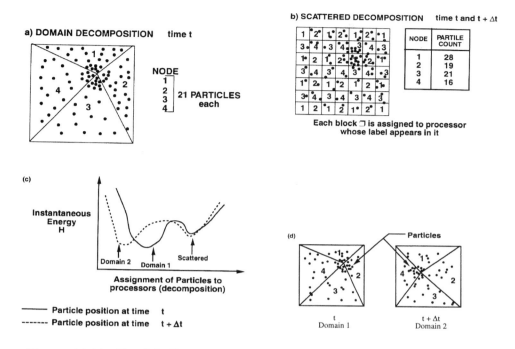

Figure 11.19: Particle Dynamics Problem on a Four-node System with Two Decompositions (a) Domain, Time t, (b) Scattered Times t and $t + \Delta t$, (c) Instantaneous Energies, (d) Domain Decomposition Changing from Time t to $t + \Delta t$

in Figure 11.19(c), which sketches the energy H as a function of the chosen decomposition. Now, suppose that the particles move in time from t to $t + \Delta t$ as shown in Figure 11.19(d). The scattered decomposition minimum is *unchanged*, but as shown in Figure 11.19(c),(d) the domain decomposition minimum moves with time.

Now, one would often be interested not in the instantaneous energy H, but rather in the average

$$\bar{H}(\Delta t) = \frac{1}{\Delta t} \int_t^{t+\Delta t} H \text{ (time value } t) \, dt \qquad (11.13)$$

For this new objective function $\bar{H}(\Delta t)$, the scattered decomposition can be the global minimum as illustrated in Figure 11.20. The domain decomposition is smeared with time and so its minimum is raised in value; the value of H at the scattered decomposition minimum is unchanged. We can

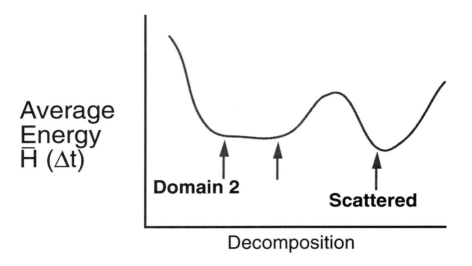

Figure 11.20: The Average Energy $\bar{H}$ of Equation 11.13

study $\bar{H}$ as a function of Δt, and the hardware ratio $\lambda = t_{\text{comm}}/t_{\text{calc}}$ used in Equation 3.10. As Δt increases or λ decreases, we move from the situation of Figure 11.19(c) to that of Figure 11.20. In physics language, Δt and λ are order parameters which control the phase transition between the two states *scattered* and *domain*. Rapidly varying systems (high T_s), rather than those with lower T_s, are more likely to see the transition as Δt increases. This agrees with physical intuition, as we now describe. When T_s is small (slowly varying system), domain decomposition is the global minimum and this switches to a scattered decomposition as T_s increases. In Figure 11.19(a),(b), we can associate with each particle in the simulation a spin value which indicates the label of the processor to which it is assigned. Then we see the direct analogy to physical spin systems. At high temperatures, we have spin waves (scattered decomposition); at low temperatures, (magnetic) domains (domain decomposition).

We end by noting that in the analogy there is a class of problems which we call *microscopically dynamic*. These are explored in [Fox:88f], [Fox:88kk;88uu]. In this problem class, the fundamental entities (particles in above analogy) move between nodes of parallel machine on a microscopic time scale. The previous discussion had only considered the *adiabatic* loosely synchronous problems where one can assume that the data elements (particles in the analogy) can be treated as fixed in a particular processor at each time instant. We will not give a general discussion here, but rather just illustrate the ideas with one example—the global sum calculation written in Fortran as

```
DO 1 I=1, LIMIT1
A(I)=0
DO 1 J=1, LIMIT2
1 A(I)=A(I) + B(I,J)
```

This is illustrated in Figure 11.21 (Color Plate) for the case LIMIT1=4 decomposed onto a four-node machine. The value of LIMIT1 is important for performance considerations but irrelevant for the discussion here. The optimal scheduling of communication and calculation is tricky and is discussed as the *fold* algorithm in [Fox:88a]. The four tasks of calculating the four A(I) cannot be viewed as particles as they move from node to node and we cannot represent this movement in the formalism used up to now. Rather, we now represent the tasks by "space-time" strings or world lines and one replaces Equation 11.9 by a Hamiltonian which describes interacting strings rather than interacting particles. This can be applied to event-driven simulations, message routing, and other microscopically dynamic problems. The strings need to be draped over the space-time grid formed by the complex computer as it evolves in time. Figure 11.21 (Color Plate) shows this compact "draping" for the fold algorithm.

We have successfully applied similar ideas to multivehicle and multi-arm robot path planning and routing problems [Chiu:88f], [Fox:90e;90k;92c], [Gandhi:90a]. Comparison of the vehicle navigation in Figure 11.22 (Color Plate) with the computational routing problem in Figure 11.21 (Color Plate) illustrates the analogy.

11.3 Physical Optimization

C^3P maintained a significant activity in optimization. There were several reasons for this, one of which was, of course, natural curiosity. Another was the importance of load balancing and data decomposition which is, as discussed previously in this chapter, "just" an optimization problem. Again, we already mentioned in Section 6.1 our interest in neural networks as a naturally parallel approach to artificial intelligence. Section 9.9 and Section 11.1 have shown how neural networks can be used in a range of optimization problems. Load balancing has the important (optimization) characteristic of NP completeness, which implies that it would take an exponential time to solve completely. Thus, we studied the travelling salesman problem (TSP) which is well known to be NP-complete and formally equivalent to other problems with this property. One important contribution of C^3P was the work of Simic [Simic:90a;91a]. [Simic:91a]

Simic derived the relationship between the neural network [Hopfield:86a] and elastic net [Durbin:87a;89a], [Rose:90f;91a;93a], [Yuille:90a] approaches to the TSP. This work has been extensively reviewed [Fox:91j;92c;92h;92i] and we will not go into the details here. A key concept is that of *physical optimization* which implies the use of a physics approach of minimizing the energy, that is, finding the ground state of a complex system set up as a physical analogy to the optimization problem. This idea is illustrated clearly by the discussion in Section 11.1.3 and Section 11.2. One can understand some reasons why a physics analogy could be useful from two possible plots of the objective function to be minimized, against the possible configurations, that is, against the values of parameters to be determined. Physical systems tend to look like Figure 11.1(a), where correlated (i.e., local) minima are "near" global minima. We usually do not get the very irregular landscape shown in Figure 11.1(b). In fact, we do find the latter case with the so-called random field Ising model, and here conventional physics methods perform poorly [Marinari:92a], [Guagnelli:92a]. Ken Rose showed how these ideas could be generalized to a wide class of optimization problems as a concept called *deterministic annealing* [Rose:90f], [Stolorz:92a]. Annealing is illustrated in Figure 11.23 (Color Plate). One uses temperature to smooth out the objective function (energy function) so that at high temperature one can find the (smeared) global minimum without getting trapped in spurious local minima. Temperature is decreased skillfully initializing the search at Temperature T_2 by the solution at the previous higher temperature T_1. This annealing can be applied either statistically [Kirkpatrick:83a] as in Sections 11.1 and 11.3 or with a deterministic iteration. Neural and elastic networks can be viewed as examples of deterministic annealing. Rose generalized these ideas to clustering [Rose:90a;90c;91a;93a]; vector quantization used in coding [Miller:92b], [Rose:92a]; tracking [Rose:89b;90b]; and electronic packing [Rose:92b]. Deterministic annealing ;has also been used for robot path planning with many degrees of freedom [Fox:90k], [Gandhi:90b] (see also Figure 11.22 (Color Plate)), character recognition [Hinton:92a], scheduling problems [Gislen:89a;91a], [Hertz:92a], [Johnston:92a], and quadratic assignment [Simic:91a].

Neural networks have been shown to perform poorly in practice on the

TSP [Wilson:88a], but we found them excellent for the formally equivalent load-balancing problem in Section 11.1. This is now understood from the fact that the simple neural networks used in the TSP [Hopfield:86a] used many redundant neural variables, and the difficulties reported in [Wilson:88a] can be traced to the role of the constraints that remove redundant variables. The neural network approach summarized in Section 11.1.6 uses a parameterization that has no redundancy and so it is not surprising that it works well. The elastic network can be viewed as a neural network with some constraints satisfied exactly [Simic:90a]. This can also be understood by generalizing the conventional binary neurons to multistate or Potts variables [Peterson:89b;90a;93a].

Moscato developed several novel ways of combining simulated annealing with genetic algorithms [Moscato:89a;89c;89d;89e] and showed the power and flexibility of these methods.

11.4 An Improved Method for the Travelling Salesman Problem

The Travelling Salesman Problem (TSP) is probably the most well-known member of the wider field of *combinatorial optimization* (CO) problems. These are difficult optimization problems where the set of feasible solutions (trial solutions which satisfy the constraints of the problem but are not necessarily optimal) is a finite, though usually very large set. The number of feasible solutions grows as some combinatoric factor such as $N!$, where N characterizes the size of the problem. We have already commented on the use of neural networks for the TSP in the previous section. Here we show how to combine problem-specific heuristics with simulated annealing, a physical optimization method.

It has often been the case that progress on the TSP has led to progress on many CO problems and more general optimization problems. In this way, the TSP is a playground for the study of CO problems. Though the present work concentrates on the TSP, a number of our ideas are general and apply to all optimization problems.

The most significant issues occur as one tries to find extremely good or exact solutions to the TSP. Many algorithms exist which are fast and find feasible solutions which are within a few percent of the optimum length. Here, we present algorithms which will usually find exact solutions to substantial instances of the TSP. We are limited by space considerations to a brief presentation of the method—more details may be found in [Martin:91a].

In a general instance of the TSP one is given N "cities" and a matrix d_{ij} giving the distance or cost function for going from city i to j. Without loss of generality, the distances can be assumed to be positive. A "tour" consists of a list of N cities, $tour[i]$, where each city appears once and only once. In the TSP, the problem is to find the tour with the minimum "length," where length is defined to be the sum of the lengths along each step of the tour,

$$length = \sum_{k=0}^{N-1} d_{tour[k],tour[k+1]},$$

and $tour[N]$ is identified with $tour[0]$ to make it periodic.

Most common instances of the TSP have a symmetric distance matrix; we will hereafter focus on this case. All CO problems can be formulated as optimizing an objective function (e.g., the length) subject to constraints (e.g., legal tours).

11.4.1   Background on Local Search Heuristics

In a local search method, one first defines a neighborhood topology on the set of all tours. For instance, one might define the neighborhood of a tour T_1 to be all those tours which can be obtained by changing at most k edges of T_1. A tour is said to be *locally opt* if no tour in its neighborhood is shorter than it. One can search for locally opt tours by starting with a random tour T_1 and performing k-changes on it as long as the tour length decreases. In this way, one constructs a sequence of tours T_1, T_2, ... Eventually the process stops and one has reached a local opt tour. Lin [Lin:65a] studied the case of $k = 2$ and $k = 3$, and showed that one could get quite good tours quickly. Furthermore, since in general there are quite a few locally opt tours, in order to find the globally optimal tour, he suggested repeating this process from random starts many times until one was confident all the locally opt tours had been found. Unfortunately, the number of local opt tours rises exponentially with N, the number of cities. Thus in general, it is more efficient to use a more sophisticated local opt (say higher k) than to try to repeat the search from random starts many times. The current state-of-the-art optimization heuristic is an algorithm due to Lin and Kernighan [Lin:73a]. It is a variable depth k-neighborhood search, and it is the benchmark against which all heuristics are tested. Since it is significantly better than three-opt, for any instance of the TSP, there are many fewer L–K-opt tours than there are three-opt tours. This postpones the problem of doing exponentially many random starts until one reaches N on the order of a few hundred. For still larger N, the number of L–K-opt tours itself gets unmanageable. Given that one really does want to tackle these larger problems, there are two natural ways to go. First, one can try to extend the neighborhood which L–K considers, just as L–K extended the neighborhood of three-changes. Second, one expects that instead of sampling the local opt tours in a random way as is done by applying the local searches from random starts many times, it might be possible to obtain local opt tours in a more efficient way, say via a sampling with a bias in favor of the shorter tours. We will see that this gives rise to an algorithm which indeed enables one to solve much larger instances.

11.4.2 Background on Markov Chains and Simulated Annealing

Given that any local search method will stop in one of the many local opt solutions, it may be useful to find a way for the iteration to escape by temporarily allowing the tour length to increase. This leads to the popular method of "simulated annealing" [Kirkpatrick:83a].

One starts by constructing a sequence of tours T_1, T_2, and so on. At each step of this chain, one does a k-change (moves to a neighboring tour). If this decreases the tour length, the change is accepted; if the tour length increases, the change is rejected with some probability, in which case one simply keeps the old tour at that step. Such a stochastic construction of a sequence of Ts is called a Markov chain. It can be viewed as a rather straightforward extension of the above local search to include "noisiness" in the search for shorter tours. Because increases in the tour length are possible, this chain never reaches a fixed point. For many such Markov chains, it is possible to show that given enough time, the chain will visit every possible tour T, and that for very long chains, the Ts appear with a calculable probability distribution. Such Markov chains are closely inspired by physical models where the chain construction procedure is called a Monte Carlo. The stochastic accept/reject part is supposed to simulate a random fluctuation due to temperature effects, and the temperature is a parameter which measures the bias towards short tours. If one wants to get to the globally optimal tour, one has to move the temperature down towards zero, corresponding to a strong bias in favor of short tours. Thus, one makes the temperature vary with time, and the way this is done is called the annealing schedule, and the result is simulated annealing.

If the temperature is taken to zero too fast, the effect is essentially the same as setting the temperature to zero exactly, and then the chain just traps at a local opt tour forever. There are theoretical results on how slowly the annealing has to be done to be sure that one reaches the globally optimum solution, but in practice the running times are astronomical. Nevertheless, simulated annealing is a standard and widely used approach for many minimization problems. For the TSP, it is significantly slower than Lin-Kernighan, but it has the advantage that one can run for long times and slowly improve the quality of the solutions. See, for instance, the studies Johnson et al. [Johnson:91a] have done. The advantage is due to the improved sampling of the short length tours: Simulated annealing is able to ignore the tours which are not near the minimum length. An intuitive way to think about it is that for a long run, simulated annealing is able to try to improve an already very good tour, one which probably has many links in common with the exact optimum. The standard Lin-Kernighan algorithm, by contrast, continually restarts from scratch, throwing away possibly useful information.

11.4.3   The New Algorithm—Large-Step Markov Chains

Simulated annealing does not take advantage of the local opt heuristics. This means that instead of sampling local opt tours as does L–K repeated from random starts, the chain samples all tours. It would be a great advantage to be able to restrict the sampling of a Markov chain to the local opt tours only. Then the bias which the Markov chain provides would enable one to sample the shortest local opt tours more efficiently than local opt repeated from random starts. This is what our new algorithm does.

To do this, one has to find a way to go from one local opt tour, T_n, to another, T_{n+1}, and this is the heart of our procedure. We propose to do a change on T_n, which we call a "kick." This can be a random p-change, for instance, but we will choose something smarter than that. Follow this kick by the local opt tour improvement heuristic until reaching a new local opt tour T_{n+1}. Then accept or reject T_{n+1} depending on the increase or decrease in tour length compared to T_n. This is illustrated in Figure 11.24. Since there are many changes in going from T_n to T_{n+1}, we call this method a "Large-Step Markov Chain." It can also be called "Iterated Local Opt," but it should be realized that it is precisely finding a way to iterate which is the difficulty! The algorithm is far better than the small-step Markov chain methods (conventional simulated annealing) because the accept/reject

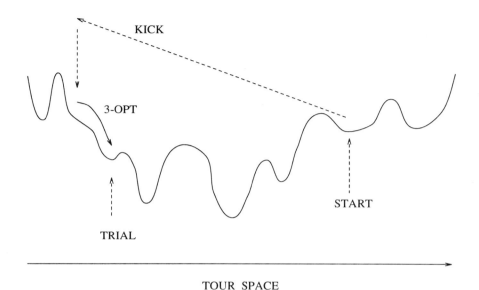

Figure 11.24: Schematic Representation of the Objective Function and of the Tour Modification Procedure Used in the Large-step Markov Chain

procedure is not implemented on the intermediate tours which are almost always of longer length. Instead, the accept/reject does not happen until the system has returned to a local minimum. The method directly steps from one local minimum to another. It is thus much easier to escape from local minima.

At this point, let us mention that this method is no longer a true simulated annealing algorithm. That is, the algorithm does NOT correspond to the simulation of any physical system undergoing annealing. The reason is that a certain symmetry property, termed "detailed balance" in the physics community, is not satisfied by the large-step algorithm. [Martin:91a] says a bit more about this. One consequence of this is that the parameter "temperature" which one anneals with no longer plays the role of a true, physical temperature—instead it is merely a parameter which controls the bias towards the optimum. The lack of a physical analogy may be the reason that this algorithm has not been tried before, even though much more exotic algorithms (such as appealing to quantum mechanical analogies!) have been proposed.

We have found that in practice, this methodology provides an efficient sampling of the local opt tours. There are a number of criteria which need to be met for the biased sampling of the Markov chain to be more efficient than plain random sampling. These conditions are satisfied for the TSP, and more generally whenever local search heuristics are useful. Let us stress before proceeding to specifics that this large-step Markov chain approach is extremely general, being applicable to any optimization problem where one has local search heuristics. It enables one to get a performance which is at least as good as local search, with substantial improvements over that if the sampling can be biased effectively. Finally, although the method is general, it can be adapted to match the problem of interest through the choice of the kick. We will now discuss how to choose the kick for the TSP.

Consider, for instance, the case where the local search is three-opt. If we used a kick consisting of a three-change, the three-opt would very often simply bring us back to the previous tour with no gain. Thus, it is probably a good idea to go to a four-change for the kick when the local search is three-opt. For more general local search algorithms, a good choice for the kick would be a k-change which does not occur in the local search. Surprisingly, it turns out that two-opt, three-opt, and especially L–K are structured so that there is one kick choice which is natural for all of them. To see this, it is useful to go back to the paper by Lin and Kernighan. In that paper, they define "sequential" changes and they also show that if the tour is to be improved, one can force all the partial gains during the k-change to be positive. A consequence of this is that the checkout time for sequential k-changes can be completed in $O(N)$ steps. It is easy to see that all two and three changes are sequential, and that the first nonsequential change occurs at $k = 4$ (Figure 2 of their paper). We call this graph a "double-bridge" change because of what it does to the tour. It can be constructed by first doing a two-change which disconnects the tour; the second two-change must then reconnect the two parts, thereby creating a bridge. Note that both of the two-changes are bridges in their own way, and that the double-bridge change is the only nonsequential four-change which cannot be obtained by composing changes which are both sequential and leave the tour connected. If we included this double-bridge change in the definition of the neighborhood for a local search, checkout time would require $O(N^2)$ steps (a factor N for each bridge essentially). Rather than doing this change as part of the local search, we include such changes stochastically as our kick. The double-bridge kick is the most natural choice for any local search method which considers only sequential changes. Because L–K does so many changes for k greater than three, but misses double-bridges, one can expect that most of what remains in excess length using L–K might be removed with our extension. The results below indicate that this is the case.

11.4.4 Results

At first we implemented the Large-Step Markov Chain for the three-opt local search. We checked that we could solve to optimality problems of sizes up to 200 by comparing with a branch and bound program. For $N = 100$, the optimum was found in a few minutes on a SUN-3, while for $N = 200$ an hour or two was required. For larger instances, we used problems which had been solved to optimality by other people. We ran our program on the Lin-318 instance solved to optimality by Padberg and Crowder. Our iterated three-opt found the optimal tour on each of five separate runs, with an average time of less than 20 hours on the SUN-3. We also ran on the AT&T-532 instance problem solved to optimality by Padberg and Rinaldi. By using a postreduction method inspired by tricks explained in the Lin-Kernighan paper, the program finds the optimum solution in 100 hours. It is of interest to ask what is the expected excess tour length for very large problems using our method with a reasonable amount of time. We have run on large instances of cities randomly distributed in the unit square. Ordinary three-opt gives an average length 3.6% above the Held-Karp bound, whereas the iterated three-opt does better than L–K (which is 2.2% above): it leads to an average of less than 2.0% above H–K. Thus we see that without much more algorithmic complexity, one can improve three-opt by more than 1.6%.

In [Martin:91a], we suggested that such a dramatic improvement should also carry over to the L–K local opt algorithm. Since then, we have implemented a version of L–K and have run it on the instances mentioned above. Johnson [Johnson:90b] and also Cook, Applegate, Chvatal [Cook:90b] have similarly investigated the improvement of iterated L–K over repeated L–K. It is now clear that the iterated L–K is a big improvement. Iterated L–K is able to find the solution to the Lin-318 instance in minutes, and the solution to the AT&T-532 problem in an hour. At a recent TSP workshop [TSP:90a], a 783-city instance constructed by Pulleyblank was solved to optimality by ourselves, Johnson, and Cook et. al., all using the large-step method.

For large instances (randomly distributed cities), Johnson finds that iterated L–K leads to an average excess length of 0.84% above the Held-Karp bound. Previously it was expected that the exact optimum was somewhere above 1% from the Held-Karp bound, but iterated L–K disproves this conjecture.

One of the most exciting results of the experiments which have been performed to date is this: For "moderate"-sized problems (such as the AT&T-532 or the 783 instance mentioned above), no careful "annealing" seems to be necessary. It is observed that just setting the temperature to zero (no uphill moves at all!) gives an algorithm which can often find the exact optimum. The implication is that, for the large-step Markov chain algorithm, the effective energy landscape has only one (or few) local minima! Almost all of the previous local minima have been modified to saddle points by the extended neighborhood structure of the algorithm.

Steve Otto had the original idea for the large-step Markov chain. Olivier Martin has made (and continues to make) many improvements towards developing new, fast local search heuristics. Steve Otto and Edward Felten have developed the programs, and are working on a parallel implementation.

Chapter 12

Irregular Loosely Synchronous Problems

12.1 Irregular Loosely Synchronous Problems Are Hard

This chapter contains some of the hardest applications we developed within C^{3}P at Caltech. The problems are still "just" data-parallel with the natural "massive" (i.e., large scale as directly proportional to the number of data elements or problem size) loosely synchronous parallelism summarized in Figure 12.1. However, the irregularity of the problem—both static and dynamic—makes the implementation technically hard. Interestingly, after this hard work, we do find very good speedups, that is, this problem class has as much parallelism as the simpler synchronous problems of Chapters 4 and 6. In fact, one finds that it is in this class of problems that parallel machines most clearly outperform traditional vector supercomputers [Fox:89i;89n;90o]. The (dynamic) irregularity makes the parallelism harder to expose, but it does not remove it; however, the irregularity of a problem can make it impossible to get good performance on (SIMD) vector processors.

The problems contained in this chapter are also typical of the hardest challenges for parallelizing compilers. These applications are not easy to write in a high-level language, such as High Performance Fortran of Chapter 13, in a way that compilers can efficiently extract the parallelism. This area is one of major research activity with interesting contributions from the groups at Yale [Bhatt:92a] and Stanford [Singh:92a] for the N-body problem described in Section 12.4.

METHODOLOGY of DATA PARALLELISM

- All successful concurrent machines with
  - Many nodes
  - High performance
        Have obtained "massive" parallelism from
        "Data Parallelism" or"Domain Decomposition."

- Problem is an algorithm or computation applied
  to a data set with macroscopic (loosely synchronous)
  or microscopic (synchronous) algorithmic synchronization

    Obtain concurrency by acting on different
    data elements concurrently.

    Different machine architectures implement
    this differently.

  - MIMD Distributed Memory   Processing and
                                     Data Distributed

  - MIMD Shared Memory   Processing Distributed

  - SIMD Distributed Memory   Synchronous Processing
                                     Distributed Data

Figure 12.1: Data Parallelism

The applications in this chapter can be summarized as follows:

1. Sections 12.2, 12.3: Adaptive unstructured meshes—the data structure is an irregular graph—where we use the DIME system of Chapter 10 to cope with the "complication." A domain-specific software tool, rather than a general compiler, has been used.

2. Section 12.6: Adaptive irregular clusters superimposed on a regular grid. This application has essentially the same parallelization issues as region finding in image processing [Copty:92a].

3. Section 12.7: Sorting features an adaptive treelike (hierarchical) data structure.

4. Sections 12.4, 12.5, 12.8: These combine a hierarchical tree structure for fast calculation of forces with the underlying geometric structure of the physical domain. The applications are either "pure" particle simulations or a mix of particle and continuum calculations. In the latter case, they generalize to irregular dynamic problems the particle in the cell methods described in Section 9.3.

We suggest that Chapters 12, 14, and 18 contain some of those applications which should be studied by computer scientists developing new software tools and parallel languages. This is where the application programmer needs help! We have separated off Chapter 14, as the violation of the loose synchronization condition in this chapter produces different complications from the dynamic irregularity that characterizes the applications of Chapter 12. Chapter 18 contains compound metaproblems combining all types of problem structure.

12.2 Simulation of the Electrosensory System of the Fish *Gnathonemus petersii*

All animals are faced with the computationally intense task of continuously acquiring and analyzing sensory data from their environment. To ensure maximally useful data, animals appear to use a variety of motor strategies or behaviors to optimally position their sensory apparatus. In all higher animals, neural structures which process both sensory and motor information are likely to exist which can coordinate this exploratory behavior for the sake of sensory acquisition.

To study this feedback loop, we have chosen the weak electric fish, which use a unique electrically based means of exploring their environment [Bullock:86a], [Lissman:58a]. These nocturnal fish, found in the murky waters of the Congo and Amazon, have developed electrosensory systems to allow them to detect objects without relying on vision. In fact, in some species this electric sense appears to be their primary sensory modality.

This sensory system relies on an electric organ which generates a weak electric field surrounding the fish's body that in turn is detected by specialized electroreceptor cells in the fish's skin. The presence of animate or inanimate objects in the local environment causes distortions of this electric field, which are interpreted by the fish. The simplicity of the sensory signal, in addition to the distributed external representation of the detecting apparatus, makes the electric fish an excellent animal through which to study the involvement in sensory discrimination of the motor system in general, and body position in particular.

Simulations in two dimensions [Bacher:83a], [Heiligenberg:75a] and measurements with actual fish have shown that body position, especially the tail angle, significantly alter the fields near the fish's skin.

To study quantitatively how the fish's behavior affects the "electric images" of objects, we are developing three-dimensional computer simulations of the electric fields that the fish generate and detect. These simulations, when calibrated with the measured fields, should allow us to identify and focus on behaviors that are most relevant to the fish's sensory acquisition tasks, and to predict the electrical consequences of the behavior of the fish with higher spatial resolution than possible in the tank.

Being able to visualize the electric fields, in false color on a simulated fish's body as it swims, may provide a new level of understanding of how these curious animals sense and respond to their world. For this simulation, we have chosen the fish *Gnathonemus petersii*.

12.2.1 Physical Model

We need to reduce the great complexity of a biological organism to a manageable physical model. The ingredients of this model are the fish body, shown in Figure 12.2, the object that the fish is sensing, and the water exterior to both the fish and the object.

The real fish has some projecting fins, and our first approximation is to neglect these because their electrical properties are essentially the same as those of water.

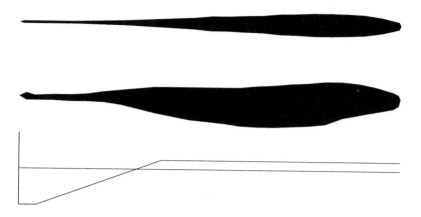

Figure 12.2: Side and Top Views of the Fish, and Internal Potential Model

We will assume that the fish is exploring a small conductive object, such as a small metal sphere. First, we reduce the geometrical aspect of the object to being pointlike, yet retaining some relevant electrical properties. Except when the object is another electric fish, we expect it to have no active electrical properties, but only to be an *induced dipole*.

We now come to the modelling of the fish body itself. This consists of a skin with electroreceptor cells which can detect potential differences, and a rather complex internal structure. We shall assume that the source voltage is maintained at the interface between the internal structure and the skin, so that we need not be concerned with the details of the internal structure. Thus, the fish body is modelled as two parts: an internal part with a given voltage distribution on its surface, and a surrounding skin with variable conductivity.

The upshot of this model is that we need to solve Laplace's equation in the water surrounding the fish, with an induced dipole at the position of the object the fish is investigating, with a mixed or Cauchy boundary condition at the surface of the fish body.

12.2.2 Mathematical Theory

The boundary element method [Brebbia:83a], [Cruse:75a] has been used for many applications where it is necessary to solve a linear elliptic partial differential equation. Because of the linearity of the underlying differential equation, there is a Green's function expressing the solution throughout the

three-dimensional domain in terms of the behavior at the boundaries, so that
the problem may be transformed into an integral equation on the boundary.

The discrete approximation to this integral equation results in the solution of a full set of simultaneous linear equations, one equation for each
node of the boundary mesh; the conventional finite-difference method would
result in solving a sparse set of equations, one for each node of a mesh-filling
space. Let us compare these methods in terms of efficiency and software
cost.

To implement the finite-difference method, we would first make a mesh
filling the domain of the problem (i.e., a three-dimensional mesh), then for
each mesh point set up a linear equation relating its field value to that of its
neighbors. We would then need to solve a set of sparse linear equations. In
the case of an exterior problem such as ours, we would need to pay special
attention to the farfield, making sure the mesh extends out far enough and
that the proper approximation is made at this outer boundary.

With the boundary element method, we discretize only the surface of the
domain, and again solve a set of linear equations, except that now they are
no longer sparse. The far field is no longer a problem, since this is taken
care of analytically.

If it is possible to make a regular grid surrounding the domain of interest,
then the finite-difference method is probably more efficient, since multigrid
methods or alternating direction methods will be faster than the solution of
a full matrix. It is with complex geometries, however, that the boundary
element method can be faster and more efficient on sequential or distributed-
memory machines. It is much easier to produce a mesh covering a curved
two-dimensional manifold than a three-dimensional mesh filling the space
exterior to the manifold. If the manifold is changing from step to step, the
two-dimensional mesh need only be distorted, whereas a three-dimensional
mesh must be completely remade, or at least strongly smoothed, to prevent
tangling. If the three-dimensional mesh is not regular, the user faces the
not inconsiderable challenge of explicit load balancing and communication
at the processor boundaries.

12.2.3   Results

Figure 12.3 shows a view of four of the model fish in some rather unlikely
positions, with natural shading.

Figure 12.4 shows a side view of the fish with the free field (no object)
shown in gray scale, and we can see how the potential ramp at the skin-body

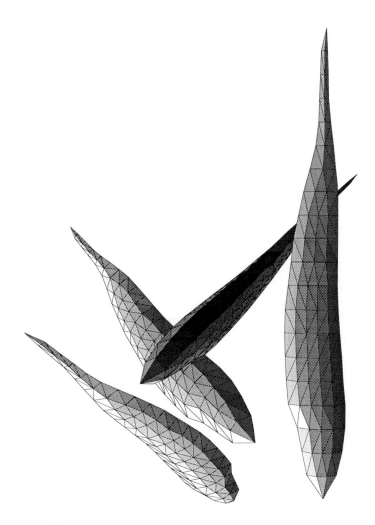

Figure 12.3: Four Fish with Simple Shading

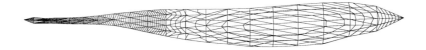

Figure 12.4: Potential Distribution on the Surface of the Fish, with No
External Object

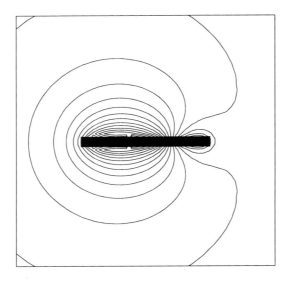

Figure 12.5: Potential Contours on the Midplane of the Fish, Showing Dipole
Distribution from the Tail

interface has been smoothed out by the resistivity of the skin. Figure 12.5
shows the computed potential contours for the midplane around the fish
body, showing the dipole field emanating from the electric organ in the tail.

Figure 12.6 (Color Plate) shows the difference field (voltage at the skin
with and without the object) for three object positions, near the tail (top),
at the center (middle) and near the head (bottom). It can be seen that
this difference field, which is the sensory input for the fish, is greatest when
the object is close to the head. A better view of the difference voltage is
shown in Figure 12.7, which shows the envelope of the difference voltage on
the midline of the fish, for various object positions. Again, we see that the
maximum sensory input occurs when the object is close to the head of the
fish, rather than at the tail, where the electric organ is.

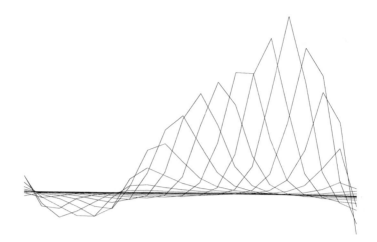

Figure 12.7: Envelope of Voltage Differences Along Midline of the Fish, for 20 Object Positions, Each 3 cm Above Mid-plane

12.2.4 Summary

The BEM algorithm was written as a DIME application [Williams:90b;90c] by Roy Williams, Brian Rasnow of the Biology Division, and Chris Assad of the Engineering Division.

12.3 Transonic Flow

Unstructured meshes have been widely used for calculations with conventional sequential machines. Jameson [Jameson:86a;86b] uses explicit finite-element-based schemes on fully unstructured tetrahedral meshes to solve for the flow around a complete aircraft, and other workers [Dannenhoffer:89a], [Holmes:86a], [Lohner:84a;85a;86a] have used unstructured triangular meshes. Jameson and others [Jameson:87a;87b], [Mavriplis:88a], [Perez:86a], [Usab:83a] have used multigrid methods to accelerate convergence. For this work [Williams:89b], we have used the two-dimensional explicit algorithm of Jameson and Mavriplis [Mavriplis:88a].

An explicit update procedure is local, and hence well matched to a massively parallel distributed machine, whereas an implicit algorithm is more difficult to parallelize. The implicit step consists of solving a sparse set of linear equations, where matrix elements are nonzero only for mesh-connected nodes. Matrix multiplication is easy to parallelize since it is also a local operation, and the solve may thus be accomplished by an iterative technique such as conjugate gradient, which consists of repeated matrix multiplications. If, however, the same solve is to be done repeatedly for the same mesh, the most efficient (sequential) method is first decomposing the matrix in some way, resulting in fill-in. In terms of the mesh, this fill-in represents nonlocal connection between nodes: indeed, if the matrix were completely filled, the communication time would be proportional to N^2 for N nodes.

12.3.1 Compressible Flow Algorithm

The governing equations are the Euler equations, which are of advective type with no diffusion,

$$\frac{\partial \mathbf{U}}{\partial l} + \nabla \cdot \mathbf{F}(\mathbf{U}) = 0, \tag{12.1}$$

where $\mathbf{U}$ is a vector containing the information about the fluid at a point. I have used bold symbols to indicate an *information* vector, or a set of fields describing the state of the fluid. In this implementation, $\mathbf{U}$ consists of density, velocity, and specific total energy (or, equivalently, pressure); it could also include other information about the state of the fluid such as chemical mixture or ionization data. $\mathbf{F}$ is the flux vector and has the same structure as $\mathbf{U}$ in each of the two coordinate directions.

The numerical algorithm is explained in detail in [Mavriplis:88a], so only an outline is given here. The method uses linear triangular elements to approximate the field. First, a time step is chosen for each node which is constrained by a local Courant condition. The calculation consists of two parts:

Advection: At each node, calculate $\mathbf{F}$ from $\mathbf{U}$. Each element then averages $\mathbf{F}$ from its neighboring nodes, and calculates the flux across each edge of the element, which is then added back into the node opposite the edge. This change in $\mathbf{U}$ is combined across the representations of the node in different processors. If the node is at a boundary which is a hard surface, a modification is made so that no flux of mass or energy occurs through the surface.

Artificial Dissipation: The artificial dissipation is calculated as a combination of approximations to the Laplacian and the double Laplacian of $\mathbf{U}$, involving a combine step for each. The double Laplacian is only used where the flow is smooth, to prevent dissipation of strong shocks.

The time stepping is done with a five-stage Runge-Kutta scheme, where the advection step is done five times, and the dissipation step is done twice. Since advection takes one communication stage and dissipation two, each full time step requires nine loosely synchronous communication stages.

12.3.2 Adaptive Refinement

After the initial transients have dispersed and the flow has settled, the mesh may be refined. The criterion used is based on the gradient of the pressure for deciding which elements are to be refined. The user specifies a percentage of elements which are to be refined, and a criterion

$$R_e = \nabla_e |\nabla p| \qquad (12.2)$$

is calculated for each element. A value R_{crit} of this criterion is found such that the given percentage of elements have a value of R_e greater than R_{crit}, and those elements are refined. The criterion is not simply the gradient of the pressure, because the strongest shock in the simulation would soak up all the refinement leaving weaker shocks unresolved. With the element area ∇_e in the criterion, regions will "saturate" after sufficient refinement, allowing weaker shocks to be refined.

12.3.3 Examples

Figures 10.8 and 10.9 (Color Plates) show the pressure and computational mesh resulting from Mach 0.8 flow over a NACA0012 airfoil at 1.25 degrees angle of attack, computed with a 32-processor nCUBE machine. This problem is that used by the AGARD working group [AGARD:83a] in their benchmarking of compressible flow algorithms. The mesh has 5135 elements after four stages of adaptive refinement. Each processor has about the same number of elements. In the pressure plot is also shown the sonic line; the plot agrees well with the AGARD data.

Note the shock about 2/3 of the way downstream from the leading edge, and the corresponding increase in mesh density there.

Figure 12.8 (Color Plate) shows pressure in a wind-tunnel with a step. A Mach 3 stream comes in from the left, with a detached bow-shock upstream from the step. A second shock is attached by a Mach stem to the bow shock, which is then reflected from the walls of the wind tunnel.

Notice how the mesh density is much greater in the neighborhood of the shocks and at the step where the pressure gradient is high. This computation was performed on 32 processors of a Symult machine.

12.3.4   Performance

The efficiency of any parallel algorithm increases as the computational load dominates the communication load [Williams:90a]. In the case of a domain-decomposed mesh, the computational time depends on the number of elements per processor, and the communication time on the number of nodes at the boundary of the processor domain. If there are N elements in total, distributed among n processors, we expect the computation to go as N/n and the communication as the square root of this, so that the efficiency should approach unity as the square root of n/N.

We have run the example described above starting with a mesh of 525 elements, and refining 50% of the elements. In fact, more than 50% will be refined because of the nature of the refinement algorithm: In practice, it is about 70%. The refinement continues until the memory of the machine runs out.

Figure 12.9 shows timing results. At top right are results for 1, 4, 16, 64, and 256 nCUBE processors. The time taken per simulation time step is shown for the compressible flow algorithm against number of elements in the simulation. The curves end when the processor memory is full. Each processor offers a nominal 512 Kb memory, but when all the software and communication buffers are accounted for, there is only about 120 Kb available for the mesh.

The top left of Figure 12.9 shows the same curves for 1, 4, 16, 64, and 128 Symult processors, and at bottom left the results for 1, 4, 16, and 32 processors of a Meiko CS-1 computing surface. For comparison, the bottom right shows the results for one head of the CRAY Y-MP, and also for the Sun Sparcstation.

Each figure has diagonal lines to guide the eye; these are lines of constant time per element. We expect the curves for the sequential machines to be parallel to these because the code is completely local and the time should be proportional to the number of elements. For the parallel machines, we expect the discrepancy from parallel lines to indicate the importance of communication inefficiency.

12.3.5   Summary

The transonic flow algorithm was written as a DIME application by Roy Williams, using the algorithm of A. Jameson of Princeton University and D. Mavriplis of NASA ICASE [Williams:89b;90a;90b].

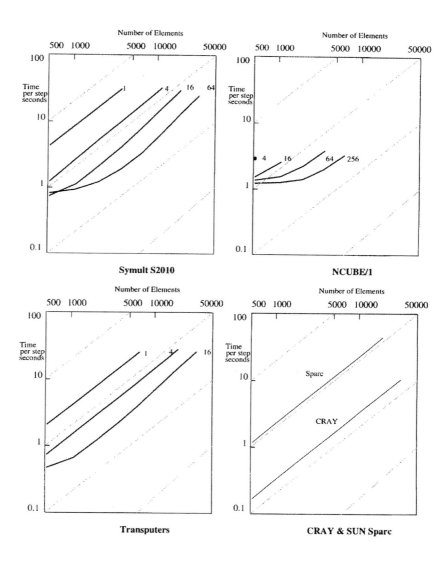

Figure 12.9: Timings for Transonic Flow

12.4   Tree Codes for N-body Simulations

Continuous physical systems must generally be "discretized" prior to analysis with a digital computer. In practice, there are relatively few ways to discretize a physical system. Finite-element and finite-difference approximations are useful for dealing with partial differential equations in a small number of dimensions (up to three). If the dimensionality of the independent variable space is large, however, discretization by finite difference or finite elements becomes unwieldy. For example, the collisionless Boltzman equation,

$$\partial_t f(\vec{x}, \vec{v}, t) + \vec{v} \cdot \partial_{\vec{x}} f(\vec{x}, \vec{v}, t) + \vec{a} \cdot \partial_{\vec{v}} f(\vec{x}, \vec{v}, t) = 0, \qquad (12.3)$$

is expressed as a partial differential equation in six independent variables. A fairly modest discretization of the domain with 100 "elements" in each dimension would result in a system with 10^{12} elements. A simulation of this size is out of the question on computers which will be available in the foreseeable future.

Fortunately, another means of discretization is available. Particle Simulation (or N-body simulation) is discussed at length by Hockney and Eastwood [Hockney:81a]. It is appropriate for systems like the collisionless and collisional Boltzman equation, and hence it is applicable to a number of outstanding problems in astrophysics, where the basic physical processes are governed by Newtonian gravity and the Boltzman equation [Binney:87a].

In such simulations, the phase-space density, f, is represented by a swarm of "particles", or "bodies" which evolve in time according to the dynamics of Newtonian gravity:

$$\frac{d^2 \vec{x}_i}{dt^2} = \sum_{j \neq i} \vec{a}_{ij} = \sum_{j \neq i} -\frac{G m_j \vec{d}_{ij}}{|d_{ij}|^3}, \qquad \vec{d}_{ij} \equiv \vec{x}_i - \vec{x}_j. \qquad (12.4)$$

The $3N$ second-order, ordinary differential equations may be integrated in time by a large number of methods, ranging from the very simple (Euler's method) to the very complex [Aarseth:85a]. The difficulty with using Equation 12.4 is that a straightforward implementation of the right-hand sides of these equations requires $O(N^2)$ operations. Each of N accelerations is the vector sum of $N - 1$ components, each of which requires a handful of floating-point operations (including at least one square-root). Even if one utilizes Newton's second law, one can cut the total number of operations by half, but the asymptotic $O(N^2)$ behavior remains unchanged. N-body

COLOR PLATES

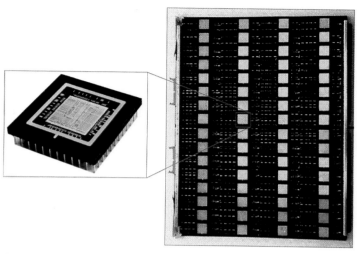

FIGURE 1.1
The nCUBE-2 node and its integration into a board. Up to 128 of these boards can be combined into a single supercomputer.

FIGURE 1.2
The CM-5 produced by Thinking Machines.

FIGURE 1.3

The *Delta Touchstone* parallel supercomputer produced by Intel and installed at Caltech.

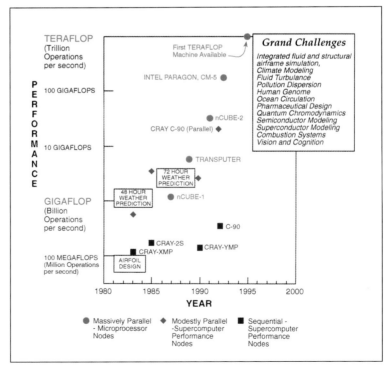

FIGURE 1.4

Grand challenge applications. Some major applications which will be enabled by parallel supercomputers. The computer performance numbers are given in more detail in color Figure 2.1.

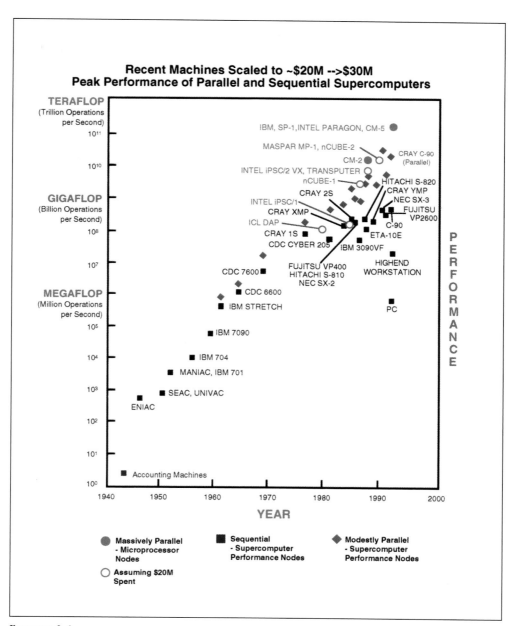

FIGURE 2.1

Historical trends of peak computer performance. In some cases, we have scaled up parallel machine performance to correspond to a configuration that would cost approximately $20 million.

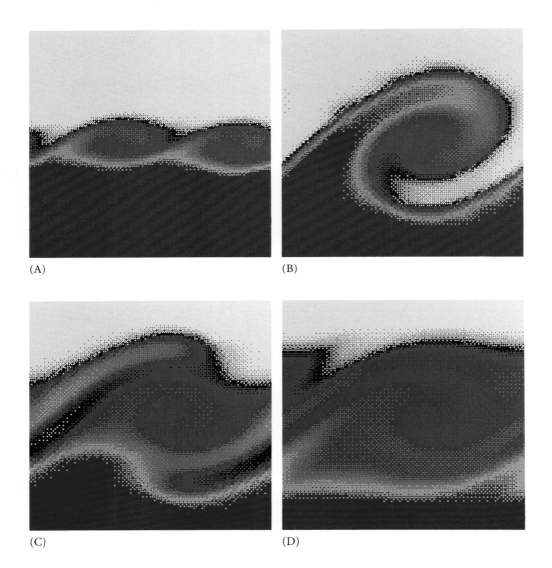

(A)

(B)

(C)

(D)

FIGURE 6.2 (A-D)
The development of the Kelvin-Helmholtz instability at the interface of two fluids in shear motion.

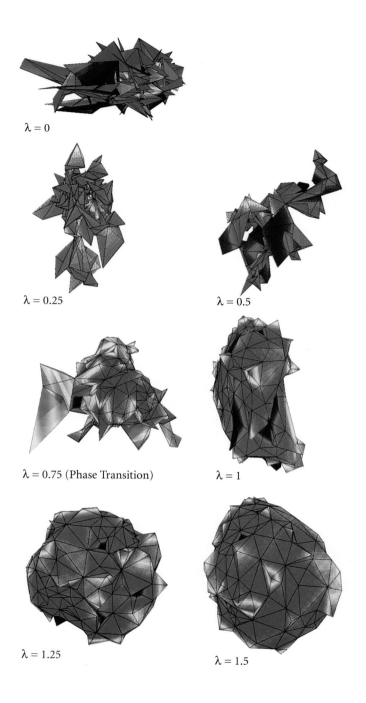

$\lambda = 0$

$\lambda = 0.25$

$\lambda = 0.5$

$\lambda = 0.75$ (Phase Transition)

$\lambda = 1$

$\lambda = 1.25$

$\lambda = 1.5$

FIGURE 7.4
A 288-node DTRS uncrumpling as λ changes from 0 to 1.5.

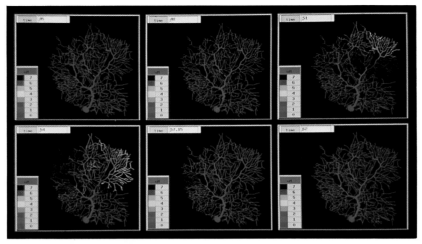

FIGURE 7.15
Cerebellar Purkinje cell model in GENESIS. Our most detailed single-cell model to date.

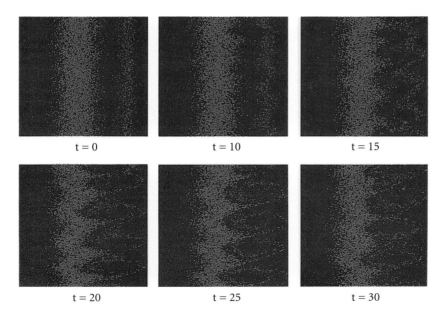

FIGURE 9.4
Time history of electron phase space in a plasma PIC simulation of an electron beam plasma instability on the Mark IIIfp hypercube. The horizontal axis is the electron velocity and the vertical axis is the position. Initially, a small population of beam electrons (green dots) stream through the background plasma electrons (magenta dots). An electrostatic wave grows, tapping the energy in the electron beam. The vortices in phase space at late times result from electrons becoming trapped in the potential of the wave. See Section 9.3 of the text for further description.

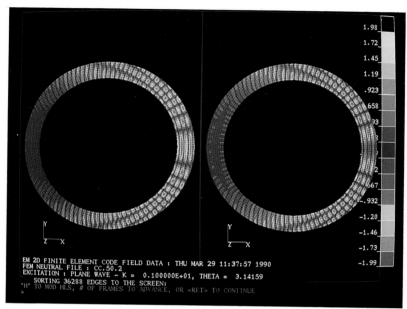

FIGURE 9.7

Results from the two-dimensional electromagnetic scalar finite-element code
described in the text.

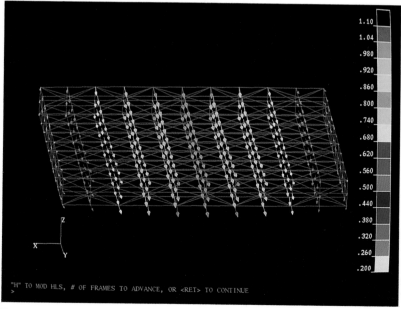

FIGURE 9.8

Test case for the electromagnetic three-dimensional code with no scatterer
described in the text.

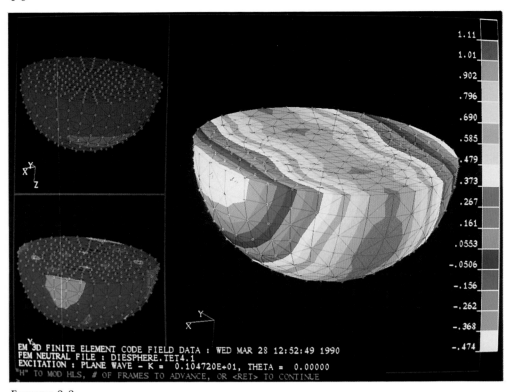

FIGURE 9.9

Test case for electromagnetic three-dimensional planewave in spherical domain with no scatterer described in the text.

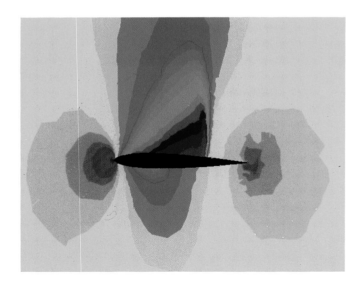

FIGURE 10.8

Pressure plot for Mach 0.8 flow over a NACA0012 airfoil, with the sonic line shown. The mesh for this computation is shown in color Figure 10.9.

FIGURE 10.9

Depiction of the mesh for the transonic flow calculation of color Figure 10.8. Each group of similarly colored triangles is owned by an individual processor. The mesh has been dynamically adapted and load-balanced. The yellow lines connect copies of nodes which are in the same geometric position, but have been separated for the purpose of the picture. The load balancing is by *orthogonal recursive bisection.*

FIGURE 11.12

A stage of eigenvalue recursive bisection. A mesh has already been split into eight pieces, which are separated by gray lines, and the eigenvector is depicted on each of these. The next split (into sixteen pieces) is shown by the black lines.

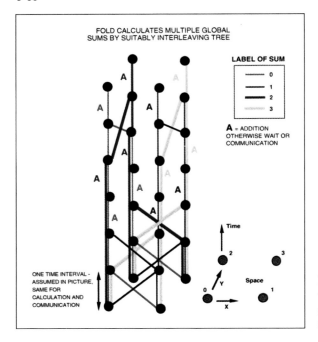

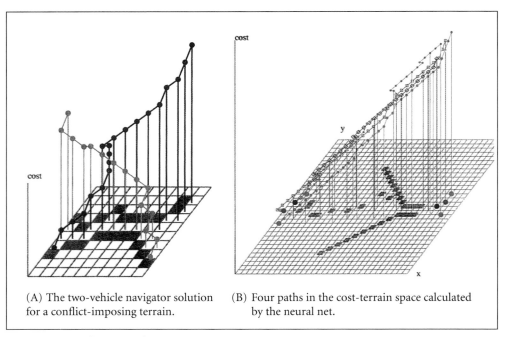

FIGURE 11.21

The Fold Algorithm. Four global sums interleaved optimally on four processors.

(A) The two-vehicle navigator solution for a conflict-imposing terrain.

(B) Four paths in the cost-terrain space calculated by the neural net.

FIGURE 11.22 (A AND B)

Two- and four-vehicle navigation problems. In each case, vehicles have been given initial and final target positions. The black squares are impassable and define a narrow pass. Physical optimization methods [Fox:88ii;90e] were used to find the solutions.

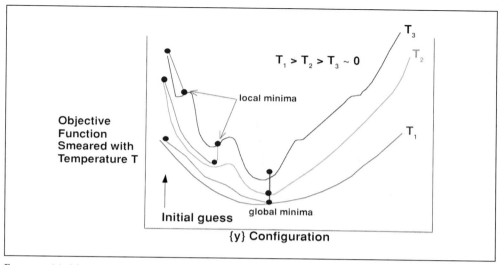

FIGURE 11.23

Annealing tracks global minima by initializing search at temperature T_i by minima found at temperature T_{i-1}.

FIGURE 12.6

Potentials on the surface of the electric fish model as a conducting object moves from head (left) to tail (right) of the fish, keeping 3 cm from the midline (above the paper).

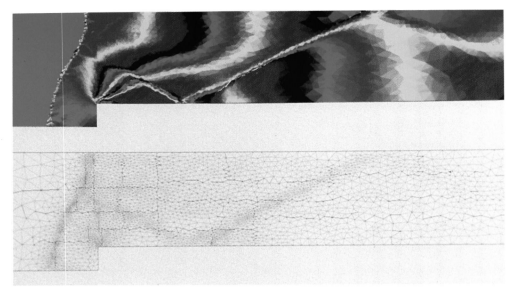

FIGURE 12.8

Pressure and mesh for a Mach 3 wind tunnel with a step. The red lines in the mesh separate processor domains. The mesh has been dynamically adapted and load-balanced with orthogonal recursive bisection.

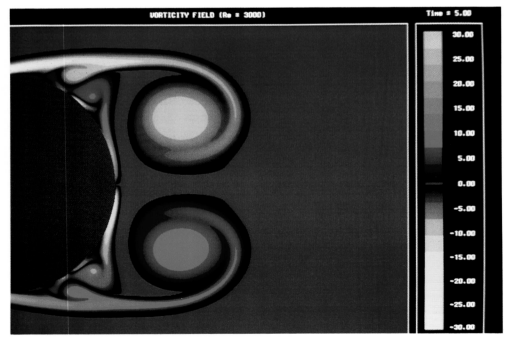

FIGURE 12.21

Vorticity field for *Re* = 3000 at time = 5.0.

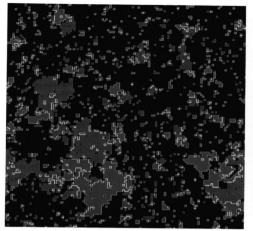

FIGURE 12.23

Initial configuration of 3-state Potts spins on which Wolff Algorithm is to be applied.

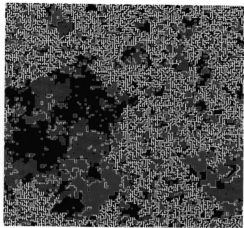

FIGURE 12.24

Configuration of Figure 12.23 with bonds of cluster constructed by Wolff Algorithm indicated in yellow.

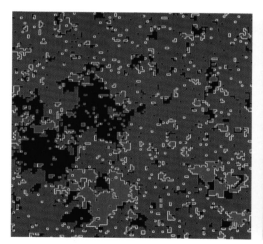

FIGURE 12.25

Result of Wolff Algorithm applied to spin configuration in color Figure 12.23—all spins in cluster flipped to same new value (in this case from blue to red).

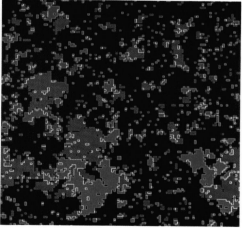

FIGURE 12.26

Result of Metropolis Algorithm applied to spin configuration in Figure 12.23—only a few single spins flipped.

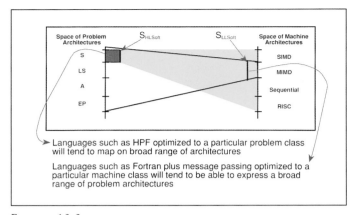

FIGURE 13.3
Problem architectures mapped into machine architecture.

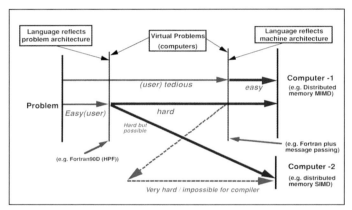

FIGURE 13.4
Migration and compilation in the map of problems to computers.

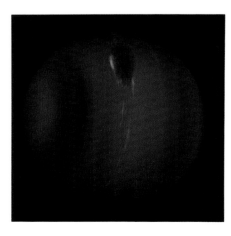

FIGURE 18.1
Neptune, taken by Voyager 2 in
1989 and processed by Mark IIIfp.

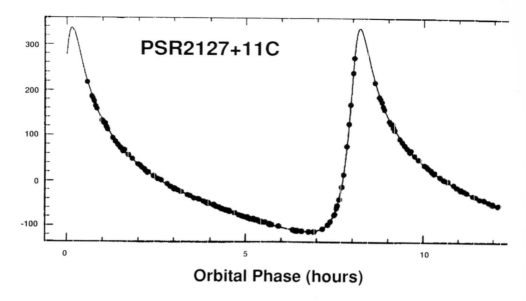

(A) Apparent pulse period of a binary pulsar in the globular cluster M15. The approximately eight-hour period (one of the shortest known) corresponds to high radial velocities that are 0.1% of the speed of light. This pulsar was discovered from analysis of radio astronomy data in 1989 by the 512-node nCUBE-1 at Caltech.

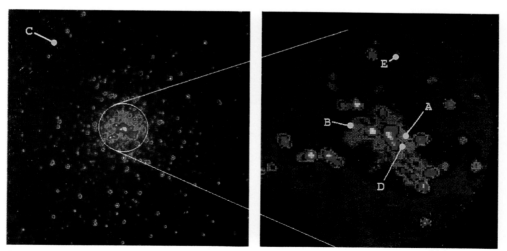

(B) Five pulsars in globular cluster M15. These were discovered or confirmed (M15 A) by analysis on the nCUBE-1 [Anderson:89d], [Fox:89i;89y;90o], [Gorham:88a].

FIGURE 18.2 (A AND B)

Globular cluster M15.

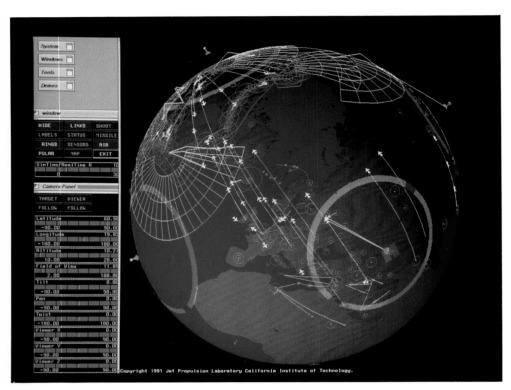

FIGURE 18.12
A complex strategic defense situation graphically summarized.

simulations using direct summation are practical up to a few tens of thousands of bodies on modern supercomputers. Even the teraflop performance promised by parallel computation would only increase this by an order of magnitude or so. Substantially larger simulations require alternative methods for evaluating the forces. The fact that gravity is "long-range," makes rapid evaluation of the forces problematical. It is not acceptable to simply disregard all bodies beyond a certain fixed cutoff, because the contribution of distant bodies does not decrease fast enough to balance the fact that the number of bodies at a given distance is an increasing function of distance.

Recent algorithmic advances [Appel:85a], [Barnes:86a], [Greengard:87b], [Jernighan:89a] however, have shown that while it is not acceptable to disregard distant collections of bodies, it is possible to accurately approximate their contribution without summing all of the individual components. It has been known since the time of Newton that the effect of the earth on an apple may be computed by replacing the countless individual atoms in the earth with a single point-mass located at the earth's center. The force calculation is then:

$$\vec{a} = \sum_{atoms} -\frac{Gm_j\vec{d_j}}{|d_j|^3} \approx -\frac{GM\vec{d}_{cm}}{d_{cm}^3}. \qquad (12.5)$$

12.4.1 Oct-Trees

There are a number of ways to utilize this fact in a computer simulation [Appel:85a], [Barnes:86a], [Greengard:87b], [Zhao:87a]. The methods differ in choice of data structure, level of mathematical rigor, and complexity of the fundamental interactions. We shall consider an adaptive tree data structure, and an algorithm that treats each body independently. The algorithm begins by partitioning space into an oct-tree, that is, a tree whose nodes correspond to cubical regions of space. Each node may have up to eight daughter nodes, corresponding to the eight subcubes that are obtained by dividing in half in each Cartesian direction. The tree is defined by the following properties:

1. All terminal nodes of the tree have either one or zero bodies.

2. All nodes with one or zero bodies are terminal.

Oct-trees are somewhat difficult to draw on two-dimensional paper. The corresponding analog in two dimensions is a quad-tree. Figure 12.10a shows a very shallow quad-tree, with each of the square cells explicitly represented. Figure 12.10b shows the same tree in a more compact, "flattened" representation. The "flattened" representation has a tendency to de-emphasize the

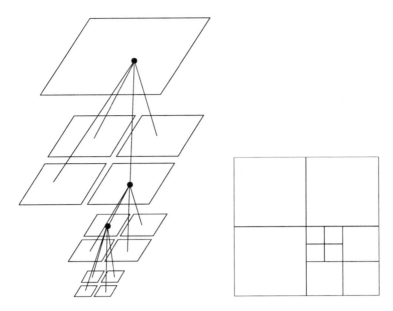

Figure 12.10: (a) Expanded and (b) Flat Representation of an Adaptive Tree

importance of the higher levels of the tree. This is purely an artifact of the graphical representation. In all cases, the tree consists of both terminal nodes and internal nodes. Figure 12.11 shows a quad-tree derived from 10,000 bodies distributed at random on a disc.

The oct-tree provides a convenient data structure which allows us to record the properties of the matter distribution on all length scales. It is especially convenient for astrophysical systems because it is adaptive. That is, the depth of the tree adjusts itself automatically to the local particle density. In order to use an approximation like Equation 12.5, we need to know certain properties of the matter distribution in each cell. In the simplest case, these properties are the mass and center-of-mass of the matter distribution, but it is possible to use quadrupole moments [Hernquist:87a], or higher-order moments [Salmon:90a] for added accuracy. All of these properties may be computed by a bottom-up traversal of the tree, combining the properties of the "daughters" of a node to get the properties of the node itself. The time required for this bottom-up traversal is proportional to the number of internal nodes in the tree, that is, $O(N)$.

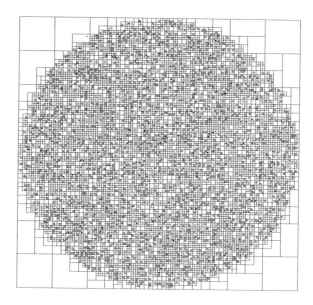

Figure 12.11: 10,000 Body Barnes-Hut Tree

12.4.2 Computing Forces

Once the distribution of matter is represented on a number of length scales, it is possible to use the approximation in Equation 12.5 to reduce the number of operations required to find the force on a body. The force on each body is computed independently by a recursive procedure that traverses the tree from the top down. Beginning at the root of the tree, we simply apply a *multipole acceptability criterion* (MAC). This tells us whether Equation 12.5 (or an appropriate higher-order approximation) is sufficiently accurate. If it is, then we evaluate the approximation, and eliminate the summation over all the bodies contained within the node. Otherwise, we proceed recursively to the eight daughter cells of the node. Whenever we reach a terminal node, we simply compute the body-body interaction. The procedure is shown schematically in Figure 12.12.

The performance of the algorithm depends on how we evaluate the MAC. For example, one could always answer "no," in which case the performance would be identical to the $O(N^2)$ case (although the bookkeeping overhead would be somewhat higher, and we would not take advantage of Newton's second law). The specifics of how best to evaluate the MAC would take us far afield [Barnes:89d], [Makino:90a], and [Salmon:92a].

The Barnes-Hut Algorithm

$$\vec{a} = \sum \frac{Gm}{r^2}\,\hat{e}$$

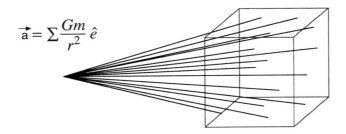

IF(Mpole approx OK?)

$$\vec{a} = \frac{Gm}{r_{\text{cm}}^2}\,\hat{e}_{\text{cm}}$$

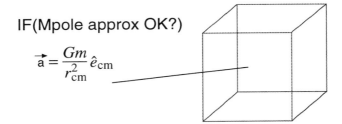

ELSE

$$\vec{a} = \sum_{subcells}$$

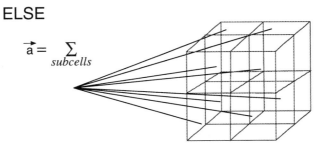

Figure 12.12: The Barnes-Hut Algorithm

Suffice it to say that all methods are based on the idea that the multipole approximation is accurate when the distance to the cell is large compared to the size of the cell. Essentially any criterion based on a ratio of size-of-cell to distance-to-cell will require $O(\log N)$-force evaluations to compute the total force on each body [Barnes:86a], [Salmon:90a]. Since the forces on all bodies are evaluated independently, the total number of evaluations is proportional to $O(N \log N)$, which is a substantial improvement over the $O(N^2)$ situation that results from a naive evaluation of Equation 12.3.

12.4.3 Parallelism in Tree Codes

Computational science advances both in hardware and algorithms. Occasionally, algorithmic advances are of such tremendous significance that they completely overshadow the striking advances constantly being made by hardware. Tree codes are just such an algorithmic advance. It is literally true that a tree code running on a modest workstation can address larger problems than can the fastest parallel supercomputer running an $O(N^2)$ algorithm. It is well known [Fox:84e], [Fox:88a] that parallel computers can efficiently evaluate the $O(N^2)$ force evaluations required by direct application of Equation 12.5. However, this fact is of limited significance now that a new class of algorithms has changed the underlying complexity of the problem. If parallel computers are to have an impact on the N-body problem, then they must be able to efficiently execute tree codes.

Parallelization of tree codes is a challenging problem. Typical astrophysical simulations are highly inhomogeneous. Spatial densities can vary by a factor of 10^6 or more through the computational domain. The tree must be adaptive to deal with such a large dynamic range in densities, that is, it must be deep in regions of high particle density, and shallow in regions of low particle density. Furthermore, the structure of the inhomogeneities is often dynamic—for example, galaxies form, move, collide, and merge in cosmological simulations. A fixed tree and/or a fixed decomposition is not suitable for such a system. Despite these problems, it is possible to find parallelism in tree codes and to run them efficiently on large parallel computers [Fox:89t], [Salmon:90a], [Warren:92a;93a].

The technique of "domain decomposition" has been applied with excellent results to a number of other problem areas. We have found that a slightly abstracted concept of domain decomposition is also applicable to tree codes. Recall that a domain decomposition usually proceeds by "assigning" spatial domains to processors. In designing a parallel program, the precise meaning

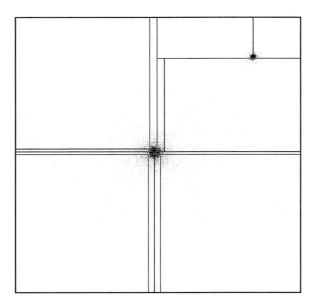

Figure 12.13: Decomposition Resulting from Orthogonal Recursive Bisection of a System with Two Galaxies

of "assign" is crucial. We adopt the following "owner-computes" definition of a domain: *A domain is a rectangular region of simulation space. Assignment of a domain to a processor implies that the processor will be responsible for updating the positions and velocities of all particles located within that region of simulation space.* We allow that processor domains might change from one time step to the next, based, presumably, on load-balancing considerations.

Processor domains are chosen using orthogonal recursive bisection, or ORB (see Section 11.1.5). Recall that ORB tries repeatedly to split some measure of the "load" in half, and assign the halves to sets of processors. In the present context, that means finding a coordinate so that half of the computational "load" is associated with particles above the split, and half is associated with particles below the split. The result of applying orthogonal recursive bisection to a system containing two "galaxies," (well-separated regions with high local particle density) is shown in Figure 12.13.

It is a simple matter to record the "load" associated with each particle. For example, one can count interactions, or one could simply read the clock before and after the force on the particle is computed. Then, in order to find the splitting coordinate, one simply executes a binary (or more sophisticated) search, seeking a value of the coordinate for which half of the per-particle work is above and half is below.

In fact, seeking the exact median coordinate of the per-particle work does not necessarily guarantee load balance. It guarantees load balance *within the force calculation*, but it does not account for load imbalance that may result during construction of the tree, or during the other phases of the computation. It is possible to account for these sources of load imbalance by seeking a coordinate which is not precisely at the median (i.e., 50th percentile), but rather at another percentile. The new target percentile is found by measuring the actual load imbalance, and adjusting the target by a small amount on each time step to reduce the observed load imbalance [Salmon:90a].

12.4.4 Acquiring Locally Essential Data

Many parallel algorithms conform to a pattern of activity that can loosely be described as:

1. Choose a decomposition—that is, determine which processor is responsible for updating which data.

2. Communicate—that is, arrange for some data to reside in several processors. Exactly which data are replicated, and how they are stored depends on the next phase.

3. Proceed with calculation using an essentially serial implementation, but restrict the data updated by each processor to those in the processor's domain.

In this volume, the techniques discussed are structured in this way. Some important advantages arise from this approach to parallelism. It leads to modularity and portability, by separating distinct functions into separate phases. It also allows reuse of sequential code (in the third phase), which is frequently highly optimized and extensively tested. One drawback of this approach is the fact that it precludes overlapping of communication and calculation. We shall not be concerned with overlap of communication and calculation because communication overhead constitutes a small part of the overall time in parallel tree code implementations [Salmon:90a].

We have already discussed decomposition, and described the use of orthogonal recursive bisection to determine processor domains. The next step is the acquisition of "locally essential data", that is, the data that will be needed to compute the forces on the bodies in a local domain. In other applications one finds that the locally essential data associated with a domain is itself local. That is, it comes from a limited region surrounding the processor domain. In the case of hierarchical N-body simulations, however, the locally essential data is not restricted to a particular region of space. Nevertheless, the hierarchical nature of the algorithm guarantees that if a processor's domain is spatially limited, then any particle within that domain will not require detailed information about the particle distribution in distant regions of space. This idea is illustrated in Figure 12.14, which shows the parts of the tree that are required to compute forces on bodies in the grey region. Clearly, the locally essential data for a limited domain is much smaller than the total data set (shown in Figure 12.11). In fact, when the grain size of the domain is large, that is, when the number of bodies in the domain is large, the size of the locally essential data set is only a modest constant factor larger than the local data set itself [Salmon:90a]. This means that the work (both communication and additional computation) required to obtain and assemble the locally essential dataset is proportional to the grain size, that is, is $O(N_{grain})$. In contrast, the work required to compute the forces in parallel is $O(N_{grain} \log N)$. The "big-O" notation can hide large constants which dominate practical considerations. Typical astrophysical simulations with 10^5–10^7 bodies perform 200500 interactions per body [Hernquist:87a], [Warren:92a], and each interaction costs from 30 to 60 floating-point operations. Thus, there is reason to be optimistic that assembly of the locally essential data set will not be prohibitively expensive.

Determining, in parallel, which data is locally essential for which processors is a formidable task. Two facts allow us to organize the communication of data into a regular pattern that guarantees that each processor receives precisely the locally essential data which it needs.

1. At each level of the orthogonal recursive bisection, the domains are always rectangles.

2. It is possible to quickly determine whether a given cell's multipole approximation is acceptable for all particles in a given rectangular domain. Or, conversely, whether the locally essential data for the domain includes information contained in the daughters of the given cell. This test is called the domain multipole acceptability criterion (DMAC).

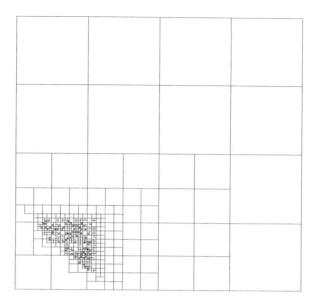

Figure 12.14: The Locally Essential Data Needed to Compute Forces in a Processor Domain, Located in the Lower Left Corner of the System

The procedure by which processors go from having only local data to having all locally essential data consists of a loop over each of the bisections in the ORB tree. To initialize the iteration, each processor builds a tree from its local data. Then, for each bisector, it traverses its tree, applying the DMAC at each node, using the *complimentary domain* as an argument, that is, asking whether the given cell contains an approximation that is sufficient for all bodies in the domain on the other side of the current ORB bisector. If the DMAC succeeds, the cell is needed on the other side of the domain, so it is copied to a buffer and queued for transmission. Traversal of the current branch can stop at this point because no additional information within the current branch of the local tree can possibly be necessary on the other side of the bisector. If the DMAC fails, traversal continues to deeper levels of the tree. This procedure is shown schematically in code in Table 12.1.

Figure 12.15 shows schematically how some data might travel around a 16-processor system during execution of the above code.

The second tree traversal in the above code conserves a processor's memory by reclaiming data which was transmitted through the processor, but which is not needed by the processor itself, or any other member of its cur-

Table 12.1: Outline of `BuildLETree` which constructs a locally essential representation of a tree.

```
BuildLETree(bodylist)
BuildTreeLocal(bodylist, Tree)
for( each bisection created by DomainDecomp )
    Traverse the Tree and queue any data which may be
        necessary to the domain on the other
        side of the bisector.
    Traverse the Tree again, and delete any data which
        can never be necessary on ''this''
        processor's side of the bisector.
    Exchange queued data with corresponding processor
        on other side of bisector, and merge it
        into the Tree.
endfor
Do any necessary housekeeping to finish the tree.
endfunc
```

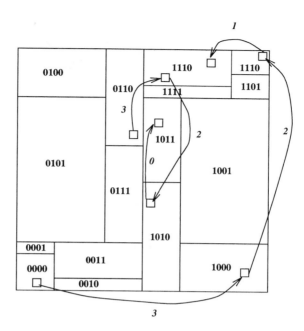

Figure 12.15: Data Flow in a 16 Processor System. Arrows indicate the flow of data and are numbered with a decreasing "channel" number corresponding to the bisector being traversed.

rent subset. In Figure 12.15, the body sent from processor 0110 through 1110 and 1010 to 1011 would likely be deleted from processor 1110's tree during the pruning on channel 2, and from 1010's tree during the pruning on channel 0.

The Code requires the existence of a DMAC function. Obviously, the DMAC depends on the details of the MAC which will eventually be used to traverse the tree to evaluate forces. Notice, however, that the DMAC must be evaluated *before* the entire contents of a cell are available in a particular processor. (This happens whenever the cell itself extends outside of the processor's domain). Thus, the DMAC must rely on purely geometric criteria (the size and location of the cell), and cannot depend on, for example, the exact location of the center-of-mass of the cell. The DMAC is allowed, however, to err on the side of caution. That is, it is allowed to return a negative result about a cell even though subsequent data may reveal that the cell is indeed acceptable. The penalty for such "false negatives" is de-

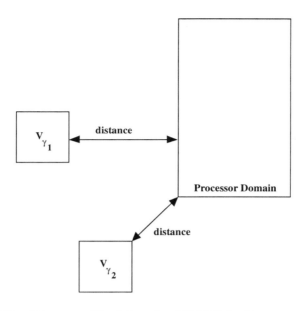

Figure 12.16: The Distance Used by the DMAC is Computed by Finding the Shortest Distance Between the Processor Domain and the Boundary of the Cell.

graded performance, as they cause data to be unnecessarily communicated and assembled into locally essential data sets.

Because the DMAC must work with considerably less information than the MAC, it is somewhat easier to categorically describe its behavior. Figure 12.16 shows schematically how the DMAC is implemented. Recall that the MAC is based on a "distance-to-size" ratio. The distance used by the DMAC is the shortest distance from the cell to the processor domain. The "min-distance" MAC [Salmon:90a;92a] uses precisely this distance to decide whether a multipole approximation is acceptable. Thus, in a sense, the min-distance MAC is best suited to parallelization because it is equivalent to its own DMAC. The DMAC generates fewer false-positive decisions. Fortunately, the min-distance MAC also resolves certain difficulties associated with more commonly used MACs, and is arguably the best of the "simple" MACs [Salmon:92a].

12.4.5 Comments on Performance

It is possible to generate a huge amount of data related to parallel performance. One can vary the size of the problem, and/or the number of processors. Performance can be related to various problem parameters, for example, the nonuniformity of the particle distribution. Parallel overheads can be identified and attributed to communication, load imbalance, synchronization, or additional calculation in the parallel code [Salmon:90a]. All these provide useful diagnostics and can be used to predict performance on a variety of machines. However, they also tend to obscure the fact that the ultimate goal of parallel computation is to perform simulations larger or faster than would otherwise be possible.

Rather than analyze a large number of statistics, we restrict ourselves to the following "bald" facts.

In 1992, the 512-processor Intel Delta at Caltech evolved two astrophysical simulations with 17.15 million bodies for approximately 600 time steps. The machine ran at an aggregate speed exceeding 5000 MFLOPS/sec. The systems under study were simulated regions of the universe 100 Mpc (megaparsec) and 25 Mpc in diameter, which were initialized with random-density fluctuations consistent with the "cold dark matter" hypothesis and the recent results on the anisotropy of the microwave background radiation. The data from these runs exceeded 25 Gbytes, and is analyzed in [Zurek:93a]. Salmon and Warren were recipients of the 1992 Gordon Bell Price for performance in practical parallel processing research.

12.5 Fast Vortex Algorithm and Parallel Computing

Vortex methods are a powerful tool for the simulation of incompressible flows at high Reynolds number. They rely on a discrete Lagrangian representation of the vorticity field to approximately satisfy the Kelvin and Helmholtz theorems which govern the dynamics of vorticity for inviscid flows. A timesplitting technique can be used to include viscous effects. The diffusion equation is considered separately after convecting the particles with an inviscid vortex method. In our work, the viscous effects are represented by the so-called deterministic method. The approach was extended to problems where a flux of vorticity is used to enforce the no-slip boundary condition.

In order to accurately compute the viscous transport of vorticity, gradients need to be well resolved. As the Reynolds number is increased, these gradients get steeper and more particles are required to achieve the requisite resolution. In practice, the computing cost associated with the convection step dictates the number of vortex particles and puts an upper bound on the Reynolds number that can be simulated with confidence. That threshold can be increased by reducing the asymptotic time complexity of the convection step from $\mathcal{O}(N^2)$ to $\mathcal{O}(N \log N)$. The nearfield of every vortex particle is identified. Within that region, the velocity is computed by considering the pairwise interaction of vortices. The speedup is achieved by approximating the influence of the rest of the domain, the farfield. In that context, the interaction of two vortex particles is treated differently depending on their spatial relation. The resulting computer code does not lend itself to vectorization but has been successfully implemented on concurrent computers.

12.5.1   Vortex Methods

Vortex methods (see [Leonard:80a]) are used to simulate incompressible flows at high Reynolds number. The two-dimensional inviscid vorticity equation,

$$\frac{\partial \omega}{\partial t} + \mathbf{u} \cdot \nabla \omega = 0,$$

is solved by discretizing the vorticity field into Lagrangian vortex particles,

$$\omega(\mathbf{x}, t) = \sum_{j}^{N} \Gamma_j(t)\, \delta\left(\mathbf{x} - \mathbf{x}_j(t)\right),$$

where α_j is the strength or the circulation of the jth particle. For an incompressible flow, the knowledge of the vorticity is sufficient to reconstruct the velocity field. Using complex notation, the induced velocity is given by

$$\mathrm{w}(z, t) = \frac{i}{2\pi} \sum_{j}^{N} \frac{\Gamma_j}{(z - z_j)^*}.$$

The velocity is evaluated at each particle location and the discrete Lagrangian elements are simply advected at the local fluid velocity. In this way, the numerical scheme approximately satisfies Kelvin and Helmholtz theorems that govern the motion of vortex lines. The numerical approximations have transformed the original partial differential equation into a set of $2N$ ordinary differential equations, an N-body problem. This class of problems is encountered in many fields of computational physics, for example, molecular dynamics, gravitational interactions, plasma physics and, of course, vortex dynamics.

12.5.2 Fast Algorithms

When each pairwise interaction is considered, distant and nearby pairs of vortices are treated with the same care. As a result, a disproportionate amount of time is spent computing the influence of distant vortices that have little influence on the velocity of a given particle. This is not to say that the far field is to be totally ignored since the accumulation of small contributions can have a significant effect. The key element in making the velocity evaluation faster is to approximate the influence of the far field by considering groups of vortices instead of the individual vortices themselves. When the collective influence of a distant group of vortices is to be evaluated, the very accurate representation of the group provided by its vortices can be overlooked and a cruder description that retains only its most important features can be used. These would be the group location, circulation, and, possibly, some coarse approximation of its shape and vorticity distribution.

A convenient approximate representation is based on multipole expansions. It would be possible to build a fast algorithm by evaluating the multipole expansion at the location of particles that do not belong to the group. This is basically the scheme used by Barnes and Hut [Barnes:86a] (the concurrent implementation of this algorithm is discussed in Section 12.4). Greengard and Rokhlin [Greengard:87b] went a step further by proposing group-to-group interactions. In this case, the multipole expansion is transformed into a Taylor series around the center of the second group, where the influence of the first one is sought. The expansions provide an accurate representation of the velocity field when the distance between the groups is large compared to their radii.

One now needs a data structure that is going to facilitate the search for acceptable approximations. As proposed by Appel [Appel:85a], a binary tree is used. In that framework, a giant cluster sits on top of the data structure; it includes all the vortex particles. It stores all the information relevant to the group, that is, its location, its radius, and the coefficients of the multipole expansion. In addition, it carries the address of its two children, each of them responsible for approximately half of the vortices of the parent group. Whenever smaller groups are sought, these pointers are used to rapidly access the relevant information. The children carry the description of their own group of vortices and are themselves pointing at two smaller groups, their own children, the grandchildren of the patriarchal group. More subgroups are created by equally dividing the vortices of the parent groups along the "x" and "y" axis alternatively. This splitting process stops when all groups have approximately $J_{\min}$ vortices. Then, instead of pointing toward two smaller groups, the parent node points toward a list of vortices. This data structure provides a quick way to access groups, from the largest to the smallest ones, and ultimately to the individual vortices themselves. Appel's data structure is Lagrangian since it is built on top of the vortices and moves with them. As a result, it can be used for many time steps.

Comparing the speed of this algorithm with the classical $\mathcal{O}(N^2)$ approach, the crossover occurs for as few as 150 vortices. At this point, the extra cost of maintaining the data structure is balanced by the savings associated with the approximate treatment of the far field. When N is increased further, the savings outweigh the extra bookkeeping and the proposed algorithm is faster than its competitor by a margin that increases with the number of vortices.

12.5.3   Hypercube Implementation

The global nature of the N^2 approach has made its parallel implementation fairly straightforward (see [Fox:88a]). However, as we have already seen in Section 12.4, that character was drastically changed by the fast algorithm as it introduced a strong component of locality. Globality is still present since the influence of particle is felt throughout the domain, but more care and computational effort is given to its near field. The fast parallel algorithm has to reflect that dual nature, otherwise an efficient implementation will never be obtained. Moreover, the domain decomposition can no longer ignore the spatial distribution of the vortices. Nearby vortices are strongly coupled computationally, so it makes sense to assign them to the same processor. Binary bisection is used in the host to spatially decompose the domain. Then, only the vortices are sent to the processors where a binary tree is locally built on top of them. For example, Figure 12.17 shows the portion of the data structure assigned to processor 1 in a 4-processor environment.

In a fast algorithm context, sending a copy of local data structure to half the other processors does not necessarily result in a load balanced implementation. The work associated with processor-to-processor interactions now depends on their respective location in physical space. A processor

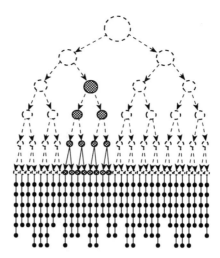

Figure 12.17: Data Structure Assigned to Processor 1

whose vortices are located at the center of the domain is involved in more costly interactions than a peripheral processor. To achieve the best possible load balancing, that central processor could send a copy of its data to more than half of the other processors and hence itself be responsible for a smaller fraction of the work associated with its vortices.

Before a decision is made on which one is going to visit and which to receive, we minimize the number of pairs of processors that need to exchange their data structure. Following the domain decomposition, the portion of the data structure that sits above the subtrees is not present anywhere in the hypercube. That gap is filled by broadcasting the description of the largest group of every processor. By limiting the broadcast to one group per processor, a small amount of data is actually exchanged but, as seen on Figure 12.18, this step gives every processor a coarse description of its surroundings and helps it find its place in the universe.

If the vortices of processor A are far enough from those of processor B, it is even possible to use that coarse description to compute the interaction of A and B without an additional exchange of information. The far field of every processor can be quickly disposed of. After thinking globally, one now has to act locally; if the vortices of A are adjacent to those of B, a more detailed description of their vorticity field is needed to compute their mutual influence.

This requires a transfer of information from either A to B or from B to A. In

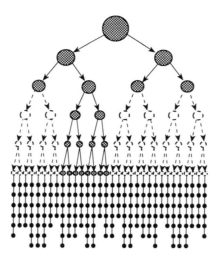

Figure 12.18: Data Structure Known to Processor 1 After Broadcast

the latter case, most of the work involved in the A–B interaction takes place in processor A. Obviously, processor B should not always send its information away since it would then remain idle while the rest of the hypercube is working. Load-balancing concerns will dictate the flow of information.

12.5.4 Efficiency of Parallel Implementation

Since our objective is to compute the flow around a cylinder, the efficiency of the parallel implementation was tested on such a problem. The region for which $1 < r < 1.6$ is uniformly covered with N particles. The parallel efficiency is shown on Figure 12.19 as a function of the hypercube size. The parallel implementation is fairly robust: The parallel efficiency, ϵ, remains larger than 0.7. The number of vortices per processor was kept roughly constant at 1500 even if the parallel efficiency is not a strong function of the size of the problem. It is, however, much more sensitive to the quality of the domain decomposition. The fast parallel algorithm performs better when all the subdomains have approximately the same squarish shape or in other words, when the largest group assigned to a processor is as compact as possible.

The results of Figure 12.19 were obtained at early times when the Lagrangian particles are still distributed evenly around the cylinder which makes the domain decomposition an easier task. At later times, the dis-

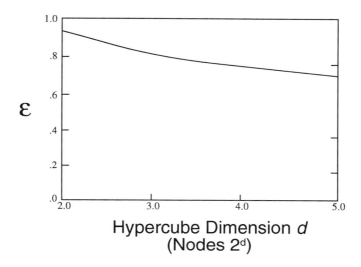

Figure 12.19: Parallel Efficiency of the Fast Algorithm

tribution of the vortices does not allow the decomposition of the domain in groups having approximately the same radius and the same number of vortices. Some subdomains cover a larger region of space and as a result, the efficiency drops to approximately 0.6. This is mainly due to the fact that more processors end up in the near field of a processor responsible for a large group; the request lists are longer and more data has to be moved between processors.

The sources of overhead corresponding to Figure 12.19 are shown on Figure 12.20 normalized with the useful work. Load imbalance, the largest overhead contributor, is defined as the difference between the maximum useful work reported by a processor and the average useful work per processor. Further, the extra work includes the time spent making a copy of one's own data structure, the time required to absorb the returning information, and the work that was duplicated in all processors, namely, the search for acceptable interactions in the upper portion of the tree and the subsequent creation of the request lists. The remaining overhead has been lumped under communication time although most of it is probably idle time (or synchronization time) that was not included in the definition of load imbalance.

We expected that as P increases, the near field of a processor would eventually contain a fixed number of neighboring processors. The number of messages and the load imbalance would then reach an asymptote and

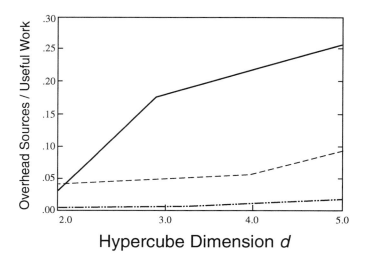

Figure 12.20: Load Imbalance (solid), Communication and Synchronization Time (dash), and Extra Work (dot-dash) as a Function of the Number of Processors

the loss of efficiency would be driven by the much smaller communication and extra times. However, this has yet to happen at 32 processors and the communication time is already starting to make an impact.

Nevertheless, the fast algorithm, its reasonably efficient parallel implementation and the speed of the Mark III have made possible simulations with as many as 80,000 vortex particles.

12.5.5   Results

These 80,000 particles were used to compute the flow past an impulsively started cylinder. Figure 12.21 (Color Plate) shows the vorticity field after five time units, meaning that the cylinder has been displaced by five radii; the Reynolds number is 3000. The pair of primary eddies induced by the body's motion is clearly visible along with a number of small structures produced by the interaction of the wake with the rear portion of the cylinder. It should be noted that symmetry has been enforced in the simulation. Streamlines derived from this vorticity distribution are presented in Figure 12.22 and compared with Bouard and Coutanceau's flow visualization [Bouard:80a] obtained at the same dimensionless time and Reynolds number.

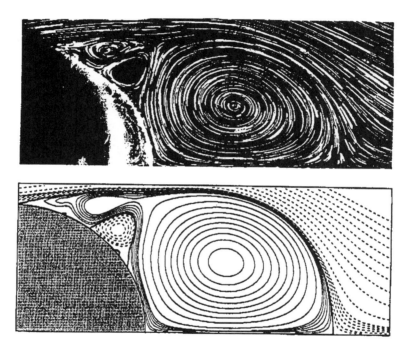

Figure 12.22: Comparison of Computed Streamlines with Bouard and Coutanceau Experimental Flow Visualization at $Re = 3000$ and $T = 5.0$

12.6   Cluster Algorithms for Spin Models

12.6.1   Monte Carlo Calculations of Spin Models

The goal of computer simulations of spin models is to generate configurations of spins typical of statistical equilibrium and measure physical observables on this ensemble of configurations. The generation of configurations is traditionally performed by Monte Carlo methods such as the Metropolis algorithm [Metropolis:53a], which produce configurations with a probability given by the Boltzmann distribution $e^{-\beta S(\phi)}$, where $S(\phi)$ is the action, or energy, of the system in configuration ϕ, and β is the inverse temperature. One of the main problems with these methods in practice is that successive configurations are not statistically independent, but rather are correlated with some autocorrelation time, τ, between effectively independent configurations.

A key feature of traditional (Metropolislike) Monte Carlo algorithms is that the updates are *local* (i.e., one spin at a time is updated), and its new value depends only on the values of spins which affect its contribution to the action, that is, only on local (usually nearest neighbor) spins. Thus, in a single step of the algorithm, information about the state of a spin is transmitted only to its nearest neighbors. In order for the system to reach a new effectively independent configuration, this information must travel a distance of order the (static or spatial) correlation length ξ. As the information executes a random walk around the lattice, one would suppose that the autocorrelation time $\tau \sim \xi^2$. However, in general, $\tau \sim \xi^z$, where z is called the dynamical critical exponent. Almost all numerical simulations of spin models have measured $z \approx 2$ for local update algorithms. (See also Sections 4.3, 4.4, 7.3, 12.6, and 14.2).

For a spin model with a phase transition, as the inverse temperature β approaches the critical value, ξ diverges to infinity so that the computational efficiency rapidly goes to zero! This behavior is called *critical slowing down* (CSD), and until very recently it has plagued Monte Carlo simulations of statistical mechanical systems, in particular spin models, at or near their phase transitions. Recently, however, several new "cluster algorithms" have been introduced which decrease z dramatically by performing *nonlocal* spin updates, thus reducing (or even eliminating) CSD and facilitating much more efficient computer simulations.

12.6.2   Cluster Algorithms

The aim of the cluster update algorithms is to find a suitable collection of spins which can be flipped with relatively little cost in energy. We could obtain nonlocal updating very simply by using the standard Metropolis Monte Carlo algorithm to flip randomly selected bunches of spins, but then the acceptance would be tiny. Therefore, we need a method which picks sensible bunches or clusters of spins to be updated. The first such algorithm was proposed by Swendsen and Wang [Swendsen:87a], and was based on an equivalence between a Potts spin model [Potts:52a], [Wu:82a] and percolation models [Stauffer:78a], [Essam:80a], for which cluster properties play a fundamental role.

The Potts model is a very simple spin model of a ferromagnet, in which the spins can take q different values. The case $q = 2$ is just the well-known Ising model. In the Swendsen and Wang algorithm, clusters of spins are created by introducing bonds between neighboring spins with probability $1 - e^{-\beta}$ if the two spins are the same, and zero if they are not. All such clusters are created and then updated by choosing a random new spin value for each cluster and assigning it to all the spins in that cluster.

A variant of this algorithm, for which only a single cluster is constructed and updated at each sweep, has been proposed by Wolff [Wolff:89a]. The implementation of this algorithm is shown in Figures 12.23 through 12.25 (Color Plates), which show a $q = 3$ Potts model at its critical temperature, with different colors representing the three different spin values. From the starting configuration (Figure 12.23 (Color Plate)), we choose a site at random, and construct a cluster around it by bonding together neighboring sites with the appropriate probabilities (Figure 12.24 (Color Plate)). All sites in this cluster are then given the same new spin value, producing the new configuration shown in Figure 12.25 (Color Plate), which is obviously far less correlated with the initial configuration than the result of a single Metropolis update (Figure 12.26 (Color Plate)). Although Wolff's method is probably the best *sequential* cluster algorithm, the Swendsen and Wang algorithm seems to be better suited for parallelization, since it involves the entire lattice rather than just a single cluster. We have, therefore, concentrated our attention on parallelizing the method of Swendsen and Wang, where *all* the clusters must be identified and labelled.

First we outline a sequential method for labelling clusters, the so-called "ants in the labyrinth" algorithm. The reason for its name is that we can visualize the algorithm as follows [Dewar:87a]. An ant is put somewhere on the lattice, and notes which of the neighboring sites are connected to the site it is on. At the next time step, this ant places children on each of these connected sites which are not already occupied. The children then proceed to reproduce likewise until the entire cluster is populated. In order to label all the clusters, we start by giving every site a negative label, set the initial cluster label to be zero, and then loop through all the sites in turn. If a site's label is negative, then the site has not already been assigned to a cluster so we place an ant on this site, give it the current cluster label, and let it reproduce, passing the label on to all its offspring. When this cluster is identified, we increment the cluster label and carry on repeating the ant-colony birth, growth, and death cycle until all the clusters have been identified.

12.6.3 Parallel Cluster Algorithms

As with the percolation models upon which the cluster algorithms are based, the phase transition in a spin model occurs when the clusters of bonded spins become large enough to span the entire lattice. Thus, near criticality (which in most cases is where we want to perform the simulation), clusters come in all sizes, from order N (where N is the number of sites in the lattice) right down to a single site. The highly irregular and nonlocal nature of the clusters means that cluster update algorithms do not vectorize well and hence give poor performance on vector machines. On this problem, a CRAY X-MP is only about ten times faster than a Sun 4 workstation. The irregularity of the clusters also means that SIMD machines are not well suited to this problem [Apostolakis:92a;93a], [Baillie:91a], [Brower:91a], whereas for the Metropolis type algorithms, they are perhaps the best machines available. It therefore appears that the optimum performance for this type of problem will come from MIMD parallel computers.

A parallel cluster algorithm involves distributing the lattice onto an array of processors using the usual domain decomposition. Clearly, a sequential algorithm can be used to label the clusters on each processor, but we need a procedure for converting these labels to their correct *global* values. We need to be able to tell many processors, which may be any distance apart, that some of their clusters are actually the same, to agree on which of the many different local labels for a given cluster should be assigned to be the global cluster label, and to pass this label to all the processors containing a part of that cluster. We have implemented two such algorithms, "self-labelling" and "global equivalencing" [Baillie:91a], [Coddington:90a].

12.6.4   Self-labelling

We shall refer to this algorithm as "self-labelling," since each site figures out which cluster it is in by itself from local information. This method has also been referred to as "local label propagation" [Brower:91a], [Flanigan:92a]. We begin by assigning each site, i, a unique cluster label, S_i. In practice, this is simply chosen as the position of that site in the lattice. At each step of the algorithm in parallel, every site looks in turn at each of its neighbors in the positive directions. If it is bonded to a neighboring site, n, which has a different cluster label, S_n, then both S_i and S_n are set to the minimum of the two. This is continued until nothing changes, by which time all the clusters will have been labelled with the minimum initial label of all the sites in the cluster. Note that checking termination of the algorithm involves each processor sending a termination flag (finished or not finished) to every other processor after each step, which can become very costly for a large processor array. This is an SIMD algorithm and can, therefore, be run on machines like the AMT DAP and TMC Connection Machine. However, the SIMD nature of these computers leads to very poor load balancing. Most processors end up waiting for the few in the largest cluster which are the last to finish. We implemented this on the AMT DAP and obtained only about 20% efficiency.

We can improve this method on a MIMD machine by using a faster sequential algorithm, such as "ants in the labyrinth," to label the clusters in the sublattice on each processor, and then just use self-labelling on the sites at the edges of each processor to eventually arrive at the global cluster labels [Baillie:91a], [Coddington:90a], [Flanigan:92a]. The number of steps required to do the self-labelling will depend on the largest cluster which, at the phase transition, will generally span the entire lattice. The number of self-labelling steps will therefore be of the order of the maximum distance between processors, which for a square array of P processors is just $2\sqrt{P}$. Hence, the amount of communication (and calculation) involved in doing the self-labelling, which is proportional to the number of iterations times the perimeter of the sublattice, behaves as L for an $L \times L$ lattice; whereas, the time taken on each processor to do the local cluster labelling is proportional to the area of the sublattice, which is L^2/P. Therefore, as long as L is substantially greater than the number of processors, we can expect to obtain a reasonable speedup. Of course, this algorithm suffers from the same type of load imbalance as the SIMD version. However, in this case, it is much less severe since most of the work is done with "ants in the labyrinth," which is well load balanced. The speedups obtained on the Symult 2010, for a variety

Self - labelling

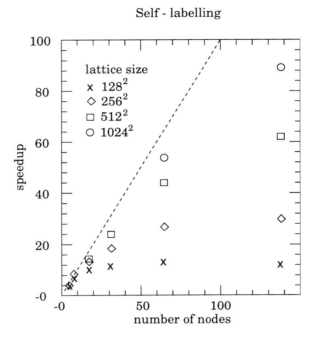

Figure 12.27: Speedups for Self-Labelling Algorithm

of lattice sizes, are shown in Figure 12.27. The dashed line indicates perfect speedup (i.e., 100% efficiency). The lattice sizes for which we actually need large numbers of processors are of the order of 512^2 or greater, and we can see that running on 64 nodes (or running multiple simulations of 64 nodes each) gives us quite acceptable efficiencies of about 70% for 512^2 and 80% for 1024^2.

12.6.5   Global Equivalencing

In this method we again use the fastest sequential algorithm to identify the clusters in the sublattice on every processor. Each processor then looks at the labels of sites along the edges of the neighboring processors in the positive directions, and works out which ones are connected and should be matched up. These lists of "equivalences" are all passed to one of the processors, which uses an algorithm for finding equivalence classes [Knuth:68a], [Press:86a] (which, in this case, are the global cluster labels) to match up the connected clusters. This processor then broadcasts the results back to all the other

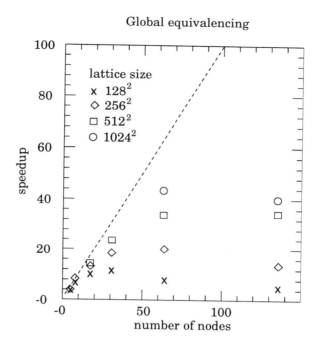

Figure 12.28: Speedups for Global Equivalencing Algorithm

processors.

This part of the algorithm is purely sequential, and is thus a potentially disastrous bottleneck for large numbers of processors. It also requires this processor to have a large amount of memory in which to store all the labels from every other processor. The amount of work involved in doing the global matchup is proportional to P times the perimeter of the sublattice on each processor, or $L\sqrt{P}$ so that the efficiency should be less than for self-labelling; although, we might still expect reasonable speedups if the number of processors is not extremely large. The speedups obtained on the Symult 2010 for a variety of lattice sizes are shown in Figure 12.28. The figure for 512^2 on 128 processors is missing due to memory constraints. Global equivalencing gives about the same speedups as self-labelling for small numbers of processors, but as expected self-labelling does much better as the number of processors increases.

12.6.6   Other Algorithms

The problem of labelling clusters of spins is an example of a standard graph problem known as *connected component labelling* [Horowitz:78a]. Another important instance occurs in image analysis, in identifying and labelling the connected components of a binary or multicolored image composed of an array of pixels [Rosenfeld:82a]. There have been a number of parallel algorithms implemented for this problem [Alnuweiri:92a] [Cypher:89a], [Embrechts:89a], [Woo:89a]. The most promising of these parallel algorithms for spin models has a hierarchical divide-and-conquer approach [Baillie:91a], [Embrechts:89a]. The processor array is divided up into smaller subarrays of, for example, 2×2 processors. In each subarray, the processors look at the edges of their neighbors for clusters which are connected across processor boundaries. As in global equivalencing, these equivalences are all passed to one of the nodes of the subarray, which places them in equivalence classes. The results of these partial matchings are similarly combined on each 4×4 subarray, and this process is continued until finally all the partial results are merged together on a single processor to give the global cluster values.

Finally, we should mention the trivial parallelization technique of running independent Monte Carlo simulations on different processors. This method works well until the lattice size gets too big to fit into the memory of each node. In the case of the Potts model, for example, only lattices of size less than about 300^2 or 50^3 will fit into 1 Mbyte, though most other spin models are more complicated and more memory-intensive. The smaller lattices which are seen to give poor speedups in Figure 12.27 and Figure 12.28 can be run with 100% efficiency in this way. Note, of course, that this requires an MIMD computer. In fact, we have used this method to calculate the dynamical critical exponents of various cluster algorithms for Potts models [Baillie:90m;91b], [Coddington:92a] (see Section 4.4.3).

12.6.7   Summary

This research was performed by C. F. Baillie, P. D. Coddington, J. Apostolakis, and E. Marinari.

12.7   Sorting

This section discusses *sorting*: the rearrangement of data into some set sequential order. Sorting is a common component of many applications and so it is important to do it well in parallel. Quicksort (to be discussed below) is fundamentally a divide-and-conquer algorithm and the parallel version is closely related to the recursive bisection algorithm discussed in Section 11.1. Here, we have concentrated on the best general-purpose sorting algorithms: *bitonic*, *shellsort*, and *quicksort*. No special properties of the list are exploited. If the list to be sorted has special properties, such as a known distribution (e.g., random numbers with a flat distribution between 0 and 1) or high degeneracy (many redundant items, e.g., text files), then other strategies can be faster. In the case of known data distribution, a bucketsort strategy (e.g., radix sort) is best, while the case of high degeneracy is best handled by the distribution counting method ([Knuth:73a, pp. 379-81]).

The ideas presented here are appropriate for MIMD machines and are somewhat specific to hypercubes (we will assume 2^d processors), but can easily be extended to other topologies.

There are two ways to measure the quality of a concurrent algorithm. The first may be termed "speed at any cost," and here one optimizes for the highest absolute speed possible for a fixed-size problem. The other we can call "speed per unit cost," where one, in addition to speed, worries about efficient use of the parallel machine. It is interesting that in sorting, different algorithms are appropriate depending upon which criterion is employed. If one is interested only in absolute speed, then one should pay for a very large parallel machine and run the bitonic algorithm. This algorithm, however, is inefficient. If efficiency also matters, then one should only buy a much smaller parallel machine and use the much more efficient shellsort or quicksort algorithms.

Another way of saying this is: for a *fixed-size* parallel computer (the realistic case), quicksort and shellsort are actually the *fastest* algorithms on all but the smallest problem sizes. We continue to find the misconception that "Everyone knows that the bitonic algorithm is fastest for sorting." This is *not* true for most combinations of machine size and list size.

The data are assumed to initially reside throughout the parallel computer, spread out in a random, but load-balanced fashion (i.e., each processor begins with an approximately equal number of datums). In our experiments, the data were positive integers and the sorting key was taken to be simply their numeric value. We require that at the end of the sorting process, the data residing in each node are sorted internally and these sublists are also sorted globally across the machine in some way.

12.7.1   The Merge Strategy

In the merging strategy to be used by our sorting algorithms, the first step is
for each processor to sort its own sublist using some fast algorithm. We take
for this a combined quicksort/insertion sort which is described in detail as
Algorithm Q by Knuth ([Knuth:73a, pp. 118-9]). Once the local (processor)
sort is complete, it must be decided how to merge all of the sorted lists in
order to form one globally sorted list. This is done in a series of compare-
exchange steps. In each step, two neighboring processors exchange items so
that each processor ends up with a sorted list and all of the items in one
processor are greater than all of the items in the other. Thus, two sorted lists
of m items each are merged into a sorted list of $2m$ items (stored collectively
in the memory of the two processors). The compare-exchange algorithm is
interesting in its own right, but we do not have the space here to discuss it.
The reader is referred to Chapter 18 of [Fox:88a] for the details.

12.7.2   The Bitonic Algorithm

Many algorithms for sorting on concurrent machines are based upon
Batcher's bitonic sorting algorithm ([Batcher:68a], [Knuth:73a, pp.232-3]).
The first step in the merge strategy is for each processor to internally sort
via quicksort. One is then left with the problem of constructing a series
of compare-exchange steps which will correctly merge $N = 2^d$ sorted sublists. This problem is completely isomorphic to the problem of sorting a list
of 2^d items by pairwise comparisons between items. Each one of our sublist compare-exchange operations is equivalent to a single compare-exchange
between two individual items. The pattern of compare-exchanges for the
bitonic algorithm for the $d = 3$ case is shown in Figure 12.29. More details
and a specification of the bitonic algorithm can be found in Chapter 18 of
[Fox:88a].

Table 12.2 shows the actual times and efficiencies for our implementation
of the bitonic algorithm. Results are shown for sorting lists of sizes 1 K
to 2048 K items on hypercubes with dimensions, d, ranging from one (2
nodes) to seven (128 nodes). Efficiencies are computed by comparing with
single-processor times to quicksort the entire list (we take quicksort to be
our benchmark sequential algorithm). The same information is also shown
graphically in Figure 12.30.

Clearly, the efficiencies fall off rapidly with increasing d. From the standpoint of cost-effectiveness, this algorithm is a failure. On the other hand,

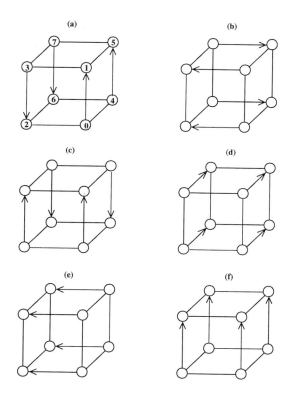

Figure 12.29: Bitonic Scheme for $d = 3$. This figure illustrates the six compare-exchange steps of the bitonic algorithm for $d = 3$. Each diagram illustrates four compare-exchange processes which happen simultaneously. The arrows represent a compare-exchange between two processors. The largest items go to the processor at the point of the arrow, and the smallest items to the one at the base of the arrow.

Table 12.2: Bitonic sort on a hypercube. The rows are labelled by hypercube size ($N_{\text{proc}} = 2^d$), the columns by number of items to sort.

Total List Size

	Execution times (sec)										
d	1K	2	4	8	16	32	64	128	256	512	1024	2048K
1	.25	.54	1.19	2.52	5.50	11.72						
2	.15	.33	.71	1.49	3.24	6.66	13.92					
3	.10	.20	.44	.92	1.95	3.98	8.41	17.56				
4	.07	.14	.29	.60	1.26	.260	5.39	11.31	23.11			
5	.05	.10	.20	.40	.82	1.71	3.50	7.15	14.80	30.34		
6	.03	.06	.13	.26	.53	1.08	2.20	4.48	9.15	18.74	38.26	
7	.03	.04	.09	.17	.33	.67	1.35	2.77	5.60	11.37	23.22	47.00
	Efficiency ε										
d	1K	2	4	8	16	32	64	128	256	512	1024	2048K
1	.92	.94	.93	.95	.94	.94						
2	.77	.77	.78	.80	.80	.83	.85					
3	.58	.63	.63	.65	.66	.69	.70	.71				
4	.41	.45	.48	.50	.51	.53	.55	.55	.57			
5	.29	.32	.35	.37	.39	.40	.42	.44	.45	.46		
6	.24	.26	.27	.29	.30	.32	.34	.35	.36	.37	.39	
7	.12	.20	.19	.22	.24	.26	.27	.28	.30	.31	.32	.33

*In units of 1K=1024 items. Divide by 2^d for items per processor.

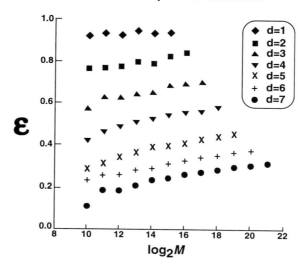

Figure 12.30: The Efficiency of the Bitonic Algorithm Versus List Size for Various Size Hypercubes—Labelled by Cube Dimension d.

Table 12.2 shows that for fixed-list sizes and increasing machine size, the execution times continue to decrease. So, from the speed-at-any-cost point of view, the algorithm is a success. We attribute the inefficiency of the bitonic algorithm partly to communication overhead and some load imbalance during the compare-exchanges, but mostly to nonoptimality of the algorithm itself. In our definition of efficiency we are comparing the parallel bitonic algorithm to sequential quicksort. In bitonic, the number of cycles grows quadratically with d. This suggests that efficiency can be improved greatly by using a parallel algorithm that sorts in fewer operations without sacrificing concurrency.

12.7.3 Shellsort or Diminishing Increment Algorithm

This algorithm again follows the merge strategy and is motivated by the fact that d compare-exchanges in the d different directions of the hypercube result in an almost-sorted list. Global order is defined via *ringpos*, that is, the list will end up sorted on an embedded ring in the hypercube. After the d compare-exchange stages, the algorithm switches to a simple mopping-up stage which is specially designed for almost-sorted lists. This stage is optimized for moving relatively few items quickly through the machine and amounts to a parallel bucket brigade algorithm. Details and a specification of the parallel shellsort algorithm can be found in Chapter 18 of [Fox:88a].

It turns out that the mop-up algorithm takes advantage of the MIMD nature of the machine and that this characteristic is crucial to its speed. Only the few items which need to be moved are examined and processed. The bitonic algorithm, on the other hand, is natural for a SIMD machine. It involves much extra work in order to handle the worst case, which rarely occurs.

We refer to this algorithm as shellsort ([Shell:59a], [Knuth:73a] pp. 84-5, 102-5) or a diminishing increment algorithm. This is not because it is a strict concurrent implementation of the sequential namesake, but because the algorithms are similar in spirit. The important feature of Shellsort is that in early stages of the sorting process, items take very large jumps through the list reaching their final destinations in few steps. As shown in Figure 12.31, this is exactly what occurs in the concurrent algorithm.

The algorithm was implemented and tested with the same data as the bitonic case. The timings appear in Table 12.3 and are also shown graphically in Figure 12.32. This algorithm is much more efficient than the bitonic algorithm, and offers the prospect of reasonable efficiency at large d. The remaining inefficiency is the result of both communication overhead and algorithmic nonoptimality relative to quicksort. For most list sizes, the mop-up time is a small fraction of the total execution time, though it begins to dominate for very small lists on the largest machine sizes.

12.7.4 Quicksort or Samplesort Algorithm

The classic quicksort algorithm is a divide-and-conquer sorting method ([Hoare:62a], [Knuth:73a] pp.118-23). As such, it would seem to be amenable to a concurrent implementation, and with a slight modification (actually an improvement of the standard algorithm) this turns out to be the case.

The standard algorithm begins by picking some item from the list and using this as the splitting key. A loop is entered which takes the splitting key and finds the point in the list where this item will ultimately end up once the sort is completed. This is the first splitting point. While this is being done, all items in the list which are less than the splitting key are placed on the low side of the splitting point, and all higher items are placed on the high side. This completes the first divide. The list has now been broken into two independent lists, each of which still needs to be sorted.

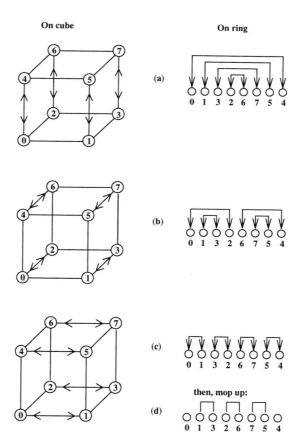

Figure 12.31: The Parallel Shellsort on a $d = 3$ Hypercube. The left side shows what the algorithm looks like on the cube, the right shows the same when the cube is regarded as a ring.

Table 12.3: Shellsort

Total List Size

d	1K	2	4	8	16	32	64	128	256	512	1024	2048K
					Execution times (sec)							
1	.25	.54	1.20	2.52	5.51	11.73						
2	.15	.31	.68	1.43	3.13	6.40	13.44					
3	.07	.16	.36	.76	1.62	3.30	7.03	14.96				
4	.04	.09	.19	.40	.85	1.82	3.70	7.91	16.66			
5	.05	.07	.11	.23	.44	.91	1.93	4.01	8.47	17.51		
6	.07	.08	.09	.16	.27	.52	1.05	2.12	4.36	9.15	18.81	
7	.21	.16	.06	.17	.23	.37	.67	1.30	2.44	5.23	10.22	21.03

d	1K	2	4	8	16	32	64	128	256	512	1024	2048K
					Efficiency ε							
1	.92	.94	.92	.95	.94	.94						
2	.77	.82	.81	.84	.82	.86	.88					
3	.82	.79	.77	.79	.80	.84	.84	.84				
4	.72	.70	.73	.75	.76	.76	.80	.79	.80			
5	.29	.45	.63	.65	.73	.76	.76	.78	.78	.80		
6	.10	.20	.38	.47	.60	.66	.70	.74	.76	.77	.78	
7	.02	.05	.11	.22	.35	.47	.55	.60	.68	.67	.72	.74

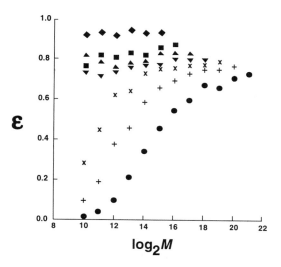

Figure 12.32: The Efficiency of the Shellsort Algorithms Versus List Size for Various Size Hypercubes. The labelling of curves and axes is as in Figure 12.30.

Quicksort

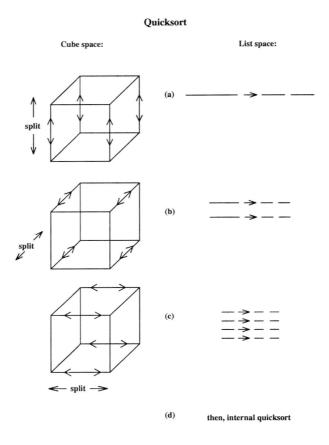

Figure 12.33: An Illustration of the Parallel Quicksort

The essential idea of the concurrent (hypercube) quicksort is the same. The first splitting key is chosen (a global step to be described below) and then the entire list is split, in parallel, between two halves of the hypercube. All items higher than the splitting key are sent in one direction in the hypercube, and all items less are sent the other way. The procedure is then called recursively, splitting each of the subcubes' lists further. As in Shellsort, the ring-based labelling of the hypercube is used to define global order. Once d splits occur, there remain no further interprocessor splits to do, and the algorithm continues by switching to the internal quicksort mentioned earlier. This is illustrated in Figure 12.33.

So far, we have concentrated on standard quicksort. For quicksort to

Parallel Quicksort vs Sequential Quicksort

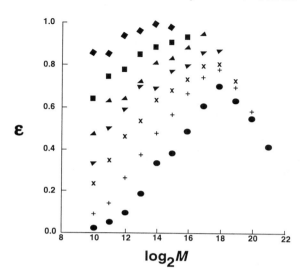

Figure 12.34: Efficiency Data for the Parallel Quicksort described in the Text. The curves are labelled as in Figure 12.30 and plotted against the logarithm of the number of items to be sorted.

work well, even on sequential machines, it is essential that the splitting points land somewhere near the median of the list. If this isn't true, quicksort behaves poorly, the usual example being the quadratic time that standard quicksort takes on almost-sorted lists. To counteract this, it is a good idea to choose the splitting keys with some care so as to make evenhanded splits of the list.

This becomes much more important on the concurrent computer. In this case, if the splits are done haphazardly, not only will an excessive number of operations be necessary, but large load imbalances will also occur. Therefore, in the concurrent algorithm, the splitting keys are chosen with some care. One reasonable way to do this is to randomly sample a subset of the entire list (giving an estimate of the true distribution of the list) and then pick splitting keys based upon this sample. To save time, all $2^d - 1$ splitting keys are found at once. This modified algorithm should perhaps be called *samplesort* and consists of the following steps:

- each processor picks sample of l items at random;

- sort the sample of $l\ 2^d$ items using the parallel shellsort;

- choose splitting keys as if this was the entire list;

- broadcast splitting keys so that all processors know all splitting keys;

- perform the splits in the d directions of the hypercube;

- each processor quicksorts its sublist.

Times and efficiencies for the parallel quicksort algorithm are shown in Table 12.4. The efficiencies are also plotted in Figure 12.34. In some cases, the parallel quicksort outperforms the already high performance of the parallel shellsort discussed earlier. There are two main sources of inefficiency in this algorithm. The first is a result of the time wasted sorting the sample. The second is due to remaining load imbalance in the splitting phases. By varying the sample size l, we achieve a trade-off between these two sources of inefficiency. Chapter 18 of [Fox:88a] contains more details regarding the choice of l and other ways to compute splitting points.

Before closing, it may be noted that there exists another way of thinking about the parallel quicksort/samplesort algorithm. It can be regarded as a bucketsort, in which each processor of the hypercube comprises one bucket. In the splitting phase, one attempts to determine reasonable limits for the 2^d buckets so that approximately equal numbers of items will end up in each bucket. The splitting process can be thought of as an optimal routing scheme on the hypercube which brings each item to its correct bucket. So, our version of quicksort is also a bucketsort in which the bucket limits are chosen dynamically to match the properties of the particular input list.

The sorting work began as a collaboration between Steve Otto and summer students Ed Felten and Scott Karlin. Ed Felten invented the parallel Shellsort; Felten and Otto developed the parallel Quicksort.

12.8 Hierarchical Tree-Structures as Adaptive Meshes

12.8.1 Introduction

Two basic types of simulations exist for modelling systems of many particles: grid-based (point particles indirectly interacting with one another through the potential calculated from equivalent particle densities on a mesh) and

Table 12.4: Quicksort

Total List Size

d						Execution times (sec)						
	1K	2	4	8	16	32	64	128	256	512	1024	2048K
1	.27	.60	1.18	2.51	5.24	11.37						
2	.18	.34	.71	1.41	2.93	6.10	12.71					
3	.12	.20	.43	.83	1.59	3.32	6.69	13.25				
4	.09	.13	.24	.44	.96	1.83	3.80	7.46	15.64			
5	.06	.09	.15	.28	.51	1.02	2.02	3.94	8.26	19.45		
6	.08	.11	.13	.20	.34	.61	1.11	2.12	4.26	10.11	25.87	
7	.20	.16	.18	.20	.24	.45	.76	1.29	2.38	5.59	13.66	37.91

d						Efficiency ε						
	1K	2	4	8	16	32	64	128	256	512	1024	2048K
1	.85	.84	.94	.95	.98	.97						
2	.64	.75	.78	.85	.88	.91	.93					
3	.48	.63	.64	.72	.81	.83	.88	.95				
4	.32	.49	.58	.68	.67	.76	.78	.84	.85			
5	.24	.35	.46	.53	.63	.68	.73	.80	.80	.72		
6	.09	.14	.27	.37	.47	.57	.66	.74	.78	.69	.57	
7	.02	.05	.10	.19	.34	.38	.49	.61	.70	.63	.54	.41

particle-based (point particles directly interacting with one another through potentials at their positions calculated from the other particles in the system). Grid-based solvers traditionally model continuum problems, such as fluid and gas systems like the one described in Section 9.3, and mixed particle-continuum systems. Particle-based solvers find more use modeling discrete systems such as stars within galaxies, as discussed in Section 12.4, or other rarefied gases. Many different physical systems, including electromagnetic interactions, gravitational interactions, and fluid vortex interactions all are governed by Poisson's Equation:

$$\nabla^2 \phi = -4\pi G \rho, \tag{12.6}$$

for the gravitational case. To evolve N particles in time, the exact solution to the problem requires calculating the force contribution to each particle from all other particles at each time step:

$$\mathbf{F}_i = \sum_{j \neq i}^{N} \frac{G m_i m_j (\mathbf{x}_j - \mathbf{x}_i)}{|\mathbf{x}_j - \mathbf{x}_i|^3}. \tag{12.7}$$

The $O(N^2)$ operation count is prohibitive for simulations of more than a few thousand particles commonly required to represent astrophysical and vortex configurations of interest.

One method of decreasing the operation count utilizes grid-based solvers which translate the particle problem into a continuum problem by interpolating the particles onto a mesh representing density and then solve the discretized equation. Initial implementations were based upon *fast fourier transform* (FFT) and *cloud-in-cell* (CIC) methods which can calculate the potential of a mass distribution on a three-dimensional grid with axes of length M in $O(M^3 \log M^3)$ operations, but at the cost of lower accuracy in the force resolution. All of these algorithms are discussed extensively by Hockney and Eastwood [Hockney:81a].

A newer type of grid-based solver for discretized equations classified as a multilevel or multigrid method has been in development for over a decade [Brandt:77a], [Briggs:87b]. Frequently, the algorithm utilizes a hierarchy of rectangular meshes on which a traditional relaxation scheme may be applied, but multiscale methods have expanded beyond any particular type of solver or even grids, per se. Relaxation methods effectively damp oscillatory error modes whose wave numbers are comparable to the grid size, but most of the iterations are spent propagating smooth, low-wave number corrections throughout the system. Multigrid utilizes this property by resampling the low-wave number residuals onto secondary, lower-resolution meshes, thereby shifting the error to higher wave numbers comparable to the grid spacing where relaxation is effective. The corrections computed on the lower-resolution meshes are interpolated back onto the original finer mesh and the combined solutions from the various mesh levels determine the result.

Many grid-based methods for particle problems have incorporated some form of local direct-force calculation, such as the *particle-particle/particle-mesh* (PPPM) method or the *method of local corrections* (MLC), to correct the force on a local subset of particles. The grid is used to propagate the far-field component of the force while direct-force calculations provide the near-field component either completely or as a correction to the "external" potential. The computational cost strongly depends on the criterion used to distinguish near-field objects from far-field objects. Extremely inhomogeneous systems of densely clustered particles can deteriorate to nearly $O(N^2)$ if most of the particles are considered neighbors requiring direct force computation.

A class of alternative techniques which have been implemented with great success utilize methods to efficiently calculate and combine the coefficients of an analytic approximation to the particle forces using spherical harmonic multipole expansions in three dimensions.

$$
\begin{aligned}
\phi_\gamma(\mathbf{r}) &= \int_{V_\gamma} d^3x\, G(\mathbf{r} - \mathbf{x})\rho(\mathbf{x}) \\
&= \sum_{n=0}^{\infty} \phi_{\gamma(n)}(\mathbf{r}) \\
&= M_{\gamma(0)} G|_{\mathbf{r}-\mathbf{r}_\gamma} - M_{\gamma(1)}^i \partial_i G|_{\mathbf{r}-\mathbf{r}_\gamma} \\
&\quad + \frac{1}{2} M_{\gamma(2)}^{ij} \partial_i \partial_j G|_{\mathbf{r}-\mathbf{r}_\gamma} - \frac{1}{6} M_{\gamma(3)}^{ijk} \partial_i \partial_j \partial_k G|_{\mathbf{r}-\mathbf{r}_\gamma} \cdots,
\end{aligned}
\tag{12.8}
$$

where the multipole moments

$$
M_{\gamma(n)}^{i_1 \cdots i_n} = \int_{V_\gamma} d^3x\, (\mathbf{x} - \mathbf{r}_\gamma)^{i_1} (\mathbf{x} - \mathbf{r}_\gamma)^{i_2} \cdots (\mathbf{x} - \mathbf{r}_\gamma)^{i_n} \rho(\mathbf{x}),
\tag{12.9}
$$

V_γ are the disjoint spatial regions, and $G(r)$ is the Green's function. Instead of integrating G over the volume V_γ, one may compute the potential (and, in a similar manner, the gradient) at any position by calculating the multipole moments which characterize the density distribution in each region, evaluating G and its derivatives at $\mathbf{r} - \mathbf{r}_\gamma$, and summing over indices. This algorithm is described more extensively in Section 12.4.

Not only does spatially sorting the particles into a tree-type data structure provide an efficient database for individual and collective particle information [Samet:90a], but the various algorithms require and utilize the hierarchical grouping of particles and combined information to calculate the force on each particle from the multipole moments in $O(N \log N)$ operations or less.

Implementations for three-dimensional problems frequently use an oct-tree—a cube divided into eight octants of equal spatial volume which contain subcubes similarly divided. The cubes continue to nest until, depending on the algorithm, the cube contains either zero or one particles or a few particles of equal number to the other "terminal" cells. Binary trees which subdivide the volume with planes chosen to evenly divide the number of particles instead of the space also have been used [Appel:85a]; a single bifurcation separates two particles spaced arbitrarily close together while the oct-tree would require arbitrarily many subcubes refining one particular region. This approach may produce fewer artifacts by not imposing an arbitrary rectangular structure onto the simulation, but construction is more difficult and information about each cut must be stored and used throughout the computation.

Initial implementations for both grid-based and multipole techniques normally span the entire volume with a uniform resolution net in which to catch the result. While this is adequate for homogeneous problems, it either wastes computational effort and storage or sacrifices accuracy for problems which exhibit clustering and structure. Many of the algorithms described above provide enough flexibility to allow adaptive implementations which can conform to complicated particle distribution or accuracy constraints.

12.8.2   Adaptive Structures

Mesh-based algorithms have started to incorporate adaptive mesh refinement to decrease storage and wasted computational effort. Instead of solving the entire system with a fixed resolution grid designed to represent the finest structures, local regions may be refined adaptively depending on accuracy requirements such as the density of particles. Unlike finite-element and finite-volume algorithms, which deform a single grid by shifting or adding vertices, *adaptive mesh refinement* (AMR) algorithms simply overlay regions of interest with increasingly fine rectangular meshes. Berger, Colella, and

Oliger have pioneered application of this method to hyperbolic partial differential equations [Berger:84a;89a]. Almgren recently has extended AMR for multigrid to an MLC implementation [Almgren:91a].

Adaptive mesh refinement traditionally has been limited to rectangular regions. McCormick and Quinlan have extended their very robust, inherently conservative adaptive mesh multilevel algorithm called *asynchronous fast adaptive composite* (AFAC) [McCormick:89a] to relax nonrectangular subregions directly between two grid levels. The algorithm is a true multiscale solver not limited to relaxation-type solvers. AFAC provides special benefits for parallel implementations because the various levels in a single multigrid cycle may be scheduled in any convenient order and combined at the end of the cycle instead of the traditional, sequentially-ordered V-cycle.

In the particle-based solver regime, the Barnes-Hut [Barnes:86a] method utilizes an adaptive tree to store information about one particle or the collective information about particles in the subcubes. Each particle calculates the force on itself from all of the other particles in the simulation by querying the hierarchical database, descending each branch of the tree until a user-specified accuracy criterion has been met. The accuracy is determined by the solid angle subtended by the cluster of particles within the cube from the vantage point of the particle calculating the force. If the cube contains a single particle or if all of the particles in the cube can be approximated by the center of mass, the force is computed using a multipole expansion; otherwise, each of the eight subcubes is examined in turn using the same criterion. By utilizing combined information instead of the individual data at the terminal node of each branch, the algorithm requires $O(N \log N)$ operations. Section 12.4 provides additional explanation while describing a parallel implementation of this method.

The Fast Multipole Method(FMM) developed by Greengard and Rokhlin [Greengard:87b] utilizes new techniques to quickly compute and combine the multipole approximations in $O(N)$ operations. Initial implementations sorted the particles into groups on a fixed level of the tree with the hierarchical pyramid structure providing the communication network used to combine and repropagate the multipole-calculated potential. Recent enhancements include adaptive refinement of the hierarchy-creating structures similar to a Barnes-Hut tree [Greengard:91a].

Both Katzenelson and Anderson have noted the applicability of a variety of "tree algorithms" to the N-body problem. Katzenelson utilizes the common structure of the Barnes-Hut and FMM algorithms to study how this problem can be mapped to a variety of parallel computer designs

[Katzenelson:89a]. Anderson utilizes the multigrid framework as a basis for communication in his FMM implementation which substitutes Poisson integrals for spherical harmonic multipole expansions [Anderson:90b].

12.8.3   Tree as Grid

We propose that the exact same hierarchical structure used by particle-based methods now may be effectively utilized in adaptive mesh refinement implementation. The spatially structured cubic volumes into which the mass-points are sorted are inherently situated, sized, and ordered as an efficient adaptive mesh representing the system of interest. Instead of interpreting the hierarchy as a graphical representation of the tree-shaped database, it can function as the physical mesh which links the grid resolution with the particle density. Figures 12.10(a) and 12.35 represent a two-dimensional tree-structure from a particle simulation (simplified for ease of presentation). Figures 12.36 and 12.37 show the configuration in Figure 12.35 represented by a composite grid. The similarity between Figures 12.35 and 12.36 demonstrates the convergence of these two different approaches. Tree levels and cells may not directly correspond with grid levels and zones, that is, multiple particles (and cells) from multiple levels would be collected to form a single grid level of appropriate resolution aligned with the tree cells. Figure 12.11 shows a larger, more realistic two-dimensional tree for which we can give a similar discussion.

This relationship stems from the grid-based algorithm's reliance on the locality of the discrete operator and the particle-based schemes' similar utilization of locality to efficiently collect, combine, and redistribute the multipole moments. In the Poisson case, the locality stems from the regularity of harmonic functions which allow accurate approximation of the smooth, far-field solution by low-order representations [Almgren:91a]. Barnes-Hut requires the locality of the tree not just as a framework for the algorithm but to provide the ability to selectively descend into subcubes as needed during the computation, allowing Salmon to create "locally essential" data sets per processor [Salmon:90a]. Locality is common to and useful for many loosely synchronous parallel algorithms [Fox:88a].

This union of hierarchies provides opportunities beyond similar programming structure [Anderson:90b], [Katzenelson:89a]: It allows easier synthesis of combined particle and mesh algorithms and allows hierarchy-building developments to benefit both simulation methods. An additional advantage of the oct-tree over the binary tree (recursive bisection) for dividing space

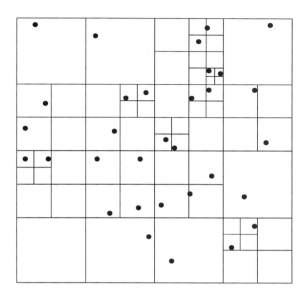

Figure 12.35: A Collapsed Representation of a Small, Two-dimensional Barnes-Hut Tree Containing 32 Particles

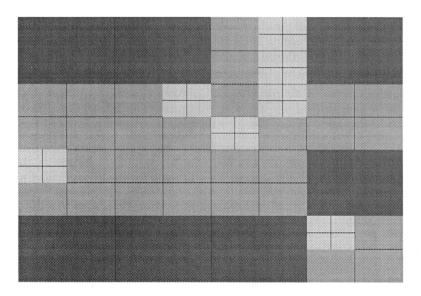

Figure 12.36: The Flattened Tree in Figure 12.35 Interpreted as a Composite Grid

Figure 12.37: Another View of the Composite Grid in Figure 12.36 Showing the Individual Grid Levels from Which it is Constituted

is evident when combining particle and mesh algorithms: The spatially divided oct-tree allows for easy alignment with a mesh while the the binary tree does not easily overlay a mesh or another tree [Samet:88a]. The parallel implementation of the Barnes-Hut code by Salmon [Salmon:90a], including domain decomposition and tree construction, provides insights applicable to adaptive mesh refinement on massively parallel, multiple-instruction multiple-data (MIMD) computers. The locality of the algorithms precisely provide the structure necessary for efficient parallel domain decomposition and ordered, hypercubelike communication on MIMD architectures.

An astrophysical model combining a smooth fluid for gas dynamics with discrete particles representing massive objects can occur entirely on a mesh or using a mixed simulation. The block structures available in the AFAC algorithm allow arbitrarily shaped, nested regions of rectangular meshes to be used as the relaxation grid for a multilevel algorithm; these regions can directly represent the partially complete subcubes present in oct-tree data structures frequently used in three-dimensional particle simulations. When combining both methods, the density of mass points is no longer sufficient as an estimate for necessary grid resolution, so additional criteria based upon acceptable error in other aspects of the simulation, for example, accurately reproducing shocks, will affect the construction of the mesh. But the grid can adapt to these constraints and the hierarchy still provides the multipole information at points of interest.

If the method of local corrections is incorporated to provide greater accuracy for local interactions, the neighboring regions requiring correction can utilize the Barnes-Hut test of opening angle or the Salmon test of cumulative error contribution [Salmon:92a] instead of a direct proximity calculation. The correction can be calculated using a multipole expansion instead of the direct particle-particle interaction, which improves efficiency for the worst-case scenario of dense clusters. While the same machinery can be used to solve the entire particle problem with a multipole method, some boundary conditions may be much harder to implement, necessitating the use of a local correction grid method.

12.8.4 Conclusion

Grid-based particle simulation algorithms continue to provide an effective technique for studying systems of pointlike particles in addition to continuum systems. These methods are a useful alternative to grid-less simulations which cannot incorporate fluid interactions or complicated boundary conditions as easily or effectively. While the approach is quite different, the tree-structure and enhanced accuracy criterion which are the bases of multipole methods are equally applicable as the fundamental structure of an adaptive refinement mesh algorithm. The two techniques complement each other well and can provide a useful environment both for studying mixed particle-continuum systems and for comparing results even when a mesh is not necessitated by the physically interesting aspects of the modelled system. The hierarchical structure naturally occurs in problems which demonstrate locality such as systems governed by Poisson's Equation.

Implementations for parallel, distributed-memory computers gain direct benefit from the locality. Because both the grid-based and particle-based methods form the same hierarchical structure, common data partitioning can be employed. A hybrid simulation using both techniques implicitly has the information for both components—particle and fluid—at hand on the local processor node, simplifying the software development and increasing the efficiency of computing such systems.

Considerations such as the efficiency of a deep, grid-based hierarchy with few or even one particle per grid cell need to be explored. Current particle-based algorithm research comparing computational accuracy against grid resolution (i.e., one can utilize lower computational accuracy with a finer grid or less refinement with higher computational accuracy), will strongly influence this result. Also, the error created by interpolating the particles onto a grid and then solving the discrete equation must be addressed when comparing gridless and grid-based methods.

Chapter 13

Data Parallel C and Fortran

13.1 High-Level Languages

13.1.1 High Performance Fortran Perspective

Essentially, all the work of C^3P used the message-passing model with the application scientist decomposing the problem by hand and generating C (and sometimes Fortran) plus message-passing code to express the parallel program. This book is designed to show that this message-passing model is effective. It gets good performance and experienced users find it convenient to use as it is the most powerful approach that can express essentially all problems as long as the software is suitably embellished—with, if necessary, the functionality described in Chapters 15, 16, and 17. However, we can regard the success of message passing for parallel computing as comparable to the success of machine language programming for conventional machines. This was how early computers were programmed, and is still used today to get optimal performance for computational kernels and libraries. However, the overwhelming majority of lines of sequential code are developed, not with machine language but with high-level languages such as Fortran, C, or even higher level object-oriented systems. There are at least two reasons to seek a higher level approach than message passing for parallel computing, reasons that are shared by the machine language analogy.

- First, higher level software should be more portable as it is less tailored to a particular machine.

- Second, the adoption of parallel machines by a broad range of users will be enhanced if we can offer easy to learn and productive parallel

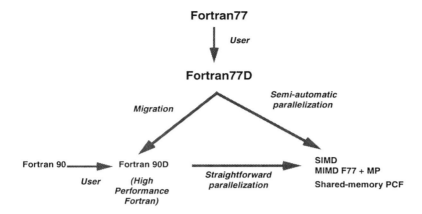

Figure 13.1: The Initial Integrated FortranD Environment

software environments. Parallel computers are sufficiently powerful that one can afford to "throw away" modest factors (e.g., a factor of two) in performance to obtain a more productive software environment.

We can illustrate the portability issues with two anecdotes from C^3P. Our original (Cosmic Cube and Mark II) hypercubes did not allow the overlap of communication and calculation. However, we carefully designed the Mark IIIfp to allow the performance enhancement offered by this overlap. However, we made little use of this hardware feature because all our codes, algorithms and software support (CrOS) had been developed for the original hardware. Even the "Marine Corps" of C^3P was not willing to recode applications and systems software to gain the extra performance. Our software did port between MIMD machines as they evolved and in this sense message passing is portable. However, the "optimal" message-passing implementation is hardware dependent and nonportable. The goal of higher level software systems is to rely on compilers and runtime systems to provide such optimization. As a second anecdote, we note that C^3P shared a 16 K CM-2 with Argonne National Laboratory. C^3P's use of this was disappointing even though several of our applications, such as QCD in Chapter 4, were very suitable for this SIMD architecture. We had excellent parallel (QCD) codes, which we ran in production, but these were written with message passing and this could not run on the CM-2. We were not willing to recode in CMFortran to use the SIMD machine for this problem.

Table 13.1: Reasons to build parallel languages on top of existing languages—especially Fortran, C, C++

- Experience of users
- Good sequential node compilers exist.
- Migration of existing codes
- Hard to build a new language as we need all the features/libraries of Fortran/C implemented well. This is why one uses Fortran 90 and not APL.
- Fortran and C are good (OK) for a class of applications
- No compelling new language that supports parallel computing better than extension of old languages

---

C^3P was correct to concentrate on message passing on its MIMD machines; this is the only way to good performance on most (excepting the CM-5) MIMD machines even in 1992—ten years after we started. However, the enduring lesson of C^3P was that "Parallel Computing Works." There is no reason that our particular software approach should endure in the same fashion. Rather, we wish to embody the lessons of C^3P's work into better and higher level software systems.

In 1987, Fox and Kennedy shared a crowded Olympus Airways flight from Athens to New York. Their conversations were key in establishing the collaboration on FortranD [Bozkus:93a;93b], [Choudhary:92c;92d;92e], [Fox:91e], [Ponnusamy:92c]. This combined the parallel compiler expertise of Kennedy [Callahan:88e], [Hiranandani:91a;91b], with C^3P's wisdom in practical use of parallel machines. Again, Fox's move to Syracuse allowed him to compare the successes of CMFortran on the SIMD CM-2 with those of message passing on the C^3P MIMD emporium. He concluded that one could use high-level data-parallel Fortran for both SIMD and MIMD machines. This evolved FortranD from its initial Fortran 77D implementation to include a Fortran 90D version [Wu:92a], illustrated in Figure 13.1. Section 13.3 describes some of the experiments leading to this realization. We will not describe data-parallel Fortran in detail because the situation is still quite fluid and this is an area that has grown spectacularly since 1990 when C^3P

Table 13.2: Features of the Fortran(C) Plus Message-Passing Paradigm

- Natural MIMD model of programming
- Used in vast majority of current successful MIMD programming
- Each node has program which controls and calculates updates of its own data (owner-computes "rule")
        CALL READ (for nonlocal data)
        Do i run over local data
        CALCULATE update of local data i
- In simplest form, one program per node of computer (SPMD)
- Advantages
    - Portable to MIMD distributed- and shared-memory machines—should scale to future machines with some difficulties (such as overlapping communication with itself and calculation)
    - Available now
    - There will be industry standards (MPI) for message-passing libraries
    - "All Problems" can be written in it
- Disadvantages
    - Can be hard work for user inserting communication calls
    - Optimizations not portable
    - Only MIMD

finished its project.

Section 13.2 describes a prototype software tool built at Caltech and Rice by Vas Balasundaram and Uli Kremer to enable users to experiment with different decompositions. This was a component of the FortranD project set up as part of the NSF Center for Research in Parallel Computation (CRPC). FortranD was set up as a scalable language, that is,

"We may need to rewrite our code for a parallel machine, but the resulting scalable (FortranD) code should run with high efficiency on 'all' current and future anticipated machines."

Many new parallel languages have been proposed—OCCAM is a well known example [Pritchard:91a]—but none are "compelling" that is, they do not solve enough parallel issues to warrant adoption. Thus, the recent trend has been to adapt existing languages such as Fortran [Brandes:92a], [Callahan:88e], [Chapman:92a], [Chen:92b], [Gerndt:90a], [Merlin:92a], [Zima:88a], C++ [Bodin:91a], C [Hamel:92a], [Hatcher:91a;91b], and Lisp. The latter is illustrated by the successful *Lisp, parallel Lisp implementation available on the CM-1, 2, and 5. Table 13.1 summarizes some of the issues involved in choosing to adopt a new language rather than modifying an old one. Table 13.2 summarizes the message-passing approach and why we might choose to replace it by a higher level system, such as data-parallel C or Fortran as summarized in Table 13.3. We were impressed by the C* language offered on the CM-2; Section 13.6 describes an early experiment to develop a loosely synchronous version of this. We should probably have explored this more thoroughly, although at the time we did not perceive this as our mission and realized this project would require major resources to develop a system with good performance. Indeed, the performance of the early CM-2 C* compiler was poor and this also discouraged us. Quinn and Hatcher implemented a similar but more restrictive C* MIMD compiler [Hatcher:91a]. ASPAR, in Section 13.5, had similar goals to Fortran 77D, although it was targeted more as a migration tool than an efficient complete compiler.

FortranD extends Fortran with a set of directives [Fox:91e], which help the compiler produce good code on a parallel machine. These directives include those specifying the decomposition of the data-parallel arrays onto the target hardware. The language includes forms of parallel loop (*Forall* and *DO independent*) for which parallelization can be asserted without a difficult dependence analysis. The run time library implements optimized parallel functions operating on the data-parallel arrays. Fortran 90D also includes the parallelism implied by the explicit array notation, for example, if A, B, and C are arrays of the same size, $A = B + C$ is executed in parallel. This CRPC research was based in important ways on the research of C^3P. Further during 1992, an informal forum representing all the major players in the parallel computing arena agreed on a new industry-standard language, *High Performance Fortran* or HPF [Kennedy:93a]. This embodies all the essential ideas of FortranD—including the full Fortran 90 syntax. We have modified FortranD so that HPF is a subset of FortranD. The CRPC FortranD project continues as a research compiler to investigate extensions of HPF to handle more general problems and unsolved issues such as parallel

Table 13.3: Issues in Data-Parallel Fortran Programming Paradigm

- Program represented as sequence of functions (run time library) operating on arrays

  e.g., Dimension: $A(100, 100)$, $B(100, 100)$, $C(100, 100)$

  $\qquad A = B + C$

  $\qquad A = B + \text{Shift in } x, y(C)$

  $\qquad \text{forall } i, j$

  $\qquad\qquad A(i, j) = B(i, j) + C(i - 1, j) + \ldots$

  using an APL, Fortran90–like syntax or with explicit parallel loops
- All data owned by a particular processor
- Owner computes rules: for an expression $A(i, j) = \ldots$,

  Processor holding (owning) $A(i, j)$ calculates expression after communication of any data needed because right-hand side uses data not owned by processor
- Similar concepts in C, C++, LISP, ADA ...
- Advantages
  - Very portable and scalable to both SIMD and MIMD architectures
  - Should be able to eventually handle essentially all synchronous and loosely synchronous problems, including ones that only run well on MIMD machines
  - Industry Standard "High Performance Fortran" will be adopted, which include major features of CMFortran, Vienna Fortran, and FortranD
- Disadvantages
  - Need to wait for good compiler
  - Not all problems can be expressed in it

Table 13.4: High Performance Fortran (HPF) and its extensions

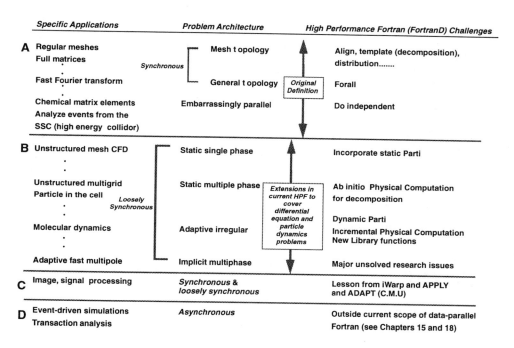

I/O [Bordawekar:93a], [Rosario:93a]. We expect that data-parallel languages should be able to eventually express nearly all loosely synchronous problems, that is, the vast majority of scientific and engineering computations.

The scope of HPF and FortranD is summarized in Table 13.4. Table 13.4(a) roughly covers both the synchronous and embarrassingly parallel calculations of Chapters 4, 6, 7, and 8. Note that we include computations such as the Kuppermann and McKoy chemical reaction problems in Chapter 8, which mix the synchronous and embarrassingly parallel classes. The original FortranD [Fox:91e] and the initial HPF language [Kennedy:93a] should be able to express these two problem classes in such a way that the compiler will get good performance on MIMD and, for synchronous problems, SIMD machines [Choudhary:92d;92e]. Table 13.4(b) covers the loosely synchronous problems of Chapters 9 and 12, which need HPF extensions to express the irregular structure. We intend to incorporate the ideas of PARTI [Berryman:91a], [Saltz:91b] into FortranD as a prototype of an extended HPF that could handle loosely synchronous problems. The difficult applications in Sections 12.4, 12.5, 12.7, and 12.8 have a hierarchical tree structure that is not easy to express [Bhatt:92a], [Blelloch:92a], [Mou:90a], [Singh:92a]. Table 13.4(c) indicates that we have not yet studied HPF and FortranD for signal processing applications, although the iWarp group at Carnegie Mellon University has developed high level languages APPLY and ADAPT for this problem class [Webb:92a]. Table 13.4(d) notes that we cannot express in FortranD and HPF the difficult asynchronous applications introduced in Chapter 14.

We expect this study and implementation of data-parallel languages to be a growing and critical area of parallel computing.

In Section 13.7, we contrast hierarchical and distributed memory systems. Both require data locality and we expect that data parallel languages such as High Performance Fortran will be able to use the HPF directives to improve performance of sequential machines by exploiting the cache and other levels of memory hierarchy better.

13.1.2   Problem Architecture and Message-Passing Fortran

Here we discuss the trade off between message-passing and data-parallel languages from the problem architecture point of view developed in Chapter 3.

We return to Figure 3.4, which expressed computation as a sequence of maps. We elaborate this in Figure 13.2, concentrating on the map of the (numerical formulation of the) problem S_{num} onto the computer S_{comp}. This map could be performed in several stages reflecting the different software levels. Here, we are interested in the high-level software map $S_{num} \rightarrow S_{HLSoft}$. One often refers to S_{HLSoft} as the virtual machine (VM), since one can think of it as abstracting the specific real machine into a generic VM. One could perhaps more accurately consider it as a virtual problem, since one is expressing the details of a particular problem in the language of a general problem of a certain class. Naively, one can say in Figure 13.2 that S_{HLSoft} is "nearer" the problem than the computer. One often thought of CMFortran as a language for SIMD machines. This is not accurate—rather, it is a language for synchronous problems (i.e., a particular problem architecture) which can be executed on all machine architectures. This is illustrated by the use of CMFortran on the MIMD CM-5 and the HPF (FortranD) discussion of the previous subsection. These issues are summarized in Table 13.5. Generally, we believe that high-level software systems should be based on a study of problems and their architectures rather than on machine characteristics.

Figure 13.3 (Color Plate) illustrates the map of problem onto machine,

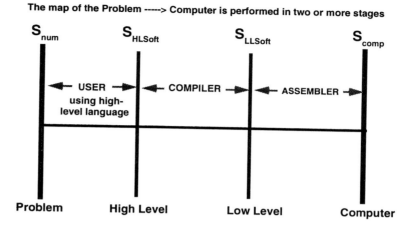

The map of the Problem -----> Computer is performed in two or more stages

S_{num} S_{HLSoft} S_{LLSoft} S_{comp}

◀— USER —▶   ◀— COMPILER —▶   ◀— ASSEMBLER —▶
using high-
level language

Problem   **High Level**   **Low Level**   **Computer**

Figure 13.2: Architecture of "Virtual Problem" Determines Nature of High-Level Language

emphasizing the different architectures of both. Here we regard message passing as a (low-level S_{LLSoft}) paradigm that is naturally associated with a particular machine architecture, that is, it does reflect a virtual machine— the generic MIMD architecture. One has a trade off in languages between features optimized for a particular problem class against those optimized for particular machine architectures. This figure is also drawn so as to emphasize that HPF corresponds to a S_{HLSoft} "near" the problem and Fortran-plus message passing is a paradigm "near" the computer.

Figure 13.4 (Color Plate) illustrates the compilation and migration processes from this point of view. HPF is a language that reflects the problem structure. It is difficult but possible to produce a compiler that maps it onto the two machine (SIMD and MIMD) architectures in the figure. Fortran-plus message passing expresses the MIMD computer architecture. It is typically harder for the user to express the problem in this paradigm than in the higher level HPF. However, it is quite easy for the operating system to map explicit message passing efficiently onto a MIMD architecture. However, this is not true if one wishes to map message passing to a different architecture (such as a SIMD machine) where one must essentially convert ("compile") the message passing back to the HPF expression of the problem. This is typically impossible as the message-passing formulation does not have all the necessary information contained in it. Expressing a problem in a specific language often "hides" information about the problem that is

Table 13.5: Message Passing, Data-Parallel Fortran, Problem Architectures

---

- Note: Distinguish
    - programming model (architecture of virtual problem S_{HLSoft})
    - machine model (generalization of architecture of real machine S_{comp})
- We can adopt data-parallel Fortran as a programming model for all machines. (It is specialized to certain problems, not to certain machines.)
- Fortran-plus Message Passing
    - naturally maps onto MIMD machines
    - very hard for SIMD real machines
    - can represent SIMD (synchronous) and MIMD (loosely synchronous, asynchronous) problems
- Data-Parallel Fortran (HPF, FortranD)
    - can map onto SIMD and MIMD machines
    - easiest for SIMD (synchronous) problems
    - can be extended to some MIMD (loosely synchronous) problems

---

essential for parallelization. This is why much of the existing Fortran 77 sequential code cannot be parallelized. Critical information about the underlying problem cannot be discovered except at run time when it is hard to exploit. We discuss this point in more detail in the following subsection.

13.1.3 Problem Architecture and Fortran 77

In Section 3.3, we noted that the concept of space and time are not preserved in the mappings between complex systems defined in Equation 3.1. We can use this to motivate some advantage in using the array notation used in Fortran 90. Consider a complex problem whose data domain is expressed in two Fortran arrays A and B with, say,

$$\text{DIMENSION} \quad A(100, 100), \quad B(100, 100).$$

Suppose some part of the program involves adding the arrays, which is expressed as

$$A = A + B \qquad (13.1)$$

in Fortran 90 and

$$
\begin{array}{ll}
\text{DO 1} \ I & = 1,100 \\
\text{DO 1} \ J & = 1,100 \\
1 \quad A(I,J) & A(I,J) + B(I,J)
\end{array}
\qquad (13.2)
$$

in Fortran 77. In this last equation, the data-parallel spatial manipulation of Equation 13.1 is converted into 10,000 time steps. In other words, Fortran 77 has not preserved the spatial structure of the problem. The task of a parallelizing Fortran 77 compiler is to reverse this procedure by recognizing that the sequential (time-stepped) DO loops are "just" a spatially (data)-parallel expression. We find mappings:

$$
\begin{aligned}
\text{Fortran 90:} \quad & \text{Space (problem)} \to \text{Space}(S_{\text{HLSoft}}) \\
& \to \text{Space and Time (parallel computer)} \qquad (13.3)
\end{aligned}
$$

$$
\begin{aligned}
\text{Fortran 77:} \quad & \text{Space (problem)} \to \text{Time}(S_{\text{HLSoft}}) \\
& \to \text{Space and Time (parallel computer)} \qquad (13.4)
\end{aligned}
$$

Note that the final parallel computer implementation maps the original spatial structure into a combination of time (the "node" program) and space (distribution) over nodes.

We can attribute some of the difficulties in producing an effective Fortran 77 compiler to the unfortunate mapping of space into time (control) shown in Equation 13.4. In the trivial example of Equation 13.3, one can undo this "wrong," but in general there is not enough compile time information in a Fortran 77 code to recover the original spatial parallelism. In this language, Fortran-plus message passing also does not preserve the spatial structure, but rather maps into a mix of space (the message-passing parallelism) and time (node Fortran).

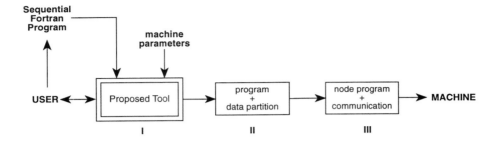

Figure 13.5: The Program Development Process

13.2 A Software Tool for Data Partitioning and Distribution

Programming a distributed-memory parallel computer is a complicated task. It involves two basic steps: (1) specifying the partitioning of the data, and (2) writing the communication that is necessary in order to preserve the correct data flow and computation order. The former requires some intellectual effort, while the latter is straightforward but tedious work.

We have observed that programmers use several well-known tricks to optimize the communication in their programs. Many of these techniques are purely mechanical, relying more on clever juxtapositions and transformations of the code rather than on a deep knowledge of the algorithm. This is not surprising, since once the data domain has been partitioned, the data dependences in the program completely define the communication necessary between the separate partitions. It should, therefore, be possible for a software tool to automate step (2), once step (1) has been accomplished by the programmer.

This would allow the program to be written in a traditional sequential language extended with annotations for specifying data distribution, and have a software tool or compiler mechanically generate the node program for the distributed-memory computer. This strategy, illustrated by stages II and III in Figure 13.5, is being studied by several researchers [Callahan:88d], [Chen:88b], [Koelbel:87a;90a], [Rogers:89b], [Zima:88a].

What is missing in this scheme? Although the tedious step has been automated, the hard intellectual step of partitioning the data domain is still left entirely to the programmer. The choice of a partitioning strategy often involves some deeper knowledge of the algorithm itself, so we clearly cannot hope to automate this process completely. We could, however, provide some assistance in the data partitioning process, so that the programmer can make a better choice of partitioning schemes from all the available options. This section describes the design of an interactive data partitioning tool that provides exactly this kind of assistance.

13.2.1 Is Any Assistance Really Needed?

The ultimate goal of the programmer is peak performance on the target computer. The realization of peak performance requires the understanding of many subtle relationships between the algorithm, the program, and the target machine architecture. Factors such as input data size, data dependences in the code, target machine characteristics, and the data partitioning scheme are related in very nonintuitive ways, and jointly determine the performance of the program. Thus, a data partitioning scheme that is chosen purely on the basis of some algorithmic property, may not always be the best choice.

Let us examine the relationship between these aspects more closely, to illustrate the subtle complexities that are involved in choosing the partitioning of the data domain. Consider the following program:

```
subroutine example (A, B, N)
    double precision A(N, N), B(N, N)

    do k=1, cycles
        do j=1,N
            do i=2,N-1
                A(i, j) = F ( B(i-1, j), B(i+1, j) )
            enddo
        enddo
        do j=2,N-1
            do i=2,N-1
                B(i,j) = F' ( A(i-1, j), A(i+1, j), A(i, j),
                    A(i, j-1), A(i, j+1) )
            enddo
        enddo
    enddo
end
```

$\mathcal{F}$ and $\mathcal{F}'$ represent functions with 4 and 10 double-precision floating-point operations, respectively. This program segment does not represent any particular realistic computation; rather, it was chosen to illustrate all the

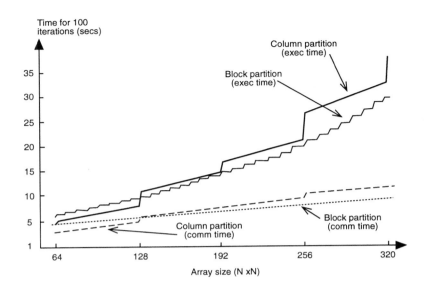

Figure 13.6: Timing results on an nCUBE, using 64 processors.

aspects of our argument using a small piece of code. The program segment
was executed on 64 processors of an nCUBE, with array sizes ranging from
$N = 64$ to $N = 320$. A and B were first partitioned as columns, so that each
processor was assigned $N/64$ successive columns. The program was then
run once again, this time with A and B partitioned as blocks, so that each
processor was assigned a block of $N^2/64$ elements. The resulting execution
and communication times for column and block partitioning schemes are
shown in Figure 13.6. The communication time was measured by removing
all computation in the loops.

When employing a column partitioning scheme for arrays A and B, communication is only necessary after the first j loop. Each processor has to
exchange boundary values with its left and right neighbor. In a block partitioning scheme, each processor has to communicate with its four neighbors
after the first loop and with its north and south neighbors after the second
loop. For small message lengths, the communication cost is dominated by
the message startup time, whereas the transmission cost begins to dominate
as the messages get longer (i.e., more data is exchanged at each communication step). This explains why communication cost for the column partition
is greater than for the block partition for array sizes larger than 128×128.
It is clear from the graph that column partitioning is preferable when the

array sizes are less than 128×128, and block partitioning is preferable for larger sizes.

The steps in the execution time graphs are caused mainly by load imbalance effects. For example, the step between $N = 128$ and $N = 129$ for the column partition is due to the fact that for size 129 one subdomain has an extra column, so that the processor assigned to that subdomain is still busy after all the others have finished, causing load imbalance in the system. Similar behavior can be observed for the block partition, but here the steps occur at smaller increments of the array size N. The steps in the communication time graphs are due to the fact that the packet size on the nCUBE is 1 Kbyte, so that messages that are even a few bytes longer need an extra packet to be transmitted.

The above example indicates that several factors contribute to the observed performance of a chosen partitioning scheme, making it difficult for a human to predict this behavior statically. Our aim is to make the programmer aware of these performance effects without having to run the program on the target computer. We hope to do this by providing an interactive tool, that can give performance estimates in response to a data layout specification. The tool's performance estimates will allow the programmer to gauge the effect of a data partitioning scheme and thus provide some guidance in making a better choice.

13.2.2 Overview of the Tool

When using the tool we envision, the programmer will select a program segment for analysis, and the system will provide assistance in choosing an efficient data partitioning for the computation in that program segment, for various problem sizes. In a first step, the user determines a set of reasonable partitionings based on the data dependence information and interprocedural analysis information provided by the tool. An important component of the system is the performance estimation module, which is subsequently used to select the best partitionings and distributions from among those examined. In the present version, the do loop is the only kind of program segment that can be selected. For simplicity, the set of possible partitions of an array is restricted to regular rectangular patterns such as by row, by column, or by block for a two-dimensional array and their higher dimensional analogs for arrays of larger dimensions. This permits the examination of all reasonable partitionings of the data in an acceptable amount of time.

The tool will permit the user to generalize from local partitionings to layouts for an entire program in easy steps, using repartitioning and redistribution whenever it leads to a better performance overall. In addition, the tool will support many program transformations that can lead to more efficient data layouts.

The principal value of such an environment for data partitioning and distribution is that it supports an exploratory programming style in which the user can experiment with different data partitioning strategies, and estimate the effect of each strategy for different input data sizes or different target machines without having to change the program or run the program each time.

13.2.3 Dependence-based Data Partitioning

Given a sequential Fortran program and a selected program segment (which in the preliminary version can only be a loop nest), the tool provides assistance in deriving a set of reasonable data partitions for the arrays accessed in that segment. The assistance is given in the form of data dependence information for variables accessed within the selected segment. When partitioning data, we must ensure that the parallel computations done by all the processors on their local partitions preserve the data dependence relations in the sequential program segment. If the computations done by the processors on the distributed data satisfy all the data dependences, the results of the computation will be the same as those produced by a sequential execution of the original program segment. There are two ways to achieve this: (1) by "internalizing" data dependences within each partition, so that all values required by computations local to a processor are available in its local data subdomain; or (2) by inserting appropriate communication to get the nonlocal data.

Let us consider a sample program segment and see how data dependence information can be used to help derive reasonable data partitionings for the arrays accessed in the segment.

P1. Example program segment.

```
do j = 1, n
    do i = 1, n
        A(i, j) = F( A(i-1, j) )
        B(i, j) = F'( A(i, j), B(i, j-1), B(i, j) )
    enddo
enddo
```

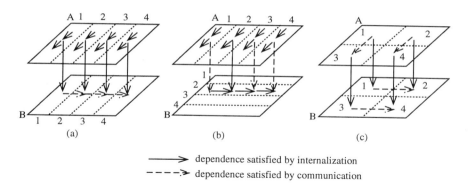

(a)   (b)   (c)

———————➤ dependence satisfied by internalization

- - - - ➤ dependence satisfied by communication

Figure 13.7: Data Dependences Satisfied by Internalization and Communication for the Partitioning Schemes (a) A by Column, B by Column (b) A by Column, B by Row and (c) A by Block, B by Block. Dotted lines represent partition boundaries and numbers indicate virtual processor ids (the figures are shown for $p = 4$ virtual processors). For clarity, only a few of the dependences are shown.

$\mathcal{F}$ and $\mathcal{F}'$ represent arbitrary functions, and their exact nature is irrelevant to this discussion. When the programmer selects the "do i" loop, the tool indicates that there is one data dependence that is carried by the i loop: the dependence of $A(i, j)$ on $A(i - 1, j)$. This dependence indicates that the computation of an element of A cannot be started until the element immediately above it in the previous row has been computed. The programmer then selects the outer "do j" loop to get the data dependences that are carried by the j loop. There is one such dependence, that of $B(i, j)$ on $B(i, j - 1)$. This dependence indicates that the computation of an element of B cannot be started until the computation of the element immediately to the left of it in the previous column has been computed. Figure 13.7(a) illustrates the pattern of data dependences for the above program segment.

The pattern of data dependences between references to elements of an array gives the programmer clues about how to partition the array. It is usually a good strategy to partition an array in a manner that internalizes all data dependences within each partition, so that there is no need to move data between the different partitions that are stored on different processors. This avoids expensive communication via messages. For example, the data dependence of $A(i, j)$ on $A(i - 1, j)$ can be satisfied by partitioning A in a columnwise manner, so that the dependences are "internalized" within each partition. The data dependence of $B(i,j)$ on $B(i,j-1)$ can be satisfied by partitioning B row-wise, since this would internalize the dependences within each partition.

It is not enough to examine only the dependences that arise due to references to the same array. In some cases, the data flow in the program implicitly couples two different arrays together, so that the partitioning of one affects the partitioning of the other. In our example, each point $B(i,j)$ also requires the value $A(i,j)$. We treat this as a special data dependence (3) called a *value* dependence (read "B is value dependent on A"), to distinguish it from the traditional data dependence that is defined only between references to the same array. This value dependence must also be satisfied either by internalization or by communication. Internalization of the value dependence is possible only by partitioning B in the same manner as A, so that each $B(i,j)$ and the $A(i,j)$ value required by it are in the same partition.

Based on the pattern of data dependences in the program segment, the following are a possible list of partitioning choices that can be derived:

1. Partition A by column and B by column. This satisfies the dependences within A and the value dependences of B on A by internalization but communication is required to satisfy the data dependences within B (Figure 13.7(a)). An analogous case is to partition both A and B by row. This would require communication to satisfy dependences within A.

2. Partition A by column and B by row. Dependences within B are now satisfied by internalization, but communication is needed to satisfy the value dependence of B on A (Figure 13.7(b)).

3. Partition both A and B as two-dimensional blocks. This would result in communication to satisfy dependences within both A and B, while the value dependence of B on A is satisfied by internalization (Figure 13.7(c)).

The partitioning of A by row and B by column was not considered among the possible choices because, in this scheme, none of the dependences are internalized, thus requiring greater communication compared to (1), (2) or (3). Communication overhead is a major cause of performance degradation on most machines, so a reasonable first choice would be the partitioning scheme that requires the least communication. This can be determined either by analyzing the number of dependences that are cut by the partitioning (indicating the need for communication), or more accurately using the performance estimation module that is described in the next section.

13.2.4 Mapping Data to Processors

For the selected program segment, the programmer picks one of the choices (1) through (3), and specifies the data partitioning via an interface provided by the tool. The tool responds by creating an internal data mapping that specifies the mapping of the data to a set of virtual processors. The number of virtual processors is equal to the number of partitions indicated by the data partitioning. The mapping of the virtual processors onto the physical processors is assumed to be done by the run time system, and this mapping is unspecified in the software layer. Henceforth, we will use the term "processor" synonymously with "virtual processor." The internal data mapping is used by the performance estimator to compute an estimate of communication and other costs for the program segment. It is also used by the tool to determine the data that needs to be communicated between the processors.

Let us continue with our example program segment, and see how the internal mapping is constructed for partitioning (2), that is, A partitioned by column and B by row. The data mappings for the other two cases can be constructed in a similar manner. Let A and B be of size $n \times n$ and the number of (virtual) processors be p. For simplicity we assume that p divides n. The following two data mappings are computed:

- $A(1:n, 1:n)$ partitioned by column: Create a virtual array $A\$(1:p)$, where $A\$(k)$ represents the kth column partition of A, that is, A\$ consists of the elements $A(1:n, (n/p)(k-1)+1:(n/p)k)$. The virtual array is only an internal entity, used within the tool to maintain the mapping of data to (virtual) processors. It does not have any physical storage on the machine. The partition of A represented by $A\$(k)$ is assumed to be mapped onto the kth processor by default.

- $B(1:n, 1:n)$ partitioned by row: Create a virtual array $B\$(1:p)$, where $B\$(k)$ represents the ith row partition of B, that is, B\$ consists of the elements $B((n/p)(k-1)+1:(n/p)k, 1:n)$. $B\$(k)$ is assigned to the kth processor by default.

The internal data mapping is used to solve the following two problems:

1. Given a processor q, what part of A is local to it? This is given by the section of A that belongs to the partition A(q).

2. Given a section A($x1 : x2, y1 : y2$), what processors contain elements of this section? This is given by the set of processors $\{q|A\$(q) \cap A(x1 : x2, y1 : y2) \neq \phi\}$.

The values n and p are assumed to be known statically.

A useful technique that we will subsequently use on these sections is called "translation." Translation refers to the conversion of an accessed section computed with respect to a particular loop to the section accessed with respect to an enclosing loop. For example, consider a reference to a two-dimensional array within a doubly nested loop. The section of the array accessed within each iteration of the innermost loop is a single element. The same reference, when evaluated with respect to the entire inner loop (i.e., all iterations of the inner loop) may access a larger section, such as a column of the array. If we evaluated the reference with respect to the outer loop (i.e., all iterations of the outer loop), we may notice that the reference results in an access of the entire array in a columnwise manner. Translation is thus a method of converting array sections in terms of enclosing loops, and we will denote this operation by the symbol "⇑".

The tool uses (1) to determine which processors should do what computations. The general rule used is: each processor executes only those program statements whose l-values are in its local storage. The l-values computed by a processor are said to be *owned* by the processor. In order to compute an l-value, several r-values may be required, and not all of them may be local to that processor. The inverse mapping (2) is used to determine the set of processors that own the desired r-values. These processors must send the r-value they own to the processor that will execute the statement.

The data mapping scheme described above works only for arrays. Scalar variables are assumed to be replicated, that is, every processor stores a copy of the scalar variable in its local memory. By the rule stated earlier, this implies that any statement that computes the value of a scalar is executed by all the processors.

13.2.5　Communication Analysis and Performance Improvement Transformations

The communication analysis algorithm takes the internal data mappings, the dependence graph, and the loop nesting structure of the specified program segment as its input. For each processor the algorithm determines information about all communications the processor is involved in. We will now illustrate the communication analysis algorithm using the example program segments P1, P2, and P3, where P2 is derived from P1, and P3 from P2, respectively, by a transformation called *loop distribution*.

Substantial performance improvement can be achieved by performing various code transformations on the program segment. For example, the *loop-distribution* transformation [Wolfe:89a] often helps reduce the overhead of communication. Loop distribution splits a loop into a set of smaller loops, each containing a part of the body of the original loop. Sometimes, this allows communication to be done between the resulting loops, which may be more efficient than doing the communication within the original loop.

Consider the program segment P1. If A is partitioned by column and B by row, communication will be required within the inner loop to satisfy the value dependence of B on A. Each message communicates a single element of A. For small message sizes and a large number of messages, the fraction of communication time taken up by message startup overhead is usually quite large. Thus, program P1 will most likely give poor performance because it involves the communication of a large number of small messages.

However, if we loop-distributed the inner do i loop over the two statements, the communication of A from the first do i loop to the second do i loop can be done between the two new inner loops. This allows each processor to finish computing its entire column partition of A in the first do i loop, and then send its part of A to the appropriate processors as larger messages, before starting computation of a partition of B in the second do i loop. This communication is done only once for each iteration of the outer do j loop, that is, a total of $O(n)$ communication steps. In comparison, program P1 requires communication within the inner loop, which gives a total of $O(n^2)$ communication steps:

P2. After loop distribution of i loop.

```
do j = 2, n
    do i = 2, n
        A(i, j) = F( A(i−1, j) )
    enddo
    do i = 2, n
        B(i, j) = F'( A(i, j), B(i, j−1), B(i, j) )
    enddo
enddo
```

The reduction in the number of communication steps also results in greater parallelism, since the two inner `do i` loops can be executed in parallel by all processors without any communication. This effect is much more dramatic if we apply loop distribution once more, this time on the outer `do j` loop:

P3. After loop distribution of j loop.

```
do j = 2, n
    do i = 2, n
        A(i, j) = F( A(i−1, j) )
    enddo
enddo
do j = 2, n
    do i = 2, n
        B(i, j) = F'( A(i, j), B(i, j−1), B(i, j) )
    enddo
enddo
```

For the same partitioning scheme (i.e., A by column and B by row), we now need only $O(1)$ communication steps, which occur between the two outer `do j` loops. The computation of A in the first loop can be done in parallel by all processors, since all dependences within A are internalized in the partitions. After that, the required communication is performed to satisfy the value dependence of B on A. Then the computation of B can proceed in parallel, because all dependences within B are internalized in the partitions. The absence of any communication within the loops considerably improves efficiency.

Currently, the tool provides a menu of several program transformations, and the programmer can choose which one to apply. When a particular transformation is chosen by the programmer, the tool responds by automatically performing the transformation on the program segment, and updating all internal information automatically.

13.2.6   Communication Analysis Algorithm

For the sake of illustration, let the size of A and B be 8×8 (i.e., $n = 8$), and let the number of (virtual) processors be $p = 4$. The following is a possible sequence of actions that the programmer could do using the tool.

After examining the data dependences within the program segment as reported by the tool, let us assume that the programmer decides to partition A by column and B by row. The tool computes the internal mapping:

A$(1) = A(1:8, 1:2) and B$(1) = B(1:2, 1:8).
A$(2) = A(1:8, 3:4) and B$(2) = B(3:4, 1:8).
A$(3) = A(1:8, 5:6) and B$(3) = B(5:6, 1:8).
A$(4) = A(1:8, 7:8) and B$(4) = B(7:8, 1:8).

To determine the communication necessary, the tool uses Algorithm COMM, shown in Figure 13.8. For simple partitioning schemes as found in many applications, the communication computed by algorithm COMM can be parameterized by processor number, that is, evaluated once for an arbitrary processor. In addition, we are also investigating other methods to speed up the algorithm.

Consider program P1 for example. According to algorithm COMM, when the kth processor executes the first statement, the required communication is given by

$$\{(q, \lambda)|\lambda = \text{A\$}(q) \cap \text{A}(i-1, j) \neq \phi\}$$

where the range of i and j are determined by the section of the LHS owned by processor k, in this case $i = 2 : 8$ and $j = 2(k - 1) + 1 : 2k$ (since A is partitioned columnwise). But the partitioning of A ensures that $\forall k$, the data $\text{A}(*, 2(k - 1) + 1 : 2k)$ is always local to k. The set of (q, λ) pairs will, therefore, be an empty set for any k. Thus, the execution of the first statement with A partitioned by column requires no communication.

When the kth processor executes the second statement, the communication as computed by algorithm COMM is given by

$$\begin{aligned} &\{(q, \lambda)|\lambda = \text{A\$}(q) \cap \text{A}(i, j) \neq \phi\} \\ \cup \quad &\{(q, \lambda)|\lambda = \text{B\$}(q) \cap \text{B}(i, j - 1) \neq \phi\} \\ \cup \quad &\{(q, \lambda)|\lambda = \text{B\$}(q) \cap \text{B}(i, j) \neq \phi\}. \end{aligned}$$

The ranges of i and j are determined by the section of the LHS that is owned by processor k: in this case $i = 2(k - 1) + 1 : 2k$ and $j = 2 : 8$ (since B is partitioned rowwise). The second and third terms will be ϕ, because the row partitioning of B ensures that $\forall k$, the data $\text{B}(2(k-1)+1 : 2k, *)$ is always local to k. The first term can be a nonempty set, because processor k owns a column of A (i.e., j in the range $2(k-1)+1 : 2k$)), while the range of j in the first term is $2 : 8$. Thus, communication may be required to get the nonlocal element of A before the kth processor can proceed with the computation of its $\text{B}(i, j)$. The dependence from the definition of $\text{A}(i, j)$ to its use is loop-independent. Algorithm COMM therefore computes `commlevel`, the common nesting level of the source and sink of the dependence, to be the

Algorithm COMM

Input: The data mapping specified by the chosen partitioning scheme,
the dependence graph, and the selected loop.
Output: A set of pairs (q, λ), indicating that processor q must send the section λ of
data that it owns, to processor k, and the level at which the communication occurs.

for each processor k **do**
    for each statement **do**
        Let def(X) be the section of the LHS array X that is owned by the kth processor;
        for each RHS array reference Y **do**
            Let use(Y) be the section of the RHS array Y that is needed to compute
            each element of def(X);
            We need to determine the communication required, if any, to get use(Y)
            from all processors $q \neq k$;
            Define `commlevel` of a dependence to be:
$$\begin{cases} \text{level of the dependence,} & \text{if it is loop-carried} \\ \text{common nesting level of src} & \text{if it is loop-independent} \\ \text{and sink of dependence,} & \end{cases}$$
            Let `lmax` = max(`commlevels` of all dependences with Y as sink reference);
            Let ⇑use(Y) be the section use(Y) "translated" to the level `lmax`;
            Then, the set of all (q, λ) pairs is given by
                $\{(q, \lambda), q \neq k \mid \lambda = Y\$(q) \cap \Uparrow use(Y) \neq \phi\}$,
                with the communications occurring at level `lmax`;
        endfor
    endfor
endfor

Figure 13.8: Algorithm to Determine the Communication Induced by the
Data Partitioning Scheme

level of the inner i loop. The section $A(i, j)$ translated to the level of the inner i loop is simply the single element $A(i, j)$. Thus, each message communicates this single element and the communication occurs within the inner i loop.

The execution of program P1 results in a large number of messages because each message only communicates a single element of A, and the communication occurs within the inner loop. Message startup and transmission costs are specified by the target machine parameters, and the average cost of each message is determined from the performance model. The tool computes the communication cost by multiplying the number of messages by the average cost of sending a single element message. This cost estimate is returned to the programmer.

Now consider the program P2, with the same partitioning scheme for A and B. When the kth processor executes the first statement, the required communication as determined by algorithm COMM is given by

$$\{(q, \lambda) | \lambda = A\$(q) \cap A(1 : 7, j) \neq \phi\},$$

where the range of j is determined by the section of the LHS owned by processor k, in this case $j = 2(k-1) + 1 : 2k$ (since A is partitioned columnwise). Note that in this case, $\Uparrow A(i-1, j) = A(1 : 7, j)$. This is because $\mathtt{commlevel}$ is now the level of the outer j loop, so that the section $A(i-1, j)$ must be translated to the level of the j loop. In other words, the reference to $A(i-1, j)$ in the first statement results in an access of the first seven elements of the jth column of A, during each iteration of the j loop. Since A is partitioned columnwise, this section will always be available locally in each processor, so that the above set is empty and no communication is required.

When processor k executes the second statement, the communication required is given by

$$\begin{aligned} & \{(q, \lambda) | \lambda = A\$(q) \cap A(2(k-1) + 1 : 2k, j) \neq \phi\} \\ \cup \ & \{(q, \lambda) | \lambda = B\$(q) \cap B(2(k-1) + 1 : 2k, j-1) \neq \phi\} \\ \cup \ & \{(q, \lambda) | \lambda = B\$(q) \cap B(2(k-1) + 1 : 2k, j) \neq \phi\} \end{aligned}$$

The second and third terms will be empty sets since the required part of B is local to each k (because B is partitioned rowwise). The first term will be nonempty, because each processor owns $A(*, 2(k-1)+1 : 2k)$, and the range of j in the first term is outside the range $2(k-1)+1 : 2k$. The data required by processor k from processor q will therefore be a strip $A(2(k-1)+1 : 2k, j)$, from each $q \neq k$.

This data can be communicated between the two inner $\mathtt{do\ i}$ loops. Each message will communicate a 2×1 size strip of A. Fewer exchanges will be required compared to program P1, because each exchange now communicates a strip of A, and the communication occurs outside the inner loop. Once again, the performance model and target machine parameters are used by the tool to estimate the total communication cost, and this cost is returned to the programmer.

For most target machines, the communication cost in program P2 will be considerably less than in program P1, because of larger message size and fewer messages.

Next, let us consider program P3. Assuming that the same partitioning scheme is used for A and B, the execution of the first loop by the kth processor will require communication given by

$$\{(q, \lambda) | \lambda = A\$(q) \cap A(1 : 7, 2(k - 1) + 1 : 2k)\}.$$

But this is an empty set because of the column partitioning of A. Here $\Uparrow A(i - 1, j) = A(1 : 7, 2(k - 1) + 1 : 2k)$, because `commlevel` for this case is the level of the subroutine that contains the two loops. The section is, therefore, translated to this level by substituting the appropriate bounds for i and j. The translated section indicates that the reference $A(i - 1, j)$ in the first statement results in an access of the section $A(1 : 7, 2(k - 1) + 1 : 2k)$ during all iterations of the outer j loop that are executed by processor k.

When the kth virtual processor executes the second loop, the required communication is

$$\begin{aligned} &\{(q, \lambda) | \lambda = A\$(q) \cap A(2(k - 1) + 1 : 2k, 2 : 8) \neq \phi\} \\ \cup\ &\{(q, \lambda) | \lambda = B\$(q) \cap B(2(k - 1) + 1 : 2k, 1 : 7) \neq \phi\} \\ \cup\ &\{(q, \lambda) | \lambda = B\$(q) \cap B(2(k - 1) + 1 : 2k, 2 : 8) \neq \phi\}. \end{aligned}$$

The second and third terms will be empty sets because of the row partitioning of B. The first term will be nonempty, and the data required by processor k from processor q will be the block $A(2(k - 1) + 1 : 2k, 2(q - 1) + 1 : 2q)$, for each $q \neq k$. This block can be communicated between the two **do** j loops.

This communication can be done between the two loops, allowing computation within each of the two loops to proceed in parallel. The number of messages is the fewest for this case because a 2×2 block of A is communicated during each exchange. Program P3 is thus likely to give superior performance compared to P1 or P2, on most machines. We ran programs P1, P2 and P3 with A partitioned by column and B by row, on 16 processors of the nCUBE at Caltech. The functions $\mathcal{F}$ and $\mathcal{F}'$ consisted of one and two

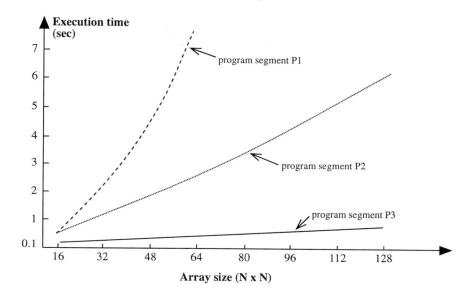

Figure 13.9: Timing Results for Programs P1, P2 and P3 on the nCUBE, Using 16 Processors.

double-precision floating-point operations, respectively. The results of the experiment are shown in Figure 13.9. The graphs clearly illustrate the performance improvement that occurs due to reduction in number of messages and increase in length of each message.

13.2.7   Static Performance Estimator

Given the results of the communication analysis in a program segment, the performance estimator can be used to predict the performance of that program segment on the target machine. The realization of such an estimator requires a simple static model of performance that is based on (1) target machine parameters such as the number of processors, the message startup and transmission costs, and the average times to perform different floating-point operations; (2) the size of the input data set; and (3) the data partitioning scheme.

We undertook a study of published performance models [Chen:88b], [Fox:88a], [Gustafson:88a], [Saltz:87b] for use in the performance estimator, and noticed that these theoretical models did not give accurate predictions in many cases. We concluded that the theoretical models suffered from the following deficiencies:

1. Most of the models suggested in the literature were aimed at being "general-purpose," that is, intended to model the performance of any distributed-memory MIMD computer. This generality created problems in some cases, when machine-specific peculiarities tended to skew the observed results from the ones predicted by the model.

2. The models also did not account for all of the software overhead involved in implementing the low-level communication utilities on the machine. While the models accounted for things like message startup costs and packetizing costs, they often ignored factors such as internal buffer sizes, peculiarities of the algorithms used to implement the message passing protocols, and so on.

Our effort to correct these defects resulted in an increased complexity of the model, and also necessitated the introduction of several machine-specific features. We felt that this was undesirable, and decided to investigate alternative methods [Balasundaram:90d].

We constructed a program that tested a series of communication patterns using a set of basic low-level portable communication utilities. This program, called a "training set," is executed once on the target machine. The program computes timings for the different communication operations and averages them over all the processors. These timings are determined for a sequence of increasing data sizes. Since the graph of communication cost versus data size is usually a linear function, it can easily be described by specifying a few parameters (e.g., the slope). The training set thus generates a table whose entries contain the minimal information necessary to completely define the performance characteristic for each communication utility. This table is used in place of the theoretical model for the purposes of performance prediction.

Figure 13.10 shows some communication cost characteristics created using a part of our training set on 32 processors of an nCUBE. The data space was assumed to be a two-dimensional array that was partitioned column-wise; that is, each processor was assigned a set of consecutive columns. The communication utilities tested here are:

1. iSR: nearest-neighbor individual element send and receive, using the EXPRESS calls exwrite() and exread().

2. vSR: nearest-neighbor vector send and receive along one direction, using the EXPRESS calls exvwrite() and exvread().

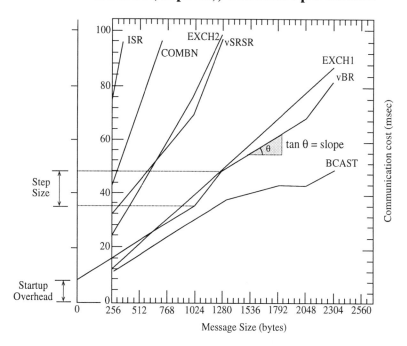

Figure 13.10: Communication cost characteristics of some EXPRESS utilities on the nCUBE

3. **EXCH1**: nearest-neighbor vector exchange along one direction, using the EXPRESS call exvchange().

4. **vSRSR**: nearest-neighbor vector sends and receives along two directions, using the EXPRESS calls exvwrite() and exvread().

5. **EXCH2**: nearest-neighbor vector exchange along two directions, using two calls to exvchange().

6. **COMBN**: combine operation over all processors, using the EXPRESS call excombine().

7. **BCAST**: one to all broadcast, using the EXPRESS call exbroadcast().

The table generated by the training set for the characteristics shown in Figure 13.10 is:

comm type	startup overhead (msec)	slope	step size (msec)
iSR	11.5	3.58	—
vSR	8.0	0.77	13.0
EXCH1	1.0	0.64	0.0
vSRSR	16.0	1.54	26.0
EXCH2	2.0	1.15	0.0
COMBN	5.2	2.05	—
BCAST	3.0	0.51	6.0

The communication cost estimate for a particular data size is then calculated using the formula:

$$T^{\mathrm{comm}} = \text{startup overhead} + (x * \text{slope}) + (\text{step size} * \lfloor \text{msg length/pkt size} \rfloor)$$

where "pkt size" is the size of each message packet, which on the nCUBE is 1024 bytes (1 Kbyte).

The static performance model is meant primarily to help the programmer discriminate between different data partitioning schemes. Our approach is to provide the programmer with the necessary tools to experiment with several data partitioning strategies, until he can converge on the one that is likely to give him a satisfactory performance. The tool provides feedback information about performance estimates each time a partitioning is done by the programmer.

13.2.8 Conclusion

Our emphasis in this work has been to try to recognize *collective* communication patterns rather than generate sequences of individual element sends and receives. Algorithm COMM determines this in a very natural way. This is especially important for loosely synchronous problems which represent a large class of scientific computations [Fox:88a]. Several communication utilities have been developed that provide optimal message-passing communication for such problems, provided the communication is of a regular nature and occurs collectively [Fox:88h].

We believe that our approach can be extended to derive partitioning schemes automatically. Data dependence and other information can be used to compute a fairly restricted set of reasonable data partitioning schemes for a selected program segment. The performance estimation module can then be applied in turn to each of the partitionings in the computed set.

The work described in this section was a joint effort between Caltech and Rice University, as part of the Center for Research on Parallel Computation (CRPC) research collaboration [Balasundaram:90a]. The principal researchers were Vasanth Balasundaram and Geoffrey Fox at Caltech, and Ken Kennedy and Ulrich Kremer at Rice. The data partitioning tool described here is being implemented as part of the ParaScope parallel programming environment under development at Rice University [Balasundaram:89c].

13.3 Fortran 90 Experiments

Near the end of the C^{3}P work at Caltech, we did some important experiments using Fortran 90 which formed the basis of the aspects of the FortranD project overviewed in Section 13.1. These were partly motivated by Fox's change of architectural environment. At Caltech, he was surrounded by MIMD machines and the associated culture; at Syracuse's NPAC facility, the centerpiece in 1990 was a 32 K-node SIMD CM-2. In reading the CMFortran (Fortran 90) manual, Fox noted that the Fortran 90 run time support included all the important collective communication primitives (such as combine and broadcast) we had found important in CrOS and Express.

The first experiment involved a climate modelling code using spectral methods [Keppenne:89a;90a]. We had rashly promised a TRW group that we would be able to easily parallelize such a code. However, we had not realized that the code was written in C with extensive C++-like use of pointers. ParaSoft—responsible for the code conversion—was horrified and the task seemed daunting! However, Keppenne was interested in rewriting the code in Fortran 90, which was a "neat" language like C++. ParaSoft found that the resultant Fortran 90 code was straightforward to port to a variety of parallel machines, as shown in Tables 13.6 and 13.7. Note that the new version of the code had an order-of-magnitude-higher performance than the original one on a single CPU CRAY Y-MP. The discipline implied by Fortran 90 allowed both "outside computational scientists" and the Cray compiler to "understand" the code. We analyzed this process and believe that we could indeed replace our friends at ParaSoft for this problem by a compiler—initially Fortran 90D—which could generate good SIMD and MIMD code. This is, of course, the motivation of use of the array syntax feature in High Performance Fortran as it captures the parallelism in a transparent fashion.

This experiment motivated the Fortran 90D language [Fox:91f], [Wu:92a], and we followed up the climate experiments with some other simple exam-

Table 13.6: Logistics of Migration Experiment on Climate Code

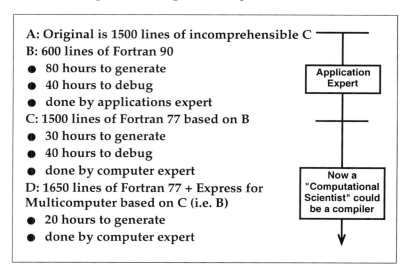

ples, which are summarized in Table 13.8. This compares "optimal hand-coded" Fortran-plus message-passing code with what we expect a good Fortran 90D (HPF) compiler could produce from the (annotated) Fortran 90 source. The results are essentially perfect for the Gaussian elimination example and reasonable for the FFT. These estimates were borne out in practice [Bozkus:93a;93b] and the prototype Fortran 90D compiler developed at Syracuse produced code that was about 10% slower than the optimal node Fortran 77+ message-passing version.

13.4   Optimizing Compilers by Neural Networks

The ability of neural networks to compute solutions to optimization problems has been widely appreciated since Hopfield and Tank's work on the travelling salesman problem [Hopfield:85b]. Chapter 11 reviews the general work in C^3P on optimization and physical and neural approaches. We have examined whether neural network optimization can be usefully applied to compiler optimizations. The problem is nontrivial because compiler optimizations usually involve intricate logical reasoning, but we were able to find an elegant formalism for turning a set of logical constraints into a neural network [Fox:89l]. However, our conclusions were that the method will only

Table 13.7: Performance of a Climate Modelling Computational Kernel. In each case, only minor (obviously needed) optimizations were performed.

Code	Machines	Performance **MFLOPS**	
Original C	CRAY Y-MP (1 head)	1.5	Old Code
Fortran 90 (CM Fortran)	8K CM-2	66 (problem too small)	New
Fortran 77 Generated from Fortran 90	CRAY Y-MP	20	
Fortran 77 + Message Passing Generated from Fortran 90	NCUBE-2 (16-node) hypercube	3.3	Portable
	NCUBE-2 (16-node) hypercube	20	code
	Intel i860 (16-node) hypercube	80	

Table 13.8: Effectiveness of Fortran 90 on Two Simple Kernels. The execution time is given as a function of the number of nodes used in the iPSC2 multicomputer.

iPSC2 (# of nodes)	Hand Coded F77 + Message Passing		Fortran 90 Estimate of what the Fortran 90D compiler will do on conversion to F77 + Message Passing
256×256 matrix Gaussian Elimination			
1	85.4	73.4	80
2	58.1	50.1	50.2
4	31.1	26.1	26.6
8	16	13.8	13.8
16	8.42	7.53	7.72
	(original)	(better)	
Fast Fourier Transform (2^{14} points)			
1	16.8		20.7
2	7.97		11
4	3.35		5.85
8	1.96		3.08
16	0.98		1.62

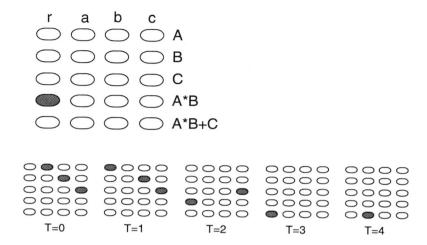

Figure 13.11: A Neural Network Can Represent Machine States (top) and Generate Correct Machine Code for Simple Computations (bottom).

be viable if and when large hierarchically structured neural networks can be built. The neural approach to compiler optimization is worth pursuing, because such a compiler would not be limited to a finite set of code transformations and could handle unusual code routinely. Also, if the neural network were implemented in hardware, a processor could perform the optimizations at run time on small windows of code.

Figure 13.11 shows how a simple computation of $A = A * B + C$ is scheduled by a neural network. The machine state is represented at five consecutive cycles by five sets of 20 neurons. The relevant portion of the machine comprises the three storage locations a, b, c and a register r, and the machine state is defined by showing which of the five quantities A, B, C, $A * B$ and $A * B + C$ occupies which location. A firing neuron (i.e., shaded block) in row $A * B$ and column r indicates that $A * B$ is in the register. The neural network is set up to "know" that computations can only be done in the register, and it produces a firing pattern representing a correct computation of $A = A * B + C$.

The neural compiler was conceived by Geoffrey Fox and investigated by Jeff Koller [Koller:88c], [Fox:891;90nn].

13.5   ASPAR

ASPAR was developed by Ikudome from C^{3}P [Ikudome:90a] in collaboration with ParaSoft. It was aimed at aiding the conversion of existing Fortran codes and embodies the experience especially of Flower and Kolawa. AS-PAR is aimed at those applications involving particular stencil operation on arrays—noting that many sequential stencils need modification for parallel execution. In this way, ASPAR involves a collaboration between user and compiler in the parallelization process. The discussion in this section is due to Flower and Kolawa, and we include some of the introductory material as a contrast to the discussion given in the introductory sections of each chapter in this book, which largely reflect Fox's prejudice.

It is now a widely accepted fact that parallel computing is a successful technology. It has been applied to problems in many fields and has achieved excellent results on projects ranging in scope from academic demonstrations to complete commercial applications, as shown by other sections of this book.

Despite this success, however, parallel computing is still considered something of a "black art" to be undertaken only by those with intimate knowledge of hardware, software, physics, computer science and a wealth of other complex areas. To the uninitiated there is something frightening about the strange incantations that abound in parallel processing circles—not just the "buzz words" that come up in polite conversation but the complex operations carried out on a once elegant piece of sequential code in order for it to successfully run on a parallel processing system.

13.5.1   Degrees of Difficulty

It is easy to define various "degrees of difficulty" in parallel processing. One such taxonomy might be as follows:

1. Extremely difficult (*Asynchronous*)

   In this category fall the complex, asynchronous, real-time applications. A good example of such a beast is "parallel chess" [Felten:88h] of Section 14.3, where AI heuristics must be combined with real-time constraints to solve the ill-posed problem of searching the "tree" of potential moves.

2. Complex (*Compound Metaproblems*)

   In this area one might put the very large applications of fairly straightforward science. Often, algorithms must be carefully constructed, but the greatest problems are the large scale of the overall system and the fact that different "modules" must be integrated into the complete system. An example might be the SDI simulation "Sim88" and its successors [Meier:90a] described in Section 18.3. The parallel processing issues in such a code require careful thought but pose no insurmountable problems.

3. Hard (*Loosely Synchronous*)

   Problems such as large-scale fluid dynamics or oceanography [Keppenne:90b] mentioned in Section 13.3 often have complex physics but fairly straightforward and well-known numerical methods. In these cases, the majority of the work involved in parallelization comes from analysis of the individual algorithms which can then often be parallelized separately. Each submodule is then a simpler, tractable problem which often has a "well-known" parallel implementation.

4. Straightforward but Tedious (*Synchronous*)

   The simplest class of "interesting" parallel programs are partial differential equations [Brooks:82b], [Fox:88a] and the applications of Chapters 4 and 6. In these cases the parallel processing issues are essentially trivial but the successful implementation of the algorithm still requires some care to get the details correct.

5. Trivial

   The last class of problems are those with "embarrassing parallelism" such as in Chapter 7—essentially uncoupled loop iterations or functional units. In these cases, the parallel processing issues are again trivial but the code still requires care if it is to work correctly in all cases.

The "bottom line" from this type of analysis is that all but the hardest cases pose problems in parallelization which are, at least conceptually, straightforward. Unfortunately, the actual practice of turning such concepts into working code is never trivial and rarely easy. At best it is usually an error-prone and time-consuming task.

This is the basic reason for ASPAR's existence. Experience has taught us that the complexities of parallel processing are really due not to any inherent problems but to the fact that human beings and parallel computers don't speak the same language. While a human can usually explain a parallel algorithm on a piece of paper with great ease, it is often a significant task to convert that picture to functional code. It is our hope that the bulk of the work can be automated by the use of "parallelizing" technologies such as ASPAR. In particular, we believe (and our results so far bear out this belief) that problems in all the previous categories (except possibly (1) above), can be either completely or significantly automated.

13.5.2   Various Parallelizing Technologies

To understand the issues involved in parallelizing codes and the difference between ASPAR and other similar tools, we must examine two basic issues involved in parallelizing code: the local and the global views.

The local view of a piece of code is restricted to one or more loops or similar constructs upon which particular optimizations are to be applied. In this case little attention is paid to the larger scale of the application.

The global view of the program is one in which the characteristics of a particular piece of data or a function are viewed as a part of the complete algorithm. The impact of operating on one item is then considered in the context of the entire application. We believe that ASPAR offers a completely new approach to both views.

13.5.3   The Local View

"Local" optimization is a method which has been used in compilers for many years and whose principles are well understood. We can see the evolutionary path to "parallelizing compilers" as follows.

1. Vectorizing Compilers

   The goal of automatic parallelization is obviously not new, just as parallel processors are not new. In the past, providing support for advanced technologies was in the realm of the compiler, which assumed the onus, for example, of hiding vectorizing hardware from the innocent users.

   Performing these tasks typically involves a fairly simple line of thought shown by the "flow diagram" in Figure 13.12. Basically the simplest idea is to analyze the dependences between data objects within loops. If there are no dependences, then "kick" the vectorizer into performing all, or as many as it can handle, of the loop iterations at once. Classic vector code therefore has the appearance

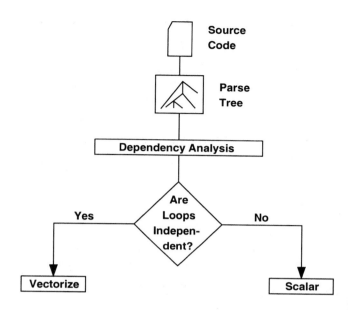

Figure 13.12: Vectorizability Analysis

```
DO 10 I=1,10000
      A(I) = B(I) + C(I)*D(I)
10 CONTINUE
```

2. Parallelizing Compilers

We can easily derive parallelizing compilers from this type of technology by changing the box marked "vectorize" in Figure 13.12 to one marked "parallelize." After all, if the loop iterations are independent, parallel operation is straightforward. Even better results can often be achieved by adding a set of "restructuring operations" to the analysis as shown in Figure 13.13.

The idea here is to perform complex "code transformations" on cases which fail to be independent during the first dependence analysis in an attempt to find a version of the same algorithm with fewer dependences. This type of technique is similar to other compiler optimizations such as *loop unrolling* and *code inlining* [Zima:88a], [Whiteside:88a]. Its goal is to create new code which produces exactly the same result when executed but which allows for better optimization and, in this case, parallelization.

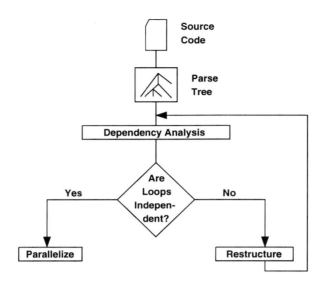

Figure 13.13: A Parallelizing Compiler

3. ASPAR

The emphasis of the two previous techniques is still on producing exactly the same result in both sequential and parallel codes. They also rely heavily on sophisticated compiler technology to reach their goals.

ASPAR takes a rather different approach. One of its first assumptions is that it may be okay for the sequential and parallel codes to give different answers!

In technical terms, this assumption removes the requirement that loop iterations be independent before parallelization can occur. In practical terms, we can best understand this issue by considering a simple example: image analysis.

One of the fundamental operations of image analysis is "convolution." The basic idea is to take an image and replace each pixel value by an average of its neighbors. In the simplest case we end up with an algorithm that looks like

```
DO 10 I = 2,N-1
DO 20 J = 2,N-1
          A(I,J)=0.25*(A(I+1,J)+A(I-1,J)+A(I,J+1)+A(I,J-1))
20 CONTINUE
```

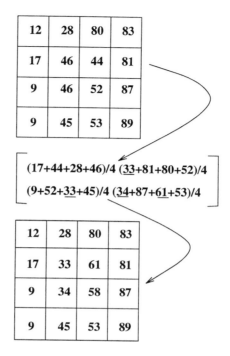

Figure 13.14: A Sequential Convolution

10 CONTINUE

To make this example complete, we show in Figure 13.14 the results of applying this operation to an extremely small (integer-valued) image.

It is crucial to note that the results of this operation are not as trivial as one might naively expect. Consider the value at the point (I=3, J=3) which has the original value 52. To compute this value we are instructed to add the values at locations A(2,2), A(2,4), A(3,2), and A(3,4). If we looked only at the original data from the top of the figure, we might then conclude that the correct answer is $(46 + 87 + 44 + 53)/4 = 57$.

Note that the source code, however, modifies the array A while simultaneously using its values. As a result, the above calculation accesses the correct array elements, but by the time we get around to computing the value at $(3,3)$ the values to the left and above have already been changed by previous loop iterations. As a result the correct value at $(3,3)$ is given by $(\underline{34} + 87 + \underline{61} + 53)/4 = 58$, where the underlined values are those which have been calculated on previous loop iterations.

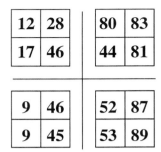

Figure 13.15: Data Distributed for Four Processors

Obviously, this is no problem for a sequential program because the algorithm, as stated in the source code, is translated correctly to machine code by the compiler, which has no trouble executing the correct sequence of operations; the problems with this code arise, however, when we consider its parallelization.

The most obvious parallelization strategy is to simply partition the values to be updated among the available processors. Consider, for example, a version of this algorithm parallelized for four nodes.

Initially we divide up the original array A by assigning a quadrant to each processor. This gives the situation shown in Figure 13.15. If we divide up the loop iterations in the same way, we see that the process updating the top-left corner of the array is to compute $(17 + 28 + 46 + 44)/4$ where the first two values are in its quadrant and the others lie to the right and below the processor boundary. This is not too much of a problem—on a shared-memory machine, we would merely access the value "44" directly, while on a distributed-memory machine, a message might be needed to transfer the value to our node. In neither case is the procedure very complex; especially since we are having the compiler or parallelizer do the actual communication for us.

The first problem comes in the processor responsible for the data in the top-right quadrant. Here we have to compute $(?? + 81 + 80 + 52)/4$ where the values "80" and "81" are local and the value "52" is in another processor's quadrant and therefore subject to the same issues just described for the top-left processor.

The crucial issue surrounds the value "??" in the previous expression. According to the sequential algorithm, this processor should wait for the top-left node to compute its value and then use this new result to compute the

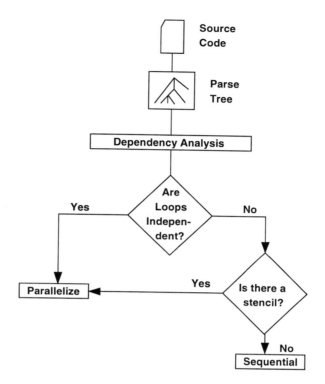

Figure 13.16: ASPAR's Decision Structure

new data in the top-right quadrant. Of course, this represents a serialization of the worst kind, especially when a few moments' thought shows that this delay propagates through the other processors too! The end result is that no benefit is gained from parallelizing the algorithm.

Of course, this is not the way image analysis (or any of the other fields with similar underlying principles such as PDEs, Fluid mechanics, and so on) is done in parallel. The key fact which allows us to parallelize this type of code despite the dependences is the observation that: *A large number of sequential algorithms contain data dependences that are not crucial to the correct "physical" results of the application.*

In this case, the data dependence that appears to prevent parallelization is also present in the sequential code but is typically irrelevant. This is not to say that its effects are not present but merely that the large-scale behavior of our application is unchanged by ignoring it. In this case, therefore, we allow the processor with the top-right quadrant of the image to use the "old" value of the cells to its left while computing new values, even though the processor with the top-left quadrant is actively engaged in updating them at the very same time that we are using them!

While this discussion has centered on a particular type of application and the intricacies of parallelizing it, the arguments and features are common to an enormous range of applications. For this reason ASPAR works from a very different point of view than "parallelizing" compilers: its most important role is to find data dependences of the form just described—and break them! In doing this, we apply methods that are often described as *stencil* techniques.

In this approach, we try to identify a relationship between a new data value and the old values which it uses during computation. This method is much more general than simple dependence analysis and leads to a correspondingly higher success rate in parallelizing programs. The basic flow of ASPAR's deliberations might therefore be summarized in Figure 13.16.

It is important to note that ASPAR provides options to enforce strict dependence checking as well as to override "stencil-like" dependences. By adopting this philosophy of checking for simple types of dependences, ASPAR more nearly duplicates the way humans address the issue of parallelization and this leads to its greater success. The use of advanced compilation techniques could also be useful, however, and there is no reason why ASPAR should "give up" at the point labelled "Sequential" in Figure 13.16. A similar "loopback" via code restructuring, as shown in Figure 13.13, would also be possible in this scenario and would probably yield good results.

13.5.4 The "Global" View

Up to now, the discussion has rested mainly on the properties of small portions of code—often single or a single group of nested loops in practical cases. While this is generally sufficient for a "vectorizing" compiler, it is too little for effective parallelization. To make the issues a little clearer, consider the following piece of code:

```
   DO 10 I=1,100
         A(I) = B(I) + C(I)
10 CONTINUE
   DO 20 I=1,100
         D(I) = B(I) + C(100-I+1)
20 CONTINUE
```

Taken in isolation (the local view), both of these loop constructs are trivially parallelizable and have no dependences. For the first loop, we would assign the first few values of the arrays A, B, and C to the first processor, the next few to the second, and so on until we had accounted for each loop iteration. For the second loop, we would assign the first few elements of A and B and the last few of C to the first node, and so on. Unfortunately, there is a conflict here in that one loop wants to assign values from array C in increasing order while the other wants them in decreasing order. This is the *global decomposition* problem.

The simplest solution in this particular case can be derived from the fact that array C only appears on the right-hand side of the two sets of expressions. Thus, we can avoid the problem altogether by not distributing array C at all. In this case, we have to perform a few index calculations, but we can still achieve good speedup in parallel.

Unfortunately, life is not usually as simple as presented in this case. In typical codes, we would find that the logic which led to the "nondistribution" of array C would gradually spread out to the other data structures with the final result that we end up distributing nothing and often fail to achieve any speedup at all.

13.5.5 Global Strategies

Addressing the global decomposition problem poses problems of a much more serious nature than the previous dependence analysis and local stencil methods because, while many clever compiler-related tricks are known to help the local problems, there is little theoretical analysis of more global problems. Only very recently, for example, do we find compilers that perform any kind of interprocedural analysis at all.

As a result, the resolution of this problem is really one which concerns the parallel programming model available to the parallelization tools. Again, ASPAR is unique in this respect.

To understand some of the possibilities, it is again useful to create a classification scheme for global decomposition strategies. It is interesting to note that, in some sense, the complexity of these strategies is closely related to our initial comments about the "degree of difficulty" of parallel processing.

1. Functional Decomposition

   This style is the simplest of all. We have a situation in which there are no data dependences among functional units other than initial and final output. Furthermore, each "function" can proceed independently of the others. The global decomposition problem is solved by virtue of never having appeared at all.

In this type of situation, the run-time requirements of the parallel processing system are quite small—typically, a "send" and "receive" paradigm is adequate to implement a "master-slave" processing scenario. This is the approach used by systems such as Linda [Padua:86a] and Strand [Foster:90a].

Of course, there are occasional complexities involved in this style of programming, such as the use of "broadcast" or data-reduction techniques to simplify common operations. For this reason higher level systems such as Express are often easier to use than their "simpler" contemporaries since they include standard mechanisms for performing commonly occurring operations.

2. Global Static Decomposition

This type of application is typified by areas such as numerical integration or convolution operations similar to those previously described.

Their characteristic is that while there are data dependences among program elements, these can be analyzed symbolically at compile time and catered for by suitable insertion of calls to a message-passing (for distributed-memory) or locking/unlocking (for shared-memory) library.

In the convolution case, for example, we provide calls which would arrange for the distribution of data values among processors and the communication of the "boundary strip" which is required for updates to the local elements.

In the integration example, we would require routines to sum up contributions to the overall integral computed in each node. For this type of application, only simple run time primitives are required.

3. Global, "Oscillating" Decompositions

Problems such as those encountered in large-scale scientific applications typically have behavior in which the global decomposition schemes for data objects vary in some standard manner throughout the execution of the program, but in a deterministic way which can be analyzed at compile-time: One routine might require an array to be distributed row-by-row, for example, while another might require the same array to be partitioned by columns or perhaps not at all.

These issues can be dealt with during the parallelization process but require much more sophisticated run-time support than those previously described. Particularly if the resulting programs are to scale well on larger numbers of nodes, it is essential that run-time routines be supplied to efficiently perform matrix transposition or boundary cell exchange or global concatenation operations. For ASPAR, these operations are provided by the Express run-time system.

4. The "Hard" Case

The three categories of decomposition described so far can deal with a significant part of a large majority of "real" applications. By this we mean that good implementations of the various dependence analysis, dependence "breaking" and run-time support systems can correctly parallelize 90% of the code in any application that is amenable to automatic parallelization. Unfortunately, this is not really good enough.

Our real goal in setting out to produce automatic parallelization tools is to relieve the user of the burden of performing tricky manipulations by hand. Almost by definition, the 10% of each application left over by the application of the techniques described so far is the most complex part and probably represents about 95% of the complexity in parallelizing the original code by hand! So, at this point, all we have achieved is the automatic conversion of the really easy parts of the code, probably at the expense of introducing messy computer-generated code, which makes the understanding of the remaining 10% very difficult.

The solution to this problem comes from the adoption of a much more sophisticated picture of the run time environment.

13.5.6 Dynamic Data Distribution

The three decomposition methods already described suffer from the defect that they are all implemented, except in detail, during the compile-time "parallelization" of the original program. Thus, while the particular details of "which column to send to which other processor" and similar decisions may be deferred to the runtime support, the overall strategy is determined from static analysis of the sequential source code. ASPAR's method is entirely different.

Instead of enforcing global decomposition rules based on static evaluation of the code, ASPAR leaves all the decisions about global decomposition to the run time system and offers only hints as to possible optimizations, whenever they can safely be determined from static analysis. As a result, ASPAR's view of the previously troublesome code would be something along the lines of

```
C-- I need B and C to be distributed in increasing order.
            DO 10 I=1,100
            A(I) = B(I) + C(I)
  10     CONTINUE
C-- I need B to increase and C to decrease.
         DO 20 I=1,100
               D(I) = B(I) + C(100-I)
  20     CONTINUE
```

where the "comments" correspond to ASPAR's hints to the run time support.

The advantages of such an approach are extraordinary. Instead of being stymied by complex, dynamically changing decomposition strategies, ASPAR proceeds irrespective of these, merely expecting that the run time support will be smart enough to provide whatever data will be required for a particular operation.

As a result of this simplification in philosophy, ASPAR is able to successfully parallelize practically 100% of any application that can be parallelized at all, with no user intervention.

13.5.7 Conclusions

The success of ASPAR relies on two crucial pieces of technology:

- the ability to recognize and work around "irrelevant" data dependences by virtue of "stencils," and

- avoiding global decomposition issues by invoking a sophisticated run time support.

It is interesting that neither of these is the result of any extensions to existing compiler technology but are derived from our experience with parallel computers. This is consistent with our underlying philosophy of having ASPAR duplicate the methods which real programmers use to successfully parallelize code by hand. Obviously not all problems are amenable to this type of automatic parallelization but we believe that of the cases discussed in the opening paragraphs of this section we can usefully address all but the "Extremely Difficult."

In the simpler cases, we believe that the goal of eliminating the role of "human error" in generating correctly functioning parallel code has been accomplished.

The price that has been paid, of course, is the requirement for extremely smart runtime systems. The use of Express as the underlying mechanism for ASPAR has proved its value in addressing the simpler types of decomposition scheme.

The development of the dynamic data-distribution mechanisms required to support the more complex applications has led to a completely new way of writing, debugging, and optimizing parallel programs which we believe will become the cornerstone of the next generation of Express systems and may revolutionize the ways in which people think about parallel processing.

13.6   Coherent Parallel C

Coherent Parallel C (CPC) was originally motivated by the fact that for many parallel algorithms, the Connection Machine can be very easy to program. The work of this section is described in [Felten:88a]. Parallel to our efforts, Philip Hatcher and Michael Quinn have developed a version of C*, now called Data-Parallel C, for MIMD computers. Their work is described in [Hatcher:91a].

The CPC language is not simply a C with parallel `for` loops; instead, a data-parallel programming model is adopted. This means that one has an entire process for each data object. An example of an "object" is one mesh point in a finite-element solver. How the processes are actually distributed on a parallel machine is transparent—the user is to imagine that an entire processor is dedicated to each process. This simplifies programming tremendously: complex `if` statements associated with domain boundaries disappear, and problems which do not exactly match the machine size and irregular boundaries are all handled transparently. Figure 13.17 illustrates CPC by contrasting "normal" hypercube programming with CPC programming for a simple grid-update algorithm.

The usual communication calls are not seen at all at the user level. Variables of other processes (which may or may not be on another processor) are merely accessed, giving global memory. In our nCUBE implementation, this

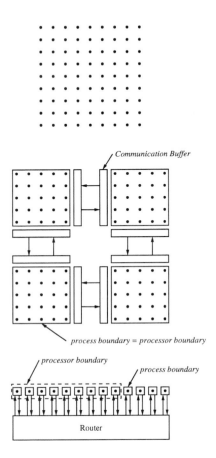

Figure 13.17: Normal Hypercube Programming Model versus CPC Model for the Canonical Grid-based Problem. The upper part of the figure shows a two-dimensional grid upon which the variables of the problem live. The middle portion shows the usual hypercube model for this type of problem. There is one process per processor and it contains a subgrid. Some variables of the subgrid are on a process boundary, some are not. Drawn explicitly are communication buffers and the channels between them which must be managed by the programmer. The bottom portion of the figure shows the CPC view of the same problem. There is one data object (a grid point) for each process so that all variables are on a process boundary. The router provides a full interconnect between the processes.

was implemented using the efficient global communications system called the *crystal_router* (see Chapter 22 of [Fox:88a]).

An actual run-time system was developed for the nCUBE and is described in [Felten:88a]. Much work remains to be done, of course. How to optimize in order to produce an efficient communications traffic is unexplored; a serious attempt to produce a fine-grained MIMD machine really involves new types of hardware, somewhat like Dally's J-machine.

Ed Felten and Steve Otto developed CPC.

13.7   Hierarchical Memory

In this section, we review some ideas of Fox, dating from 1987, that unify the decomposition methodologies for hierarchical- and distributed-memory computers [Fox:87b]. For a modern workstation, the hierarchical memory is formed by the cache and main memory. One needs to minimize the cache misses to ensure that, as far as possible, we reference data in cache and not in main memory. This is often referred to as the need for "data locality." This term makes clear the analogy with distributed-memory parallel computers. As shown in this book, we need data locality in the latter case to avoid communications between processors. We put the discussion in this chapter because we anticipate an important application of these ideas to data-parallel Fortran. The directives in High Performance Fortran essentially specify data locality and we believe that an HPF compiler can use the concepts of this section to optimize cache use on hierarchical-memory machines. Thus, HPF and similar data-parallel languages will give better performance than conventional Fortran 77 compilers on *all* high-performance computers, not just parallel machines.

Figures 13.18 and 13.19 contrast distributed-memory multicomputers, shared-memory, and sequential hierarchical-memory computers. In each case, we denote by a black square the amount of data which can fit into the lowest level of the memory hierarchy. In machines such as the nCUBE-1,2 with a simple node, illustrated in Figure 13.18(a), this amount is just what can fit into the node of the distributed-memory computers. In the other architectures shown in Figures 13.18 and 13.19, the data corresponding to the black square represents what can fit into the cache. There is one essential difference between cache and distributed memory. Both need data locality, but in the parallel case the basic data is static and fetches additional information as necessary. This gives the familiar surface-over-volume

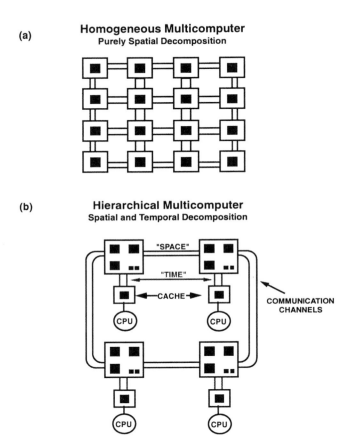

Figure 13.18: Homogeneous and Hierarchical-Memory Multicomputers. The black box represents the data that fit into the lowest level of the memory hierarchy.

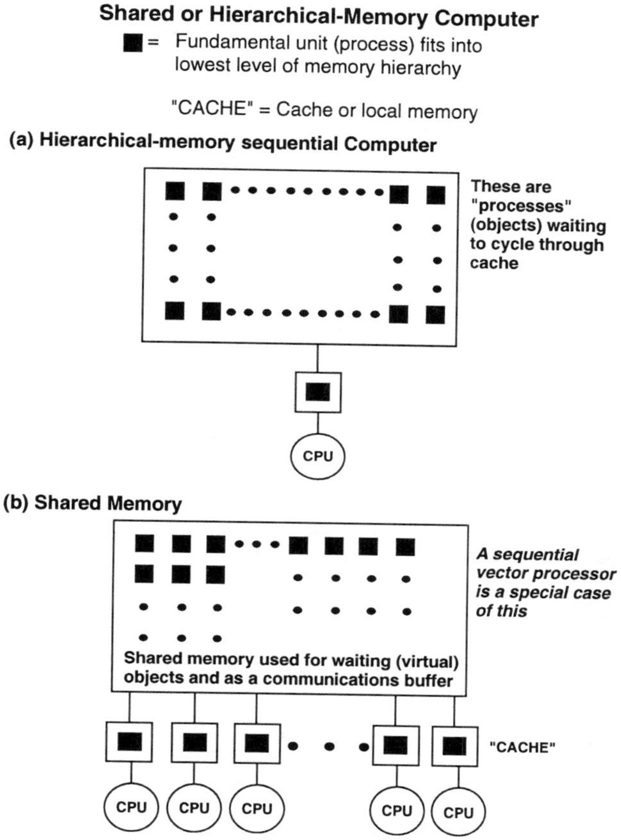

Shared or Hierarchical-Memory Computer

■ = Fundamental unit (process) fits into
lowest level of memory hierarchy

"CACHE" = Cache or local memory

(a) Hierarchical-memory sequential Computer

These are
"processes"
(objects) waiting
to cycle through
cache

CPU

(b) Shared Memory

A sequential
vector processor
is a special case
of this

Shared memory used for waiting (virtual)
objects and as a communications buffer

"CACHE"

CPU CPU CPU   CPU CPU

Figure 13.19: Shared Hierarchical-Memory Computers. "Cache" could either be a time cache or local (software-controlled) memory.

communication overheads of Equation 3.10. However, in the case of a cache, all the data must stream through it and not just the data needed to provide additional information. For distributed-memory machines, we minimize the need for information flow into and out of a grain as shown in Figure 3.9. For hierarchical-memory machines, we need to maximize the number of times we access the data in cache. These are related but not identical concepts which we will now compare. We can use the space-time complex system language introduced in Chapter 3.

Figure 13.20 introduces a new time constant, t_{mem}, which is contrasted with t_{comm} and t_{calc} introduced in Section 3.5. The constant t_{mem} represents

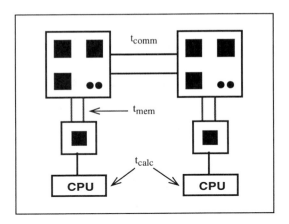

CACHE LOADING TIME = t_{mem} **x object spatial size**

TIME SPENT IN CACHE = t_{calc} **x temporal extent (computational extent)**
of object x spatial size

Memory overhead is generally

1 / (OBJECT or GRAIN SIZE) $^{1/d}$ **x** t_{mem} / t_{calc} **hierarchical memory**

d = information dimension t_{comm} / t_{calc} **distributed memory**

Figure 13.20: The Fundamental Time Constants of a Node. The information dimension represented by d is discussed in Section 3.5.

the time it takes to load a word into cache. As shown in this figure, the cache overhead is also a "surface-over-volume" effect just as it was in Section 3.5, but now the surface is measured in the temporal direction and the volume is that of a domain in space and time. We find t_{mem}, time, and memory hierarchy are analogous to t_{comm}, space, and distributed memory.

Space-time decompositions are illustrated in Figure 13.21 for a simple one-dimensional problem. The decomposition in Figure 13.21(a) is fine for distributed-memory machines, but has poor cache performance. It is blocked in space but not in time. The optimal decompositions are "space-time" blocked and illustrated in Figure 13.21(b) and (c).

A "space-time" blocking is a universal high-performance implementation of data locality. It will lead to good performance on both distributed- and hierarchical-memory machines. This is best known for the use of the BLAS-3 matrix-matrix primitives in LAPACK and other matrix library projects (see Section 8.1) [Demmel:91a]. The next step is to generate such optimal

(a) A Purely SPATIAL Blocking
A high edge/area ratio in the time direction

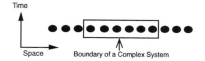

(b,c) Two Space-Time Blockings
(b) Approximately best edge/area ratio with small communication

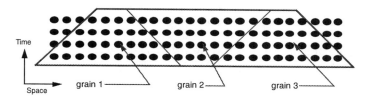

(c) A more practical space-time decomposition with more but modest communication

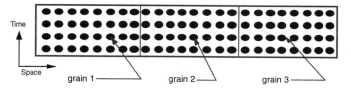

Figure 13.21: Decompositions for a simple one-dimensional wave equation.

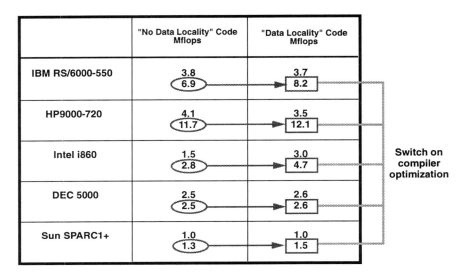

Figure 13.22: Performance of a Random Surface Fortran Code on Five RISC Architecture Sequential Computers. The optimizations are described in the text.

decompositions from a High Performance Fortran compiler.

We can illustrate these ideas with the application of Section 7.2 [Coddington:93a]. Table 7.1 records performance of the original code used, but this C version was improved by an order of magnitude in performance in a carefully rewritten Fortran code. The relevance of data locality for this *new* code is shown in Figure 13.22. For each of a set of five RISC processors, we show four performance numbers gotten by switching on and off "system Fortran compiler optimization" and "data locality." As seen from Section 7.2, this application is naturally very irregular and normal data structures do not express this locality and preserve it. Even if one starts with neighboring points in the simulated space, "near" each other also in the computer, this is not easily preserved by the dynamic retriangulation. In the "data locality" column, we have arranged storage to preserve locality as far as possible; neighboring physical points are stored near each other in memory. A notable feature of Figure 13.22 is that the Intel i860 shows the largest improvement from forcing data locality—even after compilation optimization, this action improves performance by 70%. A similar result was found in [Das:92c] for an unstructured mesh partial differential equation solver. Other architectures such as the HP9000–720 with large caches show smaller effects. In Figure 13.22, locality was achieved by user manipulation—as discussed, a next step is to put such intelligence in parallel compilers.

Chapter 14

Asynchronous Applications

14.1 Asynchronous Problems and a Summary of Basic Problem Classes

The two applications in this chapter fall into the *asynchronous* problem class of Section 3.4. This class is caricatured in Figure 14.1 and is the last and hardest to parallelize of the basic problem architectures introduced in Section 3.4. Thus, we will use this opportunity to summarize some issues across all problem classes. It would be more logical to do this in Chapter 18 where we discuss the compound metaproblem class, which we now realize is very important. However, the discussion here is based on a survey [Fox:88b], [Angus:90a] undertaken from 1988 to 1989, at which time we had not introduced the concept of compound or hierarchical problem architectures.

Table 14.1 divides 84 application areas into eight (academic) disciplines. Examples of the areas are given in the table—essentially each application section in this book would lead to a separate area for the purposes of this table. These areas are listed in [Angus:90a], [Fox:88b;92b] and came a reading in 1988 of about 400 papers which had developed quite seriously a parallel application or core nontrivial algorithm. In 1988, it was possible to read essentially all such papers—the field has grown so much in the following years that a complete survey would now be a daunting task. Table 14.2 divides these application areas into the basic problem architectures used in the book. There are several caveats to be invoked for this table. As we have seen in Chapters 9 and 12, the division between synchronous and loosely synchronous is not sharp and is still a matter of important debate. The synchronous problems are naturally suitable for SIMD architectures, while properly

ASYNCHRONOUS PROBLEMS

For example:

The world looked at macroscopically in terms of interactions between irregular inhomogeneous objects evolved as an event-driven simulation

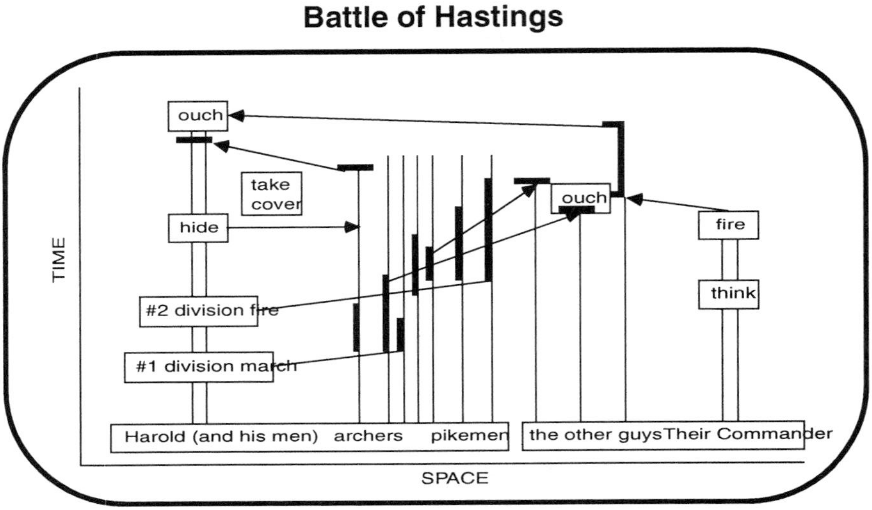

Battle of Hastings

- Parallelize by "data parallelism" over space of events but no automatic algorithmic synchronization

- Need sophisticated software built on top of message passing between events to ensure synchronization

- Speedup very problem-dependent

- MIMD architectures essential

Figure 14.1: The Asynchronous Problem Class

Table 14.1: 84 Application Areas Used in a Survey 1988–89 from 400 Papers

84	Total Application Areas
9	Biology
4	Chemistry and Chemical Engineering
14	Engineering
10	Geology and Earth Science
13	Physics
5	Astronomy and Astrophysics
11	Computer Science
18	Numerical Algorithms

e.g.   Calculate Proton Mass   Evolution of the Universe
        Seismic Modeling   Optimization of Oil Well Placement
        Image Processing   Voyager Data from Neptune
        Multiple Target Tracking   Computer Chess

loosely synchronous and asynchronous problems require MIMD hardware. This classification is illustrated by a few of the more major C^3P applications in Table 14.3 [Fox:89t], which also compares performance on various SIMD and MIMD machines in use in 1989.

Table 14.2 can be interpreted as follows: 90% of application areas (i.e., all except the asynchronous class) naturally parallelize to large numbers of processors.

Forty-seven percent of applications will run well on SIMD machines while 43% need a MIMD architecture (this is a more precise version of Equation 3.21).

These numbers are rough for many reasons. The grey line between synchronous (perhaps generalized to autonomous SIMD in Maspar language of Section 6.1) and loosely synchronous means that the division between SIMD and MIMD fractions is uncertain. Further, how should one weight each area? QCD of Section 4.3 is one of the application areas in Table 14.1, but this uses an incredible amount of computer time and is a synchronous problem. Thus, weighting by computer cycles needed or used could also change the ratios significantly.

Table 14.2: Classification of 400 Applications in 84 Areas from 1989. 90% of applications scale to large SIMD/MIMD machines.

Problem Architecture	Number	Fraction	
Synchronous	34	0.4	Total S+LS
Loosely Synchronous	30	0.36	0.76
(not Synchronous)			
Embarrassingly Parallel			
(Synch) runs on SIMD	6	0.07	
(Asynch) need MIMD	6	0.07	
Truly Asynchronous	8	0.1	Unclear
			Scaling

These tables can also be used to discuss software issues as described in Sections 13.1 and 18.2. The synchronous and embarrassingly parallel problem classes (54%) are those directly supported by the initial High Performance Fortran language [Fox:91e], [Kennedy:93a]. The loosely synchronous problems (34%) need run-time and language extensions, which we are currently working on [Berryman:91a], [Saltz:91b], [Choudhary:92d], as mentioned in Section 13.1 (Table 13.4). With these extensions, we expect High Performance Fortran to be able to express nearly all synchronous, loosely synchronous, and embarrassingly parallel problems.

The fraction (10%) of asynchronous problems is in some sense pessimistic. There is one very important asynchronous area—event driven simulations—where the general scaling parallelism remains unclear. This is illustrated in Figure 14.1 and briefly discussed in Section 15.3. However, the two cases described in this chapter parallelize well—albeit with very hard work from the user! Further, some of the asynchronous areas in Tables 14.1 and 14.2 are of the compound class of Chapter 18 and these also parallelize well.

The two examples in this chapter need different algorithmic and software support. In fact, as we will note in Section 15.1, one of the hard problems in parallel software is to isolate those issues that need to be supported over and above those needed for synchronous and loosely synchronous problems. The

Table 14.3: Classification of some C^3P applications from 1989 and their performances on machines at that time [Fox:89t]. A question mark indicates the performance is unknown whereas an X indicates we expect or have measured poor performance.

Application/ Section	1 head CRAY X-MP	1024-node nCUBE-1 Hypercube	128-node Mark IIIfp Hypercube	64K CM-2	*Problem Architecture
QCD 4.3	1	1	6	50	S
Continuous Spin (High T_c) 4.4	1	1	6	20	S
Ising/Potts Models 4.4	1	32	10	30	S
Strings 7.2	1	8	6	X	A but EP(A)
Particle Dynamics $O(N \log N)$ 12.4,12.5,12.8	1	4	16	X	LS
$O(N*N)$ [Fox:88a]	1	1	6	?	S
Astronomical Data Analysis [Fox:89i][Fox:89y] [Fox:90o]	IBM 3090 2 pulsars (1989)	nCUBE 5 pulsars (1989)	?	X	LS
Chemical Reactions H + H_2 Scattering 8.2	1	?	1.5	?	S (matrix solve)
e^- + CO Scattering 8.3	1	?	13	?	EP(A) (matrix element calculation)
Grain Dynamics 4.5, 9.2	1	1	6	15–30	S or LS
Plasma Physics 9.3	1	?	2	?	LS
Neural Networks 9.9	1	1	6	15–30	S or LS
Computer Chess 14.3	1	2.5	?	X	A
Multitarget Tracking 9.8, 18.4	1	X	12	X	LS

*A=Asynchronous, EP=Embarrassingly Parallel, LS=Loosely Synchronous, S=Synchronous software models needed for irregular statistical mechanics (Section 14.2), chess (Section 14.3), and event-driven simulations (Section 15.3) are quite different.

In Section 14.2, the need for a sequential ordering takes the normally loosely synchronous time-stepped particle dynamics into an asynchronous class. Time-stamping the updates provides the necessary ordering and a "demand-driven processing queue" provides scaling parallelism. Communication must be processed using interrupts and the loosely synchronous communication style of Section 9.1 will not work.

Another asynchronous application developed by C^3P was the ray-tracing algorithm developed by Jeff Goldsmith and John Salmon [Fox:87c], [Goldsmith:87a;88a]. This application used two forms of parallelism, with both the pixels (rays) and the basic model to be rendered distributed. This allows very large models to be simulated and the covers of our earlier books [Fox:88a], [Angus:90a] feature pictures rendered by this program. The distributed-model database requires software support similar to that of the application in Section 14.2. The rays migrate from node to node as they traverse the model and need to access data not present in the node currently responsible for ray. This application was a great technical success, but was not further developed as it used software (MOOSE of Section 15.2) which was only supported on our early machines. The model naturally forms a tree with the scene represented with increasing spatial resolution as you go down the different levels of the tree. Goldsmith and Salmon used a similar strategy to the hierarchical Barnes-Hut approach to particle dynamics described in Section 12.4. In particular, the upper parts of the tree are replicated in all nodes and only the lower parts distributed. This removes "sequential bottlenecks" near the top of the tree just as in the astrophysics case. Originally, Salmon's thesis intended to study the computer science and science issues associated with hierarchical data structures. Multiscale methods are pervasive to essentially all physical systems. However, the success of the astrophysical applications led to this being his final thesis topic. Su, another student of Fox, has just finished his Ph.D. on the general mathematical properties of hierarchical systems [Su:93a].

In Section 14.3, we have a much more irregular and dynamic problem, computer chess, where statistical methods are used to balance the processing of the different branches of the dynamically pruned tree. There is a shared database containing previous evaluation of positions, but otherwise the processing of the different possible moves is independent. One does need a clever ordering of the work (evaluation of the different final positions) to

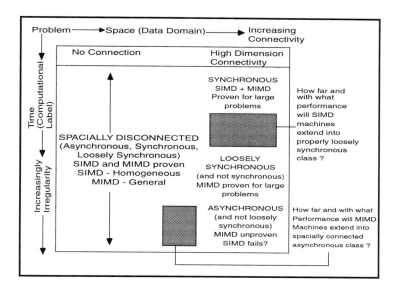

Figure 14.2: Issues Affecting Relation of Machine, Problem, and Software Architecture

avoid a significant number of calculations being wasted because they would "later" be pruned away by a parallel calculation on a different processor. Branch and bound applications [Felten:88c], [Fox:87c;88v] [Fox:87c] have similar parallelization characteristics to computer chess. This was implemented in parallel as a "best-first" and not a "depth-first" search strategy and was applied to the travelling salesman problem (Section 11.4) to find exact solutions to test the physical optimization algorithms. It was also applied to the 0/1 knapsack problem, but for this and TSP, difficulties arose due to insufficient memory for holding the queues of unexplored subtrees. The depth-first strategy, used in our parallel computer chess program and sequential branch and bound, avoids the need for large memory. On sequential machines, virtual memory can be used for the subtree queues, but this was not implemented on the nCUBE-1 and indeed is absent on most current multicomputers.

The applications in this chapter are easier than a full event-driven simulation because enough is known about the problem to find a reasonable parallel algorithm. The difficulty then, is to make it efficient. Figure 14.2 is a schematic of problem architectures labelled by spatial and temporal properties. In general, the temporal characteristics—the problem architec-

Table 14.4: Criterion for success in parallelizing a particular problem on a particular machine.

- Software powerful enough to express natural parallelism of problem (e.g., High Performance Fortran expresses data parallelism)
- Problem is "large" so grains are large enough on each node
- Architecture of computer at least as "rich" as architecture of problem
  - Temporal (control) structure
    - Synchronous versus Loosely Synchronous versus Asynchronous
    - SIMD versus MIMD
    - This is a strong constraint
    - Mismatches lead to essentially no parallelism, that is, very bad performance, speedup ~ 1
  - Spatial (topology) structure
    - "Weak" constraint
    - Mismatches "only" affect performance by "factors of two"

---

tures (synchronous, loosely synchronous and asynchronous)—determine the nature of the parallelism. One special case is the *spatially disconnected* problem class for which the temporal characteristic is essentially irrelevant. For the general *spatially connected* class, the nature of this connection will affect performance and ease, but not the nature of their parallelism. These issues are summarized in Table 14.4. For instance, spatially irregular problems, such as those in Chapter 12, are particularly hard to implement although they have natural parallelism. The applications in this chapter can be viewed as having little spatial connectivity and their parallelism comes because, although asynchronous, they are "near" the spatially disconnected class of Figure 14.2.

14.2 Melting in Two Dimensions

14.2.1 Problem Description

Although we live in a three-dimensional world, many important processes involve interactions on surfaces, which are effectively two-dimensional. While experimental studies of two-dimensional systems have been successful in probing some aspects of such systems, computer simulation is another powerful tool that can be used to measure their properties. We have used a computer simulation to study the melting transition of a two-dimensional system of interacting particles [Johnson:86a;86b]. One purpose of the study is to investigate whether melting in two dimensions occurs through a qualitatively different process than it does it three dimensions. In three dimensions, the melting transition is a first-order transition which displays a characteristic latent heat. Halperin and Nelson [Halperin:78a], [Nelson:79a] and Young [Young:79a] have raised the possibility that melting in two dimensions could occur through a qualitatively different process. They have suggested that melting could consist of a pair of higher-order phase transitions, which lack a latent heat, that are driven by topological defects in the two-dimensional crystal lattice.

We studied a two-dimensional system of particles interacting through a truncated Lennard-Jones potential. The Lennard-Jones potential is

$$\phi = 4\epsilon \left[\left(\frac{\sigma}{r} \right)^{12} - \left(\frac{\sigma}{r} \right)^{6} \right]$$

where ϵ is the energy parameter, σ is the length parameter, and r is the distance between two particles. The potential is attractive at distances larger than σ and repulsive smaller distances. The potential energy of the whole system is the sum of the potential energies of each pair of interacting particles. In order to ease the computational requirements of the simulation, we have truncated the potential at a particle separation of 3σ.

Mark A. Johnson wrote the Monte Carlo simulation of melting in two dimensions for his Ph.D. research at Caltech.

14.2.2 Solution Method

We chose to use a Monte Carlo method to simulate the interaction of the particles. The method consists of generating a sequence of configurations in such a way that the probability of being in configuration r, denoted as P_r, is

$$P_r \propto e^{-\beta E_r}$$

where E_r is the potential energy of configuration r and $\beta = 1/kT$. A configuration refers collectively to the positions of all the particles in the simulation. The update procedure that we describe in the next section generates such a sequence of configurations by repeatedly updating the position of each of the particles in the system. Averaging the values of such quantities as potential energy and pressure over the configurations gives their expected values in such a system.

The process of moving from one configuration to another is known as a Monte Carlo update. The update procedure we used involves three steps that allow the position of one particle to change [Metropolis:53a]. The first step is to choose a new position for the particle with uniform probability in a region about its current position. Next, the update procedure calculates the difference in potential energy between the current configuration and the new one. Finally, the new position for the particle is either accepted or rejected based on the difference in potential energy and rules that generate configurations with the required probability distribution.

The two-dimensional system being studied has several characteristics that must be considered in designing an efficient algorithm for implementing the Monte Carlo simulation. One of the most important characteristics is that the interaction potential has a short range. The Lennard-Jones potential approaches zero quickly enough that the effect of distant particles can be safely ignored. We made the short-range nature of the potential precise by truncating it at a distance of 3σ. We must use the short-range nature of the potential to organize the particle positions so that the update procedure can quickly locate the particles whose potential energy changes during an update.

Another feature of the system that complicates the simulation is that the particles are not confined to a grid that would structure the data. Such irregular data make simultaneously updating multiple particles more difficult. One result of the irregular data is that the computational loads of the processors are unbalanced in a distributed-memory, MIMD processor. In order to minimize the effect of the load imbalance, the nodes of the concurrent processor must run asynchronously. We developed an interrupt-driven communication system [Johnson:85a] that allows the nodes to implement an asynchronous update procedure. This "`rdsort`" system is described in Section 5.2.5 and has similarities to the current active message ideas [Eiken:92a].

The interrupt-driven communication system allows a node to send requests for contributions to the change in potential energy that moving its particle would cause. Nodes receiving such requests compute the contribution of their particles and send a response reporting their result. This operating system was sophisticated but only used for this application. However, as described in Chapter 5, these ideas formed the basis of both MOOS II and the evolution of CrOS III into Express. Interestingly, Mark Johnson designed the loosely synchronous CrOS III message-passing system as part of his service for C³P even though his particular application was one of the few that could not benefit from it.

14.2.3 Concurrent Update Procedure

Performing Monte Carlo updates in parallel requires careful attention to ensuring that simultaneous updates do not interfere with each other. Because the basic equations governing the Monte Carlo method remain unchanged, performing the updates in parallel requires that a consistent sequential ordering of the updates exists. No *particular* ordering is required; only the existence of such an ordering is critical. Particles that are farther apart than the range of the interaction potential cannot influence each other, so any arbitrary ordering of their updates is always consistent. However, if some of the particles being updated together are within the range of the potential, they cannot be updated as if they were independent because the result of one update affects the others. Fortunately, the symmetry of the potential guarantees that all of the affected particles are aware that their updates are interdependent.

Note that the Monte Carlo approach to melting or, more generally, any particle simulation is often much harder to parallelize than the competitive time-stepped evolution approach. The latter would be loosely synchronous with natural parallelism. The need for a consistent sequential ordering in the Monte Carlo algorithm leads to the asynchronous temporal structure. It is interesting that on a sequential machine, both time-stepped and Monte Carlo methods would be equally easy to implement. However, even here the sequential ordering for the Monte Carlo would make it hard to vectorize the algorithm on a conventional supercomputer. In discussing regular Monte Carlo problems such as QCD in Section 4.3, the sequential ordering constraint is there but trivial to implement, as the regular spatial structure allows one to predetermine a consistent update procedure. In particular, the normal red-black update structure achieves this. In the melting problem, one has a dynamically varying irregularity that allows no simple way of predetermining a consistent Monte Carlo update schedule.

Each node involved in the conflicting updates must act to resolve the situation by making one of only two possible decisions. For each request for contributions to the difference in potential energy of an update, a node can either send a response immediately or delay the response until its own update finishes. If the node sends the response immediately, it must use the old position of the particle that it is updating. If the node instead delays the response while waiting for its own update to finish, it will use the new position of the particle when its update finishes. If all of the nodes involved in the conflicting updates make consistent decisions, a sequential ordering of the updates will exist, ensuring the correctness of the Monte Carlo procedure. However, if two nodes both decide to send responses to each other based on the current positions of the particles they are updating, no such ordering will exist. If two nodes both decide to delay sending responses to each other, neither will be able to complete their update, causing the simulation to deadlock.

Several features of the concurrent update procedure make resolving such interdependent updates difficult. Each node must make its decision regarding the resolution of the conflicting updates in isolation from the other nodes because all of the nodes are running asynchronously to minimize load imbalance. However, the nodes cannot run completely asynchronously because assigning a consistent sequential ordering to the updates requires that the update procedure impose a synchronizing condition on the updates. Still, the condition should be as weak as possible so that the decrease in processing efficiency is minimized.

One solution to the problem of correctly ordering interdependent updates requires that a clock exist in each of the nodes. The update procedure records the time at which it begins updating a particle and includes that time with each of its requests for contributions to the difference in potential energy. When a node determines that its update conflicts with that of another node, it uses the times of the conflicting updates to resolve the dependence. The node sends a response immediately if the request involves an update that precedes its own. The node delays sending a response if its own update precedes the one that generated the request. Should the times be exactly equal, the unique number associated with each node provides a means of consistently ordering the updates. When each of the processors involved in the conflicting updates use such a method to resolve the situation, a consistent sequential ordering must result. Using the time of each of the conflicting updates to determine their ordering allows the earliest updates to finish first, which achieves good load balance in the concurrent algorithm.

Although delaying a response to a conflicting update is a synchronizing condition, it is sufficiently weak that it does not seriously degrade the performance of the concurrent algorithm. A node can respond to other nodes' requests while waiting for responses to requests that it has generated. The node that delays sending a response can perform most of the computation to generate the response while it is waiting for responses to its own requests, because the position of only one particle is in question. In fact, the current implementation simply generates the two possible responses so that it can send the correct response immediately after its own update completes.

An interesting feature of the concurrent update algorithm is that it produces results that are inherently irreproducible. If two simulations start with exactly the same initial data, including random number seeds, the simulations will eventually differ. The source of the irreproducible behavior is that all components of the concurrent processor are not driven by the same clock. For instance, the communication channels that connect the nodes contain an asynchronous loop that allows the arrival times of messages to differ by arbitrarily small amounts. Such differences can affect the order in which requests are received, which in turn determines the order in which a node generates responses. Once such differences change the outcome of a single update, the two simulations begin to evolve independently. Both simulations continue to generate configurations with the correct probability distribution, so the statistical properties of the simulations do not change. However, the irreproducible behavior of the concurrent update algorithm can make debugging somewhat more difficult.

14.2.4 Performance Analysis

Because a complete performance analysis of the Monte Carlo simulation is rather lengthy, we provide only a summary of the analysis here. Calculating the efficiency of the concurrent update algorithm is relatively simple because it requires only measurements of the time an update takes on one node and on multiple nodes. A more difficult parameter to calculate is the load balance of the update procedure. In order to calculate the load balance, we measured the time required to send each type of message that the update uses. The total communication overhead is the sum of the overheads for each type of message, which is the product of the time to send that type of message and the number of such messages. We calculated the number of each type

Table 14.5: Simulations on the 64-node Caltech Hypercube

Particles	Update Time	Efficiency	Load Balance
1024	1.33	0.477	0.713
4096	4.00	0.634	0.808
16384	13.52	0.750	0.858
65536	48.04	0.844	0.907

of message by assuming a uniform distribution of particles. Because the update algorithm contains no significant serial components, we attributed to load imbalance the parallel overhead remaining after accounting for the communication overhead. The load balance is a factor that can range from $1/N$, where N is the number of nodes, to 1, which occurs when the loads are balanced perfectly. We give the update time in seconds, the efficiency, and the load balance for several simulations on the 64-node Caltech hypercube in Table 14.5 ([Johnson:86a] p. 73).

14.3   Computer Chess

As this book shows, distributed-memory, multiple-instruction stream (MIMD) computers are successful in performing a large class of scientific computations. As discussed in Section 14.1 and the earlier chapters, these synchronous and loosely synchronous problems tend to have regular, homogeneous data sets and the algorithms are usually "crystalline" in nature. Recognizing this, C^3P explored a set of algorithms which had irregular structure (as in Chapter 12) and asynchronous execution. At the start of this study, we were very unclear as to what parallel performance to expect. In fact, we achieved good speedup even in these hard problems.

Thus, as an attempt to explore a part of this interesting, poorly understood region in algorithm space, we implemented chess on an nCUBE-1 hypercube. Besides being a fascinating field of study in its own right, computer chess is an interesting challenge for parallel computers because:

- It is not clear how much parallelism is actually available—the important method of alpha-beta pruning conflicts with parallelism.

- Some aspects of the algorithm require a globally shared data set.

- The parallel algorithm has dynamic load imbalance of an extreme nature.

One might also ask the question, "Why study computer chess at all?" We think the answer lies in the unusual position of computer chess within the artificial intelligence world. Like most AI problems, chess requires a program which will display seemingly intelligent behavior in a limited, artificial world. Unlike most AI problems, the programmers do not get to make up the rules of this world. In addition, there is a very rigorous procedure to test the intelligence of a chess program—playing games against humans. Computer chess is one area where the usually disparate worlds of AI and high-performance computing meet.

Before going on, let us state that our approach to parallelism (and hence speed) in computer chess is not the only one. Belle, Cray Blitz, Hitech, and the current champion, Deep Thought have shown in spectacular fashion that fine-grained parallelism (pipelining, specialized hardware) leads to impressive speeds (see [Hsu:90a], [Frey:83a], [Marsland:87a], [Ebeling:85a], [Welsh:85a]). Our coarse-grained approach to parallelism should be viewed as a complementary, not a conflicting, method. Clearly the two can be combined.

14.3.1 Sequential Computer Chess

In this section we will describe some basic aspects of what constitutes a good chess program on a sequential computer. Having done this, we will be able to intelligently discuss the parallel algorithm.

At present, all competitive chess programs work by searching a tree of possible moves and countermoves. A program starts with the current board position and generates all legal moves, all legal responses to these moves, and so on until a fixed depth is reached. At each leaf node, an evaluation function is applied which assigns a numerical score to that board position. These scores are then "backed up" by a process called minimaxing, which is simply the assumption that each side will choose the line of play most favorable to it at all times. If positive scores favor white, then white picks the move of maximum score and black picks the move of minimum score. These concepts are illustrated in Figure 14.3.

The evaluation function employed is a combination of simple material balance and several terms which represent positional factors. The positional

Full-Width Tree:

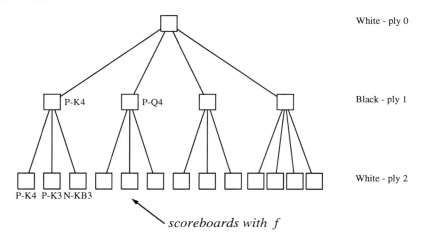

scoreboards with f

Minimaxing:

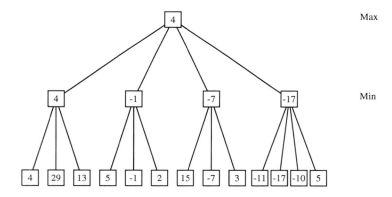

Figure 14.3: Game Playing by Tree Searching. The top half of the figure illustrates the general idea: Develop a full-width tree to some depth, then score the leaves with the evaluation function, f. The second half shows minimaxing—the reasonable supposition that white (black) chooses lines of play which maximize (minimize) the score.

terms are small in magnitude but are important since material balance rarely changes in tournament chess games.

The problem with this brute-force approach is that the size of the tree explodes exponentially. The "branching factor" or number of legal moves in a typical position is about 35. In order to play master-level chess a search of depth eight appears necessary, which would involve a tree of 35^8 or about 2×10^{12} leaf nodes.

Fortunately, there is a better way. Alpha-beta pruning is a technique which always gives the same answer as brute-force searching without looking at so many nodes of the tree. Intuitively, alpha-beta pruning works by ignoring subtrees which it knows cannot be reached by best play (on the part of both sides). This reduces the effective branching factor from 35 to about 6, which makes strong play possible.

The idea of alpha-beta pruning is illustrated in Figure 14.4. Assume that all child nodes are searched in the order of left to right in the figure. On the left side of the tree (the first subtree searched), we have minimaxed and found a score of +4 at depth one. Now, start to analyze the next subtree. The children report back scores of +5, −1, ... The pruning happens after the score of −1 is returned: since we are taking the minimum of the scores +5, −1, ... , we immediately have a bound on the scores of this subtree—we know the score will be no larger than −1. Since we are taking the maximum at the next level up (the root of the tree) and we already have a line of play better than −1 (namely, the +4 subtree), we need not explore this second subtree any further. Pruning occurs, as denoted by the dashed branch of the second subtree. The process continues through the rest of the subtrees.

The amount of work saved in this small tree was insignificant but alpha-beta becomes very important for large trees. From the nature of the pruning method, one sees that the tree is not evolved evenly downward. Instead, the algorithm pursues one branch all the way to the bottom, gets a "score to beat" (the alpha-beta bounds), and then sweeps across the tree sideways. How well the pruning works depends crucially on move ordering. If the best line of play is searched first, then all other branches will prune rapidly.

Actually, what we have discussed so far is not full alpha-beta pruning, but merely "pruning without deep cutoffs." Full alpha-beta pruning shows up only in trees of depth four or greater. A thorough discussion of alpha-beta with some interesting historical comments can be found in Knuth and Moore [Knuth:75a].

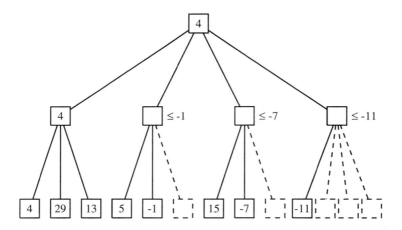

Figure 14.4: Alpha-Beta Pruning for the Same Tree as Figure 14.3. The tree is generated in left-to-right order. As soon as the score -1 is computed, we immediately have a bound on the level above (≤ -1) which is below the score of the $+4$ subtree. A cutoff occurs, meaning no more descents of the ≤ -1 node need to be searched.

The Evaluation Function

The evaluation function of our program is similar in style to that of the Cray Blitz program [Welsh:85a]. The most important term is material, which is a simple count of the number of pieces on each side, modified by a factor which encourages the side ahead in material to trade pieces but not pawns. The material evaluator also recognizes known draws such as king and two knights versus king.

There are several types of positional terms, including pawn structure, king safety, center control, king attack, and specialized bonuses for things like putting rooks on the seventh rank.

The pawn structure evaluator knows about doubled, isolated, backward, and passed pawns. It also has some notion of pawn chains and phalanxes. Pawn structure computation is very expensive, so a hash table is used to store the scores of recently evaluated pawn structures. Since pawn structure changes slowly, this hash table almost always saves us the work of pawn structure evaluation.

King safety is evaluated by considering the positions of all pawns on the file the king is occupying and both neighboring files. A penalty is assessed if any of the king's covering pawns are missing or if there are holes (squares which can never be attacked by a friendly pawn) in front of the king. Additional penalties are imposed if the opponent has open or half-open files near the king. The whole king safety score is multiplied by the amount of material on the board, so the program will want to trade pieces when its king is exposed, and avoid trades when the opponent's king is exposed. As in pawn structure, king safety uses a hash table to avoid recomputing the same information.

The center control term rewards the program for posting its pieces safely in the center of the board. This term is crude since it does not consider pieces attacking the center from a distance, but it can be computed very quickly and it encourages the kind of straightforward play we want.

King attack gives a bonus for placing pieces near the opposing king. Like center control, this term is crude but tends to lead to positions in which attacking opportunities exist.

The evaluation function is rounded out by special bonuses to encourage particular types of moves. These include a bonus for castling, a penalty for giving up castling rights, rewards for placing rooks on open and half-open files or on the seventh rank, and a penalty for a king on the back rank with no air.

Quiescence Searching

Of course it only makes sense to apply a static evaluation function to a position which is quiescent, or tactically quiet. As a result, the tree is extended beyond leaf nodes until a quiescent position is reached, where the static evaluator is actually applied.

We can think of the quiescence search as a dynamic evaluation function, which takes into account tactical possibilities. At each leaf node, the side to move has the choice of accepting the current static evaluation or of trying to improve its position by tactics. Tactical moves which can be tried include pawn promotions, most capture moves, some checks, and some pawn promotion threats. At each newly generated position the dynamic evaluator is applied again. At the nominal leaf nodes, therefore, a narrow (small branching factor) tactical search is done, with the static evaluator applied at all terminal points of this search (which end up being the true leaves).

Iterative Deepening

Tournament chess is played under a strict time control, and a program must make decisions about how much time to use for each move. Most chess programs do not set out to search to a fixed depth, but use a technique called iterative deepening. This means a program does a depth two search, then a depth three search, then a depth four search, and so on until the allotted time has run out. When the time is up, the program returns its current best guess at the move to make.

Iterative deepening has the additional advantage that it facilitates move ordering. The program knows which move was best at the previous level of iterative deepening, and it searches this principal variation first at each new level. The extra time spent searching early levels is more than repaid by the gain due to accurate move ordering.

The Hash Table

During the tree search, the same board position may occur several times. There are two reasons for this. The first is transposition, or the fact that the same board position can be reached by different sequences of moves. The second reason is iterative deepening—the same position will be reached in the depth two search, the depth three search, and so on. The hash table is a way of storing information about positions which have already been searched; if the same position is reached again, the search can be sped up or eliminated entirely by using this information.

The hash table plays a central role in a good chess program and so we will describe it in some detail. First of all, the hash table is a form of content-addressable memory—with each chess board (a node in the chess tree) we wish to associate some slot in the table. Therefore, a hashing function h is required, which maps chess boards to slots in the table. The function h is designed so as to scatter similar boards across the table. This is done because in any single search the boards appearing in the tree differ by just a few moves and we wish to avoid collisions (different boards mapping to the same slot) as much as possible. Our hash function is taken from [Zobrist:70a]. Each slot in the table contains

- the known bounds on the score of this position;

- the depth to which these bounds are valid;

- a suggested move to try;

- a staleness flag; and

- a 64-bit collision check

Instead of just blindly generating all legal moves at a position and then going down these lines of play, the hash table is first queried about the position. Occasionally, the hash table bounds are so well-determined as to cause an immediate alpha-beta cutoff. More often, the hash table has a suggested move to try and this is searched first. The 64-bit collision check is employed to ensure that the slot has information about the same position that the program is currently considering (remember, more than one chess board can map to the same slot in the table).

Whenever the program completes the search of a subtree of substantial size (i.e., one of depth greater than some minimum), the knowledge gained is written into the hash table. The writing is not completely naive, however. The table contains only a finite number of slots, so collisions occur; writeback acts to keep the most valuable information. The depth field of the slot helps in making the decision as to what is most valuable. The information coming from the subtree of greater depth (and hence, greater value) is kept.

The staleness flag allows us to keep information from one search to the next. When time runs out and a search is considered finished, the hash table is not simply cleared. Instead, the staleness flag is set in all slots. If, during the next search, a read is done on a stale slot the staleness flag is cleared, the idea being that this position again seems to be useful. On writeback, if the staleness flag is set, the slot is simply overwritten, without checking the depths. This prevents the hash table from becoming clogged with old information.

Proper use of an intelligent hash table such as the one described above gives one, in effect, a "principal variation" throughout the chess tree. As discussed in [Ebeling:85a], a hash table can effectively give near-perfect move ordering and hence, very efficient pruning.

The Opening

The opening is played by making use of an "opening book" of known positions. Our program knows the theoretically "best" move in about 18,000 common opening positions. This information is stored as a hash table on disk and can be looked up quickly. This hash table resolves collisions through the method of chaining [Knuth:73a].

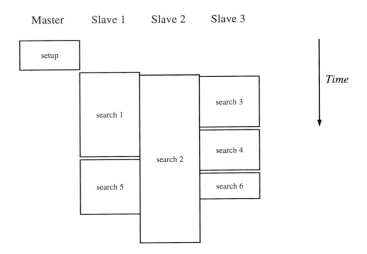

Figure 14.5: Slaves Searching Subtrees in a Self-scheduled Manner. Suppose one of the searches—in this case search two—takes a long time. The advantage of self-scheduling is that, while this search is proceeding in slave two, the other slaves will have done all the remaining work. This very general technique works as long as the dynamic range of the computation times is not too large.

The Endgame

Endgames are handled by using special evaluation functions which contain knowledge about endgame principles. For instance, an evaluator for king and pawn endgames may be able to directly recognize a passed pawn which can race to the last rank without being caught by the opposing king. Except for the change in evaluation functions, the endgame is played in the same fashion as the middlegame.

14.3.2   Parallel Computer Chess: The Hardware

Our program is implemented on an nCUBE/10 system. This is an MIMD (multiple instruction stream, multiple data stream) multicomputer, with each node consisting of a custom VLSI processor running at 7 MHz, 512 Kbytes of memory, and on-chip communication channels. There is no shared memory—processors communicate by message-passing. The nodes are connected as a hypercube but the VERTEX message-passing software [nCUBE:87a] gives the illusion of full connectivity. The nCUBE system at

Caltech has 512 processors, but systems exist with as many as 1024 processors. The program is written in C, with a small amount of assembly code.

14.3.3 Parallel Alpha-Beta Pruning

Some good chess programs do run in parallel (see [Finkel:82a], [Marsland:84a], [Newborn:85a], [Schaeffer:84a;86a]), but before our work nobody had tried more than about 15 processors. We were interested in using hundreds or thousands of processors. This forced us to squarely face all the issues of parallel chess—algorithms which work for a few processors do not necessarily scale up to hundreds of processors. An example of this is the occurrence of sequential bottlenecks in the control structure of the program. We have been very careful to keep control of the program decentralized so as to avoid these bottlenecks.

The parallelism comes from searching different parts of the chess tree at the same time. Processors are organized in a hierarchy with one master processor controlling several teams, each submaster controlling several subteams, and so on. The basic parallel operation consists of one master coming to a node in the chess tree, and assigning subtrees to his slaves in a self-scheduled way. Figure 14.5 shows a timeline of how this might happen with three subteams. Self-scheduling by the slaves helps to load-balance the computation, as can be seen in the figure.

So far, we have defined what happens when a master processor reaches a node of the chess tree. Clearly, this process can be repeated recursively. That is, each subteam can split into sub-subteams at some lower level in the tree. This recursive splitting process, illustrated in Figure 14.6, allows large numbers of processors to come into play.

In conflict with this is the inherent sequential model of the standard alpha-beta algorithm. Pruning depends on fully searching one subtree in order to establish bounds (on the score) for the search of the next subtree. If one adheres to the standard algorithm in an overly strict manner, there may be little opportunity for parallelism. On the other hand, if one is too naive in the design of a parallel algorithm, the situation is easily reached where the parallel program searches an impressive number of board positions per second, but still does not search much more deeply than a single processor running the alpha-beta algorithm. The point is that one should not simply split or "go parallel" at every opportunity—as we will see below, it is sometimes better to leave processors idle for short periods of time and then do work at more effective points in the chess tree.

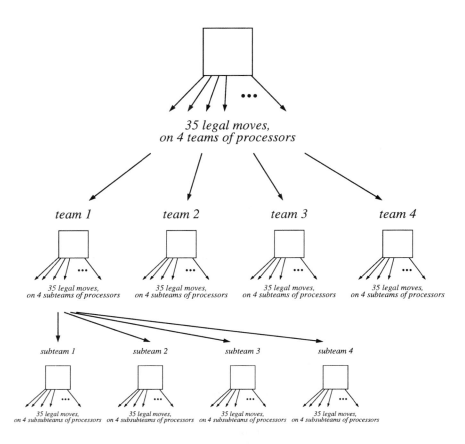

Figure 14.6: The Splitting Process of Figure 14.5 is Now Repeated, in a Recursive Fashion, Down the Chess Tree to Allow Large Numbers of Processors to Come into Play. The topmost master has four slaves, which are each in turn an entire team of processors, and so on. This figure is only approximate, however. As explained in the text, the splitting into parallel threads of computation is not done at every opportunity but is tightly controlled by the global hash table.

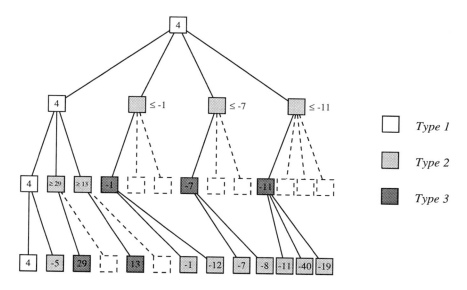

Figure 14.7: Pruning of a Perfectly Ordered Tree. The tree of Figures 14.3 and 14.4 has been extended another ply, and also the move ordering has been rearranged so that the best move is always searched first. By classifying the nodes into types as described in the text, the following pattern emerges: All children of type one and three nodes are searched, while only the first child of a type two node is searched.

Analysis of Alpha-Beta Pruning

The standard source on mathematical analysis of the alpha-beta algorithm is the paper by Knuth and Moore [Knuth:75a]. This paper gives a complete analysis for perfectly ordered trees, and derives some results about randomly ordered trees. We will concern ourselves here with perfectly ordered trees, since real chess programs achieve almost-perfect ordering.

In this context, perfect move-ordering means that in any position, we always consider the best move first. Ordering of the rest of the moves does not matter. Knuth and Moore show that in a perfectly ordered tree, the nodes can be divided into three types, as illustrated by Figure 14.7. As in previous figures, nodes are assumed to be generated and searched in left-to-right order. The typing of the nodes is as follows. Type one nodes are on the "principal variation." The first child of a type one node is type one and the rest of the children are type two. Children of type two nodes are type three, and children of type three nodes are type two.

How much parallelism is available at each node? The pruning of the perfectly ordered tree of Figure 14.7 offers a clue. By thinking through the alpha-beta procedure, one notices the following pattern:

- All children of type one nodes are searched,

- Only the first child of a type two node is searched—the rest are pruned; and

- All children of type three nodes must be searched.

This oscillating pattern between the node types is, of course, the reason for distinguishing them as different types in the first place.

The implications of this for a parallel search are important. To efficiently search a perfectly ordered tree in parallel, one should perform the following algorithm.

- At type one nodes, the first child must be searched sequentially (in order to initialize the alpha-beta bounds), then the rest can be searched in parallel.

- At type two nodes, there is no parallelism since only one child will be searched (time spent searching other children will be wasted).

- Type three nodes, on the other hand, are fully parallel and all the children can be searched independently and simultaneously.

The key for parallel search of perfectly ordered chess trees, then, is to stay sequential at type two nodes, and go parallel at type three nodes. In the non-perfectly ordered case, the clean distinction between node types breaks down, but is still approximately correct. In our program, the hash table plays a role in deciding upon the node type. The following strategy is used by a master processor when reaching a node of the chess tree:

> Make an inquiry to the hash table regarding this position. If the hash table suggests a move, search it first, sequentially. In this context, "sequentially" means that the master takes her slaves with her down this line of play. This is to allow possible parallelism lower down in the tree. If no move is suggested or the suggested move fails to cause an alpha-beta cutoff, search the remaining moves in parallel. That is, farm the work out to the slaves in a self-scheduled manner.

This parallel algorithm is intuitively reasonable and also reduces to the correct strategy in the perfectly ordered case. In actual searches, we have explicitly (on the nCUBE graphics monitor) observed the sharp classification of nodes into type two and type three at alternate levels of the chess tree.

Global Hash Table

The central role of the hash table in providing refutations and telling the program when to go parallel makes it clear that the hash table must be shared among all processors. Local hash tables would not work since the complex, dynamically changing organization of processors makes it very unlikely that a processor will search the same region of the tree in two successive levels of iterative deepening. A shared table is expensive on a distributed-memory machine, but in this case it is worth it.

Each processor contributes an equal amount of memory to the shared hash table. The global hash function maps each chess position to a global slot number consisting of a processor ID and a local slot number. Remote memory is accessed by sending a message to the processor in which the desired memory resides. To insure prompt service to remote memory requests, these messages must cause an interrupt on arrival. The VERTEX system does not support this feature, so we implemented a system called *generalized signals* [Felten:88b], which allows interrupt-time servicing of some messages without disturbing the running program.

When a processor wants to read a remote slot in the hash table, it sends a message containing the local slot number and the 64-bit collision check to the appropriate processor. When this message arrives the receiving processor is interrupted; it updates the staleness flag and sends the contents of the desired slot back to the requesting processor. The processor which made the request waits until the answer comes back before proceeding.

Remote writing is a bit more complicated due to the possibility of collisions. As explained previously, collisions are resolved by a priority scheme; the decision of whether to overwrite the previous entry must be made by the processor which actually owns the relevant memory. Remote writing is accomplished by sending a message containing the new hash table entry to the appropriate processor. This message causes an interrupt on arrival and the receiver examines the new data and the old contents of that hash table slot and decides which one to keep.

Since hash table data is shared among many processors, any access to the hash table must be an atomic operation. This means we must guarantee that two accesses to the same slot cannot happen at the same time. The generalized signals system provides a critical-section protection feature which can be used to queue remote read and write requests while an access is in progress.

Experiments show that the overhead associated with the global hash table is only a few percent, which is a small price to pay for accurate move ordering.

14.3.4   Load Balancing

As we explained in an earlier section, slaves get work from their masters in a self-scheduled way in order to achieve a simple type of load balancing. This turns out not to be enough, however. By the nature of alpha-beta, the time necessary to search two different subtrees of the same depth can vary quite dramatically. A factor of 100 variation in search times is not unreasonable. Self-scheduling is somewhat helpless in such a situation. In these cases, a single slave would have to grind out the long search, while the other slaves (and conceivably, the entire rest of the machine) would merely sit idle. Another problem, near the bottom of the chess tree, is the extremely rapid time scales involved. Not only do the search times vary by a large factor, but this all happens at millisecond time scales. Any load-balancing procedure will therefore need to be quite fast and simple.

These "chess hot spots" must be explicitly taken care of. The master and submaster processors, besides just waiting for search answers, updating alpha-beta bounds, and so forth, also monitor what is going on with the slaves in terms of load balance. In particular, if some minimum number of slaves are idle and if there has been a search proceeding for some minimum amount of time, the master halts the search in the slave containing the hot spot, reorganizes all his idle slaves into a large team, and restarts the search in this new team. This process is entirely local to this master and his slaves and happens recursively, at all levels of the processor tree.

This "shoot-down" procedure is governed by two parameters: the minimum number of idle slaves, and the minimum time before calling a search a potential hot spot. These parameters are introduced to prevent the halting, processor rearrangement, and its associated overhead in cases which are not necessarily hot spots. The parameters are tuned for maximum performance.

The payoff of dynamic load balancing has been quite large. Once the load-balancing code was written, debugged, and tuned, the program was approximately three times faster than before load balancing. Through observations of the speedup (to be discussed below), and also by looking directly at the execution of the program across the nCUBE (using the parallel graphics monitor, also to be discussed below) we have become convinced that the program is well load balanced and we are optimistic about the prospects for scaling to larger speedups on larger machines.

An interesting point regarding asynchronous parallel programming was brought forth by the dynamic load-balancing procedure. It is concerned with the question, "Once we've rearranged the teams and completed the search, how do we return to the original hierarchy so as to have a reasonable starting point for the next search?" Our first attempts at resetting the processor hierarchy met with disaster. It turned out that processors would occasionally not make it back into the hierarchy (that is, be the slave of someone) in time for another search to begin. This happened because of the asynchronous nature of the program and the variable amount of time that messages take to travel through the machine. Once this happened, the processor would end up in the wrong place in the chess tree and the program would soon crash. A natural thing to try in this case is to demand that all processors be reconnected before beginning a new search but we rejected this as being tantamount to a global resynchronization and hence very costly. We therefore took an alternate route whereby the code was written in a careful manner so that processors could actually stay disconnected from the processor tree, and the whole system could still function correctly. The disconnected processor would reconnect eventually—it would just miss one search. This solution seems to work quite well both in terms of conceptual simplicity and speed.

14.3.5 Speedup Measurements

Speedup is defined as the ratio of sequential running time to parallel running time. We measure the speedup of our program by timing it directly with different numbers of processors on a standard suite of test searches. These searches are done from the even-numbered Bratko-Kopec positions [Bratko:82a], a well-known set of positions for testing chess programs. Our benchmark consists of doing two successive searches from each position and adding up the total search time for all 24 searches. By varying the depth of search, we can control the average search time of each benchmark.

The speedups we measured are shown in Figure 14.8. Each curve corresponds to a different average search time. We find that speedup is a strong function of the time of the search (or equivalently, its depth). This result is a

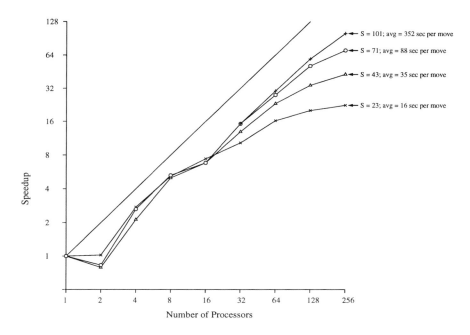

Figure 14.8: The Speedup of the Parallel Chess Program as a Function of Machine Size and Search Depth. The results are averaged over a representative test set of 24 chess positions. The speedup increases dramatically with search depth, corresponding to the fact that there is more parallelism available in larger searches. The uppermost curve corresponds to tournament play—the program runs more than 100 times faster on 256 nodes as on a single nCUBE node when playing at tournament speed.

reflection of the fact that deeper search trees have more potential parallelism and hence more speedup. Our main result is that at tournament speed (the uppermost curve of the figure), our program achieves a speedup of 101 out of a possible 256. Not shown in this figure is our later result: a speedup estimated to be 170 on a 512-node machine.

The "double hump" shape of the curves is also understood: The location of the first dip, at 16 processors, is the location at which the chess tree would like the processor hierarchy to be a one-level hierarchy sometimes, a two-level hierarchy at other times. We always use a one-level hierarchy for 16 processors, so we are suboptimal here. Perhaps this is an indication that a more flexible processor allocation scheme could do somewhat better.

14.3.6 Real-time Graphical Performance Monitoring

One tool we have found extremely valuable in program development and tuning is a real-time performance monitor with color-graphics display. Our nCUBE hardware has a high-resolution color graphics monitor driven by many parallel connections into the hypercube. This gives sufficient bandwidth to support a status display from the hypercube processors in real time. Our performance-monitoring software was written by Rod Morison and is described in [Morison:88a].

The display shows us where in the chess tree each processor is, and it draws the processor hierarchy as it changes. By watching the graphics screen we can see load imbalance develop and observe dynamic load balancing as it tries to cope with the imbalance. The performance monitor gave us the first evidence that dynamic load balancing was necessary, and it was invaluable in debugging and tuning the load balancing code.

14.3.7 Speculation

The best computer chessplayer of 1990 (Deep Thought) has reached grandmaster strength. How strong a player can be built within five years, using today's techniques?

Deep Thought is a chess engine implemented in VLSI that searches roughly 500,000 positions per second. The speed of Chiptest-type engines can probably be increased by about a factor of 30 through design refinements and improvements in fabrication technology. This factor comes from assuming a speed doubling every year, for five years. Our own results imply that an additional factor of 250 speedup due to coarse-grain parallelism is plausible. This is assuming something like a 1000-processor machine with each processor being an updated version of Deep Thought. This means that a machine capable of searching 3.75 billion ($30 \times 250 \times 500,000$) positions per second is not out of the question within five years.

Communication times will also need to be improved dramatically over the nCUBE-1 used. This will entail hardware specialization to the requirements of chess. How far communication speeds can be scaled and how well the algorithm can cope with proportionally slower communications are poorly understood issues.

The relationship between speed and playing strength is well-understood for ratings below 2500. A naive extrapolation of Thompson's results [Thompson:82a] indicates that a doubling in speed is worth about 40 rating points in the regime above 2500. Thus, this machine would have a rating somewhere near 3000, which certainly indicates world-class playing strength.

Of course nobody really knows how such a powerful computer would do against the best grandmasters. The program would have an extremely unbalanced style and might well be stymied by the very deep positional play of the world's best humans. We must not fall prey to the overconfidence which led top computer scientists to lose consecutive bets to David Levy!

14.3.8   Summary

Steve Otto and Ed Felten were the leaders of the chess project and did the majority of the work. Eric Umland began the project and would have been a major contributor but for his untimely death. Rod Morison wrote the opening book code and also developed the parallel graphics software. Summer students Ken Barish and Rob Fätland contributed chess expertise and various peripheral programs.

Chapter 15

High-Level Asynchronous Software Systems

15.1 Asynchronous Software Paradigms

There is not now nor will there be a single software paradigm that applies to all parallel applications. The previous chapters have shown one surprising fact. At least 90% of all scientific and engineering computations can be supported by loosely synchronous message-passing systems, such as CrOS (Express) at a low level and data-parallel languages such as High Performance Fortran at a higher and somewhat less general level. The following chapters contain several different software approaches that sometimes are alternatives for synchronous and loosely synchronous problems, and sometimes are designed to tackle more general applications.

Figures 3.11(a) and 3.11(b) illustrate two compound problem architectures—one of which the battle management simulation of Figure 3.11(b) is discussed in detail in Sections 18.3 and 18.4. MOVIE, discussed in Chapter 17, and the more ad hoc heterogeneous software approach described in Section 18.3 are designed as "software glue" to integrate many disparate interconnected modules. Each module may itself be data-parallel. The application of Figure 3.11(b) involves signal processing, for which data parallelism is natural, and linking of satellites, for which a message-passing system is natural. The integration needed in Figure 3.11(a) is of different modules of a complex design and simulation environment—such as that for a new aircraft or automobile described in Chapter 19. We redraw the application of Figure 3.11(a) in Figure 15.1 to indicate that one can view the

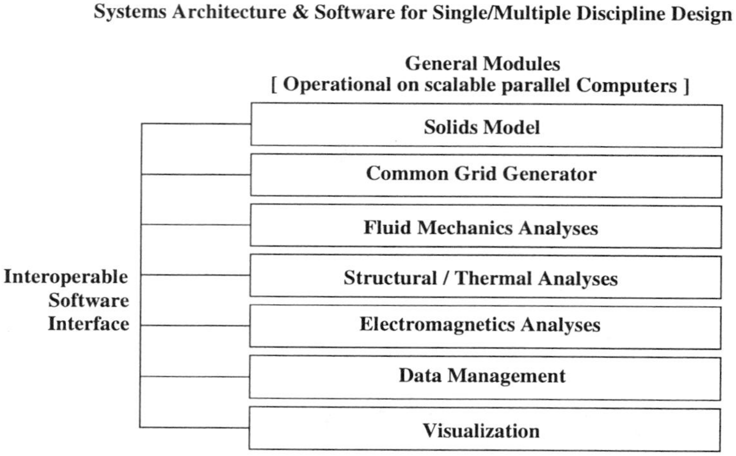

Systems Architecture & Software for Single/Multiple Discipline Design

Figure 15.1: General Software Structure for Multidisciplinary Analysis and Design

software infrastructure in this case as forming a software "bus" or backbone into which one can "plug" application modules. This software integration naturally involves an interplay between parallel and distributed computing. This is graphically shown in Figure 15.2, which redisplays Figures 3.10 and 3.11(a) to better indicate the analogy between a software network (bus) and a heterogeneous computer network. The concept of metacomputer has been coined to describe the integration of a heterogeneous computer network to perform as a single system. Thus, we can term the systems in Chapter 17 and Section 18.3 as *metasoftware systems*, and so on, software for implementing metaproblems on metacomputers.

The discussion in Chapter 16 shows how different starting points can lead to similar results. Express, discussed in Chapter 5, can be viewed as a flexible (asynchronous) evolution of the original (loosely) synchronous CrOS message-passing system. Zipcode, described in Chapter 16, starts with a basic asynchronous model but builds on top of it the structure necessary to efficiently represent loosely synchronous and synchronous problems.

MOOSE, described in the following section, was in some sense a dead end, but the lessons learned helped the evolution of our later software as described in Chapter 5. MOOSE was designed to replace CrOS but users found it unnecessarily powerful for the relatively simple (loosely) synchronous problems being tackled by C^3P at the time.

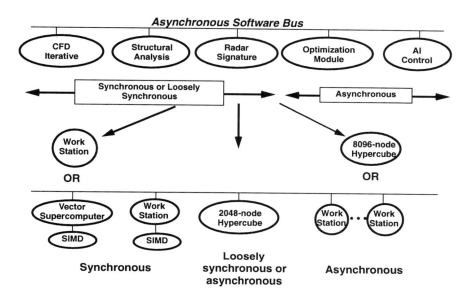

Figure 15.2: The Mapping of Heterogeneous Problems onto Heterogeneous Computer Systems combining Figure 3.10 and Figure 3.11(a).

The Time Warp operating system described briefly in Section 15.3 is an important software approach to the very difficult asynchronous event-driven simulations described in Section 14.1. The simulations described in Section 18.3 also used this software approach combined in a heterogeneous environment with our fast, loosely synchronous system CrOS. This illustrates the need for and effectiveness of software designed to support a focussed subclass of problems. The evolution of software support for asynchronous problems would seem to need a classification with the complete asynchronous class divided into subclasses for which one can separately generate appropriate support. The discussions of Sections 14.2, 14.3, 15.2, 15.3, and 18.3 represent C^3P's contributions to this isolation of subclasses with their needed software. Chapters 16 and 17 represent a somewhat different approach in developing general software frameworks which can be tailored to each problem class.

15.2   MOOS II: An Operating System for Dynamic Load Balancing on the iPSC/1

Applications involving irregular time behavior or dynamically varying data structures are difficult to program using the crystalline model or its variants. Examples are dynamically adaptive grids for studying shock waves in fluid dynamics, N-body simulations of gravitating systems, and artificial intelligence applications, such as chess. The few applications in this class that have been written typically use custom designed operating systems and special techniques.

To support applications in this class, we developed a new, general-purpose operating system called MOOSE for the Mark II hypercube [Salmon:88a], and later wrote an extended version called MOOS II for the Intel iPSC/1 [Koller:88b]. While the MOOSE system was fairly convenient for some applications, it became available at a time when the Mark II and iPSC/1 were falling into disuse because of uncompetitive performance. The iPSC/1 was used for MOOS II for two reasons: It had the necessary hardware support on the node, and, because of low performance, it had little production use for scientific simulation. Thus, we could afford to devote the iPSC/1 to the "messy" process of developing a new operating system which rendered the machine unusable to others for long periods of time. Only one major application was ever written using MOOSE (Ray tracing, [Goldsmith:88a], mentioned in Section 14.1 [Salmon:88c]), and only toy applications were written using MOOS II. Its main value was therefore as an experiment in operating system design and some of its features are now incorporated in Express (Section 5.2). The lightweight threads pioneered in MOOSE are central to essentially all new distributed- and shared-memory computing models—in particular MOVIE, described in Chapter 17.

15.2.1   Design of MOOSE

The user writes a MOOSE program as a large collection of small tasks that communicate with each other by sending messages through pipes, as shown in Figure 15.3. Each task controls a piece of data, so it can be viewed as an object in the object-oriented sense (hence the name Multitasking Object-oriented OS). The tasks and pipes can be created at any time by any task on any node, so the whole system is completely dynamic.

The MOOS II extensions allow one to form groups of tasks called teams that share access to a piece of data. Also, a novel feature of MOOS II is that

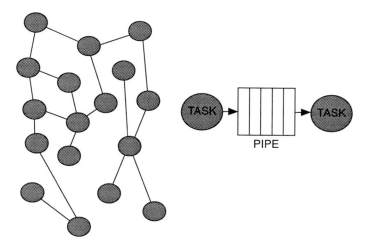

Figure 15.3: An Executing MOOSE Program Is a Dynamic Network (left) of Tasks Communicating Through FIFO Buffers Called Pipes (right).

teams are relocatable, that is, they can be moved from one node to another while they are running. This allows one to perform dynamic load balancing if necessary.

The various subsystems of MOOS II, which together form a complete operating system and programming environment, are shown in Figure 15.4. For convenience, we attempted to preserve a UNIX flavor in the design and were also able to provide support for debugging and performance evaluation because the iPSC/1 hardware has built-in memory protection. Easy interaction with the host is achieved using ICubix, an asynchronous version of Cubix (Section 5.2) that gives each task access to the Unix system calls on the host. The normal C-compilers can be used for programming, and the only extra utility program required is a binder to link the user program to the operating system.

Despite the increased functionality, the performance of MOOS II on the iPSC/1 turned out to be slightly better than that of Intel's proprietary NX system.

15.2.2 Dynamic Load-Balancing Support

Our plan was to use MOOS II to study dynamic load balancing (Chapter 11), and eventually incorporate a dynamic load balancer in the MOOSE system. However, our first implementation of a dynamic load balancer, along the

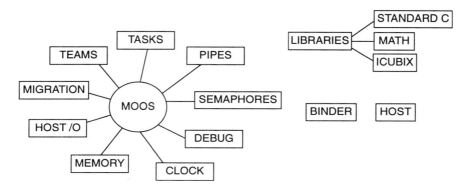

Figure 15.4: Subsystems of the MOOS II Operating System

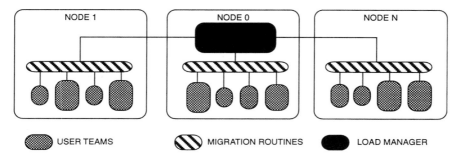

Figure 15.5: One Simple Load-Balancing Scheme Implemented in MOOS II

lines of [Fox:86h], convinced us that dynamic load balancing is a difficult and many-faceted issue, so the net result was a better understanding of the subject's complexities rather than a general-purpose balancer.

The prototype dynamic load balancer worked as shown in Figure 15.5 and is appropriate for applications where the number of MOOSE teams in an application is constant. However, the amount of work performed by individual teams changes slowly with time. A centralized load manager on node 0 keeps statistics on all the teams in the machine. At regular intervals, the teams report the amount of computation and communication they have done since the last report, and the central manager computes the new load balance. If the balance can be improved significantly, some teams are relocated to new nodes, and the cycle continues.

This centralized approach is simple and successful in that it relocates as few teams as possible to maintain the balance; its drawback is that computing which teams to move becomes a sequential bottleneck. For instance, for 256 teams on 16 processors, a simulated annealing optimization takes about 1.2 seconds on the iPSC/1, while the actual relocation process only takes about 0.3 seconds, so the method is limited to applications where load redistribution needs only to be done every 10 seconds or so. The lesson here is that, to be viable, the load optimization step itself must be parallelized. The same conclusion will also hold for any other distributed-memory machine, since the ratio of computation time to optimization time is fairly machine-independent.

15.2.3   What We Learned

Aside from finding some new reasons not to use old hardware, we were able to pinpoint issues worthy of further study, concerning parallel programming in general and load balancing in particular.

1. In the MOOSE programming style, it is messy and expensive for user tasks to find out when other groups of tasks have terminated. In our defense, the same unsolved problem exists in ADA.

2. There are serious ambiguities in the meaning of parallel-file IO for asynchronous systems like MOOSE, which are exacerbated when tasks can move from node to node. When writing, does each task have a block in the file, and if so, how do we correlate tasks with blocks? There are hints that a hypertext-like system is more suitable than a linear file for parallel IO, but we were unable to obtain completely satisfactory semantics.

3. It is not clear that there is a general solution to the dynamic load-balancing problem. The issue may be as resistant to classification as, say, the general nonlinear PDE problem. A better solution may be to provide language support so that the programmer can control the load distribution as part of the program. Existing applications that load-balance successfully (e.g., chess [Felten:87a] in Section 14.3 or the N-body solver [Salmon:89a] in Section 12.4) compute and use load information on the fly in ways that a general-purpose method could not.

4. As the number of tasks grows, the amount of load information grows enormously, and we have to be selective about what we record. The best choice seems to be application- and machine-dependent.

5. In irregular problems, having a large number of tasks does not automatically solve the load-balancing problem. Unforeseen correlations between tasks tend to appear that confound naive balancing schemes. The load-balancing problem must be tackled on many scales simultaneously.

Future work will therefore have to focus less on the mechanism of moving tasks around and more on how to communicate load information between user and system.

MOOSE was written by John Salmon, Sean Callahan, Jon Flower and Adam Kolawa. MOOS II was written by Jeff Koller.

The C^3P references are: [Salmon:88a], [Koller:88a;88b;88d;89a], [Fox:86h].

15.3   Time Warp

Discrete-event simulations are among the most expensive of all computational tasks. With current technology, one sequential execution of a large simulation can take hours or days of sequential processor time. For example, many large military simulations take days to complete on standard single processors. If the model is probabilistic, many executions will be necessary to determine the output distributions. Nevertheless, many scientific, engineering, and military projects depend heavily on simulation because experiments on real systems are too expensive or too unsafe. Therefore, any technique that speeds up simulations is of great importance.

We designed the Time Warp Operating System (TWOS) to address this problem. TWOS is a multiprocessor operating system that runs parallel discrete-event simulations. We developed TWOS on the Caltech/JPL Mark III Hypercube. We have since ported it to various other parallel architectures, including the Transputer and a BBN Butterfly GP1000. TWOS is not intended as a general-purpose multiuser operating system, but rather as an environment for a single concurrent application (especially a simulation) in which synchronization is specified using virtual time [Jefferson:85c].

The innovation that distinguishes TWOS from other operating systems is its complete commitment to an optimistic style of execution and to processing rollback for almost all synchronization. Most distributed operating systems either cannot handle process rollback at all or implement it as a rarely used mechanism for special purposes such as exception handling, deadlock, transaction abortion, or fault recovery. But the Time Warp Operating System embraces rollback as the normal mechanism for process synchronization, and uses it as often as process blocking is used in other systems. TWOS contains a simple, general distributed rollback mechanism capable of undoing or preventing any side effect, direct or indirect, of an incorrect action. In particular, it is able to control or undo such troublesome side effects as errors, infinite loops, I/O, creation and destruction of processes, asynchronous message communication, and termination.

TWOS uses an underlying kernel to provide basic message-passing capabilities, but it is not used for any other purpose. On the Caltech/JPL Mark III Hypercube, this role was played by *Cubix*, described in Section 5.2. The other facilities of the underlying operating system are not used because rollback forces a rethinking of almost all operating system issues, including scheduling, synchronization, message queueing, flow control, memory management, error handling, I/O, and commitment. All of these are handled by TWOS. Only the extra work of implementing a correct message-passing facility prevents TWOS from being implemented on the bare hardware.

We have been developing TWOS since 1983. It is now an operational system that includes many advanced features such as dynamic creation and destruction of objects, dynamic memory management, and dynamic load management. TWOS is being used by the United States Army's Concept and Analysis Agency to develop a new generation of theater-level combat simulations. TWOS has also been used to model parallel processing hardware, computer networks, and biological systems.

Figure 15.6 shows the performance of TWOS on one simulation called STB88. This simulation models theater-level combat in central Europe [Wieland:89a]. The graph in Figure 15.6 shows how much version 2.3 of TWOS was able to speed up this simulation on varying numbers of nodes of a parallel processor. The speedup shown is relative to running a sequential simulator on a single node of the same machine used for the TWOS runs. The sequential simulator uses a splay tree for its event queue. It never performs rollback, and hence has a lower overhead than TWOS. The sequential simulator links with exactly the same application code as TWOS. It is intended to be the fastest possible general-purpose discrete-event simulator that can handle the same application code as TWOS.

Figure 15.6 demonstrates that TWOS can run this simulation more than 25 times faster than running it on the sequential simulator, given sufficient numbers of nodes. On other applications, even higher speedups are possible. In certain cases, TWOS has achieved up to 70% of the maximum theoretical

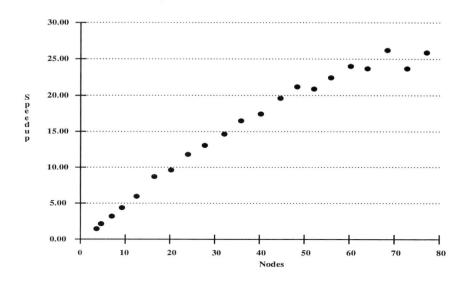

Figure 15.6: Performance of TWOS on STB88

speedup, as determined by critical path analysis.

Research continues on TWOS. Currently, we are investigating dynamic load management [Reiher:90a]. Dynamic load management is important for TWOS because good speedups generally require careful mapping of a simulation's constituent objects to processor nodes. If the balance is bad, then the run is slow. But producing a good static balance takes approximately the same amount of work as running the simulation on a single node. Dynamic load management allows TWOS to achieve nearly the same speed with simple mappings as with careful mappings.

Dynamic load management is an interesting problem for TWOS because the utilizations of TWOS' nodes are almost always high. TWOS optimistically performs work whenever work is available, so nodes are rarely idle. On the other hand, much of the work done by a node may be rolled back, contributing nothing to completing the computation. Instead of balancing simple utilization, TWOS balances effective utilization, the proportion of a node's work that is not rolled back. Use of this metric has produced very good results.

Future research directions for TWOS include database management, real-time user interaction with TWOS, and the application of virtual time synchronization to other types of parallel processing problems. [Jefferson:87a] contains a more complete description of TWOS.

Participants in this project were David Jefferson, Peter Reiher, Brian Beckman, Frederick Wieland, Mike Di Loreto, Philip Hontalas, John Wedel, Paul Springer, Leo Blume, Joseph Ruffles, Steven Belenot, Jack Tupman, Herb Younger, Richard Fujimoto, Kathy Sturdevant, Lawrence Hawley, Abe Feinberg, Pierre LaRouche, Matt Presley, and Van Warren.

Chapter 16

The Zipcode Message-Passing System

16.1 Overview of *Zipcode*

Zipcode is a message-passing system developed originally by Skjellum, beginning at Caltech in the Summer of 1988 [Skjellum:90a], [Skjellum:91c], [Skjellum:92c] and [Skjellum:91a]. *Zipcode* was created to address features and issues absent in then-existing message-passing systems such as CrOS/Express, described in Section 5.2. In particular, *Zipcode* was based on an underlying reactive asynchronous low-level message-passing system. CrOS was built on top of loosely synchronous low-level message-passing systems, which reflected C^3P's initial hardware and applications. Interestingly, both *Zipcode* and Express have evolved from their starting to quite similar high-level functionality. Currently, *Zipcode* continues to serve as a vehicle to demonstrate high-level message-passing research concepts and, more importantly, to provide the basis for supporting vendor-independent scalable concurrent libraries; notably, the *Multicomputer Toolbox* [Falgout:92a], [Skjellum:91b;92a;92d]. The basic assertion of *Zipcode* is that carefully managed, expressive message-passing is an effective way to program multicomputers and distributed computers, while low-level message passing is admittedly both error-prone and difficult.

The purpose of *Zipcode* is to manage the message-passing process within parallel codes in an open-ended way. This is done so that large-scale software can be constructed in a multicomputer application, with reduced likelihood that software so constructed will conflict in its dynamic resource use, thereby

647

avoiding potentially hard-to-resolve, source-level conflicts. Furthermore, the message-passing notations provided are to reflect the algorithms and data organizations of the concurrent algorithms, rather than predefined tagging strategies. Tagging, while generic and easy to understand, proves insufficient to support manageable application development. Notational abstractions provide a means for the user to help *Zipcode* make runtime optimizations when a code runs on systems with specific hardware features. Abstraction is therefore seen as a means to higher performance, and notation is seen as a means towards more understandable, easier-to-develop-and-maintain concurrent software. Context allocation (see below) provides a "social contract" within which multiple libraries and codes can coexist reasonably. Contexts are like system-managed "hypertag"; contexts here are called "Zipcodes".

Safety in communication is achieved by *context* control; the main process data structure is the process list (a collective of processes that are to communicate). These constructs are handled dynamically by the system. Contexts are needed so that diverse codes can be brought together and made to work without the possibility of message-passing conflicts, and without the need to globalize the semantic and syntactic issues of message passing contained in each separate piece of code. For instance, the use and support of independently conceived concurrent libraries requires separate communication space, which contexts support. As applications mature, more contexts are likely to be needed, especially if diverse libraries are linked into the system, or a number of (possibly overlapping) process structures are needed to represent various phases of a calculation. In purely message-passing instances within *Zipcode*, contexts control the flow of messages through a global messaging resource. In more complex hierarchies, contexts will manage channel and/or shared-memory blocks in the user program, while the notation remains message-passing-like to the user. This evolution is transparent to the user.

Concurrent mathematical libraries are well supported by the definition of multidimensional, logical-process-grid primitives, as provided by *Zipcode*; one-, two- and three-dimensional grids are currently supported (grid *mail classes*, also known as virtual topologies). Grids are used to assign machine-independent naming to the processes participating in a calculation, with a shape chosen by the user. Such grids form the basis for higher level data structures that describe how matrices and vectors are shared across a set of processes, but these descriptors are external to *Zipcode*. New grids may be aligned to existing grids to provide nesting, partitioning, and other desired subsetting of process grids, all done in the machine-independent notation of the parent grid. The routine *whoami* and associated routines, described in Section 5.2, provide this capability in CrOS/Express.

Mail classes (such as new grid structures) may be added statically to the system; because code cannot move with data in extant multicomputers, mail classes have to be enumerated at compile-time. Because we at present retain a C implementation, rather than C++, the library must currently be modified explicitly to add new classes of mail, rather than by inheritance. Fortunately, the predefined classes (grids, tagged messages) address a number of the situations we have encountered thus far in practical applications. Non-mathematically oriented users may conceive of mail classes that we have not as yet imagined, and which might be application-specific.

Recently, we have evolved the *Zipcode* system to provide higher level application interfaces to the basic message-passing contexts and classes of mail. These interfaces allow us to unify the notions of heterogeneity and non-uniform memory access hierarchy in a single framework, on a context-by-context basis. For instance, we view a homogeneous collection of multicomputer nodes as a particular type of memory hierarchy. We see this unification of heterogeneity and memory hierarchy in our notation as an important conceptual advance, both for distributed- and concurrent-computing applications of *Zipcode*. Mainly, heterogeneity impacts transmission bandwidth and should not have to be treated as a separate feature in data transmission, nor should it be explicitly visible in user-defined application code or algorithms, except perhaps in highly restricted method definitions, for performance' sake.

For instance, the notations currently provided by *Zipcode* support writing application programs so that the same message-passing code can map reasonably well to heterogeneous architectures, to those with shared memory between subsets of nodes, and to those which support active-message strategies. Furthermore, it should be possible to cache limited internode channel resources within the library, transparent to the user. This is possible because the gather-send and scatter-receive notations remove message formatting from the user's control. We provide general gather/scatter specifications through persistent *invoice* data types. This notation is available both to C and Fortran programmers. As a side effect, we provide a clean interface for message passing in the Fortran environment. If compilers support code inlining and other optimizations, we are convinced that overheads can be drastically reduced for systems with lighter communication overheads than heretofore developed. Cheap dynamic allocation mechanisms also help in this regard, and are easily attainable. In all cases, the user will have to map the process lists to processors to take advantage of the hierarchies, but this can be done systematically using *Zipcode*.

We define message-passing operations on a context-by-context basis (methods), so that the methods implementing send, receive, combine, broadcast, and so on, are potentially different for each context, reflecting optimizations appropriate to given parts of a hierarchy (homogeneity, power-of-two, flat shared memory, and so on). We have to rely on the user to map the problem to take advantage of such special contexts, but we provide a straightforward mechanism to take advantage of hierarchy through the gather/scatter notation. When compilers provide inlining, we will see significant improvements in performance for lower latency realizations of the system. Higher level notation, and context-by-context method definitions are key to optimizing for memory hierarchy and heterogeneity. Because the user provides us with information on the desired operations, rather than instructions on how to do them, we are able to discover optimizations. Low-level notations cannot hope to achieve this type of optimization, because they do not expose the semantic information in their instructions, nor work over process lists, for which special properties may be asserted (except with extensive compile-time analysis).

This evolutionary process implies that *Zipcode* has surpassed its original *Reactive Kernel/Cosmic Environment* platform; it is now planned that *Zipcode* implementations will be based on one or more of the following in a given implementation:

- Hardware-based shared memory (with and/or without an intervening CE/RK layer),

- Active-message strategies (cf., [Eiken:92a]),

- Pure message passing (with and/or without an intervening CE/RK layer),

- Control-network operations definable on process lists (subsets of processes or processors).

Heterogeneous translation can be by one of several translation mechanisms. For instance, XDR [XDR:87a], ELROS [Branstetter:91a;92a] or other strategies (that appropriately balance the work of the sender and recipient in the translation process as a function of their computational bandwidth for such translations). Because invoices are persistent objects, the possibility of nodal vectorization of translated objects is possible, using ELROS or other machine-specific strategies (perhaps user-defined); XDR is not currently amenable to vectorization. Such translation strategies will also be held transparent to the user, except when the user chooses to intervene, by providing a submethod that implements part of an invoice translation. With this approach, we can take advantage of the architectures presented at run time, on a context-by-context basis.

Importantly, when a code is moved to a system that does not have special features (e.g., a purely message-passing system), the user code's calls to *Zipcode* will compile down to pure message-passing, whereas the calls compile down to faster schemes within special hierarchies. This multifaceted approach to implementing *Zipcode* follows its original design philosophy; originally, the CE/RK primitives upon which *Zipcode* is based were the cheapest available primitives for system-level message-passing, and hence the most attractive to build higher level services like *Zipcode*. Today, vendor operating systems are likely to provide additional services in the other categories mentioned above which, if used directly in applications, would prove unportable, unmanageable, or too low level (like direct use of CE/RK primitives). If a user needs to optimize a code for a specific system, he or she works in terms of process lists and contexts to get desirable mappings from which *Zipcode* can effect runtime optimizations.

The CE/RK primitives (originally central to *Zipcode*) manage memory as well as message-passing operations. This is an important feature, carried into the *Zipcode* system, which is helpful in reducing the number of copies needed to pass a message from sender to recipient in basic message (hence, less wasted bandwidth). In CE/RK the system provides message space, which is freed upon transmission and allocated upon receipt. This approach removes the need for complicated strategies involving asynchronous sends, in which the user has to poll to see when his or her buffer is once again usable. Since the majority of transmissions in realistic applications involve a gather before send (and scatter on receive), rather than block-data transmission, these semantics provide, on the whole, good notational and performance benefits, while retaining simplicity. *Zipcode* extends the concept of the CE/RK-managed messages to include buffered messages (for global operations) and synchronizations. These three varieties of primitives make different assumptions about how memory is allocated (and by whom), and are implemented with the most efficient available system calls in a given *Zipcode* implementation. In all cases, actual memory allocation can be effected using lightweight allocation procedures in efficient implementations, rather than heavyweight mallocs. Therefore, the dynamic nature of the allocations need not imply significant performance penalties.

When moving *Zipcode* to a new system, the CE/RK layer will normally be the first interface provided, with additional interfaces provided if the hardware's special properties so warrant. In this way, user codes and libraries will come up to speed quickly, yet attain better performance as the *Zipcode* port is optimized for the new system. We see this as a desirable mode of operation, with the highest initial return on investment.

16.2   Low-Level Primitives

16.2.1   CE/RK Overview

To appreciate the model upon which current *Zipcode* implementations are built, one needs to understand the scope and expressivity of the low-level CE/RK system.

16.2.2   Interface with the CE/RK system

Implementations of *Zipcode* todate interface to primitives of the CE/RK, a portable, lightweight multicomputer node operating system, which provides untyped blocked and unblocked message passing in a uniform host/node model, including type conversion primitives for heterogeneous host-node communications. Presently, the Reactive Kernel is implemented for Intel iPSC/1, iPSC/2, Sequent Symmetry, Symult S2010, and Intel iPSC860 Gamma prototype multicomputers, with emulations provided for the Intel Delta prototype, Thinking Machines CM-5, and nCUBE/2 6400 machines. Furthermore, Intel provides the CE/RK primitives at the lowest level (read: highest performance) on its Paragon system. CE/RK is also emulated on shared-memory computers such as the BBN TC2000 as well as networks of homogeneous NFS-connected workstations (e.g., Sun clusters). We see CE/RK primitives as a logical, flexible platform for our work, and for other message-passing developers, and upon which higher level layers such as *Zipcode* can be ported. Because most tagged message-passing systems with restrictive typing semantics do not provide quite enough receipt selectivity directly to support *Zipcode*, we find it often best to implement untagged primitives as the interface to which *Zipcode* works. The CE/RK emulations, built most often on vendor primitives, make use of any available tagging for bookkeeping purposes, and allow users of a specific vendor system to mix vendor-specific message passing with CE/RK- or *Zipcode*-based messaging.

One should view the CE/RK system as the default message-space management system for *Zipcode* (in C++ parlance, default constructor/new, destructor/free mechanisms), with the understanding that future implementations of *Zipcode* may prefer to use more primitive calls (e.g., packet protocols or active messages) to gain even greater performance. (Alternatively, if Paragon or similar implementations are very fast, such shortcuts will have commensurately less impact on performance.) Via the shortcut approach, *Zipcode* analogs of CE/RK calls will become the lowest level interface of message passing in the system, and become a machine-dependent layer.

16.2.3 CE Functions

The *Cosmic Environment* (CE) provides control for concurrent computation through a "cube dæmon." This resource manager allows multiple real and emulated concurrent computers to be space-shared [Seitz:88a]. The following functions are provided, and we emulate these on systems that provide analogous host functionality (this emulation can be done efficiently on the nCUBE/2, almost trivially on the Gamma, and not at all on the Delta and CM-5):

- `getmc` gets multicomputer resource by type and size for space-sharing (also called `getcube`);

- `freemc` frees multicomputer resource currently in use (also called `freecube`);

- `spawn` spawns one or more node processes to a previously allocated multicomputer partition;

- `ckill` kills one or more extant processes on a previously allocated multicomputer partition.

CE Programs

To support *Zipcode*, we normally emulate the CE functions below. Again, some of these functions, particularly `getmc()`, `freemc()`, `spawn()`, and `ckill()`, are not available on all implementations (for instance, the Delta) and are restricted to the host program:

- `getmc(char *computer_name, int nnodes)` allocates a multicomputer;

- `freemc(void)` deallocates the allocated multicomputer;

- `spawn(char *prog, int node, int pid, char *state)`   spawns processes on one or more nodes;

- `ckill(int node, int pid)` kills processes on one or more nodes;

- `cosmic_init(void)` starts the environment in a process;

- `cosmic_exit(void)` ends the environment in a process;

- `mynode(void)` returns the current process's logical node; number;

- `mypid(void)` returns the current process's identification number (pid);

- `nnodes(void)` returns the number of nodes in the multicomputer allocation;

- `print(char *fmt, ...)`   resembles the standard C function `printf()`, except that the output is preceded by {`node`,`pid`} identification and terminated by a newline, with the output buffer automatically flushed; and

- `clock()` returns the running nodal clock value in microseconds.

16.2.4   RK Calls

The RK calls required by *Zipcode* are as follows:

- `msg = xmalloc(int length)` allocates a message buffer of `length` bytes and returns a pointer `msg` to it;

- `xfree(char *msg)` deallocates the message buffer pointed to by `msg`;

- `xlength(char *msg)` determines the length (in bytes) of a previously allocated or received message `msg`;

- `msg = xrecv()` receives a message without blocking, returning a pointer to the message if a message can be received and NULL if there is no message queued to the calling process;

- `msg = xrecvb()` blocks until a message can be received and returns a pointer to the message;

- `xsend(char *msg, int node, int pid)` sends a message pointed to by `msg` to the process `pid` on node `node`; and

- `xmsend(char *msg, int count, int *dest)` sends a message `msg` to multiple destinations specified by the integer array `dest` of length `2*count` in the form { `node0, pid0, node1, pid1, ...` } .

It is important to note that `xsend()` and `xmsend()` deallocate the message buffer after sending the message; they are semantically analogous to `xfree()`. The receive functions `xrecv()` and `xrecvb()` are semantically analogous to `xmalloc()`.

Zipcode-based programs are not to call any of these CE or RK functions directly. Both message passing and environment control are represented in *Zipcode*.

16.2.5   *Zipcode* Calls

Zipcode Class-Independent Calls

Mailer Creation

Mailers maintain contexts and process lists. All communication operations use mailers. Mailers are created through a loose synchronization between the members of the proposed mailer's process list. A single process creates the process list, placing itself first in the list, and initiates the "mailer-open" call with this process information; it's called the "Postmaster" for the mailer, as initiator. The other participants receive the process list as part of the synchronization procedure. A special reactive process, the "Postmaster General," maintains and distributes zip codes as mailers are opened; essentially the zip code count is a single location of shared memory. Below, each class defines an "open" function to create its mailer.

Predefined Mailer Classes

Y-Class   mail is used mainly for *Zipcode* internal mechanisms. The PO Box information is a single short-integer type. Global operations are not implemented for this class, because of its (intentional) simplicity.

Z-Class   mail is a general-purpose class. Process names are abstracted to a single integer (based on position in the process list); receipt-selectivity is based on that source name. Global operations are implemented for this class, with analogous calling sequences to the G2-Class two-dimensional-grid global operations noted below.

L-Class   mail is used to support emulation of typed message notations such as Intel's NX or PICL [Geist:92b]. Process names are not abstracted, and receipt selectivity is based on the source name (as { `node,pid`} pair) plus a type.

We have been able to classify a number of message-passing systems in [Skjellum:92c], though specific differences in sending, and receiving strategies exist between common tagged-message-passing systems. In *Zipcode*, we define the L-class, which provides for receipt selectivity based on message source in unabstracted {`node,pid`} notation, and on a long-integer tag. This class can be used to define one or more contexts of tagged message systems, that call the primitives described fully in [Skjellum:92b]. However, and perhaps more interestingly, these L-class calls can be used to generate wrappers for all the major tagged message-passing systems. In the *Zipcode* manual we illustrate how this is done by showing a few of the wrappers for the PICL, NX, and Vertex system [Skjellum:92b]. We also have a long-standing *Zipcode*-based emulation for the Livermore Message Passing System (LMPS) [Welcome:92a].

Furthermore, for each context a user declares, he or she is guaranteed that the L-class messages will not be mixed up, so that if vendor-style calls are used in different libraries, then these will not interfere with other parts of a program. This allows several existing tagged subroutines or programs to be brought together and face-lifted easily to work together, without changing tags or seeing when/where the message passing resources might conflict. In short, this provides a general means to ensure tagged-message safety, as contemplated in [Hart:93a].

G1-Class   mail is a one-dimensional-grid-abstraction class, similar to Z-Class mail. For brevity, we omit the calls supported by this class, which are simplified notations of the G2 and G3 classes.

G2-Class   mail is a two-dimensional-grid-abstraction class. A $P \times Q$ grid naming abstraction is attached to the process list; each process is specified by a (p, q) pair (e.g., in the PO Box). Through inheritance, row and column mailers are defined in each process as the appropriate subsets of the two-dimensional grid. This class has received the most extensive use because of the natural application to linear algebra and related computations.

Class-specific primitives for G2-Class mail have been defined for both higher efficiency and better abstraction. Small-g calls require mailer specification while big-G calls do not, analogous to the y- and Y-type calls defined generically above.

Letter-Generating Primitives

```
char *letter = g2_Recv(ZIP_MAILER *mailer, int p, int q);
               /* unblocked: */
       letter = g2_Recvb(ZIP_MAILER *mailer, int p, int q);
               /* blocked: */
```

Letter-Consuming Primitives

```
void g2_Send(ZIP_MAILER *mailer, char *letter, int p, int q);
```

Collective operations *combine*, *broadcast* (fanout), and *collapse* (fanin) are defined and have been highly tuned for this class (see schematics in [Skjellum:90c]).

Combines and fanins are over arbitrary associative-commutative operators specified by (*comb_fn)(). Broadcasts share data of arbitrary length, assuming all participants know the source. Collapses combine information assuming all participants know the destination:

```
int error =
    g2_combine(ZIP_MAILER *mailer, /* 2D grid mailer */
         void *buffer,        /* where result is accumulated */
         void (*comb_fn)(), /* operator for combine */
         int size           /* size of buffer items in bytes */
         int items);        /* number of buffer items */

    error = g2_fanout(ZIP_MAILER *mailer,
         void **data,               /* data/result */
         int *length,               /* data length */
         int orig_p, int orig_q); /* grid origin of data */

    error = g2_fanin(ZIP_MAILER *mailer,
         int dest_p, int dest_q,  /* destination on grid */
```

```
     void *buffer, void (*comb_fn)(),
     int size, int nitems);
```

Shorthands provide direct access to row and column children mailers, tersely providing common communication patterns within the two-dimensional grid:

```
g2_row_combine(mailer, buffer, comb_fn, size, items);
g2_col_combine(mailer, buffer, comb_fn, size, items);

g2_row_fanout(mailer, &data, &length, orig_q);
g2_col_fanout(mailer, &data, &length, orig_p;
```

and

```
g2_row_fanin(mailer, dest_q, buffer, comb_fn, size, items);
g2_col_fanin(mailer, dest_p, buffer, comb_fn, size, items);
```

The row/column instructions above compile to G1-grid calls, since rows and columns of G2 mailers are implemented via G1 mailers.

G2-Grid mailer creation:

```
ZIP_MAILER *mailer = g2_grid_open(int *P, int *Q,
                                  ZIP_ADDRESSEES *addr);
```

Once a G2 grid mailer has been established, it is possible to derive subgrid mailers by a cooperative call between all the participants in the original g2_grid_open(). In normal applications, this will result in a set of additional mailers in the postmaster (usually host program) process, and one additional G2 grid mailer in each node process. This call allows subgrids to be aligned to the original grid in reasonably general ways, but requires a basic cartesian subgridding, in that each subgrid defined must be a rectangular collection of processes.

The postmaster of the original mailer (often the host process), initiates the subgrid open request as follows:

```
/* array of pointer to subgrid mailers: */
ZIP_MAILER **subgrid_mailers =
    g2_subgrid_open(ZIP_MAILER *mailer,
            /* mailer already opened */
            /* for each (p,q) on original grid,
```

```
                    marks its subgrid: */
     int (*select_fn)(int p, int q, void *extra),
     void *select_extra;   /* extra data needed by select_fn() */
     int *nsubgrids);      /* the number of subgrids created    */
```

while each process in the original g2_grid_open() does a second, standard g2_grid_open():

```
     ZIP_MAILER *subgrid_mailer = g2_grid_open(&P, &Q, NULL);
```

Each subgrid so created has its own unique contexts of communication.

Finally, it is often necessary to determine the grid shape $P \times Q$, as well as the current process's location on the grid (p, q), when using two-dimensional logical grids. Often this information is housed only in the mailer (though some applications may choose to duplicate this information). The following calls provide simple access to these four quantities.

```
int p,q, P, Q; ZIP_MAILER *mailer;


/* set variables (P,Q) to grid shape: */
void g2_PQ(ZIP_MAILER *mailer, int P, int Q);


/* set variables (p,q) to grid position: */
void g2_pq(ZIP_MAILER *mailer, int p, int q);
```

These are the preferred forms for accessing grid information from G2-Class mailers.

G3-Class   mail is a three-dimensional-grid-abstraction class. A $P \times Q \times R$ grid naming abstraction is attached to the process list, analogously to the G2-Class two-dimensional-grid primitives. This class is interesting for problems where there are three logical "axes" of concurrency. Children of a G3 mailer are G2 mailers representing planes within the three-dimensional grid. Operations analogous to the two-dimensional case have been extended to the three-dimensional grid case and are not detailed here (see [Skjellum:92b;c]).

Shorthands provide access to the PQ-plane, QR-plane, and PR-plane children to which G2 grid operations may be applied, as above.

```
ZIP_MAILER *mailer;   /* 3D grid mailer */
ZIP_MAILER *PQ_plane_mailer, QR_plane_mailer, PR_plane_mailer;
```

```
PQ_plane_mailer = g3_PQ_plane(mailer);
QR_plane_mailer = g3_QR_plane(mailer);
PR_plane_mailer = g3_PR_plane(mailer);
```

16.3   High-Level Primitives

In order to facilitate easier use and the possibility of heterogeneous parallel computers, *Zipcode* provides a mechanism to pack and unpack buffers and letters. Buffers are unstructured arrays of data provided by the user; they are applicable with buffer-oriented *Zipcode* commands. Letters are unstructured arrays of data provided by *Zipcode* based on user specification; they are tied to specific mail contexts and are dynamically allocated and freed.

Pack (gather) and unpack (scatter) are implemented with the use of Zip_Invoices. The analogy is taken from invoices or packing slips used to specify the contents of a postal package. An invoice informs *Zipcode* what variables are to be associated with a communication operation or communication buffer. This invoice is subsequently used when zip_pack() (zip_unpack()) is called to copy items from the variables specified into (out of) the communication buffer space to be sent (received); this implements gather-on-send- and scatter-on-receive-type semantics. In a heterogeneous environment, pack/unpacking will allow data conversions to take place without user intervention. Users who code with zip_pack()/zip_unpack() will have codes that are guaranteed to work in heterogeneous implementations of *Zipcode*.

16.3.1   Invoices

The zip_new_invoice() call creates new invoices:

```
voidzip_new_invoice(Zip\_invoice const char *format, va_list ap)
```

The call zip_new_invoice() creates an invoice (**inv), while taking a variable number of arguments, starting with a format string (**format**) similar to the commonly used **printf()** strings. The format string contains one or more conversion specifications. A conversion specification is introduced by a percent sign ("%") and is followed by:

- a positive integer indicating the number of items to convert, or a "*" or "&" indicating argument-list specification of an integer expression or address (see below). If no integer is specified the default is one item.

- an optional stride factor indicated by a "." followed by a positive integer indicating the stride; optionally a "*" or "&" may be specified, signifying argument-list specification of an integer expression or address (see below). If no stride is specified the default is one.

- an optional "-" character indicating that the indicated space is to be reserved but not packed (ignore-space option).

- a character specifying an internal type or a string indicating a user type.

For both the number of items to convert and stride, "*" or "&" can replace the hard-coded integer. If '*' is used, then the next argument in the argument list is used as an integer expression specifying the size of the conversion (or stride). Both the number of items to convert and the stride factor can be indirected by using "&" instead of an integer. The "&" indicates that a pointer to an integer should be stored, which will address the size of the invoice item (or stride) when it is packed. When "&" is used, the size is not evaluated immediately but is deferred until the actual packing of the data occurs. The "&" indirection consequently allows variable-size invoices to be constructed at runtime; we call this feature *deferred sizing*. The "*" allows the size of an invoice item (or stride) to be specified at run time.

One must be cautious of the scope of C variables when using "&." For example, it is improper to create an invoice in a subroutine that has a local variable as a stride factor and then attempt to pass this invoice out and use it elsewhere, since the stride factor points at a variable that is no longer in scope. Unpredictable things will happen if this is attempted.

The single character types that are supported are as follows:

"c" character,
"s" short,
"i" int,
"l" long,
"f" float, and
"d" double.

For each conversion specification, a pointer to an array of that type must be passed as an argument.

User-defined types may be added to the system to ease the packing of complicated data structures. An extra field (for passing whatever the user wants) may be passed to the conversion routines by adding "(*)" to the end of the user-type name. The "-" character can be used to skip space so that one can selectively push/pull things out of a letter. This allows for unpacking part of a letter and then unpacking the rest based on the part unpacked.

The following code would pack variable i followed by elements $0, 2, 4, \ldots 18$ of the double_array.

```
/* Example 1 */
ZIP_MAILER *mlr;
char *letter;
...

Zip_Invoice*invoice;
int i = 20;
double double_array[20];

zip_new_invoice(''*invoice,%i%10.2d'', &i, double_array);
...

/* use the invoice (see below) */
letter = zip_malloc(mlr, zip_sizeof_invoice(mlr, invoice));
length = zip_pack(mlr, invoice, ZIP_LETTER,
                  &letter, ZIP_IGNORE);

if(length == -1)        /* an error occurred */
    ...
```

The second example is a variant of the first. The first pack call is the same, while the second packs the first five elements of the double_array.

```
/* Example 2 */
int len = 10, stride = 2;
zip_new_invoice(''*invoice,%i%&.&d'', &i, &len, &stride,
                               double_array);

/* use the invoice */
letter = zip_malloc(mlr, zip_sizeof_invoice(mlr, invoice));
length = zip_pack(mlr, invoice, ZIP_LETTER, &letter,
```

```
                        ZIP_IGNORE);
    . . .
    len = 5;   /* set the length and stride for this use
                  of the invoice */
    stride = 1;

    /* use the invoice */
    letter = zip_malloc(mlr, zip_sizeof_invoice(mlr, invoice));
    length = zip_pack(mlr, invoice, ZIP_LETTER, &letter,
                      ZIP_IGNORE);
```

If a user-defined type `matrix` has been added to the system to pack matrix structures, then the following example shows how `matrix`-type data can be used in an invoice declaration. See also below on how to add a user-defined type.

```
    /* Example 3 */
    struct matrix M;   /* some user-defined type */
    int i;
    Extra extra; /* contains some special info on packing a  */
                 /* 'matrix'; often this will not be needed, */
                 /* but this feature is provided for */
                 /* flexibility */

    zip_new_invoice(''*invoice,%i%matrix(*)%20d'', &i, &M,
                    &extra, double_array);
```

At times it might be useful to know the size (in bytes) that is needed to hold the variables specified by an invoice. `zip_sizeof_invoice` returns the size (in bytes) that the invoice will occupy when packed. We have already used this in several examples above.

```
int zip_sizeof_invoice(ZIP_MAILER *mailer, Zip_Invoice *inv)
```

To delete an existing invoice when there is no more need for it use `zip_free_invoice()`:

```
    void zip_free_invoice(Zip_Invoice **inv)
```

This will free up the specified invoice and set `*inv = NULL` to help flag accidental access.

User-defined types for pack and unpack routines are defined using a registry mechanism provided by *Zipcode*.

```
int zip_register_invoice_type(char *name, Method *in, Method
                              *out, Method *len, Method *align)
```

The structure `Method` is a composite of a pointer-to-function, and additional state information for a function call. The details of `Method` declarations are beyond the scope of this presentation.

In the above, `name` is the user-defined name for the auxiliary type. User-defined names follow the ANSI standard for C identifiers. They begin with a nondigit (characters "A" through "Z," "a" through "z," and the underscore "_"), followed by one or more nondigits or digits. User-defined type names currently have global scope so beware of name conflicts. User-defined types cannot be the same as one of the built-in types specified above. The `in`, `out`, `len`, and `align` are the `Methods` used to pack/unpack the user-defined type. They must have the following parameter lists

```
    int in(ZIP_MAILER *mailer, void *src, void *dest,
                        int num_items, int stride,
                        Extra *extra)

    int out(ZIP_MAILER *mailer, void *src, void *dest,
                int num_items, int stride, Extra *extra)

    int align(ZIP_MAILER *mailer, void *dest, Extra *extra)

    int len(ZIP_MAILER *mailer, int num_items, int stride,
                Extra *extra)
```

Here, `src` is a pointer to the items to be converted and the `dest` parameter is a pointer to the space where converted items are stored. In addition, `num_items` is the number of items to be converted, `stride` is a stride factor for striding through arrays, and `extra` is used to pass any miscellaneous information that is needed by the conversion. The user can pass an extra using the '%user-type(*)' notation discussed in `zip_new_invoice`.

The `align` variable returns the number of bytes to be added to `dest` to align the value properly. The purpose of `len` is to return the total size of `num_items`, in bytes; the `in()` and `out()` functions perform the conversion.

Finally, to remove a user-defined type from the system use the

```
int zip_unregister_invoice_type(char *name)
```

call. Invoking `zip_unregister_invoice_type` deletes the entry for the named type, which cannot be used after this call has been made.

16.3.2 Packing and Unpacking

Packing is done when one wishes to copy the variables into the communications buffer space prior to transmission; to access the contents of a packed buffer, one must unpack it first.

```
int zip_pack(ZIP_MAILER *mailer, Zip_Invoice *inv,
                 int buffer_type, char **ptr, int len)
```

This command packs the invoice. The meaning of `buffer_type` is either "ZIP_BUFFER" or "ZIP_LETTER," indicating whether we are packing into a buffer (say for a combine or fanout) or a letter (for sends/receives).

If one is packing a buffer and has preallocated the buffer space, then `len` must be set to the size of this allocated buffer space. If the invoice is too large to fit in this buffer space, an error occurs. By specifying `*ptr = NULL` and `len = ZIP_IGNORE`, the pack routine will allocate the space for the buffer based on the size of the invoice to be packed. Alternatively, if a preallocated letter is being packed, then pack will fill in the letter by using the invoice. If the letter provided is not large enough, then an error will occur. If no preallocated letter is available, the pack routine can create one automatically, provided `*ptr = NULL`. Note that `len` is ignored when letters are involved, as the size of letters can be determined with `Zip_length()`; `len` should always be `ZIP_IGNORE` when packing letters. For either case, `zip_pack()` returns the number of bytes that the data from the invoice occupies in the communication space (letter or buffer).

To unpack a letter, use

```
int zip_unpack(ZIP_MAILER *mailer, Zip_Invoice *inv,
                 int buffer_type, char *ptr)
```

As in `zip_pack()`, `inv` is the invoice to unpack. The `buffer_type` parameter indicates the type of communication space being used; that is, whether we are unpacking a letter (`buffer_type = ZIP_LETTER`) or a buffer

(`buffer_type` = `ZIP_BUFFER`). The parameter `ptr` is a pointer to the communication space. Unlike `zip_pack()`, we pass a pointer to the communication space to `zip_unpack()`, not a pointer to a pointer. The communication space must be freed by the caller after it is unpacked.

16.3.3   The Packed-Message Functions

As may be apparent, many packs are followed almost immediately by sends, while corresponding receives are followed closely by unpacks. Not only is this notationally somewhat tedious, but it also limits the optimizations that can be done by *Zipcode*. To create a more flexible system, *Zipcode* provides the capability to do both the pack and communications in a single call. For instance,

```
g3_pack_send(ZIP_MAILER *g3mailer, int d1, d2, d3,
Zip_Invoice
     *invoice)
```

takes care of creating the letter, packing the invoice, and sending it to grid location specified by {`d1`,`d2`,`d3`}. Whenever possible, use pack_send-style routines, as they will generally be more run time optimizable than pack calls followed by send calls.

Packed versions of collective operations are also provided. Here is the specific syntax for the G2, two-dimensional-grid pack combine:

```
int g2_pack_combine(ZIP_MAILER *g2mlr, Zip_Invoice *invoice,
                    void (*func()) )
```

16.3.4   Fortran Interface

The Fortran (F77) interface is provided, but certain features have necessarily been omitted (awaiting Fortran 90). The syntax is different since there are no pointers in F77. There are no user-defined types provided in the Fortran interface as Fortran does not provide structures. Once Fortran 90 has been adopted, user-defined types will likely appear in the Fortran interface.

Since Fortran does not allow variable argument functions, the construction of invoices differs from that of the C interface. An invoice is built up over several function calls, each one specifying the next field in the invoice.

```
C       Example 1F
        integer mailer
```

```
      integer letter
      ...
      integer invoice
      integer i, length
      double double_array(20)

      call ZIP_INV_NEW(invoice)
      call ZIP_INV_ADD_INT(invoice, i, 1, 1, .false., .false.)
      call ZIP_INV_ADD_DBLE(invoice, double_array, 10, 2,
                            .false., .false.)

C     use the invoice
      CALL ZIP_SIZEOF_INVOICE(mailer, invoice, length)
      CALL YMALLOC(mailer, length, letter)
      CALL ZIP_PACK(mailer, invoice, ZIP_LETTER, letter,
                    ZIP_IGNORE, length)

   if(length .eq. -1) then
C     an error occurred
      ...
```

The above example packs the same invoice that Example 1 does in C. The last two arguments to ZIP_INV_ADD_INT() and ZIP_INV_ADD_DBLE() are the "ignore-space" and "deferred-sizing" logicals, respectively, to be explained via examples below. They also appear in the C syntax, but as part of the argument string via special characters.

```
C     Example 2F

      integer invoice
      integer i, len, stride
      DOUBLE double_array(20)

      i      = 20
      len    = 10
      stride =  2

      call ZIP_INV_NEW(invoice)
      call ZIP_INV_ADD_INT(invoice, i, 1, 1, .false.,
```

```
                               .false.)
C
C The .true. argument invokes deferred sizing of the data:
          call ZIP_INV_ADD_DBLE(invoice, double_array, len,
                                 stride, .false., .true.)

C         pack or unpack call is made...

          len    = 5
          stride = 1

C         pack or unpack call is made...
```

This example performs the same work the C Example 2 did. To ignore space in a pack or unpack call, the ignore-space logical is set true. For instance:

```
          call ZIP_INV_ADD_INT(invoice, 1, 1, .true., .false.)
```

To ignore space and use deferred-sizing evaluation, both flags are set true:

```
call ZIP_INV_ADD_INT(invoice, len, stride, .true., .true.)
```

Other *Zipcode* calls are very similar in Fortran to the C versions. A preprocessor is used to create some definitions for use by the Fortran programmer.

The following conventions are followed in the Fortran interface.

- No functions. This avoids some problems on various machines with returning C values to Fortran code. Return values from C routines are passed as an extra argument to the Fortran interface.

- All items that are pointers in C are declared in Fortran as type integer.

A few other minor changes appear because of case-sensitivity issues. See [Skjellum:92b] for the definitive list.

16.4   Details of Execution

In this section, we cover the initialization and termination protocols, and discuss how to get node processes spawned in the *Zipcode* model of multicomputer programming. Within this model, the user is not allowed to call CE/RK functions directly.

16.4.1 Initialization/Termination

Each host program and node program must call the appropriate initialization function to initialize *Zipcode* for their process:

```
int error = Zip_init(void);
            /* assume default mode for initialization */
    error = Zip_global_init(void);
            /* assume a simpler host-master model */
    void zip_exit(void);
            /* terminate Zipcode session */
```

16.4.2 Process Creation/Destruction

The basic mailer manipulation commands (such as `g1_grid_open()`) require the specification of process lists, currently as ordered pairs of nodes and process IDs packaged within a `ZIP_ADDRESSEES` structure. For application convenience, we supply optional commands to support the creation of such collections. One common collection is a *cohort*, a set of processes with the same process ID, distributed across a number of nodes. A cohort is often used to formulate a single-program, multiple-data (SPMD) calculation. Cohort list creation:

```
    ZIP_ADDRESSEES *addressees =
        zip_new_cohort(int N,
                /* number of processes involved */
                int node_bias,
                /* node number of zeroth entry in list */
                int cohort_pid,
                /* process ID of entire collection of processes */
                int host_flag);
                /* flags whether host process participates */
```

Additionally, we provide a *Zipcode*-level spawn mechanism:

```
    int result = zip_spawn(
                char *prog_name,
                /* ASCII name of program to spawn */
                ZIP_ADDRESSEES *addressees,
                /* addressee list to spawn */
                void *state,
```

```
/* future expansion */
int pm_flag);
/* flags if program is spawned on zeroth
   addressee */
```

where `result` is nonzero on failure. Most implementations require that this spawning function be effected in the host process, although the original CE/R system did not make this restriction. A compatible `zip_kill()` is also defined:

```
result = zip_kill(addressees);
```

With the addition of these functions, *Zipcode* specifies an entire programming environment that can be completely divorced, if desired, from its original foundations in the CE/RK. This is possible so long as one can emulate appropriate CE/RK functions for *Zipcode* to use. This has been accomplished in release 2.0 of nCUBE's 6400 system software, for instance.

16.5 Conclusions

Zipcode currently provides portable message-passing capability on a number of multicomputers. It also works on homogeneous networks of workstations and will soon be supported on heterogeneous networks and for heterogeneous multicomputers, when such systems are created. The key benefits of *Zipcode* are its ability to work over process lists designated by the user, to define separate contexts of communication so that message-passing complexity can be managed, and to allow different notations of message-passing appropriate to the concurrent algorithms being implemented. Tagged message passing is seen as a special case of the notations supported by *Zipcode*.

We see notational abstraction as helpful in dealing with issues of non-uniform memory access hierarchy and heterogeneity in multicomputers and distributed computers. Abstraction is a way to help *Zipcode* find additional runtime optimizations, rather than a tacit source of inefficiency. We believe that *Zipcode* implementations will be competitive in performance to tagged message systems whenever vendors make low-level access to their hardware and system calls available to us during our implementation phase.

Chapter 17

MOVIE — Multitasking Object-oriented Visual Interactive Environment

17.1 Introduction

17.1.1 The Beginning

The software system described here—*MOVIE* (Multitasking Object-oriented Visual Interactive Environment)—is the most sophisticated developed by C^3P. Indeed, it is sufficiently complicated that the project led by Wojtek Furmanski didn't finish the first prototype until two years after the end of C^3P and Furmanski's move to Syracuse. MOVIE is designed to address the general *compound* problem class introduced in Section 3.6 and illustrated in Chapter 18. Sections 17.3 and 17.2.10 describe current and potential MOVIE applications, and so provide an interesting discussion of many examples of this complex problem class. MOVIE is a new software system, integrating High Performance Computing (HPC) with the Open Systems standards for graphics and networking. The system was designed and prototyped by Furmanski at Caltech within the Caltech Concurrent Computation Program and it is currently in the advanced implementation stage at Northeast Parallel Architectures Center (NPAC), Syracuse University [Furmanski:93a]. The MOVIE System is structured as a multiserver network of interpreters of the high-level object-oriented programming language MovieScript. MovieScript derives from PostScript and extends it in the C++

syntax-based, object-oriented, interpreted style towards high-performance computing, three-dimensional graphics, and general-purpose high-level communication protocol for distributed and MIMD-parallel computing. The present paper describes the overall design of the system with the focus on the HPC component and it discusses in more detail one current application (Terrain Map Understanding) and one planned application area (Virtual Reality).

The concept of the MOVIE System emerged in a series of computational experiments with various software models and hardware environments, performed by Furmanski during the last few years. His attitude was that of a computational scientist who tries to find the shortest path towards a functional (HPC) environment which would be both dynamic enough to fully utilize the hardware and software technology advances and stable enough to support reusable programming, resulting in extendible, backward-compatible and integrable application software.

MOVIE concepts derive from the computational science research within C^3P, such as optimal communication [Fox:88h] and load-balancing [Fox:88e] algorithms for loosely synchronous problems and, in the application sector, matrix algebra [Furmanski:88b], neural network [Nelson:89a], and machine vision [Furmanski:88c] algorithms. As a next step, we started to develop the high-performance software environment for neural networks and machine vision and we realized that the full model in such areas must go beyond the regular HPC domain. New required components included dynamic interactive Graphical User Interfaces (GUI), support for irregular, dynamic computing which emerges, for example, in higher, AI-based layers of machine vision, and support for system integration in the heterogeneous computational model involving diverse components such as regular massively parallel image processing and irregular, symbolic expert system techniques. This complex structure—a "system of systems"—is typical of the compound problem class.

Furmanski's work decoupled therefore for some time from the main C^3P/NPAC thrust and, assuming tentatively that we "understand" the regular HPC components, he followed an independent exploratory route, making a series of computational experiments and identifying components of the "next-step" broader model for HPC, which would integrate all elements discussed above.

17.1.2 Towards the MOVIE System

The communication and load-balancing algorithms were implemented on Caltech/JPL hypercube Mark II. The need for interactive GUIs emerged for the first time during our work on parallel implementation of a neurophysiological model for olfactory cortex [Furmanski:87a] and, in the next, step, in the machine vision research [Furmanski:88c]. At that time (1988), we were using the nCUBE1 system at C^3P and also the "personal hypercube" system based on IBM AT under XENIX with the 4-node nCUBE1 add-on board. The graphics support in the latter environment was nonexistent and we constructed from scratch the GUI system based on the interpreted language g [Furmanski:88a], custom designed and coupled with the regular parallel computing software components. The language g was 80286 assembly-coded and XENIX kernel-based and hence very fast. However, it couldn't be ported anywhere beyond this environment, which clearly became obsolete before the g-based implementation work was even fully completed. Some design concepts and implementation techniques from this first experiment survived and are now part of the MOVIE System, but the major lesson learned was that GUIs for HPC must be based on portable graphics standards rather than on custom-made or vendor-specific models.

It was at about the same time (late 1980s) that the major multivendor effort started towards standardizing computer graphics in the UNIX environment. We were participating actively in this process, experimenting with subsequent models such as SunView, X10, X11, NeWS, XView, OpenLook, Motif, DPS, and finally PHIGS/PEX/GL. It was very difficult to build a stable graphics-intensive system for HPC during the period of the last four years, when the standardization efforts were competing with the vendor-specific customization efforts. However, certain generic concepts and required features of such a system gradually started to emerge in the course of my experiments with subsequent standard candidates.

For example, it became clear, with the onset of network-extensible server-based graphics models such as X or NeWS, that any solid HPC environment must include the distributing computing model as well and to unify it with the SIMD- and MIMD-parallel models. Also, to cope with portability issues in the emerging heterogeneous HPC environments, such a system must include appropriate high-level software abstraction layers, supporting Virtual Machine-based techniques. A network of compute servers, tightly/loosely coupled in MIMD-parallel/distributed mode, with each server following the high-level Virtual Machine design, appeared to be the natural overall software architecture. Modern software techniques such as preemptive multi-threading and object orientation are required to assure appropriate dynamics and functionality of such a server in diverse tasks involving graphics, computation, and communication. Among the emerging standards, the design closest to the above specification was offered by the NeWS (Network-extensible Window System) [Gosling:89a] server, developed by Sun. Following NeWS ideas, we adopted PostScript [Adobe:87a] syntax for the server language design, extending it appropriately to support object-oriented techniques and enhancing substantially its functionality towards the HPC domain.

The resulting system was called MOVIE, due both to its adequate acronym and its stress on the relevance of interactive graphics in the system design. The server language, integrating computation, graphics, and communication, was called MovieScript. The first implementation of the MOVIE Server was done at Caltech [Furmanski:89d] on a Sun workstation and then the system was ported to the DEC environment at Syracuse University [Furmanski:90b]. Here, we learned about virtual reality [Furmanski:91g] which we now consider the ultimate GUI model for MOVIE, "closing" the system design. In the fall of 1991, the MOVIE group was formed and the "individual researcher" period of the system development is now followed by the team development period [Furmanski:93a].

17.1.3 Current Status and Outlook

Currently, MOVIE is in the advanced design and development process, organized as a sequence of internal prereleases of the system code and documentation. At the time of preparing this document (April 1992), MOVIE 0.4 has been released internally at NPAC. The associated technical documentation now contains manual drafts [Furmanski:92a;92b] and some 25 internal reports (about 700 pages total). The current total size of the MOVIE code, including source, binaries, and custom CASE tools, is on the order of 40 Mb. Both documentation and code will evolve during the next months towards the first external release MOVIE 1.0, planned for the fall 1993. MOVIE 1.0 will be associated with the set of reference/programming manual pairs for all basic system components, discussed later in this paper (MetaShell, MOVIE Server, MovieScript). Starting from MOVIE 1.0, we intend to provide user support, assure backward compatibility, and initiate a series of MOVIE application projects.

This paper discusses the MOVIE System and is considered as a summary of the design and prototype development stage (Section 17.2). It also contains a brief description of the current status and the planned near-term applications. A more complete description can be found in [Furmanski:93a] (see also [Furmanski:93b;93d] for recent overview reports). Here we concentrate on one current application—Terrain Map Understanding (Section 17.3) (see also [Cheng:92a]) and on one planned application area—virtual reality (Section 17.4) (see [Furmanski:92g] for an overview and [Furmanski:93c;93e;93f] for the current status).

17.2 System Overview

17.2.1 The MOVIE System in a Nutshell

MOVIE System is a network of MOVIE servers. MOVIE Server is an interpreter of MovieScript. MovieScript is a high-level object-oriented programming language derived from PostScript. PostScript is embedded in the larger language model of MovieScript. This includes new types and operators as well as syntax extension towards the C++ style object-oriented model with dynamic binding and multiple inheritance. MOVIE Server is based on the custom-made high-performance MovieScript interpreter. Some design concepts of MovieScript are inherited from the NeWS model developed by Sun. C-shell-based CASE tools are constructed for automated server language extension. MOVIE 1.0 will offer uniform MovieScript interface to all major components of the Open Systems software such as X/Motif/OpenLook, DPS/NeWS, PEX/GL, UNIX socket library-based networking, and Fortran90-style index-free matrix algebra. Subsequent releases will build on top of these standards and extend the model by more advanced modules such as database management, expert systems and virtual reality. The language extensibility model is based on the concept of *inheritance forest*, which allows us to enlarge both the functional and object-oriented components of MovieScript, both in the system and application sector and at the compiled and interpreted level. The default development model for MOVIE applications is based on MovieScript programming. System integration tools are also provided which allow to incorporate third-party software into the system and to structure it as suitable language extensions. Integrated visualization model is provided, unifying two-dimensional pixel and vector graphics, three-dimensional graphics, and GUI toolkits. Interfaces to AVS-style dataflow-based visualization servers are also provided. MOVIE Server is a single C program, single UNIX process, and single X client. The server dynamics are governed by preemptive multithreading with real-time support. Threads, which are MovieScript light-weighted processes, compute by interpreting MovieScript and communicate by sending/receiving MovieScript. A uniform model for networking and message passing is provided. Various forms of concurrency can be naturally implemented in MOVIE, such as single-server multitasking or multiserver networks for MIMD-parallel or heterogeneous distributed computing. Multiserver systems of multithreading language interpreters offer a novel approach to parallel processing, integrating data-parallel and dynamic, irregular components. Due to such system features as rapid prototyping, extensibility, modularity, and "in large" programming model, MOVIE lends itself to building large, modern software applications of the compound or metaproblem class.

17.2.2   MovieScript as Virtual Machine Language

The server design, summarized in the previous section, can be conveniently formulated in terms of a Virtual Machine (VM) model. Our goal in MOVIE is to provide a uniform integration and development platform for diverse hardware architectures and software models. The natural strategy is to enforce homogeneity in such a heterogeneous collection by constructing an abstract software layer, implementing the VM "assembler" such that diverse software components are mapped on a consistent VM "instruction set" and diverse hardware architectures follow a uniform VM "processor" model.

Our initial hardware focus is a UNIX workstation and the target software volume is provided by the present set of Open Systems standards. This includes subsystems such as X for windowing, Motif/OpenLook for XtIntrinsics-based GUI toolkits, DPS/NeWS for PostScript graphics, PEX/GL for network-extensible three-dimensional graphics, AVS/Explorer-style dataflow-based visualization models, and C/C++ and Fortran77/Fortran90 as the major low-level programming languages. In the next stage, this environment will be extended by more advanced software models such as database management systems, expert systems, virtual reality operating shells, and so on. Massively parallel systems are considered in this approach as the "special hardware" extensions and will be discussed in the next sections.

The concept of Open Systems is to enforce interoperability among various vendors, but in practice the standardization efforts are often accompanied by the vendor-specific customization, driven by the marketing mechanisms. Examples include competing GUI toolkits such as Motif and OpenLook or three-dimensional graphics protocols such as PEX or GL. There are also deficiencies of the current integration models within the single-vendor software volume. The only currently existing fully consistent integration platform for the Open Systems software is provided at the level of the C programming language. However, C is not suitable for "in large" programming due to lack of rapid prototyping and "impedance mismatch" [Bancilhon:88a], generated by C interfaces to dedicated modules based on higher level languages (e.g., SQL-based DBMSs or PostScript-based vector graphics servers). In the HPC domain, the current standardization efforts are Fortran-based, which is an even less adequate language model for compound problems. In consequence, there is now an urgent need for the vendor-independent high-level integration platform of the VM type for the growing volume of the standard Open Systems software, also capable of incorporating the HPC component into the model. MOVIE System can be considered an attempt in this direction.

The choice of PostScript as the integration language represents a natural and in some sense unique minimal solution. A stack-based model, PostScript lends itself ideally as a Virtual Machine "assembler." An interpreted high-level extensible model, it provides natural rapid prototyping capabilities. A Turing-equivalent model, it provides an effective integration factor between code and data and hence between computation and communication. Finally, the graphics model of PostScript is already a de facto standard for electronic printing/imaging and part of the Open Systems software in the form of DPS/NeWS servers.

The concept of the multithreading programmable server based on extended PostScript derives from the NeWS (Network-extensible Window System) server [Gosling:89a], developed by Sun in the late 1980s. The seminal ideas of NeWS for client-server-based device-independent windowing are substantially extended in MOVIE towards multiserver-based, Open System-conforming, device-independent, high-performance distributed computing.

Within the VM model, the C code for the MOVIE Server can be viewed as "hardware" material used to build the virtual processor. The MOVIE Server illustrated in Figure 17.1 is a virtual processor and MovieScript plays the role of virtual assembler. Continuing the VR analogy, we can consider MovieScript objects as VM "words" and the physical memory storing the content of objects as the VM "registers." VM "programs", and so on, MovieScript ASCII files, are typically stored on disks, which play the role of VM memory.

The MovieScript "machine word" or object handle is represented as a 64-bit-long C structure, referred to as *item*, composed of a 32-bit-long tag field and a 32-bit-long value field. The tag field decomposes into a 16-bit-long

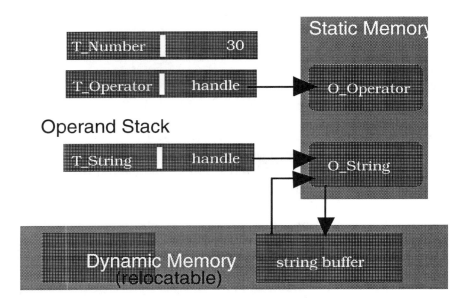

Figure 17.1: Elements of the MOVIE Server Virtual Machine Involved in Executing the Script { **30 string** }. The number**30** is represented as an atomic item with the *T_Number* tag, *FMT_Integer* mask ON in the status flag vector, and with the value field = 30. The operator **string** is represented as a static composite item with the value field pointing to the header which is given by the object structure *O_Operator*, stored in the static memory and containing the specific execution instruction—in this case a pointer to the appropriate C method. As a result of this method of execution, the item **30** is popped and the string object is created and pushed on the operand stack. String object is represented as a dynamic composite item with the value field pointing to the *O_String* header. The header contains object attributes such as, string length value, whereas the string character buffer is stored in the dynamic memory.

object identifier field and a 16-bit-long status flag vector. The value field contains either the object value for atomic types (such as numbers) or the object pointer for composite types (such as strings or arrays). MovieScript array objects and stacks are implemented as vectors of items. Composite objects are handled by the custom Memory Manager. Each composite object contains the header with object attributes and (optionally) the data buffer. MOVIE memory consists of two sectors—*static* and *dynamic*—each implemented as a linked list of contiguous segments. Headers/buffers are located in static/dynamic memory. Static memory pointers are "physical" (time-independent), whereas buffers in the dynamic memory can be dynamically relocated by the heap fragmentation handler. Headers are assumed to be "small" (i.e., of fixed maximal size, much smaller than the memory segment size) and hence the static memory is assumed to never fragment in the nonrecoverable fashion.

The persistence of the memory objects is controlled by the reference count mechanism. Buffer relocation is controlled by the lock counter. Each reference to the object buffer must be preceded/followed by the appropriate *open/close* commands which increment/decrement the lock count. Only the buffers with zero lock count are relocated during the heap compaction process. Item, header, and buffer components of an object are represented by three separate chunks of physical memory. The connectivity is provided by three pointers: item points to the header, header points to the buffer, and buffer points back to the header (the last pointer is used during the heap compaction).

The inner loop of the interpreter is organized as a large C switch with the case values given by the identifier fields of the object items. Some performance-critical primitive operators are built into the inner loop as explicit switch cases, while others are implemented as C functions or MovieScript procedures. Convenient CASE tools are constructed for automatic insertion of new primitives into the inner loop switch.

A single cycle of the interpreter contains the following steps: Check the software interrupt vector, take the next object from the execution stack, push it on the operand stack (if the object is literal), or jump to the switch case, given by the object identifier (if the object is executable). The interrupt vector is used to handle the system-clock-based requests such as thread switching, event handling, or network services, as well as the user requests such as debugging, monitoring, and so on.

Both the MOVIE memory and the inner loop of the interpreter are performance-optimized and supported by internal caches, for example, to speedup the systemdict requests or small object creation. MOVIE Server is faster than NeWS or DPS servers in most basic operations such as control flow or arithmetic, often by a factor two or more.

17.2.3 Data-Parallel Computing

A currently popular approach to portable data-parallel computing is based on the Fortran90 model, which extends the scalar arithmetic of Fortran77 towards the index-free matrix arithmetic. This concept, originally implemented as CM Fortran by TMC on CM-2, is now extended as in Chapter 13 in the form of Fortran90D and High Performance Fortran model towards the MIMD-parallel systems as well.

The Fortran90-based data-parallel model allows us to treat massively parallel machines as superfast mathematical co-processors/accelerators for matrix operations. The details of the parallel hardware architecture and even its existence are transparent to the Fortran programmer. Good programming practice is simply to minimize explicit loops and index manipulations and to maximize the use of matrices and index-free matrix arithmetic, optionally supported by the compiler directives to optimize data decompositions. The resultant product is a metaproblem programming system having as its core, for synchronous and loosely synchronous problems, an *interpreter* of High Performance Fortran.

The index-free vector/matrix algebra constructs appear in various languages, starting from the historically first APL model [Brown:88b]. Also, database query languages such as SQL can be viewed as vector models, operating on table components such as rows or columns. In interpreted languages, vector operations are useful also in sequential implementations since they allow reduction of the interpreter overhead. For example, scalar arithmetic in MovieScript is slower by a factor of five or more than the C arithmetic—the C-coded interpreter performs the actual arithmetical operation and additionally a few control and stack manipulation operations. The absolute value of such overhead is similar for scalar and vector operands and hence it becomes relatively negligible with the increasing vector size.

In MovieScript, the numerical computing is implemented in terms of the following types: *number*, *record*, and *field*. MovieScript numbers extend the PostScript model by adding the formatted numbers such as *Char*, *Short*, *Double*, *Complex*, and so on. The original PostScript arithmetic preserves value (e.g., an integer result is converted to real in case of overflow), whereas the extended formatted arithmetic preserves format as in the C language.

Record is the interpreted abstraction of the C language structure. The MovieScript interface is similar to that for dictionary objects. The memory layout of the record buffer coincides with the C language layout of the corresponding structure. This feature is C compiler-dependent and it is parametrized in the MOVIE Server code in terms of a few typical alignment models, covering all currently popular 32-bit processors.

Field is an n-dimensional array of numbers, records, or object handles. All scalar arithmetic operators are polymorphically extended to the field domain in a way similar to Fortran90. This basic set of field operators is then further expanded to provide vectorial support for domains such as imaging, neural nets, databases, and so on.

Images are represented as two-dimensional fields of bytes, and the image-processing algorithms can typically be reduced to the appropriate field algebra. Since the interpreter overhead is negligible for large fields, MovieScript offers natural rapid prototyping tools for experimentation with the image-processing algorithms and with other regular computational domains such as PDEs or neural networks.

A table in the relational database can be represented as a one-dimensional field of records, with the record elements used as column labels. Most of the basic SQL commands can be expressed again in terms of the suitably extended field algebra operators.

PostScript syntax provides flexible language tools for manipulating field objects and it facilitates operations such as constructing regions (object-oriented version of sections in Fortran90) or building multi-dimensional fields. The MovieScript **field** operator creates an instance of the field type. For example,

/image Byte [256 512] field def

creates a 256×512 image (array of bytes) and

/cube Bit [10 { 2 } repeat] field def

creates a 10-dimensional binary hypercube. Regions are created by the **ptr** operator. For example,

/p image [[0 2 $] [1 2 $]] ptr def

creates a "checkerboard pattern" pointer **p**, and

/c image [[1[ ]1] [1[ ]1]] ptr def

creates the "central region" pointer **c** containing the original image excluding the one-pixel wide boundaries. Pointers can be moved by the **move** operator, for example, one can move the central pointer **c** to the right by one pixel as follows:

/r c [1 0] move def.

To act with the Laplace operator on the original image, we construct the right, left, up, and down shifts as above, denoted by **r**, **l**, **u**, **d**. We store the content of **c** in the temporary field **t** and then we perform the following data-parallel arithmetic operation:

t 4 mul [r l u d] { sub } forall,

which is equivalent to the set of scalar arithmetic operations $t = 4 * c - \{l + r + u + d\}$ for each pixel in t.

The above examples illustrate the way new components of MovieScript are cooperating with the existing PostScript constructs. For example, we use literal PostScript arrays to define grid pointers and we extend polymorphic PostScript operators such as mul or sub to the field domain. New operators such as ptr are also polymorphic; for example, a two-dimensional region can be pointed to by either a two-element array or a two-component field, and so on. Array objects used as pointers can also be manipulated by appropriate language tools (e.g., they can be generated in the run time, concatenated, superposed, and so on), which provides flexibility in handling more complex matrix operations.

All section operations from the Fortran90 model are supported and appropriately encoded in terms of literal array pointers. Some of the resulting regions, such as rows, columns, scattered or contiguous windows, and so on, are shown in Figure 17.2. Furthermore, there is nothing special about rectangular regions in the Postscript model, which is armed with the vector graphics operators. Hence, the ptr operator can also be polymorphically extended to select arbitrary irregular regions, such as illustrated in Figure 17.2—for example, by allowing the PostScript path as a valid pointer object argument. This is a simple example of the uniform high-level design which crosses the boundaries of matrix algebra and graphics. Another example is provided by allowing the PostScript vector (and hence data-parallel) drawing operators to act on field objects. A diagonal two-dimensional array

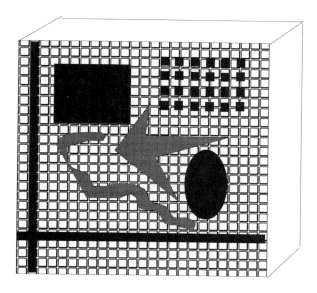

Figure 17.2: Some Data-Parallel Pointers in the MovieScript Model, Created by the `ptr` Operator. Row, column, contiguous, and scattered rectangle correspond to various Fortran90 style sections, here appropriately encoded as grid pointers in terms of literal array objects. Other irregular regions in the figure can be generated by using the corresponding PostScript graphics path objects as arguments of the `ptr` operator. The n-dim grid pointer is given as an n-element array of 1–dim axis pointers. Axis pointers are given by numbers or arrays. A number pointer selects the corresponding single element along the axis and the 1, 2, or 3-element array selects 1–dim region. If all elements of such an array are numbers, they are interpreted as *min, step,* and *max* offset values. If one (central) element is an array itself, the other elements are interpreted as the left/right margins and the array corresponds to the axis interior and is interpreted recursively according to the above rules. Special convenience symbols $ and [ ] stand for "infinity" and "full span."

can then be constructed, for example, by "drawing" a diagonal line across the corresponding field "canvas."

Unlike the Fortran90 model where the arithmetic is part of the syntax design, there is nothing special about the arithmetic operators such as `mul` or `add` in MovieScript. New, more specialized and/or more complex regular field operators can be smoothly added to the design, extending the index-free arithmetic and supporting computational domains such as signal processing, neural networks, databases, and so on.

The implementation of data-parallel operations in MovieScript is clearly hardware-dependent. The regular, grid-based component of the design is functionally equivalent to Fortran90 and its implementation can directly benefit from the existing or forthcoming parallel Fortran support. Some more specialized operators can in fact be difficult or impractical to implement on particular systems, such as, for example, data-parallel PostScript drawing on some SIMD-parallel processor arrays. In such cases, only the restricted regular subset of the language will be supported. The main strength of the concurrent MOVIE model is in the domain of MIMD-parallel computing discussed below.

17.2.4   Model for MIMD-parallelism

The MIMD MOVIE model is illustrated in Figure 17.3. Basically, MOVIE Server plays the role of the general purpose node program or, rather, node operating shell. The MovieScript-based communication model is constructed on top of the compiled language-based communication library, provided either directly by the hardware vendor or by one of the portable low-level models such as the commercial Express package [ParaSoft:88a] or the public domain PICL package [Geist:90b] described in Chapters 5 and 16. The MIMD operation of MOVIE can both support the asynchronous problem class and mimic the message-passing model for loosely synchronous applications.

The interesting features of such a model stem from the multithreading character of the node program. The MIMD mesh of node servers can be configured either in the fully asynchronous or the regular mode. Various intermediate and/or mixed modes are also possible and useful. The default mode is asynchronous—each server maintains its own thread queue, executing individual thread programs and serving the communication requests according to the software-clock-based preemptive scheduling model. The system operation in this mode is similar to the distributed computing model

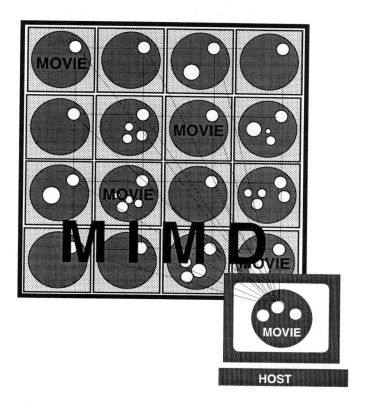

Figure 17.3: Elements of the MIMD MOVIE Model. Each node runs asynchronously an identical, independent copy of the multithreading MOVIE Server, interpreting (a priori distinct) node MovieScript programs and communicating with other modes via MovieScript messages. Regular and irregular components can be time-shared as illustrated in the figure. A single unique thread has been selected in each node (the one in the upper right corner) for regular processing and the other threads are participating in some independent or related irregular tasks. The regular thread processing is based on the "MovieScript + message passing" model, that is, all node programs are given by the same code which depends only parametrically on the node number. The mesh of regular threads is mapped on a single host thread which can be considered, for example, as a matrix algebra accelerator "board" within some sequential or distributed Virtual Machine model, involving the host server.

and is discussed in more detail in Section 17.2.5.

The simplest way to enforce the regular mode is by retaining only one thread in each node server and by following the conventional "MovieScript + message passing" loosely synchronous programming techniques. A more advanced, but also often more useful configuration is when the regular and asynchronous modes are time-shared. This is illustrated in Figure 17.3, where a unique thread has been selected in each node to implement some regular algorithm and all other threads are involved in some irregular processing. The communication messages are thread-specific and hence the regular component is processed in a transparent way, without any conflicts with the irregular traffic. MovieScript scheduling is programmable and hence the system can adjust and control dynamically the time slices assigned to individual components.

The code development process for multicomponent algorithms factorizes into modular programs for individual threads or groups. In consequence, all techniques such as optimal regular communication or matrix algebra algorithms, constructed previously in compiled models (see, e.g., [Fox:88h], [Furmanski:88b]), can be easily reconstructed in MovieScript and organized as appropriate language extension.

A natural next step is to construct the Fortran90-style matrix algebra by using the physical communication layer and the already existing single node support in terms of the field objects now playing the role of node sections of the domain-decomposed global fields. Such construction represents the run-time interpreted version of the High Performance Fortran (Fortran90D) model [Fox:91e]. Compiler directives are replaced by "interpreter directives," that is, MovieScript tools for data decomposition which can be employed in the dynamic real-time mode. Various interface models to the compiled Fortran90D environment can also be constructed. Furthermore, since arithmetic doesn't play any special role in the MovieScript syntax, the matrix algebra model can be naturally further extended by new, more complex and specialized regular operators, emerging in the application areas such as image processing, neural networks, and so on.

The advantage of the concurrent multithreading model is that the regular sector can be time-shared with the dynamic, irregular algorithms. The need for such configurations appears in complex applications such as machine vision, Command and Control, or virtual reality where the massively parallel regular algorithms (early vision, signal processing, rendering) are to be time-shared and often coupled by pipelines or feedback loops with the irregular components (AI, event-driven, geometry modeling).

Such problems can hardly be handled exclusively in the data-parallel, Fortran90-style model. The conventional, more versatile but less portable "Fortran77 or C + message-passing" techniques can be used, but then one effectively starts building the custom multithreading server for each large multicomponent application. In the MIMD MOVIE model, we reverse this process by first constructing the general-purpose multithreading services, organized as the user-extensible node operating shell.

Many other interesting features emerge in such a model. High-level Post-Script messages can be dynamically created and destroyed. Dynamic point-like debugging and monitoring can be realized in a straightforward way at any time instance by sending an appropriate query script to the selected node. Longer chunks of the regular MovieScript code can be stored in a distributed fashion and broadcast only when synchronously invoked, that is, one can work with both distributed data and code. Static load-balancing and resource allocation techniques developed for compiled models (see, e.g., [Fox:88e;88tt;88uu]) apply, and can be significantly enhanced by new dynamic algorithms, utilizing the thread mobility features in the distributed MovieScript environment.

17.2.5 Distributed Computing

Distributed computing is the most natural environment for the MOVIE System. The communication model for MOVIE networks is based on one simple principle, uniform for distributed and MIMD-parallel architectures: nodes of such network communicate by sending MovieScript. This model unifies communication and computation: Computing in MOVIE is when a server interprets MovieScript, whereas communication occurs when a server sends MovieScript to be interpreted by another server on the network.

Social human activities provide adequate analogies here. One can think of MOVIE network as a society of autonomous intelligent agents, capable of internal information processing and of information exchange, both organized in terms of the same high-level language structures. The processing capabilities of such a system are in principle unlimited. Detailed programming paradigms for distributed computing are not specified initially at the MovieScript level and can be freely selected depending on the application needs. Successful computation/communication patterns with some reusability potential can then be retained within the system in the form of appropriate MovieScript extensions.

The MovieScript-based user-level model for MOVIE networks is uniform, elegant, and appealing. Its detailed technical implementation, however, is a complex task. Communication services must be included at the lowermost level of the inner loop of the MovieScript interpreter and coordinated with scheduling, event handling, software interrupts, and other dynamic components of the server. Also, when building interfaces to existing Open Systems components, we have to cope with various existing network and message-passing protocols. In the networking domain, we use the UNIX socket library as the base-C-level platform, but then the question arises of how to handle higher protocols such as NFS, RPC, XDR and a variety of recent "open" models (see, e.g. Figure 17.4). Similar uncertainties arise in handling and integrating various message-passing protocols for MIMD-parallel computing.

Since the consistent implementation of the MovieScript-based communication is one of the most complex tasks in the MOVIE development process, we adopted the following evolutionary and self-supporting approach. The system design was started in the single-node, single-thread configuration. The notion of multithreading was built into the design from the beginning by adopting consistent thread-relative addressing modes. In consequence, the detailed model for scheduling, networking, and message passing factorized as an independent sector of MovieScript and it was initially postponed. The base interpreter loop was developed first. In the next stage, we constructed the field algebra for regular matrix processing, interpreted object-oriented model with rapid prototyping capabilities and graphics/visualization/windowing layers with the focus on interpreted GUI interfaces.

These layers are currently in the mature stage and they can now be used to provide GUI support for prototyping multithreading distributed MOVIE networks, starting with the regular modules for concurrent matrix algebra and signal processing. The current status of the design and implementation work on scheduling, networking and message passing is described in [Niemiec:92a], [Niemiec:92b] and [Furmanski:93a].

17.2.6   Object Orientation

Most of the MovieScript components discussed so far, such as Fortran90-style matrix algebra or communication, are implemented in terms of extended sets of Postscript types and operators. In the area of data-parallel computing, based on a finite set of generic operations, the distinction between language models such as Fortran, C, C++, Lisp, or PostScript is largely a matter of

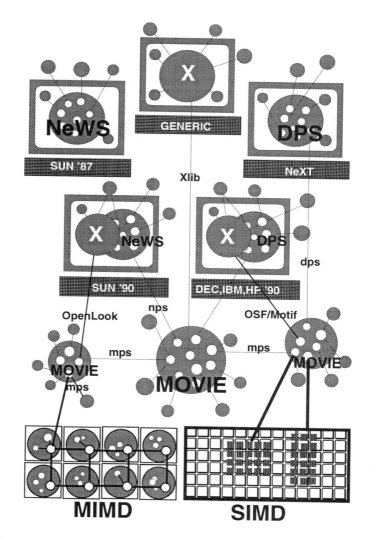

Figure 17.4: An Example of the Distributed MOVIE Environment. The figure illustrates various network-extensible graphics protocols used in implementing the uniform high-level MovieScript protocol. We denote by *mps*, *nps*, and *dps*, respectively, the MOVIE, NeWS, and Display PostScript protocols. MOVIE servers communicate directly via *mps*, whereas MovieScript messages sent to NeWS/DPS/X servers are internally translated by the MOVIE server to the remote server-specific protocols.

taste. However, with the growing structural complexity of a given domain, typically associated with irregular, dynamic computational complexity, both the compiled imperative languages such as Fortran or C/C++ as well as the interpreted functional languages such as Lisp of PostScript become impractical. The best techniques invented so far to handle such complex problems are provided by the interpretive object-oriented models.

MovieScript extends PostScript by the full object-oriented sector with all "orthodox" components such as polymorphism, encapsulation, data abstraction, dynamic binding, and multiple inheritance. This extension process is organized structurally in the form of a two-dimensional inheritance forest which provides a novel design platform for integrating functional and object-oriented language structures.

All the original PostScript types such as *array*, *string*, *dict*, and so on. are retained and included in the topmost "horizontal" layer of *primitive types* in MovieScript. This layer is further extended by new computation, graphics, and communication primitives. The design objectives of this language sector are optimized performance, structural simplicity, and enforced polymorphism of the operator set. The group of primitive types within the inheritance forest plays the role of the root class in conventional object-oriented models.

At the same time, the PostScript syntax itself is also extended within the MovieScript design to support the C++-style, "true" object-oriented model with dynamic binding and multiple inheritance. The *derived types*, constructed via the inheritance mechanism starting from the primitive functional types, extend the inheritance forest in the "vertical" direction towards more composite, complex, and abstract language structures. A finite set of primitive types is constructed in C and hardwired into the server design. Other primitive types and all derived types are constructed at run time at the interpreted level. Some elements of the inheritance forest model are illustrated in Figure 17.5.

The integration of the PostScript-style functional layer with the C++-style object-oriented layer, as well as the "in large" extensibility model which defines a suitable balance between both layers, are considered distinctive features of MovieScript. The idea is to encapsulate the structural complexity in the form of methods for derived types and to maintain a finite set of maximally polymorphic operators in the functional sector. The resulting organization is similar to the way complexity is handled by natural languages and human practices. The world is described by a large number of "things" (objects, words) and a relatively small number of "rules" (polymorphic op-

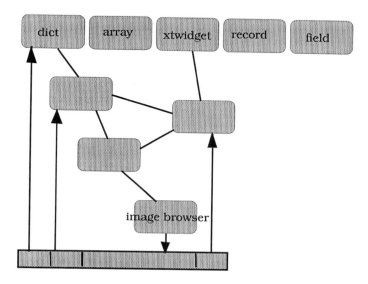

Figure 17.5: Elements of the Inheritance Forest Model. The upper horizontal axis represents primitive MovieScript types such as *dict, array, xtwidget,* and so on. The forest of derived types extends down and follows the multiple inheritance model. Closed loops in the inheritance network are allowed and resolved by maintaining only a single copy of a degenerate superinstance. The figure illustrates the *image browser* class which can be thought of as being both a dictionary (of image names) and a widget (such as a selection list). An instance of a derived type is represented by a noncontiguous collection of superinstance headers and buffers, with each buffer maintaining a list of pointers to its superinstance headers, as illustrated in the figure.

erators, relations). We could define "common English" as a set of rules and
a very restricted subset of objects. The "expert English" dialects are constructed by extending the vocabulary by more specialized and/or abstract
objects with complex methods and inheritance patterns. The process of
building expert extensions is graded and consistent with the human learning
process.

Our claim is that the good "in large" computer language design should
contain a nontrivial "common English" part, useful by itself for a broad
set of generic tasks, and it should offer a graded, multiscale extensibility
model towards specialized expert dialects. Indeed, we program by building
reusable associations between software entities and names. Each "in large"
programming model unavoidably contains a large number of names. The
disciplined and structured process of naming software entities is crucial for
successful complexity control. In languages such as C or Fortran, the "common English" part is reduced to arithmetic and simple control structures
such as *if*, *for*, *switch*, and so on. All other names are simply mapped on
a huge and ever-growing linear chain of library functions. The original language syntax, based on mathematics notation, degenerates towards a poorly
organized functional programming style. "In large" programming in such
languages becomes very complex.

More abstract models such as functional, object-oriented and dataflow
modular programming are more useful, but there are usually some structure
versus function trade-offs in the individual language designs and the optimal
choice for "in large" model is all but obvious. A few examples of various
language models are sketched in Figure 17.6. In our approach, we consider
the object-oriented techniques as the best available tool for building expert
extensions (with the expert knowledge encapsulated in methods) and the
functional model of PostScript as the best way of encoding the common
part of the language. PostScript operators play the role of rules and Postscript primitive types represent the common vocabulary. Inheritance forest
of MovieScript allows for smooth transition from common to expert types.

The complexity of "expert English" is encapsulated in methods for derived types, and general-purpose functionality of "common English" is exposed in terms of restricted set of polymorphic operators, processing objects
of all granularities. A multiscale language development model, supported by
such organization, is discussed in Section 17.2.8.

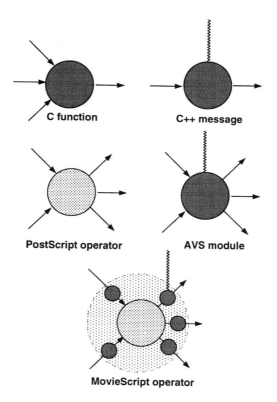

Figure 17.6: Computational Vertices in Various Language Models. Solid arrows indicate input/output arguments or objects. Wavy lines indicate messages sent to objects. Dark blobs represent nonsyntactic components of the language. Light blobs represent polymorphic operators, considered as syntactic identifiers/keywords. Among the models illustrated in the figure, we consider MovieScript organization of computational vertices as most adequate for "in large" programming. C, AVS, and PostScript have a poor encapsulation model. C and C++ are not convenient for dynamic dataflow programming as they don't offer any universal mechanism for multi-object/argument output. MovieScript vertices are constructed by superposition of the C++ style encapsulation model and PostScript-style multiobject interaction model. Large MovieScript operators are functionally similar to AVS modules but they follow a multiscale structural design which enforces software economy and reusability.

17.2.7   Integrated Visualization Model

Support for graphics is currently the most elaborate sector of the Open Systems software. It is also the sector which varied most vigorously during last years. The current standard environment, based on a collection of subsystems such as X, Motif/OpenLook, PHIGS/PEX/GL, and AVS/Explorer, offers broad functionality and diversity of visualization tools, but it is still difficult to use in application programming. The associated C libraries are huge and the C-language-based development and integration model generates severe compilation/linking time bottleneck. The most extreme case is the PHIGS library, which is on an order of 8 Mb and generates binaries of that size even for modest three-dimensional graphics applications. Furthermore, the competing subsystems, grouped in the list above—for example, Motif and OpenLook—are typically available only in exclusive mode on a particular hardware platform and hence the associated C language application codes are nonportable.

DPS/NeWS

Our approach in MOVIE is to design an integrated MovieScript-based model for graphics, GUIs and visualization. We adopt the original PostScript model for scalable two-dimensional graphics as defined in [Adobe:87a] and we extend it by including other graphics subsystems. Even in the PostScript domain, however, we face uncertainties due to competing models offered by the DPS server from Adobe Systems, Inc. and the NeWS server from Sun. Since none of these Postscript extension models is complete (e.g., none offers the model for three-dimensional graphics), we don't follow any of them in building the MovieScript extension. Only the intersection of both models, given by the original PostScript model for printers, is adopted "as is" in MOVIE, and we build custom extensions towards windowing and event handling, compatible with other Open Systems components. The conflicting extension models of DPS and NeWS are not part of the MovieScript design but these language sectors can be accessed from the MovieScript code since the MOVIE→DPS/NeWS interface model supports programmability of remote PostScript servers.

Remote PostScript devices such as NeWS or DPS servers are accessed from the MovieScript code by the operators gop and gdef. The syntax of gop is the following:

$$key \ \#_{in} \ code \ \#_{out} \ \textbf{gop} \ \Rightarrow \ key \ rop$$

where *key* is the literal name, $\#_{in}$ and $\#_{out}$ are numbers, *code* is a MovieScript object capable of defining some remote PostScript code, and *rop* is the MovieScript operator (with the prefix "r" standing for "remote"). Here, gop installs the user-defined graphics operator (implemented as a PostScript procedure) in the remote PostScript server and it also creates the local MovieScript operator *rop* associated with this remote operator. Both local and remote operators are associated with the common name, specified by *key*. The code object can be a MovieScript procedure or string. The execution of *rop* consists of sending $\#_{in}$ arguments from the MOVIE operand stack to the NeWS/DPS operand stack, executing remote procedure in NeWS/DPS, associated with *key* and previously installed in NeWS/DPS by gop, finally transporting back $\#_{out}$ output objects from NeWS/DPS to MOVIE.

The associated gdef operator is simply a sequence: { gop def }, that is, it installs *rop* in the local dictionary under the name *key*. In other words, the action of gdef is fully symmetric on local (MOVIE) and remote (NeWS/DPS) servers. The gop output format can be used to handle *rop* differently—for example, by installing it as an instance method within the MovieScript class model.

MovieScript support is also provided to control the connection status and buffering modes along the PostScript-based communication lines.

The interface model described above was developed first for the NeWS server [Furmanski:92d], and it is now ported to DPS [Podgorny:92b].

X/Motif/OpenLook

MovieScript windowing is constructed by building the interface to the XtIntrinsics-based GUI toolkits. The generic interface model is constructed and so far explicitly implemented for Motif [Furmanski:92e]. The OpenLook implementation is in progress. Mechanisms are provided for combining various toolkit components into the global GUI toolkit. The minimal set of components consists of the XtIntrinsics subtree provided by the X Consortium and the vendor-specific subtree such as Motif or OpenLook. This two-component model can be further extended by new user-provided components. Each toolkit component is implemented as individual MovieScript shell. In particular, the shell Xi defines the intrinsic widgets, the shell Xm defines the Motif widgets, and so on. There is also a toolkit integration shell Xt which provides tools for combining toolkit components (e.g., $Xt = Xi + Xm$). The implementation of OpenLook interface in this model is reduced to specifying the shell Xol with the OpenLook widgets and building the full toolkit $Xt = Xi + Xol$.

The object-oriented model of XtIntrinsics is based on static binding and single inheritance. As such, it doesn't contain enough dynamics and functionality to motivate the faithful embedding in terms of derived types in MovieScript. Instead, we implement the widget classes as parametric modules in terms of a few primitive MovieScript types such as *xtclass* (widget class), *xtwidget* (widget instance), *xtattr* (widget attribute), and *xtcallback* (widget callback). The types *xtclass* and *xtattr* play the role of static containers of the corresponding Xlib information and they are supported only by a set of query/browse methods. The types *xtwidget* and *xtcallback* are dynamic, that is, their instances are created/destroyed in the run time.

The operator `xtwidget` creates an instance of the widget class, taking as input two objects: the parent widget and the array of attribute-value pairs. Attributes are specified by literal MovieScript names, coinciding with the corresponding Motif names. The Motif attribute set is suitably extended. For example, the widget class name itself is a special attribute, to be specified first in the attribute-value array. The associated value is the widget instance name as referred to by the X Resource Manager. Another special attribute is represented by the MovieScript atomic item `$` which indicates the nested child widget. Its corresponding value is the attribute-value array for this child widget. The `$[...]` pairs of this type can be nested, which allows for creating trees of nested widgets linked by the parent-child relations. This construct is extensively used in building GUI interfaces. We illustrate it below on a simple example:

```
xtinit
$ [/MainShell   /main
  $ [/XmRowColumn    /panel
          /orientation    /Vertical
    $ [/XmPushButton    /red
          /background [ 1.0 0.0 0.0 ]
          /activateCallback { (red) run }
      ]
    $ [/XmPushButton    /green
          /background [ 0.0 1.0 0.0 ]
          /activateCallback { (green) run }
      ]
    $ [/XmPushButton    /blue
```

```
        /background [ 0.0 0.0 1.0 ]
        /activateCallback { (blue) run }
    ]
  ]
] xtwidget realize
xtmainloop
```

As a result of executing the MovieScript program above, the main application window will be created with three buttons, labelled by *color = red, green, blue* strings and colored accordingly. By pressing a selected *color* button, the ./color file in the current directory will be executed, that is, interpreted as a MovieScript code. In this example, the nested widget tree is constructed with the depth three: *Main* is created as a child of the root window, *panel* is created as a child of *main*, and, finally *red, green, blue* buttons are created as panel children.

The GUI in this example is provided in terms of the button widgets and the associated *callback* procedures. The /activateCallback attribute for the button widget expects as value the MovieScript procedure (executable array), to be executed whenever the X event ButtonPress is generated, that is, whenever the user presses this button. Callback procedure in MovieScript is a natural interpreted version of the conventional C language interface, in which one registers the callback functions to be invoked as a response to the appropriate X events, created by the GUI controls. The advantage of the MovieScript-based GUI model is the support for rapid prototyping. After constructing the control panel as in the example above, one can now easily develop, modify, and test the scriptable callback procedures simply by editing the corresponding *red, green, and blue* files in the run-time mode.

AVS/Explorer

A new model for visual distributed computing is proposed by the present generation of high-end dataflow-based visualization systems such as AVS from AVS, Inc. (formerly Stardent Computer, Inc.), Explorer from SGI, or public domain packages such as apE from OSC or Khoros from UNM.

The computational model of AVS is based on a collection of parametric modules, that is, autonomous building blocks which can be connected to form processing networks. Each module has definite I/0 dataflow properties, specified in terms of a small collection of data structures such as *field, colormap*, or *geometry*. The Network Editor, operating as a part of the AVS kernel, offers interactive visual tools for selecting modules, specifying connectivity and designing convenient GUIs to control module parameters. A set of base modules for mapping, filtering, and rendering is built into the AVS kernel. The user extensibility model is defined at the C/Fortran level— new modules can be constructed and appended to the system in the form of independent UNIX processes, supported by appropriate dataflow interface.

From the MOVIE perspective, we see AVS-type systems as providing the interesting model for "coarse grain" modular extensibility of MovieScript, augmenting the native "fine grain" extensibility model discussed in Section 17.2.6. An AVS module interpolates between the concepts of a Post-Script operator (since it "consumes" a set of input objects and "produces" a set of output objects) and a class instance (since it also contains GUI-based "methods" to control internal module parameters). This is illustrated in Section 17.6 where we compare various language models in the context of "in large" programming. Consequently, AVS-style modules can be used to extend both the functional and object-oriented layers of MovieScript towards the UNIX domain in the form of user-provided independent UNIX processes. Also, any third-party source or "dusty deck" software package can be converted to the appropriate modular format and appended to the MOVIE system in terms of similar interface libraries as developed for AVS modules. The advantage of the AVS extensibility model is maximal "external" software economy due to easy connectivity to third-party packages. The advantage of the MOVIE model, based on the MovieScript language extensibility, is maximal "internal" software economy within the native code volume, generated by MOVIE developers. The merging of both techniques is particularly natural in the MovieScript context since PostScript itself can be viewed as a dataflow language.

An independent near-term issue is designing MOVIE interfaces to current and competing packages such as AVS and Explorer. Various possible interface models can be constructed in which MOVIE server either plays the role of the compute server, offering high-level language tools for building AVS modules or it takes over the control and AVS is used as a high-quality rendering device.

3D MOVIE

Scientific visualization systems such as AVS or Explorer offer sufficient functionality for relatively static graphics needs but they are not very useful for dynamic real-time graphics—for example, those required in virtual reality environments. Features of MOVIE such as interpretive multithreading, object orientation and rapid prototyping are crucial in building such advanced interfaces, where the high-quality graphics support must be tightly coupled with high-performance computing and with the high-level-language-based development tools.

We are currently in the design and implementation process of the custom three-dimensional graphics model in MovieScript which will be fully portable across various platforms such as PHIGS, PEX, and GL and which will make full use of the functionality available in these protocols. The low-level component of this model is structurally similar to the Motif interface described above, that is, it is based on parametric modules implemented as primitive types with attribute-value input arrays. As in the Motif case, the purpose of this layer is to provide portable low-level interpreted interfaces to the appropriate C libraries and to facilitate further high-level design of derived types in the rapid prototyping mode. The initial design ideas and the current implementation status of this work is described in [Faigle:92b], [Faigle:92c], and [Furmanski:93a].

Integration

The integrated graphics model in MovieScript is simple at the user level and complex at the implementation level, as illustrated in Figure 17.7.

Our main goal is to bring the heterogeneous collection of present standard subsystems (X, Motif/OpenLook, DPS/NeWS, PHIGS/PEX/GL) to the uniform sector of a high-level language. Interfaces to individual subsystems were discussed above. The overall strategy is to build first a uniform set of low-level primitive types for GUI toolkits and three-dimensional servers, structured as smooth extensions of the DPS/NeWS server-based Postscript graphics model for the two-dimensional vector graphics. This interpreted layer is then used in the next stage to design the high-level object-oriented graphics world in terms of more complex derived types. The resulting graphics support is very powerful and unique in some sense: It utilizes fully the available Open Systems graphics software resources; it conforms to one of the standards (PostScript) at the level of primitives; and finally, it provides the user-friendly, intuitive, and complete programming interface for modern graphics applications.

As an independent component, we provide also the MovieScript interface to dataflow packages such as AVS/Explorer. Both coroutine and sub-

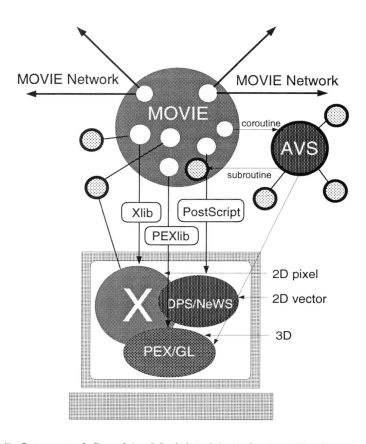

Figure 17.7: Integrated Graphics Model in MovieScript. Uniform interface in terms of primitive types is constructed to X, DPS/NeWS, and PEX/GL components of the Open Systems software and implemented, correspondingly, in terms of the Xlib, GL/PEXlib and PostScript communication protocols. Additionally, an interface to the AVS server is constructed, supporting both the subroutine and coroutine operation modes. The AVS-style extensibility model in terms of the UNIX dataflow processes is illustrated both for AVS and MOVIE servers. Within this model, one can also import other graphics models and applications to the MOVIE environment. This is illustrated on the example of the third-party X Window application which is configured as a MovieScript object or operator.

routine models for MOVIE-based AVS modules are supported, which allows for diverse interaction patterns between MOVIE and AVS servers. The AVS interface is redundant since the graphics functionality of systems such as AVS/Explorer will soon be included in the PEX/GL-based 3D MOVIE model, but it is useful in the current stage where various components of the 3D MOVIE model are still in the implementation process. In particular, the AVS interface was used in the Map Separates application, providing high-quality three-dimensional display tools for the MovieScript field algebra-based imaging and histogramming. We discuss this application in Chapter 3.

17.2.8 "In Large" Extensibility Model

MOVIE 1.0 will represent the minimal closed design of the MOVIE server, defined as the uniform object-oriented interpreted interface to all Open Systems resources defined in Section 17.2.1. Such a model can then be further expanded both at the system level (i.e., by adding new emerging standards or by creating and promoting new standard candidates) and at the application level (i.e., by building MOVIE based application packages).

Two basic structural entities used in the extension process are *types* and *shells*. Typically, types for the system extensions and shells are used for building MOVIE applications. In fact, however, both type- and shell-based extensibility models, as well as system and application level extensions, can be mixed within "in large" programming paradigms.

Both type- and shell-based extensions can be implemented at the compiled or interpreted level. At the current stage, the compiled extensibility level is fully open for MOVIE developers. The detailed user-level extensibility model will be specified starting from MOVIE 1.0. Explicit user access to the C code server resources will be restricted and the dominant extension mode will be provided at the interpreted MovieScript level. The C/Fortran-based user-level extensions as well as the extensibility via the third party software will be supported in the encapsulated, "coarse-grain" modular form similar to the AVS/Explorer model (see Section 17.2.7).

The type extension model is based on the inheritance forest and it was discussed in Section 17.2.3. The shell extension model utilizes PostScript-style extensibility and is described below.

Structurally, a MovieScript shell is an instance of the *shell type*. Its special functional role stems from the fact that it provides mechanisms for extending the system dictionary by new types and the associated polymorphic operators. In consequence, types and shells are in a dual relationship—examples would be nodes and links in a network or nouns and verbs in a sentence. In a simple physical analogy, types play the role of particles, i.e. some elementary entities in the computational domain and shells provide interactions between particles. In conventional object-oriented models, objects—that is, particles—are the only structural entities and the interactions are to be constructed as special kind of objects. The organization in MOVIE is similar at the formal structural level since MovieScript shells are instances of the MovieScript type, but there is functional distinction between object-based and shell-based programming. The former is following the message-passing-based C++ syntax and can be visualized as "particle in external field" type interaction. The latter follows the dataflow-based PostScript syntax and can be visualized as multiparticle processes such as scattering, creation, annihilation, decay, fusion and so on.

An appealing high-level language design model can be constructed by iterating the dual relation between types and shells in the multiscale fashion. Composite types of generation $N+1$ are constructed in terms of interactions involving types and shells of generation N. The ultimate structural component, that is, the system-wide type dictionary, is expected to be rich and diverse to match the complexity of the "real world" computational problems. The ultimate functional component, that is, some very high level language defined by the associated shells is expected to be simple, polymorphic and easy to use ("common English"), with all complexity hidden in methods for specialized types ("expert English").

In our particle physics analogy, this organization could be associated with the real-space renormalization group techniques. New composite types play the role of new collective variables at larger spatial scale, polymorphic operators correspond to the scale-invariant interaction vertices, and MovieScript shells contribute new effective interaction terms. Good high-level language design corresponds to the critical region, in which the number of effective "relevant" interactions stabilizes with increasing system size. Our conjecture is that natural languages can be viewed as such fixed points in some grammar space, and hence the best we can do to control computational complexity is to evolve in a similar direction when designing high-level computer languages.

17.2.9 CASE Tools

MOVIE Server is a large C program and it requires appropriate software engineering tools for its development.

Commercial software systems are usually developed in terms of sophisticated commercial CASE tools. In the academic environment, one rarely builds large production systems and one usually uses simpler, lower level tools based on dialects of the UNIX shell, most typically the C shell which forms now the standard text-mode UNIX interface on most workstations. The C-shell-based environment is most natural in the research working mode where the code is usually of small or moderate size, its typical lifetime is short, and it undergoes a series of major changes during the development cycle. These changes are often of unpredictable character and hence difficult to parametrize a priori in the form of some high-level CASE tools.

MOVIE project aims at the large, commercial quality production system, and yet it is created in the academic environment and contains substantial research components in the domain of HPDC. We therefore decided to select a compromise strategy and to start the MOVIE Server development process in terms of simple, custom-made, C-shell-based CASE tools. More explicitly, the current generation of CASE tools for MOVIE is structured as the interpreter of a very simple high level object-oriented language called MetaShell, designed as a superset of the C-shell. In this way, we assure the compatibility with the standard academic environment and, at the same time, we provide somewhat more powerful software development tools than those offered by the plain text-mode UNIX environment.

A more functional language model for the CASE tools in MOVIE would be provided by the MovieScript itself due to its high-level features and the built-in GUI support but we need a consistent bootstrap scheme in such a process. A natural approach is to use C shell to build MOVIE 1.0, then use its MovieScript to build MOVIE 2.0, and so on. Alternatively, we can consider the task of building high-quality visual "intelligent" CASE tools as one of the MOVIE 1.0-based application projects. We discuss these future plans is Section 17.2.10 and here we present the current MetaShell model from the MOVIE developer's point of view. The detailed technical documentation of the MetaShell tools can be found in [Furmanski:92c].

The entire code volume associated with MOVIE is stored in the directory $MOVIEHOME, shown in Figure 17.8 installed as the UNIX environment variable and used as the base pathname for the MetaShell addressing modes. The most relevant nodes in this directory are: *bin, sys,* and *M.* The *bin* di-

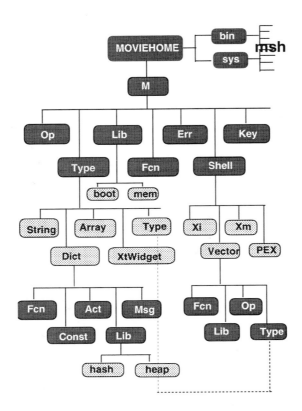

Figure 17.8: Sample Elements of the $MOVIEHOME Directory Tree. Dark blobs represent system nodes/names, shaded blobs represent user-provided nodes/names within the M-tree model. For example, each new type, such as *Dict*, automatically generates its subtree containing the following directories: *Fcn* (low-level object functions, used for implementing other object components), *Act* (object-dependent methods for polymorphic operators), *Msg* (methods implementing object messages), *Const* (predefined default instances of a given type), *Lib*, and (C libraries of object functions).

rectory, to be included in the developer's path, contains the external binaries such as the main MetaShell script and the MOVIE Server binary. The *sys* directory contains diverse system-level support tools—for example, the C and C-shell code implementing the MetaShell model. The server code starts in the subdirectory *M* and we will refer to the associated directory tree, starting at *M*, as the *M − tree*.

M branches into a set of base software categories such as, for example: *Op* (C or MovieScript source files implementing methods for the MovieScript operators), *Lib* (C language libraries), *Err* (MovieScript error operators), *Key* (system name objects), *Type* (MovieScript types), *Shell* (MovieScript shell objects) and so on.

Some of these nodes are simple, that is, they contain only a set of regular files (e.g., M/Op); some are composite, that is, they branch further into subdirectories (e.g., M/Lib which branches into system libraries). In the current implementation, the maximal branching level is five (e.g., directory M/Type/String/Lib/regex, which contains the *string* type library functions for handling regular expressions). Many structural aspects of the system can be presented in the form of some suitable *M-tree* mappings, listed below:

MetaDictionary

There is a one-to-one mapping between an *M-tree* directory and a MovieScript dictionary. The dictionary tree starts from the MetaDictionary *M*, which contains keys *Op*, *Lib*, and so on, associated with appropriate dictionaries as values. The *Op* dictionary contains MovieScript operators as values, the *Lib* dictionary contains the dictionaries of library functions as values, and so on. MetaDictionary mapping provides run-time interpreted access to all resources within the *M-tree*, and it can be used, for example, for building more advanced MovieScript-based CASE tools for the server development.

C Language Naming Conventions

There is a one-to-one correspondence between the C names of various software entities (functions, structures, macros, and so on) and the location of the corresponding code within the *M-tree*. In consequence, the whole server code has a hypertext-style organization which facilitates software understanding, documentation, upgrades, and maintenance in the group development mode.

MetaIndex

There is a unique 32-bit integer called MetaIndex associated with each software entity contributing to the server, such as functions, structures, or individual structure elements. The overall index is constructed by concatenating subindices along the *M-tree* path which allows for fast encoding/decoding between the binary (MetaIndex-based) and ASCII (pathname-based) addressing modes for the server code entities. Since the MovieScript itself can be viewed structurally as a subset of *M-tree*, one can construct a compact binary network protocol equivalent to the ASCII representation of the MovieScript code and more suitable for the high-speed communication purposes.

Makefile Model

The Makefile for the server binary is distributed along the *M-tree* in the form of independent modularized components for all functions, structures, and macros. The global Makefile is constructed from these components by a set of nested make-include directives.

Documentation Model

The organization of the MOVIE Server Reference Manual mirrors the structure of the *M-tree*, with the appropriate M-nodes represented as nested parts, chapters, sections, and so on. There is a corresponding detailed manual page for each elementary component of the server such as function, structure, or method, and an overview page for each composite component such as type, shell, or library. The interactive documentation browser is available, currently based on the WYSIWYG Publisher program from Arbor Text, Inc. [Podgorny:92a].

MetaShell tools operate on nodes of the *M-tree* and its mappings in a way similar to how the query language operates on its database. Atomicity and integrity of all operations is assured. A typical command, creating new C function *foo* in the library M/Type/String/Lib/regex, implies the following actions, performed automatically by MetaShell:

- The full C name for this function (*o_string_regex_foo*) is constructed based on the C naming rules for the server entities;

- files *foo.c* (C-source), *foo.h* (C-include), and *foo.mk* (make-include) are created in the library directory M/Type/String/Lib/regex from suitable templates;

- the name *foo* is appended to the system name dictionary M/Key;

- new MetaIndex slot is assigned for this function in the appropriate descriptor table and the MetaIndex is computed;

- *foo* entry is appended to the MovieScript dictionary *T_String_Lib_regex*, maintaining all functions in this library and installing itself as appropriate node in the MetaDictionary tree; and

- the manual page for this function is created.

MetaShell commands are organized in the object-oriented style, with each directory/file node of the M-tree represented as a MetaShell class/instance. The basic methods supported for all MetaShell objects are: Create, destroy, and query/browse. More sophisticated CASE tools, useful in the group development mode are currently under construction, such as a class corresponding to the whole $MOVIEHOME (with instances represented by individual developers' copies of the system) or the server class (with instances representing the customized versions of the MOVIE server).

17.2.10 Planned MOVIE Applications

Starting from the first external release MOVIE 1.0 of the system, we intend to initiate a series of application projects in various computational domains. Below, we list and briefly describe some of the near-term applications which are currently in the planning stage. In each case, we expose the elements of the MOVIE System which are most adequate in a given domain.

Machine Vision

This problem provided the initial motivation for developing MOVIE. Vision involves diverse computational modules, ranging from massively parallel algorithms for image processing to symbolic AI techniques and coupled in the real time via feedforward and feedback pathways. In consequence, the corresponding software environment needs to support both the regular data-parallel computing and the irregular, dynamic processing, all embedded in some uniform high-level programming model with consistent data structures and communication model between individual modules. Furmanski started the vision research within the Computation and Neural Systems (CNS) program at Caltech and then continued experiments with various image-processing and early/medium vision algorithms (Sections 6.5, 6.6, 6.7,

9.9) with the terrain Map Understanding project (Section 17.3). The most recent framework is the new Computational Neuroscience Program (CNP) at Syracuse University, where various elements of our previous work on vision algorithms and the software support could be augmented by new ideas from biological vision and possibly integrated towards some more complete machine vision system. We are also planning to couple some aspects of the vision research with the design and development work for virtual reality environments.

Neural Networks

A broad class of neural network algorithms [Grossberg:88a], [Hopfield:82a], [Kohonen:84a], [Rumelhart:86a] can be implemented in terms of a suitable set of data-parallel operators [Fox:88g], [Nelson:89a]. Rapid prototyping capabilities of MOVIE, combined with the field algebra model, offer a convenient experimentation and portable development environment for neural network research. In fact, the need for such tools, integrated with the HPC support, was one of the original arguments driving the MOVIE project. We plan to continue our previous work on parallel neural network algorithms [Fox:88e], [Ho:88c], [Nelson:89a], now supported by rapid prototyping and visualization tools.

Within CNP, we also plan to continue our exploration of methods in computational neurobiology [Furmanski:87a], [Nelson:89a]. We want to couple MOVIE with popular neural network simulation systems such as Aspirin from MITRE or Genesis from Caltech and to provide the MOVIE-based HPC support for the neuroscience community. Another attractive area for neural network applications is in the context of load-balancing algorithms for the MIMD-parallel and distributed versions of the system. We plan to extend our previous algorithms for neural net-based static load balancing [Fox:88e] to the present, more dynamic MOVIE model and to construct "neural routing" techniques for MovieScript threads.

This class of neural net applications can be viewed as an instance of a broader domain referred to as *physical computation*, illustrated in Chapter 11—that is, using methods and intuitions of physics to develop new algorithms for hard problems in combinatorial optimization [Fox:88kk;88tt;88uu;90nn], [Koller:89b]. We also plan to continue this promising research path.

Databases

The new nCUBE2-based parallel Oracle system (currently version 7.0) is installed at NPAC within the joint JPL/NPAC database project sponsored by ASAS. The MIMD Oracle model is based on a mesh of SQL interpreters and hence it follows an organization similar to the MIMD MOVIE model. We plan to develop the "server parallel" coupling between Oracle and MOVIE systems, for example, by locating them on parallel subcubes and linking, via the common hypercube channel. This would allow for smooth integration of high-performance database with high-performance computing and also for extending the restricted parallelism of the current MIMD Oracle model by the Fortran90–style data-parallel support for processing large distributed tables.

We also plan to experiment with object-oriented [Zdonik:90a] and intelligent [Parsaye:89a] database models in MOVIE and to develop MovieScript tools for integrating heterogeneous distributed database systems. MovieScript offers adequate language tools to address these modern database issues and to develop a bridge between relational and object-oriented techniques. For example, a table in the relational database can be represented in terms of MovieScript objects (fields of records) and then extended towards more versatile abstract data structures by using the inheritance mechanism.

Global Change

The Global Change federal initiative raises unprecedented challenges in various associated technology areas such as parallel processing [Rosati:91a] and large object-oriented databases [Stonebraker:91a]. The complexity of this domain is due both to the huge data sizes/rates to be processed and to the diversity of involved research and simulation areas ranging from climate modelling to economics. In collaboration with the Bainbridge Technology Group, Ltd. (BTGL) [Rosati:91b], we are planning to evaluate MOVIE in the context of various computational tasks associated with Global Change, with the focus on advanced visualization, animation, and large system integration.

High Energy Physics Data Analysis

Another computationally intensive domain is experimental High Energy Physics (HEP) at the Superconducting Super Collider (SSC) energy range. This accelerator (SSC) is now cancelled, but similar challenges exist at

CERN (Geneva) and Fermilab near Chicago. We are examining areas such as high-end visualization and virtual reality (for event display and virtual detector engineering) [Haupt:92a], [Skwarnicki:92a], MIMD-parallel computing (e.g., for parallel GEANT-style Monte Carlo simulations) [Fox:90bb], and databases (parallel computing support, integration tools in the heterogeneous distributed environment). HEP is a computationally intensive discipline based on mature and advanced but so far custom-made Fortran-based software environment. The computational challenges of the next high-energy experiments require modern software technology insertions such as HPC, advanced visualization and rapid prototyping tools. We see the MOVIE model, appropriately interfaced to the existing Fortran77-based HEP systems and offering convenient Fortran90–style portable extension towards HPC, as an attractive development and integration platform for the software environment at current and future experiments [Furmanski:92f].

Expert Systems

Using our work on Terrain Map Understanding (Section 17.3), we plan to build the expert system support in MovieScript to be used in late vision tasks such as proximity analysis, GIS knowledge-based processing, and object recognition. This project, also a part of the ASAS Map separates program, is planned with Coherent Research, Inc., Syracuse NY, where a similar expert system capability is being developed for analyzing black-and-white handmade maps used by the local electric company (Niagara Mohawk).

We are also planning to build the knowledge-based "intelligent" CASE tools to enforce economy and to accelerate the MOVIE development process. Typical examples include smart-class browsers or automated interface builders based on "fuzzy" specification of user requests. This approach is in the spirit of the Knowledge Based Software Engineering (KBSE) technology, recently advocated by DARPA on the basis of comprehensive analysis of software costs [Boehm:90a] as the efficient economy measure for the next generation software processes. Implementation of the KBSE concepts requires integrating expert system techniques with conventional software engineering practices. Since PostScript derives from Lisp, its appropriate extension in MovieScript towards symbolic processing offers a natural integration platform for KBSE tools.

Command and Control

Dynamic and integrative features of the MOVIE environment are optimally suited for modelling and prototyping various aspects and components of the new generation of C^3I systems. The new objectives in this area are to cope efficiently with potentially smaller but more diversified and less predictable threats, and to operate in a robust, adaptive fashion in the dynamic heterogeneous distributed environment. Dynamic topology of the MOVIE network, supporting adaptive routing schemes to recover from network damages is useful for such C^3I functions as *information transmission* and *battle management*. High-quality dynamic visualization services of the MOVIE model, evolving towards hypermedia navigation and virtual reality are suitable for such C^3I functions as *planning* and *evaluation*. Finally, the integrative high-level language model of MovieScript, supporting both the data parallel and irregular object-oriented computing, is adequate for such C^3I functions as *fusion* and *detection*.

MOVIE is planned as one of the candidate software models for the C^3I simulation, modelling and prototyping, to be evaluated within the new cooperative on parallel software engineering industrial CRDA (Cooperative Research and Development Agreement), starting in summer 1992 and coordinated by Rome Laboratory.

Virtual Reality

We see virtual reality as a promising candidate for the "ultimate" human-machine interface technology and also as the most challenging system component of the MOVIE model, playing the role of the global integration and synchronization platform for all major design concepts of the system, including interpretive multiserver networking, preemptive multithreading with the real-time aspects, object-oriented three-dimensional graphics model, and support for high-performance computing. We describe this application area in more detail in Section 17.4.

17.3 Map Separates

17.3.1 Problem Specification

Analysis of terrain maps, digitized as (noisy) full-color images, is the first MOVIE application, funded by the ASAS agency in parallel with the base system development project.

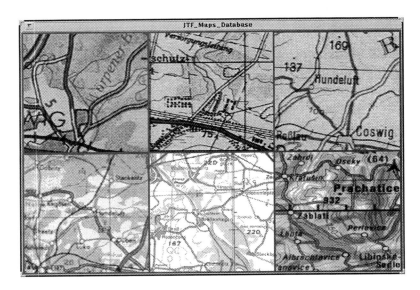

Figure 17.9: A Sample Set of RGB Images of Terrain Maps, Provided to Us by ASAS/JPL. Maps are of various sizes, scales, resolutions, saturation, and intensity ranges. They also contain diverse topographic elements and cartographic techniques.

A sample set of map images, provided to us by ASAS/JPL, is presented in Figure 17.9. The project has been split by the agency into the following stages:

- *Map separates*, where the goal is to reduce the 24-bit color images (inflicted with noise due to the cartographic and digitization processes) to clean separated (segmented) images containing only a small set (typically eight) of the original base colors.

- *Map understanding*, where the color-separated images are converted to the high-level database with all characters and symbols recognized and all elements and patches such as roads, rivers, urban, or vegetation areas uniquely identified.

This problem, posed by the DMA and addressed by several groups within the ASAS TECHBASE program (Cartography group at JPL, MOVIE group at NPAC, Coherent Research, Inc. (CRI) at Syracuse), turns out to be highly nontrivial, especially above certain critical accuracy level of order 80%.

The JPL approach to Map Separates is based on the back-propagation techniques. The CRI approach to map understanding is based on the expert systems techniques. Our MOVIE group approach is based on machine vision techniques. Our goal is to construct the complete map recognition system, including both separation and understanding components, structured as low- and high-level layers of the vision system and coupled by the feedforward and feedback pathways.

The problem involves diverse computational domains such as image processing, pattern recognition, and AI, and it provided the initial driving force for developing the general-purpose MOVIE system based support. At the current stage, we have completed the implementation of a class of early/medium vision algorithms for map separates, based on zero-crossings for edge detection and RGB clustering for segmentation. The resulting techniques are comparable in quality and give higher performance than the backpropagation-based approach.

Our conclusion from this stage is that further quality improvement in the separation process can be achieved only by coupling the low-level pixel-based techniques with the high-level approaches, based on symbolic representations, and by providing the feedback loop from the recognition layers to the separation layer.

From the computational perspective, the currently implemented layers are based on the MOVIE field algebra support for image processing. Two trial user interfaces constructed so far were based on the X/Motif interface for two-dimensional graphics and on the AVS interface for three-dimensional graphics. In preparation is a more complete tool, based on uniform two- and three-dimensional graphics support in MOVIE and providing the testbed environment for evaluating various techniques, employed so far to handle this complex problem. As part of this testbed program, we have also recently implemented the backpropagation algorithm for map separates [Simoni:92a], following the techniques developed originally by the JPL group.

In the following, we discuss in more detail various algorithms involved in this problem, with the focus on the RGB clustering techniques. The material presented here is based on an internal report [Fox:93b].

17.3.2   Test Case

We will use the map image in Figure 17.10 to illustrate concepts and algorithms discussed in this section.

This image, referred to as *ad250*, was given to us by the JPL group as

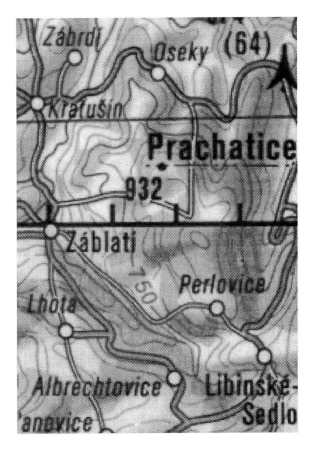

Figure 17.10: Map Image, Referred to in the Text as ad250 and Given to Us by the JPL Group as the Test Case for the Backpropagation Algorithm. The original image is of size 305×200 in pixel units with 24 bits of color per pixel.

the test case of their backpropagation algorithm. The ad250 is a relatively complex image since it involves shaded relief, color saturation is poor, and there are a lot of isoclines represented by a broad spectrum of a brown tint, fluctuating and intermixed on boundaries with white, grey (= white+relief), green, and dark green (= green + relief).

The color separation of this image is not unique unless some human guidance is involved. For example, gray shaded relief can either be considered independent color or ignored, that is, identified as white. Also, isoclines with various tints of brown can be labelled by either different colors or a single effective brown. We obtained from JPL their results from the backpropagation algorithm for this image. The color selection ambiguities were resolved there by the map analyst during the network training stage and since these decisions can be deduced from the final result, we adopted the same color mapping rules in our work.

The rules are as follows:

- Ignore shaded relief, that is, identify both true white and grey as *white* and both true green and dark green as *green*;

- identify all isocline lines with various tint of brown as single *brown*;

- identify all road boundaries (which are medium to dark grey) and city names (which are "almost" black) as single *black*; and

- other colors in the image to be separated are: *magenta* (interior color of the road, say from Kratusin to Zablati), *blue* (the river and also the horizontal line just below Kratusin name), and *purple* (an arrow and number (64) in the upper right corner).

To summarize, the image in Figure 17.10 is to be separated into seven base colors: white, green, brown, magenta, blue, purple, and black. Having done this, we can easily declutter it within the contextual regions of these colors, that is, we can distinguish isoclines from roads (but we cannot, for example, distinguish a city name from the road boundary).

The separation results obtained at JPL using the backpropagation algorithm for the ad250 image are presented in Figure 17.11.

17.3.3 Segmentation via RGB Clustering

Our approach is to explore the computer vision techniques for map separates. This requires more labor and investment than the neural network

Figure 17.11: Image *ad250* from Figure 17.10, Separated into Seven Base Colors Using the JPL Backpropagation Algorithm. The net is trained on a subset of the image pixels. A set of 27 color values for the 3×3 image window is provided each time and the required output is enforced for the central pixel. Ten hidden neurons are used.

method which has the advantage of the "black box"-type approach, but one expects that the vision based strategy will be eventually more successful. The disadvantage of the backpropagation approach is that it doesn't leave much space for major improvements—it delivers reasonable quality results for low-level separation but it can hardly be improved by including more insights from higher level reasoning modules since some information is already lost inside the backpropagation "black-box." On the contrary, machine vision is a hierarchical, coupled system with feedback which allows for systematic improvements and provides the proper foundation for the full map understanding program.

The map separates problem translates in the vision jargon into segmentation and region labelling. These algorithms are somewhere on the border of the early and medium vision modules. We have analyzed the RGB clustering algorithm for the map image segmentation. In this method, one first constructs a three-dimensional histogram of the image intensity in the unit RGB cube. For a hypothetical "easy" image composed of a small, fixed number of colors, only a fixed number of histogram cells will be populated. By associating distinct labels with the individual nonempty cells, one can then filter the image, treating the histogram as a pixel→label look-up table—that is, assigning for each image pixel the corresponding cell label. For "real world" map images involving color fluctuation and diffusion across region boundaries, the notion of the isolated histogram cells should be replaced by that of the color clusters. The color image segmentation algorithm first isolates and labels individual clusters. The whole RGB cube is then separated into a set of nonoverlapping polyhedral regions, specified by the cluster centers. More explicitly, for each histogram cell, a label is assigned given by the label of the nearest cluster, detected by the clustering algorithm. The pixel→region look-up table constructed this way is then used to assign region labels for individual pixels in the image.

As a first test of the RGB clustering, we constructed a set of color histograms with fixed bin sizes and various resolutions (Figure 17.12). Even with such a crude tool, one can observe that the clustering method is very efficient for most image regions and when appropriately extended to allow for irregular bin volumes, it will provide a viable segmentation and labelling algorithm. The interactive tool in Figure 17.12 also provided a nice test of rapid prototyping capabilities of MOVIE. The whole MovieScript code for the demo is on the order of only 40 K and it was created interactively based on the integrated scriptable tools for Motif, field algebra, and imaging.

The simple, regular algorithm in Figure 17.12 cannot cope with problems

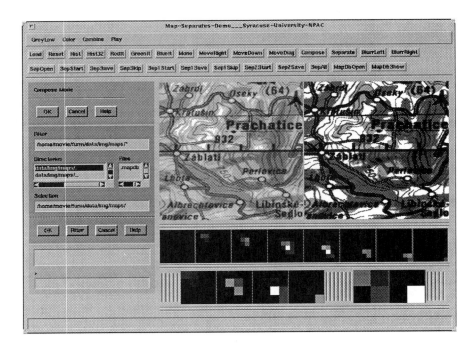

Figure 17.12: Map Separates Tool Constructed in MovieScript in the Rapid Prototyping Mode to Test the RGB Clustering Techniques. The left image represents the full color source, the right image is separated into a fixed number of base colors. Three RGB histograms are constructed with the bin sizes $2 \times 2 \times 2$, $4 \times 4 \times 4$, and $8 \times 8 \times 8$, correspondingly. Each histogram is represented as a sequence of RG planes, parametrized by the B values. The first row under the image panel contains eight blue planes of the $8 \times 8 \times 8$ histogram, the second row contains $4 \times 4 \times 4$ and $2 \times 2 \times 2$ histograms. The content of each bin is encoded as an appropriate shade of gray. A mouse click into the selected square causes the corresponding separate to be displayed in the right image window, using the average color in the selected bin. In the *separate* mode, useful for previewing the histogram content, subsequent separates overwrite the content of the right window. In the *compose* mode, used to generate this snapshot, subsequent separates are superimposed. Tools are also provided for displaying all separates for a given histogram in the form of an array of images.

such as shaded relief, non-convex clusters, and color ambiguities, discussed above. To handle such problems, we need interactive tools to display, manipulate, and process three-dimensional histograms. The results presented below were obtained by coupling MOVIE field algebra with the AVS visualization modules. In preparation is the uniform MovieScript-based tool with similar functionality, exploiting the currently developed support for the three-dimensional graphics in MOVIE.

The RGB histogram for the ad250 image is presented in Figure 17.13. Each nonempty histogram cell is represented as a sphere, centered at the bin center, with the radius proportional to the integrated bin content and with the color given by the average RGB value of this cell. Poor color separation manifests as cluster concentration along the R = G = B axis. Two large clusters along this diagonal correspond to white and grey patches on the image. A "pipe" connecting these two clusters is the effect of shaded relief, composed of a continuous band of shades of gray. Three prominent off-diagonal clusters, forming a strip parallel to the major white-gray structure, represent two tints of true green and dark green, again with the shaded relief "pipe." Brown isoclines are represented by an elongated cloud of small spheres, scattered along the white-gray structure.

The separation of these three elongated structures—white, green, and brown—represents the major complexity since all three shapes are parallel and close to each other. The histogram in Figure 17.13 is constructed with the $32 \times 32 \times 32$ resolution, which is slightly too low for numerical analysis (discussed below) but useful for graphical representation as a black-and-white picture. The $64 \times 64 \times 64$ histogram, used in actual calculations, contains too many small spheres to create any compelling three-dimensional sensation without the color cues and interactive three-dimensional tools (however, it looks impressive and spectacular on a full-color workstation with 3D graphics accelerator). By working interactively with the $64 \times 64 \times 64$ histogram, one can observe that all three major clusters are in fact reasonably well separated.

All remaining colors separate in an easy way: Shades of black again form a scattered diagonal strip which is far away from the three major clusters and separates easily from a similar, smaller parallel strip of shades of purple; red separates as a small but prominent cluster (close to the central gray blob in Figure 17.13); finally, blue is very dispersed and manifests as a broad cloud or dilute gas of very small spheres, invisible in Figure 17.13 but again separating easily into an independent polyhedral sector of the RGB cube.

The conclusion from this visual analysis, only partially reproduced by

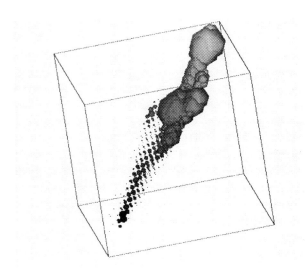

Figure 17.13: Color histogram of the ad250 image (see Figure 17.10) in the unit RGB cube. Histogram resolution is $32 \times 32 \times 32$. Each bin is represented by a sphere with the radius proportional to the bin content and with the average color value in this bin.

the picture in Figure 17.13, is that RGB clustering is the viable method for separating ad250 into the seven indicated base colors. As mentioned above, this separation process requires human guidance because of the color mapping ambiguities. The nontrivial technical problem from the domain of human-machine interface we are now facing is how to operate interactively on complex geometrical structures in the RGB cube. A map analyst should select individual clusters and assign a unique label/color with each of them. As discussed above, these clusters are separable but their shapes are complex, of them given as clouds of small spheres, some others elongated, non-convex, and so on.

Virtual reality-type interface with the glove input and the three-dimensional video output could offer a natural solution for this problem. For example, an analyst could encircle a selected cluster by a set of hand movements. Also, the analyst's presence inside the RGB cube, implemented in terms of the immersive video output, would allow for fast and efficient identification of various geometric structures.

Right now, we adopted a more cumbersome but also more realistic approach, implementable in terms of conventional GUI tools. Rather than

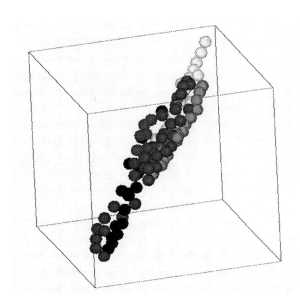

Figure 17.14: A set of ~ 80 Color Values, Selected Interactively and Mapped on the Specified Set of Seven Base Colors as Described in the Text

separate clusters, we *reconstruct* them from a set of small spheres. An interactive tool was constructed in which an analyst can select a small region or even a single pixel in the image and assign an effective color/label to it. This procedure is iterated some number of times. For example, we click into some white areas and say: white. Then we click into few levels of a shaded relief and we say again: white. Finally, we click into the gray region and we also say: white. In a similar way, we click into some number of isoclines with various tints of brown and we say: brown. Each point selected in this way becomes a center of a new cluster.

The set of clusters selected this way defines the partition of the RGB cube into a set of nonoverlapping polyhedral regions. Each such region is convex and therefore the number of small clusters to be selected in this procedure must be much larger than the number of "real" clusters (which is seven in our case), since the real clusters often have complex, nonconvex shapes.

A sample selection of this type is presented in Figure 17.14. It contains about 80 small spheres, each in one of the seven base colors. Separation of "easy" colors such as blue or red can be accomplished in terms of a few clusters. Complex structures such as white, green, and brown require about

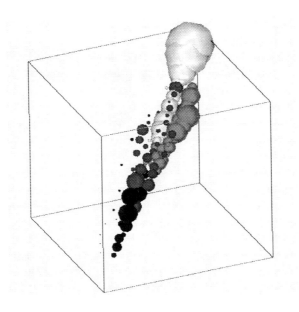

Figure 17.15: The Same Set of Selected Color Values as in Figure 17.14 But Now with the Radius Proportional to the Integrated Content of Each Polyhedral Cell with the Center Specified by the Selected RGB Value.

20 clusters each to achieve satisfactory results. The image is then segmented using the color look-up table constructed in this way and the weight is assigned to each small cluster, proportional to the integrated content of the corresponding polyhedral region. The same selection as in Figure 17.14, but now with the sphere radii proportional to this integrated content, is presented in Figure 17.15.

As seen, we have effectively reconstructed a shape with topology roughly similar to the original histogram in Figure 17.13 but now separated into the seven base colors.

The resulting separated image is presented in Figure 17.16 and compared with the JPL result in Figure 17.11 in the next section.

17.3.4   Comparison with JPL Neural Net Results

The quality of the separation algorithms in Figure 17.16 (RGB clustering) and in Figure 17.11 (neural network) is roughly similar. The RGB cluster-based result contains more high-frequency noise since the algorithm is based on the point-to-point look-up table approach and it doesn't perform any

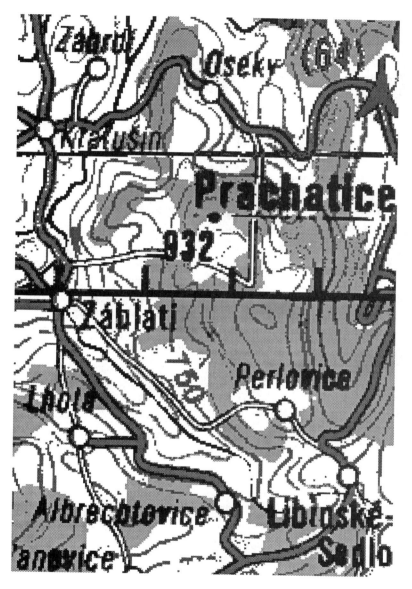

Figure 17.16: Image ad250 from Figure 17.10, Separated into Seven Base Colors Using the RGB Clustering Algorithm with the Clusters and Colors Selected as in Figure 17.15.

neighborhood analysis. This noise could easily be cleaned up by a simple postprocessor, eliminating isolated pixels, but we didn't perform it so far. In our approach, image smoothness analysis is represented by another class of algorithms, discussed in Section 17.3.5.

The most important point to stress is that the RGB cluster-based method is much faster than the backpropagation method. Indeed, in the RGB clustering algorithm, the pixel→label assignment is performed by a simple local look-up table computation which involves five numerical operations per pixel. The JPL backpropagation algorithm, employed in computing the result in Figure 17.11, contains 27 input neurons, 10 hidden neurons, and 7 output neurons, requiring about 700 numerical operations per pixel. The neural network chip speeds up the backpropagation-based separation algorithm by a factor of 10. In consequence, our algorithm is faster by a factor of 100 than the JPL software algorithm and it is still faster by a factor of 10 when compared with the JPL hardware implementation.

Our interpretation of these results and understanding of the backpropagation approach in view of our experience based on numerical/graphical experiments described above is as follows. Both algorithms contain similar components. In both cases, we enter some color mapping information into the system during the "training" stage and we construct some internal look-up table. In our case, this look-up table is constructed as a set of labelled polyhedral regions, realizing a partition of the RGB cube, whereas in the backpropagation case it is implemented in terms of the hidden units. Our look-up table is optimal for the problem at hand, whereas backpropagation uses the "general-purpose" look-up table offered by its general-purpose input→output mapping capabilities. It is therefore understandable that our algorithm is much faster.

Still, both algorithms are probably functionally equivalent, that is, the backpropagation algorithm effectively constructs a very similar look-up table, performing RGB clustering in terms of hidden units and synaptic weights. But it does this in a very inefficient way. One says that neural network is always the "second best" solution of the problem. In complex perceptual or pattern matching problems, this truly best solution is often unknown and the neural network approach is useful, whereas in the early/medium vision problems such as map separates, the machine vision techniques are competitive in quality and more efficient. However, we stress that backpropagation, even if less efficient, is a convenient way to get reasonable results quickly as far as user development time is concerned. It maximizes initial user productivity—not algorithmic performance.

Figure 17.17: Three-dimensional Surface Representing a Selected Color Plane (Red) for a Region of the ad250 Image from Figure 17.10 (Includes Letter "P" from "Prachatice" in the Upper Right Corner). X, Y of the surface correspond to pixel coordinates and the Z value of the surface is proportional to the image intensity.

The backpropagation algorithm produces a cleaner separated image as seen in Figures 17.11 and 17.16. This is due to the fact that the backpropagation operates on a 3×3 input window and the RGB clustering uses 1×1 window—that is, just a single pixel. Some smearing is therefore built into the neural network during the training period. The corresponding vision algorithms, involving the neighborhood analysis based on image smoothness, are discussed in the next Section.

17.3.5 Edge Detection via Zero Crossing

Figure 17.17 presents a region from the ad250 image, displayed as a three-dimensional surface. The image pixel coordinates X, Y are mapped on the surface X, Y coordinates, whereas the Z value of the surface for a given X, Y is proportional to the local intensity value of a given color plane. In Figure 17.17, the red plane was taken; similar pictures can be obtained for green, blue, luminance, and any other plane filter. To identify the displayed region on the image, note the letter P—the first character in the "Prachatice" name in the upper-right corner of the surface and the number "932" below and left of it.

As seen, even if there are some local intensity fluctuations in the image, the resulting surface is reasonably smooth and the segmentation problem can also be addressed by using suitable edge detection techniques.

On an "ideal" map image, edges could be detected simply by identifying color discontinuities. On the "real world" map images, the edges are typically not very abrupt due to the A/D conversion process—it is more appropriate to think in terms of smooth surface fitting and analyzing rapid changes of the first derivatives or zeros of the second derivative. These types of techniques were developed originally by Marr and Hildreth [Marr:80a] and most recently by Canny [Canny:87a].

The single step of this algorithm looks as follows:

- Smooth the image using the Gaussian filter with some fixed width σ;

- compute local gradient G;

- compute second directional derivative D in the direction of local gradient;

- identify *zero crossings* of D, that is, closed contours defined by $D = 0$; and

- accept or reject the resulting edges based on some signal-to-noise evaluation technique.

The result of the *Canny filter* applied to the ad250 image is presented in Figure 17.18. Each pixel is represented there as a 4×4 color square and the neighboring squares are separated by a one-pixel-wide black background. Zero crossings of D are marked as white segments and they always form closed contours.

As seen, the brown isoclines which required substantial labor to be separated by the RGB clustering techniques are now detected in a very easy and clean way. However, there is also some number of spurious contours in Figure 17.18 which are to be rejected. The simplest signal-to-noise-based selection technique could be as follows:

- compute average global gradient in the image;

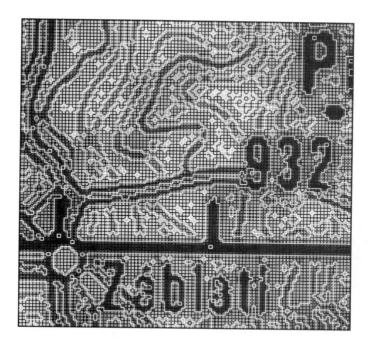

Figure 17.18: Output of the Canny Edge Detector Filter, Applied to a Region of the Image ad250 from Figure 17.10. Closed contours are zero crossings of the second directional derivative, taken in the direction of local intensity gradient.

- for each contour, compute the integrated value of the gradient as a line integral along the contour; and

- reject all contours with the integrated gradient value lower than some standard deviation times the global average gradient.

A natural use of the Canny filter in Figure 17.18 could be as follows. The image is first segmented into Canny contours which are threshold as above and then labelled. For each contour, an average color is computed by integrating the color context enclosed by this contour. This reduced color palette is then used as input to the RGB clustering. Such an approach would guarantee, for example, that all brown isoclines in Figure 17.10 will be detected as smooth lines, contrary to both RGB clustering and neural network algorithms, which occasionally fail to reconstruct continuous isoclines.

Consider, however, a "Mexican hat"-shaped green patch in Figure 17.10, located in the upper left part of the image, between Prachatice name and 932 number. This patch was very easily and correctly detected by both RGB clustering and by the neural net, but we would fail to detect it by the single step Canny filter described above. Indeed, after careful inspection of the contours in Figure 17.18, one can notice that there is no single closed zero crossing line encircling this region. In consequence, any contour-based color averaging procedure as above would result in some green color "leakage." Within the Canny edge detection program, such edges are detected using the multiscale approach. The base algorithm outlined above is iterated with the increasing value of the Gaussian width σ and some multiscale acceptance/rejection method is employed. The green patch would eventually manifest as a low-frequency edge for some sufficiently large value of σ.

We intend to investigate in more detail such multiresolution edge-detection strategies. In our opinion, however, a more attractive approach is based on hybrid techniques, discussed in the next Section.

17.3.6   Towards the Map Expert System

The output of the Canny edge detector, composed of a set of non-overlapping contiguous regions covering the whole image, is precisely of the format provided as input to the expert system, constructed by Coherent Research, Inc. in their SmartMaps system. This expert system performs such high-level tasks as object grouping, proximity analysis, Hough transforms, and so on. The output of an RGB clustering and/or neural network can also be structured in such format. Probably the best strategy at this point is to extend this expert system so that it would select the best ultimate separation pattern using a set of trial candidates. A genetic algorithm type philosophy could be used as a guiding technique. Each low-level algorithm is typically successful within a certain image region and it fails for some other regions. A smart split-and-merge approach, consistent with some set of common sense rules, could yield a much better low-level separation result than each individual low-level technique itself. For example, Canny edge detector would offer brown isoclines as good candidates and RGB clustering would offer the green patch as a good candidate for a region. Both propositions would be cross-checked and accepted as reasonable by both algorithms and the final result would contain both types of regions, separated with high fidelity. This type of medium-level geometrical reasoning could then be augmented and enforced by the high-level contextual reasoning within the full map understanding program.

17.3.7 Summary

We have described in this chapter our current results for map separates, based on the RGB clustering algorithm. This method results in a comparable or somewhat lower quality separation then the backpropagation algorithm, but it is faster by a factor of 100. It is suggested that our RGB clustering algorithm is in fact essentially equivalent to a backpropagation algorithm. In the neural network jargon, we can say that we have found the analytic representation for the bulk of the hidden unit layer which results in dramatic performance improvement. This representation can be thought of numerically as a pixel→region look-up table or geometrically as a set of polyhedral regions covering the RGB cube. Further quality improvement of our results will be achieved soon by refining our software tools and by coupling the RGB clustering with the zero-crossing-based segmentation and edge detection algorithms. Zero crossing techniques provide in turn a natural algorithmic connectivity for our intended collaboration with Coherent Research, Inc. on high-level vision and AI/expert systems techniques for map understanding.

17.4 The Ultimate User Interface: Virtual Reality

17.4.1 Overall Assessment

Virtual reality (VR) is a new human-machine interface technology based on the full sensory *immersion* of participants in the virtual world, generated in real time by the high-performance computer. Virtual worlds can range from physical spaces such as those modelled by dynamic terrain viewers or architectural walk-through tools, through a variety of "fantasy lands" to entirely abstract cognitive spaces, generated by dynamic visualization of low-dimensional parametric subspaces, extracted from complex nontopographic databases.

The very concept of the immersive interface and the first prototypes were already known in 1960s [Sutherland:68a] and 1970s [Kilpatrick:76a]. In the 1990s, VR technology is becoming affordable. Most current popular hardware implementations of the interface are based on a set exotic peripherals such as goggles for the wide solid-angle three-dimensional video output, head-position trackers, and gloves for sensory input and tactile feedback. Another immersion strategy is based on "non-encumbered" interfaces

[Krueger:91a], implemented in terms of the real-time machine vision front-end which analyzes participants' gestures and responds with the synchronized sensory feedback from the virtual world.

VR projects cover the wide range of technologies and goals, including high-end scientific visualization (UNC), high-end space applications (NASA Ames), base research and technology transfer (HIT Lab), and low-end consumer market products (AGE).

The VR domain is growing vigorously and already has reached the mass media, generating the current "VR hype." According to VR enthusiasts, this technology marks the new generation of computing and will start a revolution comparable in scope to personal computing in the early 1980s. In our opinion, this might be the correct assessment since VR seems to be the most natural logical next step in the evolution of human-machine interfaces and it might indeed become the "ultimate solution" for using computers because of its potential for maximal sensory integration with humans. However, the explicit implementations of VR will most probably vary very rapidly in the coming years, in parallel with the progress of technology, and most of the current solutions, systems, and concepts will become obsolete very soon.

Nevertheless, one is tempted to immediately start exploring this exciting field, additionally encouraged by the rapidly increasing affordability of VR peripherals. The typical cost of a peripheral unit for a VR environment has gradually decreased from $1M (Super Cockpit) in the 1970s through $100K in the 1980s (NASA) down to $10K (VPL DataGlove) in the early 1990s. The new generation of low-cost "consumer VR" systems which will reach the broad market in the mid-1990s comes with a price tag of about $100. This clearly indicates that the time to get involved in VR is—now!

VR opponents predict that VR will have its major impact in entertainment rather than R&D or education. However, there is already a new buzzword in VR newspeak, suggesting a compromise solution: *edutainment*! From the software engineering perspective, the edutainment argument can be formulated as follows: the software models and standards generated today will mature perhaps five to ten years from now and hence they will be used by the present "Nintendo generation." There is no reason to expect that these kids will accept anything less intuitive and natural for user interfaces than the current Nintendo standards, which will evolve rapidly during the coming years towards the full-blown VR interfaces.

Leaving aside longer term prognoses, we would expect that a few years from now, VR will be available on all systems in the form of an add-on option, more or less as the mouse was for personal computers a few years ago.

We will be witnessing soon the new generation of consumer VR products for the broad entertainment market and, in the next stage, the transfer of this technology to the computer interface domain. These low-cost gloves and headsets will probably appear more and more frequently attached to conventional monitors and easy to use. VR applications will coexist with standard applications within the existing windowing systems. We will still be using conventional text editors and other window tools, whereas the add-on VR peripherals and software layers will allow us to enter virtual worlds (i.e., dynamic three-dimensional-intensive applications) through conventional two-dimensional windows.

17.4.2 Markets and Application Areas

Matrix Information Services, Inc. (MIS) recently finished an extensive survey of emerging VR programs, firms and application areas [MIS:91a]. Some 40 sites have been identified. The claim is, however, that the actual number of new VR initiatives is much larger since many large firms do not disclose any information about their VR startups. The first generation of commercial VR products identified by MIS include applications in medical imaging, aerospace, business, engineering, transportation, architecture and design, law enforcement, education, tours and travel, manufacturing and training, personal computing, entertainment, and the arts. In fact, when Bill Bricken, HIT Lab's Chief Scientist, was asked to estimate the VR market some 20 years from now, he replied: "Just the Gross National Product." Statements like this are clearly made to amplify the current VR hype for fund-raising purposes. Nevertheless, the diversity of emerging application areas might indeed suggest that VR is capable of embracing a substantial portion of today's computer market in the next decade.

Furmanski often met such enthusiastic opinions during his VR trip in the summer of 1991 [Furmanski:91g] with representatives of BTGL through the West Coast labs and companies. However, the same companies admit that the real VR market in the U.S. as of today is—virtual.... The bulk of their sales is in Japan where the investments in VR R&D are an order of magnitude higher than in the U.S. We don't hear much about Japan's progress in VR since their approach is very different. Still, some of their latest achievements, like commercial products with nonencumbered, machine vision-based VR interfaces have found the way into the media. In the U.S., this technology has been researched for years in the academic and then small business mode by Myron Krueger, a true pioneer of artificial reality.

There is much less VR hype in Japan and the VR technology is viewed there in a more modest fashion as a natural next generation of GUIs. It is intended to be fully integrated with existing computing environments rather then an entirely new computing paradigm. It is therefore very plausible that, due to this more organized, long-range approach, Japan will take the true leadership role in VR. This issue has been raised by then-Senator Gore, who advocated increasing R&D funds for VR in this country. One should also notice that the federal support for virtual reality needs to be associated with similar ongoing efforts towards maintaining U.S. dominance in the domain of High Performance Computing, since we expect both technologies to become tightly coupled in the near future.

17.4.3   VR at Syracuse University

There is a campuswide interest in multimedia/VR at Syracuse University, involving labs and departments such as the CASE Center, NPAC, School of Information Studies, Multimedia Lab and Advanced Graphics Research Lab. A small scope virtual reality Lab has been started, sponsored by the CASE Center and Chris Gentile from AGE, Inc., who is an SU alumnus and partner in the successful NYS startup focused on low-end broad-market consumer VR products. New planned collaborations with the corporate sponsors include joint projects with SimGraphics Engineering, Inc., a California-based company developing high-quality graphics software for simulation, animation, and virtual engineering, and with virtual reality, Inc., a new East Coast startup interested in developing high-end VR systems with high-performance computing support.

On the base VR research side, there is a planned collaboration with Rome Laboratories [Nilan:91a] aimed at designing the VR-based group decision support for the modern C^3I systems. The project also involves evaluating MOVIE as a candidate for the high-end VR operating shell. Within the new multidisciplinary Computational Neuroscience Program at Syracuse University, we are also planning to couple some vision and neutral network research issues with the design issues for VR environments such as "nonencumbered" machine vision-based interfaces, VR-related perception limits, or neural net-based predictive tracking techniques for fast VR rendering.

Multimedia is a discipline closely associated with VR and strongly represented at Syracuse University by the Multimedia Lab within the CASE Center and by the Belfer Audio Lab. Some of the multimedia applications are more static and/or text-based than the dynamic three-dimensional VR environments. The borderline between both disciplines is usually referred to as hypermedia navigation—that is, dynamic real-time exploration of multimedia databases. Large, complex databases and associated R&D problems of integration, transmission, data abstraction, and so on, represent the common technology area connecting multimedia and VR projects.

Our interests at NPAC are towards high-performance VR systems, based on parallel computing support. A powerful VR environment could be constructed by combining the computational power and diverse functionality of new parallel systems at NPAC: CM-5, nCUBE2, and DECmpp, connected by fast HIPPI networks. A natural VR task assignment would be: modeller/simulator on CM-5, parallel database server on nCUBE2, and renderer on DECmpp—which basically exhausts all major computational challenges of virtual reality.

The relevance of parallel computing for VR is both obvious and yet largely unexplored within the VR community. The popular computational engine for high-end VR is provided currently by the Silicon Graphics machines and these systems are in fact custom parallel computers. But it remains to be seen if this is the most cost-effective or scalable solution for VR. The most natural testbed setup for exploring various forms of parallelism for VR can be provided by general-purpose systems. The distributed environment described above and based on a heterogeneous collection of general-purpose parallel machines would provide us with truly unique capabilities in the domain of high-end parallel/distributed VR. We intend to develop VR support in MOVIE and to use it as the base infrastructure system for high-end VR at NPAC. We discuss MOVIE's role in the VR area in more detail in the next section.

17.4.4 MOVIE as VR Operating Shell

VR poses a true challenge for the underlying software environment, usually referred to as the VR *operating shell.* Such a system must integrate real-time three-dimensional graphics, in large object-oriented modelling and database techniques, event-driven simulation techniques, and the overall dynamics based on multithreading distributed techniques. The emerging VR operating shells, such as Trix at Autodesk, Inc., VEOS at HIT Lab, and Body Electric at VPL, Inc., share many design features with the MOVIE system. A multiserver network of multithreading interpreters of high-level object-oriented language seems to be the optimal software technology in the VR domain.

We expect MOVIE to play an important role in the planned VR projects at Syracuse University, described in the previous section. The system is capable of providing both the overall infrastructure (VR operating shell) and the high-performance computational model for addressing new challenges in computational science, stimulated by VR interfaces. In particular, we intend to address research topics in biological vision on visual perception limits [Farell:91a], [Verghese:92a], in association with analogous constraints on VR technology; research topics in machine vision in association with high-performance support for the "non-encumbered" VR interfaces [Krueger:91a]; and neural network research topics in association with the tracking and real-time control problems emerging in VR environments [Simoni:92b].

From the software engineering perspective, MOVIE can be used both as the base MovieScript-based software development platform and the integration environment which allows us to couple and synchronize various external VR software packages involved in the planned projects.

Figure 17.19 illustrates the MOVIE-based high-performance VR system planned at NPAC and discussed in the previous section. High-performance computing, high-quality three-dimensional graphics, and VR peripherals modules are mapped on an appropriate set of MovieScript threads. The overall synchronization necessary, for example, to sustain the constant frame rate, is accomplished in terms of the real-time component of the MovieScript scheduling model. The object-oriented interpreted multithreading language model of MovieScript provides the critical mix of functionalities, necessary to cope efficiently with prototyping in such complex software and hardware environments.

The MOVIE model-based high-performance VR server at NPAC could be employed in a variety of visualization-intensive R&D projects. It could also provide a powerful shared VR environment, accessible from remote sites. MovieScript-based communication protocol and remote server programmability within the MOVIE network assure satisfactory performance of shared distributed virtual worlds also for low-bandwidth communication media such as telephone lines.

From the MOVIE perspective, we see VR as an asymptotic goal in the GUI area, or the "ultimate" user interface. Rather than directly build the specific VR operating shell, which would be short-lived given the current state of the art in VR peripherals, we instead construct the VR support in the graded fashion, closely following existing and emerging standards. A natural strategy is to extend the present MovieScript GUI sector based on Motif and three-dimensional servers by some minimal VR operating shell

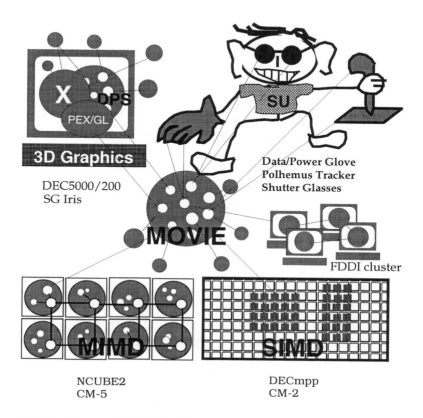

Figure 17.19: Planned High-End Virtual Reality Environment at NPAC. New parallel systems: CM-5, nCUBE2 and DECmpp are connected by the fast HIPPI network and integrated with distributed FDDI clusters, high-end graphics machines, and VR peripherals by mapping all these components on individual threads of the VR MOVIE server. Overall synchronization is achieved by the real-time support within the MOVIE scheduling model. Although the figure presents only one "human in the loop," the model can also support in a natural way the multiuser, shared virtual worlds with remote access capabilities and with a variety of interaction patterns among the participants.

support.

Two possible public domain standard candidates in this area to be evaluated are VEOS from HIT Lab and MR (Minimal Reality) from the University of Alberta. We also plan to experiment with the Presence toolkit from DEC and with the VR_Workbench system from SimGraphics, Inc.

Parallel with evaluating emerging standard candidates, we will also attempt to develop a custom MovieScript-based VR operating shell. Present VR packages typically split into the static CAD-style authoring system for building virtual worlds and the dynamic real-time simulation system for visiting these worlds. The general-purpose support for both components is already present in the current MovieScript design: an interpretive object-oriented model with strong graphics support for the authoring system and a multithreading multiserver model for the simulation system.

A natural next step is to merge both components within the common language model of MovieScript so that new virtual worlds could also be designed in the dynamic immersive mode. The present graphics speed limitations do not currently allow us to visit worlds much more complex than just Boxvilles of various flavors, but this will change in coming years. Simple solids can be modelled in the conventional mouse-based CAD style, but with the growing complexity of the required shapes and surfaces, more advanced tools such as VR gloves become much more functional. This is illustrated in Figure 17.20, where we present a natural transition from the CAD-style to VR-style modelling environment. Such VR-based authoring systems will dramatically accelerate the process of building virtual worlds in areas such as industrial or fashion design, animation, art, and entertainment. They will also play a crucial role in designing nonphysical spaces—for example, for hypermedia navigation through complex databases where there are no established VR technologies and the novel immersion ideas can be created only by active, dynamic human participation in the interface design process.

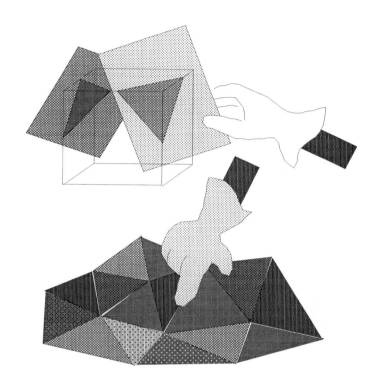

Figure 17.20: Examples of the Glove-Based VR Interfaces for CAD and Art Applications. The upper figure illustrates the planned tool for interactive sculpturing or some complex, irregular CAD tasks. A set of "chisels" will be provided, starting from the simplest "cutting plane" tool to support the glove-controlled polygonal geometry modelling. The lower figure illustrates a more advanced interface for the glove-controlled surface modelling. Given the sufficient resolution of the polygonal surface representation and the HPC support, one can generate the illusion of smooth, plastic deformations for various materials. Typical applications of such tools include fashion design, industrial (e.g., automotive) design, and authoring systems for animation. The ultimate goal in this direction is a virtual world environment for creating new virtual worlds.

Chapter 18

Complex System Simulation and Analysis

18.1 MetaProblems and MetaSoftware

18.1.1 Applications

In this chapter, we discuss some large-scale applications involving a mixture of several computational tasks. The ISIS system described in Section 18.2 grew out of several smaller C^3P projects undertaken by Rob Clayton and Brad Hager in Caltech's Geophysics Department. These are described in [Clayton:87a;88a], [Clayton:88a] [Gurnis:88a], [Lyzenga:85a;88a], [Raefsky:88b]. The geophysics applications in C^3P covered a broad range of topics and time scales. At the longest time scale (10^7 to 10^8 years), Hager's group used finite-element methods to study thermal convection processes in the Earth's mantle to understand the dynamics of plate tectonics. A similar algorithm was used to study the processes involved in earthquakes and crustal deformation over periods of 10 to 100 years. On a shorter time scale, Clayton simulated acoustic waves, such as those generated by an earth tremor in the Los Angeles basin. The algorithm was finite difference using high-order approximation. This (synchronous) regular grid was implemented using vector operations as the basic primitive so that Clayton could easily use both Cray and hypercube machines. This strategy is a forerunner of the ideas embodied in the data-parallel High Performance Fortran of Chapter 13. Tanimoto developed a third type of geophysics application with the MIMD hypercube decomposed as a pipeline to calculate the different resonating eigenmodes of the Earth, stimulated after an earthquake.

Sections 18.3 and 18.4 discuss a major series of simulations that were developed under U. S. Air Force sponsorship at the Jet Propulsion Laboratory in collaboration with Caltech. The application is caricatured in Figure 3.11(b), and Section 18.3 describes the overall architecture of the simulation. The major module was a sophisticated parallel Kalman filter and this is described in Section 18.4. Other complex applications developed by C^3P included the use of the Mark IIIfp at JPL in an image processing system that was used in real time to analyze images sent down by the space probe Voyager as it sped past Neptune. One picture produced by the hypercube at this encounter is shown in Figure 18.1 (Color Plate) [Groom:88a], [Lee:88a;89b]. Another major data analysis project in C^3P involved using the 512-node nCUBE-1 to look at radio astronomy data to uncover the signature of pulsars. As indicated in Table 14.3, this system "discovered" more pulsars in 1989 than the original analysis software running on a large IBM-3090. This measure (black holes located per unit time) seems more appropriate than megaflops for this application. A key algorithm used in the signal processing was a large, fast Fourier transform that was hand-coded for the nCUBE. This project also used the concurrent I/O subsystem on the nCUBE-1 and motivated our initial software work in this area, which has continued with software support from ParaSoft Corporation for the Intel Delta machine at Caltech. Figure 18.2 (Color Plate) illustrates results from this project and further details will be found in [Anderson:89c;89d;89e;90a], [Gorham:88a;88d;89a].

Another interesting signal-processing application by the same group was the use of high-performance computing in the removal of atmospheric disturbance from astronomical images, as illustrated by Figure 18.3. This combines parallel multidimensional Fourier transform of the bispectrum with conjugate gradient [Gorham:88d] minimization to reconstruct the phase. Turbulence, as shown in Figure 18.3(a), broadens images but one exploits the approximate constancy of the turbulence due to atmospheric patches over a 10 to 100 millisecond period. The 200″ Mount Palomar telescope is used an an interferometer by dividing it spatially onto one thousand "separate" small telescopes. Then standard astronomical interferometry techniques based on the bispectrum can be used to remove the turbulence effects, as shown in Figure 18.3(b), where one has increased statistics by averaging over 6,000 time slices [Fox:89i;89n;89y;90o].

An important feature of these applications is that they are built up from a set of modules as exemplified in Figures 3.10, 3.11, 15.1, and 15.2. They fall

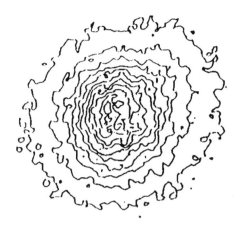

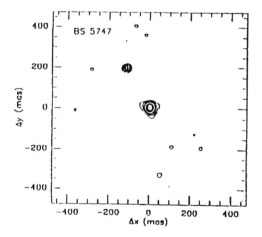

Figure 18.3: Optimal Binary Star Before (a) and After (b) Atmospheric Turbulence Removed. (a) Raw data from a six second exposure of BS5747 (β Corona Borealis) with a diameter of about 1 arcsecond. (b) The reconstructed image on the nCUBE-1 on the same scale as (a) using an average over 6,000 frames, each of which lasted 100 milliseconds. Each figure is magnified by a factor of 1000 over the physical image at the 200″ Palomar telescope focus.

into the compound problem class defined in Section 3.6. We had originally
(back in 1989, during a survey summarized in Section 14.1) classified such
metaproblems as asynchronous. We now realize that metaproblems have
a hierarchical structure—they are an asynchronous collection of modules.
However, this asynchronous structure does *not* lead to the parallelization
difficulties illustrated by the applications of Chapter 14. Thus, the "massive" parallelism does not come from the difficult synchronization of the
asynchronously linked modules but rather from internal parallelization of
the modules, which are individually synchronous (as, for example, with the
FFT mentioned above), or loosely synchronous (as in the Kalman Filter of
Section 18.4). One can combine data parallelism inside each module with
the functional asynchronous parallelism by executing each module concurrently. For example, in the SIM 87, 88, 89 simulations of Section 18.3, we
implemented this with an effective but crude method. We divided the target
machine—a 32-node to 128-node Mark IIIfp hypercube—into "subcubes"—
that is, the machine was statically partitioned with each module in Figure 3.11(b) assigned to a separate partition. Inside each partition, we used
a fast optimized implementation of CrOS, while the parallelism between
partitions was implemented by a variation of the Time Warp mechanism
discussed briefly in Sections 15.3 and 18.3. In the following subsections, we
discuss these software issues more generally.

18.1.2   Asynchronous versus Loosely Synchronous?

This is the last chapter on our voyage through the space of problem
classes. Thus, we will use this opportunity to wrap up some general issues.
We will, in particular, summarize the hardware and software architectures
that are suitable for the different problem classes that are reviewed in Table 18.1. We will first sharpen the distinction between loosely synchronous
and asynchronous problems. Let us compare,

1. Topology is an irregular two- or three-dimensional graph.

   Loosely Synchronous: Solution of partial differential equation with an
   unstructured mesh, as in Figure 12.8 (Color Plate).

   Asynchronous: Communication linkage between satellites in three dimensions, as in Figure 3.11(b).

2. Topology is an irregular tree (hierarchical structure).

Table 18.1: Summary of Problem Classes

- *Synchronous: Data Parallel*
  Tightly coupled and software needs to exploit features of problem structure to get good performance. Comparatively easy as different data elements are essentially identical.

- *Loosely Synchronous:*
  As above but data elements are not identical. Still parallelizes due to macroscopic time synchronization.

- *Asynchronous:*
  Functional (or data) parallelism that is irregular in space and time. Often loosely coupled and so need not worry about optimal decompositions to minimize communication. Hard to parallelize (massively) unless ...

- *Embarrassingly parallel:*
  Independent execution of disconnected components.

- *Compound MetaProblems:*
  Asynchronous collection of (loosely) synchronous components where these programs themselves can be parallelized. Metaproblems can also include asynchronous components and be defined hierarchically (recursively).

Loosely Synchronous: Fast multipole approach to N-body problem, as in Figure 12.11.

Asynchronous: α-β pruned game tree coming from computer chess, as in Figure 14.4.

These examples show that asynchronous and loosely synchronous problems are represented by similar underlying irregular graphs. What are the differences? Notice that we can always treat a loosely synchronous problem as asynchronous and indeed many approaches do this. One just needs to ignore the macroscopic algorithmic synchronization present in loosely synchronous problems. When is this a good idea? One would treat loosely synchronous problems as asynchronous when:

- The resultant (parallel) asynchronous implementation had sufficient performance. The loosely synchronous feature, if exploited, would lead to better and scaling parallel performance. Asynchronous problems, or asynchronous programming paradigms applied to loosely synchronous problems, typically do not have scaling parallel speedup proportional to number of nodes used.

- The easier (to use) asynchronous software paradigm led to a quicker implementation.

- The underlying target hardware could not exploit the performance gains of the loosely synchronous paradigm. For instance, a distributed computer network, such as that in Figures 3.10 or 15.2, might have latencies and bandwidth deficiences so that the asynchronous software paradigm performed as well as the loosely synchronous approach.

Thus, we see that loosely synchronous problems have an irregular underlying graph, but the underlying macroscopic synchronicity allows either the user or compiler to achieve higher performance. This is an opportunity (to achieve better performance), but also a challenge (it is not easy to exploit). Typically, asynchronous problems—or at least asynchronous problems that will get reasonable parallelism—have as much irregularity as loosely synchronous problems. However, they have larger grain size and lower communication-to-calculation ratios (f_C in Equation 3.10), so that one can obtain good performance without the loosely synchronous constraint. For instance, the chess tree of Figure 14.4 is more irregular and dynamic than the Barnes-Hut tree of Figure 12.11. However, the leaves of the Barnes-Hut are more tightly coupled than those of the chess tree. In Figure 3.11(b)

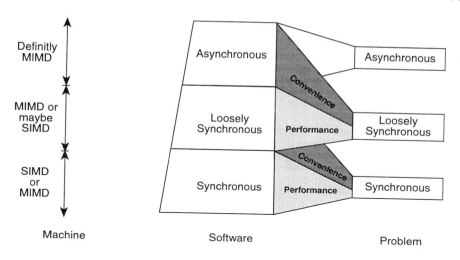

Figure 18.4: Mapping of Asynchronous, Loosely Synchronous, and Synchronous Levels or Components of Machine, Software and Problem. Each is pictured hierarchically with the asynchronous level at the top and synchronous components at lowest level. Any one of the components may be absent.

the satellites represent much larger grain size (and hence lower f_C values in Equation 3.10) than the small (in computational load) finite-element nodal points in Figure 12.8 (Color Plate).

As illustrated in Figure 18.4, one must implement asynchronous levels of a problem with asynchronous software paradigms and execute on a MIMD machine. Synchronous and perhaps loosely synchronous components can be implemented with synchronous software paradigms and executed with good performance on SIMD architectures; however, one may always choose to use a more flexible software model and if necessary a more flexible hardware architecture. As we have seen, MIMD architectures support both asynchronous and the more restricted loosely synchronous class; SIMD machines support synchronous and perhaps some loosely synchronous problems. These issues are summarized in Tables 18.2 and 18.3.

The approaches of Sections 12.4 and 12.8 exemplify the different choices that are available. In Section 12.8, Edelsohn uses an asynchronous system to control the high level of the tree with the lower levels implemented loosely synchronously for the particle dynamics and the multigrid differential equation solver. Warren and Salmon use a loosely synchronous system at each level. Software support for such structured adaptive problems is discussed

Table 18.2: What is the "correct" machine architecture for each problem class?

Problem Class	*Machine*
Synchronous	SIMD, MIMD
Loosely Synchronous	MIMD, maybe SIMD
Asynchronous	MIMD, but may not perform well without special hardware features
Compound (Metaproblems)	Heterogeneous network (see Figure 15.2)
Embarrassingly Parallel	Network of workstations MIMD, sometimes SIMD

in [Choudhary:92d] as part of the plans to add support of properly loosely synchronous problems to FortranD and High Performance Fortran (HPF).

In a traditional Fortran or HPF compiler, the unit of computation is the program or perhaps subroutine. Each Fortran statement (block) is executed sequentially (possibly with parallelism implied internally to statement (block) as in HPF), with synchronization at the end of each block. However, one could choose a smaller unit with loosely synchronous implementation of blocks and an overall asynchronous system for the statements (blocks). We are currently using this latter strategy for an HPF interpreter based on the MOVIE technology of Chapter 17. This again illustrates that in a hierarchical problem, one has many choices at the higher level (coarse grain) of the problem. The parallel C++ system Mentat developed by Grimshaw [Grimshaw:93b] uses similar ideas.

18.1.3   Software for Compound Problems

We have already described how the application of Section 18.3 illustrates a compound or metaproblem. The software support is that of an adaptive asynchronous high-level system controlling data parallel (synchronous

Table 18.3: Candidate Software Paradigms for each problem architecture.

- *Synchronous*: High Performance Fortran, Fortran 77D, Fortran 90D, C*, Crystal, APL

- *Loosely Synchronous*: Extensions of the above

- *Asynchronous*: MOVIE, PCN, Linda, C++, Time Warp (specialized application), object-oriented approaches

- *Compound Metaproblems*: MOVIE, AVS, PCN, Linda, extensions of ADA, Fortran or C++, controlling modules written in synchronous or loosely synchronous approach

- *Embarrassingly Parallel*: Several approaches work?
  - MOVIE, PCN, Linda, Network Express, ISIS, PVM

Note: Citations are given in the text, except for Crystal [Chen:88b], ISIS [Birman:87a;87b;91a], parallel C++ [Bodin:91a], [Chandy:92a], and PVM [Geist:92a], [Sunderam:90a].

or loosely synchronous) modules. Perhaps the best developed system of this type is AVS, which was originally developed for visualization but can be used to control computational modules as well [Cheng:92a]. Examples of such use of AVS are [Mills:92a;92b] for financial modelling, [Cheng:93a] for electromagnetic simulation, and the NPSS system at NASA Lewis [Claus:92a] for multidisciplinary optimization, as in Figures 3.11(a), 15.1, and 15.2. As summarized in Table 18.3, MOVIE, described in Chapter 17, was designed precisely for such metaproblems with the original target problem that of the many linked modules needed in large-scale image processing. Linda [Gelertner:89a] and its extension Trellis [Factor:90a], [Factor:90b] is one attractive commercial system which has been used for data fusion applications that fall into the problem class. The recent work on PCN [Chandy:90a] and its extensions CC++ [Chandy:92a] and Fortran-M [Foster:92a] were first implemented as reactive (asynchronous) software systems. However, it is planned to extend them to support the data-parallel modules needed for metaproblems.

The simulation systems of Sections 15.3 and 18.3 illustrate that one may need special functionality (in the cited cases, the support of event-driven simulation) in the high-level asynchronous component of the software system.

Clearly, this area is still poorly understood, as we have little experience. However, we expect such metaproblems to be the norm and not the exception as we tackle the large, complex problems needed in industry (Chapter 19).

18.2   ISIS: An Interactive Seismic Imaging System

The design goals and a prototype multicomputer implementation of an Interactive Seismic Imaging System (ISIS) are presented. The purpose of this system is to change the manner in which images of the subsurface are developed, by allowing the geologist/analyst to interactively observe the effects of changing focusing parameters, such as velocity. This technique leads to improved images and, perhaps more importantly, to an understanding of their accuracy.

18.2.1   Introduction

ISIS is a multicomputer-based interactive system for the imaging of seismic reflection data. In the sense used here, *interactive* means that when the seismic analyst makes an adjustment to an imaging parameter, the displayed image is updated rapidly enough to create a feedback loop between the analyst and the imaging machine. This interactive responsiveness allows a much greater use of the analyst's talents and training than conventional seismic processing systems do. To carry out the interactive imaging, we introduce a set of conceptual tools for the analyst to exploit, and also suggest a new role for the structural geologist—who is usually charged with interpreting a seismic image—as geologist/analyst.

18.2.2   Concepts of Interactive Imaging

The task of the seismic analyst is twofold: to select the proper imaging steps for a given data set, and the proper imaging parameters to produce an accurate image of the subsurface. The ideal imaging system would allow the analyst to inspect every datum for the effects of parameter selections and to adjust those parameters for best results. In conventional practice, such a task would be extremely cumbersome, requiring the generation of hundreds of plots and dozens of passes through the data. ISIS, however, provides an efficient mechanism for accomplishing this task. The system keeps the entire data volume on-line and randomly accessible; thus, any gather may be assembled and displayed on the monitor very rapidly. A sequential series of gathers may be displayed at a rate of several per second, a feature we refer to as a *movie*. Movies provide an opportunity to inspect and edit the data and to adjust the imaging parameters on the data groupings that most naturally display the effects of those parameters. For example, a movie of shot gathers enables the analyst to quickly identify bad shots or to inspect the accuracy of the ground roll mutes. A movie of the midpoint gathers allows for the inspection of the normal moveout correction and the stretch mutes. A movie of receiver gathers permits the analyst to detect problematic surface conditions, and a movie of constant-offset gathers allows the analyst to study various offset-dependent characteristics. In this way, the analyst may inspect the entire data volume in various groupings in a few minutes and may stop at any point to interactively adjust the imaging parameters.

Some parameters have effects that manifest themselves more clearly in the composite image than they do in raw data gathers. For instance, the effects of the migration velocity are only apparent in the migrated image. Ideally, the analyst would adjust the imaging parameters and immediately see the effect on the image. We refer to this ability as *interactive focusing*, an analogy to a photographer focusing a camera while viewing an image through the viewfinder. A typical focusing technique is to alternate an image back and forth between under-focus and over-focus in diminishing steps until the point of optimal focus is reached. Any seismic analyst can easily recognize an over- or under-migrated image, but the ability to smoothly pass from one to the other allows for the fine-tuning of the velocity model. This process also allows the analyst to test the robustness of the reflectors and their orientation in the image. Other parameters, such as those used in deconvolution, for instance, may also be tuned interactively.

Another task of the analyst is to diagnose problems in the seismic image and take corrective action. An image may be contaminated by a variety of artifacts; it is important to eliminate them if possible, or identify them if not. To aid the analyst in this task, ISIS provides a feature called *image deconstruction*. Consider an analyst studying a stacked section. Image deconstruction allows the analyst to point the cursor to a feature on the image and call up the midpoint gather(s) that produced it. In the same way the analyst may display any of the shot or receiver gathers that provided traces to the midpoint gather(s). At this point, the analyst may use movies of the gathers to study the features of interest. By tying the image points back to the raw data through image deconstruction, the analyst has an additional tool for distinguishing true reflectors from processing artifacts.

18.2.3 Geologist-As-Analyst

In traditional practice, a seismic analyst will produce an image that is then sent to a structural geologist for interpretation and the construction of a geologic cross-section. A problem with that practice is that the features that are important to the geologist—relationships between geologic beds, the dip on structures, the thickness of beds, and so on—may have been given little consideration by the analyst. Similarly, the analyst may have little information as to the geologic constraints of the region being imaged—information that would aid in producing a more accurate image. The ISIS project was originally conceived in an attempt to blend the roles of analyst and geologist. In the role of geologist the user can make use of the interactive imaging facilities to gain useful information about the character and robustness of the imaged structure. A structural geologist provided with an interactive processing system can develop a much more thorough, dynamic understanding of the image than would ever be possible through the examination of a static section produced through some unknown processing sequence. In the role of analyst the user may apply geologic constraints and intuition to improve the imaging process. While we will continue to refer to the seismic analyst throughout this paper, we believe that through the use of interactive imaging the distinction between geologist and analyst will disappear.

As mentioned above, the principal task of the structural geologist is to interpret a seismic section and produce a geologic cross-section of a prospect. The act of making this interpretation also implicitly creates a seismic model. It should therefore be possible to use this as the input model in the imaging process. An image produced in this way should be very similar to the image from which the interpretation was originally made; if not, there is reason to suspect the accuracy of the model. A future addition to ISIS will allow the geologist to make interpretations as the imaging system honors the interpretation in recomputing the image. This process will further break down the barrier between imaging and interpretation, and between geologist and analyst.

18.2.4   Why Interactive Imaging?

It would be difficult to conceive of a fully automated system to process seismic data. The enormous complexity of geologic structures and the recorded data make such a system an unlikely near-term development. Similarly, it is difficult to imagine a generalized inversion formula for seismic reflection data, since the trade-off between the reflectivity and velocity structures of the subsurface is generally not completely constrained by the data. Now and for the foreseeable future, the expertise of a human analyst will be required for the accurate imaging of seismic data. This fact does not mean that the role of the machine will be minimized, however, as advances in imaging technique have more than kept pace with advances in hardware capability. But, until recently, the batch-processing paradigm in seismic imaging has been the only option. Currently, the seismic analyst uses his or her extensive experience and training only when the latest plot is generated by the processing software. ISIS is an attempt to change that paradigm by allowing for a much greater utilization of the analyst's abilities.

Other advantages of interactive imaging include the ability to process a seismic survey in just one or two days, and the generation of a self-documenting history of the imaging sequence (with the ability to return to any stage of the processing). ISIS should be an excellent educational tool, not only by providing students the ability to interact with data and imaging parameters, but also because it is programmable, providing a good platform for experimental algorithms.

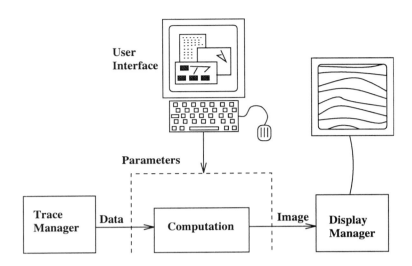

Figure 18.5: Imaging Tasks. The four principal divisions of the ISIS system are shown. The dotted lines represent software layers that insulate the computational processes from the other functions.

18.2.5   System Design

ISIS consists of four main parts (Figure 18.5): a parallel, on-line seismic trace manager, a high-performance parallel computational engine, a parallel graphics display manager, and a window-based, interactive user interface. The data from a seismic survey are stored across an array of trace manager processes. These processes are responsible for providing seismic traces to the computational processes at transfer rates sufficiently high to keep the computational processes from being idle. The computational processes generate an image and deliver it to the display manager for display on a monitor. The user triggers this processing sequence by adjusting an imaging parameter. The system is designed to minimize the delay between the user's action and the refreshing of the image—if the delay is short enough, the imaging will be truly interactive.

ISIS was designed to be a flexible, programmable imaging system. As described here, ISIS is actually two systems. The first is a set of system-level programs accessible through simple library interfaces. This software was designed to conceal implementation-specific details from the applications programmer. The trace manager and the display manager are part of the system-level software. The second level of ISIS, the applications level, is built upon the first. The user interface and seismic processing functions are part of the applications level. The system software was designed to minimize the effort needed to develop custom user interface and processing functions. We have developed both levels; the ISIS presented here is a processing system built upon the system software.

The advantages of the division between system and applications software are numerous: 1) the system is customizable, allowing for the addition of new imaging techniques or user interface technology; 2) the system will be portable with a minimal effort at the applications end—for instance, the application interface to the trace manager would be the same regardless of whether the platform was a message-passing multicomputer, a shared-memory multicomputer, a network of workstations, or a single uniprocessor machine; and 3) the parallelism of the trace manager and display manager are concealed from the applications programmer, greatly simplifying the programming effort.

18.2.6 Performance Considerations

To provide the interactive imaging capabilities discussed above, the imaging hardware must provide certain minimum levels of performance. Figure 18.5 schematically represents data flowing from the trace manager to the computational processes and the image generated there being sent to the display manager for eventual display on the monitor. To perform the interactive focusing discussed above, the computational engine must deliver approximately 200 to 300 MFLOPS. While this number may be difficult and expensive to obtain in a single-processor system, it is easily obtainable in parallel systems. Likewise, in order to satisfy the demands of interactive stacking, the trace manager is required to deliver many thousands of traces per second (approximately 4 to 8 Kbytes/trace) to the computational processes. Since these traces are essentially randomly ordered throughout a multigigabyte data volume, a simple calculation will show that, for current disk drive technology, the limiting factor in supplying the data is the disk seek time, not the aggregate transfer rate. Again, a solution to the problem is for a number of disks working in parallel to provide the needed performance. Finally, in order to display movies of seismic gathers at eight frames per second, the graphics processors must be able to absorb and display eight megabytes of data per second. Once again, this requirement may be satisfied by multiple nodes working in parallel.

In addition to the general performance issues, which could be achieved by the creation of a specially built machine, or the addition of custom I/O devices to an existing supercomputer, we chose to use only commercially available hardware. The reasons for this choice are twofold: We wanted other interested researchers to be able to duplicate our efforts, and we wanted the system to be reasonably affordable.

18.2.7   Trace Manager

From the point of view of the applications programmer, the trace manager consists of two principal functions: The first, datarequest, is a request for the trace manager to deliver certain data to the requesting process (e.g., a shot gather); the other function, *getdata*, is called repeatedly after a call to datarequest, each call returning a single trace until no traces remain and the request is satisfied. Because of the simplicity of this interface, the applications programmer need know nothing of the implementation details of the trace manager.

Each instance of the trace manager consists of an archive containing some portion of the data from a seismic survey, and a list containing information on the archived traces. In this implementation of ISIS, the archive takes the form of magnetic disk drives, but in other implementations the data may be stored or staged in process memory. A single copy of the data from a seismic survey is spread evenly among all the instances of the trace manager process.

When a computational process calls *datarequest*, each instance of the trace manager searches its trace list and generates a secondary list of traces that satisfy the request. Because there may be multiple computational processes, there may be several active request lists—at most, one for each computational process. The trace manager retrieves the listed traces from the archive and prepares them for delivery to the requesting process. Before delivering the traces, the trace manager may, at the behest of the requesting process, perform some simple object-oriented preprocessing, such as applying statics, mutes, and NMO.

18.2.8   Display Manager

The display manager, like the trace manager, is designed to conceal implementation details from the applications programmer. It consists of two calls: one for delivering a trace to the display manager for plotting, and another

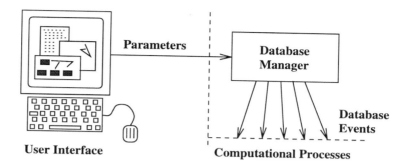

Figure 18.6: The User Interface/Database

to inform the display manager that the image is complete. Each instance of the display manager buffers images until a signal from the user interface notifies it to copy or assemble an image in video memory and display it. This interface with the application allows the user to have complete control over what is displayed and the movie display rate.

18.2.9 User Interface

At the system level, no hardware or software specification of the user interface is made; it is left to the applications designer to select an appropriate interface. The necessary communication between the user interface and the computational processes is accomplished through a system-level parameter database. The database manager maintains multiple user-defined databases and stores information in key/content pairs. When an imaging parameter is selected or modified, the user interface packs the parameter into a byte stream and stores it in a database (Figure 18.6).

The database manager then generates database events which are sent, along with the data, to the computational processes where they are dealt with as discussed in the next section.

This event-driven mechanism has several advantages over other means of managing control flow. It allows the system-level software to provide the communication between the user interface and the computational processes without the system needing any knowledge of the content of the messages, and without the user knowing the communications scheme. The data is packed and unpacked from user-defined structures only within the user-provided processes. Our implementation of ISIS uses Sun's XDR routines for

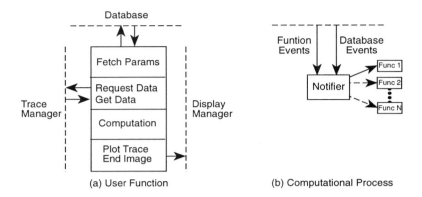

Figure 18.7: An Instance of a Computational Process: (a) a User-Defined Function; (b) the Controlling Process with Several User Functions in Place. The bold arrow running from the notifier to the user function "Func 1" indicates the currently active function.

packaging the data, which has the added advantage that it also resolves the byte-ordering differences between the host machine and the computational processors.

18.2.10   Computation

The computational process consists of two parts: the system-level framework, and the user-defined, application-level processing functions. The user-defined functions perform the seismic imaging tasks and are free to pursue that end by whatever means the applications programmer finds appropriate, as long as the functions return normally and in a timely fashion. Figure 18.7a is a schematic example of a typical user-defined function. The user function, when called, first retrieves any relevant parameters from the database. These parameters may be processing parameters, such as the velocity model, or they may be special information, such as a specification of the data to be processed. After retrieving the parameters, the function requests the appropriate data from the trace manager through a call to datarequest. It then loops over calls to getdata, performs computations, and executes the appropriate calls to plot the processed traces. The function may loop over several data requests if multiple gathers are needed, for instance, to build a stacked section. The function notifies the display manager when the image is complete, and the user function returns to the calling process.

While the parallelism of the computational process cannot be hidden from the applications programmer, the programming task is made much simpler by concealing the implementation details of the trace manager, display manager, and database. To help facilitate parallelization, each instance of a computational process is provided with the total number of computational processes, as well as its own logical position in that number. With this information, most seismic imaging tasks can be easily parallelized by either data or domain decomposition.

The system-level software for the computational processes (Figure 18.7b) consists of a main notifier loop that handles the database events and distributes control to the user-defined functions. The programmer is provided with functions for registering the processing functions with the notifier, along with the databases of interest to those functions. For instance, a function to plot shot gathers may depend on the statics database only, while a function to produce a stacked section may depend on the velocity database and the statics database. The applications programmer is also provided with an interface for selecting the active function. No more than one function may be active at any given time. Incoming database events are consumed by the notifier, the data are stored in the local database, and the notifier will call the active function if and only if that function has registered an interest in that particular database. This interface simplifies adding a new processing function or parameter to the existing system.

18.2.11 Prototype System

ISIS is implemented on a multicomputer manufactured by Meiko Scientific Ltd. Figure 18.8 is a schematic representation of the prototype ISIS hardware. The trace manager is implemented on eight nodes, each with an Inmos T800 processor and a SCSI controller responsible for two 1.2-gigabyte disk drives. Two of the trace manager nodes also control 8mm tape drives used for initial loading of data into the system. The computational processes reside on eight nodes with Intel i860 processors. The display manager is mapped onto two T800 nodes with video RAM and an RGB analog output that drives a color monitor. The user interface resides on a Sun SPARCstation that serves as the host machine for the Meiko system.

It should be noted that, because the i860 is nearly an order of magnitude faster than the T800, many of the functions of the trace manager and the display manager are actually performed on the computational nodes, but this detail is completely hidden from the applications programmer.

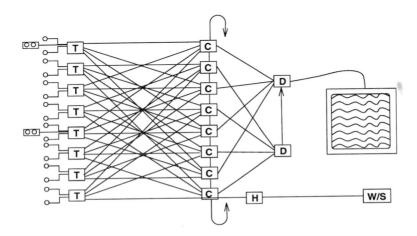

Figure 18.8: Layout of Processes on the Meiko Multicomputer. Each box enclosing a letter represents a node: trace manager processes are marked "T," computational processes "C," and display manager processes "D." "H" is the system host board, and "W/S" represents the Sun workstation, where the user interface resides. Each trace manager has access to two disk drives (small circles), and two processors also have 8mm tape drives. The lines between nodes represent communications channels.

We consider this system a prototype. A simple evaluation of the capabilities of the hardware will show that it cannot provide the performance described in Section 18.2.6. While this machine has proven to be extremely useful, a complete system would be two to four times the size. The system software is designed to be scalable, as is the hardware. In fact, if the size of the machine were doubled, the ISIS software would run as is, without requiring recompilation.

18.2.12 Conclusions

Because of the recent and ongoing advances in computer technology, interactive seismic imaging will become an increasingly powerful and affordable tool. It is only within the last two years that machines with all the capabilities necessary to perform interactive seismic imaging have been commercially available. In another ten years, machines with all the necessary capabilities will be no larger than a workstation and will be affordable even within the budget of the smallest departments. Because of the availability of these machines, interactive imaging will certainly replace the traditional methods. It is our hope that the success of the ISIS project will continue the trend toward true interactive imaging, and provide a model for systems of the future.

We have introduced several concepts that we believe will be important to any future systems: movies, interactive focusing, and image deconstruction. These tools provide the means for the analyst to interactively image seismic data. We also introduce the idea of geologist-as-analyst to extend the range of the imaging machine into the interpretation of the image, and to allow the geologist a better understanding of the image itself.

The design of ISIS concentrated on providing the building blocks of an interactive imaging system, and on the implementation of a prototype system. The imaging task is divided into four main parts: trace manager, display manager, computational engine, and user interface. Each part is implemented in a way that makes it scalable on multiprocessor systems, but conceals the implementation details from the applications programmer. Interfaces to the different parts are designed for simplicity and portability.

18.3 Parallel Simulations that Emulate Function

Increasingly, computer simulation is directed at predicting the behavior and performance of large manmade systems that themselves include multiple instances of imbedded digital computers. Often the computers are distributed, sometimes over wide geographic distances, and the system modelling becomes largely a combination computer/communication simulation. The type of simulation needed here can be characterized as having some elements that are *simulated* in a conventional sense where a statistical or descriptive model of the element is used. But other elements, particularly the imbedded computers, are *emulated*, which is to say that the computations performed nearly duplicate the functionality of that real-world element. For example, a "tracker" really tracks. It does not simply provide results that are in conformance with how a tracker *should* track.

In this manner, the simulator becomes both a predictor of system performance and an active participant in the system development as the behavior of the emulated elements is refined and evolved.

In 1987, the Mark III Hypercube Applications group at JPL undertook the most computationally demanding simulation of this type yet proposed: the detailed simulation of the global Strategic Defense Initiative System—sometimes known as Star Wars [Meier:89a;90a], [Warren:88a], [Zimmerman:89a].

A parallel processor was chosen to perform the simulation both because of its ability to deliver the computational power required and because it was closely reflective of the class of machines that might be used for the imbedded computers in the SDI System—that is, the simulation was helping to prove the applicability of parallel processing for complex real-time system applications. The Mark IIIfp Hypercube was the host machine of choice at the time (1987–1989).

18.3.1   The Basic Simulation Structure

The basic structure of the simulation—first called Simulation87—is shown in Figure 18.9. Here, an otherwise monolithic hypercube is subdivided into subcubes, each containing a data-parallel subapplication of typically synchronous character. Shown in this early and greatly simplified view are

- a pair of multitarget trackers—described in detail later on in this Chapter

- Battle Management—a computation that takes the tracking output, assesses the overall situation, and assigns the defensive assets to the targets [Payne:90a]

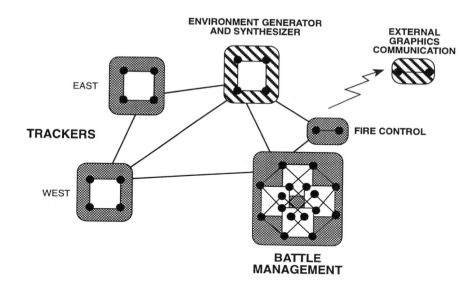

Figure 18.9: Basic Simulation87 Structure

- Fire Control—carries out the details of "shooting" the assigned targets

- Environment Generation—provides the housekeeping computations: timekeeping, flying the threats (ICBMs), defensive satellite orbits, and so on, and overall simulation synchronization and control

The details of each module are not important for our discussions here. What is pertinent is that each involves a substantial computation that runs on a parallel machine using standard data-parallel techniques. The inter-module communications take place over the normal hypercube communications channels in a (rather low-fidelity) emulation of the communications necessary in the real-world system. The execution of the simulation as a whole can then exploit two classes of parallelism: the multiple modules or functions execute concurrently and each function is itself a data-parallel process. Load balancing is done on a coarse level as shown by the size of the subcube allocations to each function. Emphasis was also placed on communicating information to graphics workstations that helped visualize and interpret the progress of the simulation.

This is a rather general structure for an emerging class of simulation that seeks to model large-scale system performance and employ elements both of pure computer simulation and this relatively unique element of emulation.

18.3.2   The Run-Time Environment—the Centaur Operating System

The most productive and efficient run-time environment interior to each subcube was that of CrOS—described above in Chapter 5—since the applications typically hosted were of the synchronous type. But the intermodule communications needed were definitely asynchronous. For them, the communications primitives needed were those that had already been developed in the Mercury OS [Burns:88a] and similar to those described in Chapter 16. The system-level view was one of needing "loosely coupled sets of tightly coupled multiprocessors." That is, a single node needed to be tightly coupled, using CrOS, to nearest neighbors in its local subcube, yet loosely coupled, using Mercury or other asynchronous protocol, to other subcubes working on other tasks. Of course, it would have been possible to use Mercury for communications of both types, but on the Mark III level of hardware implementation, the performance penalty for using the asynchronous protocol where a synchronous protocol would suffice was factor of nearly five.

The CrOS latency of nearest-neighbor messaging on the Mark III is $100\,\mu sec$; for Mercury it is $520\,\mu sec$—both adequate numbers for the 2-Mip 68020 data processors used on the Mark III, but often strained by the Weitek 16-MFLOPS floating-point accelerator. Messaging latency still is a key problem, even on the most recent machines. For example, on the Delta machine, NX delivers a nearest-neighbor message in $60\,\mu sec$; Express takes $112\,\mu sec$. About the same, but now supporting a 120-Mip, 60-MFLOPS data processor.

To meet these hybrid needs and preserve maximum performance, a dual-protocol messaging system—called Centaur for its evocation of duality—was developed [Lee:89a]. To implement the disparate protocols involved—Mercury is interrupt driven whereas CrOS uses polled communications—it was determined that all messages would initially be assumed to be asynchronous and first handled as Mercury messages. A message that was actually synchronous contained a signal to that effect in its first packet header. Upon reading this signal, Mercury would disable interrupts and yield to the much faster CrOS machinery for the duration of the CrOS message. This scheme yielded synchronous and asynchronous performance only about 30% degraded from their counterparts in a nonmixed context.

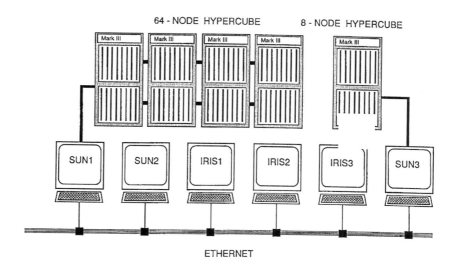

Figure 18.10: Typical Sim89 Hardware Configuration

18.3.3 SDI Simulation Evolution

Three separate versions of the SDI simulations were constructed: Sim87, Sim88, and Sim89. Each was more elaborate and used more capable hardware than its predecessor. Sim87, for example, executed on a single 32-node Mark III; Sim89, in contrast, was implemented to run on the 128-node Mark IIIfp. Configuration was flexible; Figure 18.10 shows a typical example using two hypercubes and a network of Ethernet-connected workstations. The internal structure of the simulation showed similar evolution. Sim87 was not much more elaborate than indicated in Figure 18.9 but it evolved to the much more capable version shown in Figure 18.11 for Sim89 [Meier:90a], [Yeung:90a].

Features of Sim89 included more elaborate individual modules, outlined below.

- The intermediate abstraction of "platform" was introduced and platforms became hosts to instances of multiple modules as shown. The importance of the platform beyond that of definitional convenience was that a platform in general becomes associated with a satellite whose

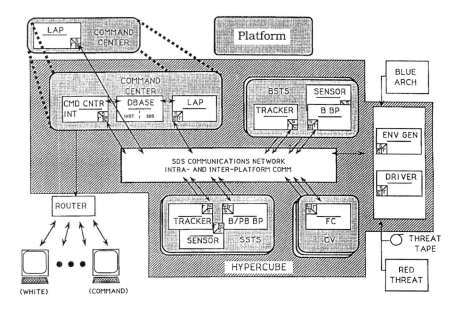

Figure 18.11: An Evolved SDI Simulation, Sim89

location and trajectory with respect to the emerging scenario determine its view and computational progress. A typical platform might host a sensor, a tracker, and a battle planner of some type and consist of as many subcubes. Multiple platforms of each type were permitted and multiple platform types could be created; communication links between the platforms completed the constellation and determined the flow of information.

- An important platform class was the simulated Ground Command Center, included in the Simulation to model the effects that the human command element could have on the progress and outcome of the scenarios being simulated. The Command Center included the elements of:

  1. Graphics interpretations of the progress of the simulation (Figure 18.12 (Color Plate)).

  2. A fully concurrent database that received, processed, and made

pertinent data available to other command center elements.

3. A Look Ahead Planner which in itself was a medium-fidelity simulation, capable of projecting the current state of the simulation forward rapidly and analyzing the prospective results of various command options.

The Command Center was an important conceptual step. It repositioned the role of the workstations from one of passive display of the activities occurring internally to the hypercube, to the role of the key user interface into a network computing environment assisted by large-scale parallel machines. It, in effect, helped us merge our own mental picture of the paradigm of network computing with that of parallel processing and into the more unifying view of cooperative, high-performance computing.

18.3.4 Simulation Framework and Synchronization Control

The original structure of multiple data-parallel function emulations executing concurrently was left intact by this evolution. The supporting services and means of synchronizing the various activities have evolved considerably, however.

The execution of the simulation as shown in Figure 18.9 is synchronized rather simply. Refer now to Figure 18.13. By the structure of the desired activities, sensor data are sent to the Trackers, their tracks are sent to the Battle Planner, and the battle plans are returned to the Environment Generator (which calculates the effects of any defensive actions taken). The exchange of mono tracks shown is a communication internal to the Tracker's two subcubes.

The simulation initiates by having each module forward its data to the next unit in the pipeline and then read its input data as initialization for the first set of computations. At initialization, all messages are null except the sensor messages from the Environment Generator. In the first computation cycle, only the Tracker is active; the Battle Planner has no tracks. After the tracker completes its initial sensor data processing (described in detail later in the chapter), the resulting tracks are forwarded to the Battle Planner, which starts computing its first battle plan while the Tracker is working on the second set of sensor data—a computational pipeline, or round, has been established. When an element finishes with a given work segment, the results are forwarded and that element then waits if necessary for the data that initiates the next work segment. Convenient, effective, but hardly of

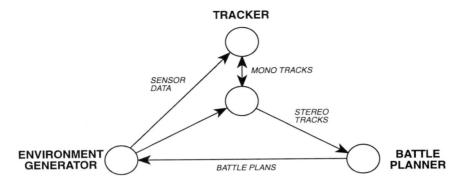

Figure 18.13: The Simulation of Figure 18.9 is Controlled by a Pipeline Synchronization

the generality of, say, Time Warp (described in Section 15.3) as a means of concurrency control.

Yet a full implementation of Time Warp is not necessarily required here even in the most general circumstances. Remember that Time Warp implements a general but pure discrete event simulation. Its objective—speedup— is achieved by capitalizing on the functional parallelism inherent in all the multiple objects, analogous to the multiple functions being described here. It permits the concurrent execution of the needed procedures and ensures a correct simulation via rollback when the inevitable time accidents occur. In the type of simulation discussed here, not only is speedup often not the goal, but when it is, it is largely obtained via the data parallelism of each function and load-balanced by the judicious assignment of the correct number of processors to each. The speedup due to functional parallelism can be small and good performance can still result. A means of assuring a correct simulation, however, is crucial.

We have experimented with several synchronization schemes that will ensure this correctness even when the simulation is of a generality illustrated by Figure 18.11. The most straightforward of these is termed *time buckets* and is useful whenever one can structure a simulation where activities taking place in one time interval, or bucket, can only have effects later on in the next or succeeding time buckets.

The initial implementation of the time bucket approach was in conjunction with an SDS communications simulation, one that sought to treat in higher fidelity the communications activities implicit in Figure 18.11. In this simulation, the emulators of the communications processors aboard each

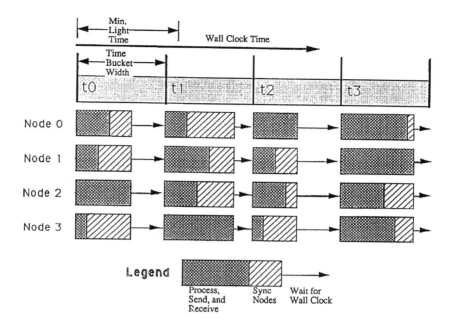

Figure 18.14: The Time Bucket Approach to Synchronization Control

satellite and the participating ground stations were distributed across the nodes of the Mark III hypercube. In the most primitive implementation, each node would emulate the role of a single satellite's comm processor; messages would be physically passed via the hypercube comm channels and a rather complete emulation would result.

Since the correspondence to the real world is not perfect—actual hypercube comm delays are not equal to the satellite-to-satellite light time delays, for example, this emulation must be controlled and synchronized just like a conventional discrete-event parallel simulation if time accidents are not to occur and invalidate the results. Figure 18.14 shows the use of the time bucket approach for synchronization in this situation. The key is to note that, because of the geometries involved there is a minimum light time delay between any two satellites. If the processing is done in time steps—time buckets, if you will—of less than this delay, it is possible to ensure that accidents will never occur.

Referring to Figure 18.14, assume each of the processors is released at time t_0 and is free to process all messages in its input queue up to and including the time bucket's duration without regard to any coordination of the progress of simulation time in the other nodes. Since the minimum light time delay is longer than this bucket, it is not possible for a remote node to send a message and have it received (in simulation time) interior to the free processing time; no accidents can occur. Each node then processes all its events up to a simulation time advance of one time bucket. It waits until all processors have reached the same point and all messages—new events from outside nodes—have been received and placed properly in their local event queues. When all processors have finished, the next time bucket can be entered.

The maximum rate that simulation time can advance is, of course, determined by the slowest node to complete in each time bucket. If proceeding is desired, not as rapidly as possible but in real time (i.e., maintaining a close one-to-one correspondence between elapsed wall clock and simulation time), the nodes can additionally wait for the wall clock to catch up to simulation time before proceeding; this behavior is illustrated in Figure 18.4.

While described as a communication simulation, this is a rather general technique. It can be used whenever the simulation modules can reasonably obey the constraint that they not schedule events shorter than Δt into the future for objects external to the local node. It can work efficiently whenever the density of events/processor is significantly greater than unity for this same Δt. A useful view of this technique is that the simulation is fully parallel and event-driven interior to a time bucket, but is controlled by an implicit global controller and is a time-stepped simulation with respect to coarser time resolutions.

Implementation varies. The communication simulation just described was hosted on the Mark III and took advantage of the global lines to coordinate the processor release times. In more general circumstances where globals are not available, an alternative *time service* [Li:91a] has been implemented and is currently used for a network-based parallel Strategic Air Defense simulation.

Where a fixed time step does not give adequate results, an alternate technique implementing an adaptive Δt has been proposed and investigated [Steinman:91a]. This technique, termed *breathing time buckets*, is notionally diagrammed in Figure 18.15. Pictured there are the local event queues for two nodes. These event queues are complete and ordered at the assumed synchronized *start of cycle* simulation time. The object of the initial pro-

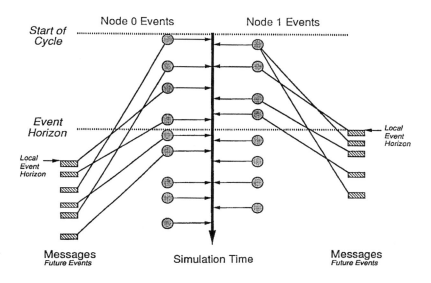

Figure 18.15: Breathing Time Buckets as a Means of Synchronization Control

cessing is to determine a "global event horizon" which is defined as the time of the earliest new event that will be generated by the subsequent processing. Current events prior to that time may be processed in all the nodes without fear of time accidents. This time is determined by having each node optimistically process its own local events, but withhold the sending of messages, until it has reached a simulation time where the next event to be processed is a "new" event. The time reached is called the "local event horizon." Once every node has determined its local horizon, a global minimum is determined and equated to the global event horizon. All nodes then roll back their local objects to that simulation time (easy since no messages have been sent) send the messages that are valid, and commit to the event processing up to that point.

In implementation, there are many refinements and extensions of these basic ideas in order to optimize performance, but this is the fundamental construct. It is proving to be relatively easily implemented, gives good per-

formance in a variety of circumstances, and has even outperformed Time
Warp in some cases [Steinman:92a].

Synchronization control is but one issue, albeit the most widely discussed
and debated, in building a general framework to support this class of simulation. Viewed from the perspective of cooperative high performance computing, the Simulation Framework can be seen as services needed by the
individual applications programmer, but not provided by the network or
parallel computer operating system. Providing support for:

- object-oriented programming including distributed objects

- data-parallel programming

- interprocess communications

- remote procedure calls

- global naming services

- distributed database as simulation resource

- parallel proximity detection

- simulation checkpointing

- interactive simulation control

- provisions for interface to real-world systems (e.g., people)

in addition to synchronization control, are all important issues currently
under active investigation and implementation.

18.4   Multitarget Tracking

18.4.1   Nature of the Problem

Sim89, described broadly in the previous section, is designed to process a
so-called mass raid scenario, in which a few hundred primary threats are
launched within a one- to two-minute time window, together with about 40
to 60 secondary, anti-satellite launches. The primary targets boost through
two stages of powered flight (total boost time is about 300 seconds), with
each booster ultimately deploying a single *post boost vehicle* (PBV). Over
the next few hundred seconds, each PBV in turn deploys 10 *re-entry vehicles*

(RVs). The Sim89 environment does not yet include the factor of 10 to 100 increase in object counts due to decoys, as would be expected in the "real world."

The data available for the tracking task consist, essentially, of line-of-sight measurements from various sensing platforms to individual objects in the target ensemble at (fairly) regular time intervals. At present, all sensing platforms are assumed to travel in circular orbits about a spherically symmetric earth (neither of these assumptions/simplifications is essential). The current program simulates two classes of sensors: GEO platforms, in geostationary, equatorial orbits, and MEO platforms in polar orbits at altitude 2000 km. The scan time for GEO sensors is typically taken to be $\Delta T = 5$ sec, with $\Delta T = 10$ sec for MEO platforms.

Figure 18.16 shows a small portion of the field of view of a MEO sensor at a time about halfway through the RV deployment phase of a typical Sim89 scenario. The circles are the data seen by the sensor at one scan and the crosses are the data seen by the same sensor at a time $\Delta T = 10$ sec later. Given such data, the primary tasks of the tracking program are fairly simple to state:

1. Determine which data at one scan are associated with data from previous scans.

2. For associated data points over several scans, determine the trajectory of the underlying targets.

Moreover, these tasks must be done in an extremely timely fashion. For example, the ASATs mentioned at the beginning of this subsection have burn times of order 100 seconds, and can hit a space-based asset in less that 250 seconds after launch. In order to allow self/mutual defense among the space-based assets, the tracker must provide good three-dimensional tracks for ASATs within about 60 seconds of launch.

In order to (in principle) process data from a wide variety of sensors, the Sim89 tracker adopts a simple unified sensing formalism. For each sensor, the *standard reference plane* is taken to be the plane passing through the center of the earth, normal to the vector from the center of the earth to the (instantaneous) satellite position. Note that these standard frames are *not* inertial. The two-dimensional data used by the tracking algorithm are the coordinates of the intersection of the reference plane and the line of sight from the sensor to the target. The intersection coordinates are defined in terms of a standard Cartesian basis in the reference frame, with one axis

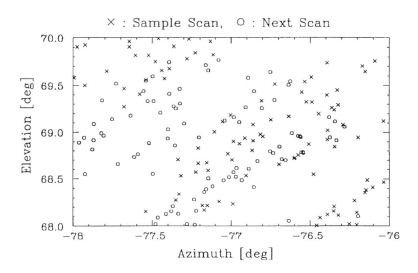

Figure 18.16: Typical Midcourse Data Sets, Consecutive Scans

along the normal to the sensor's orbital plane, and the other parallel to the projection of the platform velocity onto the reference plane.

18.4.2   Tracking Techniques

The task of interpreting data such as those shown in Figure 18.16 is clearly rather challenging. The tracking algorithm described in the next section is based on a number of elementary building blocks, which are now briefly described [Baillie:88f], [Gottschalk:87f;88a;90a;90b].

Single-Target Tracking

In order to associate observations from successive scans, a model for the expected motion of the underlying target is required. The system model used throughout the Sim89 tracker is based on a simple kinematic Kalman filter. Consider, for the moment, motion in one dimension. The model used to describe this motion is

$$\frac{d}{dt}\begin{pmatrix} x \\ v \\ a \\ j \end{pmatrix} = \begin{pmatrix} v \\ a \\ j \\ 0 \end{pmatrix} + \begin{pmatrix} 0 \\ 0 \\ 0 \\ w_q \end{pmatrix} \qquad (18.1)$$

where x, v, a and j are position, velocity, acceleration and jerk ($j = da/dt$) and w_q is a stochastic (noise) contribution to the jerk. The Kalman filter based on Equation 18.1 is completely straightforward, and ultimately depends on a single parameter

$$q \equiv \langle w_q^2 \rangle \approx \frac{10^{-8}\,\mathrm{km}^2}{sec^7} \qquad (18.2)$$

The system model of Equation 18.1 is appropriate for describing targets travelling along trajectories with unknown but approximately smooth accelerations. The size of the noise term in Equation 18.2 determines the magnitude of abrupt changes in the acceleration which can be accommodated by the model without loss of track. For the typical noise value quoted in Equation 18.2, scan-to-scan variations $|\Delta a| \leq 1 - 2\,\mathrm{g}$ are easily accommodated.

During boost phase, the actual trajectories of the targets are, in principle, not known, and the substantial freedom for unanticipated maneuvering implicit in Equations 18.1 and 18.2 is essential. On the other hand, the exact equation of motion for ballistic target (i.e., RVs) is completely known, so that the uncertainties in predicted positions according to the kinematic model are much larger than is necessary. Nonetheless, Equation 18.1 is maintained as the primary system model throughout *all* phases of the Sim89 tracker. This choice is based primarily on considerations of speed. Evaluations of predicted positions according to Equation 18.1 require only polynomial arithmetic and are much faster than predictions done using the exact equations of motion. Moreover, for the scan times under consideration, the differences between exact and polynomial predictions are certainly small compared to expected sensor measurement errors.

While "exact" system models for target trajectories are not used in the tracker per se, they are used for the collection of tracking "answers" which are exchanged between tracking systems or between trackers and other elements in the full Sim89 environment. (This "handover" issue is discussed in more detail in the next section.)

Multitarget Tracking

Given the preceding prescription for estimating the state of a single target from a sequence of two-dimensional observations, the central issue in multi-target tracking is that of associating observations with tracks or observations on one scan with those of a subsequent scan (e.g., in Figure 18.16, which x is paired with which o). There are, in a sense, two extreme schemes for attempting this track↔hit association:

Track splitting: All *plausible* associations of existing tracks with new data are maintained in the updated track file.

Optimal associations: Only a single global association of tracks with incoming data is selected.

Each of these prescriptions has advantages and disadvantages.

The track splitting model is robust in the sense that the correct track↔hit association is very likely to be generated and maintained at any step in track processing. The track extension task is also extremely "localized," in the sense that splittings of any one track can be done independently of those for other tracks. This makes concurrent implementations of track splitting quite simple. The primary objections to track splitting are twofold:

1. Track splitting does not provide an easily interperted "answer" as to the actual nature of the underlying scenario.

2. Without (sometimes) elaborate mechanisms to identify and delete poor or duplicate entries in the track file, track splitting leads to an essentially exponential explosion in the track file size in dense target environments.

Track splitting is particularly useful at early times in the evolution of a target scenario, when the available data are too sparse to determine the "correctness" of any candidate track. As is discussed in more detail in Section 18.4.3, the primary role of Track Splitting in the Sim89 tracker is that of track initiation.

The optimal association prescription is orthogonal to track splitting in the sense that the single "best" pairing is maintained in place of all plausible pairings. This best Track↔Hit association is determined by a global optimization procedure, as follows. Let $S_A = \{a_i\}$ and $S_B = \{b_j\}$ be two lists of items (e.g., actual data and predicted data values). Let

$$d_{ij} \equiv d[a_i, b_j] \tag{18.3}$$

be a cost for associating items a_i and b_j (e.g., the cartesian distance between predicted and actual data positions for the data coordinates defined above). The optimal association of the two lists is that particular permutation,

$$i \mapsto j = \Pi(i) \tag{18.4}$$

such that the total association score,

$$S_{TOT} \equiv \sum_i d[a_i, b_{\Pi(i)}] \tag{18.5}$$

is minimized over all permutations Π of Equation 18.4.

Leaving aside, for now, the question of computational costs associated with the minimization of Equation 18.5, there are some fundamental difficulties associated with the use of optimal associators in multitarget tracking models. In particular

1. Optimal associators perform poorly if the two lists S_A and S_B do not correspond to the *same* sets of underlying targets.

2. Poor entries in the cost matrix $\{d_{ij}\}$ can lead to global distortions of the globally optimal association.

The purely mathematical solution to the problem of minimizing Equation 18.5 need not be a *reasonable* solution to the problem of finding the best pairings of the two lists, and the points just noted are canonical failure modes by which blind optimal associations yield miserable solutions to "real" problems. Nonetheless, if one requires the ultimate output of the tracking function to be the single "best guess" as to the actual nature of the underlying target scenario, then some suitably massaged form of optimal association is clearly required.

18.4.3 Algorithm Overview

The manner in which the elements of the preceding section are combined into an overall tracking algorithm is governed by two fundamental assumptions:

1. For substantial fractions of the scenarios under consideration, the actual trajectories of the targets of interest are not fully constrained.

2. The densities of targets are not so large as to preclude the separation of individual targets over some/most of the time interval in question.

The first assumption requires *stereo tracking*. Target motion along the line of sight from any one sensor is assumed to be sufficiently "unknowable" that cooperative tracking from pairs of sensors is required to determine the full three-dimensional state of a target. The second assumption is, in essence, a statement of limitations of the entire Sim89 approach. The Sim89 tracker is ultimately a *point tracker* in the sense that the algorithm attempts to associate targets with individual data points provided by the sensors. This approach makes sense only if the sensor can actually resolve individual targets for most/much of the time. If the nature of the sensor and underlying targets is such that a cluster of real targets is seen only as an ill-defined 'clump' by the sensor, the overall Sim89 prescription is inappropriate, and more imaginative solutions to the tracking problem (e.g., track density estimation by neural network techniques) would be required.

Given these assumptions on the nature of the tracking problem, the overall form of the Sim89 tracking model is as illustrated in Figure 18.17. The basic elements are a pair of two-dimensional trackers, each receiving and processing data from its own sensor, a three-dimensional tracking module which combines information from the two two-dimensional systems, and a 'Handover' module. The handover module controls both the manner in which the three-dimensional tracker sends its answers to whomever is listening and the way in which tracks from other systems are entered into the existing three-dimensional track files. The following subsections provide brief descriptions of the algorithms used in each of these component subtasks.

18.4.4 Two-dimensional Mono Tracking

The primary function of the two-dimensional tracking module is fairly straightforward: Given two-dimensional data sets arriving at reasonably regular time intervals (scans) from the sensors, construct a big set of "all" plausible two-dimensional tracks linking these observations from scan-to-scan. This is done by way of a simple track-splitting module. The tracks from the two two-dimensional trackers in Figure 18.17 are the fundamental inputs to the three-dimensional track initialization algorithm described in the next subsection.

The adoption of track splitting in place of optimal association for the two-dimensional trackers is largely a consequence of assumption (A1) above. Without a restrictive model for the (unseen) motion along the sensor line of sight, the information available to the two-dimensional tracker is not sufficient to differentiate among plausible global track sets through the data

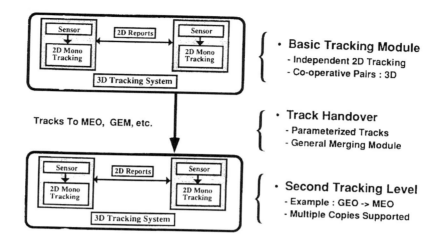

Figure 18.17: Gross Structure of Sim89 Tracking Model

points. Instead, the two-dimensional tracker attempts to form all plausible "tracks" through its own two-dimensional data set, with the distinction between real and phantom tracks deferred to the three-dimensional track initiation and association modules described in the next section.

With the receipt of a new data set from the sensors, the action of the two-dimensional tracker consists of several simple steps:

1. Extend existing tracks to new data, as possible.

2. Redistribute the global track file among the nodes (concurrent execution).

3. Collect and sort "good" two-dimensional tracks into a global two-dimensional report list.

4. Initialize new entries for the track file.

This algorithm flow is illustrated in Figure 18.18. Discussions of the track file redistribution in Step 2 (as well as concurrent aspects of the other steps) are deferred. The following subsections describe track extensions, report collection, and track initiation.

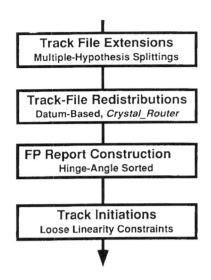

Track File Extensions
Multiple-Hypothesis Splittings

Track-File Redistributions
Datum-Based, *Crystal_Router*

FP Report Construction
Hinge-Angle Sorted

Track Initiations
Loose Linearity Constraints

- **All-Options Approach**
  - Initiate All Plausible Tracks
  - Recognize/Delete Bad Options

- **Concurrent Implementation**
  - Datum-Based Tracks -> Nodes
  - Redistributions : *Crystal_Router*

- **Track-File Prunings**
  - Merging : Same 4-Scan History
  - Restrict N[Tracks] *per* Datum
  - Restrict Local Track File Size

Figure 18.18: Processing Flow for two-dimensional Mono Tracking

Two-dimensional Track Extensions

An item in the two-dimensional track file is described by an eight-component state vector

$$\vec{x} \equiv \left(\begin{array}{c} \vec{x}_y \\ \vec{x}_z \end{array} \right) \tag{18.6}$$

where the component vectors on the RHS of Equation 18.6 are four-element kinematic state vectors as defined for Equation 18.1, referred to the standard measurement axes:

$\hat{y}$: Unit vector along the projected sensor velocity

$\hat{z}$: Unit vector along the normal to the orbital plane

defined in Section 18.4.1. (Recall that the "massaged" data used in the tracker are the projections of the true target positions onto these axes.) The axis $\hat{y}$ is noninertial, so that the state in Equation 18.6 has substantial "contaminations" from motion of the sensor.

In principle, each track described by Equation 18.6 has an associated co-variance matrix with 36 independent elements. In order to reduce the storage and CPU resource requirements of two-dimensional tracking, a simplifying assumption is made. The measurement error matrix for a two-dimensional datum

$$\vec{z} \equiv \begin{pmatrix} \rho_y \\ \rho_z \end{pmatrix}, \tag{18.7}$$

is taken to have the simple form

$$M \equiv E[\vec{z}\vec{z}^T] \equiv \begin{bmatrix} \sigma_M^2 & 0 \\ 0 & \sigma_M^2 \end{bmatrix} \tag{18.8}$$

with the *same* effective value σ_M^2 used to describe the measurement variance for each projection, and no correlation of the measurement errors. The assumption in Equations 18.7 and 18.8 is reasonable, provided the effective measurement error σ_M is made large enough, and reduces the number of independent components in the covariance matrix from 36 to 10.

The central task of the two-dimensional track extension module is to find all plausible track↔hit associations, subject to a set of criteria which define "plausible." The primary association criterion is based on the track association score

$$S \equiv |\vec{y}|^2 / [2(P_{xx} + \sigma_M^2)], \tag{18.9}$$

where P_{xx} is the variance of the prediced data position along a reference axis and

$$\vec{y} \equiv \vec{z}_{DATA} - \vec{z}_{PREDICTED} \tag{18.10}$$

is the difference between the actual data value and that predicted by Equation 18.6 for the time of the datum. Equation 18.9 is simply a dimensionless measure of the size of the mismatch in Equation 18.10, normalized by the expected prediction error.

The first step in limiting Track↔Hit associations is a simple cut $S < S_{MAX}$ on the association score of Equation 18.9. For the dense, multitarget environments used in Sim89, this simple cut is not sufficiently restrictive, and a variety of additional heuristic cuts are made. The most important of these are

1. *Approximate data linearity:* The data point of a proposed association must represent 'forward' motion relative to the last two data included in the track.

2. *Vertical motion cuts (optional):* The projected two-dimensional motion must be consistent with underlying three-dimensional motion away from the earth.

These cuts are particularly important at early stages in *boost-phase* tracking, when scan-to-scan target motion is not large compared to measurement errors, and the sizes of the prediction gates according to the tracking filter are large.

The actual track scoring cut is a bit more complicated than the preceding paragraph implies. Let S_{EXT} denote the nominal extension score of Equation 18.9. In addition, define a cumulative association score S_{TOT} which is updated on associations in a fading memory fashion

$$S_{TOT} \mapsto \alpha S_{TOT} + (1 - \alpha)S_{EXT} \qquad (18.11)$$

with (typically) $\alpha \approx 0.5$. An extension is accepted only if S_{EXT} is below some nominal cutoff (typically 3–4σ) *and* S_{TOT} is below a more restrictive cut (2–3σ). This second cut prevents creation of poor tracks with barely acceptable extension scores at each step.

The preceding rules for Track↔Hit associations define the basic two-dimensional track extension formalism. There are, however, two additional problems which must be addressed:

- The prescription can generate duplicate tracks (meaning identical associated data sets over some number of scans).

- The size of the track file can increase without bounds.

These problems are particularly acute in dense target environments.

In regard to the first problem, two entries in the track file are said to be *equivalent* if they involve the same associated data points over the past four scans. If an equivalent track pair is found in the track file, the track with a higher cumulative score S_{TOT} is simply deleted. The natural mechanism for track deletion in a track-splitting model is based on the track's data association history. If no data items give acceptable association scores over some preset number of scans (typically 0–2), the track is simply discarded.

The equivalent-track merging and poor track deletion mechanisms are not sufficient to prevent track file "explosions" in truly dense environments. A final track-limiting mechanism is simply a hard cutoff on the number of tracks maintained for any item in the data set (this cut is typically $N_{MAX} = 8$). If more than N_{MAX} tracks give acceptable association scores to a particular datum, only the N_{MAX} pairings with the lowest total association scores S_{TOT} are kept.

The complexity of the track extension algorithm is nominally $N_{DATA} \times N_{TRACKS}$ for N_{DATA} new data items and N_{TRACKS} existing tracks. This

$O(N^2)$ computational burden is easily reduced to something closer to $O(NlogN)$ by sorting both the incoming data and the predicted data values for existing tracks.

Two-dimensional Report Formation

The *report formation* subtask of the two-dimensional tracker collects/organizes established two-dimensional tracks into a list to be used as input for three-dimensional track initiations, where "established" simply means tracks older than some minimum cutoff age (typically seven hits). The task of initiating three-dimensional tracks from lists of two-dimensional tracks consists of two parts:

1. Determining which items from the two lists are to be associated.

2. Constructing three-dimensional state information for associated pairs.

The second task is straightforward geometry. The report function for two-dimensional tracking is intended to aid in the more difficult association task.

The essential element in two $-$ dimensional $+$ two $-$ dimensional $\rightarrow$ three $-$ dimensional associations is the so-called *hinge angle* illustrated in Figure 18.19. Consider a single target viewed *simultaneously* by two different sensors. Assuming that each two-dimensional tracker knows the orbits of the other tracker's sensor, each tracker can independently reconstruct two reference planes in three-dimensional inertial space:

SSE: The plane containing the two sensors and the center of the earth.

SST: The plane containing the two sensors and the target.

The hinge angle

$$\chi = \chi(t) \equiv \Theta(SSE, SST) \qquad (18.12)$$

is simply the angle between these two planes.

Once the time for the two-dimensional report has been specified, the steps involved in the report function are relatively straightforward:

1. Select all tracks satisfying the minimum age requirement.

2. Use the state model in Equation 18.6 to propagate these tracks to the reference time

3. Evaluate both χ *and* its time derivative $d\chi/dt$ at the reference time

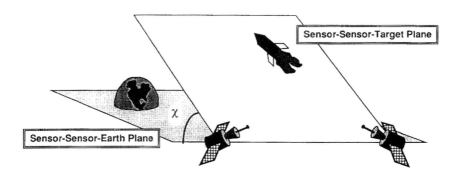

Figure 18.19: Definition of the Stereo Association Angle χ

4. Sort the list of reported tracks by χ values.

The state model in Equation 18.6 not only provides the mechanism for synchronizing the report items but also the additional variable $d\chi/dt$, which ultimately aids in the associations of report lists from two two-dimensional systems.

Track Initialization

The algorithm described in Section 18.4.4 is only applicable for extending tracks which already exist in the track file. The creation of new entries is done by a separate track initiation function.

The track initiator involves little more than searches for nearly colinear triples of data over the last three scans. A triplet

$\vec{z}_1$: two-dimensional datum, current scan

$\vec{z}_2$: two-dimensional datum, prior scan

$\vec{z}_3$: two-dimensional datum, two scans back

is a candidate new track if

$$S_{INIT} \equiv \left(\frac{1}{12\sigma_M^2} \right) \left[\frac{\vec{z}_1 - \vec{z}_2}{t_1 - t_2} - \frac{\vec{z}_2 - \vec{z}_3}{t_2 - t_3} \right] \leq S_{CUT}, \qquad (18.13)$$

where the cutoff is generally fairly loose (e.g., $S_{CUT} \approx 16$). In addition, a number of simple heuristic cuts (maximum speed) are applied.

The initiator searches for all approximately linear triples over the last three scans, subject to the important additional restriction that *no* initiations to a particular item $\vec{z}_1$ of the current data set are attempted if *any* established track (minimum age cut) already exists ending at that datum. The nominal $O(N^3)$ complexity of the initiator is reduced to approximately $O(N \log N)$ by exploiting the sorted dature on the incoming data sets.

18.4.5 Three-dimensional Tracking

Unlike the two-dimensional tracking module, the three-dimensional stereo tracker attempts to construct a single track for each (perceived) underlying target. The fundamental algorithm element for this type of tracking is the optimal associator described in Section 18.4.2. A single pass through the three-dimensional tracker utilizes optimal associations for two distinct subtasks:

Track extensions Data from a sensor are associated with predicted data positions for existing three-dimensional tracks. This task is performed twice per scan, once for each two-dimensional subsystem of Figure 18.17.

Track initiation Two-dimensional report lists are associated and new three-dimensional tracks are initiated for correlations to data points not used in the preceding track extension step.

As was noted in Section 18.4.2, a canonical problem with optimal associators is the possibility of globally poor associations due to incompatible lists or poor distance information for some of the entries in either lists. These problems are addressed as follows:

1. Evaluations of individual distances for the cost matrix include relatively restrictive cuts which prohibit poor associations. The nominal cost for such associations is set to an "infinite" token and the association is simply ignored if selected in the course of minimization of Equation 18.5.

2. Additional "quality control" modules are used to assess feasibility of proposed associations; tracks failing the quality constraints are deleted from the system.

The associators for track extensions and initiations and the quality control modules are described in the following subsections.

Track Extension Associations

Given a list of existing three-dimensional tracks and a set of observations from a particular sensor, the track extension task nominally consists of three basic steps:

1. Evaluate the cost matrix for associating individual tracks with entries from the data set.

2. Find the optimal association by minimization of the global score of Equation 18.5.

3. Update each track according to its associated data item, using a full three-dimensional kinematic Kalman filter.

This nominal algorithm is hopelessly slow. If the track file and data set each have a characteristic size N, Step 1 requires N^2 operations and Step 2 requires N^3. The reduction of the unacceptable polynomial complexities of Steps 2 and 3 to something approaching $O(N \log N)$ is done as follows.

A list of predicted data values for existing tracks is evaluated and is sorted using the same key as was used sorting the data set. The union of the sorted prediction and data sets is then broken into some number of gross subblocks, defined by appropriately large gaps in values of the sorting key. This reduces the single large association problem into a number of smaller subproblems.

For each subproblem, a pruned distance matrix is evaluated, subject to two primary constraints:

- Individual associations are considered only if the association score is less than some maximum allowed score value.

- The number of data value to be associated with any one track prediction is limited to some preset maximum.

The score for an individual association is the distance between prediction and datum, weighted by the prediction uncertainty:

$$d[\text{Track,Datum}] \equiv \frac{\Delta z^2}{\hat{P}_{zz}} + \frac{\Delta y^2}{\hat{P}_{yy}} \tag{18.14}$$

where, for $i = y, z$,

$$\Delta x_i \equiv x_i[\text{Datum}] - x_i[\text{Prediction}] \qquad (18.15)$$

and $\hat{P}_{ii}$ is the predicted variance for Equation 18.15 according to the three-dimensional tracking filter. The score is essentially a χ^2 for the proposed association, and the cutoff value is typically of order $\chi^2 \leq 16$. The maximum allowed number of associations for any single prediction is typically $N_{MAX} = 6$–8. If more than N_{MAX} data give acceptable association scores, the possible pairings are sorted by the association score and only the N_{MAX} best fits (lowest scores) are kept.

The preceding scoring algorithm leads to a (generally) sparse distance matrix for the large subblocks defined through gaps in the sorting keys. The next step in the algorithm is a quick block diagonalization of the distance matrix through appropriate reorderings of the rows and columns. By this point, the original large association problem has been reduced to a large number of modest sized subproblems and Munkres algorithm for minimizing the global cost in Equation 18.5 is (finally) used to find the optimal pairings.

Chapter 19

Parallel Computing in Industry

19.1 Motivation

Now at Syracuse University, Fox has set up a new program ACTION (Advanced Computing Technology is an Innovative Opportunity Now). This is funded by New York State to accelerate the introduction of parallel computing into the State's industry. The methodology is based directly on that proven successful in C^3P. The applications scientists are now in different industries—not in different Caltech or JPL departments. There are many differences in detail between the projects. The basic hardware is now available commercially and need not be developed concurrently with applications and systems software. However, the applications are much harder. In C^3P, a typical code was at most a few thousand lines long and often developed from scratch by each new graduate student. In ACTION, the codes are typically larger (say 100,000 lines) and longer lived.

We also find differences when we analyze the problem class. There are fewer regular synchronous problems in industry than in academia and many more of the metaproblem class with several different interrelated functions.

Table 19.1 presents some initial results of a survey of industrial applications [Fox:92e]. Note that we are at the stage analogous to the beginnings of C^3P when we first wandered around Caltech talking to computational scientists.

In general, we find that the central parallel algorithms needed in industry have usually already been studied by the research community. Thus, again

Table 19.1: An Initial Survey of Industry and Government Opportunities for High-Performance (Parallel) Computing

Item	Company/ Agency	Applications	Current Big Computer	*Problem Class	Can One Use HPC?	Relevant Dusty Decks Exist?
1	General Electric (Syracuse)	Acoustic Beam Forming	Special & iWarp	S	yes	no
2	General Electric (Syracuse)	Ocean Environmental Modeling	many	LS	yes	maybe
3	Grumman United Technologies	CFD & Structures Electromagnetic Simulations	Cray & CM-2	S/LS	yes	yes
4	Grumman Par Systems	Avionics & Command and Control (JointStars)	Special & VAX	M	yes	probably not
5	Otis	Manage Repair Database	Not Yet Implemented	M	yes	no
6	Lamson (small Syracuse Company)	Design Exhaust Pump	None	LS	?	yes
7	Carrier	Design Air Conditioners	VAX	LS	?**	yes
8	Atlantic Research (ARC)	Antenna Fields	VAX	EP	yes	yes (little change)
9	Niagara Mohawk	Control and Plan Electrical Power Grid	IBM 3090	LS	yes	no
10	MONY Insurance Co.	Process Insurance Policies	IBM 3090	EP	no	yes
11	Blue Cross/ Blue Shield	Process Medicare Claims	IBM 3090	EP	no	yes
12	Wall Street Brokers	Predict Values of Securities	Maspar, iPSC/860 & Hypercube	Some EP	?	yes (small)
13	SIAC	Control Trading on Floor of NY and American Stock Exchange	Tandem & PC	EP	?	yes
14	Electronic Systems Div. ESD (USAF)	Command and Control & Battle Management for SDI	Many	M	yes	probably not
15	Army ASAS Project	Data Fusion	VAX	M	yes	somewhat
16	Par Systems	Infrared Sensors in Aircraft	Special Purpose	S	yes	no
17	AGE	Entertainment, Toys, Theme Parks, Virtual Reality	Must be low cost (toys) Supercomputer (theme park)	M	yes	no

*S=Synchronous, LS=Loosely Synchronous, EP=Embarrassingly Parallel, M=Metaproblem
**(is physics or noise understood?)

we find that, "in principle," parallel computing works. However, we have an even harder software problem and it is not clear that the software issues key to the research applications are the same for industry. As described in Chapter 14 for High Performance Fortran, software standards are critical so companies can be assured that their parallel software investment will be protected as hardware evolves.

One interesting initial conclusion about the industrial opportunities for parallel computers concerns the type of applications. Simulations of various sorts dominated the previous chapters of this book and most academic computing. However, we find that the industrial applications show that simulation, while very promising, is not the largest market in the long run. Rather, we live in the "information area" and it is in the processing of information that parallel computing will have its largest opportunity. This is not (just) transaction processing for the galaxywide network of automatic teller machines; rather, it is the storage and access of information followed by major processing ("number-crunching"). Examples include the interpretation of data from NASA's "mission to planet Earth" where the processing is large-scale image analysis; the scanning and correlation of technical and electronic information from the world's media to give early warning for economic and social crises; the integration of medicaid databases to lower the burden on doctors and patients and identify inefficiencies. Interestingly, such information processing is currently not stressed in the national high-performance computing initiative.

19.2 Examples of Industrial Applications

In the following, we refer to the numerical label (item number) in the first column of Table 19.1.

Items 1, 4, 14, 15, and 16 are typical of major signal processing and feature identification problems in defense systems. Currently, special purpose hardware—typically with built-in parallelism—is used for such problems. We can expect that use of commercial parallel architectures will aid the software development process and enhance reuse. Parallel computing in acoustic beam forming (item 1) should allow adaptive on-line signal processing to maximize signal-to-noise ratio dynamically as a function of angle and time. Currently, the INTEL iWarp is being used, although SIMD architectures would be effective in this and most low-level signal processing problems. A SIMD initial processor would be augmented with a MIMD machine to do the higher level vision functions. Currently, JointStars (item 4) uses a VAX for the final tracking stage of their airborne synthetic aperture radar system. This was used very successfully in the Gulf War. However, parallel computing could enhance the performance of JointStars and allow it to track many moving targets—one may remember the difficulties in following the movement of SCUD launchers in the Gulf War. As shown in Chapter 18, we already know good MIMD algorithms for multitarget tracking [Gottschalk:88a;90b].

We can expect the Defense Department to reduce the purchases of new planes, tanks, and ships. However, we see a significant opportunity to integrate new high-performance computer systems into existing systems at all levels of defense. This includes both avionics and mission control in existing aircraft and the hierarchy of control centers within the armed services. High-performance computing can be used both in the delivered systems and perhaps even more importantly in the simulation of their performance.

Modelling of the ocean environment (item 2) is a large-scale partial differential equation problem which can determine dynamically the acoustic environment in which sonar signals are propagating. Large scale (teraflop) machines would allow real-time simulation in a submarine and lead to dramatic improvement in detection efficiency.

Computational fluid dynamics, structural analysis, and electromagnetic simulation (item 3) are a major emphasis in the national high-performance computing initiative—especially within NASA and DOE. Such problems are described in Chapter 12. However, the industries that can use this application are typically facing major cutbacks and the integration of new technology faces major hurdles. How do you use parallelism when the corporation would like to shut down its current supercomputer center and, further, has a hiring freeze preventing personnel trained in this area from entering the company? We are collaborating with NASA in helping industry with a new consortium where several companies are banding together to accelerate the integration of parallelism into their working environment in the area of multidisciplinary design for electromagnetics, fluids, and structures. An interesting initial concept was a consortium project to develop a nonproprietary software suite of generic applications which would be modified by each company for their particular needs. One company would optimize the CFD code for a new commercial transport, another for aircraft engine design, another for automobile air drag simulation, another for automobile fan design, another for minimizing noise in air conditioners (item 7) or more efficient exhaust pumps (item 6). The electromagnetic simulation could be optimized either for stealth aircraft or the simulation of electromagnetics properties for a new high-frequency printed circuit board. In the latter case, we use simulation to identify problems which otherwise would require time-consuming fabrication cycles. Thus, parallel computing can accelerate the introduction of products to market and so give competitive edge to corporations using it.

Power utilities (item 9) have several interesting applications of high-performance computing, including nuclear power safety simulation, and gas and electric transmission problems. Here the huge dollar value of power implies that small percentage savings can warrant large high-performance computing systems. There are many electrical transmission problems suitable for high-performance computing which are built around sparse matrix operations. For Niagara Mohawk, a New York utility, the matrix has about 4000 rows (and columns) with approximately 12 nonzero elements in each row (column). We are designing a parallel transient stability analysis system now. This would have some features described in DASSL (Section 9.6). Niagara Mohawk's problem (matrix size) can only use a modest (perhaps 16-node) parallel system. However, one could use large teraflop machines (10,000 nodes?) to simulate larger areas—such as the sharing of power over a national grid.

In a completely different area, the MONY Insurance Company (item 10) spends $70 million a year on data processing—largely on COBOL applications where they have some 15 million lines of code and a multi-year backlog. They see no immediate need for high-performance computing, but surely a more productive software environment would be a great value! Similarly, Empire Blue Cross/Blue Shield (item 11) processes 6.5 million medical insurance transactions every day. Their IBM 3090-400 handles this even with automatic optical scanning of all documents. Massively parallel systems could only be relevant if one could develop a new approach, perhaps with parallel computers examining the database with an expert system or neural network to identify anomalous situations. The states and federal government are burdened by the major cost of medicaid and small improvements would have great value.

The major computing problem for Wall Street (items 12, 13) is currently centered on the large databases. SIAC runs the day-to-day operation of the New York and American Stock exchanges. Two acres (about 300) of Tandem computers handle the calls from brokers to traders on the floor. The traders already use an "embarrassingly parallel" decomposition with some 2000 stocks of the New York Stock Exchange decomposed over about 500 personal computers with about one PC per trader. For SIAC, the major problem is reliability and network management with essentially no down time "allowed." High-performance computers could perhaps be used as part of a heterogeneous network management system to simulate potential bottlenecks and strategies to deal with faults. The brokerages already use parallel computers for economic modelling [Mills:92a;92b], [Zenios:91b]. This is obviously glamorous, with integration of sophisticated optimization methods very promising.

As our final example (item 17), we have the entertainment and education industries. Here high-performance computing is linked to areas such as multimedia and virtual reality with high bandwidth and sophisticated visualization and delivery systems. Some applications can be viewed as the civilian versions of military flight simulators, with commercial general-purpose parallel computers replacing the special-purpose hardware now used. Parallelism will appear in the low end with future extensions of Nintendo-like systems; at a medium scale for computer-generated stages in a future theater; at the high end with parallel supercomputers controlling simulations in tomorrow's theme parks. Here, a summer C^3P project lead by Alex Ho with three undergraduates may prove to be pioneering [Ho:89b], [Ho:90b]. They developed a parallel video game *Asteroids* on the nCUBE-1 and transputer systems [Fox:88v]. This game is a space war in a three-dimensional toroidal space with spacecrafts, missile, and rocks obeying some sort of laws of physics. We see this as a foretaste of a massively parallel *supergame* accessed by our children from throughout the globe with high-speed lines and consumer virtual reality interfaces. A parallel machine is a natural choice to support the realism and good graphics of the virtual worlds that would be demanded by the Nintendo generation. We note that, even today, the market for Nintendo and Sega video entertainment systems is an order of magnitude larger than that for supercomputers. High-performance computers should also appear in all major sports stadiums to perform image analysis as a training aid for coaches or providing new views for cable TV audiences. We can imagine sensors and tracking systems developed for Strategic Defense Initiative being adapted to track players on a football field rather than a missile launch from an unfriendly country. Many might consider this appropriate with American football being as aggressive as many military battles!

Otis (item 5) is another example of information processing, discussed generally in Section 19.1. They are interested in setting up a database of elevator monitoring data which can be analyzed for indicators of future equipment problems. This would lead to improved reliability—an area where Otis and Japanese companies compete. In this way, high-performance computing can lead to competitive advantage in the "global economic war."

Chapter 20

Computational Science

20.1 Lessons

The C³P program, from its very initial proposal and project implementation, was designed to directly answer such questions as:

- Does parallel computing work?

- What are the needed software and hardware?

The contents of this book illustrate our answers to these questions with such results as:

- Large synchronous and loosely synchronous problems parallelize in a scalable fashion.

- Domain decomposition is a universal methodology for massive parallelism.

- C, Fortran-plus message-passing is a powerful but low-level software model of general effectiveness.

- Data-parallel languages are probably more attractive to most users. These languages are much harder to implement (requiring sophisticated compilers) and not quite as general as message passing. The latter handles functional parallelism and asynchronous computations outside the scope of data parallelism.

As in all research projects, we made many unexpected discoveries. One of the most interesting was Computational Science. Namely, much of the work described in this book is clearly interdisciplinary. It mixes physics, chemistry, engineering and other applications with mathematics and computer science. The national high performance computing initiative has stressed interdisciplinary teams in both its planning documents [FHPCP:89a] and implementations in federal proposal (Commerce Business Daily) solicitations. This idea was indeed part of the initial makeup and proposals of C^3P. However, this is not actually what happened in many cases. Probably the most important work in C^3P was not from teams of individuals—each with their own specialized skills. Rather, C^3P relied on the research of individuals and each individual possessed a mix of skills. We can give some examples.

Otto developed the initial QCD codes (Chapter 4.3) for the Cosmic Cube and its prototype. This required intricate knowledge of both the best physics and its numerical formulations. However, Otto also participated in the design and implementation of the hardware and its support software which later became Express. Otto obtained a physics Ph.D., but is now on the computer science faculty at the Oregon Graduate Center.

As a different example, we can quote the research in Chapter 11 which uses physics methods (such as simulated annealing) to solve a mathematics problem (optimization) for a computer science application (load balancing). Again, the design of higher level languages (Chapters 13, 15 through 17) requires deep computer science compiler and operating system expertise, as well as application understanding to design, say, the high-performance Fortran directives or MOVIE functionality. This mix of interests, which combines the skills of a computer scientist with those of an application area such as physics, was the rule and not the exception in C^3P. In the following, we comment on some general implications of this.

20.2 Computational Science

C^3P trained computational scientists "accidentally" by involving faculty, students, and staff in a research program whose success demanded interdisciplinary knowledge and work. Most of our students were at the Ph.D. level, although some undergraduates were involved through NSF REU (Research Experience for Undergraduates) and other research support. For instance, Felten made significant discoveries in new sorting algorithms (Section 12.7) while a physics undergraduate at Caltech. This work was awarded the prize for the best undergraduate research at Caltech during 1984. Felten is now in the Computer Science Ph.D. program at Washington University, Seattle.

We can ask the question of whether such interdisciplinary computational science can be incorporated in the academic curriculum as well as appearing in leading edge research projects? We can also ask if there is a role for a computational science at Ph.D., Masters, Undergraduate, and in K–12 precollege education.

We believe that computational science should be taught academically at all levels and not confined to research projects [Fox:92d]. We believe that there is an interdisciplinary core of knowledge for computational science. Further, this core contains fundamental issues and is far more than a programming course in Fortran, Lotus 1-2-3 or even more sophisticatedly, Express or MOVIE.

An education in computational science would include the basics of applied computer science, numerical analysis, and simulation. Computational scientists need a broader education than the typical physicist or computer scientist. Their training in basic computer science, and how to apply it, must be joined with an understanding of one or more application areas, such as physics and the computational approach to physics. Computational scientists will need a computer laboratory course so they become facile with the use of computers. These must be modern parallel supercomputers, and not just the personal computers or workstations now used for students in most universities. This broad education will only be possible if existing fields can teach their material more concisely. Considering a computational physicist, for example, the courses in applied computer science could substitute, for instance, advanced courses in quantum theory, or the parallel computer laboratory for an experimental physics lab. Thus, we could train a computational physicist with a reasonable knowledge of both physics and computation. Although the details of parallel computing are changing rapidly, the graduate of such an education will be able to track future changes. Computational science naturally links scientific fields to computer science. Here again, a specialization in computational science is an attractive option for computer scientists. An understanding of applications will allow computer scientists to develop better hardware and software. Computational scientists, whether in computer science or in an application field such as physics, will benefit directly from technology that improves the performance of computers by a factor of two or so each year. Their theoretical colleagues will not be assisted as well by technological improvements, so computational science can be expected to be a field of growing rewards and opportunities, as compared to traditional areas.

We believe that students educated in computational science will find it a rewarding and exciting experience, which should give them excellent job opportunities. Only a few universities offer such a degree, however, and often only at the Ph.D. level. Fledgling programs exist at Caltech, Cornell, Clemson, Denver, Illinois, Michigan, North Carolina, Princeton, Rice, Stanford, Syracuse, and U.C. Davis. The Caltech and Syracuse programs are both based in lessons from C^3P. These programs are diverse, and no national consensus as to the core knowledge of computational science has been developed. The NSF Supercomputer Centers at Cornell, Illinois, Pittsburgh, and San Diego have played a major role in enhancing the visibility and progress of computational science. However, these centers are set up outside of the academic framework of universities and do not contribute directly to developing computational science as an academic area. These centers, industry, the National laboratories, and indeed the federal government with its new high-performance computing and communication initiative, are all driving computational science forward. Academia is behind. Not only are there few computational science education programs, but few faculty who could teach such a curriculum. The poor job opportunities for computationalists in leading universities naturally discourages students entering the field and so again hinders the development of new educational programs. It will not be an easy issue to address, and probably only slow progress will be made as computational science gradually gains recognition in universities as a fundamentally exciting field. The inevitable dominance of parallel computing will help, as will the use of parallel computers in the NSF centers that have provided such a critical stimulus for computational science. Industry and the National laboratories already offer computational scientists excellent job opportunities, and the demand for such training will grow. Hopefully, this market pressure will lead to initiatives from within universities to hire, encourage, and promote new computational faculty, and educate students in computational science.

Consider the issues controlling the development of computational science in universities. As this field borrows and extends ideas from existing fields—computer science, biology, chemistry, physics, and so on—it will naturally face campus political hurdles as it challenges traditional and firmly held beliefs. These inevitable difficulties are exacerbated by administrative problems; many universities are facing a scenario of no growth, or even of declining funding and faculty size. This will mean that creation of new areas implies reductions in other areas. Computational science shares difficulties with other interdisciplinary areas, such as those associated with the growing interest in Planet Earth. The peer referee system used in the hiring and promoting of new faculty is perfect for ensuring high standards within the referees' domain of expertise. This tends to lead to very high-quality but isolated departments that find it hard to move into new areas. The same effect is seen in the peer review system used for the refereeing of scholarly papers and federal grants. Thus, universities find it hard to change, making it difficult for computational science to grow in academia. A key hurdle will be the development of some consensus in the community that computational science is, as we have asserted, fundamental and exciting. This needs to be quantified academically with the development of a core curriculum—a body of knowledge on which one can build computational science as an academic discipline.

There are two obvious approaches to filling the academic void identified as computational science. The boldest and simplest approach is to create an entirely new academic degree, "Computational Science," administered by a new university department. This would give the field great visibility, and, once created, the independent department would be able to develop its educational program, research, and faculty hiring without direct interference from existing academic fields. Such a department would need strong support from the university administration to flourish, and even more so for its creation. This approach would not be easy to implement. There would be natural opposition from existing academic units for both good and not-so-good reasons. A telling critic could argue that a freestanding Computational Science program is premature; there is as yet no agreement on a core body of knowledge that could define this field. Students graduating from this program might find it hard to progress up the academic ladder at the vast majority of universities that do not have such a department.

These difficulties are avoided by the second strategy for computational science, which, rather than filling the void with a new department, would broaden the existing fields to "meet in the middle." Students could graduate with traditional degrees and have a natural academic future. This is the approach taken by the existing university Computational Science and Engineering programs. For example, consider the two fields of chemistry and computer science. A computational scientist would graduate with either a Chemistry or Computer Science degree. Later academic progress would be judged by the scientist's contributions to the corresponding base field. We have already argued that such an interdisciplinary education would allow the student to be a better chemist or a better computer scientist, respectively. Naturally, the chemistry graduate from the Computational Science program would not have received as complete an education in chemistry as is traditional for theoretical or experimental chemists. Some of the chemistry elective courses would have been replaced by computational science requirements. This change would need to be approved and evaluated by the Chemistry faculty, who would also need to identify key chemistry requirements to be satisfied by computational scientists. New courses might include computational chemistry and those covering the basics of computer science, numerical analysis, and simulation. The latter set would be taught either by computer scientists or interdisciplinary Computational Science faculty. The education of a computational scientist within a Computer Science department could be handled similarly. This would have an emphasis on applied computer science, and a training in at least one application area.

In this scenario, a degree in Computational Chemistry is equivalent to one in "Chemistry within the Computational Science program." On the computer science side, one could see degrees in "Computer Science with a minor in Chemistry," or a "Ph.D. in Computer Science with a master's degree in Chemistry." At the academic level, we see an interdisciplinary program in computational science, but no separate department; faculty are appointed and students admitted to existing academic units. This approach to computational science allows us to develop and understand the core knowledge curricula in an evolutionary fashion. Implementing this more modest plan is certainly not easy, as one must modify the well-established degree requirements for the existing fields, such as chemistry and computer science. These modifications are easiest at the master's and especially at the Ph.D. level, and this is where most of the new programs have been established.

These seem to be very good reasons to establish undergraduate level Computational Science programs. We also need to create an awareness in the (K–12) educational system of the importance of computation, and the possibility of Computational Science degrees. In this way, more high school students may choose Computational Science educational programs and careers. Further, in K–12 one emphasizes a general education without the specialization normal in college. The breadth of computational science makes this very suitable for pre-college education. We also expect that high-technology environments—such as virtual reality front ends to an interactive fluid flow or other physical simulation on a parallel supercomputer—will prove to be a valuable teaching tool for today's Nintendo generation. Kids with a background in computational science will interact better with this modern computer environment and so learn more about traditional fields—for example, more about the physics of fluid flow in the sample simulation mentioned above.

Eventually, everybody will learn computational science—it will be part of any general education. When all students take two years at college of basic applied computer science—including but not at all limited to programming—then it will be natural to define computational science in all its flavors as an extension of these two years of base courses. Computation, like mathematics, chemistry, physics, and humanities, is essential in the education of tomorrow's scientists and engineers.

Appendix A: C3P Reports

These and other C^{3}P reports in the bibliography may be obtained by contacting Fox at Syracuse (email gcf@npac.syr.edu) or by email to c3prequest@ccsf.caltech.edu).

[Aldcroft:88a] Please see Bibliography for citation.

[Alkalaj:88a] Alkalaj, L., and Bond, A. H. "The use of parallel logic programming in CAD/CAM applications." Technical Report C3P-682, California Institute of Technology, Pasadena, CA, October 1988.

[Aloisio:87b] Aloisio, G., Fox, G. C., Kim, J. S., and Veneziani, N. "Digital real-time SAR processing: Partitioning alternatives." Technical Report C3P-485, California Institute of Technology, Pasadena, CA, 1987.

[Aloisio:88a] Please see Bibliography for citation.

[Aloisio:89b] Please see Bibliography for citation.

[Aloisio:90b] Please see Bibliography for citation.

[Aloisio:90c] Please see Bibliography for citation.

[Aloisio:90d] Please see Bibliography for citation.

[Aloisio:91a] Please see Bibliography for citation.

[Aloisio:91b] Please see Bibliography for citation.

[Aloisio:91c] Aloisio, G., Bochicchio, M., Fox, G. C., Albrizio, R., Mazzone, A., and Veneziani, N. "The design of a parallel/pipeline multiprocessor system for fast DFT algorithms computation," in P. Messina and

A. Murli, editors, *Proceedings of the International Conference on Parallel Computing: Problems, Methods and Applications*, pages 1–15. Elsevier Science Publishers, North-Holland, Amsterdam, 1991. Held in Anacapri, Italy, June 3–7, 1990. Caltech Report C3P-918.

[Amaldi:89a] Amaldi, E., and Nicolis, S. "Stability—capacity diagram of a neural network with Ising couplings," *Journal of Physics A: Mathematical and General*, 50(89):2333–2345, September 1989. Caltech Report C3P-679.

[Anderson:89b] Anderson, C. H., and Proia, S. L. "Complex pattern recognition utilizing neural systems with dynamic routing circuits." JPL Task Plan No. 80-3062, Broad Agency Announcement No. 89-03 C3P-747, JPL/Caltech, Pasadena, CA, February 1989. Defense Advanced Research Projects Agency, Defense Science Office, Arlington, Virginia.

[Anderson:89c] Please see Bibliography for citation.

[Anderson:89d] Please see Bibliography for citation.

[Anderson:89e] Please see Bibliography for citation.

[Anderson:90a] Please see Bibliography for citation.

[Angus:88a] Angus, I. G. "FORTRAN CUBIX: definition and implementation," in G. C. Fox, editor, *The Third Conference on Hypercube Concurrent Computers and Applications, Volume 1*, pages 787–791. ACM Press, New York, January 1988. Caltech Report C3P-575.

[Angus:88b] Angus, I. G. "NSIM: A hypercube simulator." Technical Report C3P-654, California Institute of Technology, Pasadena, CA, August 1988.

[Angus:90a] Please see Bibliography for citation.

[Apostolakis:88d] Please see Bibliography for citation.

[Apostolakis:89a] Apostolakis, J., Baillie, C., Clayton, R. W., Ding, H., Flower, J., Fox, G. C., Gottschalk, T. D., Hager, B. H., Keller, H. B., Kolawa, A. K., Otto, S. W., Tanimoto, T., Van de Velde, E. F., Barhen, J., Einstein, J. R., and Jorgensen, C. C. "Supercomputer applications of the hypercube," in S. Kartashev and S. Kartashev, editors, *Supercomputing Systems: Architectures, Design, and Performance*, chapter 11, pages 480–577. Van Nostrand Reinhold, New York, 1989. Caltech Report C3P-550.

[Apostolakis:91a] Apostolakis, J., Baillie, C., and Fox, G. C. "Investigation of the two-dimensional O(3) model using the overrelaxation algorithm," *Physical Review D*, 43(8):2687–2693, April 1991. COLO-HEP-231, CRPC-TR90078. Caltech Report C3P-943b.

[Baillie:87a] Baillie, C., Felten, E., Flower, J., and Otto, S. "CrOS III+ on nCUBE—CrOS III plus a library of super-fast functions." Technical Report C3P-434, California Institute of Technology, Pasadena, CA, June 1987.

[Baillie:87b] Baillie, C., and Flower, J. "CrOS III on nCUBE—the limits." Technical Report C3P-492, California Institute of Technology, Pasadena, CA, November 1987.

[Baillie:87c] Baillie, C., and Flower, J. "CrOS III and Cubix on the nCUBE." Technical Report C3P-432, California Institute of Technology, Pasadena, CA, May 1987.

[Baillie:87d] Baillie, C., and Flower, J. "nCUBE at Caltech: An interim report." Technical Report C3P-410, California Institute of Technology, Pasadena, CA, March 1987.

[Baillie:87e] Baillie, C., Felten, E., and Walker, D. "Benchmarking the Connection Machine." Technical Report C3P-443, California Institute of Technology, Pasadena, CA, July 1987.

[Baillie:88c] Baillie, C. F. "Comparing communication in concurrent processor operating systems," in G. C. Fox, editor, *The Third Conference on Hypercube Concurrent Computers and Applications, Volume 1*, pages 167–172. ACM Press, New York, January 1988. Caltech Report C3P-569.

[Baillie:88d] Baillie, C. F., Johnsson, S. L., Ortiz, L., and Pawley, G. S. "QED on the Connection Machine," in G. C. Fox, editor, *The Third Conference on Hypercube Concurrent Computers and Applications, Volume 2*, pages 1288–1295. ACM Press, New York, 1988. Caltech Report C3P-572.

[Baillie:88f] Please see Bibliography for citation.

[Baillie:88h] Please see Bibliography for citation.

[Baillie:88i] Baillie, C. F. "Visit to SCRI at FSU to benchmark ETA^{10}." Technical Report C3P-657b, California Institute of Technology, Pasadena, CA, August 1988.

[Baillie:88j] Baillie, C. F. "Using a shared memory computer as a distributed memory computer." Technical Report C3P-658, California Institute of Technology, Pasadena, CA, September 1988.

[Baillie:88m] Baillie, C. F. "Comparing shared and distributed memory computers," *Parallel Computing 8*, pages 101–110, 1988. Caltech Report C3P-719.

[Baillie:88p] Baillie, C. F., and Felten, E. W. "Benchmarking concurrent supercomputers," in E. Gelenbe, editor, *High Performance Computer Systems*, pages 93–102. Elsevier Science Publishers, North-Holland, Amsterdam, 1988. Caltech Report C3P-453.

[Baillie:89d] Baillie, C. F., and Johnston, D. A. "Metropolis and Langevin Time," *Phys. Rev. D.*, 39(4):1246–1248, 1989. Caltech Report C3P-680.

[Baillie:89e] Please see Bibliography for citation.

[Baillie:89n] Baillie, C. F., and Pawley, G. S. "A comparison of the CM with the DAP for lattice gauge theory," *Parallel Computing*, 12:209–220, 1989. Caltech Report C3P-530.

[Baillie:89o] Baillie, C. F., and Walker, D. W. "Lattice QCD—as a large scale scientific computation," in J. Dongarra, I. Duff, P. Gaffney, and S. McKee, editors, *Proceedings of International Conference on Vector and Parallel Computing*, pages 21–35. Ellis Horwood Limited, December 1989. Held in Tromso, Norway, June 6–10, 1988. Caltech Report C3P-641.

[Baillie:89p] Baillie, C. F., Gupta, R., Kilcup, G., Patel, A., and Sharpe, S. "QCD with dynamical Wilson fermions," *Phys. Rev. D*, 40:2072–2084, 1989. Caltech Report C3P-674.

[Baillie:90a] Baillie, C. F. "Lattice spin models and new algorithms—a review of Monte Carlo computer simulations," *International Journal of Modern Physics C*, 1(1):92–117, 1990. Caltech Report C3P-854.

[Baillie:90c] Please see Bibliography for citation.

[Baillie:90d] Please see Bibliography for citation.

[Baillie:90e] Please see Bibliography for citation.

[Baillie:90f] Baillie, C. F. "Lattice QCD: Commercial versus home-grown parallel computers," in D. W. Walker and Q. F. Stout, editors, *The Fifth Distributed Memory Computing Conference, Volume I*, pages 397–405. IEEE Computer Society Press, Los Alamitos, CA, 1990. Held April 9–12, Charleston, SC. Caltech Report C3P-878.

[Baillie:90g] Baillie, C. F., and Williams, R. D. "Numerical simulations of dynamically triangulated random surfaces on parallel computers and 100% speedup," in D. W. Walker and Q. F. Stout, editors, *The Fifth Distributed Memory Computing Conference, Volume II*, pages 1246–1254. IEEE Computer Society Press, Los Alamitos, CA, 1990. Held April 9–12, Charleston, SC. Caltech Report C3P-879.

[Baillie:90h] Baillie, C. F. "Using SIMD massively-parallel computers for lattice calculations in physics," in *Parallel Computing '89*, pages 201–207. Elsevier Science Publishing Company, Inc., New York, 1990. Caltech Report C3P-829.

[Baillie:90j] Please see Bibliography for citation.

[Baillie:90m] Please see Bibliography for citation.

[Baillie:90n] Please see Bibliography for citation.

[Baillie:90o] Baillie, C. F., and Fox, G. C. "Parallel computing comes of age: Supercomputer calculations for lattice QCD and spin models on advanced architecture computers," in J.-L. Delhaye and E. Gelenbe, editors, *High Performance Computing*. Elsevier Science Publishers, North-Holland, Amsterdam, 1990. European Symposium held in Montpellier, France, March, 22–24, 1989. Caltech Report C3P-711.

[Baillie:90p] Baillie, C. F. "Lattice spin models and new algorithms," *International Journal of Modern Physics C*, 1:91–117, 1990. Caltech Report C3P-777.

[Baillie:90q] Baillie, C. F., Barish, K. N., Gupta, R., and Pawley, G. S. "A new MCRG calculation of the critical behavior of the 3D Ising model— preliminary results," *Nuclear Physics B (Proc. Suppl.)*, pages 323– 327, 1990. Presented at International Workshop, Lattice '89, Capri, September 1989. Caltech Report C3P-831.

[Baillie:91a] Please see Bibliography for citation.

[Baillie:91b] Please see Bibliography for citation.

[Baillie:91c] Please see Bibliography for citation.

[Baillie:91d] Please see Bibliography for citation.

[Balasundaram:90a] Please see Bibliography for citation.

[Balasundaram:90b] Balasundaram, V. "A meeting of minds: The parallelization process as a joint endeavor by the programmer and the compiler." Technical Report C3P-884, California Institute of Technology, Pasadena, CA, March 1990. Presented at the Ohio State University Workshop on Parallel Computing, Columbus, Ohio, March 21–23, 1990.

[Balasundaram:90c] Balasundaram, V. "Deriving communication from data layout specifications and optimizing it for the Connection Machine." Technical Report C3P-885, California Institute of Technology, Pasadena, CA, April 1990. Invited presentation at the Parallel Computation Workshop on the Connection Machine, UCLA, Los Angeles.

[Balasundaram:90d] Please see Bibliography for citation.

[Balasundaram:90e] Balasundaram, V. "A mechanism for keeping useful internal information in parallel programming tools: The data access descriptor," *Journal of Parallel and Distributed Computing*, 9:154–170, 1990. Caltech Report C3P-843.

[Balasundaram:90f] Balasundaram, V. "A static performance estimator." Technical Report C3P-941, California Institute of Technology, Pasadena, CA, August 1990.

[Barajas:87a] Please see Bibliography for citation.

[Barhen:87a] Barhen, J., Einstein, J. R., and Jorgensen, C. C. "Advances in concurrent computation for machine intelligence and robotics," in *Proceedings of the Second International Conference on Supercomputing.* International Supercomputing Institute, Inc., St. Petersberg, FL, May 1987. Caltech Report C3P-418.

[Barhen:88a] Please see Bibliography for citation.

[Barish:87a] Barish, K. "Caltech Lattice QCD program conversion from parallel C to parallel Fortran for performance comparisons." Technical Report C3P-471, California Institute of Technology, Pasadena, CA, September 1987.

[Barish:89a] Barish, K. N. "A computer simulation of the 3D Ising model: Two methods to determine critical exponents." Technical Report C3P-819, University of California, Santa Cruz, March 1989. Undergraduate Project.

[Barnes:89a] Please see Bibliography for citation.

[Barnes:89b] Please see Bibliography for citation.

[Barnes:89c] Please see Bibliography for citation.

[Barnes:91a] Please see Bibliography for citation.

[Barr:87a] Barr, A. H., Clayton, R. W., Kuppermann, A., Leal, L. G., Leonard, A., and Prince, T. A. "Caltech supercomputer initiative: A commitment to leadership and excellence." Technical Report C3P-394, California Institute of Technology, Pasadena, CA, December 1987.

[Battiti:87a] Battiti, R. "A back propagation approach to shifts in selective visual attention." Technical Report C3P-436, California Institute of Technology, Pasadena, CA, June 1987.

[Battiti:88a] Please see Bibliography for citation.

[Battiti:89a] Please see Bibliography for citation.

[Battiti:89f] Battiti, R. "Low level image processing with high level "Emergent Properties": Color based segmentation using the heat diffusion equation," in *IEEE Proc. Int. Workshop on Ind. Appl. of Machine Intelligence and Vision*, pages 128–132, 1989. Held in Tokyo, Japan. Caltech Report C3P-776b.

[Battiti:89g] Please see Bibliography for citation.

[Battiti:90a] Please see Bibliography for citation.

[Battiti:90c] Battiti, R. "An adaptive multiscale scheme for real-time motion field estimation," in D. W. Walker and Q. F. Stout, editors, *The Fifth Distributed Memory Computing Conference, Volume I*, pages 194–203. IEEE Computer Society Press, Los Alamitos, CA, 1990. Held April 9–12, Charleston, SC. Caltech Report C3P-933.

[Battiti:90d] Please see Bibliography for citation.

[Battiti:91a] Please see Bibliography for citation.

[Battiti:91b] Please see Bibliography for citation.

[Beigie:89a] Beigie, D., Leonard, A., and Wiggins, S. "Chaotic advection and dynamical systems analysis using Caltech/JPL hypercubes," in J. L. Gustafson, editor, *The Proceedings of the Fourth Conference on Hypercubes, Concurrent Computers and Applications*, page 941. Golden Gate Enterprises, Los Altos, CA, March 1989. Caltech Report C3P-752.

[Berry:89a] Berry, M., Chen, D., Koss, P., Kuck, D., Lo, S., Pang, Y., Roloff, R., Samey, A., Clementi, E., Chin, S., Scheider, D., Fox, G., Messina, P., Walker, D., Hsiung, C., Schwarzmeier, J., Lue, K., Orszag, S., Seidl, F., Johnson, O., Goodrum, R., and Martin, J. "The Perfect Club benchmarks: Effective performance evaluation of supercomputers," *International Journal for Supercomputing Applications*, 3(3):5, 1989. C3P-942b.

[Bond:88a] Bond, A. H., and Fashena, D. "Parallel vision techniques on the hypercube computer," in G. C. Fox, editor, *The Third Conference on Hypercube Concurrent Computers and Applications, Volume 2*, pages 1007–1010. ACM Press, New York, January 1988. Caltech Report C3P-632.

[Bond:88d] Bond, A. H., and Gasser, L. "A subject-indexed bibliography of distributed artificial intelligence," in *Readings in Distributed Artificial Intelligence*. Morgan Kaufmann, San Mateo, California, 1988. Caltech Report C3P-661.

[Bond:88e] Bond, A. H., and Ricci, R. J. "The development and coordination of models in aircraft design." Technical Report C3P-688, California Institute of Technology, Pasadena, CA, September 1988.

[Bond:88f] Bond, A. H. "The cooperation of experts in manufacturing." Technical Report C3P-689, California Institute of Technology, Pasadena, CA, September 1988.

[Bond:88g] Bond, A. H., and Gasser, L. "A survey of distributed artificial intelligence," in *Readings in Distributed Artificial Intelligence*. Morgan Kaufmann, San Mateo, California, 1988. Caltech Report C3P-407b.

[Bond:88h] Bond, A. H., and Gasser, L. "Multiple perspective organizational analysis of distributed artificial intelligence." Technical Report C3P-494b, California Institute of Technology, Pasadena, CA, 1988.

[Bond:88i] Bond, A. H., and Gasser, L. *Readings in Distributed Artificial Intelligence*. Morgan Kaufmann, San Mateo, CA, 1988.

[Bond:90a] Bond, A. H. "A computational model for organizations of co-operating intelligent agents." Technical Report C3P-923, California Institute of Technology, Pasadena, CA, April 1990.

[Bond:90b] Bond, A. H., and Austel, V. "Toward a parallel CAD/CAM system." Technical Report C3P-924, California Institute of Technology, Pasadena, CA, June 1990.

[Breaden:86a] Breaden, M., Chang, D., Chen, S., and O'Dea, J. "SURFCUBE: The development of a small hypercube for personal computers." Technical Report C3P-374, California Institute of Technology, Pasadena, CA, October 1986.

[Brickner:89a] Brickner, R. G., and Baillie, C. F. "Pure gauge QCD on the Connection Machine," in H. D. Simon, editor, *Scientific Applications of the Connection Machine*, pages 234–251. World Scientific Publishing Co. Pte. Ltd., Singapore, 1989. Held at NASA Ames Research Center, Moffett Field, CA, September 12–14, 1988. Caltech Report C3P-710.

[Brickner:89b] Please see Bibliography for citation.

[Brickner:91a] Please see Bibliography for citation.

[Briggs:87a] Briggs, D. "Ph 76/98 project a Monte-Carlo study of the H_2 molecule with algorithmic considerations to a parallel processor." Technical Report C3P-444, California Institute of Technology, Pasadena, CA, June 1987.

[Brochard:89a] Brochard, L. "Implementation and performance evaluation of multigrid methods on hypercubes," in J. L. Gustafson, editor, *The Proceedings of the Fourth Conference on Hypercubes, Concurrent Computers and Applications*, page 1263. Golden Gate Enterprises, Los Altos, CA, March 1989. Caltech Report C3P-771.

[Brochard:89c] Brochard, L., Prost, J.-P., and Faurie, F. "Synchronization and load unbalance effects of parallel iterative algorithms," in *International Conference on Parallel Processing*. ACM Press, New York, 1989. Caltech Report C3P-783.

[Brooks:81a] Brooks, E., Fox, G. C., Gupta, R., Martin, O., Otto, S. W., and De Benedictis, E. "Nearest neighbor concurrent processor." Technical Report C3P-001, California Institute of Technology, Pasadena, CA, September 1981.

[Brooks:82a] Brooks, E., and Fox, G. C. "A simple mail box communications package for the NNCP." Technical Report C3P-002, California Institute of Technology, Pasadena, CA, April 1982.

[Brooks:82b] Please see Bibliography for citation.

[Brooks:83a] Please see Bibliography for citation.

[Brooks:84a] Brooks, E. I., Fox, G. C., Johnson, M., Otto, S. W., Stolorz, P., Athas, W., DeBenedictis, E., Faucette, R., Seitz, C., and Stack, J. "Pure gauge SU(3) lattice gauge theory on an array of computers," *Phys. Rev. Lett.*, 52:2324, 1984. Caltech Report C3P-065.

[Brown:89b] Brown, M. L. "A hypercube image processing language," in J. L. Gustafson, editor, *The Proceedings of the Fourth Conference on Hypercubes, Concurrent Computers and Applications*, page 1013. Golden Gate Enterprises, Los Altos, CA, March 1989. Caltech Report C3P-754.

[Burns:88a] Please see Bibliography for citation.

[Calalo:86a] Calalo, R. H. "Binary pattern matching on Mark II hypercube." Technical Report C3P-322, California Institute of Technology, Pasadena, CA, June 1986.

[Calalo:86b] Calalo, R. H. "Selected summing algorithm on Mark II hypercube." Technical Report C3P-323, California Institute of Technology, Pasadena, CA, June 1986.

[Calalo:86c] Calalo, R. H. "Eleventh bit algorithm on Mark II hypercube." Technical Report C3P-324, California Institute of Technology, Pasadena, CA, June 1986.

[Calalo:86d] Calalo, R. H. "Compressing algorithm on Mark II hypercube." Technical Report C3P-325, California Institute of Technology, Pasadena, CA, June 1986.

[Calalo:86e] Calalo, R. H. "Right justifying algorithm on Mark II hypercube." Technical Report C3P-326, California Institute of Technology, Pasadena, CA, June 1986.

[Calalo:87a] Calalo, R. H. "Hypercube connectivity, processor numbers, channel masks and channel numbers ...." JPL/Caltech Hypercube Course C3P-419.9, California Institute of Technology, Pasadena, CA, March 1987.

[Calalo:88a] Calalo, R. H., Lyons, J. R., and Imbriale, W. A. "Finite difference time domain solution of electromagnetic scattering on the hypercube," in G. C. Fox, editor, *The Third Conference on Hypercube Concurrent Computers and Applications, Volume 2*, pages 1088–1100. ACM Press, New York, January 1988. Caltech Report C3P-596.

[Calalo:89a] Calalo, R. H., Imbriale, W. A., Jacobi, N., Liewer, P. C., Lockhart, T. G., Lyzenga, G. A., Lyons, J. R., Manshadi, F., and Patterson, J. E. "Hypercube matrix computation task report for 1986–1988." Technical Report C3P-743, California Institute of Technology/JPL, Pasadena, CA, 1989. JPL Publication 88–31.

[Callahan:85a] "Baby SMP: A sequential and parallel algorithm." Term Paper on Computer Algebra C3P-234, California Institute of Technology, Pasadena, CA, December 1985.

[Callahan:88a] Please see Bibliography for citation.

[Callahan:88b] Callahan, S. Please see Bibliography for citation.

[Cao:88a] Cao, H. T., and Baillie, C. F. "Caltech missile tracking program—
a benchmark comparison: nCUBE and T800 versus Sequent Balance
and Symmetry." Technical Report C3P-673, California Institute of
Technology, Pasadena, CA, October 1988.

[Chen:87a] Chen, M., DeBenedictis, E., Fox, G., Li, J., and Walker,
D. "Hypercubes are general-purpose multiprocessors with high
speedup." Technical Report C3P-499, California Institute of Technology, Pasadena, CA, 1987.

[Chiu:88b] Chiu, T. W. Please see Bibliography for citation.

[Chiu:88c] Chiu, T. W. Please see Bibliography for citation.

[Chiu:88d] Chiu, T. W. "A parallel computer for lattice gauge theories,"
in G. C. Fox, editor, *The Third Conference on Hypercube Concurrent
Computers and Applications, Volume 1*, pages 81–91. ACM Press, New
York, January 1988. Caltech Report C3P-584.

[Chiu:88e] Please see Bibliography for citation.

[Chiu:88f] Please see Bibliography for citation.

[Chiu:89a] Please see Bibliography for citation.

[Chiu:89b] Please see Bibliography for citation.

[Chiu:90a] Please see Bibliography for citation.

[Chow:87a] Chow, E., Maden, H., Peterson, J., Grunwald, D., and Reed, D.
"Hyperswitch network for the hypercube computer," in H. J. Siegel,
editor, *Proceedings of the 15th Annual International Symposium on
Computer Architecture*. IEEE Computer Society Press, Los Alamitos,
May 1987. Computer Architecture News, Volume 16, Number 2. Cal-
tech Report C3P-484.

[Chu:88b] Chu, D. "SURF report—three-dimensional asteroid on hyper-
cube." Technical Report C3P-677, California Institute of Technology,
Pasadena, CA, November 1988. Summer Undergraduate Research
(SURF) Report.

[Chua:88a] Chua, K., Leonard, A., Pepin, F., and Winckelmans, G. "Robust vortex methods for three-dimensional incompressible flows," in *Proc. Sym. on Recent Advances in Computational Fluid Dynamics.* ASME Winter Meeting, December 1988. Caltech Report C3P-690.

[Cisneros:85a] Cisneros, A. "Scalar products on the hypercube." Technical Report C3P-199, California Institute of Technology, Pasadena, CA, 1985. A tutorial on minimizing the time of interprocessor communications.

[Cisneros:86a] Cisneros, A., and Kolawa, A. "Switching between interrupt driven and polled communication systems on a hypercube," in M. T. Heath, editor, *Proceedings of the Second Conference on Hypercube Multiprocessors*, pages 239–243. SIAM, Philadelphia, 1986. Held in Knoxville, Tennessee, September 29–October 1. Caltech Report C3P-277.

[Cisneros:86b] Cisneros, A. "Irregular regions and multigrid on the hypercube." Technical Report C3P-318, California Institute of Technology, Pasadena, CA, July 1986.

[Cisneros:87a] Cisneros, A. "A communications system for irregular local interaction problems on a concurrent computer," *Comp. Phys. Comm.*, 46(1):35–41, 1987. Caltech Report C3P-317.

[Clayton:83a] Clayton, R., Hager, B., Fox, G. C., Kuppermann, A., Keller, H., Saffman, P., Johnsson, L., Martin, A., and Seitz, C. "Caltech scientific computing group." Technical Report C3P-023, California Institute of Technology, Pasadena, CA, January 1983.

[Clayton:84a] Clayton, R. W. "Finite difference solutions of the acoustic wave equation on a concurrent processor." Technical Report C3P-089, California Institute of Technology, Pasadena, CA, 1984.

[Clayton:87a] Please see Bibliography for citation.

[Clayton:88a] Please see Bibliography for citation.

[Coddington:90a] Please see Bibliography for citation.

[Coddington:91a] Coddington, P. D., and Baillie, C. F. "Parallel cluster algorithms," *Nuclear Physics B (Proc. Suppl.)*, 20:76, 1991. Proceedings of the International Conference on Lattice Field, Theory, Tallahassee, Florida, October 8–12, 1990. SCCS-102. Caltech Report C3P-946.

[Crichton:85a] Crichton, J., and Enguehard, S. "Using the Mark II hypercube symbolic debugger." Technical Report C3P-220b, California Institute of Technology, Pasadena, CA, 1985. Corrected April 30, 1986.

[Cuccaro:89a] Please see Bibliography for citation.

[Cuccaro:89b] Please see Bibliography for citation.

[Curkendall:85a] Curkendall, D. "Hypercube research project: Annual report." Technical Report C3P-245, Jet Propulsion Laboratory/California Institute of Technology, Pasadena, CA, November 1985.

[Curkendall:85b] Curkendall, D. "Hypercube research project—quarterly progress letter." Technical Report C3P-195, Jet Propulsion Laboratory/California Institute of Technology, Pasadena, CA, April 1985.

[Curkendall:85d] Curkendall, D. "Hypercube research project: Mark III core engineering notebook." Technical Report C3P-176b, Jet Propulsion Laboratory/California Institute of Technology, Pasadena, CA, December 1985. JPL D-2431.

[DeForest:88a] DeForest, D., Faustini, A., and Lee, R. A. "Hyperflow," in G. C. Fox, editor, *The Third Conference on Hypercube Concurrent Computers and Applications, Volume 1*, pages 482–488. ACM Press, New York, January 1988. Caltech Report C3P-504.

[Dembart:84a] Please see Bibliography for citation.

[Ding:88a] Please see Bibliography for citation.

[Ding:88b] Please see Bibliography for citation.

[Ding:88c] Ding, H. Q. "Performance of a QCD code on the Mark II-Ifp." Technical Report C3P-624, California Institute of Technology, Pasadena, CA, April 1988.

[Ding:88d] Please see Bibliography for citation.

[Ding:89e] Ding, H.-Q. "64-bit Mark IIIfp hypercube: A preliminary performance evaluation." Technical Report C3P-847, California Institute of Technology, Pasadena, CA, November 1989.

[Ding:90a] Ding, H.-Q., and Makivić. "Spin correlations in the antiferromagnetic crystals $La_2 CuO_4$ and $K_2 N_i F_4$," *Modern Physics Letters B*, 4(11):697–701, 1990. Caltech Report C3P-896.

[Ding:90b] Please see Bibliography for citation.

[Ding:90c] Please see Bibliography for citation.

[Ding:90d] Ding, H.-Q. "Quark potential at large distance: Evidence of scaling from lattice gauge simulations on a hypercube supercomputer." Technical Report C3P-914, California Institute of Technology, Pasadena, CA, June 1990.

[Ding:90e] Ding, H.-Q. "Phase transitions in two-dimensional quantum spin systems—Monte Carlo simulations on a hypercube supercomputer." Technical Report C3P-915, California Institute of Technology, Pasadena, CA, June 1990.

[Ding:90f] Ding, H.-Q. "Asymptotic scaling of the heavy quark potential in lattice QCD," *Physical Review D*, 42(7):2350–2354, October 1990. Caltech Report C3P-916.

[Ding:90g] Please see Bibliography for citation.

[Ding:90h] Please see Bibliography for citation.

[Ding:90i] Ding, H.-Q. "Antiferromagnetic transitions in the High-T_c materials," *J. Phys. Condensed Matter*, 2:7979–7984, 1990. Caltech Report C3P-953.

[Ding:90j] Ding, H.-Q., and Makivic, M. S. "On the quantum nature of the spin-1/2 antiferromagnetics—a reply to a comment," *Phys. Rev. Letters*, 65:1520, 1990. Caltech Report C3P-954.

[Ding:90k] Please see Bibliography for citation.

[Ding:91a] Ding, H.-Q. "Improved determination of the heavy quark potential in lattice QCD," *Physical Review D*, 44:2200–2202, October 1991. Caltech Report C3P-970.

[Ding:91b] Ding, H.-Q. "Heavy quark potential in lattice QCD: a review of recent progress at Caltech," *International Journal of Modern Physics C*, 2(2):637–658, 1991. Caltech Report C3P-963b.

[Ding:91c] Ding, H.-Q. "Computing quark potential on a parallel supercomputer," *Computer Physics Communications*, 65:92–99, 1991. Caltech Report C3P-949.

[Ding:91d] Ding, H.-Q. "Simulating lattice QCD on a Caltech/JPL hypercube," *The International Journal of Supercomputer Applications*, 5(2):73–80, 1991. Caltech Report C3P-951.

[Ding:91e] Ding, H.-Q. "2D quantum antiferromagnet at low temperatures," *Phys. Lett. A*, 159:355–357, 1991. Caltech Report C3P-975.

[Ding:92a] Please see Bibliography for citation.

[Ding:92b] Ding, H.-Q., and Makivic, M. S. "A reply to comments on quantum *XY* model," *Phys. Rev. B*, 45(1), 1992. Caltech Report C3P-977.

[Dunbar:88a] Dunbar, S., Chi, C. Y., and Hsiao, S. V. "Parallel implementations of wind retrieval algorithms for spaceborne radar scatterometers." Proposal C3P-666, California Institute of Technology, Pasadena, CA, August 1988.

[Eng:85a] Eng, S. T., and Fox, G. C. "A study of optically interconnected concurrent computers." Technical Report C3P-185b, California Institute of Technology, Pasadena, CA, December 1985. Proposal to President's Fund.

[Enguehard:85a] Enguehard, S., and Crichton, G. "Using the Mark II hypercube symbolic debugger." Technical Report C3P-220, California Institute of Technology, Pasadena, CA, November 1985.

[Fatland:87a] Fatland, R., and Morison, R. "Profiling C programs on the nCUBE." Technical Report C3P-456, California Institute of Technology, Pasadena, CA, August 1987.

[Felten:85a] Please see Bibliography for citation.

[Felten:85b] Please see Bibliography for citation.

[Felten:85c] Felten, E., Karlin, S., and Otto, S. "Sorting on a hypercubic, MIMD computer." Technical Report C3P-092b, California Institute of Technology, Pasadena, CA, February 1985.

[Felten:87a] Please see Bibliography for citation.

[Felten:87b] Felten, E. "Parallel branch and bound algorithms." Technical Report C3P-457, California Institute of Technology, Pasadena, CA, 1987.

[Felten:87d] Felten, E. "Message passing on RP3 and other shared-memory machines." Technical Report C3P-448, California Institute of Technology, Pasadena, CA, July 1987.

[Felten:88a] Please see Bibliography for citation.

[Felten:88b] Please see Bibliography for citation.

[Felten:88c] Please see Bibliography for citation.

[Felten:88f] Felten, E. W., and Otto, S. W. "A safe vertex," in G. C. Fox, editor, *The Third Conference on Hypercube Concurrent Computers and Applications, Volume 1*, pages 560–562. ACM Press, New York, January 1988. Caltech Report C3P-614.

[Felten:88g] Felten, E. W., and Otto, S. W. "Chess on a hypercube," in G. C. Fox, editor, *The Third Conference on Hypercube Concurrent Computers and Applications, Volume 2*, pages 1329–1341. ACM Press, New York, January 1988. Caltech Report C3P-579.

[Felten:88h] Please see Bibliography for citation.

[Felten:88i] Felten, E. W., and Otto, S. W. "A highly parallel chess program," in *Proceedings of International Conference on Fifth Generation Computer Systems 1988*, pages 1001–1009. ICOT, November 1988. Tokyo, Japan, November 28 – December 2. Caltech Report C3P-579c.

[Felten:88l] Felten, E., Fox, G., and Otto, S. "A uniform programming environment for synchronous and loosely synchronous problems: SIMD and MIMD parallel computers." Technical Report C3P-656, California Institute of Technology, Pasadena, CA, August 1988.

[Felten:89a] Felten, E., Messina, P., and Williams, R. "Parallelizing a real application code: Is it worth it?." Technical Report C3P-713, California Institute of Technology, Pasadena, CA, February 1989.

[Felten:90a] Please see Bibliography for citation.

[Ferraro:90a] Ferraro, R. D., Cwik, T., Jacobi, N., Liewer, P. C., Lockhart, T. G., Lyzenga, G. A., Parker, J., and Patterson, J. E. "Parallel finite elements applied to the electromagnetic scattering problem," in D. W. Walker and Q. F. Stout, editors, *The Fifth Distributed Memory Computing Conference, Volume I*, pages 417–420. IEEE Computer Society Press, Los Alamitos, CA, 1990. Held April 9–12, Charleston, SC. Caltech Report C3P-903.

[Ferraro:90b] Please see Bibliography for citation.

[Flower:85a] Please see Bibliography for citation.

[Flower:85b] Flower, J. "Parallelism for the intermediate host." Technical Report C3P-235, California Institute of Technology, Pasadena, CA, December 1985.

[Flower:85c] Flower, J. "Concurrent crossword generation." Proposal C3P-202, California Institute of Technology, Pasadena, CA, September 1985.

[Flower:86b] Please see Bibliography for citation.

[Flower:86c] Please see Bibliography for citation.

[Flower:87a] Please see Bibliography for citation.

[Flower:87b] Flower, J. *Lattice Gauge Theory on a Parallel Computer*. PhD thesis, California Institute of Technology, 1987. Caltech Report C3P-411.

[Flower:87c] Please see Bibliography for citation.

[Flower:87d] Flower, J. "Debugging aids on the nCUBE." Technical Report C3P-491, California Institute of Technology, Pasadena, CA, December 1987.

[Flower:87e] Please see Bibliography for citation.

[Flower:88a] Flower, J., and Williams, R. "Parallel programming in comfort," in G. C. Fox, editor, *The Third Conference on Hypercube Concurrent Computers and Applications, Volume 1*, pages 811–822. ACM Press, New York, January 1988. Caltech Report C3P-531.

[Flower:88b] Flower, J., Apostolakis, J., Baillie, C., and Ding, H. Q. "Lattice gauge theory on the hypercube," in G. C. Fox, editor, *The Third Conference on Hypercube Concurrent Computers and Applications, Volume 2*, pages 1278–1287. ACM Press, New York, January 1988. Caltech Report C3P-605.

[Fox:82a] Please see Bibliography for citation.

[Fox:83a] Fox, G. C. "Decomposition of scientific problems for concurrent processors." Technical Report C3P-028, California Institute of Technology, Pasadena, CA, 1983. CALT-68-986.

[Fox:83b] Fox, G. C., and Seitz, C. "Concurrent processing and the decomposition of problems." Proposal C3P-034, California Institute of Technology, Pasadena, CA, 1983.

[Fox:83c] Fox, G. C., "Scientific calculations with ensemble computers," March 1983. Invited talk at Padua High Energy Physics Microprocessor Conference. Caltech Report C3P-037.

[Fox:84a] Please see Bibliography for citation.

[Fox:84b] Fox, G. "Use of concurrent processors in (high energy physics) data analysis." Technical Report C3P-129, California Institute of Technology, Pasadena, CA, 1984.

[Fox:84c] Fox, G. "On the sequential component of computation." Technical Report C3P-130, California Institute of Technology, Pasadena, CA, 1984.

[Fox:84d] Fox, G. "Square matrix decomposition: Symmetric, local, scattered." Technical Report C3P-097, California Institute of Technology, Pasadena, CA, 1984.

[Fox:84e] Please see Bibliography for citation.

[Fox:84f] Fox, G. C. "The cyclic Jacobi method for eigenvalues of symmetric matrices." Technical Report C3P-082, California Institute of Technology, Pasadena, CA, July 1984.

[Fox:84g] Please see Bibliography for citation.

[Fox:84h] Please see Bibliography for citation.

[Fox:84i] Fox, G. C. "LU decomposition for banded matrices." Technical Report C3P-099, California Institute of Technology, Pasadena, CA, August 1984.

[Fox:84j] Please see Bibliography for citation.

[Fox:84k] Please see Bibliography for citation.

[Fox:85a] Fox, G., Otto, S. W., and Umland, E. A. "Monte Carlo physics on a concurrent processor," *Journal of Statistical Physics*, 43(5/6):1209–1237, June 1986. Proceedings of the Conference on Frontiers of Quantum Monte Carlo, September 3–6, 1985 at Los Alamos. Caltech Report C3P-214.

[Fox:85b] Please see Bibliography for citation.

[Fox:85c] Please see Bibliography for citation.

[Fox:85d] Please see Bibliography for citation.

[Fox:85e] Please see Bibliography for citation.

[Fox:85g] Fox, G. C., "Summary of the Cosmic Cube as a prototype of the future general purpose supercomputer," April 1985. Layman's description of Invited Talk at APS meeting in Crystal City, VA. Caltech Report C3P-153b.

[Fox:85i] Please see Bibliography for citation.

[Fox:85j] Fox, G. C. "Use of the Caltech hypercube," *IEEE Software*, 2:73, July 1985. Caltech Report C3P-162.

[Fox:85k] Please see Bibliography for citation.

[Fox:85l] Fox, G. C. "Concurrent scalar products on the hypercube." Technical Report C3P-173, California Institute of Technology, Pasadena, CA, June 1985.

[Fox:85m] Fox, G. C., "BBC science now radio program," July 1985. Cassette which includes "Layman's" discussion. Caltech Report C3P-187.

[Fox:85o] "The Caltech Concurrent Computation Program—a multidisciplinary research group in concurrent computation for scientific and engineering problems." Proposal to the Department of Energy, March 1985. Caltech Report C3P-156.

[Fox:85p] "Appendices D and E and Tables 1 and 2 of C^{3}P-156," January 1985. Summary of Caltech/JPL Applications on Hypercube. Caltech Report C3P-156b.

[Fox:86a] Please see Bibliography for citation.

[Fox:86c] Fox, G., and Furmanski, W. "Communication algorithms for regular convolutions and matrix problems on the hypercube," in M. T. Heath, editor, *Hypercube Multiprocessors*, pages 223–238. SIAM, Philadelphia, 1987. Caltech Report C3P-329.

[Fox:86e] Fox, G. "Iterative full matrix-vector multiplication on the hypercube." Technical Report C3P-336, California Institute of Technology, Pasadena, CA, 1986.

[Fox:86f] Please see Bibliography for citation.

[Fox:86h] Please see Bibliography for citation.

[Fox:86k] Fox, Geoffrey, C., and Kolawa, A. "Implementation of high performance crystalline operating system on the Intel iPSC hypercube." Technical Report C3P-247, California Institute of Technology, Pasadena, CA, January 1986.

[Fox:86m] Fox, Geoffrey, C., "Caltech Concurrent Computation Program," June 1986. Talk given at Aerospace Corporation. Caltech Report C3P-294.

[Fox:86n] Fox, Geoffrey, C. VHS Tape. Text is Fox:86m. Caltech Report C3P-294b.

[Fox:86q] Fox, Geoffrey, C. "Lattice gauge theory on the hypercube." Technical Report C3P-309, California Institute of Technology, Pasadena, CA, June 1986.

[Fox:86r] Fox, Geoffrey, C. "An overview of ten challenge problems on the hypercube." Technical Report C3P-338, California Institute of Technology, Pasadena, CA, 1986.

[Fox:87b] Please see Bibliography for citation.

[Fox:87c] Please see Bibliography for citation.

[Fox:87d] Please see Bibliography for citation.

[Fox:87f] Fox, G. C. "The hypercube as a supercomputer." Technical Report C3P-391, California Institute of Technology, Pasadena, CA, January 1987. Presented at the Second International Conference on Supercomputing at Santa Clara, May 1987; published by the International Supercomputing Institute, Inc., St. Petersburg, Florida, May 1987.

[Fox:87g] Fox, G. C. "Concurrent supercomputer initiative at Caltech." Technical Report C3P-409, California Institute of Technology, Pasadena, CA, January 1987. Presented at the Second International Conference on Supercomputing at Santa Clara, May 1987. Published by the International Supercomputing Institute, Inc., St. Petersburg, FL, May 1987.

[Fox:87j] Fox, G. C., Clayton, R., Kuppermann, A., Leonard, A., Keller, H., and Prince, T. "A research proposal to NSF by The Concurrent Supercomputing Initiative at Caltech—Facilities and Computational Science." Technical Report C3P-435, California Institute of Technology, Pasadena, CA, June 1987.

[Fox:87k] Fox, G. C., Clayton, R., Kuppermann, A., Leonard, A., Keller, H., Prince, T., and Messina, P. "A pilot project in performance evaluation of scientific programs on selected advanced architecture computers. A research proposal to NSF from the California Institute of Technology." Technical Report C3P-439, California Institute of Technology, Pasadena, CA, July 1987.

[Fox:87l] Fox, G. C., Clayton, R., Kuppermann, A., Leonard, A., Keller, H., Prince, T., and Messina, P. "The concurrent supercomputing initiative at Caltech—overview for performance analysis project." Technical Report C3P-440, California Institute of Technology, Pasadena, CA, July 1987.

[Fox:88a] Please see Bibliography for citation.

[Fox:88b] Please see Bibliography for citation.

[Fox:88c] Fox, G. C., editor. *The Third Conference on Hypercube Concurrent Computers and Applications.* Jet Propulsion Laboratory of the California Institute of Technology, ACM Press, New York, January 1988. Volume 1 - Architecture, Software, Computer Systems and General Issues; Volume 2 - Applications.

[Fox:88d] Fox, G. C., and Frey, A. "Problems and approaches for a teraflop processor," in G. C. Fox, editor, *The Third Conference on Hypercube Concurrent Computers and Applications, Volume 1*, pages 21–25. ACM Press, New York, January 1988. Caltech Report C3P-606.

[Fox:88e] Please see Bibliography for citation.

[Fox:88f] Please see Bibliography for citation.

[Fox:88g] Please see Bibliography for citation.

[Fox:88h] Please see Bibliography for citation.

[Fox:88u] Fox, G. C. "Issues in software development for concurrent computers," in G. J. Knafl, editor, *Proceedings of The Twelfth Annual International Computer Software and Applications Conference*, pages 302–305. Computer Society Press of the IEEE, Washington, D.C., October 1988. Caltech Report C3P-640.

[Fox:88v] Please see Bibliography for citation.

[Fox:88w] Fox, G. C. "Theory and practice of concurrent systems," in *Proceedings of International Conference on Fifth Generation Computer Systems 1988*, pages 157–160. ICOT, November 1988. Caltech Report C3P-664.

[Fox:88dd] Fox, G. C., and Walker, D. "Concurrent supercomputers in science," in E. F. Redish and J. S. Risley, editors, *Proceedings of the Conference on Computers in Physics Instruction*, pages 346–361. Addison-Wesley, 1989. Conference held in Raleigh, NC, August 1–5, 1988. Caltech Report C3P-646.

[Fox:88gg] Fox, G. C. "A plan for parallel programming." Technical Report C3P-672, California Institute of Technology, Pasadena, CA, October 1988.

[Fox:88ii] Fox, G. C. "Introductory material on parallel computers for a course in computational science." Technical Report C3P-678, California Institute of Technology, Pasadena, CA, November 1988.

[Fox:88kk] Please see Bibliography for citation.

[Fox:88mm] Please see Bibliography for citation.

[Fox:88nn] Please see Bibliography for citation.

[Fox:88oo] Please see Bibliography for citation.

[Fox:88tt] Please see Bibliography for citation.

[Fox:88uu] Please see Bibliography for citation.

[Fox:89b] Fox, G. C. "Experience on the hypercube." Technical Report C3P-716, California Institute of Technology, Pasadena, CA, February 1989.

[Fox:89f] Fox, G. C. "Caltech-Hughes Aircraft Neural Valley, California Competitive Technology Program." Proposal C3P-728, California Institute of Technology, Pasadena, CA, March 1989.

[Fox:89h] Fox, G. C. "A note on neural networking for trackfinding." Technical Report C3P-748, California Institute of Technology, Pasadena, CA, March 1989. Unpublished.

[Fox:89i] Please see Bibliography for citation.

[Fox:89l] Please see Bibliography for citation.

[Fox:89n] Please see Bibliography for citation.

[Fox:89t] Please see Bibliography for citation.

[Fox:89u] Fox, G. C., and Prince, Thomas, A. "CISE research instrumentation for a program in physical computation and complex systems." NSF Proposal C3P-814, California Institute of Technology, Pasadena, CA, August 1989.

[Fox:89x] Fox, G. C., Ho, A. W., Messina, P., and Cole, T. "Hands-on parallel processing," *BYTE*, 14(10):287–293, October 1989. Caltech Report C3P-828.

[Fox:89y] Please see Bibliography for citation.

[Fox:89aa] Fox, G. C., Gurewitz, E., and Wong, Y. "A neural network approach to multi-vehicle navigation." Technical Report C3P-833, California Institute of Technology, Pasadena, CA, October 1989. Published in Proceedings of SPIE Conference, Philadelphia.

[Fox:90e] Please see Bibliography for citation.

[Fox:90k] Please see Bibliography for citation.

[Fox:90l] Fox, G. C. "A complex system model for Eastern Europe." Technical Report C3P-931, California Institute of Technology, Pasadena, CA, June 1990. Unpublished.

[Fox:90o] Please see Bibliography for citation.

[Fox:90nn] Please see Bibliography for citation.

[Fox:91e] Please see Bibliography for citation.

[Fox:91f] Please see Bibliography for citation.

[Fox:91j] Please see Bibliography for citation.

[Fox:92b] Please see Bibliography for citation.

[Fox:92c] Please see Bibliography for citation.

[Fox:92d] Please see Bibliography for citation.

[Fox:92i] Please see Bibliography for citation.

[Fox:92k] Fox, G. C., and Balasundaram, V. "Parallel programming as an optimization problem," in *Expert Systems for Scientific Computing*, pages 125–156. Elsevier Science Publishers B.V., North-Holland, Amsterdam, 1992. Invited talk given at Second International Conference on Expert Systems for Scientific Computing, Purdue University, April 24, 1990. SCCS-110, CRPC-TR90161. Caltech Report C3P-891.

[Frankel:86a] Frankel, A., and Clayton, R. W. "Finite difference simulations of seismic scattering: Implications for the propagation of shortperiod seismic waves in the crust and models of crustal heterogeneity," *J. Geophys. Res.*, 91:64–65, 1986. Caltech Report C3P-203.

[Frey:86a] Frey, A. H. "Hypercube architectures and their application to signal processing," in *Proceedings of S.P.I.E., The International Society for Optical Engineering, Vol. 614*, January 1986. Talk given at session: Highly Parallel Signal Processing Architectures: Critical Review of Technology. Caltech Report C3P-250.

[Fucito:84a] Please see Bibliography for citation.

[Fucito:84b] Fucito, F., and Solomon, S. "Long range forces on the NNCP." Technical Report C3P-080, California Institute of Technology, Pasadena, CA, 1984.

[Fucito:85a] Please see Bibliography for citation.

[Fucito:85b] Please see Bibliography for citation.

[Fucito:85c] Please see Bibliography for citation.

[Fucito:85d] Please see Bibliography for citation.

[Fucito:85e] Fucito, F., and Solomon, S. "A concurrent pseudo Fermion algorithm," *Computer Physics Comm.*, 36:141, 1985. Caltech Report C3P-118.

[Fucito:85f] Please see Bibliography for citation.

[Fucito:86a] Please see Bibliography for citation.

[Furmanski:87a] Please see Bibliography for citation.

[Furmanski:87c] Please see Bibliography for citation.

[Furmanski:88a] Please see Bibliography for citation.

[Furmanski:88b] Please see Bibliography for citation.

[Furmanski:88c] Please see Bibliography for citation.

[Furmanski:89d] Please see Bibliography for citation.

[Furmanski:90a] Furmanski, W. "MOVIE—a system overview." Technical Report C3P-888, California Institute of Technology, Pasadena, CA, March 1990.

[Gates:86a] Gates, D. A. "An IBM PC-AT raster graphics display station." Technical Report C3P-351, California Institute of Technology, Pasadena, CA, November 1986.

[Ghil:89a] Ghil, M., and Dickey, J. O. "Application of the UCLA general circulation model to global atmospheric studies on the Caltech/JPL hypercube." President's Fund Proposal C3P-709, UCLA and JPL, January 1989.

[Goldsmith:85a] Goldsmith, J., and Salmon, J. "A ray tracing system for the hypercube." Technical Report C3P-154, Jet Propulsion Laboratory/California Institute of Technology, Pasadena, CA, 1985.

[Goldsmith:86a] Please see Bibliography for citation.

[Goldsmith:86b] Goldsmith, J. "Structure of a computer graphics system." Technical Report C3P-384, California Institute of Technology, Pasadena, CA, November 1986.

[Goldsmith:87a] Please see Bibliography for citation.

[Goldsmith:88a] Please see Bibliography for citation.

[Gorham:88a] Please see Bibliography for citation.

[Gorham:88b] Gorham, P. W. "Computational aspects of bispectral analysis in interferometric imaging." Technical Report C3P-637, California Institute of Technology, Pasadena, CA, June 1988.

[Gorham:88c] Gorham, P. W. "Speckle/bispectrum results." Technical Report C3P-705, California Institute of Technology, Pasadena, CA, December 1988.

[Gorham:88d] Please see Bibliography for citation.

[Gorham:89a] Please see Bibliography for citation.

[Gorham:89b] Gorham, P. W., Ghez, A. M., and Prince, T. A. "Recovery of diffraction-limited object autocorrelations from astronomical speckle interferograms using the CLEAN algorithm." Technical Report C3P-804, California Institute of Technology, Pasadena, CA, 1989.

[Gottschalk:86a] Gottschalk, T. D., Angus, I., and Fox, G. C. "Booster trajectory calculations." Technical Report C3P-387, California Institute of Technology, Pasadena, CA, November 1986.

[Gottschalk:86b] Gottschalk, T. D., Angus, I., and Fox, G. C. "Hypercube tracking: A preliminary status report." Technical Report C3P-388, California Institute of Technology, Pasadena, CA, November 1986.

[Gottschalk:87a] Gottschalk, T. D. "CALTRAX: The tracking program for Simulation87." Technical Report C3P-478, California Institute of Technology, Pasadena, CA, October 1987.

[Gottschalk:87b] Gottschalk, T. D. "Precision filters for boost phase tracking." Technical Report C3P-479, California Institute of Technology, Pasadena, CA, October 1987.

[Gottschalk:87c] Gottschalk, T. D. "A new multi-target tracking model." Technical Report C3P-480, California Institute of Technology, Pasadena, CA, October 1987.

[Gottschalk:87d] Gottschalk, T. D. "Concurrent stereo tracking and the assignment problem." Technical Report C3P-481, California Institute of Technology, Pasadena, CA, Oct 1987.

[Gottschalk:87e] Gottschalk, T. "A new multi-target tracking model." Technical Report C3P-442, California Institute of Technology, Pasadena, CA, July 1987.

[Gottschalk:87f] Please see Bibliography for citation.

[Gottschalk:88a] Please see Bibliography for citation.

[Gottschalk:89c] Gottschalk, T. D., and Nolty, R. "Identification of physics processes using neural network classifiers." Technical Report C3P-842, California Institute of Technology, 1989.

[Gottschalk:90a] Please see Bibliography for citation.

[Gottschalk:90b] Please see Bibliography for citation.

[Griffiths:88a] Griffiths, M. "Ada tasking on the Sequent Balance," in G. C. Fox, editor, *The Third Conference on Hypercube Concurrent Computers and Applications, Volume 1*, pages 409–416. ACM Press, New York, January 1988. Caltech Report C3P-577.

[Griffiths:88b] Griffiths, M. "Ada tasking on the Sequent Balance," *International CIS*, 2(3):4–19, July 1988. Caltech Report C3P-626.

[Groom:88a] Please see Bibliography for citation.

[Groom:89a] Groom, S. L. "A better host interface for the Mark III hypercube," in J. L. Gustafson, editor, *The Proceedings of the Fourth Conference on Hypercubes, Concurrent Computers and Applications*, page 145. Golden Gate Enterprises, Los Altos, CA, March 1989. Caltech Report C3P-809.

[Gupta:85a] Gupta, R., Otto, S. W., and Patel, A. "Implementation of the $\sqrt{3}$ blocking scheme on the hypercube." Technical Report C3P-135, California Institute of Technology, Pasadena, CA, January 1985.

[Gupta:88a] Please see Bibliography for citation.

[Gupta:89a] Gupta, R., Patel, A., Baillie, C. F., Guralnik, G., Kilcup, G. W., and Sharpe, S. R. "QCD with dynamical Wilson Fermions," *Physical Review D*, 40(6):2072–2084, September 1989. Caltech Report C3P-674b.

[Gupta:90a] Gupta, R., Patel, A., Baillie, C. F., Kilcup, G., and Sharpe, S. "Exploring glueball wavefunctions on the lattice." Technical Report C3P-943, California Institute of Technology, Pasadena, CA, 1990.

[Gupta:91a] Gupta, R., Baillie, C. F., Brickner, R. G., Kilcup, G. W., Patel, A., and Sharpe, S. R. "QCD with Dynamical Wilson Fermions II." Technical Report C3P-969, California Institute of Technology, Pasadena, CA, June 1991. LA-UR-91-528, COLO-HEP-254, UW DOES/ER/40614-4.

[Gurewitz:89b] Gurewitz, E., Fox, G. C., and Wong, Y.-F. "Parallel algorithm for one- and two-vehicle navigation." Technical Report C3P-852, California Institute of Technology, 1989. Published in the Proceedings of the 1990 IEEE International Workshop on Intelligent Robots and Systems, IROS '90 held in Tsuchiura, Ibaraki, Japan, July 1990.

[Gurewitz:90a] Gurewitz, E., Fox, G. C., and Wong, Y.-F. "Parallel algorithm for one and two-vehicle navigation," in D. W. Walker and Q. F. Stout, editors, *The Fifth Distributed Memory Computing Conference, Volume I*, pages 140–147. IEEE Computer Society Press, Los Alamitos, CA, 1990. Held April 9–12, Charleston, SC. Caltech Report C3P-876.

[Gurnis:88a] Please see Bibliography for citation.

[Gutt:89a] Please see Bibliography for citation.

[Gutt:90a] Gutt, G. M. "An automata model of granular materials," in D. W. Walker and Q. F. Stout, editors, *The Fifth Distributed Memory Computing Conference, Volume I*, pages 522–529. IEEE Computer Society Press, Los Alamitos, CA, 1990. Held April 9–12, Charleston, SC. Caltech Report C3P-890.

[Harstad:87a] Please see Bibliography for citation.

[Hipes:85a] Hipes, P., and Kuppermann, A. "Atom-diatom cross section calculations on concurrent computers: Matrix inversion." Technical Report C3P-094b, California Institute of Technology, Pasadena, CA, January 1985.

[Hipes:86a] Hipes, P., and Kuppermann, A. "Gauss-Jordan matrix inversion with pivoting on the hypercube." Technical Report C3P-347, California Institute of Technology, Pasadena, CA, 1986. Unpublished.

[Hipes:87a] Please see Bibliography for citation.

[Hipes:88a] Please see Bibliography for citation.

[Hipes:88b] Please see Bibliography for citation.

[Hipes:89b] Please see Bibliography for citation.

[Hipes:89c] Hipes, P. G. "Brief report on parallel electron-molecule scattering program." Technical Report C3P-815, California Institute of Technology, Pasadena, CA, August 1989.

[Hipes:89d] Please see Bibliography for citation.

[Hipes:90a] Please see Bibliography for citation.

[Ho:86c] Ho, F. "Pawn endgames for the concurrent chess program." Technical Report C3P-364, California Institute of Technology, Pasadena, CA, November 1986.

[Ho:88a] Ho, A., Fox, G. C., Walker, D., Snyder, S., Chang, D., Chen, S., Breaden, M., and Cole, T. "PC-CUBE, a personal computer based hypercube," in G. C. Fox, editor, *The Third Conference on Hyper-cube Concurrent Computers and Applications, Volume 1*, pages 92–97. ACM Press, New York, January 1988. Caltech Report C3P-587.

[Ho:88b] Ho, A., Breaden, M., and Chen, S. "Mac-CUBE user's guide." Technical Report C3P-582, California Institute of Technology, December 1988.

[Ho:88c] Please see Bibliography for citation.

[Ho:88d] Ho, A., Fox, G., Walker, D., Breaden, W., Chen, S., Knutson, A., and Kuwamato, S. "Mac-CUBE, the Macintosh-based hypercube," in G. C. Fox, editor, *The Third Conference on Hypercube Concurrent Computers and Applications, Volume 1*, pages 98–103. ACM Press, New York, January 1988. Caltech Report C3P-573.

[Ho:88f] Ho, A., and Snyder, S. "CXLISP—a concurrent XLISP interpreter on the hypercube." Technical Report C3P-559, California Institute of Technology, Pasadena, CA, March 1988.

[Ho:88g] Ho, A., Snyder, S., and Chang, D. "User's guide for PC-Cube, the IBM PC-based hypercube." Technical Report C3P-563, California Institute of Technology, Pasadena, CA, March 1988.

[Ho:88h] Ho, A., Fox, G. C., Snyder, S., Chu, D., and Mlynar, T. "Parallel 3D asteroids, a status report." Technical Report C3P-681, California Institute of Technology, Pasadena, CA, November 1988. Summer Undergraduate (SURF) Report.

[Ho:89a] Ho, A. "A back-prop controller for land and space vehicles." Technical Report C3P-735, California Institute of Technology, Pasadena, CA, March 1989.

[Ho:89b] Please see Bibliography for citation.

[Ho:90a] Ho, A. W. "Parallel neural-net path-planner on hypercube and transputer," in R. Eckmiller, G. Hartmann, and G. Hauske, editors, *Parallel Processing in Neural Systems, and Computers*, pages 421–426. Elsevier Science Publishers, North-Holland, Amsterdam, 1990. Caltech Report C3P-848.

[Ho:90b] Please see Bibliography for citation.

[Ho:90c] Ho, A. W., and Fox, G. C. "Learning to plan near-optimal, collision-free paths," in D. W. Walker and Q. F. Stout, editors, *The Fifth Distributed Memory Computing Conference, Volume I*, pages 131–139. IEEE Computer Society Press, Los Alamitos, CA, 1990. Held April 9–12, Charleston, SC. Caltech Report C3P-881.

[Ho:90d] Ho, A. W., and Fox, G. C. "Neural network near-optimal motion planning for a mobile robot on binary and varied terrains," in *IEEE International Workshop on Intelligent Robots and Systems '90*, volume 2, pages 593–600, 1990. Caltech Report C3P-882.

[Ho:90e] Ho, A. W., and Fox, G. C. "Multi-scale, vision-based navigation on distributed-memory MIMD computers," in S. I. Sayegh, editor, *Proceedings of the Third Conference on Neural Networks and Parallel Distributed Processing*, pages 39–46. Indiana University/Purdue University at Fort Wayne, 1990. Caltech Report C3P-911.

[Ho:91a] Ho, A. W., and Fox, G. C. "Competitive-cooperative system of distributed artificial neural agents," in P. Messina and A. Murli, editors, *Proceedings of the International Conference on Parallel Computing: Problems, Methods and Applications*, page 721. Elsevier Science Publishers, North-Holland, Amsterdam, 1991. Held in Anacapri, Italy, June 3–7, 1990. Caltech Report C3P-925.

[Hood:86a] Please see Bibliography for citation.

[Horvath:89a] Horvath, J. C., and Cole, R. C. "Spacecraft sequencing on the hypercube concurrent processor," in J. L. Gustafson, editor, *The Proceedings of the Fourth Conference on Hypercubes, Concurrent Computers and Applications*, page 1181. Golden Gate Enterprises, Los Altos, CA, March 1989. Caltech Report C3P-756.

[Horvath:90a] Horvath, J. C., Tang, T., Perry, L. P., and Cole, R. C. "Hypercubes for critical space flight command operations," in D. W. Walker and Q. F. Stout, editors, *The Fifth Distributed Memory Computing Conference, Volume I*, pages 2–10. IEEE Computer Society Press, Los Alamitos, CA, 1990. Held April 9–12, Charleston, SC. Caltech Report C3P-898.

[Ikudome:90a] Please see Bibliography for citation.

[Jefferson:85a] Jefferson, D., and Beckman, B. "Implementation of time warp on the Caltech hypercube." Technical Report C3P-141, California Institute of Technology, Pasadena, CA, January 1985. Presented with a group from JPL at the SCG Conference on Distributed Simulation in San Diego, California.

[Jefferson:88a] Jefferson, D., Beckman, B., Blume, L., Diloreto, M., Hontalas, P., Reiher, P., Sturdevant, K., Tupman, J., Wedel, J., Wieland, F., and Younger, H. "The status of the Time Warp operating system," in G. C. Fox, editor, *The Third Conference on Hypercube Concurrent Computers and Applications, Volume 1*, pages 738–744. ACM Press, New York, January 1988. Caltech Report C3P-627.

[Jennings:86a] "Support material for second hypercube class," 1986. The course is available on 1/2" VHS Videotapes (see also Patterson:85a). Caltech Report C3P-297.

[Johnson:85a] Please see Bibliography for citation.

[Johnson:86a] Please see Bibliography for citation.

[Johnson:86b] Please see Bibliography for citation.

[Johnson:86c] Please see Bibliography for citation.

[JPL:87a] Jet Propulsion Laboratory. "Electronic Systems Division (ESD) BM/C3 Hypercube Applications FY '87 Final Report." Technical Report C3P-517, December 1987.

[Karlin:85a] Karlin, S., and Suggs, B. "A 68010 based concurrent processor." EE91 Term Project C3P-246, California Institute of Technology, Pasadena, CA, 1985.

[Keller:88a] Fox, G. C., Seitz, C., and Keller, H. "Caltech Center for Concurrent Computation." Proposal C3P-514, California Institute of Technology, Pasadena, CA, January 1988.

[Kennedy:88a] Kennedy, K., Dongarra, J. J., and Fox, G. C. "Center for Scientific Parallel Programming." Proposal C3P-518, California Institute of Technology, Pasadena, CA, January 1988.

[Kochanek:88a] Please see Bibliography for citation.

[Kolawa:85a] Kolawa, A., and Otto, S. W. "Performance of the Mark II and Intel hypercubes," in M. T. Heath, editor, *Hypercube Multiprocessors*, page 272. SIAM, Philadelphia, 1986. Caltech Report C3P-254.

[Kolawa:85b] Kolawa, A., and Otto, S. W. "Performance of the Intel iPSC hypercube." Technical Report C3P-205, California Institute of Technology, Pasadena, CA, October 1985.

[Kolawa:86b] Please see Bibliography for citation.

[Kolawa:86c] Kolawa, A. "The crystalline operating system programmer's manual for Intel iPSC." Technical Report C3P-287, California Institute of Technology, Pasadena, CA, May 1986.

[Kolawa:86d] Please see Bibliography for citation.

[Kolawa:88a] Please see Bibliography for citation.

[Kolawa:89a] Kolawa, A. "Using Centaur on Express systems." Technical Report C3P-825, California Institute of Technology, Pasadena, CA, August 1989. ParaSoft Corporation.

[Koller:88a] Koller, J. "A dynamic load balancer on the Intel hypercube," in G. C. Fox, editor, *The Third Conference on Hypercube Concurrent Computers and Applications, Volume 1*, pages 279–284. ACM Press, New York, January 1988. Caltech Report C3P-497.

[Koller:88b] Please see Bibliography for citation.

[Koller:88c] Please see Bibliography for citation.

[Koller:88d] Koller, J., Fox, G. C., and Furmanski, W. "Physical optimization and dynamic load balancing." Technical Report C3P-670, California Institute of Technology, Pasadena, CA, October 1988.

[Koller:89a] Koller, J. "The MOOS II operating system and dynamic load balancing," in J. L. Gustafson, editor, *The Proceedings of the Fourth Conference on Hypercubes, Concurrent Computers, and Applications*, pages 599–602. Golden Gate Enterprises, Los Altos, CA, March 1989. Caltech Report C3P-730.

[Koller:89b] Please see Bibliography for citation.

[Kuppermann:86a] Please see Bibliography for citation.

[Kuyper:88a] Kuyper, James, J. "nCUBE simulation of polymer rings." Technical Report C3P-749, California Institute of Technology, December 1988.

[Lee:88a] Please see Bibliography for citation.

[Lee:89a] Please see Bibliography for citation.

[Lee:89b] Please see Bibliography for citation.

[Leonard:88a] Leonard, A., and Chua, K. "Three-dimensional interactions of vortex tubes," in *Proc. Symposium on Advances in Fluid Turbulence*, May 1988. Los Alamos. Caltech Report C3P-691.

[Leong:86a] Leong, H. "Frequency dependent electromagnetic fields: Models appropriate for the brain." Technical Report C3P-278, California Institute of Technology, Pasadena, CA, April 1986. Calculations of integrals using the hypercube.

[Li:90a] Li, P., and Tung, Y.-W. "Parallel sorting on Symult 2010," in D. W. Walker and Q. F. Stout, editors, *The Fifth Distributed Memory Computing Conference, Volume I*, pages 224–229. IEEE Computer Society Press, Los Alamitos, CA, 1990. Held April 9–12, Charleston, SC. Caltech Report C3P-901.

[Liewer:88a] Liewer, P. C., and Dawson, J. M. "Application of hypercube computers to space plasma modeling." Proposal C3P-503, California Institute of Technology, January 1988.

[Liewer:88b] Liewer, P. C., Decyk, V. K., Dawson, J. D., and Fox, G. C. "A universal concurrent algorithm for plasma particle-in-cell simulation codes," in G. C. Fox, editor, *The Third Conference on Hypercube Concurrent Computers and Applications, Volume 2*, pages 1101–1107. ACM Press, New York, January 1988. Caltech Report C3P-562.

[Liewer:88f] Liewer, P. C., Fox, G. C., Decyk, V. K., and Dawson, J. "Plasma particle simulations on the Mark III hypercube," in *Proceedings of the Sixth International Conference on Mathematical Modeling*. Permagon Press, 1988. Caltech Report C3P-460.

[Liewer:89a] Liewer, P. C., Zimmerman, B. A., Decyk, V. K., and Dawson, J. M. "Application of hypercube computers to plasma particle-in-cell simulation codes." Technical Report C3P-717, California Institute of Technology, Pasadena, CA, 1989.

[Liewer:89c] Please see Bibliography for citation.

[Liewer:90a] Please see Bibliography for citation.

[Liewer:91a] Please see Bibliography for citation.

[Lorenz:87a] Please see Bibliography for citation.

[Lorenz:89a] Please see Bibliography for citation.

[Lyzenga:85a] Please see Bibliography for citation.

[Lyzenga:88a] Lyzenga, G. A., Raefsky, A., and Nour-Omid, B. "Implementing finite element software on hypercube machines," in G. C. Fox, editor, *The Third Conference on Hypercube Concurrent Computers and Applications, Volume 2*, pages 1755–1761. ACM Press, New York, January 1988. Caltech Report C3P-594.

[Ma:85a] Ma, T. "Mark II board level diagnostic disclosure." Technical Report C3P-201, California Institute of Technology, Pasadena, CA, September 1985.

[Makivic:90a] Makivić, M. S., and Ding, H.-Q. "Two dimensional spin-$\frac{1}{2}$ Heisenberg antiferromagnet: A quantum Monte Carlo study." Technical Report C3P-897, California Institute of Technology, May 1990.

[Makivic:91a] Makivić, M. S., and Ding, H.-Q. "Two dimensional spin-$\frac{1}{2}$ Heisenberg antiferromagnet: A quantum Monte Carlo study," *Physical Review B*, 43(4):3562–3574, February 1991. Caltech Report C3P-897b.

[Martin:91a] Please see Bibliography for citation.

[Mazer:88a] Mazer, A. S. "A dataflow-based APL for the hypercube," in G. C. Fox, editor, *The Third Conference on Hypercube Concurrent Computers and Applications, Volume 1*, pages 505–512. ACM Press, New York, January 1988. Caltech Report C3P-598.

[McBryan:85a] McBryan, O., and Van de Velde, E. F. "Parallel algorithms for elliptic equations," *Communications in Pure and Applied Mathematics*, 2:311–316, 1985. Caltech Report C3P-488.

[McBryan:87a] McBryan, O., and Van de Velde, E. F. "Hypercube algorithms and implementations," *SIAM Journal on Scientific and Statistical Computing*, 8(2):227–287, 1987. Caltech Report C3P-266.

[McKoy:90a] McKoy, V., and Shing, Y. "Highly parallel computing and modelling of electron cyclotron resonance plasmas for diamond film deposition." 1990 President's Fund Proposal C3P-935, California Institute of Technology, June 1990.

[Meier:84a] Meier, D. "Two-dimensional one-fluid hydrodynamics: An astrophysical test problem for the nearest neighbor concurrent processor." Technical Report C3P-090, California Institute of Technology, Pasadena, CA, 1984. Unpublished.

[Meier:84b] Please see Bibliography for citation.

[Meier:85b] Meier, D. L., and Cloud, K. "The C3PO manual: A shell program for driving hypercube applications." Technical Report C3P-134, California Institute of Technology, Pasadena, CA, July 1985.

[Meier:88a] Please see Bibliography for citation.

[Meier:89a] Please see Bibliography for citation.

[Meier:90a] Please see Bibliography for citation.

[Meredith:83a] Meredith, D. Caltech Press Release on Project, November 1983. Caltech Report C3P-049.

[Meredith:84a] Please see Bibliography for citation.

[Messina:87a] Please see Bibliography for citation.

[Messina:87b] Messina, P. C. "Emerging supercomputer architectures." Chapter in the U.S. Supercomputer Industry C3P-449, California Institute of Technology, Pasadena, CA, July 1987. Report by Subcommittee on Science and Engineering Computing of the Committee on Computer Research and Applications of the Federal Coordinating Council on Science, Engineering and Technology, DOE/ER-0362, December 1987.

[Messina:90a] Please see Bibliography for citation.

[Miller:89a] Miller, G. F., Todd, P. M., and Hegde, S. U. "Designing neural networks using genetic algorithms," in J. D. Schaffer and C. Morgan Kaufmann, San Mateo, editors, *Proceedings of the Third International Conference on Genetic Algorithms*, pages 379–384. George Mason University, June 1989. Caltech Report C3P-797.

[Moore:89a] Moore, A. *A Computation and Neural Systems Approach to Color Constancy*. PhD thesis, California Institute of Technology, August 1989. Caltech Report C3P-824.

[Moore:91a] Moore, A., Fox, G. C., Allman, J., and Goodman, R. "A VLSI neural network for color constancy," in D. S. Touretzky and R. Lippman, editors, *Advances in Neural Information Processing Systems 3*. Morgan Kaufmann, San Mateo, CA, 1991. SCCS-48. Caltech Report C3P-956.

[Morison:86a] Please see Bibliography for citation.

[Morison:88a] Please see Bibliography for citation.

[Morison:89a] Morison, R. "CCSF visualization lab: Guide to facilities and reference manual." Technical Report C3P-849, California Institute of Technology, Pasadena, CA, November 1989.

[Moscato:88a] Moscato, P. "The t-expansion at low orders: Ground state energy density calculations in lattice systems." Technical Report C3P-684, California Institute of Technology, Pasadena, CA, December 1988.

[Moscato:89a] Please see Bibliography for citation.

[Moscato:89b] Moscato, P., and Riveros, C. "t-expansion and the Mathieu equation." Technical Report C3P-782, California Institute of Technology, Pasadena, CA, May 1989.

[Moscato:89c] Please see Bibliography for citation.

[Moscato:89d] Please see Bibliography for citation.

[Moscato:89e] Please see Bibliography for citation.

[Mudge:88a] Mudge, T., Horvath, J., and Anderson, C. "Computer vision on the hypercube concurrent processor." Proposal C3P-515, University of Michigan, Ann Arbor, MI, January 1988.

[Nakajima:89a] Nakajima, T., Kulkarni, S. R., Gorham, P. W., Ghez, A. M., Neugebauer, G., Oke, J. B., Prince, T. A., and Readhead, A. C. S. "Diffraction-limited imaging II: Optical aperture-synthesis imaging of two binary stars," *The Astronomical Journal*, 97(5):1510–1521, May 1989. Caltech Report C3P-805.

[Nelson:89a] Please see Bibliography for citation.

[Nelson:90a] Nelson, M. E., and Bower, J. M. "Computational efficiency: A common organizing principle for parallel computer maps and brain maps?," in D. S. Touretzky, editor, *Advances in Neural Network Information Processing Systems, Vol. 2*. Morgan Kaufmann, San Mateo, CA, 1990. Caltech Report C3P-863.

[Newhall:89a] Newhall, D. S., and Horvath, J. C. "Analysis of text using a neural network: A hypercube implementation," in J. L. Gustafson, editor, *The Proceedings of the Fourth Conference on Hypercubes, Concurrent Computers and Applications*, page 1119. Golden Gate Enterprises, Los Altos, CA, March 1989. Caltech Report C3P-770.

[Noerdlinger:86a] Noerdlinger, P. D., and Walker, D. W. "Discrete Fourier transforms on the Mark II hypercube." Technical Report C3P-337, California Institute of Technology, Pasadena, CA, 1986. Unpublished.

[Noerdlinger:86b] Noerdlinger, P. D. "An overview of the challenge problems #11–24 for the hypercube." Technical Report C3P-339, California Institute of Technology, Pasadena, CA, August 1986.

[Noerdlinger:86c] Noerdlinger, P. D. "Inversion of matrices over the field of integers modulo 2." Technical Report C3P-340, California Institute of Technology, Pasadena, CA, August 1986.

[Nour-Omid:87a] Nour-Omid, B., and Park, K. C. "Solving structural mechanics problems on the Caltech hypercube machine," *Computer Methods in Applied Mechanics and Engineering*, 61:161–176, 1987. North-Holland. Caltech Report C3P-273a.

[Nour-Omid:87b] Please see Bibliography for citation.

[Otto:83a] Please see Bibliography for citation.

[Otto:83b] Please see Bibliography for citation.

[Otto:84a] Please see Bibliography for citation.

[Otto:84d] Otto, S. W. "Lattice gauge theories on a hypercube computer,"
in C. Zachos, W. Celmaster, E. Kovacs, and D. Sivers, editors, *Gauge
Theory on a Lattice: 1984*, pages 12–20. Argonne National Laboratory
Workshop, Argonne National Laboratory, April 1984. Available from
NTIS as CONF-8404119. Caltech Report C3P-184.

[Otto:85b] Please see Bibliography for citation.

[Otto:85d] Otto, S. W. "Special purpose computers for lattice gauge theories." Technical Report C3P-153, California Institute of Technology,
February 1985. Layman's description of three high-energy physical
projects to build concurrent processors for use in lattice gauge theory
calculations.

[Otto:85e] Otto, S. W. "Binary trees on the hypercube." Technical Report
C3P-168, California Institute of Technology, Pasadena, CA, May 1985.

[Otto:85f] Otto, S. W., Kolawa, A., and Hey, A. "Performance of the Mark II
Caltech/JPL hypercube." Technical Report C3P-188, California Institute of Technology, Pasadena, CA, August 1985.

[Otto:87a] Otto, S. W., Baillie, Clive, F., Ding, H.-Q., Apostolakis, J.,
Gupta, R., Kilcup, G., Patel, A., and Sharpe, S. "Lattice gauge the-
ory benchmarks." Technical Report C3P-450, California Institute of
Technology, Pasadena, CA, 1987.

[Parker:90a] Parker, J. W., Ferraro, R. D., and Liewer, P. C. "An examination of finite element formulations and parameters for accurate parallel
solution of electromagnetic scattering problems," in D. W. Walker and
Q. F. Stout, editors, *The Fifth Distributed Memory Computing Conference, Volume I*, pages 421–423. IEEE Computer Society Press, Los
Alamitos, CA, 1990. Held April 9–12, Charleston, SC. Caltech Report
C3P-904.

[Patel:85a] Please see Bibliography for citation.

[Patterson:85a] Patterson, J. "Support material for videotapes of first JPL
hypercube course." Technical Report C3P-198, Jet Propulsion Labo-
ratory/California Institute of Technology, Pasadena, CA, September
1985. The course itself is available on 3/4" Umatic or 1/2" VHS Videotapes.

[Patterson:86a] Please see Bibliography for citation.

[Patterson:88a] Patterson, J. E., and Zimmerman, B. A. "Hypercube workstations for real-time signal processing and analysis." Proposal C3P-516, California Institute of Technology, Pasadena, CA, January 1988.

[Pawley:89a] Pawley, G. S., Baillie, C. F., Tenenbaum, E., and Celmaster, W. "The BBN Butterfly used to simulate a molecular liquid," *Parallel Computing*, 11:321–329, 1989. Caltech Report C3P-529.

[Pepin:90a] Pépin, F., and Leonard, A. "Concurrent implementation of a fast vortex method," in D. W. Walker and Q. F. Stout, editors, *The Fifth Distributed Memory Computing Conference, Volume I*, pages 453–462. IEEE Computer Society Press, Los Alamitos, CA, 1990. Held April 9–12, Charleston, SC. Caltech Report C3P-906.

[Pepin:90b] Pépin, F. *Simulation of the Flow Past an Impulsively Started Cylinder using a Discrete Vortex Method.* PhD thesis, California Institute of Technology/Graduate Aeronatical Laboratories, 1990. Caltech Report C3P-920.

[Peterson:85a] Please see Bibliography for citation.

[Peterson:88a] Peterson, J., Chow, E., and Madan, H. "A high-speed message-driven communication architecture," in *The International Conference on Supercomputing*, pages 355–366. Association for Computing Machinery, New York, July 1988. St. Malo, France, July 4–8. Caltech Report C3P-628.

[Pfeiffer:90a] Please see Bibliography for citation.

[Pollara:85a] Please see Bibliography for citation.

[Pollara:86a] Please see Bibliography for citation.

[Quinn:86a] Quinn, P. J., Salmon, J. K., and Zurek, W. H. "On the structure of galactic halos." Technical Report C3P-316, California Institute of Technology, Pasadena, CA, 1986.

[Quinn:86b] Quinn, P. J., Salmon, J. K., and Zurek, W. H. "Primordial density fluctuations and the structure of galactic haloes," *Nature*, 322:329, 1986. Caltech Report C3P-316b.

[Quinn:87a] Quinn, P. J., Salmon, J. K., and Zurek, W. H. "Numerical experiments on galactic halo formation," in *Proceedings of the Use of SuperComputers in Stellar Dynamics*. Princeton University Press, Princeton, NJ, 1987. Caltech Report C3P-745.

[Raefsky:88a] Raefsky, A., Gurnis, M., Hager, B. H., and Lyzenga, G. A. "Finite element solutions of thermal convection on a hypercube concurrent computer," *EOS, Trans. Amer. Geophy. Union*, 69:463, 1988. Caltech Report C3P-737.

[Raefsky:88b] Please see Bibliography for citation.

[Rose:89b] Please see Bibliography for citation.

[Rose:90a] Please see Bibliography for citation.

[Rose:90b] Please see Bibliography for citation.

[Rose:90c] Please see Bibliography for citation.

[Rose:90f] Please see Bibliography for citation.

[Rose:91a] Please see Bibliography for citation.

[Rose:91b] Rose, K., Gurewitz, E., and Fox, G. C. "Multi-target tracking by graduated nonconvexity." Technical Report C3P-968, California Institute of Technology, Pasadena, CA, 1991.

[Rose:92a] Please see Bibliography for citation.

[Rose:93a] Please see Bibliography for citation.

[Salmon:84a] Please see Bibliography for citation.

[Salmon:84b] Please see Bibliography for citation.

[Salmon:86a] Please see Bibliography for citation.

[Salmon:86b] Please see Bibliography for citation.

[Salmon:87a] Please see Bibliography for citation.

[Salmon:88a] Please see Bibliography for citation.

[Salmon:88b] Salmon, J. "A mathematical analysis of the scattered decomposition," in G. C. Fox, editor, *The Third Conference on Hypercube Concurrent Computers and Applications, Volume 1*, pages 239–240. ACM Press, New York, January 1988. Caltech Report C3P-591.

[Salmon:89a] Please see Bibliography for citation.

[Salmon:89b] Salmon, J., Quinn, P., and Warren, M. "Using parallel computers for very large N-body simulations: formation using 180K particles," in A. Toomre and R. Wielen, editors, *Proceedings of the Heidelberg Conference on the Dynamics and Interactions of Galaxies.* Springer-Verlag, April 1989. Caltech Report C3P-780b.

[Salmon:90a] Please see Bibliography for citation.

[Saltz:89a] Saltz, J., Mirchandaney, R., Fox, G., and Nicol, D. "The design of a run-time system integrable with programming environments for distributed memory machines." Technical Report C3P-700, California Institute of Technology, Pasadena, CA, January 1989.

[Sammes:87a] Royal Military College of Science. *First US/UK Workshop Parallel Processing*, Shrivenham, UNITED KINGDOM, October 1987. edited by A. J. Sammes. Volume 1—C3P-482.1; Volume 2—C3P-482.2. Caltech Report C3P-482.

[Scholl:88a] Scholl, M., and Dumont, P. "Hypercube implementation of Raleigh-Sommerfeld diffraction integral." Proposal C3P-665, California Institute of Technology, Pasadena, CA, August 1988.

[Simic:90a] Please see Bibliography for citation.

[Simic:91a] Please see Bibliography for citation.

[Simoni:89a] Please see Bibliography for citation.

[Skjellum:88a] Please see Bibliography for citation.

[Skjellum:88b] Skjellum, A., Morari, M., Mattisson, S., and Peterson, L. "Highly concurrent dynamic simulation in chemical engineering: Issues, methodologies, model problems, progress." Technical Report C3P-692, California Institute of Technology, Pasadena, CA, 1988. Presented at the AIChE 1988 Annual Meeting, Washington DC, December 1988.

[Skjellum:88d] Skjellum, A., Peterson, L., Mattisson, S., and Morari, M. "Application of multicomputer to large-scale dynamic simulation in chemical and electrical engineering: Unifying themes, software tools, progress." Technical Report C3P-750, California Institute of Technology, Pasadena, CA, October 1988. Presented at the IFIP 11th World computer Conference, San Francisco, August 1989.

[Skjellum:89a] Please see Bibliography for citation.

[Skjellum:89b] Skjellum, A., Leung, A. P., and Morari, M. "Experience with LU factorization of sparse, unsymmetric Jacobian matrices on multicomputers." Technical Report C3P-839, California Institute of Technology, Pasadena, CA, 1989.

[Skjellum:90a] Please see Bibliography for citation.

[Skjellum:90b] Skjellum, A., and Morari, M. "Concurrent DASSL: applied to dynamic distillation column simulation," in D. W. Walker and Q. F. Stout, editors, *The Fifth Distributed Memory Computing Conference, Volume I*, pages 595–604. IEEE Computer Society Press, Los Alamitos, CA, 1990. Held April 9–12, Charleston, SC. Caltech Report C3P-892.

[Skjellum:90c] Please see Bibliography for citation.

[Skjellum:90d] Please see Bibliography for citation.

[Solomon:84a] Solomon, J., Lee, M., and Fox, G. "Image processing and the hypercube-analysis of initial implementation." Technical Report C3P-132, California Institute of Technology, Pasadena, CA, 1984. Unpublished.

[Stolorz:86a] Stolorz, P. E. *Numerical Simulations of Lattice QCD*. PhD thesis, California Institute of Technology, Pasadena, CA, July 1986. Caltech Report C3P-352.

[Stolorz:86b] Please see Bibliography for citation.

[Su:89a] Su, Z., and Fox, G. C. "High performance of cellular automata fluids on Connection Machine." Technical Report C3P-811, California Institute of Technology, Pasadena, CA, June 1989.

[Synnott:89a] Synnott, S. P., Riedel, J. E., Stuve, J. A., Halamek, P., and Lehr, W. J. "Three dimensional geometry from image processing on the JPL/CIT hypercube," in J. L. Gustafson, editor, *The Proceedings of the Fourth Conference on Hypercubes, Concurrent Computers and Applications*, page 1053. Golden Gate Enterprises, Los Altos, CA, March 1989. Caltech Report C3P-763.

[Synnott:90a] Please see Bibliography for citation.

[Szpunar:90a] Szpunar, B. "Numerical studies in high temperature superconductivity: Band structure calculations." Technical Report C3P-872, Queen's University, April 1990. preprint.

[Tang:90a] Tang, T. "Parallel sorting on the hypercube concurrent processor," in D. W. Walker and Q. F. Stout, editors, *The Fifth Distributed Memory Computing Conference, Volume I*, pages 237–240. IEEE Computer Society Press, Los Alamitos, CA, 1990. Held April 9–12, Charleston, SC. Caltech Report C3P-934.

[Theiler:86a] Theiler, J. "Spurious dimension from correlation algorithms applied to limited time-series data," *Phys. Rev. A*, 34:2427, 1986. Caltech Report C3P-274a.

[Theiler:86b] Theiler, J. "Quantifying chaotic motion: Using the Caltech hypercube to compute the dynamical dimension of a physical system." Technical Report C3P-274b, California Institute of Technology, Pasadena, CA, March 1986.

[Theiler:87a] Please see Bibliography for citation.

[Theiler:87b] Please see Bibliography for citation.

[Thole:85b] Thole, C. "Experiments with the multigrid methods on the Caltech hypercube." Technical Report C3P-177b, California Institute of Technology, Pasadena, CA, 1985. GMD-Studien Nr. 103.

[Thole:86a] Thole, C.-A. "Performance of a multigrid method on a parallel architecture." Technical Report C3P-272, California Institute of Technology, Pasadena, CA, 1986. GMD D-5205.

[Tuazon:85a] Please see Bibliography for citation.

[Tuazon:85b] Tuazon, J. O. "Documentation of design of Caltech/JPL concurrent processor." Technical Report C3P-175, Jet Propulsion Laboratory/California Institute of Technology, Pasadena, CA, August 1985. Details of Mark II Design.

[Tuazon:88a] Tuazon, J., Peterson, J., and Pniel, M. "Mark IIIfp hypercube concurrent processor architecture," in G. C. Fox, editor, *The Third Conference on Hypercube Concurrent Computers and Applications, Volume 1*, pages 71–80. ACM Press, New York, January 1988. Caltech Report C3P-602.

[Upchurch:89a] Upchurch, E., Curkendall, D., Cloud, K., Loomis, A., and Geiselman, J. "Parallel joins on the Mark III hypercube," in J. L. Gustafson, editor, *The Proceedings of the Fourth Conference on Hypercubes, Concurrent Computers and Applications*, page 453. Golden Gate Enterprises, Los Altos, CA, March 1989. Caltech Report C3P-765.

[Velde:87a] Please see Bibliography for citation.

[Velde:87b] Please see Bibliography for citation.

[Velde:88a] Please see Bibliography for citation.

[Velde:88c] Van de Velde, E. F. "The formal correctness of an LU decomposition algorithm." Technical Report C3P-625, California Institute of Technology, Pasadena, CA, April 1988.

[Velde:88e] Van de Velde, E. "Implementation of linear algebra computations on multicomputers." Technical Report C3P-687, California Institute of Technology, Pasadena, CA, October 1988. To appear in Introduction to Concurrent Scientific Computing (1992).

[Velde:89b] Please see Bibliography for citation.

[Velde:90a] Please see Bibliography for citation.

[Velde:90b] Please see Bibliography for citation.

[Velde:90c] Please see Bibliography for citation.

[Walker:86a] Walker, D., Montry, G., Fox, G., and Ho, A. "A comparison of the performance of the Caltech Mark II Hypercube and the Elxsi 6400," in M. T. Heath, editor, *Hypercube Multiprocessors*, pages 210–219. SIAM, Philadelphia, 1987. Caltech Report C3P-356.

[Walker:88a] Walker, D. W., Messina, P., and Baillie, C. F. "Performance evaluation of scientific programs on advanced architecture computers," in G. C. Fox, editor, *The Third Conference on Hypercube Concurrent Computers and Applications, Volume 1*, pages 173–179. ACM Press, New York, January 1988. Caltech Report C3P-580.

[Walker:88b] Please see Bibliography for citation.

[Walker:88c] Walker, D. W. "Performance of a QCD code on the nCUBE hypercube," in G. C. Fox, editor, *The Third Conference on Hypercube Concurrent Computers and Applications, Volume 1*, pages 180–187. ACM Press, New York, January 1988. Caltech Report C3P-490b.

[Walker:88d] Walker, D. W. "Portable programming within a message-passing model: the FFT as an example," in G. C. Fox, editor, *The Third Conference on Hypercube Concurrent Computers and Applications, Volume 2*, pages 1438–1450. ACM Press, New York, January 1988. Caltech Report C3P-631.

[Walker:88e] Walker, D. W., and Fox, G. C. "A portable programming environment for multiprocessors," in R. Vichnevetsky, P. Borne, and J. Vignes, editors, *12th IMACS World Congress*, pages 475–478. IMACS, July 1988. Paris, France. Caltech Report C3P-496.

[Walker:89a] Walker, D. W. "The implementation of a three-dimensional PIC code on a hypercube concurrent processor," in J. L. Gustafson, editor, *The Proceedings of the Fourth Conference on Hypercubes, Concurrent Computers and Applications*, pages 1255–1261. Golden Gate Enterprises, Los Altos, CA, March 1989. Caltech Report C3P-739.

[Walker:90b] Please see Bibliography for citation.

[Warren:88a] Please see Bibliography for citation.

[Warren:88b] Warren, M., and Salmon, J. "An O(N log N) hypercube N-body integrator," in G. C. Fox, editor, *The Third Conference on Hypercube Concurrent Computers and Applications, Volume 2*, pages 971–975. ACM Press, New York, January 1988. Caltech Report C3P-593.

[Warren:88c] Warren, M. "An $O(N \log N)$ hypercube N-body integrator." Technical Report C3P-639, California Institute of Technology, Pasadena, CA, May 1988. Caltech Undergraduate Senior Thesis.

[Warren:91a] Warren, M. S., Zurek, W. H., Quinn, P. J., and Salmon, J. K. "The shape of the invisible halo: N-Body simulations on parallel supercomputers." Technical Report C3P-961, California Institute of Technology, Pasadena, CA, 1991. submitted to Proceedings of After the First Three Minutes, ed. S. Holt, V. Trimble, and C. Bennetti, AIP, 1991; Los Alamos Technical Report LA-UR-90-3915.

[Wasson:87a] Please see Bibliography for citation.

[Werner:84a] Werner, B. T., and Haff, P. K. "Grain dynamics simulations on the Caltech concurrent processor." Technical Report C3P-088, California Institute of Technology, Pasadena, CA, July 1984.

[Werner:85a] Werner, B. T., and Haff, P. K. "Dynamical simulations of granular materials using concurrent processing computers." Technical Report C3P-242, California Institute of Technology, Pasadena, CA, 1985. Unpublished.

[Werner:86b] Werner, B. T., and Haff, P. K. "A simulation study of the low energy ejecta resulting from single impacts in Eolian saltation," in *Proceedings of ASCE Conference on Advancements in Aerodynamics, Fluid Mechanics and Hydraulics*, pages 337–345. ASCE, Minneapolis, 1986. Caltech Report C3P-243.

[Werner:87a] Please see Bibliography for citation.

[Werner:88a] Please see Bibliography for citation.

[Werner:88b] Please see Bibliography for citation.

[Werner:90a] Please see Bibliography for citation.

[Werner:91a] Please see Bibliography for citation.

[White:87a] White, T. "Hidden surface removal on the Mark III hypercube." Technical Report C3P-477, California Institute of Technology, Pasadena, CA, October 1987.

[Wieland:88a] Wieland, F., Hawley, L., and Feinberg, A. "Implementing a distributed combat simulation on the Time Warp operating system," in G. C. Fox, editor, *The Third Conference on Hypercube Concurrent Computers and Applications, Volume 2*, pages 1269–1276. ACM Press, New York, January 1988. Caltech Report C3P-601.

[Wieland:89a] Please see Bibliography for citation.

[Wieland:90a] Wieland, F., Hawley, L., and Blume, L. "An empirical study of data partitioning and replication in parallel simulation," in D. W. Walker and Q. F. Stout, editors, *The Fifth Distributed Memory Computing Conference, Volume II*, pages 915–921. IEEE Computer Society Press, Los Alamitos, CA, 1990. Held April 9–12, Charleston, SC. Caltech Report C3P-907.

[Williams:86a] Williams, R. "Contouring in parallel." Technical Report C3P-284, California Institute of Technology, Pasadena, CA, May 1986.

[Williams:86b] Please see Bibliography for citation.

[Williams:86c] Williams, R. D. "Optimization by a computational neural net." Technical Report C3P-371, California Institute of Technology, Pasadena, CA, December 1986. CALT-68-1409.

[Williams:87a] Please see Bibliography for citation.

[Williams:87b] Please see Bibliography for citation.

[Williams:87c] Williams, R. D. "Three-dimensional plotting with the painter's algorithm." Technical Report C3p-455, California Institute of Technology, Pasadena, CA, August 1987.

[Williams:88a] Please see Bibliography for citation.

[Williams:88d] Please see Bibliography for citation.

[Williams:89a] Please see Bibliography for citation.

[Williams:89b] Please see Bibliography for citation.

[Williams:89c] Please see Bibliography for citation.

[Williams:90a] Please see Bibliography for citation.

[Williams:90b] Please see Bibliography for citation.

[Williams:90c] Please see Bibliography for citation.

[Williams:91a] Please see Bibliography for citation.

[Winstead:91d] Please see Bibliography for citation.

[Witkowski:88a] Witkowski, A., Chandrakumar, K., and Macchio, G. "Concurrent I/O systems for the hypercube multiprocessor," in G. C. Fox, editor, *The Third Conference on Hypercube Concurrent Computers and Applications, Volume 2*, pages 1398–1407. ACM Press, New York, January 1988. Caltech Report C3P-611.

[Wong:89a] Wong, Y.-F., and Fox, G. "Use of neural networks for path planning." Technical Report C3P-784, California Institute of Technology, May 1989.

[Wu:90a] Please see Bibliography for citation.

[Zamani:89a] Zamani, E. B., George, J. R., Collins, C. E., and Zimmerman, B. A. "Spacecraft activity planning in a multiprocessor environment." Technical Report C3P-744, California Institute of Technology/JPL, March 1989. Submitted for OOPSLA '89 Conference on Object Oriented Programming Systems Ofc., New Orleans, Louisiana, October 1989.

[Zimmerman:88a] Zimmerman, B. A., and Crichton, G. A. "A programming model for the Mark III hypercube with multiple processor nodes," in G. C. Fox, editor, *The Third Conference on Hypercube Concurrent Computers and Applications*, pages 528–535. ACM Press, New York, January 1988. Caltech Report C3P-597.

[Zimmerman:89a] Please see Bibliography for citation.

[Zurek:88a] Zurek, W. H., Quinn, P. J., and Salmon, J. K. "Rotation of halos in open and closed universes: Differentiated merging and natural selection of galaxy types," *Astrophysical Journal*, 330:519–534, 1988. Caltech Report C3P-736.

Appendix B

Selected Biographic Information

This includes many, but certainly not all, of the key C^{3}P participants. The bibliography and Appendix A cites the full set of C^{3}P reports and authors.

Giovanni Aloisio
Dipartimento di Elettrotecnica ed Elettronica
Facolta di Ingegneria-Politecnico di Bari (Italy)
Via Orabona, 4
70125 Bari (Italy)
Aloisio@vaxle.le.infn.it

Worked from (11/86–end of project): Investigating the efficiency of the Hypercube architecture in Real-Time SAR data processing ("SAR Hypercube Project"). Non traditional FFT algorithms, such as the Prime Factor, have been coded to run on the nCUBE, iPSC, and Mark IIIfp hypercubes. The optimal decomposition, on a specific hypercube system, of a complete software package for digital SAR data processing has been determined. This package has been implemented in the sequential version on a VAX-780 at IESI/CNR (Bari-Italy) and has been tested on digital raw data obtained by JPL (SIR-B space Shuttle mission).

Now works on: High Performance Distributed Computing (porting of several applications under PVM and Net-EXPRESS. Parallel compilers, such as HPF, will also be tested). A joint project with CCSF is in progress.

Ian Angus
Research Scientist
Boeing Computer Services
P. O. Box 24346, MS 7L-48
Seattle, WA 98124-0346
angus@atc.boeing.com

Worked from (1986–1987): Involved primarily with the implementation of a Hypercube simulator and with the design and first implementation of the Fortran Cubix programming system.

Now works on: Programming tools and environments, object oriented approaches to scientific and parallel computing, and compilation of object oriented languages.

John Apostolakis
CERN
CN Division, 513-R-024
CH 1211 GENEVA 23, Switzerland
japost@dxcern.cern.ch

Worked from (9/86–end of project): With lattice gauge theory, lattice spin models, and gravitational lenses and the issues involved in developing efficient parallel programs to simulate them.

Now works on: Implementing experimental high energy physics applications on Massively Parallel Processors.

• Contributed Section 7.4, Statistical Gravitational Lensing

Clive F. Baillie
Research Fellow
Computer Science Department
Campus Box 430
University of Colorado
Boulder CO 80309
clive@kilt.cs.colorado.edu

Worked from (9/86–end of project): Implementations of physics problems, particularly clustering methods and performance studies. Large-scale Monte-Carlo simulations of QCD, XY and O(3) models, 3D Ising model, 2D Potts model and dynamically triangulated random surfaces (DTRS).

Now works on: Further work on DTRS, making them self-avoiding to simulate superstrings, and adding Potts models to simulate quantum gravity coupled to matter.

• Contributed Sections 4.3, Quantum Chromodynamics; 4.4, Spin Models; 7.2, Dynamically Triangulated Random Surfaces; and 12.6, Cluster Algorithms for Spin Models

Vasanth Bala
Member of the Technical Staff
Kendall Square Research
170 Tracer Lane
Waltham, Massachusetts 02154
vas@ksr.com

Worked from (8/89–end of project): With the design of software tools, compiler optimizations, and communication libraries for scalable parallel computers.

Now works on: Speculative instruction scheduling for superscalar RISC processors, and general compiler optimization of C, Fortran90/HPF and C++ programs for RISC-based parallel computers. After leaving Caltech C^3P, was a research staff member at IBM T. J. Watson Research Center (Yorktown Heights, NY) involved in the design of the IBM SP1 parallel computer.

• Contributed Section 13.2, A Software Tool

Ted Barnes
Staff Physicist
Theoretical Physics Division
Oak Ridge National Laboratory
Oak Ridge, Tennessee 37831-8083

  and

Associate Professor of Physics
Department of Physics
University of Tennessee
Knoxville, Tennessee 37996

Worked from (1987–1989): Monte Carlo calculations to simulate high-temperature superconductivity.

Now works on: QCD spectroscopy, couplings and decays of hadrons, high-temperature superconductivity.

• Contributed Section 7.3, Numerical Study of High-T_c Spin Systems

Roberto Battiti
Assistant Professor of Physics
Universita' di Trento
Dipartimento di Matematica
38050 Povo (Trento), Italy
battiti@itnvax.cineca.it

Worked from (1986–end of project): Parallel implementation of neural nets and vision algorithms; computational complexity of learning algorithms.

Now works on: Constructive and destructive learning methods for neural nets, "natural" problem solving such as genetic algorithms; application of neural nets in financial and industrial areas.

• Contributed Sections 6.5, A Hierarchical Scheme for Surface Reconstruction and Discontinuity Detection; 6.7, An Adaptive Multiscale Scheme for Real-Time Motion Field Estimation; 6.8, Collective Stereopsis, and 9.9, Optimization Methods for Neural Nets: Automatic Parameter Tuning and Faster Convergence

Jim Bower
Associate Professor of Biology
Computation and Neural Systems Program
California Institute of Technology
Mail Code 216-76
Pasadena, California 91125
jbower@smaug.bbb.caltech.edu

Worked from (1988–end of project): Using concurrent computers to build large-scale realistic models of the nervous system. We recognized early on that truely realistic models of these complex systems would require the power present in parallel computation. This, in fact, is reflected in the fact that the nervous system itself is probably a parallel device. Leader of GENESIS project described in Section 7.6.

Now works on: Current interest remains understanding the relationships between the structure and the function of the nervous system. We have recently published several scientific papers that would have not been possible without the use of the concurrent machines at Caltech.

Eugene D. Brooks, III
Deputy Associate Director
Advanced Technologies Computation Organization
Lawrence Livermore National Laboratory
P. O. Box 808, L-66
Livermore, CA 94550
brooks3@llnl.gov

Worked from (1981–1983): The use of parallel computing to supply a new computational capability for computational physics tasks.

Now works on: Parallel computer architecture, parallel languages, computational physics algorithms, and parallelization of computational physics algorithms.

Robert W. Clayton
Professor of Geophysics
California Institute of Technology
Geophysics, 350 S. Mudd
Mail Code 252-21
Pasadena, CA 91125
clay@seismo.gps.caltech.edu

Worked from (1983–end of project): Finite-difference solutions of wave phenomena. Imaging with seismic reflection data.

Now works on: Finite-difference solutions of wave phenomena. Imaging with seismic reflection data.

- Contributed Section 18.2, ISIS: An Interactive Seismic Imaging System

Paul Coddington
Syracuse University
Northeast Parallel Architectures Center
111 College Place, 3-228 CST
Syracuse, New York 13244-4100
paulc@npac.syr.edu

Worked from (1988–end of project): Developed parallel implementations of non-local Monte Carl algorithms for spin models of magnetism.

Now works on: From 1990–92, worked as a Research Associate at NPAC on computational physics applications, including new sequential and parallel Monte Carlo algorithms for spin models and dynamically triangulated random surface models of quantum gravity, as well as parallel algorithms for connected component labeling and graph coloring. Also worked on improved stochastic optimization techniques, such as simulated annealing.

From 1992 until the present, worked as a Research Scientist at NPAC leading a project on the use of parallel computing in the power utility industry. This involves porting existing code to parallel computers, and developing parallel algorithms for sparse matrix computations and differential-algebraic equation solvers.

Dave Curkendall
ALPHA Project Manager and
Advanced Parallel Processing Program Manager
Jet Propulsion Laboratory
4800 Oak Grove Drive, MC 138-310
Pasadena, California 91109
DAVE_CURKENDALL@macq_smtp.Jpl.Nasa.Gov

Worked from (8/84–end of project): As Hypercube Task Manager and later as Hypercube Project Manager, was interested in the hypercube hardware development, its operating system, particularly the asynchronous message-passing developments of Mercury and Centaur, and in the development of large-scale simulations.

Now works on: The development of discrete event simulation software for parallel machines and techniques for the remote, interactive exploration of large, image and geographical databases.

- Contributed Section 18.3, Parallel Simulations that Emulate Function

Hong-Qiang Ding
Member of Technical Staff
Jet Propulsion Laboratory
4800 Oak Grove Drive
Mail Stop 169-315
Pasadena, California 91109
hding@redwood.jpl.nasa.gov

Worked from (8/87–end of project): Extensive and large-scale simulations QCD and quantum spin models.

Now works on: Developing efficient methods for long-range interactions and molecular simulations; simulate model superconductors with parallel machines.

- Contributed Sections 6.3, Magnetism in the High-Temperature Superconductor Materials; and 6.4, Phase Transitions in Two-dimensional Quantum Spin Systems

David Edelsohn
IBM T. J. Watson Research Center
P. O. Box 218
Yorktown Heights, NY 10598-0218
c1dje@watson.ibm.com

Worked from (1989–end of project): Computational astrophysics simulations of galaxy formation and evolution, and cosmology using concurrent, multiscale, hierarchical N-body and adaptive mesh refinement algorithms.

Now works on: As a doctoral candidate at the Northeast Parallel Architectures Center, Syracuse University, his research interests include computational astrophysics simulations of galaxy formation and evolution, and cosmology using concurrent, multiscale, hierarchical N-body and adaptive mesh refinement algorithms; and object-oriented concurrent languages. He is visiting IBM as an IBM Computational Science Graduate Fellow.

• Contributed Section 12.8, Hierarchical Tree-Structures as Adaptive Meshes

Ed Felten
Assistant Professor
Department of Computer Science
Princeton University
35 Olden Street
Princeton, New Jersey 08544
felten@cs.princeton.edu

Worked from (1984–end of project): Research interests included a variety of issues surrounding how to implement irregular and non-numerical applications on distributed-memory systems.

Now works on: How to build system software for parallel machines, and how to construct parallel programs to use this system software. More generally, my research interests include parallel and distributed computing, operating systems, architecture, and performance modeling.

Jon Flower
President
ParaSoft Corporation
2500 E. Foothill Blvd.
Pasadena CA 91107
jwf@parasoft.com

Worked from (1983–end of project): High-energy physics simulations; programming tools, debugging and visualization. Founder and President of ParaSoft Corporation

Now works on: Programming environments, tools, libraries for parallel computers.

• Contributed Sections 5.2, A "Packet" History of Message-passing Systems; 5.3, Parallel Debugging; 5.4, Parallel Profiling; and 13.5, ASPAR

Geoffrey C. Fox
Professor of Computer Science and Physics
Director, Northeast Parallel Architectures Center
Syracuse University
111 College Place
Syracuse, New York 13244-4100
gcf@npac.syr.edu

Worked from (1981–end of project): Involved as Principal Investigator with particular attention to applications, algorithms, and software. Developed the theory of problem architecture to describe and classify results of C^3P. Developed concepts in computational science education based on student involvement in C^3P and implemented new curricula initially at Caltech and later at Syracuse University.

Now works on: From 1990 until the present, directs the project at Syracuse University, which has a similar spirit to C^3P, but is aimed more at industry than at academic problems.

• Contributed Chapters 1, 3, 19, and 20; Sections 4.1, 4.2, 5.1, 6.1, 7.1, 9.1, 11.2, 11.3, 12.1, 13.1, 13.3, 13.7, 14.1, 15.1, and 18.1

Sandy Frey
President, Reliable Distributed Information Corporation
Pasadena, CA 91107
sandy@ccsf.caltech.edu

Worked from (1984–1988): Studying the system problems of implementing a teraflop machine with 1980s technology, and the data management problems involved in implementing massive data intensive applications in parallel processing environments, such as hypercubes.

Now works on: Data management problems involved in implementing massive data intensive applications in parallel processing environments, such as hypercubes.

Wojtek Furmanski
Research Professor of Physics
Syracuse University
201 Physics Building
Syracuse, New York 13244-1130
furm@npac.syr.edu

Worked from (1986–end of project): Developed a class of optimal collective communication algorithms implemented on Caltech hypercubes, and applied in parallel implementation of neuroscience simulations and machine vision algorithms.

Now works on: Based on lessons learned in these early parallel simulations, developed MOVIE system aimed at a general purpose platform for interactive HPCC environments. MOVIE, initially used for terrain image analysis, is now further developed at NPAC. Recently, the HPF interpreter has been constructed on top of MOVIE, and the MOVIE system is now further developed with the aim of integrating HPCC and Virtual Reality software technologies towards the broadband network based televirtuality environment.

• Contributed Chapter 17, MOVIE — Multitasking Object-oriented Visual Interactive Environment

Jeff Goldsmith
California Institute of Technology
Mail code 350-74
Pasadena, California 91125
jeff@gg.caltech.edu

Worked from (1985–end of project): Computer Graphics.

Now works on: Computer Graphics, in particular, computer-designed motion.

Peter Gorham
Project Manager
University of Hawaii at Manoa
Honolulu, Hawaii 96822
gorham@fermion.phys.Hawaii.Edu

Worked from (1987–end of project): My work with C^3P came about through Tom Prince's involvement with the project. Tom hired me as a postdoc in 1987 and I arrived in February of that year. Tom was beginning a collaboration with Shri Kulkarni of the Caltech Astronomy Department in two areas: first, a program to develop code for bispectral anlaysis of astronomical speckle interferograms taken with the Hale 5 m telescope; and second, a search for new radio pulsars using the Arecibo Observatory's 300 m transit telescope. In both cases, the telescopes involved were among the largest of their class and the data sets to be produced could only be managed with a supercomputer. Also in both cases, the data analysis lent itself very well to parallel processing techniques.

Both programs were very successful and Tom and I had the pleasure of seeing two graduate students complete their PhD requirements in each of the research areas (Stuart Anderson, pulsars; and Andrea Ghez, infrared speckle interferometry). Something of order a dozen research papers came out of this effort before I left for my present position in July of 1991, and a steady stream of results have come out since.

Now works on: The Deep Underwater Muon and Neutrino Detector (DUMAND) project. This project is developing a large, deep ocean Cherenkov detector which will be sensitive to high energy neutrino interactions and will have the capability to produce images of the sky in the "light" of neutrinos, with angular resolution of order 1 degree. The motivation behind such research arises from current belief that emission of high energy neutrinos may be a dominant process by which active galactic nuclei and QSOs release energy into their galactic environment. Detection of such neutrinos would provide unique information about the central engine of such galaxies.

Thomas D. Gottschalk
Member of the Professional Staff
California Institute of Technology
Mail code 356-48
Pasadena, California 91125
tdg@cithex.cithep.caltech.edu
tdg@bigbird.jpl.nasa.gov

Worked from (1987–end of project): Concurrent multi-target tracking for SDI scenarios/applications.

Now works on: Multi-target tracking (aircraft and space objects), surveillance systems operations, including sensor tasking, and design rule checking for VLSI systems.

• Contributed Sections 9.8, Munkres Algorithm for Assignment; and 18.4, Multi-Target Tracking

Gary Gutt
Member of the Technical Staff
Jet Propulsion Laboratory
4800 Oak Grove Drive
Mail Stop 183-401
Pasadena, California 91109
gmg@mg.jpl.nasa.gov

Worked from (4/88–5/89): Numerical simulation of granular systems using the lattice grain dynamics paradigm.

Now works on: Microgravity containerless materials processing; development of electrostatic and electromagnetic positioning techniques for use in microgravity containerless materials processing.

• Contributed Section 4.5, An Automata Model for Granular Materials

Peter Halamek
Technical Staff Member
Jet Propulsion Laboratory
Mail Stop 301-125L
Pasadena CA 91109
pxh@hamlet.caltech.edu

Worked from (6/88–1/89): Image processing; determination of 3D physical properties of objects from 2D camera images taken aboard a spacecraft.

Now works on: Optical navigation related research: improving accuracy of extended body center-finding on images of celestial bodies.

Paul G. Hipes
Vice President
Salmon Brothers, Inc.
7 World Trade Center
37th Floor
New York, New York 10048
hipes@daffy.sbi.com

Worked from (11/87–end of project): Direct solvers for dense systems of linear equations, special purpose matrix O.D.E. solvers, electron-molecule scattering problems approached with Schwinger variational methods, atom-molecule scattering problems approached by direct expansion methods, and green function Monte Carlo techniques for stationary states of many-electron systems.

Now works on: the term structure of interest rates and related topics in fixed income arbitrage.

Alex Ho
Research scientist
IBM Almaden Research Center
K54/802
650 Harry Rd.
San Jose, California 95120-6099

Worked from (7/85–end of project): Pattern recognition, artificial intelligence, neural nets, robot navigation.

Now works on: Massively parallel computing, programming models, architectures, fault-tolerance, performance evaluation.

Mark A. Johnson
Senior Engineer/Scientist
IBM Corporation
Internal Zip 4441
11400 Burnet Road
Austin, Texas 78758
maj@austin.ibm.com

Worked from (1983–1986): Pursued research that led to a Ph.D. in Statistical Physics. Primary research interests included studying melting in a two-dimensional system of interacting particles.

Now works on: System architecture in the area of High End Technical Systems of the Advanced Workstations and Systems Division of IBM.

• Contributed Section 14.2, Melting in Two Dimensions

Jai Sam Kim
Associate Professor, Department of Physics
Pohang Institute of Science and Technology
Hyoja-dong San 31
Pohang 780-784, S. KOREA
jsk@vision.postech.ac.kr

Worked from (1986–1988): Involved in the development of the hypercube simulator NSIM. Later, he parallelized the FFT codes with Italian visitors Aloisio and collaborators. Their work on the prime factor DFT code demonstrated the usefulness of Crystal_Router and also the limitations with the store-and-forward routing method. He wrote the FORTRAN application codes that were included in *Solving Problems on Concurrent Processors*, Vol. 2 [Angus:90a].

Now works on: Shortly before he returned to his home country Korea, he joined the interactive parallelizer project described in Chapter 13. He has not been heard from for some time, but has recently parallelized some working PDE codes used by mechanical engineers both on NSIM and PVM.

Adam Kolawa
Chairman/CEO ParaSoft Corporation
2500 E. Foothill Blvd., Suite 104
Pasadena, California 91107
ukola@flea.parasoft.com

Worked from (1983–end of project): Development of system software for parallel computers.

Now works on: Development of software tools.

Jeff Koller
Computer Scientist
Information Sciences Institute
4676 Admiralty Way
Marina del Rey, California 90292
koller@isi.edu

Worked from (1987–1989): MOOS II operating system, application of novel optimization techniques to dynamic load balancing and compiler optimization.

Now works on: VLSI design and system software for next-generation parallel machines.

• Contributed Sections 13.4, Optimizing Compilers by Neural Networks; and 15.2, MOOS II: An Operating System for Dynamic Load Balancing on the iPSC/1

Aron Kuppermann
Professor
California Institute of Technology
Mail Code 127-72
Pasadena, California 91125
aron@caltech.edu

Worked from (from beginning to end of project): Quantum mechanical reaction dynamics; reactive scattering methodologies suitable for MIMD machines.

Now works on: Adapting quantum mechanical reaction dynamics codes to new parallel machines.

• Contributed Section 8.2, Quantum Mechanical Reactive Scattering using a High Performance Parallel Computer

Paulette C. Liewer
Member of the Technical Staff
Jet Propulsion Laboratory
4800 Oak Grove Drive
Mail Stop 198-231
Pasadena, California 91109
pauly@hyper-spaceport.jpl.nasa.gov

    and

Visiting Associate in Applied Physics
California Institute of Technology
Mail Code 128-95
Pasadena, California 91125

Worked from (1986–end of project): Concurrent algorithms for particle-in-cell codes.

Now works on: 3D plasma particle-in-cell codes; application of concurrent PIC codes to problems in solar, space and laboratory plasmas.

• Contributed Section 9.3, Plasma Particle-in-Cell Simulation of an Electron Beam Plasma Instability

Gregory A. Lyzenga
Associate Professor of Physics
Harvey Mudd College
Physics Department
Claremont, California 91711
lyzenga@hmcvax.ac.hmc.edu

Worked from (1985–end of project): Parallel solution of fine element problems as applied to geophysics, solid mechanics, fluid mechanics, and electromagnetics.

Now works on: Solid earth geophysics; mechanics of earthquakes and tectonic deformation

Miloje Makivic
Computational Research Scientist
Northeast Parallel Architectures Center
111 College Place
Syracuse, New York 13244-4100
miloje@npac.syr.edu

Worked from (1988–end of project): As graduate student in the Division of Mathematics, Physics and Astronomy at Caltech, collaborated with the C^3P group. After 1990, used parallel resources at C^3P to develop computational physics algorithms, specifically Monte Carlo methods on parallel processors for strongly correlated quantum systems: Spin systems, high-temperature superconductors, disordered superconducting thin films, and general quantum critical phenomena. Also worked on self-consistent perturbation theory approach to heavy fermions and low-dimensional magnets.

Now works on: From 1990 until September 1993, worked as post-doctoral research in the Physics Department of Ohio State University. Presently, working at Syracuse University (NPAC) on the application of parallel computing in industry and science. Current projects include atmospheric data assimilation and financial modelling.

Vincent McKoy
Professor
California Institute of Technology
Mail Code 127-72
Pasadena, California 91125
bvm@citchem.bitnet

Worked from (3/89–9/89): Studies of collisions of electrons with polyatomic molecules.

Now works on: Using variational procedures to obtain cross-sections for electronic excitation of molecules by electron impact.

- Contributed Section 8.3, Studies of Electron-Molecule Collisions on Distributed-memory Parallel Computers

Paul Messina
CCSF Executive Director
California Institute of Technology
Mail Code 158-79
Pasadena, California 91125
messina@CCSF.Caltech.edu

Worked from (1987–end of project): Involved as Co-Investigator with particular emphasis on acquiring and managing the computing facilities, and on the systems issues of concurrent computing environments.

Now works on: From 1990 until the present, directs the Caltech Concurrent Supercomputing Facilities, which have pushed to higher limits of performance the approaches conceived in C^3P. Also, manages the CASA gigabit network testbed project, which explores issues on distributed supercomputing.

• Contributed Chapter 2, Technical Backdrop

Steve Otto
Assistant Professor
Department of Computer Science and Engineering
Oregon Graduate Institute of Science and Technology
20000 NW Walker Rd., P. O. Box 91000
Portland, Oregon 97291-1000
otto@cse.ogi.edu

Worked from (1981–1989): QCD, Computer chess, fine-grained parallel systems, combinatoric optimization schemes.

Now works on: Parallel languages and compilation techniques for scalable parallel architectures; new combinatoric optimization algorithms.

• Contributed Sections 6.6, Character Recognition by Neural Nets; 7.5, Parallel Random Number Generators; 11.4, An Improved Method for the Traveling Salesman Problem; 12.7, Sorting; 13.6, Coherent Parallel C; and 14.3, Computer Chess

Jean Patterson
Technical Group Supervisor for
Remote Sensing Analysis Systems and Modeling Group
Jet Propulsion Laboratory
4800 Oak Grove Drive
Mail Code 198-231
Pasadena, California 91109
jep@yosemite.Jpl.Nasa.Gov

Worked from (1984–end of project): Remote sensing data analysis and modeling for remote sensing applications. These applications use high-performance parallel processing systems for the analysis. In particular, involved has been with electromagnetic scattering and radiation analysis, atmospheric radiative transfer, and synthetic aperture radar processing.

Now works on: Continues with electromagnetics and atmospheric radiative transfer modeling. Key participants involved in the finite element work include Tom Cwik, Robert Ferraro, Nathan Jacobi, Paulette Liewer, Greg Lyzenga, and Jay Parker

- Contributed Section 9.4, Computational Electromagnetics

Francois Pepin
Staff Member
Canadair Aerospace Group
11324 Meunier
Montreal H3L 2Z6, Canada

Worked from (6/87–end of project): Simulation of viscous incompressible flows using vortex methods; fast algorithms for N-body problems.

Now works on: Simulation of compressible flows over transport aircraft.

- Contributed Section 12.5, Fast Vortex Algorithm and Parallel Computing

Tom Prince
Professor of Physics
California Institute of Technology
Mail Code 220-47
Pasadena, California 91125
prince@caltech.edu

Worked from (1985–end of project): Diffraction-limited imaging with large ground-based optical and infrared telescopes, very-high sensitivity searches for pulsars in globular clusters, and searches for pulsars in short-orbit binary systems.

Now works on: Very-high speed data acquisition and analysis, image enhancement of astronomical infrared maps, and pulsar search and detection.

Peter Reiher
Member of the Technical Staff
Jet Propulsion Laboratory
4800 Oak Grove Drive
Mail Stop 525-3660
Pasadena, California 91109

Worked from (11/87–1989): The TimeWarp operating system, parallel programming synchronization methods.

Now works on: Parallel and distributed operating systems.

• Contributed Section 15.3, Time Warp

Ken Rose
Assistant Professor
University of California at Santa Barbara
Department of Electrical and Computer Engineering
Santa Barbara, California 93106
rose@ece.ucsb.edu

Worked from (7/89–end of project): Combinatin of principles of information theory with tools from statistical physics for solving hard optimization problems. Particular applications included fuzzy and hard clustering (pttern recognition and neural networks), vector quantization (coding/communications), and tracking.

Now works on: Information theory (particularly rate-distortion theory), pattern recognition, source coding, communications, signal processing, and nonconvex optimization.

John Salmon
Research Fellow
California Institute of Technology
Mail Code 206-49
Pasadena, California 91125
johns@ccsf.caltech.edu

Worked from (8/83–end of project): As a graduate student and post-doc, research interests included astrophysical applications, Fourier transforms, ray-tracing, parallel I/O, and operating systems. Still working with the current incarnations of C^3P at Caltech.

Now works on: Fast tree-based methods for N-body problems and other applications (hydrodynamics, panel methods, random fields) have dominated recent attention. Work with the current incarnations of C^3P are still being continued at present.

- Contributed Section 12.4, Tree Codes for N-body Simulations

Anthony Skjellum
Assistant Professor of Computer Science
NSF Engineering Research Center for Computational Field Simulation
and Computer Science Department
Mississippi State University
P. O. Drawer CS
300 Butler Hall
Mississippi State, Mississippi 39762-5623
tony@cs.msstate.edu

Worked from (9/87–end of project): Parallel libraries, message-passing systems, portability, chemical engineering applications—flowsheeting.

Now works on: Same as above, plus standards in message passing (message-passing interface forum), heterogeneous high-performance clusters

- Contributed Sections 9.5, LU Factorization of Sparse, Unsymmetric Jacobi Matrices; 9.6, Concurrent DASSL Applied to Dynamic Distillation Column

Simulation; and Chapter 16, The Zipcode Message-passing System

Michael D. Speight
Registrar in Medical Radiodiagnosis, Royal Infirmary of Edinburgh
c/o Medical Statistics Unit
University of Edinburgh
Teviot Place
Edinburgh EH8 9AG, Scotland
mds3@edinburgh.ac.uk

Worked from (1989–end of project): Biologically realistic neural simulation on parallel computers. Most recent involvement was via Jim Bower's group doing neural simulation work on the Intel Touchstone Delta.

Now works on: Virtual reality systems and parallel computing for manipulating medical images (e.g., human brain MRI scans).

• Contributed Section 7.6, Parallel Computing in Neurobiology: The GENESIS Project

Eric Van de Velde
Senior Research Fellow
California Institute of Technology
Mail Code 217-50
Pasadena, California 91125
evdv@ama.caltech.edu

Worked from (6/86–end of project): Algorithms for concurrent scientific computing; multigrid and linear algebra algorithms.

Now works on: Multigrid, linear algebra, fluid flow, reaction-diffusion equations.

• Contributed Section 9.7, Adaptive Multigrid

David Walker
Member of the Technical Staff
Building 9207A, MS-8083
P.O. Box 2009
Oak Ridge National Laboratory
Oak Ridge, TN 37831-8083
walker@msr.epm.ornl.gov

Worked from (3/86–8/88): Parallel linear algebra, parallel CFD, benchmarking, programming paradigms, parallel FFT algorithms.

Now works on: Linear algebra software for MIMD machines, concurrent particle-in-cell algorithms for plasma simulations, benchmarking, molecular dynamics.

• Contributed Sections 6.2, Convectively-Dominated Flows and the Flux-Corrected Transport Technique; and 8.1, Full and Banded Matrix Algorithms

Brad Werner
Assistant Professor
University of California at San Diego
Scripps Institution of Oceanography
Center for Coastal Studies
Mail Code 0209
9500 Gilman Drive
La Jolla, California 92093-0209
werner@hayek.ucsd.edu

Worked from (1983–1987): Simulation of the dynamics of granular materials.

Now works on: Quantitative geomorphology, nearshore and desert processes, granular materials, computer simulation, pattern formation.

• Contributed Section 9.2, Geomorphology by Micromechanical Simulations

Roy Williams
Senior Staff Scientist
Concurrent Supercomputing Facilities
California Institute of Technology
Mail Code 206-49
Pasadena, California 91125
roy@ccsf.caltech.edu

Worked from (2/86–end of project): Programming paradigms and algorithms for unstructured triangular meshes.

Now works on: General unstructured meshes; finite-element and finite-volume methods; reaction-diffusion equations; mesh generation in complex geometries.

• Contributed Chapter 10, DIME Programming Environment; Sections 11.1, Load Balancing as an Optimization Problem, 12.2, Simulation of the Electrosensory System of the Fish *Gnathonemus petersii*; and 12.3, Transonic Flow

Carl Winstead
Assistant Scientist
California Institute of Technology
Mail Code 127-72
Pasadena, California 91125
clw@cco.caltech.edu

Worked from (3/89–9/89): Computation of electron-molecule collision cross-sections with parallel machines.

Now works on: Electron-molecule collision cross-sections relevant to low-temperature plasmas; improving methods and algorithms in such calculations.

Bibliography

[Aarseth:85a] Aarseth, S. J. "Direct methods for N-Body simulations," in J. U. Brackbill and B. I. Cohen, editors, *Multiple Time Scales*, pages 377–418. Academic Press, New York, NY, 1985.

[Aboelaze:89a] Aboelaze, M. Technical report, York University, Ontario, Canada, June 1989. Unpublished manuscript.

[Adobe:87a] Adobe Systems, Inc. *PostScript Language Reference Manual.* Addison-Wesley, Reading, MA, 1987.

[AGARD:83a] Advisory Group for Aerospace Research or Development. *Test Cases for Steady Inviscid Transonic or Supersonic Flows.* North Atlantic Treaty Organization, January 1983. AGARD FDP WG-07.

[Agarwal:91a] Agarwal, A., Chaiken, D., D'Sousa, G., Johnson, K., Kranz, D., Kubiatowicz, J., Kurihara, K., Lim, B. G., Maa, G., Nussbaum, D., Parkin, M., and Yeung, D. "The MIT Alewife machine: A large-scale distributed memory multiprocessor." Technical Report MIT/LCS TM-454, Massachusetts Institute of Technology, Boston, MA, 1991.

[Ahnert:87a] Ahnert, F. "Approaches to dynamic equilibrium in theoretical simulations of slope development," *Earth Surface Processes and Landforms*, 12:3–15, 1987.

[Aho:83a] Aho, A. V., Hopcroft, J. E., and Ullman, J. D. *Data Structures and Algorithms*, page 427. Addison-Wesley, Reading, MA, 1983.

[Ahuja:86a] Ahuja, S., Carriero, N., and Gelernter, D. "Linda and friends," *Computer*, 19(8):26–34, August 1986.

[Alaghband:89a] Alaghband, G. "Parallel pivoting combined with parallel reduction and fill-in control," *Parallel Computing*, 11:201–221, 1989.

877

[Aldcroft:88a] Aldcroft, T., Cisneros, A., Fox, G. C., Furmanski, W., and Walker, D. W. "LU decomposition of banded matrices and the solution of linear systems on hypercubes," in G. C. Fox, editor, *The Third Conference on Hypercube Concurrent Computers and Applications, Volume 2*, pages 1635–1655. ACM Press, New York, January 1988. Caltech Report C3P-348b.

[Almasi:89a] Almasi, G. S., and Gottlieb, A. *Highly Parallel Computing*. The Benjamin/Cummings Publishing Company, Inc., Redwood City, CA, 1989.

[Almgren:91a] Almgren, A. *A Fast Adaptive Vortex Method Using Local Correction*. PhD thesis, University of California at Berkeley, June 1991. Center for Pure and Applied Mathematics Technical Report 527.

[Alnuweiri:92a] Alnuweiri, H. M., and Prasanna, V. K. "Parallel architectures and algorithms for image component labeling," *IEEE Trans. Patt. Anal. Machine Intell.*, 10:1014–1034, 1992.

[Aloisio:88a] Aloisio, G., Veneziani, N., Kim, J. S., and Fox, G. C. "The prime factor non-binary discrete Fourier transform and use of Crystal_Router as a general purpose communication routine," in G. C. Fox, editor, *The Third Conference on Hypercube Concurrent Computers and Applications, Volume 2*, pages 1322–1327. ACM Press, New York, January 1988. Caltech Report C3P-523.

[Aloisio:89b] Aloisio, G., Lopinto, E., and Fox, G. C. "A method to reduce the inter-node communications for a concurrent implementation of the prime factor algorithm," in J. L. Gustafson, editor, *The Proceedings of the Fourth Conference on Hypercubes, Concurrent Computers and Applications*, page 1079. Golden Gate Enterprises, Los Altos, CA, March 1989. Caltech Report C3P-773.

[Aloisio:90b] Aloisio, G., Bochicchio, M., Fox, G. C., Albrizio, R., Mazzone, A., and Veneziani, N. "The design of a parallel/pipeline multiprocessor system for fast DFT algorithms computation." Technical Report C3P-918, California Institute of Technology, Pasadena, CA, 1990. For publication information, see Aloisio:91c.

[Aloisio:90c] Aloisio, G., Veneziani, N., Fox, G., and Milillo, G. "Computational load evaluation for the real-time compression of X-SAR raw data," *Space Technology*, 10(4):189–199, November 1990. Caltech Report C3P-740b.

[Aloisio:90d] Aloisio, G., Bochicchio, M., and Marzocca, C. "A heterogeneous hypercube based on strengthened nodes for a fast processing of SAR raw-data," in D. W. Walker and Q. F. Stout, editors, *The Fifth Distributed Memory Computing Conference, Volume II*, pages 704–712. IEEE Computer Society Press, Los Alamitos, CA, 1990. Held April 9–12, Charleston, SC. Caltech Report C3P-962.

[Aloisio:91a] Aloisio, G., Fox, G. C., Kim, J. S., and Veneziani, N. "A concurrent implementation of the prime factor algorithm on a hypercube," *IEEE Trans. ASSP*, 39(1):160–170, January 1991. Caltech Report C3P-468b.

[Aloisio:91b] Aloisio, G., Lopinto, E., Veneziani, N., Fox, G. C., and Kim, J. S. "Two approaches to the concurrent implementation of the prime factor algorithm on a hypercube," *Concurrency: Practice and Experience*, 3(5):483–495, October 1991. Caltech Report C3P-874.

[Ambjorn:85a] Ambjorn, J., Durhuus, B., and Frohlich, J. "Diseases of triangulated random surface models and possible cures," *Nucl. Phys. B*, 257:433–449, 1985.

[Ambjorn:87a] Ambjorn, J., et al. "Regularized strings with extrinsic curvature," *Nucl. Phys. B*, 290:480–506, 1987.

[Ambjorn:87b] Ambjorn, J., de Forcrand, P., Koukiou, F., and Petritis, D. "Monte Carlo simulations of regularized bosonic strings," *Phys. Lett. B*, 197:548–552, 1987.

[Ambjorn:89a] Ambjorn, J., B., D., Frohlich, J., and Jonsson, T. "A renormalization group analysis of lattice models of two-dimensional membranes," *J. Stat. Phys.*, 55:29–85, 1989.

[Ambjorn:89b] Ambjorn, J., Durhuus, B., and Jonsson, T. "Kinematical and numerical study of the crumpling transition in crystalline surfaces," *Nucl. Phys. B*, 316:526–558, 1989.

[Ambjorn:92a] Ambjorn, J., Jurkiewicz, J., Varsted, S., Irback, A., and Petersson, P. "Critical properties of the dynamical random surface with extrinsic curvature," *Phys. Lett.*, 275B:295, 1992.

[Amdahl:67a] Amdahl, G. M. "Validity of the single processor approach to achieving large-scale computing capabilities," in *AFIPS Conference Proceedings 30*, page 483. AFIPS Press, Montvale, NJ, 1967.

[AMT:87a] Technology, A. M. *Fortran-Plus Language*. Active Memory Technology, Irvine, CA, October 1987.

[Andersen:88a] Andersen, H. W., and Laroche, L. F. Private Communications on *Chemsim*, 1988–1990.

[Anderson:87a] Anderson, P. W. "The resonating valence bond state in $La_2 Cu O_4$ and superconductivity," *Science*, 235:1196–1197, 1987.

[Anderson:89c] Anderson, S., Gorham, P., Kulkarni, S., Prince, T., and Wolszczan, A. "Pulsar in globular cluster M15." Technical Report C3P-802, California Institute of Technology, Pasadena, CA, 1989. International Astronomical Union Circular 4762.

[Anderson:89d] Anderson, S., Gorham, P., Kulkarni, S., Prince, T., and Wolszczan, A. "PSR 2127+11C." Technical Report C3P-803, California Institute of Technology, Pasadena, CA, 1989. International Astronomical Union Circular 4772.

[Anderson:89e] Anderson, S., Kulkarni, S., and Prince, T. "Ten-millisecond pulsar in M13." Technical Report C3P-812, California Institute of Technology, Pasadena, CA, 1989. International Astronomical Union Circular 4819.

[Anderson:90a] Anderson, S. B., W., G. P., Kulkarni, S. R., Prince, T. A., and Wolszczan, A. "Discovery of two radio pulsars in the globular cluster M15," *Nature*, 346:42, 1990. Caltech Report C3P-864.

[Anderson:90b] Anderson, C. R. "An implementation of the fast multipole method without multipoles." Technical Report 90-14, University of California, Los Angeles, CA, July 1990. Center for Applied Mathematics.

[Anderson:90c] Anderson, E., Bai, Z., Bischof, C., Demmel, J., Dongarra, J., DuCroz, J., Greenbaum, A., Hammarling, S., McKenney, A., and Sorensen, D. "LAPACK: a portable linear algebra library for high-peformance computers," in *Proceedings of Supercmputing '90*, pages 1–10. IEEE Computer Society Press, Los Alamitos, CA, 1990.

[Andrews:91a] Andrews, G. R. *Concurrent Programming: Principles and Practice*. The Benjamin/Cummings Publishing Company, Inc., Redwood City, CA, 1991.

[Angus:90a] Angus, I. G., Fox, G. C., Kim, J. S., and Walker, D. W. *Solving Problems on Concurrent Processors: Software for Concurrent Processors*, volume 2. Prentice-Hall, Inc., Englewood Cliffs, NJ, 1990.

[Aoki:91a] Aoki, S. E., et al. "Physics goals of the QCD teraflop project," *The International Journal of Modern Physics C*, 2(4):829–948, 1991.

[Apostolakis:88d] Apostolakis, J., and Kochanek, C. S. "Statistical gravitational lensing on the Mark III hypercube," in G. C. Fox, editor, *The Third Conference on Hypercube Concurrent Computers and Applications, Volume 2*, pages 963–970. ACM Press, New York, January 1988. Caltech Report C3P-581.

[Apostolakis:92a] Apostolakis, J., Coddington, P., and Marinari, E. "A multi-grid cluster labeling scheme," *Europhysics Letters*, 17:189, 1992.

[Apostolakis:93a] Apostolakis, J., Coddington, P., and Marinari, E. "New SIMD algorithms for cluster labeling on parallel computers," *International Journal of Modern Physics C*, 4(4):749–763, August 1993.

[Appel:85a] Appel, A. W. "An efficient program for many-body simulation," *SIAM J. Sci. Stat. Comput.*, 6:85, 1985.

[Arbib:90a] Arbib, M., and Robinson, J. A., editors. *Natural and Artificial Parallel Computation*. The MIT Press, Cambridge, MA, 1990.

[Ashby:90a] Ashby, S. F., 1990. Private Communication on *Iterative DASSL*. Lawrence Livermore National Laboratory, Numerical Mathematics Group, Livermore, California.

[Athas:88a] Athas, W. C., and Seitz, C. L. "Multicomputers: Message-passing concurrent computers," *IEEE Computer*, pages 9–24, August 1988.

[Auerbach:88a] Auerbach, A., and Arovas, D. P. "Spin dynamics in the square-lattice antiferromagnet," *Phys. Rev. Lett.*, 61:617–620, 1988.

[Avico:89a] Avico, N., et al. (the APE Collaboration). "From APE to APE-100: From 1 to 100 Gflops in lattice gauge theory simulations," *Comp. Phys. Comm.*, 57:285, 1989.

[Bacher:83a] Bacher, M. "A new method for the simulation of electric fields, generated by electric fish, and their distortions by objects," *Biol. Cybern.*, 47:51–54, 1983.

[Baden:87a] Baden, S. B. *Run-Time Partitioning of Scientific Continuum Calculations Running on Multiprocessors.* PhD thesis, University of California, Berkeley, 1987.

[Bagnold:41a] Bagnold, R. A. *The Physics of Blown Sand and Desert Dunes.* Methuen, London, 1941.

[Baiardi:89a] Baiardi, F., and Orlando, S. *Strategies for a Massively Parallel Implementation of Simulated Annealing*, volume 366 of *Lecture Notes in Computer Science*, pages 273–277. Springer-Verlag, Berlin/New York, 1989.

[Baig:89a] Baig, M., Espriu, D., and Wheater, J. F. "Phase transition in random surfaces," *Nucl. Phys. B*, 314:587–608, 1989.

[Baillie:88f] Baillie, C. F., Gottschalk, T. D., and Kolawa, A. "Comparisons of concurrent tracking on various hypercubes," in G. C. Fox, editor, *The Third Conference on Hypercube Concurrent Computers and Applications, Volume 1*, pages 155–166. ACM Press, New York, January 1988. Caltech Report C3P-568.

[Baillie:88h] Baillie, C. F., and Barish, K. "Spin operators for the 3-d Ising model." Technical Report C3P-648, California Institute of Technology, Pasadena, CA, July 1988.

[Baillie:89a] Baillie, C. "Lattice gauge theory and QCD, an overview of algorithms." Seminar C3P-707, California Institute of Technology, Pasadena, CA, January 1989.

[Baillie:89e] Baillie, C. F., Brickner, R. G., Gupta, R., and Johnsson, L. "QCD with dynamical Fermions on the Connection Machine," in *Proceedings of Supercomputing '89*, pages 2–9. ACM Press, November 1989. IEEE Computer Society and ACM SIGARCH, Reno, Nevada. Caltech Report C3P-786.

[Baillie:90c] Baillie, C. F., Williams, R. D., and Johnston, D. A. "Crumpling dynamically triangulated random surfaces in higher dimensions," *Physics Letters B*, 243(4):358–364, January 1990. Caltech Report C3P-867.

[Baillie:90d] Baillie, C. F., Williams, R. D., and Johnston, D. A. "Non-universality in dynamically triangulated random surfaces with extrinsic curvature," *Mod. Phys. Lett. A*, 5(C3P-868):1671–1683, 1990. Caltech Report C3P-868.

[Baillie:90e] Baillie, C. F., Johnston, D. A., and Williams, R. D. "Computational aspects of simulating dynamically triangulated random surfaces," *Computer Physics Communications*, 58(1/2):105–117, 1990. February/March 1990. Caltech Report C3P-808.

[Baillie:90j] Baillie, C. F., Johnston, D. A., and Williams, R. D. "Crumpling in dynamically triangulated random surfaces with extrinsic curvature," *Nuclear Physics B*, 335:469–501, 1990. Caltech Report C3P-807.

[Baillie:90m] Baillie, C. F., and Coddington, P. D. "A comparison of cluster algorithms for Potts models," *Nucl. Phys. B. (Proc. Suppl.)*, 17:305–308, 1990. Proceedings of the International Workshop "Lattice 89," Capri (September 1989). Caltech Report C3P-835.

[Baillie:90n] Baillie, C. F., Johnston, D. A., and Kilcup, G. W. "Status and prospects of the computational approach to high-energy physics," *The Journal of Supercomputing*, 4:277–300, 1990. Caltech Report C3P-800b.

[Baillie:91a] Baillie, C. F., and Coddington, P. D. "Cluster identification algorithms for spin models," *Concurrency: Practice and Experience*, 3(2):129–144, April 1991. Caltech Report C3P-855.

[Baillie:91b] Baillie, C. F., and Coddington, P. "Comparison of cluster algorithms for two-dimensional Potts models," *Physical Review B*, 43:10617–10621, 1991. SCCS-12. Caltech Report C3P-945.

[Baillie:91c] Baillie, C. F., Williams, R. D., Catterall, S. M., and Johnston, D. A. "Further investigations of the crumpling transition in dynamically triangulated random surfaces," *Nuclear Physics B*, 348:543–579, 1991. Caltech Report C3P-917.

[Baillie:91d] Baillie, C. F. "A new MCRG calculation of the critical behavior of the 3D Ising model," *Comput. Phys. Comm.*, 65:17–23, 1991. in IMACS First International Conference on Computational Physics, Boulder (June 1990). Caltech Report C3P-937.

[Balasundaram:89c] Balasundaram, V., Kennedy, K., Kremer, U., and McKinley, K. "The ParaScope Editor: An interactive parallel programming tool," in *Supercomputing 89*, November 1989. Held in Reno, Nevada.

[Balasundaram:90a] Balasundaram, V., Fox, G., Kennedy, K., and Kremer, U. "An interactive environment for data parititioning and distribution," in D. W. Walker and Q. F. Stout, editors, *The Fifth Distributed Memory Computing Conference, Volume II*, pages 1160–1170. IEEE Computer Society Press, Los Alamitos, CA, 1990. Held April 9–12, Charleston, SC; CRPC-TR90047. Caltech Report C3P-883.

[Balasundaram:90d] Balasundaram, V., Fox, G., Kennedy, K., and Kremer, U. "Estimating communication costs from data layout specifications in an interactive data partitioning tool." Technical Report C3P-886, California Institute of Technology, Pasadena, CA, April 1990. Invited presentation at the Workshop on Programming Distributed Memory Machines: Language Constructs, Compilers and Run-time Environments, NASA Langley Research Center, Hampton, Virginia, May 14–16, 1990.

[Bancilhon:88a] Bancilhon, F., and Maier, D. "Multilanguage object-oriented systems: New answer to old database problems?," in K. Fuchi and L. Kott, editors, *Future Generation Computer II*. North Holland Press, 1988.

[Barajas:87a] Barajas, F., and Williams, R. "Optimization with a distributed-memory parallel processor." Technical Report C3P-465, California Institute of Technology, Pasadena, CA, September 1987.

[Barhen:88a] Barhen, J., Gulati, S., and Iyengar, S. S. "The pebble crunching model for load balancing in concurrent hypercube ensembles," in G. C. Fox, editor, *The Third Conference on Hypercube Concurrent Computers and Applications, Volume 1*, pages 189–199. ACM Press, New York, January 1988. Caltech Report C3P-610.

[Barkai:84b] Barkai, D., Moriarty, K. J. M., and Rebbi, C. "Force between static quarks," *Phys. Rev. D*, 30:1293–1304, 1984.

[Barkai:84c] Barkai, D., Moriarty, K. J. M., and Rebbi, C. "Force between static charges and universality in lattice QCD," *Phys. Rev. D*, 30:2201–2211, 1984.

[Barnard:93a] Barnard, S., and Simon, H. D. "A fast multilevel implementation of recursive spectral bisection for partitioning unstructured problems," *Concurrency: Practice and Experience*, June 1993. Accepted for publication.

[Barnes:82a] Barnes, E. R. "An algorithm for partitioning the nodes of a graph," *SIAM Journal for Algorithms and Discrete Methods*, 3:541–550, 1982.

[Barnes:86a] Barnes, J., and Hut, P. "A hierarchical $O(N \log N)$ force calculation algorithm," *Nature*, 324:446–449, 1986.

[Barnes:88c] Barnes, T., and Daniell, G. J. "Numerical solution of spin systems and the s $= 1/2$ Heisenberg antiferromagnet using guided random walks," *Phys. Rev. B.*, 37:3637, 1988.

[Barnes:89a] Barnes, T., Cappon, K. J., Dagotto, E., Kotchan, D., and Swanson, E. S. "Critical behavior of the 2D anisotropic Heisenberg antiferromagnet: A numerical test of spin-wave theory," *Phys. Rev. B.*, 40:8945, 1989. Toronto preprint UTPT-89-01. Caltech Report C3P-722.

[Barnes:89b] Barnes, T. "Numerical solution of high temperature superconductor spin systems," in C. Bottcher, M. R. Strayer, and J. B. McGrory, editors, *Nuclear and Atomic Physics at One Gigaflop*, volume 10, pages 83–106. Nuclear Science Research Conference Series, Harwood Academic, 1989. Toronto preprint UTPT-88-07. Caltech Report C3P-638.

[Barnes:89c] Barnes, T., Kotchan, D., and Swanson, E. S. "Evidence for a phase transition in the zero temperature anisotrophic 2D Heisenberg antiferromagnet," *Phys. Rev. B.*, 39:4357, 1989. Caltech Report C3P-653.

[Barnes:89d] Barnes, J. E., and Hut, P. "Error analysis of a tree code," *Astrophysical Journal (Suppl.)*, 70:389–417, June 1989.

[Barnes:90b] Barnes, T., and Kovarik, M. D. "Static hole energies in the t-j model and a t-j-e model of the high-temperature superconductors," *Phys. Rev. B*, 42:6159–6164, 1990.

[Barnes:91a] Barnes, T. "The 2D Heisenberg antiferromagnet in High-T_c superconductivity," *International Journal of Modern Physics C*, 2(2):659–709, June 1991. A Review of Numerical Techniques and Results. Caltech Report C3P-873b.

[Barron:83a] Barron, I. M., Cavill, P., May, D., and Wilson, P. "The transputer," *Electronics*, 56:109, November 1983.

[Bartschat:89a] Bartschat, K. "Excitation and ionization of atoms by interaction with electrons, positrons, protons, and photons," *Physics Reports*, 180:1–81, 1989.

[Batcher:68a] Batcher, K. E. "Sorting networks and their applications," in *AFIPS Conference Proceedings 32*, page 307. AFIPS Press, Montvale, NJ, 1968.

[Batcher:85a] Batcher, K. E. "MPP: A high speed image processor," in *Algorithmically Specialized Parallel Computers*. Academic Press, New York, 1985.

[Batrouni:85a] Batrouni, G. G., Katz, G. R., Kronfeld, A. S., Lepage, G. P., Svetitsky, B., and Wilson, K. G. "Langevin simulations of lattice field theories," *Phys. Rev. D*, 32:2736–2747, 1985.

[Battista:92a] Battista, C., Cabasino, S., Marzano, F., Paolucci, P., Pech, J., Rapuano, F., Sarno, R., Todesco, G., Torelli, M., Tross, W., Vicini, P., Cabibbo, N., Marinari, E., Parisi, G., Salina, G., Del Prete, F., Lai, A., Lombardo, M., and Tripiccione, R. "The Ape-100 computer: The architectures," *International Journal of High Speed Computing*, March 1992. Reprint in G. Parisi, "Field Theory, Disorder, and Simulations" (World Scientific, Singapore, 1992). SCCS-268.

[Battiti:88a] Battiti, R. "Collective stereopsis on the hypercube," in G. C. Fox, editor, *The Third Conference on Hypercube Concurrent Computers and Applications, Volume 2*, pages 1000–1006. ACM Press, New York, January 1988. Caltech Report C3P-583.

[Battiti:89a] Battiti, R. "Accelerated back-propagation learning: Two optimization methods," *Complex Systems*, 3(4):331–342, 1989. Caltech Report C3P-714.

[Battiti:89g] Battiti, R. *Multiscale Methods, Parallel Computation, and Neural Networks for Computer Vision.* PhD thesis, California Institute of Technology, November 1989. Caltech Report C3P-850.

[Battiti:90a] Battiti, R. "Surface reconstruction and discontinuity detection: A fast hierarchical approach on a two-dimensional mesh," in D. W. Walker and Q. F. Stout, editors, *The Fifth Distributed Memory Computing Conference, Volume I,* pages 184–193. IEEE Computer Society Press, Los Alamitos, CA, 1990. Held April 9–12, Charleston, SC. Caltech Report C3P-900.

[Battiti:90d] Battiti, R., and Masulli, F. "BFGS optimization for faster and automated supervised learning," in *Proceedings of the International Neural Network Conference INNC-90,* pages 757–760. Kluwer Academic Publishers, Dordrecht/Boston/London, 1990. held in Paris, France. Caltech Report C3P-841.

[Battiti:91a] Battiti, R. "Real-time multiscale vision on multicomputers," *Concurrency: Practice and Experience,* 3(2):55–87, 1991. Caltech Report C3P-932b.

[Battiti:91b] Battiti, R., Amaldi, E., and Koch, C. "Computing optical flow across multiple scales: An adaptive coarse-to-fine strategy," *International Journal of Computer Vision,* 6(2):133–145, 1991.

[Bayliss:80a] Bayliss, A., and Turkel, E. "Radiation boundary conditions for wave-like equations," *Commun. Pure and Appl. Math,* 33:707–725, 1980.

[BBN:87a] *Butterfly Products Overview.* BBN Advanced Computers, Inc., Cambridge, MA, 1987.

[Berger:84a] Berger, M. J., and Oliger, J. "Adaptive mesh refinement for hyperbolic partial differential equations," *Journal of Computational Physics,* 54:484, 1984.

[Berger:87a] Berger, M., and Bokhari, S. "A partitioning strategy for nonuniform problems on multiprocessors," *IEEE Trans. Computers,* C-36(5):570–580, May 1987.

[Berger:89a] Berger, M. J., and Colella, P. "Local adaptive mesh refinement for shock hydrodynamics," *Journal of Computational Physics,* 82:64, 1989.

[Berntsen:89a] Berntsen, J. "Communication efficient matrix multiplication on hypercubes," *Parallel Computing*, 12(3):335–342, December 1989.

[Berryman:91a] Berryman, H., Saltz, J., and Scroggs, J. "Execution time support for adaptive scientific algorithms on distributed memory machines," *Concurrency: Practice and Experience*, 3(3):159–178, 1991.

[Bhalla:92a] Bhalla, U. S., Bilitch, D. H., and Bower, J. M. "Rallpacks: A set of benchmarks for neuronal simulators," *Trends Neurosci.*, 15:453–458, 1992.

[Bhalla:93a] Bhalla, U. S., and Bower, J. M. "Exploring parameter space in detailed single neuron models: Simulations of the mitral and granule cells of the olfactory bulb," *Journal of Neurophysiology*, 69:1948–1965, June 1993.

[Bhatt:92a] Bhatt, S., Chen, M., Lin, Y., and Liu, P. "Abstraction for parallel N-body simulations," in J. Saltz, editor, *Proceedings of Scalable High Performance Computing Conference (SHPCC)*, pages 38–45. IEEE Press, April 1992.

[Billoire:86a] Billoire, A., and David, F. "A model of random surfaces with non-trivial critical behavior," *Nucl. Phys. B*, 275:548–552, 1986.

[Binder:86a] Binder, K., editor. *Monte Carlo Methods in Statistical Physics*. Springer-Verlag, Berlin, 1986.

[Binney:87a] Binney, J., and Tremaine, S. *Galactic Dynamics*. Princeton University Press, Princeton, NJ, 1987.

[Birgeneau:71a] Birgeneau, J., Skalyo, Jr., J., and Shirane, G. "Critical magnetic scattering in $K_2 Ni F_4$," *Phys. Rev. B*, 3:1736–1749, 1971.

[Birgeneau:90a] Birgeneau, R. J. "Spin correlations in the two dimensional $S = 1$ Heisenberg antiferromagnet," *Phys. Rev. B.*, 41:2514–2516, 1990.

[Birman:87a] Birman, K. P., and Joseph, T. "Reliable communication in the presence of failures," *ACM Trans. on Computer Systems*, 5:47–76, February 1987.

[Birman:87b] Birman, K. P., and Joseph, T. "Exploiting virtual synchrony in distributed systems," in *Proceedings of the Eleventh Symposium on Operating Systems Principles*, pages 123–138. ACM, November 1987.

[Birman:91a] Birman, K., and Cooper, R. "The ISIS project: Real experience with a fault tolerant programming system," *Operating Systems Review*, pages 103–107, April 1991. ACM/SIGOPS European Workshop on Fault-Tolerance Techniques in Operating Systems, held in Bologna, Italy (1990).

[Blackman:86a] Blackman, S. S. *Multiple-Target Tracking with Radar Applications*. Artech House, Dedham, MA, 1986.

[Blelloch:90a] Blelloch, G. E. *Vector Models for Data-Parallel Computing*. The MIT Press, Cambridge, MA/London, 1990.

[Blelloch:92a] Blelloch, G. E., Chatterjee, S., Hardwick, J., Sipelstein, J., and Zagha, M. "Implementation of a portable nested data-parallel language." Technical report, Carnegie Mellon University, Pittsburgh, PA, October 1992. NESL is high-level language on top of intermediate vector interpreter VCODE.

[Bodin:91a] Bodin, F., Beckman, P., Gannon, D., Narayana, S., and Shelby, Y. "Distributed pC++: Basic ideas for an object parallel language," in *Proceedings of Supercomputing '91*, pages 273–282. (IEEE) Computer Society and (ACM) (SIGARCH), November 1991.

[Boehm:90a] Boehm, B., and Papaccio, P. "Understanding and controlling software costs," *IEEE Transactions on Software Engineering*, pages 1462–1477, October 1990.

[Boghosian:90a] Boghosian, B. M. "Computational physics on the Connection Machine: massive parallelism—a new paradigm," *Computers in Physics*, 4:14–33, January 1990.

[Bolstadt:86a] Bolstadt, J. H., and Keller, H. "A multigrid continuation method for elliptic problems with folds," *SIAM Journal on Scientific and Statistical Computing*, 7:1081–1104, 1986.

[Boppana:87a] Boppana, R. B. "Eigenvalues and graph bisection: An average case analysis," in *28th Annual Symposium on the Foundations of Computer Science*, pages 67–75. Institute of Electrical and Electronics Engineers, New York, 1987.

[Bordawekar:93a] Bordawekar, R., Choudhary, A., and del Rosario, J. M. "An experimental performance evaluation of the Touchstone Delta concurrent file system," in *Proceedings of the International Conference on Supercomputing '93*, July 1993. Tokyo, Japan. Syracuse University Technical Report SCCS-420.

[Boris:73a] Boris, J. P., and Book, D. L. "Flux-corrected transport, I. SHASTA, a fluid transport code that works," *J. Comp. Phys.*, 11:38, 1973.

[Borsellino:61a] Borsellino, A., and Gamba, A. "An outline of a mathematical theory of PAPA," *Nuovo Cimento Suppl. 2*, 20:221–231, 1961.

[Bouard:80a] Bouard, R., and Coutanceau, M. "The early stage of development of the wake behind an impulsively started cylinder for $40 \le \mathrm{Re} \le 10^4$," *J. Fluid Mech.*, 101:583–607, 1980.

[Boulatov:86a] Boulatov, D. V., Kazakov, V. A., Kostov, I. K., and Migdal, A. A. "Analytical and numerical study of a model of dynamically triangulated random surfaces," *Nucl. Phys. B*, 275:641–686, 1986.

[Bowick:93a] Bowick, M., Coddington, P., Han, L., Harris, G., and Marinari, E. "The phase diagram of fluid random surfaces with extrinsic curvature," *Nucl. Phys. B*, 394:791, 1993.

[Bowler:85a] Bowler, K. C., et al. "The β-function and potential at $\beta = 6.0$ and 6.3 in SU(3) gauge theory," *Phys. Lett. B*, 163:367–370, 1985.

[Bowyer:81a] Bowyer, A. "Computing Direchlet tesselations," *Comp. J.*, 24:162–168, 1981.

[Boyle:87a] Boyle, J., Butler, R., Disz, T., Glickfeld, B., Lusk, E., Overbeek, R., Patterson, J., and Stevens, R. *Portable Programs for Parallel Processors*. Holt, Rinehart and Winston, 1987.

[Bozkus:93a] Bozkus, Z., Choudhary, A., Fox, G. C., Haupt, T., and Ranka, S. "Fortran 90D/HPF compiler for distributed memory MIMD computers: Design, implementation, and performance results." Technical Report SCCS-498, Syracuse University, Syracuse, NY, 1993. To appear in Proceedings of Supercomputing '93, Portland, OR, November 1993.

[Bozkus:93b] Bozkus, Z., Choudhary, A., Fox, G., Haupt, T., Ranka, S., and Wu, M.-Y. "Compiling Fortran 90D/HPF for distributed memory

MIMD computers." Technical Report SCCS-444, Syracuse University, Syracuse, NY, March 1993.

[Brandes:92a] Brandes, T. "ADAPTOR language reference manual." Technical Report ADAPTOR-3, German National Research Center for Computer Science, 1992.

[Brandt:77a] Brandt, A. "Multilevel adaptive solutions to boundary value problems," *Mathematics of Computation*, 31:333–390, 1977.

[Branstetter:91a] Branstetter, M. L., Guse, J. A., and Nessett, D. M. "ELROS—an embedded language for remote operations service." Technical Report UCRL-JC-108862, Lawrence Livermore National Laboratory, Livermore, CA, November 1991.

[Branstetter:92a] Branstetter, M. L., Guse, J. A., Nessett, D. M., and Stanberry, L. C. "An ELROS primer." Technical report, Lawrence Livermore National Laboratory, Livermore, CA, 1992.

[Braschi:90a] Braschi, B., Ferreira, A. G., and Zerovnik, J. "On the behavior of parallel simulated annealing," in D. J. Evans, G. R. Joubert, and F. J. Peters, editors, *Supercomputing 90*, pages 17–26. Elsevier Science Publishers, North-Holland, Amsterdam, 1990.

[Bratko:82a] Bratko, I., and Kopec, D. "A test for comparison of human and computer performance in chess," in M. Clarke, editor, *Advances in Computer Chess III*, pages 31–56. Pergamon Press, Oxford, 1982.

[Brawer:89a] Brawer, S. *Introduction to Parallel Programming*. Academic Press, Inc. Ltd., London, 1989.

[Brebbia:83a] Brebbia, C. A., editor. *Boundary Elements*. Springer-Verlag, Berlin, 1983.

[Brenan:89a] Brenan, K. E., Campbell, S. L., and Petzold, L. R. *Numerical Solution of Initial-Value Problem in Differential-Algebraic Equations.* Elsevier, North-Holland, Amsterdam, 1989.

[Brescansin:89a] Brescansin, L. M., Lima, M. A. P., and McKoy, V. "Cross sections for rotational excitation of CH_4 by 3–20 eV electrons," *Phys. Rev. A*, 40:5577–5582, 1989.

[Brezin:76a] Brezin, E., and Zinn-Justin, J. "Spontaneous breakdown of continuous symmetries near two dimensions," *Phys. Rev. B*, 14:3110–3120, 1976.

[Brickner:89b] Brickner, R. G., and Baillie, C. F. "Pure gauge QCD on the Connection Machine," *International Journal of High Speed Computing*, 1(2):303–320, June 1989. Caltech Report C3P-710.

[Brickner:91a] Brickner, R. G., Baillie, C. F., and Johnsson, L. "QCD on the Connection Machine: Beyond *Lisp," *Comput. Phys. Comm.*, 65:39–51, 1991. In IMACS First International Conference on Computational Physics, Boulder (June 1990). Caltech Report C3P-936.

[Brickner:91b] Brickner, R. G. "CMIS arithmetic and multiwire NEWS for QCD on the Connection Machine," *Nucl. Phys. B (Proc. Suppl.)*, 20(76):145–148, 1991. Proceedings of the International Conference on Lattice Field Theory, Tallahassee (Oct. 1990).

[Briggs:87b] Briggs, W. *A Multigrid Tutorial*. SIAM, Philadelphia, 1987.

[Bristeau:87a] Bristeau, M. O., Glowinski, R., and Periaux, J. "Numerical methods for the Navier-Stokes equations: Applications to the simulation of compressible and incompressible viscous flows," *Comp. Phys. Rep.*, 6:73–166, 1987.

[Brochard:92a] Brochard, L., and Freau, A. "Computation and data movement on RP3," *Concurrency: Practice and Experience*, 4(1):57–78, February 1992.

[Brochard:92b] Brochard, L., and Freau, A. "Designing algorithms on RP3," *Concurrency: Practice and Experience*, 4(1):79–106, February 1992.

[Brooks:82b] Brooks, E. "The Laplace equation on NNCP." Technical Report C3P-10, California Institute of Technology, Pasadena, CA, September 1982.

[Brooks:83a] Brooks, E., Fox, G., Otto, S., Randeria, M., Athas, W., DeBenedictis, E., Newton, N., and Seitz, C. "Glueball mass calculations on an array of computers," *Nucl. Phys. B.*, 220(FS8):383–400, 1983. Caltech Report C3P-027.

[Broomhead:88a] Broomhead, D. S., and Lowe, D. "Multivariable functional interpolation and adaptive networks," *Complex Systems*, 2:321–355, 1988.

[Brower:91a] Brower, R. C., Tamayo, P., and York, B. "Parallel multigrid algorithms for percolation clusters," *J. Stat. Phys.*, 63:73–88, 1991.

[Brown:87a] Brown, F., and Woch, T. J. "Over-relaxed heat bath and Metropolis algorithms for accelerating pure gauge Monte Carlo calculations," *Phys. Rev. Lett.*, 58:2394–2396, 1987.

[Brown:88b] Brown, J. A., Pakin, S., and Polivka, R. P. *APL2 at a Glance*. Prentice Hall, 1988.

[Brown:91a] Brown, P. N., and Hindmarsh, A. C. "Reduced storage matrix methods in stiff ODE systems," *J. Appl. Math. and Comp.*, 1991. To be published.

[Bullock:86a] Bullock, T. H., and Heiligenberg, W., editors. *Electroreception*. John Wiley and Sons, Ltd., New York, 1986.

[Burgeios:71a] Burgeios, F., and Lassalle, J. C. "An extension of munkres algorithm for the assignment problem to rectangular matrices," *Comm. of the ACM*, 14:802, 1971.

[Burns:88a] Burns, P., Crichton, J., Curkendall, D., Eng, B., Goodhart, C., Lee, R., Livingston, R., Peterson, J., Pniel, M., Tuazon, J., and Zimmerman, B. "The JPL/Caltech Mark IIIfp hypercube," in G. C. Fox, editor, *The Third Conference on Hypercube Concurrent Computers and Applications, Volume 1*, pages 872–884. ACM Press, New York, January 1988. Caltech Report C3P-607.

[Burt:84a] Burt, P. J. "The pyramid as a structure for efficient computation," in A. Rosenfeld, editor, *Multiresolution Image Processing and Analysis*, pages 6–35. Springer-Verlag, 1984.

[Calalo:89b] Calalo, R., Cwik, T., Ferraro, R. D., Imbriale, W. A., Jacobi, N., Liewer, P. C., Lockhart, T. G., Lyzenga, G. A., Mulligan, S., Parker, J. W., and Patterson, J. E. "Hypercube matrix computation task—research in parallel computational electromagnetics." Technical Report C3P-979, California Institute of Technology/Jet Propulsion Laboratory, Pasadena, CA, 1989.

[Callahan:88a] Callahan, S. "Non-local path integral Monte Carlo on the hypercube," in G. C. Fox, editor, *The Third Conference on Hypercube Concurrent Computers and Applications, Volume 2*, pages 1296–1302. ACM Press, New York, January 1988. Caltech Report C3P-589.

[Callahan:88b] Callahan, S. *Exchange Interactions in Solid ^{3}He on a Parallel Computer*. PhD thesis, California Institute of Technology, August 1988. Caltech Report C3P-645.

[Callahan:88d] Callahan, D., and Kennedy, K. "Compiling programs for distributed-memory multiprocessors," in *1988 Workshop on Programming Languages and Compilers for Parallel Computing*, Cornell, August 1988.

[Callahan:88e] Callahan, D., and Kennedy, K. "Compiling programs for distributed memory multiprocessors," *The Journal of Supercomputing*, pages 171–207, 1988.

[Callaway:83a] Callaway, D., and Rahman, A. "Lattice gauge theory in the microcanonical ensemble," *Phys. Rev. D*, 28:1506–1514, 1983.

[Canny:87a] Canny, J. "A computational approach to edge detection," in M. A. Fischler and O. Firschein, editors, *Readings in Computer Vision: Issues, Problems, Principles and Paradigms*. Morgan and Kaufmann, 1987.

[Catterall:89a] Catterall, S. M. "Extrinsic curvature in dynamically triangulated random surface models," *Phys. Lett. B*, 220(1–2):207–214, 1989.

[Chakravarty:88a] Chakravarty, S., Halperin, B. I., and Nelson, D. "Low-temperature behavior of two-dimensional quantum antiferromagnet," *Phys. Rev. Lett.*, 60:1057–1060, 1988.

[Chan:82a] Chan, T. F. C., and Keller, H. B. "Arc-length continuation and multi-grid techniques for nonlinear elliptic Eigenvalue problems," *SIAM Journal on Scientific and Statistical Computing*, 3:173–193, June 1982.

[Chan:86b] Chan, T. F., and Saad, Y. "Multigrid algorithms on the hypercube multiprocessor," *IEEE Trans. on Computers*, C-35(11):969–977, 1986.

[Chandy:90a] Chandy, K., and Taylor, S. "A primer for program composition notation." Technical Report CRPC-TR90056, California Institute of Technology, Pasadena, CA, June 1990.

[Chandy:92a] Chandy, K. M., and Kesselman, C., "Compositional C++: Compositional parallel programming," 1992. California Institute of Technology.

[Chapman:92a] Chapman, B. M., Mehrotra, P., and Zima, H. P. "Vienna Fortran—a Fortran language extension for distributed memory multiprocessors," in J. Saltz and P. Mehrotra, editors, *Languages, Compilers and Run-Time Environments for Distributed Memory Machines*, pages 39–62. Elsevier Science Publishers, North-Holland, Amsterdam, 1992. Advances in Parallel Computing Series, Volume 3.

[Chen:88a] Chen, W. K., and Gehringer, E. F. "A graph-oriented mapping strategy for a hypercube," in G. C. Fox, editor, *The Third Conference on Hypercube Concurrent Computers and Applications, Volume 1*, pages 200–209. ACM Press, New York, NY, January 1988.

[Chen:88b] Chen, M., Li, J., and Choo, Y. "Compiling parallel programs by optimizing performance," *Journal of Supercomputing*, 2:171–207, 1988.

[Chen:92b] Chen, M., and Wu, J. J. "Optimizing FORTRAN-90 programs for data motion on massively parallel systems." Technical Report YALEU/DCS/TR-882, Yale University, New Haven, CT, 1992. Department of Computer Science.

[Cheng:92a] Cheng, G., Faigle, C., Fox, G. C., Furmanski, W., Li, B., and Mills, K. "Exploring AVS for HPDC software integration: Case studies towards parallel suport for GIS." Technical Report SCCS-473, Syracuse University, Syracuse, NY, March 1992. Paper presented at the 2nd Annual International AVS Conference *The Magic of Science: AVS '93*, Lake Buena Vista, Florida, May 24–26, 1993.

[Cheng:93a] Cheng, G., Lu, Y., Fox, G. C., Mills, K., and Haupt, T. "An interactive remote visualization environment for an electromagnetic scattering simulation on a high performance computing system." Technical Report SCCS-467, Syracuse University, Syracuse, NY, March 1992.

[Cherkassky:88a] Cherkassky, V., and Smith, R. "Efficient mapping and implementation of matrix algorithms on a hypercube," *The Journal of Supercomputing*, 2:7–27, 1988.

[Chiu:88b] Chiu, T. W. "Shift-register sequence random number generators on the hypercube concurrent computers," in G. C. Fox, editor, *The Third Conference on Hypercube Concurrent Computers and Applications, Volume 2*, pages 1421–1429. ACM Press, New York, January 1988. Caltech Report C3P-526.

[Chiu:88c] Chiu, T. W. "Fermion propagators on a four dimensional random-block lattice," *Phys. Lett. B*, 206(3):510–516, January 1988. Caltech Report C3P-507.

[Chiu:88e] Chiu, T. W. "Vacuum polarization on 4-d random block lattice." Technical Report C3P-693, California Institute of Technology, Pasadena, CA, 1988.

[Chiu:88f] Chiu, T. W. "Field theory on the random block lattice." Technical Report C3P-694, California Institute of Technology, Pasadena, CA, 1988.

[Chiu:89a] Chiu, T. W. "Random coupling models of lattice Fermion." Technical Report C3P-813, California Institute of Technology, Pasadena, CA, August 1989.

[Chiu:89b] Chiu, T. W. "Schwinger model on the random block lattice," *Phys. Lett. B*, 217:151–156, 1989. Caltech Report C3P-647.

[Chiu:90a] Chiu, T. W. "Gauge theories on the random-block lattice," *Physics Letters B*, 245(3/4):570–574, August 1990. CRPC-TR91113, SCCS-38. Caltech Report C3P-955.

[Choi:92a] Choi, J., Dongarra, J. J., and Walker, D. W. "Level 3 BLAS for distributed memory concurrent computers," in *Proceedings CNRS-NSF Workshop on Environments and Tools for Parallel Scientific Computing*. Springer-Verlag, 1992. Held in France, September 6–8, 1992.

[Choi:92b] Choi, J., Dongarra, J. J., and Walker, D. W. "The design of scalable software libraries for distributed memory concurrent computers," in *Proceedings CNRS-NSF Workshop on Environments and Tools for*

Parallel Scientific Computing. Springer-Verlag, 1992. Held in France, September 6–8, 1992.

[Choudhary:92c] Choudhary, A., Fox, G. C., Ranka, S., Hiranandani, S., Kennedy, K., Koelbel, C., and Tseng, C. "Compiling Fortran 77D and 90D for MIMD distributed-memory machines," in *Proceedings of the Fourth Symposium on the Frontiers of Massively Parallel Computation: Frontiers '92*, pages 4–11. IEEE Computer Society Press, Los Alamitos, CA, October 1992. Syracuse University Technical Report SCCS-251. CRPC-TR92203.

[Choudhary:92d] Choudhary, A., Fox, G., Hiranandani, S., Kennedy, K., Koelbel, C., Ranka, S., and Saltz, J. "A classification of irregular loosely synchronous problems and their support in scalable parallel software systems," in *DARPA Software Technology Conference 1992 Proceedings*, pages 138–149, April 1992. Syracuse Technical Report SCCS-255.

[Choudhary:92e] Choudhary, A., Fox, G., Ranka, S., Hiranandani, S., Kennedy, K., Koelbel, C., and Saltz, J. "Software support for irregular and loosely synchronous problems," *Computing Systems in Engineering*, 3(1–4):43–52, 1992. CSE-MS 118, CRPC-TR92258.

[Chrisochoides:90a] Chrisochoides, N. P. "Communication overhead on the nCUBE-6400 hypercube." Technical report, Purdue University, West Lafayette, IN, 1990. Unpublished.

[Chrisochoides:91a] Chrisochoides, N. P., Houstis, E. N., and Houstis, C. E. "Geometry based mapping strategies for PDE computations," in *Int. Conf. on Supercomputing*, pages 115–127. ACM Press, New York, NY, 1991.

[Chrisochoides:91b] Chrisochoides, N. P., Houstis, C. E., Houstis, E. N., Papachiou, P. N., Kortesis, S. K., and Rice, J. R. "DOMAIN DECOMPOSER:a software tool for mapping PDE computations to parallel architectures," in *Domain Decomposition Methods for Partial Differential Equations*, chapter 28, pages 341–356. SIAM, 1991.

[Chrisochoides:92a] Chrisochoides, N. P., Aboelaze, M., Houstis, E. N., and Houstis, C. E. "The parallelization of some level 2 and 3 BLAS operations on distributed-memory machines," in *Advances in Computer*

Methods for Partial Differential Equations, pages 127–133. IMAC, 1992. Purdue University Technical Report CSD-TR-91-007, CAPO Report, CER-91-04.

[Chrisochoides:93a] Chrisochoides, N., Houstis, E., and Rice, J. "Mapping algorithms and software environment for data parallel PDE iterative solvers," *Parallel and Distributed Computing*, 1993. To appear in Special Issue: Data Parallel Algorithms and Programming.

[Christ:84a] Christ, N. H., and Terrano, A. E. "A very fast parallel processor," *IEEE Trans. Comput.*, 33:344–349, 1984.

[Christ:86a] Christ, N. H. "Lattice Gauge theory with a fast highly parallel computer," *Journal of Statistical Physics*, 43(5/6), June 1986. Proceedings of the Conference on Frontiers of Quantum Monte Carlo, September 3–6, 1985 at Los Alamos, edited by J. E. Gubernatis.

[Christ:90a] Christ, N. H. "Status of the Columbia 256-Node machine," *Nucl. Phys. B (Proc. Suppl.)*, 17:267–271, 1990. Proc. of the 1989 Symposium on Lattice Field Theory.

[Christ:91a] Christ, N. H. "QCD machines—present and future," *Nucl. Phys. B (Proc. Suppl.)*, 20:129–137, 1991. Proc. of the 1990 Symposium on Lattice Field Theory.

[Chu:87a] Chu, E., and George, A. "Gaussian elimination with partial pivoting and load balancing on a microprocessor," *Parallel Computing*, 5:65–74, 1987.

[Clarke:91a] Clarke, L., and Wilson, G. "Tiny: An efficient routing harness for the INMOS transputer," *Concurrency: Practice and Experience*, 3(3):221–245, 1991.

[Claus:92a] Claus, R., 1992. Private communication (NASA Lewis).

[Clayton:87a] Clayton, R., Hager, B., and Tanimoto, T. "Applications of concurrent processors in geophysics," in *Proceedings of the Second International Conference on Supercomputing*. International Supercomputing Institute Inc., St. Petersburg, FL, May 1987. Caltech Report C3P-408.

[Clayton:88a] Clayton, R. W., and Graves, R. W. "Acoustic wavefield propagation using paraxial extrapolators," in G. C. Fox, editor, *The Third Conference on Hypercube Concurrent Computers and Applications, Volume 2*, pages 1157–1175. ACM Press, New York, January 1988. Caltech Report C3P-613.

[Coddington:90a] Coddington, P. D., and Baillie, C. F. "Cluster algorithms for spin models on MIMD parallel computers," in D. W. Walker and Q. F. Stout, editors, *The Fifth Distributed Memory Computing Conference, Volume I*, pages 384–387. IEEE Computer Society Press, Los Alamitos, CA, 1990. Held April 9–12, Charleston, South Carolina. Caltech Report C3P-862.

[Coddington:92a] Coddington, P., and Baillie, C. "Empirical relations between static and dynamic exponents for Ising model cluster algorithms," *Phys. Rev. Lett.*, 68:962–965, 1992.

[Coddington:93a] Coddington, P., Fox, G. C., Han, L., Harris, G., and Marinari, E. "Optimization of a dynamic random surface code for RISC processor." Technical Report SCCS-481, Syracuse University, Syracuse, NY, April 1993.

[Coniglio:80a] Coniglio, A., and Klein, W. "Clusters and Ising critical droplets: A renoramlization group approach," *J. Phys. A*, 13:2775, 1980.

[Cook:80a] Cook, W. J. "A modular dynamic simulator for distillation systems," Master's thesis, Case Western Reserve University, 1980. Chemical Engineering.

[Cook:90b] Cook, W., Chvatal, V., and Applegate, D., 1990. TSP Workshop, Rice University, April 22–24.

[Copty:92a] Copty, N., Ranka, S., Fox, G., and Shankar, R. "A data parallel algorithm for solving the region growing problem on the Connection Machine." Technical Report SCCS-397, Syracuse University, Syracuse, NY, December 1992. To appear in *Journal of Parallel and Distributed Computing*, Special Issue: Data Parallel Algorithms and Programming.

[Couch:88a] Couch, A. L. *Seecube User's Manual.* Tufts University, January 1988.

[Couch:88b] Couch, A. L., and Krumme, D. W. "Monitoring parallel executions in real time," in D. W. Walker and Q. F. Stout, editors, *The Fifth Distributed Memory Computing Conference, Volume II*, pages 1187–1196. IEEE Computer Society Press, Los Alamitos, CA, 1990. Held April 9–12, Charleston, SC.

[Creutz:83a] Creutz, M. *Quarks, Lattices and Gluons*. Cambridge University Press, Cambridge, Great Britain, 1983.

[Creutz:87a] Creutz, M. "Over-relaxation and Monte Carlo simulation," *Phys. Rev. D*, 36:515–519, 1987.

[Cruse:75a] Cruse, T. A., and Rizzo, F. J., editors. *Boundary Integral Equation Method: Computational Applications in Applied Mechanics*. Applied Mechanics Division (ASME, Vol. 11), American Society of Mechanical Engineers, June 1975. Rensselaer Polytechnic Institute, Troy, NY, June 23–25.

[Cuccaro:89a] Cuccaro, S. A., Hipes, P. G., and Kuppermann, A. "Hyperspherical coordinate reactive scattering using variational surface functions," *Chem. Phys. Letters*, 154(2):155–164, January 1989. Caltech Report C3P-720.

[Cuccaro:89b] Cuccaro, S. A., Hipes, P. G., and Kuppermann, A. "Symmetry analysis of accurate H + H_2 resonances," *Chem. Phys. Letters*, 157(5):440–446, May 1989. Caltech Report C3P-821.

[Cundall:79a] Cundall, P. A., and Strack, O. D. L. "A discrete numerical model for granular assemblies," *Geotechnique*, 29(1):47–65, 1979.

[Cypher:89a] Cypher, R., Sanz, J. L. C., and Snyder, L. "Hypercube and shuffle-exchange algorithms for image component labeling," *J. Algorithms*, 10:140–150, 1989.

[Dahl:87a] Dahl, E. D. "Accelerated learning using the generalized delta rule," in M. Caudill and C. Butler, editors, *International Conference on Neural Networks (IEEE), Volume II*, pages 523–530. IEEE Publishers, 1987.

[Dally:90a] Dally, W. J. "Network and processor architecture for message-driven computers," in Suaya and Birtwistle, editors, *VLSI and Parallel Computation*, chapter 3. Morgan Kaufmann, San Mateo, CA, 1990.

[Dally:92a] Dally, W. J., Fiske, J., Keen, J., Lethin, R., Noakes, M., Nuth, P., Davison, R., and Fyler, G. "The message-driven processor: A multicomputer processing node with efficient mechanisms," *IEEE Micro*, 12(2):23–29, April 1991.

[Dannenhoffer:89a] Dannenhoffer, D. J., and Davis, R. L. "Adaptive grid computations for complex flows," in L. P. Kartashev and S. I. Kartachev, editors, *Proceedings of the Fourth International Conference on Supercomputing at Santa Clara, Volume II*, pages 206–209. International Supercomputing Institute, Inc., St. Petersburg, FL, 1989.

[DAP:79a] Jesshope, C. R., and Hockney, R. W., editors. *The DAP Approach*, volume 2, pages 311–329. Infotech Intl. Ltd., Maidenhead, 1979. Infotech State of the Art Report: Supercomputers.

[Darema:85a] Darema-Rogers, F., George, D. A., Norton, V. A., and Pfister, G. F. "A VM parallel environment." Technical Report RC11225, IBM Research Report, January 1985.

[Darema:87a] Darema, F. "Applications environment for the IBM research parallel processor prototype, RP3," in C. Polychronoupolos, editor, *ICS 87, International Conference on Supercomputing*. Springer-Verlag, New York, NY, 1987. Published as a Lecture Note in Computer Science.

[Darema:88a] Darema, F., George, D. A., Norton, V. A., and Pfister, G. F. "A single-program-multiple-data model for EPEX/FORTRAN," *Parallel Computing*, 7:11–24, 1988.

[Das:92c] Das, R., Mavriplis, D. J., Saltz, J., Gupta, S., and Ponnusamy, R. "The design and implementation of parallel unstructured Euler solver using software primitives," in *AIAA 30th Aerospace Sciences Meeting*, 1992. Paper AIAA-92-0562.

[David:85a] David, F. "A model of random surfaces with non-trivial critical behavior," *Nucl. Phys. B.*, 257:543–576, 1985.

[David:87a] David, F., Jurkiewicz, J., Krzywicki, A., and Petersson, B. "Critical exponents in a model of dynamically triangulated random surfaces," *Nucl. Phys. B.*, 290:218–230, 1987.

[DeForcrand:85a] DeForcrand, P., Schierholz, G., Scheider, H., and Teper, M. "The string and its tension in SU(3) lattice gauge theory: Towards definitive results," *Phys. Lett. B*, 160:137–143, 1985.

[DeJongh:74a] De Jongh, L. J., and Miedema, A. R. "Experiments on simple magnetic model systems," *Adv. Phys.*, 23:1–88, 1974.

[DeRaedt:84a] De Raedt, H., De Raedt, B., and Lagendijk, A. "Thermodynamics of the two-dimensional spin-1/2 XY model," *Z Phys. B*, 57:209–233, 1984.

[Decyk:88a] Decyk, V. K. "Benchmark timings with particle plasma simulation codes," *Supercomputer*, 27:33, 1988.

[Delves:59a] Delves, L. M. "Tertiary and general-order collisions," *Nuclear Physics*, 9:391, 1959.

[Delves:62a] Delves, L. M. "Three-particle photo-disintegration of the Triton," *Nuclear Physics*, 29:268, 1962.

[Dembart:84a] Dembart, L. Los Angeles Times Article, January 1984. Caltech Report C3P-055.

[Demmel:91a] Demmel, J. "LAPACK: A portable linear algebra library for high-performance computers," *Concurrency: Practice and Experience*, 3(6):655–666, December 1991. Special Issue: Practical Parallel Computing: Status and Prospects. Guest Editors: Paul Messina and Almerico Murli.

[Denker:86a] Denker, J. S., editor. *Neural Networks for Computing*. AIP, New York, NY, 1986. AIP Conference Proceedings 151.

[Denker:87a] Denker, J. S., Schwartz, D., Wittner, B., Solla, S., Howard, R., Jackel, L., and Hopfield, J. "Large automatic learning, rule extraction, and generalization," *Complex Systems*, 1:877–922, 1987.

[Dewar:87a] Dewar, R., and Harris, C. K. "Parallel computation of cluster properties: Application to 2-D percolation," *J. Phys. A*, 20:985–993, 1987.

[Dinar:85a] Dinar, N., and Keller, H. B. "Computations of Taylor vortex flows using multigrid continuation methods." Technical report, California Institute of Technology, Pasadena, CA, October 1985.

[Ding:88a] Ding, H. Q. "Polymer simulation on the hypercube," in G. C. Fox, editor, *The Third Conference on Hypercube Concurrent Computers and Applications, Volume 2*, pages 1044–1050. ACM Press, New York, January 1988. Caltech Report C3P-574.

[Ding:88b] Ding, H. Q. "A performance analysis of the polymer simulation on the hypercube: Mark III vs. FPS T-Series." Technical Report C3P-566, California Institute of Technology, Pasadena, CA, March 1988.

[Ding:88d] Ding, H. Q. "A fast random number generator for hypercube computers." Technical Report C3P-629, California Institute of Technology, Pasadena, CA, May 1988.

[Ding:90b] Ding, H.-Q., Baillie, C. F., and Fox, G. C. "Calculation of the heavy quark potential at large separation on a hypercube parallel computer," *Phys. Rev. D*, 41(9):2912–2916, May 1990. Caltech Report C3P-779b.

[Ding:90c] Ding, H.-Q. "The 600 megaflops performance of the QCD code on the Mark IIIfp hypercube," in D. W. Walker and Q. F. Stout, editors, *The Fifth Distributed Memory Computing Conference, Volume II*, pages 1295–1301. IEEE Computer Society Press, Los Alamitos, CA, 1990. Held April 9–12, Charleston, SC. Caltech Report C3P-799b.

[Ding:90g] Ding, H.-Q., and Makivic, M. "Spin correlations of 2d quantum antiferromagnet at low temperatures and a direct comparison with neutron scattering experiments," *Physics Review Letters*, 64(12):1449–1452, 1990. Caltech Report C3P-844.

[Ding:90h] Ding, H.-Q., and Makivic, M. S. "Kosterlitz-Thouless transition in the two-dimensional quantum XY model," *Physical Review B*, 42(10):6827–6830, October 1990. Caltech Report C3P-851b.

[Ding:90k] Ding, H.-Q., and Makivic, M. S. "Quantum spin calculations on a hypercube parallel supercomputer," in D. W. Walker and Q. F. Stout, editors, *The Fifth Distributed Memory Computing Conference, Volume I*, pages 389–396. IEEE Computer Society Press, Los Alamitos, CA, 1990. Held April 9–12, Charleston, SC. Caltech Report C3P-845b.

[Ding:92a] Ding, H.-Q. "Phase transition and thermodynamics of quantum XY model in two dimensions," *Phys. Rev. B*, 45(1), 1992. In press. Caltech Report C3P-976.

[Dongarra:90a] Dongarra, J. J., Duff, I. S., Sorensen, D. C., and van der Vorst, H. A. *Solving Linear systems on Vector and shared Memory Computers.* SIAM Press, Philadelphia, 1990.

[Doyle:91a] Doyle, J. "Serial, parallel, and neural computers," *Futures*, 23(6):577–593, 1991. (July/August).

[DSL:89a] *The Helios Operating System.* Distribute Software Limited, Bristol, England, 1989.

[Duane:85a] Duane, S. "Stochastic quantization versus the microcanonical ensemble: Getting the best of both worlds," *Nucl. Phys. B*, 257:652–662, 1985.

[Duane:87a] Duane, S., Kennedy, A. D., Pendleton, B. J., and Roweth, D. "Hybrid Monte Carlo," *Phys. Lett. B*, 195:216–220, 1987.

[Duff:77a] Duff, I. S. "MA28—a set of Fortran subroutines for sparse unsymmetric linear equations." Technical Report Technical Report R8730, AERE, HMSO, 1977. London.

[Duff:86a] Duff, I. S., Erisman, A. M., and Reid, J. K. *Direct Methods for Sparse Matrices.* Oxford University Press, Oxford, 1986.

[Duncan:90a] Duncan, R. "A survey of parallel computer architectures," *Computer*, 23(2):5–16, 1990.

[Durbin:87a] Durbin, R., and Wilshaw, D. "An analogue approach to the traveling salesman problem using an elastic net method," *Nature*, 326:689–691, 1987.

[Durbin:89a] Durbin, A., Szeliski, R., and Yuille, A. "An analysis of the elastic net approach to the Travelling Salesman Problem," *Neural Computation*, 1:348–358, 1989.

[Durhuus:84a] Durhuus, B., Frohlich, J., and Jonsson, T. "Critical behavior in a model of planar random surfaces," *Nucl. Phys. B.*, 240:453–480, 1984.

[Ebeling:85a] Ebeling, C. *All the Right Moves: A VLSI Architecture for Chess.* MIT Press, Cambridge, 1985.

[Edelman:92a] Edelman, A., "The first annual large dense linear system survey." preprint available by anonymous ftp from math.berkeley.edu.

[Eichten:80a] Eichten, E., Gottfried, K., Kinoshita, T., Lane, K. D., and Yan, T. M. "Charmonium: Comparison with experiment," *Phys. Rev. D*, 21:203–233, 1980.

[Eiken:92a] von Eiken, T., Culler, D. E., Goldstein, S. C., and Schauser, K. E. "Active messages: A mechanism for integrated communication and computation." Technical Report UCB/CSD 92/#675, UC Berkeley, Computer Science, Berkeley, CA, May 1992. In *Proceedings of the Nineteenth International Symposium on Computer Architecture*.

[Embrechts:89a] Embrechts, H., Roose, D., and Wambacq, P. "Component labeling on a distributed memory multiprocessor," in F. Andre and J. P. Verjus, editors, *Proc. First European Workshop on Hypercube and Distributed Computers*, pages 5–17. North-Holland, Amsterdam, 1989.

[Endoh:88a] Endoh, Y., Yamada, K., Birgeneau, R. J., Gabbe, D. R., Jenssen, H. P., Kastner, M. A., Peters, C. J., Picone, P. J., Thurston, T. R., Tranquada, J. M., Shirane, G., Hidaka, Y., Oda, M., Enomoto, Y., Suzuki, M., and Murakami, T. "Static and dynamic spin correlations in pure and doped La_2CuO_4," *Phys. Rev. B*, 37:7443–7453, 1988.

[Enkelmann:88a] Enkelmann, W. "Investigations of multigrid algorithms for the estimation of optical flow fields in image sequences," *Computer Vision, Graphics and Image Processing*, 43:150–177, 1988.

[Ercal:88a] Ercal, F., Ramanujam, J., and Sadayappan, P. "Task allocation onto a hypercube by recursive mincut bipartitioning," in G. C. Fox, editor, *The Third Conference on Hypercube Concurrent Computers and Applications, Volume 1*, pages 210–221. ACM Press, New York, NY, January 1988.

[Ercal:88b] Ercal, F. *Heuristic Approaches to Task Allocation for Parallel Computing*. PhD thesis, Ohio State University, 1988.

[Espriu:87a] Espriu, D. "Triangulated random surfaces," *Phys. Lett. B*, 194:271–276, 1987.

[Essam:80a] Essam, J. W. "Percolation theory," *Rep. Prog. Phys.*, 43:833–912, 1980.

[Factor:90a] Factor, M. "The process Trellis architecture for real_time monitors," in *Proceedings of the Second ACM SIGPLAN Symposium on Principles and Practice of Parallel Programming (PPOP)*, March 1990. Held in Seattle, Washington.

[Factor:90b] Factor, M., and Gelernter, D. G. "Experience with Trellis architecture." Technical Report YALEU/DCS/RR-818, Yale University, New Haven, CT, August 1990.

[Faigle:92b] Faigle, C. "3D graphics design in MOVIE." Technical Report NPAC/MOVIE/ALPHA/92-4, Northeast Parallel Architetures Center, Syracuse, NY, 1992.

[Faigle:92c] Faigle, C. "3D MOVIE extension status report." Technical Report NPAC/MOVIE/ALPH/92-18, Northeast Parallel Architectures Center, Syracuse, NY, 1992.

[Falgout:92a] Falgout, R. D., Skjellum, A., Smith, S. G., and Still, C. H. "The multicomputer toolbox approach to concurrent BLAS and LACS," in J. Saltz, editor, *Proceedings of Scalable High Performance Computing Conference (SHPCC)*, pages 121–128. IEEE Press, April 1992. LLNL Technical Report UCRL-JC-109775.

[Farell:91a] Farell, B., and Pelli, D. G. "Can we attend to large and small at the same time?." Technical report, Syracuse University, Syracuse, NY, 1991. Institute for Sensory Research Report.

[Farhat:88a] Farhat, C. "A simple and efficient automatic FEM domain decomposer," *Computers and Structures*, 28(5):579–602, 1988.

[Farhat:89b] Farhat, C. "On the mapping of massively parallel processors onto finite element graphs," *Computers and Structures*, 32(2):347–353, 1989.

[FCCSET:94a] "High performance computing and communications: Toward a national information infrastructure." Report of the FCCSET (Federal Coordinating Council for Science, Engineering, and Technology) Committee on Physical, Mathematical, and Engineering Sciences, 1994. Office of Science and Technology Policy.

[Felten:85a] Felten, E., Karlin, S., and Otto, S. "Sorting on a hypercube." Technical Report C3P-244, California Institute of Technology, Pasadena, CA, 1985.

[Felten:85b] Felten, E., Karlin, S., and Otto, S. "The traveling salesman problem on a hypercube, MIMD computer," in *Proceedings of 1985 International Conference on Parallel Processing*, pages 6–10, 1985. St. Charles, IL. Caltech Report C3P-093b.

[Felten:87a] Felten, E., Morison, R., Otto, S., Barish, K., Fätland, R., and Ho, F. "Chess on a hypercube," in M. T. Heath, editor, *Hypercube Multiprocessors*, pages 327–332. SIAM, Philadelphia, 1987. Caltech Report C3P-383.

[Felten:88a] Felten, E. W., and Otto, S. W. "Coherent parallel C," in G. C. Fox, editor, *The Third Conference on Hypercube Concurrent Computers and Applications, Volume 1*, pages 440–450. ACM Press, New York, January 1988. Caltech Report C3P-527.

[Felten:88b] Felten, E. W. "Generalized signals: An interrupt-based communication system for hypercubes," in G. C. Fox, editor, *The Third Conference on Hypercube Concurrent Computers and Applications, Volume 1*, pages 563–568. ACM Press, New York, January 1988. Caltech Report C3P-433b.

[Felten:88c] Felten, E. W. "Best-first branch-and-bound on a hypercube," in G. C. Fox, editor, *The Third Conference on Hypercube Concurrent Computers and Applications, Volume 2*, pages 1500–1504. ACM Press, New York, January 1988. Caltech Report C3P-590.

[Felten:88h] Felten, E. W., and Otto, S. W. "Chess on a hypercube," in *Proceedings of IEEE Symposium on the Design and Application of Parallel Digital Processors*, pages 30–42. IEEE Press, April 1988. Held in Lisbon. Caltech Report C3P-579b.

[Felten:90a] Felten, E., Martin, O., Otto, S., and Hutchinson, J. "Multi-scale training of large backpropagation networks," *Biological Cybernetics*, 62:503–509, 1990. Caltech Report C3P-608b.

[Ferraro:90b] Ferraro, R. D., Liewer, P. C., and Decyk, V. K. "A 2D electrostatic PIC code for the Mark III hypercube," in D. W. Walker and Q. F. Stout, editors, *The Fifth Distributed Memory Computing Conference, Volume I*, pages 440–445. IEEE Computer Society Press, Los Alamitos, CA, 1990. Held April 9–12, Charleston, SC. Caltech Report C3P-905.

[Ferraro:93a] Ferraro, R. D., Liewer, P. C., and Decyk, V. K. "Dynamic load balancing for a 2D concurrent plasma PIC code," *Computational Physics*, 109, 1993. In Press.

[Feynman:65a] Feynman, R. P., and Hibbs, A. R. *Quantum Mechanics and Path Integrals*. McGraw-Hill, New York, 1965.

[FHPCP:89a] "The federal high performance computing program." Executive Office of the President, Office of Science and Technology Policy, September 1989.

[Fiedler:75a] Fiedler, M. "Algebraic connectivity of graphs," *Czechoslovak Mathematics Journal*, 23(19/3):298–307, 1975.

[Fiedler:75b] Fiedler, M. "A property of eigenvectors of non-negative symmetric matrics and its application to graph theory," *Czechoslovak Mathematics Journal*, 25:619–627, 1975.

[Finkel:82a] Finkel, R. A., and Fishburn, J. P. "Parallelism in Alpha-Beta search," *Artificial Intelligence*, 19:89–106, 1982.

[Fischler:92a] Fischler, M. "The ACPMAPS system." Technical Report FERMILAB-TM-1780, Fermilab, Batavia, IL, 1992. Fermilab preprint.

[Fisher:67a] Fisher, M. E. *Physics*, 3:255, 1967.

[Flanigan:92a] Flanigan, M., and Tamayo, P. "A parallel cluster labeling method for Monte Carlo dynamics," *International Journal of Modern Physics C*, 3(6):1235–1249, 1992.

[Floeder:85a] Floeder, K., Fromme, D., Raith, W., Schwab, A., and Sinapius, G. "Total cross section measurements for positron and electron scattering on hydrocarbons between 5 and 400 eV," *J. Phys. B*, 18:3347–3359, 1985.

[Flower:85a] Flower, J. W., and Otto, S. "The field distribution in SU(3) lattice gauge theory," *Phys. Lett. B*, 160:128–132, 1985. Caltech Report C3P-178.

[Flower:86b] Flower, J., and Otto, S. W. "Scaling violations in the heavy quark potential," *Phys. Rev. D*, 34:1649–1650, 1986. CALT-68-1340 DOE Research and Development Report—High Energy Physics calculations on the Hypercube. Caltech Report C3P-262.

[Flower:86c] Flower, J., and Williams, R. "PLOTIX—a graphical system to run CUBIX and UNIX." Technical Report C3P-285, California Institute of Technology, Pasadena, CA, May 1986.

[Flower:87a] Flower, J., Otto, S., and Salama, M. "Optimal mapping of irregular finite element domains to parallel processors." Technical Report C3P-292b, California Institute of Technology, Pasadena, CA, August 1987. In Proceedings, Symposium on Parallel Computations and Their Impact on Mechanics, ASME Winter Meeting, Dec. 14–16, Boston, Mass.

[Flower:87c] Flower, J. "A guide to debugging with NDB." Technical Report C3P-489, California Institute of Technology, Pasadena, CA, December 1987.

[Flower:87e] Flower, J. "Baryons on the lattice," *Nucl. Phys. B*, 289(2):484–504, 1987. Caltech Report C3P-319b.

[Foster:90a] Foster, I., and Taylor, S. *Strand: New Concepts in Parallel Programming.* Prentice Hall, Englewood Cliffs, NJ, 1990.

[Foster:92a] Foster, I. T., and Chandy, K. M. "Fortran M: A language for modular parallel programming." Technical Report MCS-P327-0992, Argonne National Laboratory, Argonne, IL, June 1992. Mathematics and Computer Science Division preprint.

[Fox:82a] Fox, G. C. "Matrix operations on the homogeneous machine." Technical Report C3P-005, California Institute of Technology, Pasadena, CA, July 1982.

[Fox:84a] Fox, G., and Otto, S. "Algorithms for concurrent processors," *Physics Today*, 37(5):50, 1984. Caltech Report C3P-071.

[Fox:84e] Fox, G. C. "Concurrent processing for scientific calculations," in *Proceedings of the IEEE COMPUCON.* IEEE Computer Society Press, February 1984. Conference held in San Francisco. Caltech Report C3P-048.

[Fox:84g] Fox, G. C. "Eigenvalues of symmetric tridiagonal matrices." Technical Report C3P-095, California Institute of Technology, Pasadena, CA, July 1984.

[Fox:84h] Fox, G. C. "Householder's tridiagonalization technique." Technical Report C3P-098, California Institute of Technology, Pasadena, CA, August 1984.

[Fox:84j] Fox, G. C. "Annual report of the Caltech Concurrent Computation Project." Technical Report C3P-100, California Institute of Technology, Pasadena, CA, July 1984.

[Fox:84k] Fox, G. C. "Are concurrent processors general purpose computers?," in *IEEE Transactions of NPSS, Volume 34*. IEEE Computer Society Press, February 1985. Invited talk at IEEE Nuclear Science Symposium held October 31, 1984. Caltech Report C3P-122.

[Fox:85b] Fox, G., Hey, A. J. G., and Otto, S. "Matrix algorithms on the hypercube I: Matrix multiplication," *Parallel Computing*, 4:17–31, 1987. Caltech Report C3P-206.

[Fox:85c] Fox, G. "The performance of the Caltech hypercube in scientific calculations: A preliminary analysis," in F. A. Matsen and T. Tajima, editors, *SuperComputers—Algorithms, Architectures, and Scientific Computation*. University of Texas Press, Austin, 1987. Caltech Report C3P-161.

[Fox:85d] Fox, G. C. "Annual report 1983–1984 and recent documentation." Caltech/JPL Concurrent Computation Project, Collection of Reports C3P-166, California Institute of Technology, Pasadena, CA, 1985. Volume 1 - Tutorial and System Documentation; Volume 2 - Applications.

[Fox:85e] Fox, G. C. "Caltech Concurrent Computation Program: Annual Report 1984–1985." Technical Report C3P-179, California Institute of Technology, Pasadena, CA, July 1985.

[Fox:85h] Fox, G. C., Lyzenga, G., Rogstad, D., and Otto, S. "The Caltech Concurrent Computation Program—project description," in *ASME Conference on International Computers in Engineering*. ASME, August 1985. Caltech Report C3P-157.

[Fox:85i] Fox, G. C., and Otto, S. W. "The Caltech Concurrent Computation Program—a status report," *Computers in Mechanical Engineering*, December 1985. Published by ASME and Springer Verlag in a theme issue on supercomputing in March, 1986. Caltech Report C3P-157b.

[Fox:85k] Fox, G. C., and Jefferson, D. "Concurrent processor load balancing as a statistical physics problems." Technical Report C3P-172, California Institute of Technology, Pasadena, CA, May 1985.

[Fox:86a] Fox, G., and Otto, S. "Concurrent computation and the theory of complex systems," in M. T. Heath, editor, *Hypercube Multiprocessors*, pages 244–268. SIAM, Philadelphia, 1986. Caltech Report C3P-255.

[Fox:86f] Fox, G. "The Caltech Concurrent Computation Program," in M. T. Heath, editor, *Hypercube Multiprocessors*, pages 353–381. SIAM, Philadelphia, 1987. Caltech Report C3P-290b.

[Fox:86h] Fox, G., Kolawa, A., and Williams, R. "The implementation of a dynamic load balancer," in M. T. Heath, editor, *Hypercube Multiprocessors*, pages 114–121. SIAM, Philadelphia, 1987. Caltech Report C3P-328.

[Fox:87b] Fox, G. *Domain Decomposition in Distributed and Shared Memory Environments—I: A Uniform Decomposition and Performance Analysis for the nCUBE and JPL Mark IIIfp Hypercubes*, volume 297 of *Lecture Notes in Computer Science*, pages 1042–1073. Springer-Verlag, New York, 1987. Supercomputing, ed. E. N. Houstis, T. S. Papatheodorou, and C. D. Polychronopoulos. Caltech Report C3P-392.

[Fox:87c] Fox, G. C., and Messina, P. "The Caltech Concurrent Computation Program annual report 1986–1987." Annual Report C3P-487, California Institute of Technology, Pasadena, CA, November 1987.

[Fox:87d] Fox, G. C. "Questions and unexpected answers in concurrent computation," in J. J. Dongarra, editor, *Experimental Parallel Computing Architectures*, pages 97–121. Elsevier Science Publishers B.V., North-Holland, Amsterdam, 1987. Caltech Report C3P-288.

[Fox:88a] Fox, G. C., Johnson, M. A., Lyzenga, G. A., Otto, S. W., Salmon, J. K., and Walker, D. W. *Solving Problems on Concurrent Processors*, volume 1. Prentice-Hall, Inc., Englewood Cliffs, NJ, 1988.

[Fox:88b] Fox, G. C. "What have we learnt from using real parallel machines to solve real problems?," in G. C. Fox, editor, *The Third Conference on Hypercube Concurrent Computers and Applications, Volume 2*, pages 897–955. ACM Press, New York, January 1988. Caltech Report C3P-522.

[Fox:88e] Fox, G. C., and Furmanski, W. "Load balancing loosely synchronous problems with a neural network," in G. C. Fox, editor, *The Third Conference on Hypercube Concurrent Computers and Applications, Volume 1*, pages 241–278. ACM Press, New York, January 1988. Caltech Report C3P-363b.

[Fox:88f] Fox, G. C., and Furmanski, W. "A string theory for time dependent complex systems and its application to automatic decomposition," in G. C. Fox, editor, *The Third Conference on Hypercube Concurrent Computers and Applications, Volume 1*, pages 285–305. ACM Press, New York, January 1988. Caltech Report C3P-521.

[Fox:88g] Fox, G. C., and Furmanski, W. "Hypercube algorithms for neural network simulation the Crystal_Accumulator and the Crystal_Router," in G. C. Fox, editor, *The Third Conference on Hypercube Concurrent Computers and Applications, Volume 1*, pages 714–724. ACM Press, New York, January 1988. Caltech Report C3P-405b.

[Fox:88h] Fox, G. C., and Furmanski, W. "Optimal communication algorithms for regular decompositions on the hypercube," in G. C. Fox, editor, *The Third Conference on Hypercube Concurrent Computers and Applications, Volume 1*, pages 648–713. ACM Press, New York, January 1988. Caltech Report C3P-314b.

[Fox:88ii] Fox, G. C. "Introductory material on parallel computers for a course in computational science." Technical Report C3P-678, California Institute of Technology, Pasadena, CA, November 1988.

[Fox:88kk] Fox, G. C., Furmanski, W., Ho, A., Koller, J., Simic, P., and Wong, Y. F. "Neural networks and dynamic complex systems." Technical Report C3P-695, California Institute of Technology, Pasadena, CA, December 1988. Proceedings of 1989 SCS Eastern Conference, Tampa, Florida, March 28–31, 1989.

[Fox:88mm] Fox, G. C. "A review of automatic load balancing and decomposition methods for the hypercube," in M. Schultz, editor, *Numerical Algorithms for Modern Parallel Computer Architectures*, pages 63–76. Springer-Verlag, New York, 1988. Caltech Report C3P-385b.

[Fox:88nn] Fox, G. C. "A graphical approach to load balancing and sparse matrix vector multiplication on the hypercube," in M. Schultz, editor, *Numerical Algorithms for Modern Parallel Computer Architectures*, pages 37–62. Springer-Verlag, New York, 1988. Caltech Report C3P-327b.

[Fox:88oo] Fox, G. C. "The hypercube and the Caltech Concurrent Computation Program: A microcosm of parallel computing," in B. J. Alder, editor, *Special Purpose Computers*, pages 1–40. Academic Press, Inc., Boston, 1988. Caltech Report C3P-422.

[Fox:88tt] Fox, G. C., and Furmanski, W. "The physical structure of concurrent problems and concurrent computers," *Phil. Trans. R. Soc. Lond. A*, 326:411–444, 1988. Caltech Report C3P-493.

[Fox:88uu] Fox, G. C., and Furmanski, W. "The physical structure of concurrent problems and concurrent computers," in R. J. Elliott and C. A. R. Hoare, editors, *Scientific Applications of Multiprocessors*, pages 55–88. Prentice Hall, Englewood Cliffs, NJ, 1988. Caltech Report C3P-493.

[Fox:88v] Fox, G. C., and Messina, P. "Report for 1988 on the Caltech Concurrent Computation Program." Annual Report C3P-685, California Institute of Technology, Pasadena, CA, December 1988.

[Fox:89cc] Fox, G. C. "Caltech concurrent computation program technical bulletin." Technical Report 20, California Institute of Technology, Pasadena, CA, 1989. Editor: Mary M. Maloney.

[Fox:89dd] Fox, G. C. "Caltech concurrent computation program technical bulletin." Technical Report 21, California Institute of Technology, Pasadena, CA, 1989. Editor: Mary M. Maloney.

[Fox:89i] Fox, G. C. "1989—the first year of the parallel supercomputer," in J. L. Gustafson, editor, *The Proceedings of the Fourth Conference on Hypercubes, Concurrent Computers and Applications*, page 1. Golden Gate Enterprises, Los Altos, CA, March 1989. CRPC-TR890010, CCR-8809615. Caltech Report C3P-769.

[Fox:89l] Fox, G. C., and Koller, J. G. "Code generation by a generalized neural network: General principles and elementary examples," *Journal of Parallel and Distributed Computing*, 6(2):388–410, 1989. Caltech Report C3P-650b.

[Fox:89n] Fox, G. C. "Parallel computing comes of age: Supercomputer level parallel computations at Caltech," *Concurrency: Practice and Experience*, 1(1):63–103, September 1989. Caltech Report C3P-795.

[Fox:89t] Fox, G. C., Hipes, P., and Salmon, J. "Practical parallel supercomputing: Examples from chemistry and physics," in *Proceedings of Supercomputing '89*, pages 58–70. ACM Press, November 1989. IEEE Computer Society and ACM SIGARCH, Reno, Nevada. Caltech Report C3P-818.

[Fox:89y] Fox, G. C. "Parallel computing." Technical Report C3P-830, California Institute of Technology, Pasadena, CA, September 1989. Chapter in *Encyclopedia of Physical Science and Technology 1991 Yearbook*, Academic Press, Inc.

[Fox:90bb] Fox, G., and Goldberg, M. "Development of advanced computer methods for SSC data analysis." Technical Report SCCS-19, Syracuse University, Syracuse, NY, October 1990. Unsuccessful proposal submitted to Texas National Research Laboratory Commission.

[Fox:90e] Fox, G. C., Gurewitz, E., and Wong, Y. "A neural network approach to multi-vehicle navigation," in D. W. Walker and Q. F. Stout, editors, *The Fifth Distributed Memory Computing Conference, Volume I*, pages 148–152. IEEE Computer Society Press, Los Alamitos, CA, 1990. Held April 9–12, Charleston, SC. Caltech Report C3P-910.

[Fox:90k] Fox, G. C. "Applications of the generalized elastic net to navigation." Technical Report C3P-930, California Institute of Technology, Pasadena, CA, June 1990. Unpublished.

[Fox:90nn] Fox, G. C., Furmanski, W., and Koller, J. "The use of neural networks in parallel software systems," in *Intelligent Mathematical Software Systems*, pages 51–61. Elsevier Science Publishers B.V., North-Holland, Amsterdam, 1990. Invited talk given at First International Conference on Expert Systems for Numerical Computing, Purdue University, 1988. Caltech Report C3P-642c.

[Fox:90o] Fox, G. C. "Applications of parallel supercomputers: Scientific results and computer science lessons," in M. A. Arbib and J. A. Robinson, editors, *Natural and Artificial Parallel Computation*, chapter 4, pages 47–90. MIT Press, Cambridge, MA, 1990. SCCS-23. Caltech Report C3P-806b.

[Fox:91e] Fox, G. C., Hiranandani, S., Kennedy, K., Koelbel, C., Kremer, U., Tseng, C.-W., and Wu, M.-Y. "Fortran D language specification." Technical Report SCCS-42c, Syracuse University, Syracuse, NY, April 1991. Rice Center for Research in Parallel Computation; CRPC-TR90079.

[Fox:91f] Fox, G. C. "Achievements and prospects for parallel computing," *Concurrency: Practice and Experience*, 3(6):725–739, December 1991. Special Issue: Practical Parallel Computing: Status and Prospects. Guest Editors: Paul Messina and Almerico Murli. SCCS-29b, C3P-927b, CRPC-TR90083.

[Fox:91j] Fox, G. C. "Physical computation," *Concurrency: Practice and Experience*, 3(6):627–653, December 1991. Special Issue: Practical Parallel Computing: Status and Prospects. Guest Editors: Paul Messina and Almerico Murli. SCCS-2b, C3P-928b, CRPC-TR90090.

[Fox:92b] Fox, G. C. "Parallel supercomputers," in C. H. Chen, editor, *Computer Engineering Handbook*, chapter 17. McGraw-Hill Publishing Company, New York, 1992. Caltech Report C3P-451d.

[Fox:92c] Fox, G. C. "The use of physics concepts in computation," in B. A. Huberman, editor, *Computation: The Micro and the Macro View*, chapter 3. World Scientific Publishing Co. Ltd., 1992. SCCS-237, CRPC-TR92198. Caltech Report C3P-974.

[Fox:92d] Fox, G. C. "Parallel computing and education," *Daedalus Journal of the American Academy of Arts and Sciences*, 121(1):111–118, 1992. CRPC-TR91123, SCCS-83. Caltech Report C3P-958.

[Fox:92e] Fox, G. C. "Parallel computing in industry—an initial survey," in *Proceedings of Fifth Australian Supercomputing Conference (supplement)*, pages 1–10. Communications Services, Melbourne, December 1992. Held at World Congress Centre, Melbourne, Australia. Syracuse University Technical Report SCCS-302b. CRPC-TR92219.

[Fox:92h] Fox, G. C. "Parallel computers and complex systems," in *Complex Systems '92—From Biology to Computation*, December 1992. Syracuse University Technical Report SCCS-370.

[Fox:92i] Fox, G. C. "Approaches to physical optimization," in *Proceedings of 5th SIAM Conference on Parallel Processes for Scientific Computation*, pages 153–162, 1992. SCCS-92, CRPC-TR91124. Caltech Report C3P-959.

[Fox:92j] Fox, G. C., Mohamed, G. A., von Laszewski, G., and Parashar, M. "On the parallelization of blocked LU factorization algorithms for distributed memory architectures," in *Supercomputing '92*, pages 170–179. IEEE Computer Society Press, Inc., Minneapolis, MN, November 1992. CRPC-TR92210.

[Fox:93a] Fox, G. C., and Coddington, P. D. "An overview of high performance computing for the physical sciences," in *Proceedings of Mardi Gras Conference: High Performance Computing and Its Applications in the Physical Sciences*. World Scientific, February 1993. Syracuse University Technical Report SCCS-488.

[Fox:93b] Fox, G., Furmanski, W., and Podgorny, M. "ASAS quarterly report." Technical Report SCCS-423, Syracuse University, Syracuse, NY, February 1993. October–December 1991. WARNING: Internal

[Frederickson:88a] Frederickson, P. O., and McBryan, O. A. "Parallel superconvergent multigrid," in S. McCormick, editor, *Multigrid Methods, Proceedings of the Third Copper Mountain Conference on Multigrid Methods*, pages 195–210. Marcel-Dekker, 1988. held in Copper Mountain, CO, April 6–10, 1987.

[Frederickson:88b] Frederickson, P., and McBryan, O. "Intrinsically parallel multiscale algorithms for hypercubes," in G. C. Fox, editor, *Proceedings of the Third Conference on Hypercube Concurrent Computers and Applications, Volume 2*, pages 1726–1734. ACM Press, New York, NY, 1988.

[Frederickson:89a] Frederickson, P. O. "Totally parallel multilevel algorithms for sparse elliptic systems," in C. John L. Gustafson, Los Altos, editor, *The Proceedings of the Fourth Conference on Hypercubes, Concurrent Computers and Applications*, page 1275, March 1989.

[Frederickson:89b] Frederickson, P. O. "Totally parallel multilevel algorithms," in H. D. Simon, editor, *Proceedings of the Conference on Scientific Applications of the Connection Machine*, page 161. World

Scientific Publishing Co., Ltd., Teaneck, NJ, 1989. Held September 12–14, 1988.

[Frey:83a] Frey, P. W., editor. *Chess Skill in Man and Machine.* Springer-Verlag, New York, NY, 1983.

[Frisch:86a] Frisch, U., Hasslacher, B., and Pomeau, Y. "Lattice-gas automata for the Navier-Stokes equations," *Phys. Rev. Lett.*, 56:1505–1508, 1986.

[Fucito:81a] Fucito, F., Marinari, E., Parisi, G., and Rebbi, C. "A proposal for Monte Carlo simulations of Fermionic systems," *Nucl. Phys. B*, 180([FS2]):369–377, 1981.

[Fucito:84a] Fucito, F., Kinney, R., and Solomon, S. "On the phase diagram of finite temperature QCD in the presence of dynamical quarks," *Nucl. Phys. B.*, 248:615–628, 1984. CALT-68-1189. Caltech Report C3P-333.

[Fucito:85a] Fucito, F., and Solomon, S. "Monte Carlo parallel algorithm for long-range interactions," *Computer Physics Communications*, 34:225–230, 1985. Caltech Report C3P-079b.

[Fucito:85b] Fucito, F., and Solomon, S. "The chiral symmetry restoration transition in the presence of dynamical quarks," *Phys. Rev. Lett.*, 55:2641–2644, 1985. CALT-68-1124. Caltech Report C3P-331.

[Fucito:85c] Fucito, F., and Solomon, S. "Finite temperature QCD in the presence of dynamical quarks," *Nucl. Phys. B.*, 253:727–741, 1985. BNL 34784 CALT-68-1127. Caltech Report C3P-332.

[Fucito:85d] Fucito, F., and Solomon, S. "On the order of the deconfining transition for finite temperature QCD in the presence of dynamical quarks," *Phys. Rev. D*, 31:1460–1464, 1985. CALT-68-1285. Caltech Report C3P-334.

[Fucito:85f] Fucito, F., and Solomon, S. "On the relation between the Coulomb gas and the lattice XY model," *Journal of Physics Letters A*, Gen. 19:L739–1743, 1985. CALT-68-1114 April 10, 1984. Caltech Report C3P-076.

[Fucito:86a] Fucito, F., Moriarty, K. J. M., Rebbi, C., and Solomon, S. "The hadronic spectrum with dynamical Fermions," *Phys. Lett. B*, 172:235–241, May 1986. Caltech Report C3P-341.

[Furmanski:87a] Furmanski, W., Bower, J. M., Nelson, M. E., Wilson, M. A., and Fox, G. "Piriform (Olfactory) cortex model on the hypercube," in G. C. Fox, editor, *The Third Conference on Hypercube Concurrent Computers and Applications, Volume 2*, pages 977–999. ACM Press, New York, January 1988. Caltech Report C3P-404b.

[Furmanski:87c] Furmanski, W., and Kolawa, A. "Yang-Mills vacuum—an attempt of lattice loop calculus," *Nucl. Phys. B*, 291:594–628, 1987. CALT-68-1330. Caltech Report C3P-335.

[Furmanski:88a] Furmanski, W., and Gates, D. "g—a compact language for real-time graphics," in G. C. Fox, editor, *The Third Conference on Hypercube Concurrent Computers and Applications, Volume 1*, pages 749–759. ACM Press, New York, January 1988. Caltech Report C3P-585.

[Furmanski:88b] Furmanski, W., Fox, G. C., and Walker, D. "Optimal matrix algorithms on homogeneous hypercubes," in G. C. Fox, editor, *The Third Conference on Hypercube Concurrent Computers and Applications, Volume 2*, pages 1656–1673. ACM Press, New York, January 1988. Caltech Report C3P-386b.

[Furmanski:88c] Furmanski, W., and Fox, G. C. "Integrated vision project on the computer network," in E. Clementi and S. Chin, editors, *Biological and Artificial Intelligence Systems*, pages 509–527. ESCOM Science Publishers B.V., The Netherlands, 1988. Caltech Report C3P-623.

[Furmanski:89d] Furmanski, W., and Fox, G. C. "MOVIE—a software environment for modeling complex adaptive systems." Technical Report C3P-838, California Institute of Technology, Pasadena, CA, October 1989. Presented at Society of Photo-Optical Instrumentation Engineers Conference, Philadelphia, 1989. Syracuse University Technical Report SCCS-539.

[Furmanski:90b] Furmanski, W. "MOVIE — the system overview." Technical Report SCCS-553, Syracuse University, Syracuse, NY, 1990.

[Furmanski:91g] Furmanski, W. "Report from the virtual reality tour." Technical Report SCCS-205, Syracuse University, Syracuse, NY, September 1991.

[Furmanski:92a] Furmanski, W. "MOVIE server reference manual." Technical Report SCCS-534, Syracuse University, Syracuse, NY, 1992. NPAC/MOVIE/92–1.

[Furmanski:92b] Furmanski, W. "MOVIE server programming manual." Technical Report SCCS-535, Syracuse University, Syracuse, NY, 1992.

[Furmanski:92c] Furmanski, W. "Software development tools for the MOVIE server." Technical Report SCCS-536, Syracuse University, Syracuse, NY, 1992.

[Furmanski:92d] Furmanski, W. "Interface to NeWS in MOVIE." Technical Report SCCS-537, Syracuse University, Syracuse, NY, 1992. NPAC/MOVIE/92–10.

[Furmanski:92e] Furmanski, W. "Interface to OSF/Motif in MOVIE." Technical Report SCCS-538, Syracuse University, Syracuse, NY, 1992. NPAC/MOVIE/92–11.

[Furmanski:92f] Furmanski, W. "Proposed new computing technologies for the GEM experiment at the SSC." Technical Report SCCS-556, Syracuse University, Syracuse, NY, 1992. Internal Technical Report, HEP and NPAC.

[Furmanski:92g] Furmanski, W. "Supercomputing and virtual reality." Technical Report SCCS-394, Syracuse University, Syracuse, NY, September 1992. Talk presented at the Meckler Conference on *Virtual Reality '92*, San Jose, CA.

[Furmanski:93a] Furmanski, W., Faigle, C., Haupt, T., Niemiec, J., Podgorny, M., and D., S. "MOVIE model for open systems based high-performance distributed computing," *Concurrency: Practice and Experience*, 5(4):287–308, June 1993. Special Issue: High Performance Distributed Computing. Guest Editors: Salim Hariri and Anujan Varma. SCCS-300b.

[Furmanski:93b] Furmanski, W. "Software integration towards global computing." Technical Report SCCS-557, Syracuse University, Syracuse, NY, 1993.

[Furmanski:93c] Furmanski, W. "Integrating virtual environments with high performance computing." Technical Report SCCS-412, Syracuse University, Syracuse, NY, January 1993. Paper presented at the 1st IEEE *Virtual Reality Annual International Symposium*, VRAIS '93.

[Furmanski:93d] Furmanski, W., Faigle, C., Fox, G. C., Niemiec, J., and Simoni, D. "System requirements for dynamic load balancing in homogeneous platforms for heterogeneous HPDC: Case study using MOVIE." Technical Report SCCS-554, Syracuse University, Syracuse, NY, 1993.

[Furmanski:93e] Furmanski, W., Faigle, C., Fox, G. C., Niemiec, J., and Simoni, D. "Supercomputing and VR networking," in *Virtual Reality '93*, May 1993. Paper presented at the Meckler Conference. Syracuse University Technical Report SCCS-535.

[Furmanski:93f] Furmanski, W. "Integrating virtual reality with high performance computing using the MOVIE system," in *3rd Virtual Reality Systems '93*, October 1993. Paper to be presented in New York, NY. Syracuse University Technical Report SCCS-412b.

[Gaines:87a] Gaines, I., and Nash, T. "Use of new computer technologies in elementary particle physics," in J. D. Jackson, editor, *Ann. Rev. Nucl. Part. Sci., 37*. Annual Reviews, Inc., Palo Alto, CA, 1987.

[Gandhi:90a] Gandhi, A., and Fox, G. C. "Solving problems in navigation." Technical Report SCCS-9, Syracuse University, Syracuse, NY, 1990. Unpublished.

[Gandhi:90b] Gandhi, A., and Fox, G. C. "Physical optimization for navigation and robot manipulation." Technical Report SCCS-43, Syracuse University, Syracuse, NY, 1990. Unpublished.

[Geist:86a] Geist, G. A., and Heath, M. T. "Matrix factorization on a hypercube multiprocessor," in M. T. Heath, editor, *Hypercube Multiprocessors*, pages 161–180. SIAM, Philadelphia, 1986.

[Geist:89a] Geist, G. A. "Reduction of a general matrix to tridiagonal form using a hypercube multiprocessor," in C. John L. Gustafson, Los Altos, editor, *The Proceedings of the Fourth Conference on Hypercubes, Concurrent Computers and Applications*, pages 665–670, March 1989.

[Geist:90b] Geist, G. A., Heath, M. T., Peyton, B. W., and Worley, P. H. "PICL, a portable instrumented communication library, C reference manual." Technical Report ORNL/TM-11130, Oak Ridge National Laboratory, Oak Ridge, TN, July 1990.

[Geist:92a] Geist, G. A., and Sunderam, V. S. "Network based concurrent computing on the PVM system," *Concurrency: Practice and Experience*, 4(4):293–311, June 1992.

[Geist:92b] Geist, G. A., Heath, M. T., Peyton, B. W., and Worley, P. H. "A users' guide to PICL—a portable instrumented communication library." Technical Report ORNL/TM-11616, Oak Ridge National Laboratory, Oak Ridge, TN, May 1992.

[Gelertner:89a] Gelertner, D. *Multiple Tuple Spaces in Linda*, volume 366 of *Lecture Notes in Computer Science, Proceedings of Parallel Architectures and Languages, Europe, Volume 2*, pages 20–27. Springer-Verlag, Berlin/New York, June 1989.

[Gerasoulis:88a] Gerasoulis, A., Missirlis, N., Nelken, I., and Peskin, R. "Implementing Gauss Jordan on a hypercube multicomputer," in G. C. Fox, editor, *Proceedings of the Third Conference on Hypercube Concurrent Computers and Applications, Volume 2*, pages 1569–1576. ACM Press, New York, NY, 1988.

[Gerndt:90a] Gerndt, M. "Updating distributed variables in local computations," *Concurrency: Practice and Experience*, 2(3):171–194, 1990.

[Gilbert:58a] Gilbert, E. N. "Gray codes and paths on the N-Cube," *Bell System Technical Journal*, 37:815–826, May 1958.

[Gill:81a] Gill, P. E., Murray, W., and Wright, M. H. *Practical Optimization*. Academic Press, Inc., London, 1981.

[Gislen:89a] Gislen, L., Söderberg, C., and Peterson, B. "Teachers and classes with neural nets," *Inter. Jr. of Neural Systems*, 1:167, 1989.

[Gislen:91a] Gislen, L., Söderberg, C., and Peterson, B. "Scheduling high schools with neural nets." Technical Report LU-TP-91-9, Lund University, Lund, Sweden, 1991.

[Glazer:84a] Glaser, F. "Multilevel relaxation in low-level computer vision," in A. Rosenfeld, editor, *Multiresolution Image Processing and Analysis*, pages 312–330. Springer-Verlag, Berlin/New York, 1984.

[Gliozzi:77a] Gliozzi, F., Scherk, J., and Olive, D. "Supersymmetry, supergravity theories and the dual spinor model," *Nucl. Phys. B.*, 122:253–290, 1977.

[Glowinski:84a] Glowinski, R. *Numerical Methods for Nonlinear Variational Problems.* Springer-Verlag, New York, 1984.

[Goldsmith:86a] Goldsmith, J., and Salmon, J. "Static and dynamic database distribution for graphics ray tracing on the hypercube." Technical Report C3P-360, California Institute of Technology, Pasadena, CA, 1986.

[Goldsmith:87a] Goldsmith, J., and Salmon, J. "Automatic creation of object hierarchies for ray tracing," *IEEE Computer Graphics and Animation,* 14:14–20, 1987. Caltech Report C3P-295.

[Goldsmith:88a] Goldsmith, J., and Salmon, J. "A hypercube ray-tracer," in G. C. Fox, editor, *The Third Conference on Hypercube Concurrent Computers and Applications, Volume 2,* pages 1194–1206. ACM Press, New York, January 1988. Caltech Report C3P-592.

[Golub:83a] Golub, G. H., and van Loan, C. F. *Matrix Computations.* Johns Hopkins University Press, Baltimore, MD, 1983.

[Golub:89a] Golub, G. H., and van Loan, C. F. *Matrix Computations.* Johns Hopkins University Press, Baltimore, MD, 1989. 2nd Edition.

[Gorham:88a] Gorham, P. W., Prince, T. A., and Anderson, S. "Hypercube data analysis in astronomy: Optical interferometry and millisecond pulsar searches," in G. C. Fox, editor, *The Third Conference on Hypercube Concurrent Computers and Applications, Volume 2,* pages 957–962. ACM Press, New York, January 1988. Caltech Report C3P-571.

[Gorham:88d] Gorham, P. W. "Computational aspects of bispectral analysis in interferometric imaging," in F. Merkle, editor, *Proceedings of the NOAO-ESO Conference on High Resolution Imaging by Interferometry, Volume 1,* page 191. ESO: Garching, 1988. Caltech Report C3P-637.

[Gorham:89a] Gorham, P. W., Ghez, A. M., Kulkarni, S. R., Nakajima, T., Neugebauer, G., Oke, J. B., and Prince, T. A. "Diffraction limited imaging III: 30 milliarcsecond closure phase imaging of six binary stars with the Hale 5m telescope," *The Astronomical Journal,* 98(5):1783–1799, November 1989. Caltech Report C3P-791.

[Gorman:88a] Gorman, R. P., and Seinowski, T. J. "Analysis of hidden units in a layered network trained to classify sonar targets," *Neural Networks*, 1:75–89, 1988.

[Gosling:89a] Gosling, J., Rosenthal, D. S. H., and Arden, M. *The NeWS Book*. Springer-Verlag, 1989.

[Gottlieb:86a] Gottlieb, A. "An overview of the NYU ultracomputer project," in J. J. Dongarra, editor, *Experimental Parallel Computing Architectures*. North-Holland, Amsterdam, 1987.

[Gottschalk:87f] Gottschalk, T. D. "Multiple track initiation on a hypercube," in *Proceedings of the Second International Conference on Supercomputing*. International Supercomputing Institute Inc., St. Petersburg, FL, May 1987. Caltech Report C3P-398.

[Gottschalk:88a] Gottschalk, T. D. "Concurrent multiple target tracking," in G. C. Fox, editor, *The Third Conference on Hypercube Concurrent Computers and Applications, Volume 2*, pages 1247–1268. ACM Press, New York, January 1988. Caltech Report C3P-567.

[Gottschalk:90a] Gottschalk, T. D. "Concurrent implementation of Munkres algorithm," in D. W. Walker and Q. F. Stout, editors, *The Fifth Distributed Memory Computing Conference, Volume I*, pages 52–57. IEEE Computer Society Press, Los Alamitos, CA, 1990. Held April 9–12, Charleston, SC. Caltech Report C3P-899.

[Gottschalk:90b] Gottschalk, T. D. "Concurrent multi-target tracking," in D. W. Walker and Q. F. Stout, editors, *The Fifth Distributed Memory Computing Conference, Volume I*, pages 85–88. IEEE Computer Society Press, Los Alamitos, CA, 1990. Held April 9–12, Charleston, SC. Caltech Report C3P-908.

[Green:84a] Green, M. B., and Schwarz, J. H. "Anomaly cancellations in supersymmetric d=10 gauge theory and superstring theory," *Phys. Lett. B*, 149:117–122, 1984.

[Greengard:87b] Greengard, L., and Rokhlin, V. "A fast algorithm for particle simulations," *Journal of Computational Physics*, 73:325–348, 1987. Yale University Computer Science Research Report YALEU/DCS/RR-459.

[Greengard:91a] Greengard, L., 1991. Private communication.

[Grimshaw:93b] Grimshaw, A. S. "Easy to use object-oriented parallel programming with Mentat," *IEEE Computer*, May 1993. To appear.

[Groom:88a] Groom, S. L., Lee, M., Mazer, A. S., and Williams, W. I. "Design and implementation of a concurrent image processing workstation based on the Mark III hypercube," in G. C. Fox, editor, *The Third Conference on Hypercube Concurrent Computers and Applications, Volume 2*, pages 1320–1321. ACM Press, New York, January 1988. Caltech Report C3P-599.

[Gross:85a] Gross, D., Harvey, J., Martinec, E., and Rohm, R. "Heterotic string theory," *Nucl. Phys. B.*, 256:253–284, 1985.

[Grossberg:88a] Grossberg, S. "Nonlinear neural networks: Principles, mechanisms, and architectures," *Neural Networks*, 1:17–61, 1988.

[Guagnelli:92a] Guagnelli, M., Marinari, E., and Parisi, G. "Mean field solutions of the random Ising models." Technical Report SCCS-329, Syracuse University, Syracuse, NY, July 1992.

[Gullichsen:87a] Gullichsen, E., and Chang, E. "Pattern classification by neural network: An experimental system for icon recognition," in M. Caudill and C. Butler, editors, *International Conference on Neural Networks (IEEE), Volume IV*, pages 725–732. IEEE Publishers, 1987.

[Gupta:88a] Gupta, R., DeLapp, J., Batrouni, G., Fox, G. C., Baillie, C., and Apostolakis, J. "The phase transition in the 2-d XY model," *Phys. Rev. Lett.*, 61:1996–1999, 1988. Caltech Report C3P-643.

[Gupta:93a] Gupta, R. "Calculations of hadronic matrix elements using lattice QCD," in *Proceedings of Mardi Gras Conference: High Performance Computing and Its Applications in the Physical Sciences*. World Scientific, 1993.

[Gurnis:88a] Gurnis, M., Raefsky, A., Lyzenga, G. A., and Hager, B. H. "Finite element solution of thermal convection on a hypercube concurrent computer," in G. C. Fox, editor, *The Third Conference on Hypercube Concurrent Computers and Applications, Volume 2*, pages 1176–1179. ACM Press, New York, January 1988. Caltech Report C3P-595.

[Gustafson:88a] Gustafson, J. L., Montry, G. R., and Benner, R. E. "Development of parallel methods for a 1024-processor hypercube," *SIAM J. Sci. Stat. Comput.*, 9(4):609–638, July 1988.

[Gutt:89a] Gutt, G. M. *The Physics of Granular Systems.* PhD thesis, California Institute of Technology, May 1989. Caltech Report C3P-785.

[Hackbusch:82a] Hackbusch, W., and Trottenberg, U., editors. *Multigrid Methods.* Springer-Verlag, New York, 1982.

[Hackbusch:85a] Hackbusch, W. "Multi-grid methods and applications," in *Springer Series in Computational Mathematics.* Springer-Verlag, Berlin, 1985.

[Haff:83a] Haff, P. K. "Grain flow as a fluid-mechanical phenomena," *Journal of Fluid Mechanics*, 134:401–430, 1983.

[Haff:87a] Haff, P. K. "Micromechanical aspects of pressure waves in granular materials," in *Proceedings of Solids Transport Contractor's Review*, pages 46–67. Department of Energy, September 1987. To appear in *Particle Technology Review* (in press), Hemisphere Publishing Co., Washington, D.C., J. K. Beddow, Editor.

[Haff:87b] Haff, P. K., and Werner, B. T. "Collisional interaction of a small number of confined inelastic grains," in T. Ariman and T. N. Veziroglu, editors, *Colloidal and Interfacial Phenomena, 3*, pages 483–501. Hemisphere Publishing Co., Washington, D. C., 1987.

[Hajek:88a] Hajek, B. "Cooling schedules for optimal annealing," *Mathematics of Operational Research*, 13:311–329, 1988.

[Halperin:78a] Halperin, B. I., and Nelson, D. R. "Theory of two-dimensional melting," *Phys. Rev. Lett.*, 41:121–124, 1978.

[Hamel:92a] Hamel, L. H., Hatcher, P. J., and Quinn, M. J. "An optimizing C* compiler for a hypercube multicomputer," in J. Saltz and P. Mehrotra, editors, *Languages, Compilers and Run-Time Environments for Distributed Memory Machines*, pages 285–298. Elsevier Science Publishers, North-Holland, Amsterdam, 1992. Advances in Parallel Computing Series, Volume 3.

[Hammond:92b] Hammond, S. W. *Mapping Unstructured Grid Computations to Massively Parallel Computers.* PhD thesis, Rensselaer Polytechnic Institute, February 1992.

[Hanson:90a] Hanson, F. B., and Sorensen, D. C. "The SCHEDULE parallel programming package with recycling job queues and iterated dependency graphs," *Concurrency: Practice and Experience*, 2(1):33–53, March 1990.

[Harstad:87a] Harstad, K. "Performance of vortex flow simulation on the hypercube." Technical Report C3P-500, California Institute of Technology, Pasadena, CA, October 1987.

[Hart:93a] Hart, L., Henderson, T., and Rodriguez, B. "GP5: a software layer for portable parallel program development." Technical Report ERL FSL-7, NOAA Forecast Systems Laboratory, Boulder, CO, July 1993.

[Hatcher:91a] Hatcher, P. J., and Quinn, M. J. *Data-Parallel Programming on MIMD Computers.* MIT Press, Cambridge, Massachusetts, 1991.

[Hatcher:91b] Hatcher, P., Lapadula, A., Jones, R., Quinn, M., and Anderson, R. "A production-quality C* compiler for hypercube multicomputers," in *Third ACM SIGPLAN Symposium on PPOPP*, volume 26, pages 73–82, July 1991.

[Haupt:92a] Haupt, T. "Visualization of high energy physics data using AVS." Technical Report SCCS-243, Syracuse University, Syracuse, NY, February 1992.

[Hayes:89a] Hayes, J. P., and Mudge, T. "Hypercube supercomputers," *Proceedings of the IEEE*, 77(12):1829–1841, 1989.

[Heermann:90a] Heermann, D. W., and Burkitt, A. N. "System size dependence of the autocorrelation time for the Swendsen-Wang Ising Model," *Physica A*, 162:210–214, 1990.

[Heiligenberg:75a] Heiligenberg, W. "Theoretical and experimental approaches to spatial aspects of electrolocation," *J. Comp. Physiol.*, 103:66–72, 1975.

[Hempel:91a] Hempel, R. *The ANL/GMD Macros (PARMACS) in Fortran for Portable Parallel Programming using the Message Passing Programming Model*. November 1991. User's Guide and Reference Manual, Version 5.1.

[Hennessy:91a] Hennessy, J. J., and Jouppi, N. P. "Computer technology and architectures: An evolving interaction," *IEEE Computer*, pages 18–29, 1991.

[Hennessy:93a] Hennessy, J. "Scalable multiprocessors and the Dash approach," *Computer*, 26:134, January 1993.

[Hernquist:87a] Hernquist, L. "Performance characteristics of tree codes," *Astrophysical Journal (Suppl.)*, 64(4):715–734, 1987.

[Hertz:92a] Hertz, A. "Finding a feasible course schedule using Tabu search," *Discrete Applied Mathematics*, 35:255–270, 1992.

[Hey:88a] Hey, A. J. G. "Practical parallel processing with transputers," in G. C. Fox, editor, *Proceedings of the Third Conference on Hypercube Concurrent Computers and Applications, Volume 1*, pages 115–121. ACM Press, New York, NY, 1988.

[Higgins:88a] Higgins, S., and Cowley, R. A. "The phase transition of a disordered antiferromagnet with competing interactions," *J. Phys. C*, 21:2215–2232, 1988.

[Hillis:85a] Hillis, W. D. *The Connection Machine*. MIT Press, Cambridge, MA, 1985.

[Hillis:86a] Hillis, D., and Steele, G. "Data parallel algorithms," *Comm. ACM*, 29:1170, 1986.

[Hillis:87a] Hillis, W. D. "The Connection Machine," *Scientific American*, 256:108–115, June 1987.

[Hillis:87b] Hillis, D., and Barnes, J. "Programming a highly parallel computer," *Nature*, 326:27, 1987.

[Hinton:92a] Hinton, G. E., Williams, C. K. I., and Revow, M. D. "Adaptive elastic models for hand-printed character recognition," in *NIPS-92*, January 1992. preprint.

[Hipes:87a] Hipes, P., and Kuppermann, A. "Lifetime analysis of high energy resonances in three-dimensional reactive scattering," *Chem. Phys. Letters*, 133(1):1–7, 1987. Caltech Report C3P-382.

[Hipes:88a] Hipes, P. G., and Kuppermann, A. "Gauss-Jordan inversion with pivoting on the Caltech Mark II hypercube," in G. C. Fox, editor, *The Third Conference on Hypercube Concurrent Computers and Applications, Volume 2*, pages 1621–1634. ACM Press, New York, January 1988. Caltech Report C3P-578.

[Hipes:88b] Hipes, P., Mattson, T., Wu, M., and Kuppermann, A. "Chemical reaction dynamics: Integration of coupled sets of ordinary differential equations on the Caltech hypercube," in G. C. Fox, editor, *The Third Conference on Hypercube Concurrent Computers and Applications, Volume 2*, pages 1051–1061. ACM Press, New York, January 1988. Caltech Report C3P-570.

[Hipes:89b] Hipes, P. G. "Matrix multiplication on the JPL/Caltech Mark IIIfp Hypercube—preliminary draft." Technical Report C3P-746, California Institute of Technology, Pasadena, CA, March 1989.

[Hipes:89d] Hipes, P. G. "Comparison of LU and Gauss-Jordan system solvers for distributed memory multicomputers." Technical Report C3P-652c, California Institute of Technology, Pasadena, CA, September 1989.

[Hipes:90a] Hipes, P., Winstead, C., Lima, M., and McKoy, V. "Studies of electron-molecule collisions on the Mark IIIfp hypercube," in D. W. Walker and Q. F. Stout, editors, *The Fifth Distributed Memory Computing Conference, Volume I*, pages 498–503. IEEE Computer Society Press, Los Alamitos, CA, 1990. Held April 9–12, Charleston, SC. Caltech Report C3P-909.

[Hiranandani:91a] Hiranandani, S., Kennedy, K., and Tseng, C.-W. "Compiler optimization for Fortran D on MIMD distributed-memory machines," in *Proc. Supercomputing '91*, November 1991.

[Hiranandani:91b] Hiranandani, S., Kennedy, K., and Tseng, C.-W. "Compiler support for machine-independent parallel programming in Fortran D," *Compiler and Runtime Software for Scalable Multiprocessors*, 1991.

[Ho:88c] Ho, A., and Furmanski, W. "Pattern recognition by neural network model on hypercubes," in G. C. Fox, editor, *The Third Conference on Hypercube Concurrent Computers and Applications, Volume 2*, pages 1011–1021. ACM Press, New York, January 1988. Caltech Report C3P-528.

[Ho:89b] Ho, A., Fox, G. C., Snyder, S., Chu, D., and Mylner, T. "Three-dimensional asteroids using parallel graphics on nCUBE: A testbed for evaluating controller algorithms," in J. L. Gustafson, editor, *The Proceedings of the Fourth Conference on Hypercubes, Concurrent Computers and Applications*, page 1177. Golden Gate Enterprises, Los Altos, CA, March 1989. Caltech Report C3P-681b.

[Ho:90b] Ho, A. W., and Fox, G. C. "Portable asteroids on hypercube or transputers," in D. W. Walker and Q. F. Stout, editors, *The Fifth Distributed Memory Computing Conference, Volume I*, pages 111–116. IEEE Computer Society Press, Los Alamitos, CA, 1990. Held April 9–12, Charleston, SC. Caltech Report C3P-880.

[Hoare:62a] Hoare, C. A. R. "Quicksort," *Computer J.*, 5:10, October 1962.

[Hoare:78a] Hoare, C. A. R. "Communicating sequential processes," *Communications of the ACM*, 21(8):666–677, August 1978.

[Hockney:81a] Hockney, R. W., and Eastwood, J. W. *Computer Simulation Using Particles*, chapter 8. McGraw-Hill, New York, 1981.

[Hockney:81b] Hockney, R. W., and Jesshope, C. R. *Parallel Computers*. Adam Hilger, Ltd., Bristol, Great Britain, 1981.

[Holmes:86a] Holmes, D. G., and Lamson, S. H. "Adaptive triangular meshes for compressible flow solutions," in J. Hauser and C. Taylor, editors, *Proceedings of the International Conference on Numerical Grid Generation, Landshut*, pages 413–423. Pineridge Press, Swansea, UK, 1986.

[Hood:86a] Hood, D., and Kuppermann, A. "Hyperspherical coordinate formulation of the electron-hydrogen atom scattering problems," in D. C. Clary, editor, *Theory of Chemical Reaction Dynamics*, pages 193–214. D. Reidel, Boston, 1986. Chemistry formalism related to work in C3P-94b. Caltech Report C3P-189.

[Hopfield:82a] Hopfield, J. J. "Neural networks and physical systems with emergent collective computational abilities," *Proc. Natl. Acad. Sci. USA*, 79:2554–2558, 1982.

[Hopfield:85b] Hopfield, J., and Tank, D. ""Neural" computation of decisions in optimization problems," *Biol. Cybern.*, 52:141–152, 1985.

[Hopfield:86a] Hopfield, J. J., and Tank, D. W. "Computing with neural circuits: a model," *Science*, 233:625, 1986.

[Hord:90a] Hord, R. M. *Parallel Supercomptuing in SIMD Architectures*. CRC Press, Boca Raton, Ann Arbor, Boston, 1990.

[Horn:81a] Horn, B. K. P., and Schunck, G. "Determining optical flow," *Artificial Intelligence*, 17:185–203, 1981.

[Horn:85a] Horn, B. K. P., and Brooks, M. J. "The variational approach to shape from shading," *MIT A. T. Memo*, 813, 1985.

[Horowitz:78a] Horowitz, E., and sahni, S. *Fundamentals of Computer Algorithms*. Computer Science Press, Rockville, MD, 1978.

[Houstis:90a] Houstis, E. N., Rice, J. R., Chrisochoides, N. P., Karathonases, H. C., Papachiou, P. N., Samartzis, M. K., Vavalis, E. A., Wang, K. Y., and Weerawarana, S. "ELLPACK: A numerical simulation programming environment for parallel MIMD machines," in *International Conference on Supercomputing*, pages 96–107. ACM Press, New York, NY, June 1990. Held in Amsterdam, The Netherlands.

[Hsu:90a] Hsu, F., Anantharaman, T., Campbell, M., and Nowatzyk, A. "A grandmaster chess machine," *Scientific American*, 263(4):44–50, October 1990.

[Hui:84a] Hui, K., Haff, P. K., Ungar, J. E., and Jackson, R. "Boundary conditions for high shear rate grain flows," *Journal of Fluid Mechanics*, 145:223–233, 1984.

[Huo:87a] Huo, W. M., Lima, M. A. P., Gibson, T. L., and McKoy, V. "Schwinger multichannel study of the $^2\Pi_g$ shape resonance in N_2," *Phys. Rev. A*, 36:1632–1641, 1987.

[Huo:87b] Huo, W. M., Gibson, T. L., Lima, M. A. P., and McKoy, V. "Correlation effects in elastic e-N_2 scattering," *Phys. Rev. A*, 36:1642–1648, 1987.

[Hwang:89a] Hwang, K., and DeGroot, D., editors. *Parallel Processing for Supercomputers and Artificial Intelligence*. Supercomputing and Parallel Processing. McGraw-Hill Publishing Company, New York, 1989.

[IEEE:91a] *Proceedings of SuperComputing '91*, Los Alamitos, California, 1991. IEEE Computer Society Press.

[Ikudome:90a] Ikudome, K., Fox, G. C., Kolawa, A., and Flower, J. W. "An automatic and symbolic parallelization system for a distributed memory parallel computer," in D. W. Walker and Q. F. Stout, editors, *The Fifth Distributed Memory Computing Conference, Volume II*, pages 1105–1114. IEEE Computer Society Press, Los Alamitos, CA, 1990. Held April 9–12, Charleston, South Carolina. Caltech Report C3P-877.

[Ipsen:87a] Ipsen, I. C. F., and Jessup, E. R. "Solving the symmetric tridiagonal Eigenvalue problem on the hypercube." Technical Report YALEU/DCS/RB-548, Yale University, New Haven, CT, 1987. Yale Internal Report.

[Ipsen:87b] Ipsen, I. C. F., and Jessup, E. R. "Two methods for solving the symmetric tridiagonal eigenvalue problem on the hypercube," in M. T. Heath, editor, *Hypercube Multiprocessors*, pages 627–638. SIAM, Philadelphia, 1987.

[Ipsen:87c] Ipsen, I. C. F., and Jessup, E. R. "Solving the symmetric tridiagonal Eigenvalue problem on the hypercube," in M. T. Heath, editor, *Proceedings of the Second Conference on Hypercube Multiprocessors*, pages 627–638, 1987. Held in Knoxville, Tennessee.

[Ising:25a] Ising, E. *Z. Phys.*, 31:253, 1925.

[Iwasaki:91a] Iwasaki, Y., et al. "QCDPAX: present status and first physical results," *Nucl. Phys. B (Proc. Suppl.)*, 20:141–144, 1991. Proc. of the 1990 Symposium on Lattice Field Theory.

[Jaeger:93a] Jaeger, D. *Computation and Neural Systems*, chapter 52. Kluwer, 1993. F. Eeckman and J. Bower (eds). CNS '92 Conference held from July 26–31, 1992 in San Francisco.

[Jameson:86a] Jameson, A., and Baker, T. J. *Euler Calculations for a Complete Aircraft*, volume 264 of *Lecture Notes in Physics*, pages 334–344.

Springer-Verlag, Berlin/New York, 1986. 10th International Conference on Numerical Methods in Fluid Mechanics, ed. F. G. Zhang and Y. L. Zhu.

[Jameson:86b] Jameson, A., Baker, T. J., and Weatherill, N. P. "Calculation of inviscid transonic flow over a complete aircraft." Technical Report AIAA Paper 86-0103, American Institute of Aeronautics and Astronautics, 1986.

[Jameson:87a] Jameson, A., and Baker, T. J. "Improvements to the Aircraft Euler Method." Technical Report AIAA Paper 87-0452, American Institute of Aeronautics and Astronautics, 1987.

[Jameson:87b] Jameson, A. "Successes and challenges in computational aerodynamics." Technical Report AIAA Paper 87-1184, American Institute of Aeronautics and Astronautics, 1987.

[Jefferson:85c] Jefferson, D. "Virtual time," *ACM Transactions on Programming Languages and Systems*, 7(3):404–425, July 1985.

[Jefferson:87a] Jefferson, D., Beckman, B., Wieland, F., Blume, L., Di Loreto, M., Hontalas, P., LaRouche, P., Sturdevant, K., Tupman, J., Warren, V., Wedel, J., Younger, H., and Bellenot, S. "Distributed simulation and the time warp operating system," in *Proceedings of the 11th Annual ACM Symposium on Operating System Principles*, pages 77–93. ACM Press, New York, NY, November 1987.

[Jenkins:83a] Jenkins, J. T., and Savage, S. B. "A theory for the rapid flow of identical, smooth, nearly inelastic, spherical particles," *Journal of Fluid Mechanics*, 130:187–202, 1983.

[Jernighan:89a] Jernighan, J. G., and Porter, D. H. "A tree code with logarithmic reduction of force terms, hierarchical regularization of all variables and explicit accuracy controls," *Astrophysical Journal (Suppl.)*, 71(4):871–893, 1989.

[Johnson:73a] Johnson, B. R. "The multi-channel log-derivative method for scattering calculations," *Journal of Computational Physics*, 13:445, 1973.

[Johnson:77a] Johnson, B. R. "New numerical methods applied to solving the one-dimensional Eigenvalue problem," *J. Chem. Phys.*, 67:4086–4093, 1977.

[Johnson:79a] Johnson, B. R. "The log derivative and renormalized Numerov algorithms." Technical Report LBL 9501, Lawrence Berkeley Laboratory, Berkeley, CA, 1979. Presented at the NNCC Workshop.

[Johnson:85a] Johnson, M. A. "The interrupt-driven communication system." Technical Report C3P-137, California Institute of Technology, Pasadena, CA, 1985. Unpublished.

[Johnson:86a] Johnson, M. A. *Concurrent Computation and its Application to the Study of Melting in Two Dimensions.* PhD thesis, California Institute of Technology, 1986. Caltech Report C3P-268.

[Johnson:86b] Johnson, M. A. "Melting in two dimensions." Technical Report C3P-297.10, California Institute of Technology, Pasadena, CA, 1986. Support material for Second Hypercube class.

[Johnson:86c] Johnson, M. A. "The specification of CrOS III." Technical Report C3P-253, California Institute of Technology, Pasadena, CA, February 1986.

[Johnson:87a] Johnson, P. C., and Jackson, R. "Frictional-collisional constitutive relations for granular materials, with application to plane shearing," *Journal of Fluid Mechanics*, 176:67–93, 1987.

[Johnson:90b] Johnson, D. S. "Local optimization and the traveling salesman problem," in *Proceedings of the 17th Colloquium on Automata, Languages, and Programming.* Springer-Verlag, 1990.

[Johnson:91a] Johnson, D. S., Aragon, C. R., McGeoch, L. A., and Schevon, C., "Optimization by simulated annealing: An experimental evaluation, Part III (the traveling salesman problem)," 1991. Bell Laboratory Technical Report (unpublished).

[Johnsson:87b] Johnsson, S. L., Saad, Y., and Schultz, M. H. "Alternating direct methods on multiprocessors," *SIAM J. Sci. Stat. Comput.*, 8:686–700, 1987.

[Johnsson:89a] Johnsson, S. L., and Ho, C. "Multiplication of arbitrarily shaped matrices on Boolean cubes using the full communications bandwidth." Technical Report Yale Research Report YALEU/DCS/TR-721, Yale University, New Haven, CT, July 1989.

[Johnston:92a] Johnston, M. D., and Adorf, H.-M., "Scheduling with neural networks—the case of Hubble Space Telescope." Accepted by: *J. Computers and Operations Research*, "Neural Networks" Special Issue.

[JTIS:88a] Japan Technical Information Service, Metals Park, Ohio. *Plasma Reactions and Their Applications*, 1988.

[Jurkiewicz:86a] Jurkiewicz, J., Krzywicki, A., and Petersson, B. "A numerical study of discrete euclidean polyakov surfaces," *Phys. Lett. B*, 168:273–278, 1986.

[Jurkiewicz:86b] Jurkiewicz, J., Krzywicki, A., and Petersson, B. "A grand-canonical ensemble of randomly triangulated surfaces," *Phys. Lett. B*, 177:89–92, 1986.

[Karplus:87a] Karplus, W. J., editor. *The BBN Advanced Computer Butterfly Parallel Processor: A MIMD Computer for Simulation of Complex Systems*, volume 18/2. The Society for Computer Simulation, San Diego, 1987. Proceedings of the Third Conference on Multiprocessors and Array Processors, Simulation Series.

[Katzenelson:89a] Katzenelson, J. "Computational structure of the N-Body problem," *SIAM J. Sci. Stat. Comput.*, 10(4):787–815, July 1989.

[Kazakov:85a] Kazakov, V. A., Kostov, I. K., and Migdal, A. A. "Critical properties of randomly triangulated planar random surfaces," *Phys. Lett. B*, 157:295–300, 1985.

[Kennedy:93a] High Performance Fortran Forum, K. Kennedy, chair. "High performance Fortran language specifications." Technical Report CRPC-TR92225, Center for Research in Parallel Computing, Houston, TX, May 1993. Version 1.0. To appear in *Scientific Programming*, Volume 2, Number 1, July 1993.

[Keppenne:89a] Keppenne, C. L. *Bifurcations, Strange Attractors and Low-Frequency Atmospheric Dynamics*. PhD thesis, Universite Catholique de Louvain, 1989.

[Keppenne:90a] L., K. G., Ghil, M., Fox, G. C., Flower, J. W., Kolawa, A., Papaccio, P. N., Rosati, J. J., Shepanski, J. F., Spadaro, F. G., and Dickey, J. O. "Parallel processing applied to climate modeling." Technical Report SCCS-22, Syracuse University, Syracuse, NY, November 1990.

[Keppenne:90b] L., K. G., Ghil, M., Fox, G. C., Flower, J. W., Kolawa, A., Papaccio, P. N., Rosati, J. J., Shepanski, J. F., Spadaro, F. G., and Dickey, J. O. "Parallel processing applied to climate modeling," *TRW Quest Magazine*, 13(2):54–64, 1990/1991.

[Kilpatrick:76a] Kilpatrick, P. J. *The Use of a Kinematic Supplement in an Interactive Graphics System*. PhD thesis, University of North Carolina, 1976.

[Kirkpatrick:83a] Kirkpatrick, S., Gelatt, C. D., and Vecchi, M. P. "Optimization by simulated annealing," *Science*, 220(4598):671–680, May 1983.

[Kleinert:86a] Kleinert, H. "The membrane properties of condensing strings," *Phys. Lett. B*, 174:335–338, 1986.

[Knuth:68a] Knuth, D. E. "Fundamental algorithms," in *The Art of Computer Programming, Vol. 1*. Addison-Wesley, Reading, MA, 1968.

[Knuth:73a] Knuth, D. E. *Sorting and Searching, The Art of Computer Programming*, volume 3. Addison-Wesley, Reading, MA, 1973.

[Knuth:75a] Knuth, D. E., and Moore, R. W. "An analysis of Alpha-Beta pruning," *Artificial Intelligence*, 6:293–326, 1975.

[Koch:92a] Koch, C., and Bower, J. M. "Experimentalists and modelers: Can we all just get along?," *Trends Neurosci.*, 15:458–461, 1992.

[Kochanek:88a] Kochanek, C. S., and Apostolakis, J. "The two screen gravitational lens," *Mon. Not. R. astr. Soc.*, 235:1073–1109, 1988. Caltech Report C3P-644.

[Koelbel:87a] Koelbel, C., Mehrotra, P., and Van Rosendale, J. "Semi-automatic process partitioning for parallel computation," *International Journal of Parallel Computing*, 16(5):365–382, 1987.

[Koelbel:90a] Koelbel, C., Mehrotra, P., and Rosendale, J. V. "Supporting shared data structures on distributed memory machines," in *Proceedings of the ACM Conference on Principles and Practice of Parallel Programming (PPoPP)*, pages 177–186. ACM Press, New York, NY, March 1990. Held in Seattle, Washington.

[Kohonen:84a] Kohonen, T. *Self Organization and Associative Memory.* Springer-Verlag, Berlin, 1984.

[Kolawa:86b] Kolawa, A. *Semianalytical Calculation of the O^{++} Glueball Mass in SU(2) Gauge Theory.* PhD thesis, California Institute of Technology, March 1986. Caltech Report C3P-267.

[Kolawa:86d] Kolawa, A., and Zimmerman, B. "CrOS III Manual." Technical Report C3P-253b, California Institute of Technology, Pasadena, CA, September 1986.

[Kolawa:88a] Kolawa, A., and Fox, G. C. "Use of the hypercube for symbolic quantum chromodynamics," in G. C. Fox, editor, *The Third Conference on Hypercube Concurrent Computers and Applications, Volume 2*, pages 1408–1419. ACM Press, New York, January 1988. Caltech Report C3P-182c.

[Koller:88b] Koller, J. *The MOOS II Manual.* California Institute of Technology, 1988. Caltech Report C3P-662.

[Koller:88c] Koller, J. "Neural compiler talk." Technical Report C3P-663, California Institute of Technology, Pasadena, August 1988. foils.

[Koller:89b] Koller, J., Fox, G. C., Furmanski, W., and Simic, P. "Physical optimization and load balancing algorithms," in J. L. Gustafson, editor, *The Proceedings of the Fourth Conference on Hypercubes, Concurrent Computers, and Applications*, pages 591–598. Golden Gate Enterprises, Los Altos, CA, March 1989. Caltech Report C3P-731.

[Kosterlitz:73a] Kosterlitz, J. M., and Thouless, D. J. "Ordering, metastability and phase transitions in two-dimensional systems," *J. Phys. C*, 6:1181–1199, 1973.

[Krucken:91a] Krücken, T. C., Liewer, P. C., Ferraro, R. D., and Decyk, V. K. "A 2D electromagnetic PIC code for distributed memory parallel computers," in *Proceedings of the Sixth Distributed Memory Computing Conference*, page 451. IEEE Computer Society Press, Los Alamitos, CA, 1991. CRPC-91-5.

[Krueger:91a] Krueger, M. W. *Artificial Reality II.* Addison-Wesley, 1991.

[Kuck:86a] Kuck, D. J., Davidson, E. S., Lawrie, D. H., and Sameh, A. H. "Parallel supercomputing today and the cedar approach," *Science*, 231:967, 1986.

[Kuhn:55a] Kuhn, H. W. "The Hungarian method for the assignment problem," *Naval Research Logistics Quarterly*, 2:83, 1955.

[Kunz:81a] Kunz, P. "Use of emulating processors in high energy physics," *Physical Science*, 23:492, 1981.

[Kuppermann:75a] Kuppermann, A. "A useful mapping of the triatomic potential energy surface," *Chem. Phys. Letters*, 32:374–375, 1975.

[Kuppermann:86a] Kuppermann, A., and Hipes, P. G. "Three-dimensional quantum mechanical reactive scattering using symmetrized hyperspherical coordinates," *J. Chem. Phys.*, 84(10):5962–5964, 1986. Caltech Report C3P-343.

[Kuru:81a] Kuru, S. *Dynamic Simulation with an Equation Based Flowsheeting System*. PhD thesis, Carnegie Mellon University, 1981. Chemical Engineering Department.

[Kushner:91a] Kushner, M. J., and Graves, D. B. "Special issue on modeling collisional low-temperature plasmas," *IEEE Transactions on Plasma Science*, 19(2):63–64, 1991.

[Laksh:85a] Lakshmivarahan, S., editor. *Proceedings of the Workshop on Parallel Processing using the Heterogeneous Element Processor*. The University of Oklahoma, Norman, OK, 1985.

[Laksh:90a] Lakshmivarahan, S., and Dhall, S. K. *Analysis and Design of Parallel Algorithms: Arithmetic and Matrix Problems*. McGraw-Hill Publishing Company, 1990.

[Landau:76a] Landau, D. P. "Finite-size behavior of the Ising square lattice," *Phys. Rev. B*, 13:2997–3011, 1976.

[Landry:93a] Landry, W. L., and Werner, B. T. "Wind ripples: An example of computer simulation modelling applied to landform patterns," *Physica D*, 1993. submitted for publication.

[Lapedes:87a] Lapedes, A., and Farber, R. "Nonlinear signal processing using neural networks: Prediction and system modeling." Technical Report LA-UR-87-1662, Los Alamos National Laboratory, Los Alamos, NM, 1987. Los Alamos Preprint.

[Lazou:87a] Lazou, C. *Supercomputers and Their Use.* Oxford University Press, Oxford, Great Britain, 1987.

[Lee:86a] Lee, R. "Mercury I/O library users' guide, C language edition." Technical Report C3P-301, California Institute of Technology, Pasadena, CA, 1986.

[Lee:88a] Lee, M., Cooper, G. T., Groom, S. L., Mazer, A. S., and Williams, W. I. "Concurrent image processing executive (CIPE)." Technical Report C3P-669, California Institute of Technology, Pasadena, CA, September 1988.

[Lee:89a] Lee, R. A., and Goodhart, C. E. "Centaur: A mixed synchronous/asynchronous communication protocol for the Mark III hypercube," in J. L. Gustafson, editor, *The Proceedings of the Fourth Conference on Hypercubes, Concurrent Computers and Applications*, page 841. Golden Gate Enterprises, Los Altos, CA, March 1989. Caltech Report C3P-774.

[Lee:89b] Lee, M., Groom, S., Mazer, A., and Williams, W. "Concurrent image processing executive (CIPE)," in J. L. Gustafson, editor, *The Proceedings of the Fourth Conference on Hypercubes, Concurrent Computers and Applications*, page 1069. Golden Gate Enterprises, Los Altos, CA, March 1989. Caltech Report C3P-810.

[Lenoski:89a] Lenoski, D., Laudon, J., Gharachorloo, K., Gupta, A., Hennessy, J., Horowitz, M., and Lam, M. "Design of Stanford DASH multiprocessor." Technical Report TR 89-403, Stanford University, Palo Alto, CA, 1989. Computing Systems Laboratory.

[Lenz:20a] Lenz, W. *Z. Phys.*, 21:613, 1920.

[Leonard:80a] Leonard, A. "Vortex methods for flow simulation," *J. Computational Physics*, 37:289–335, 1980.

[Lepetit:90a] Lepetit, B., Peng, Z., and Kuppermann, A. "Calculation of bound rovibrational states on the first electronically excited state of the H_3 system," *Chem. Phys. Letters*, 166:572–580, 1990.

[Lepetit:90b] Lepetit, B., and Kuppermann, A. "Numerical study of the geometric phase in the $H + H_2$ reaction," *Chem. Phys. Letters*, 166:581–588, 1990.

[Li:87a] Li, G., and Coleman, T. F. "A parallel triangular solver for a hypercube multiprocessor," in M. T. Heath, editor, *Hypercube Multiprocessors*. SIAM, Philadelphia, 1987.

[Li:89a] Li, X., and Sokal, A. D. "Rigorous lower bound on the dynamic critical exponents of the Swendsen-Wang algorithm," *Phys. Rev. Lett.*, 63:827–830, 1989.

[Li:91a] Li, T., "Track staging suite system design notebook," 1991. Internal JPL Document.

[Liewer:89c] Liewer, P. C., and Decyk, V. K. "A general concurrent algorithm for plasma particle-in-cell simulation codes," *Journal of Computational Physics*, 85(2):302–322, 1989. Caltech Report C3P-649b.

[Liewer:90a] Liewer, P. C., Leaver, E. F., Decyk, V. K., and Dawson, J. M. "Dynamic load balancing in a concurrent plasma PIC code on the JPL/Caltech Mark III Hypercube," in D. W. Walker and Q. F. Stout, editors, *The Fifth Distributed Memory Computing Conference, Volume II*, pages 939–942. IEEE Computer Society Press, Los Alamitos, CA, 1990. Held April 9–12, Charleston, South Carolina. Caltech Report C3P-894.

[Liewer:91a] Liewer, P. C., Decyk, V. K., Dawson, J. M., and Lembège, B. "Numerical studies of electron dynamics in oblique quasi-perpendicular collisionless shock waves," *Journal of Geophys. Res.*, A6:9455–9465, 1991. Caltech Report C3P-964.

[Liewer:92a] Liewer, P. C., Krücken, T. J., and Decyk, V. K. "Two dimensional plasma PIC simulations of the dissipation of Alfvén waves," in *Solar Wind Seven*, page 481. Pergamon, Oxford, 1992. COSPAR, coloq. series.

[Lima:89a] Lima, M. A. P., Watari, K., and McKoy, V. "Polarization effects in low-energy e-CH_4 collisions," *Phys. Rev. A*, 39:4312–4315, 1989.

[Lima:90a] Lima, M. A. P., Brescansin, L. M., da Silva, A. J. R., Winstead, C., and McKoy, V. "Applications of the Schwinger multichannel method to electron-molecule collisions," *Phys. Rev. A*, 41:327–332, 1990.

[Lin:65a] Lin, S. "Computer solutions of the traveling salesman problem," *The Bell System Technical Journal*, 44:2245, December 1965.

[Lin:73a] Lin, S., and Kernighan, B. W. "An effective heuristic algorithm for the traveling salseman problem," *Operations Res.*, 21:498, 1973.

[Ling:75a] Ling, R. T., and Kuppermann, A. "Electronic and atomic collisions," in J. S. Rusley and R. Gabelle, editors, *9th International Conference on the Physics of Electronic and Atomic Collisions*, volume 1, pages 353–354. University of Washington Press, Seattle, WA, July 1975. Abstracts of papers presented in Seattle, July 24–30.

[Lipowski:91a] Lipowski, R. "The conformation of membranes," *Nature*, 349:475, 1991.

[Lissman:58a] Lissman, H. W. "On the function and evolution of electric organs in fish," *J. Exp. Biol.*, 35:156–160, 1958.

[Liu:73a] Liu, B. "Ab initio potential energy surface for linear H_3," *Chemical Physics*, 58:1925, 1973.

[Liu:91a] Liu, W. C. "Fast QCD conjugate gradient solver on the Connection Machine," *Nucl. Phys. B (Proc. Suppl.)*, 20(76), 1991. Proceedings of the International Conference on Lattice Field Theory, Tallahassee (Oct. 1990).

[Livingston:88a] Livingston, M., and Stout, Q. F. "Distributing resources in hypercube computers," in G. C. Fox, editor, *The Third Conference on Hypercube Concurrent Computers and Applications, Volume 1*, pages 222–231. ACM Press, New York, NY, January 1988.

[Loh:85a] Loh, Jr., E., Scalapino, D. J., and Grant, P. M. "Monte Carlo studies of the quantum XY model in two dimensions," *Phys. Rev. B*, 31:4712–4716, 1985.

[Lohner:84a] Löhner, R., Morgan, K., and Zienkowicz, O. C. "The solution of non-linear hyperbolic equation systems by the finite element method," *International Journal of Numerical Methodology in Engineering*, 4:1043–1053, 1984.

[Lohner:85a] Löhner, R., Morgan, K., and Zienkowicz, O. C. "An adaptive finite element procedure for compressible high speed flows," *Comp. Meth. in Appl. Mech. and Eng.*, 51:441–463, 1985.

[Lohner:86a] Löhner, R., Morgan, K., Peraire, J., Zienkowicz, O. C., and Kong, L. "Finite element methods for compressible flow," in K. W. Morton and M. J. Baines, editors, *Numerical Methods for Fluid Mechanics, II*, pages 28–53. Clarendon Press, Oxford, England, 1986.

[Lorenz:87a] Lorenz, J., and Noerdlinger, P. D. "Analysis of strange attractors on the hypercube." Technical Report C3P-400, California Institute of Technology, Pasadena, CA, 1987. Unpublished.

[Lorenz:89a] Lorenz, J., and Van de Velde, E. F. "Concurrent computations of invariant manifolds," in J. L. Gustafson, editor, *The Proceedings of the Fourth Conference on Hypercubes, Concurrent Computers and Applications*, pages 1315–1320. Golden Gate Enterprises, Los Altos, CA, March 1989. Caltech Report C3P-759.

[Lorenz:92a] Lorenz, J., and Van de Velde, E. F. "Adaptive data distributions for concurrent continuation," *Numerische Mathematik*, 62(2):269–294, 1992. CRPC-TR89013.

[Lovelace:68a] Lovelace, C. "A novel application of regge trajectories," *Phys. Lett. B*, 28:264–268, 1968.

[Lyzenga:85a] Lyzenga, G. A., Raefsky, A., and Hager, B. H. "Finite elements and the method of conjugate gradients on a concurrent processor," in *Proceedings of the 1985 ASME International Computers in Engineering*, August 1985. Boston. Caltech Report C3P-164.

[Lyzenga:88a] Lyzenga, G. A., Raefsky, A., and Nour-Omid, B. "Implementing finite element software on hypercube machines," in G. C. Fox, editor, *The Third Conference on Hypercube Concurrent Computers and Applications, Volume 2*, pages 1755–1761. ACM Press, New York, January 1988. Caltech Report C3P-594.

[Maddox:90a] Maddox, J. "Towards explaining superconductivity," *Nature*, 344:485, April 1990.

[Makino:90a] Makino, J. "Comparison of two different tree algorithms," *Journal of Computational Physics*, 88:393–408, 1990.

[Manolopoulos:86a] Manolopoulos, D. E. "An improved log derivative method for inelastic scattering," *J. Chem. Phys.*, 85:6425, 1986.

[Manos:89a] Manos, D. M., and Flamm, D. L., editors. *Plasma Etching: An Introduction.* Academic Press, San Diego, 1989.

[Mansour:91a] Mansour, N., and Fox, G. C. "A hybrid genetic algorithm for task allocation in multicomputers," in *International Conference on Genetic Algorithms*, pages 466–473. Morgan Kaufmann Publishers, San Mateo, CA, July 1991.

[Mansour:92a] Mansour, N., and Fox, G. C. "Allocating data to multicomputer nodes by physical optimization algorithms for loosely synchronous computations," *Concurrency: Practice and Experience*, 4(7):557–574, 1992.

[Mansour:92b] Mansour, N., and Fox, G. "Parallel genetic algorithms with application to load balancing for parallel computating." Technical Report SCCS-74c, Syracuse University, Syracuse, NY, June 1992. Published in Supercomputing Symposium '92, Montreal, Quebec, Canada.

[Mansour:92c] Mansour, N., and Fox, G. "A comparison of load balancing algorithms for parallel computations." Technical Report SCCS-154b, Syracuse University, Syracuse, NY, June 1992. Published in Supercomputing Symposium '92, Montreal, Quebec, Canada.

[Mansour:92d] Mansour, N. *Physical Optimization Algorithms for Mapping Data to Distributed-Memory Multiprocessors.* PhD thesis, Syracuse University, August 1992. CRPC-TR92229.

[Mansour:92e] Mansour, N., and Fox, G. C. "Parallel physical optimization algorithms for data mapping," in *Proceedings of the International Conference on Parallel Processing CONPAR '92*, June 1992.

[Mansour:93b] Mansour, N., Ponnusamy, R., Choudhary, A., and Fox, G. C. "Graph contraction for physical optimization methods: A quality-cost tradeoff for mapping data on parallel computers." Technical Report SCCS-474, Syracuse University, Syracuse, NY, March 1993.

[Margolis:86a] Margolis, N., Tommaso, T., and Vichniac, G. "Cellular-automata supercomputers for fluid-dynamics modeling," *Phys. Rev. Lett.*, 56(16):1694–1696, 1986.

[Marinari:92a] Marinari, E., and Parisi, G. "Simulated tempering: A new Monte Carlo scheme," *Europhys. Lett*, 19:451, February 1992. Syracuse University Technical Report SCCS-241.

[Marinari:93a] Marinari, E. "A review talk about computers and theoretical physics," *Nucl. Phys. B (Proc. Suppl.)*, 30:122, 1993.

[Marr:76a] Marr, D., and T., P. "Cooperative computation of stereo disparity," *Science*, 195:283–287, 1976.

[Marr:80a] Marr, D. C., and Hildreth, E. "Theory of edge detection," *Proc. Roy. Soc. London B*, 270:187–217, 1980.

[Marroquin:84a] Marroquin, J. L. "Surface reconstruction preserving discontinuities," *MIT A. I. Memo*, 792, 1984.

[Marsland:84a] Marsland, T. A., and Popowich, F. "Parallel game-tree search." Technical Report TR-85-1, University of Alberta, Edmonton, AB, 1984. Department of Computing Science.

[Marsland:87a] Marsland, T. A. "Computer chess methods," in Shapiro, editor, *Encyclopedia of Artificial Intelligence*. John Wiley and Sons, New York, NY, 1987.

[Martin:91a] Martin, O., Otto, S. W., and Felten, E. "Large-step Markov chains for the traveling salesman problem," *Complex Systems*, 5(3):299–326, 1991. Caltech Report C3P-836b.

[Matsubara:56a] Matsubara, T., and Katsuda, K. "A lattice model of liquid Helium, I," *Prog. Theo. Phys.*, 16:569–578, 1956.

[Mavriplis:88a] Mavriplis, D. J. "Accurate multigrid solution of the Euler equations on unstructured and adaptive meshes." Technical Report NASA-CR 181679/ICASE 88-40, NASA/ICASE, 1988.

[McCormick:89a] McCormick, S., and Quinlan, D. "Asynchronous multilevel adaptive methods for solving partial differential equations on multiprocessors," *Parallel Computing*, 12:145, 1989.

[Meier:84b] Meier, D. L. "C3PO: a proposed general purpose intermediate host program." Technical Report C3P-087, California Institute of Technology, Pasadena, CA, July 1984.

[Meier:88a] Meier, D. "Hypercube multicomputers and their use in observational and theoretical astrophysics," in T. J. Cornwell, editor, *The Use of Supercomputers in Observational Astronomy*, pages 53–62. National Radio Astronomy Observatory/AUI, 1988. Workshop #15, held in Minneapolis, MN, November 4–6, 1985. Caltech Report C3P-252.

[Meier:89a] Meier, D. L., Cloud, K. C., Horvath, J. C., Allan, L. D., Hammond, W. H., and Maxfield, H. A. "A general framework for complex time-driven simulations on hypercubes." Technical Report C3P-761, California Institute of Technology, Pasadena, CA, March 1989. Paper presented at the Fourth Conference on Hypercubes, Concurrent Computers and Applications.

[Meier:90a] Meier, D. L., Cloud, K. L., Horvath, J. C., Allan, L. D., Hammond, W. H., and Maxfield, H. A. "A general framework for complex time-driven simulations on hypercubes," in D. W. Walker and Q. F. Stout, editors, *The Fifth Distributed Memory Computing Conference, Volume I*, pages 117–121. IEEE Computer Society Press, Los Alamitos, CA, 1990. Held April 9–12, Charleston, South Carolina. Caltech Report C3P-960.

[Meredith:84a] Meredith, D., "Caltech Cosmic Cube performing mammoth calculations." Press Release, October 1984. Caltech Report C3P-049b.

[Merlin:92a] Merlin, J. H. "Techniques for the automatic parallelization of 'distributed Fortran 90'." Technical Report SNARC 92-02, Southampton Novel Architecture Research Centre, Southampton, UK, 1992.

[Mermin:66a] Mermin, N. D., and Wagner, H. "Absence of ferromagnetism or antiferromagnetism in one or two dimensional isotropic Heisenberg models," *Phys. Rev. Lett.*, 77:1133–1136, 1966.

[Messina:87a] Fox, G., and Messina, P. "Advanced computer architectures," *Scientific American*, 255(10), October 1987. Caltech Report C3P-476.

[Messina:90a] Messina, P., Baillie, C. F., Felten, E. W., Hipes, P. G., Walker, D. W., Williams, R. D., Pfeiffer, W., Alagar, A., Kamrath, A., Leary, R. H., and Rogers, J. "Benchmarking advanced architecture computers," *Concurrency: Practice and Experience*, 2(3):195–256, 1990. Caltech Report C3P-712b.

[Messina:91d] Messina, P., and Murli, A., editors. *Practical Parallel Computing: Status and Prospects.* John Wiley and Sons, Ltd., Sussex, England, 1991.

[Messina:92a] Messina, P. "Trends in high-performance computing environments." Technical Report CCSF-12-92, California Institute of Technology, Pasadena, CA, April 1992. Supercomputing Japan '92 Conference Textbook.

[Metropolis:53a] Metropolis, N., Rosenbluth, A. W., Rosenbluth, M. N., Teller, A. H., and Teller, E. "Equation of state calculations by fast computing machines," *J. Chem. Phys.*, 21:1087–1091, 1953.

[Mihaly:92a] Mihaly, T., and Messina, P., editors. *First Intel Delta Applications Workshop*, February 1992. CSC-2. Caltech Report CCSF-14-92.

[Mihaly:92b] Mihaly, T., and Messina, P., editors. *Touchstone Delta Grand Challenge Computing Applications*, June 1992. CSC-3. Caltech Report CCSF-22-92.

[Miller:92a] Miller, G. L., Teng, S.-H., Thurston, W., and Vavasis, S., "Automatic mesh partitioning," 1992.

[Miller:92b] Miller, D., and Rose, K. "Combined source-channel vector quantization using deterministic annealing." Technical report, University of California, Santa Barbara, CA, May 1992.

[Mills:92a] Mills, K., Vinson, M., Cheng, G., and Thomas, F. "A large scale comparison of option pricing models with historical market data," in *Proceedings of The 4th Symposium on the Frontiers of Massively Parallel Computing.* IEEE Computer Society Press, October 1992. Held in McLean, VA. SCCS-260.

[Mills:92b] Mills, K., Cheng, G., Vinson, M., Ranka, S., and Fox, G. "Software issues and performance of a parallel model for stock option pricing." Technical report, Syracuse University, Syracuse, NY, December 1992. Held in Melbourne, Australia. SCCS-273b.

[MIS:91a] Matrix Information Services, Inc. *Virtual Reality—The Next Revolution in Computer/Human Interface.* MIS, 1991.

[Moler:86a] Moler, C. "Matrix computation on distributed memory multi-processors," in M. T. Heath, editor, *Hypercube Multiprocessors*, pages 181–195. SIAM, Philadelphia, 1986.

[Morison:86a] Morison, R., and Otto, S. W. "The scattered decomposition for finite element problems," *Journal of Scientific Computing*, 2(1):59–76, March 1986. Caltech Report C3P-286.

[Morison:88a] Morison, R. "Interactive performance display and debugging using the nCUBE real-time graphics system," in G. C. Fox, editor, *The Third Conference on Hypercube Concurrent Computers and Applications, Volume 1*, pages 760–765. ACM Press, New York, January 1988. Caltech Report C3P-576.

[Moscato:89a] Moscato, P. "On genetic crossover operators for relative order preservation." Technical Report C3P-778, California Institute of Technology, Pasadena, CA, April 1989.

[Moscato:89c] Moscato, P., and Fontanari, J. F. "Stochastic versus deterministic upgrade in simulated annealing." Technical Report C3P-789, California Institute of Technology, Pasadena, CA, May 1989.

[Moscato:89d] Moscato, P., and Norman, M. "A competitive-cooperative approach to complex combinatorial search." Technical Report C3P-790, California Institute of Technology, Pasadena, CA, May 1989.

[Moscato:89e] Moscato, P. "On evolution, search, optimization, genetic algorithms and martial arts: Towards memetic algorithms." Technical Report C3P-826, California Institute of Technology, Pasadena, CA, September 1989.

[Mott:87a] Mott, N. F., and Massey, H. S. W. *The Theory of Atomic Collisions*, volume II, pages 562–564. Oxford, 3rd edition, 1987.

[Mou:90a] Mou, Z. G. "Divacon: A parallel language for scientific computing based on divide and conquer," *Frontiers 90*, pages 451–461, October 1990.

[Myczkowski:91a] Myczkowski, J., and Steele, G. "Seismic modeling at 14 gigaflops on the Connection Machine," in *Proceedings of Supercomputing '91*, pages 316–326. IEEE Computer Society Press, Los Alamitos, CA, 1991. Held in Albuquerque, NM.

[Nambu:70a] Nambu, Y. "Quark model and factorization of veneziano amplitude," in R. Chand, editor, *Symmetries and Quark Models*. Gordon and Breach, 1970.

[nCUBE:87a] nCUBE Corporation. *nCUBE Users' Handbook*. nCUBE Corporation, Beaverton, Oregon, October 1987.

[Nelson:79a] Nelson, D. R., and Halperin, B. I. "Dislocation-mediated melting in two dimensions," *Phys. Rev. B.*, 19:2457–2484, 1979.

[Nelson:89a] Nelson, M. E., Furmanski, W., and Bower, J. M. "Simulating neurons and networks on parallel computers," in C. Koch and I. Segev, editors, *Methods in Neuronal Modeling: From Synapses to Networks*, chapter 12, pages 397–437. MIT Press, Cambridge, MA, 1989. Caltech Report C3P-721.

[Nelson:90b] Nelson, M. E., Furmanski, W., and Bower, J. M. "Brain maps and parallel computers," *Trends Neurosci.*, 10:403–408, 1990.

[Neveu:71a] Neveu, A., and Schwarz, J. H. "Factorizable dual models of pions," *Nucl. Phys. B.*, B31:86–112, 1971.

[Newborn:85a] Newborn, M. "A parallel search chess program," in S. R. Oliver, editor, *Proceedings of the ACM Annual Conference*, pages 272–277. ACM Press, New York, NY, 1985.

[Newton:82a] Newton, M. "An analysis of a parallel implementation of the fast Fourier transform." Technical report, California Institute of Technology, Pasadena, CA, November 1982. Caltech Computer Science Document 5057:DF:82.

[Nielsen:70a] Nielsen, H. B. "An almost physical interpretation of the dual n-point function." Technical report, Nordita, 1970. Unpublished.

[Niemiec:92a] Niemiec, J. "Scheduling for MOVIE." Technical Report NPAC/MOVIE/92-2, Northeast Parallel Architectures Center, Syracuse, NY, 1992.

[Niemiec:92b] Niemiec, J. "Networking for MOVIE." Technical Report NPAC/MOVIE/92-2, Northeast Parallel Architectures Center, Syracuse, NY, 1992.

[Nilan:91a] Nilan, M. S., Berra, P. B., Furmanski, W., Chen, C. Y. R., and Vanhatesh, M. "Problem-structuring tools in C^3I virtual environments: Training and planning applications." Technical report, Syracuse University, Syracuse, NY, 1991. A Proposal Draft to Rome Laboratories.

[Nishimura:91a] Nishimura, H., and Tawara, H. "Some aspects of total scattering cross sections of electrons for simple hydrocarbon molecules," *J. Phys. B.*, 24:L363–L366, 1991.

[Nolting:91a] Nolting, S. "Nonlinear adaptive finite element systems on distributed memory computers," in *European Distributed Memory Computing Conference*, pages 283–293, April 1991.

[Nour-Omid:87b] Nour-Omid, B., Raefsky, A., and Lyzenga, G. "Solving finite element equations on concurrent computers," in *Proceedings of the Symposium on Parallel Computations and Their Impact on Mechanics*. ASME, December 1987. Caltech Report C3P-463.

[Onsager:44a] Onsager, L. "A 2d model with an order-disorder transition," *Phys. Rev.*, 65:117–149, 1944.

[Oran:90a] Oran, E. S., Boris, J. P., Whaley, R. O., and Brown, E. F. "Exploring fluid dynamics on a Connection Machine," *Supercomputing Review*, pages 52–60, 1990.

[Otten:89a] Otten, R. H. J. M., and van Ginneken, L. P. P. P. *The Annealing Algorithm*. Kluwer Academic, Boston, MA, 1989.

[Otto:83a] Otto, S., and Randeria, M. "Modified action glueballs," *Nucl. Phys. B.*, 225(FS9):579–589, 1983. CALT-68-1040. Caltech Report C3P-330.

[Otto:83b] Otto, S. *Monte Carlo Methods in Lattice Gauge Theories*. PhD thesis, California Institute of Technology, 1983.

[Otto:84a] Otto, S. W., and Stack, J. D. "SU(3) heavy-quark potential with high statistics," *Phys. Rev. Lett.*, 52:2328–2331, 1984. Caltech Report C3P-067.

[Otto:85b] Otto, S. W., and Stolorz, P. "An improvement for glueball mass calculations on a lattice," *Phys. Lett. B*, 151(5,6):428–432, February 1985. Caltech Report C3P-343.

[Padua:86a] Padua, D. A., and Wolfe, M. J. "Advanced compiler optimizations for supercomputers," *Communications of the ACM*, 29(12):1185, 1986.

[Palmer:86a] Palmer, J. "A VLSI parallel supercomputer," in M. T. Heath, editor, *Hypercube Multiprocessors*, pages 19–26. SIAM, Philadelphia, 1986.

[ParaSoft:88a] ParaSoft. *EXPRESS: A Communication Environment for Parallel Computers*. ParaSoft, Inc., Pasadena, CA, 1988.

[Parasoft:88f] ParaSoft. *PM: Performance Analysis for Parallel Computers*. ParaSoft, Inc., Pasadena, CA, 1988.

[Parisi:81a] Parisi, G., and Wu, Y. "Perturbation theory without gauge fixing," *Sci. Sin.*, 24:483–496, 1981.

[Parisi:83a] Parisi, G., Petronzio, R., and Rapuano, F. "A measurement of the string tension near the continuum limit," *Phys. Lett. B*, 128:418–420, 1983.

[Parker:82a] Parker, D. B. "Learning logic." Technical Report S81-64, Stanford University, Stanford, CA, 1982. Invention Report, File 1, Office of Technology Licensing.

[Parker:87a] Parker, D. B. "Optimal algorithms for adaptive networks: Second order back propagation, second order direct propagation, and second order hebbian learning," in M. Caudill and C. Butler, editors, *International Conference on Neural Networks (IEEE), Volume II*, pages 593–600. IEEE Publishers, Philadelphia, PA, 1987.

[Parlett:80a] Parlett, B. *The Symmetric Eigenvalue Problem*. Prentice-Hall, Englewood Cliffs, NJ, 1980.

[Parsaye:89a] Parsaye, K., Chignell, M., Khoshafian, S., and Wong, H. *Intelligent Databases*. John Wiley and Sons, Ltd., 1989.

[Patel:85a] Patel, A., Otto, S., and Gupta, R. "The non-perturbative β-function for SU(2) lattice gauge theory," *Phys. Lett. B.*, 159:143–147, 1985. CALT-68-1261, Calculation on the Mark I 64 Node. Caltech Report C3P-216.

[Patterson:86a] Patterson, J. "Householder transformation, decomposition, results, some observations." Technical Report C3P-297.5, California Institute of Technology, Pasadena, CA, 1986. Support material for Second Hypercube class.

[Pawley:84a] Pawley, G. S., Swendsen, R. H., Wallace, D. J., and Wilson, K. G. "Monte Carlo renormalization group calculation of the critical behavior in the simple cubix Ising Model," *Phys. Rev. B*, 29:4030–4040, 1984.

[Payne:90a] Payne, D., Leaver, E., Steinman, J., and Jai, B. "Hypercube battle management for Sim89." Technical Report C3P-978, California Institute of Technology, Pasadena, CA, 1990. Internal JPL Document.

[Perez:86a] Perez, E., Periaux, J., Rosenblum, J. P., Stoufflet, B., Derviaux, A., and Lallemand, M. H. *Adaptive Full-Multigrid Finite Element Methods for Solving the Two-Dimensional Euler Equations*, volume 264 of *Lecture Notes in Physics*, pages 523–533. Springer-Verlag, Berlin/New York, 1986. 10th International Conference on Numerical Methods in Fluid Mechanics, ed. F. G. Zhang and Y. L. Zhu.

[Peterson:85a] Peterson, J. C., Tuazon, J. T., Lieberman, D., and Pniel, M. "The Mark III hypercube ensemble concurrent computer," in *IEEE 1985 Conference on Parallel Processing*, August 1985. St. Charles, IL. Caltech Report C3P-151.

[Peterson:85c] Peterson, A. F., and Mittra, R. "Method of conjugate gradients for the numerical solution of large-body electromagnetic scattering problems," *J. Opt. Soc. Am.*, 2A:971–977, 1985.

[Peterson:86a] Peterson, A. F., and Mittra, R. "Convergence of the conjugate gradient method when applied to matrix equation representing electromagnetic scattering problems," *IEEE Trans. Antennas and Propagation*, AP-34:1447–1454, 1986.

[Peterson:89b] Peterson, C., and Söderberg, B. "A new method for mapping optimization problems onto neural networks," *Int. J. Neural Syst.*, pages 3–22, 1989.

[Peterson:90a] Peterson, C. "Parallel distributed approaches to combinatorial optimization problems—benchmark studies on TSP," *Neural Computation*, 2:261, 1990.

[Peterson:93a] Peterson, C., and Söderberg, B. "Artificial neural nets and combinatorial optimization problems," *Local Search in Combinatorial Optimization*, 1993. Edited by Aarts and Lenstra, to appear in second half of 1993.

[Petzold:83a] Petzold, L. R., "DASSL: Differential algebraic system solver." Sandia National Laboratories, Livermore, CA, Category #D2A2, 1983.

[Pfeiffer:90a] Pfeiffer, W., Alagar, A., Kamrath, A., Leary, R., and Rogers, J. "Benchmarking and optimization of scientific codes on the CRAY X-MP, CRAY-2, and SCS-40 vector computers," *The Journal of Supercomputing*, 4(2):131–152, 1990. Caltech Report C3P-699.

[Pfister:85a] Pfister, G. F., et al. "The IBM research parallel processor prototype (RP3): Introduction and architecture," in *IEEE 1985 Conference on Parallel Processing*, August 1985. St. Charles, IL.

[Podgorny:92a] Podgorny, M. "MOVIE documentation system." Technical Report NPAC/MOVIE/92–6, Northeast Parallel Architectures Center, Syracuse, NY, 1992.

[Podgorny:92b] Podgorny, M. "Status of the DPS implementation in MOVIE." Technical Report NPAC/MOVIE/92–17, Northeast Parallel Architectures Center, Syracuse, NY, 1992.

[Poggio:85a] Poggio, T., Torre, V., and Koch, C. "Computational vision and regularization theory," *Nature*, 317:314–319, 1985.

[Pollara:85a] Pollara, F. "Concurrent viterbi algorithm on a hypercube," in B. Hajek and D. C. Munson Jr., editors, *Proceedings of the 23rd Annual Allerton Conference on Communication Control and Computing*, October 1985. University of Illinois. Caltech Report C3P-208.

[Pollara:86a] Pollara, F. "Concurrent viterbi algorithm with trace-back," *Advanced Algorithms and Architectures for Signal Processing*, 696:204, 1986. In August 1986 Conference of International Society of Optical Engineering. Caltech Report C3P-462.

[Polonyi:83a] Polonyi, J., and Wyld, H. W. "Microcanonical simulation of Fermionic systems," *Phys. Rev. Lett.*, 51:2257–2260, 1983.

[Polyakov:75a] Polyakov, A. M. "Interaction of goldstone particles in 2d," *Phys. Lett. B*, 59:79–81, 1975.

[Polyakov:81a] Polyakov, A. M. "Quantum geometry of bosonic strings," *Phys. Lett. B*, 103:207–210, 1981.

[Polyakov:86a] Polyakov, A. M. "Fine structure of strings," *Nucl. Phys. B*, 268:406–412, 1986.

[Ponnusamy:92c] Ponnusamy, R., Saltz, J., Das, R., Koelbel, C., and Choudhary, A. "A runtime data mapping scheme for irregular problems," in *Proceedings of Scalable High Performance Computing Conference*. IEEE Computer Society Press, Los Alamitos, CA, April 1992. Held in Williamsburg, VA. SCCS-356, CRPC-TR92263.

[Ponnusamy:93a] Ponnusamy, R., Mansour, N., Choudhary, A., and Fox, G. C. "Mapping realistic data sets on parallel computers," in *Proceedings of International Parallel Processing Symposium, IPPS '93*, pages 123–128, April 1993. CRPC-TR92265, SCCS-366.

[Pothen:89a] Pothen, A., Simon, H. D., and Liu, K. P. "Partitioning sparse matrices with eigenvectors of graphs." Technical Report RNR-89-009, NASA Ames Research Center, July 1989.

[Pothen:90a] Pothen, A., Simon, H., and Liou, K. P. "Partitioning sparse matrices with eigenvectors of graphs," *SIAM J. Matrix Anal. Appl.*, 11(3):430–452, July 1990.

[Potts:52a] Potts, R. B. "Some generalized order-disorder transformations," *Proc. Camb. Phil. Soc.*, 48:106, 1952.

[Press:86a] Press, W., Flannery, B. P., Teukolsky, S. A., and Vetterling, W. T. *Numerical Recipes, The Art of Scientific Computing*. Cambridge, 1986.

[Pritchard:89a] Pritchard, H. P., Lima, M. A. P., and McKoy, V. "Studies of elastic e-NH_3 collisions," *Phys. Rev. A*, 39:2392–2396, 1989.

[Pritchard:91a] Pritchard, D. "Special issue: Highlights of transputer applications," *Concurrency: Practice and Experience*, 3(4), August 1991.

[Raefsky:88b] Raefsky, A., Lyzenga, G. A., Gurnis, M., and Hager, B. H. "Solid earth continuum calculations on a hypercube concurrent computer." Technical Report C3P-738, California Institute of Technology, Pasadena, CA, 1988.

[Reed:91a] Reed, D. A., Olson, R. D., Aydt, R. A., Madhyastha, T., Birkett, T., Jensen, D. W., Nazief, B. A. A., and Totty, B. K. "Scalable performance environments for parallel systems." Technical Report UIUCDCS-R-92-1673, University of Illinois, Urbana, IL, March 1991. Proceedings of the 6th Distributed Memory Computing Conference, IEEE Computer Society Press, pp. 562–569.

[Reiher:90a] Reiher, P. L., and Jefferson, D. J. "Virtual time based dynamic load management in the time warp operating system," *Transactions of the Society for Computer Simulation*, 7(2):91–120, June 1990.

[Rescigno:90a] Rescigno, T. N., Lengsfield III, B. H., and McCurdy, C. W. "Electronic excitation of formaldehyde by low-energy electrons—a theoretical study using the complex Kohn variational method," *Phys. Rev. A*, 41:2462–2467, 1990.

[Rice:85a] Rice, J., and Boivster. *Solving Elliptic Problems using Ellpack.* Springer-Verlag, 1985.

[Riedel:69a] Riedel, E., and Wegner, F. "Scaling approach to anisotropic magnetic systems statics," *Z. Physik*, 225:195–215, 1969.

[Rivara:84a] Rivara, M. "Design and data structure of fully adaptive multigrid, finite-element software," *ACM Trans. in Math. Software*, 10:242–252, 1984.

[Rivara:89a] Rivara, M. "Selective refinement/derefinement algorithms for sequences of nested triangulations," *International Journal for Numerical Methods in Engineering*, 28:2889–2906, 1989.

[Rogers:89b] Rogers, A., and Pingali, K. "Process decomposition through locality of reference," in *Proceedings of the ACM SIGPLAN 89 Conference on Programming Language Design and Implementation*, pages 69–80. ACM Press, New York, NY, June 1989.

[Rogiers:79a] Rogiers, J., Grundke, E. W., and Betts, D. D. "The spin 1/2 XY model, III, analysis of high temperature series expansions of some thermodynamic quantities in two dimensions," *Can. J. Phys.*, 57:1719–1732, 1979.

[Romine:87a] Romine, C. H. "The parallel solution of triangular systems on a hypercube," in M. T. Heath, editor, *Hypercube Multiprocessors*. SIAM, Philadelphia, 1987.

[Romine:90a] Romine, C. H., and Sigmon, K. "Reducing inner product computation in the one-sided Jacobi algorithm," in D. W. Walker and Q. F. Stout, editors, *The Fifth Distributed Memory Computing Conference, Volume I*, pages 301–310. IEEE Computer Society Press, Los Alamitos, CA, 1990. Held April 9–12, Charleston, SC.

[Rosario:93a] del Rosario, J. M., and Choudhary, A. "High performance I/O for parallel computers: Problems and prospects." Technical Report SCCS-513, Syracuse University, Syracuse, NY, 1993. Submitted to IEEE *Computer* Special Issue: The I/O Subsystem: Its Impact on Computer System Performance.

[Rosati:91a] Rosati, J. J., Papaccio, P. N., Shepanski, J. F., and Spadaro, G. "Parallel processing for global change studies," *Quest, TRW Space and Defense*, 13(2), 1991.

[Rosati:91b] Rosati, J. J., "The global change research program: Requirements, technologies and opportunities," 1991. UCLA course.

[Rose:89b] Rose, K., Gurewitz, E., and Fox, Geoffrey, C. "A nonconvex cost optimization approach to tracking multiple targets by a parallel computational network." Technical Report C3P-853, California Institute of Technology, Pasadena, CA, 1989. Published in *Proceedings of the 1990 IEEE International Workshop on Intelligent Robots and Systems*, IROS'90 held in Tsuchiura, Ibaraki, Japan, July 1990.

[Rose:90a] Rose, K., Gurewitz, E., and Fox, G. "A deterministic annealing approach to clustering," *Pattern Recognition Letters*, 11(9):589–594, September 1990. Caltech Report C3P-857.

[Rose:90b] Rose, K., Gurewitz, E., and Fox, Geoffrey, C. "A nonconvex cost optimization approach to tracking multiple targets by a parallel computational network," in D. W. Walker and Q. F. Stout, editors, *The Fifth Distributed Memory Computing Conference, Volume I*, pages 78–84. IEEE Computer Society Press, Los Alamitos, CA, 1990. Held April 9–12, Charleston, South Carolina. Caltech Report C3P-875.

[Rose:90c] Rose, K., Gurewitz, E., and Fox, G. C. "Statistical mechanics and phase transitions in clustering," *Physical Review Letters*, 65(8):945–948, August 1990. SCCS-20. Caltech Report C3P-893.

[Rose:90f] Rose, K. *Deterministic Annealing, Clustering, and Optimization.* PhD thesis, California Institute of Technology, December 1990. SCCS-32, CRPC-TR91114. Caltech Report C3P-950.

[Rose:91a] Rose, K., Gurewitz, E., and Fox, G. C. "A deterministic annealing approach to constrained clustering." Technical Report C3P-957, California Institute of Technology, Pasadena, CA, 1991. Accepted to the 1991 IEEE International Symposium on Information Theory, Budapest, June 23–28.

[Rose:92a] Rose, K., Gurewitz, E., and Fox, G. C. "Vector quantization by deterministic annealing," *IEEE Trans. on Information Theory*, 38(4), July 1992. Caltech Report C3P-895.

[Rose:92b] Rose, K., and Miller, D. "A deterministic annealing approach for module placement." Technical report, University of California at Santa Barbara, Santa Barbara, March 1991.

[Rose:93a] Rose, K., Gurewitz, E., and Fox, G. C. "Constrained clustering as an optimization method," *IEEE Trans. on Pattern Recognition and Machine Intelligence*, 15(8):785–794, August 1993. Caltech Report C3P-919.

[Rosenfeld:82a] Rosenfeld, A., and Kak, A. C. *Digital Picture Processing.* Academic Press, New York, 1982.

[Rumelhart:86a] Rumelhart, D., Hinton, G., and Williams, R. "Learning internal representations by error propagation," in *Parallel Distributed Processing: Vol 1: Foundations.* MIT Press, Boston, 1986.

[Rumelhart:86b] Rumelhart, D. E., and McClelland, J. L., editors. *Parallel Distributed Processing: Explorations in the Microstructure of Cognition*, volume 1. MIT Press, Cambridge, MA, 1986.

[Saad:85a] Saad, Y., and Schultz, M. H. "Parallel direct methods for solving banded linear systems." Technical Report Yale Research Report YALEU/DCS/RR-387, Yale University, New Haven, CT, 1985.

[Saad:88a] Saad, Y., and Shultz, M. "Topological properties of hypercubes," *IEEE Transactions on Computers*, 37(7), July 1988.

[Salmon:84a] Salmon, J. "An astrophysical N-body simulation on the hyper-cube." Technical Report C3P-078, California Institute of Technology, Pasadena, CA, July 1984.

[Salmon:84b] Salmon, J. C. "Binary gray codes and the mapping of a physical lattice into a hypercube." Technical Report C3P-051, California Institute of Technology, Pasadena, CA, January 1984.

[Salmon:86a] Salmon, J., and Hogan, C. "Correlation of QSO absorption lines in universes dominated by cold dark matter," *Monthly Notices of the Royal Astronomical Society*, 221:93–104, 1986. Caltech Report C3P-211.

[Salmon:86b] Salmon, J. "The FFT and the N-body problem on the hyper-cube." Technical Report C3P-297.7, California Institute of Technology, Pasadena, CA, November 1986. Support material for Second Hyper-cube class.

[Salmon:87a] Salmon, J. "CUBIX: Programming hypercubes without programming hosts," in M. T. Heath, editor, *Hypercube Multiprocessors*, pages 3–9. SIAM, Philadelphia, 1987. Caltech Report C3P-378.

[Salmon:88a] Salmon, J., Callahan, S., Flower, J., and Kolawa, A. "MOOSE: A multi-tasking operating system for hypercubes," in G. C. Fox, editor, *The Third Conference on Hypercube Concurrent Computers and Applications, Volume 1*, pages 391–396. ACM Press, New York, January 1988. Caltech Report C3P-586.

[Salmon:88c] Salmon, J., "Ray tracing," January 1988. Poster session presentation at The Third Conference on Hypercube Concurrent Computers and Applications, Pasadena. Caltech Report C3P-565.

[Salmon:89a] Salmon, J., Quinn, P., and Warren, M. "Using parallel computers for very large N-body simulations: Shell formation using 180K particles." Technical Report C3P-780, California Institute of Technology, Pasadena, CA, April 1989.

[Salmon:90a] Salmon, J. *Parallel Hierarchical N-Body Methods*. PhD thesis, California Institute of Technology, December 1990. SCCS-52, CRPC-TR90115. Caltech Report C3P-966.

[Salmon:92a] Salmon, J. K., and Warren, M. S. "Skeletons from the treecode closet." Technical Report CCSF-28-92, California Institute of Technology, Pasadena, CA, October 1992. CSC-7, submitted to *J. Comp. Phys.*

[Saltz:87a] Saltz, J., Mirchandaney, R., Smith, R., Nicol, D., and Crowley, K. "The PARTY parallel runtime system," in *Proceedings of the SIAM Conference on Parallel Processing for Scientific Computing.* Society for Industrial and Applied Mathematics, 1987. held in Los Angeles, CA.

[Saltz:87b] Saltz, J. H., Naik, V. K., and Nicol, D. M. "Reduction of the effects of the communication delays in scientific algorithms on message passing MIMD architectures," *SIAM Journal of Sci. and Stat. Computing*, 8(1):118–134, January 1987.

[Saltz:91b] Saltz, J., Berryman, H., and Wu, J. "Multiprocessor and runtime compilation," *Concurrency: Practice and Experience*, 3(6):573–592, December 1991. Special Issue: Practical Parallel Computing: Status and Prospects. Guest Editors: Paul Messina and Almerico Murli.

[Samet:88a] Samet, H. "An overview of hierarchical spatial data structures," in *Proceedings of the Fifth Israeli Symposium on Artificial Intelligence, Vision, and Pattern Recognition*, pages 331–351, December 1988.

[Samet:90a] Samet, H. *The Design and Analysis of Spatial Data Structures.* Addison-Wesley, Reading, MA, 1990.

[Schaeffer:84a] Schaeffer, J., Olafsson, M., and Marsland, T. A. "Experiments in distributed tree-search." Technical Report TR-84-4, University of Alberta, Edmonton, AB, 1984. Department of Computing Science.

[Schaeffer:86a] Schaeffer, J. "Improved parallel alpha-beta search," in H. Stone and S. Winkler, editors, *Proceedings of ACM-IEEE Fall Joint Computer Conference*, pages 519–527. ACM Press, New York, NY, 1986.

[Schatz:75a] Schatz, G. C., and Kuppermann, A. "Quantum mechanical reactive scattering: An accurate three-dimensional calculation," *J. Chem. Phys.*, 62:2502–2504, 1975.

[Schatz:76a] Schatz, G. C., and Kuppermann, A. "Quantum mechanical reactive scattering for three-dimensional atom plus diatom systems: I. theory," *J. Chem. Phys.*, 65:4642–4667, 1976.

[Schatz:76b] Schatz, G. C., and Kuppermann, A. "Quantum mechanical reactive scattering for three-dimensional atom plus diatom systems: II. accurate cross sections for $H + H_2$," *J. Chem. Phys.*, 65:4668–4692, 1976.

[Scherk:74a] Scherk, J., and Schwarz, J. H. "Dual models for non-hadrons," *Nucl. Phys. B*, 81:118–144, 1974.

[Schneck:87a] Schneck, P. B. *Supercomputer Architecture.* Kluwer Academic Publishers, Boston, Dordrecht, Lancaster, 1987.

[Schreiber:83a] Schreiber, R., and Keller, H. B. "Driven cavity problems by efficient numerical techniques," *J. Comp. Phys.*, 49:310–326, 1983.

[Schutter:91a] de Schutter, E., and Bower, J. M. "A computer simulation of plateau potentials and synaptic interactions in Purkinje cell spiny dendrites," *Soc. Neurosci. Abstr.*, 21:1383, 1993.

[Schutter:93a] de Schutter, E. *Computation and Neural Systems*, chapter 54. Kluwer, 1993. F. Eeckman, and J. Bower (eds). CNS '92 Conference held from July 16–31, 1992 in San Francisco.

[Schwartz:80a] Schwartz, J. T. "Ultracomputers," *ACM TOPLAS*, 2:484, 1980.

[Schwarz:85a] Schwarz, J. H. *Superstrings: The First 15 Years of Superstring Theory*, volume I and II. World Scientific, Singapore, 1985.

[Schwinger:47a] Schwinger, J. "A variational principle for scattering problems," *Phys. Rev.*, 72:742, 1947.

[Segev:89a] Segev, I., Fleshman, J. W., and Burke, R. E. "Comparmental models of complex neurons," in *Methods in Neuronal Modeling: From Synapses to Networks*, chapter 3, pages 63–96. MIT Press, Cambridge, MA, 1989.

[Seitz:85a] Seitz, C. L. "The Cosmic Cube," *Communications of the ACM*, 28(1):22–33, 1985.

[Seitz:88a] Seitz, C. L., Seizovic, J., and Su, W.-K. "The C programmer's abbreviated guide to multicomputer programming." Technical Report CS-TR-881-1, California Institute of Technology, Pasadena, CA, 1988. Caltech Computer Science Technical Report.

[Seitz:88b] Seitz, C. L., Athas, W. C., Flaig, C. M., Martin, A. J., Seizovic, J., Steele, C. S., and Su, W.-K. "The architecture and programming of the Ametek series 2010 multicomputer," in G. C. Fox, editor, *Proceedings of the Third Conference on Hypercube Concurrent Computers and Applications, Volume 1*, pages 33–36. ACM Press, New York, NY, 1988.

[Seitz:90a] Seitz, C. L. "Concurrent architectures," in Suaya and Birtwistle, editors, *VLSI and Parallel Computing*, chapter 3. Morgan Kaufmann, San Mateo, CA, 1990.

[Seitz:92a] Seitz, C. L. "Mosaic C: An experimental fine-grain multicomputer." Technical report, California Institute of Technology, Pasadena, CA, 1992.

[Sejnowski:87a] Sejnowski, T. J., and Rosenberg, C. R. "Parallel networks that learn to pronounce English text," *Complex Systems*, 1(1):145–168, 1987.

[Shanno:78a] Shanno, D. F. "Conjugate gradient methods with inexact searches," *Mathematics of Operations Research*, 3(3):244–256, 1978.

[Shell:59a] Shell, D. L. "A high-speed sorting procedure," *Communications of the ACM*, 2:30, 1959.

[Siegbahn:78a] Siegbahn, P., and Liu, B. "An accurate three-dimensional potential energy surface for H_3," *J. Chem. Phys.*, 68:2457–2465, 1978.

[Simic:90a] Simic, P. "Statistical mechanics as the underlying theory of 'elastic' and 'neural' optimizations," *Network*, 1:89–103, January 1990. Caltech Report C3P-787.

[Simic:91a] Simic, P. "Constrained nets for graph matching and other quadratic assignment problems," *Neural Computation*, 3:268–281, 1991. Caltech Report C3P-973.

[Simon:91b] Simon, H. D. "Parititioning of unstructured problems for parallel processing," *Computing Systems in Engineering*, 2(2/3):135–148, 1991.

[Simoni:89a] Simoni, D. A., Zimmerman, B. A., Patterson, J. E., Wu, C., and Peterson, J. C. "Synthetic aperture radar processing using the hypercube concurrent architecture," in J. L. Gustafson, editor, *The Proceedings of the Fourth Conference on Hypercubes, Concurrent Computers and Applications*, page 1023. Golden Gate Enterprises, Los Altos, CA, March 1989. Caltech Report C3P-775.

[Simoni:92a] Simoni, D. A. "Application of backpropagation to map separates." Technical Report SCCS-558, Syracuse University, Syracuse, NY, 1992. NPAC/MOVIE/92–18.

[Simoni:92b] Simoni, D. A. "Some nonlinear neural networks and their applications to virtual realities." Technical Report SCCS-559, Syracuse University, Syracuse, NY, 1992.

[Singh:89a] Singh, R. R. P., Fleury, P. A., Lyons, K. B., and Sulewski, P. E. "Quantitative determination of quantum fluctuations in the spin-1/2 planar antiferromagnet," *Phys. Rev. Lett.*, 62:2736–2739, 1989.

[Singh:92a] Singh, J. P., Holt, C., Totuska, T., Gupta, A., and Hennessy, J. L. "Load balancing and data locality in hierarchical N-body method," *Journal of Parallel and Distributed Computing*, to be published.

[Skerrett:92a] Skerrett, P. J. "Future computers: The tera flop race," *Popular Science*, page 55, 1992.

[Skjellum:88a] Skjellum, A., Morari, M., and Mattisson, S. "Waveform relaxation for concurrent dynamic simulation of distillation columns," in G. C. Fox, editor, *The Third Conference on Hypercube Concurrent Computers and Applications, Volume 2*, pages 1062–1071. ACM Press, New York, January 1988. Caltech Report C3P-588.

[Skjellum:89a] Skjellum, A., Morari, M., Mattisson, S., and Peterson, L. "Concurrent DASSL: structure, application and performance," in J. L. Gustafson, editor, *Proceedings of the Fourth Conference on Hypercubes, Concurrent Computers and Applications*, pages 1321–1328.

Golden Gate Enterprises, Los Altos, CA, March 1989. Caltech Report C3P-733.

[Skjellum:90a] Skjellum, A., Leung, A. P., and Morari, M. "Zipcode: A portable multicomputer communication library atop the reactive kernel," in D. W. Walker and Q. F. Stout, editors, *The Fifth Distributed Memory Computing Conference, Volume II*, pages 767–776. IEEE Computer Society Press, Los Alamitos, CA, 1990. Held April 9–12, Charleston, SC. Caltech Report C3P-870.

[Skjellum:90c] Skjellum, A. *Concurrent Dynamic Simulation: Multicomputer Algorithms Research Applied to Ordinary Differential-Algebraic Process Systems in Chemical Engineering*. PhD thesis, California Institute of Technology, July 1990. Caltech Report C3P-940.

[Skjellum:90d] Skjellum, A., and Leung, A. P. "LU factorization of sparse, unsymmetric Jacobian matrices on multicomputer: Experience, strategies, performance," in D. W. Walker and Q. F. Stout, editors, *The Fifth Distributed Memory Computing Conference, Volume I*, pages 328–337. IEEE Computer Society Press, Los Alamitos, CA, 1990. Held April 9–12, Charleston, South Carolina. Caltech Report C3P-839b.

[Skjellum:91a] Skjellum, A., and Morari, M. "Zipcode: A portable communication layer for high performance multicomputing—practice and experience." Technical Report SCCS-172, Syracuse University, Syracuse, NY, March 1991.

[Skjellum:91b] Skjellum, A., and Baldwin, C. H. "The multicomputer toolbox: Scalable parallel libraries for large-scale concurrent applications." Technical Report UCRL-JC-109251, Lawrence Livermore National Laboratory, Livermore, CA, December 1991.

[Skjellum:91c] Skjellum, A., and Still, C. H. "*Zipcode* and the Reactive Kernel for the Caltech Intel Delta prototype and nCUBE/2," in *Proceedings of the Sixth Distributed Memory Computing Conference (DMCC6)*, pages 26–33. IEEE Computer Society Press, Los Alamitos, CA, April 1991. LLNL Technical Report UCRL-JC-107636.

[Skjellum:92a] Skjellum, A., Ashby, S. F., Brown, P. N., Dorr, M. R., and Hindmarsh, A. C. "The multicomputer toolbox," in G. L. Strubble, et al., editor, *Laboratory Directed Research and Development FY91–LLNL*, pages 24–26. August 1992. Lawrence Livermore National Laboratory Technical Report UCRL-53689-91 (Rev 1).

[Skjellum:92b] Skjellum, A., Smith, S. G., and Still, C. "The Zipcode system users' guide—version 1.00." Technical report, Lawrence Livermore National Laboratory, Livermore, CA, October 1992.

[Skjellum:92c] Skjellum, A., Smith, S. G., Still, Charles, H., Leung, A. P., and Morari, M. "*Zipcode:* a portable communication layer for high performance multicomputing." Technical Report UCRL-JC-106725, Lawrence Livermore National Laboratory, Livermore, CA, 1992. To be published in *Concurrency: Practice and Experience*.

[Skjellum:92d] Skjellum, A., Baldwin, C. H., and Smith, S. G. "The multicomputer toolbox on the Delta," in T. Mihaly and P. Messina, editors, *Proceedings of the First Intel Delta Applications Workshop*, pages 263–272, February 1992. Caltech Concurrent Supercomputing Consortium.

[Skwarnicki:92a] Skwarnicki, T. "3D visualization in high energy physics." Technical Report SCCST-267, Syracuse University, Department of Physics, 1992. Foils of talk at GEM SSC Detector Meeting, Dallas, TX, March 11, 1992; and at Cornell University, May 1992.

[Smith:76a] Smith, B. T. "Matrix eigensystem routine—EISPACK guide, second edition," in *Lecture Notes in Computer Science, Vol. 6*, pages 40–43. Springer-Verlag, New York, NY, 1976.

[Smith:84a] Smith, B. T., Dongarra, J. J., and Messina, P. C., editors. *Proceedings for the Argonne Workshop on Programming the Next Generation of Supercomputers*, 1984. Argonne National Laboratory Technical Report ANL/MCS-TM-34.

[Speight:92a] Speight, M. D., and de Schutter, E. "Biologically realistic neural simulation on parallel machines," in *Proceedings of the First Intel Delta Applications Workshop*, pages 82–90. Caltech Concurrent Supercomputing Facilities, Pasadena, CA, February 1992.

[Speight:92b] Speight, M. D., and Bower, J. M., "Using parallel computers for computational neurobiology," 1992. Poster preview at CNS '92 conference held from July 26–31, 1992 in San Francisco. The First Annual Computation and Neural Systems Meeting.

[Stauffer:78a] Stauffer, D. "Scaling theory of percolation clusters," *Phys. Rep.*, 54:1–74, 1978.

[Steinman:91a] Steinman, J. "SPEEDES: synchronous parallel environment for emulation and discrete event simulation," in *Proceedings of the SCS Western Simulation Multiconference*, 1991. Held in Anaheim, California.

[Steinman:92a] Steinman, J. "SPEEDES: a unified approach to parallel simulation," in *Proceedings of the SCS Western Simulation Multiconference*, 1992. Held in Anaheim, California.

[Stolorz:86b] Stolorz, P. "Microcanonical renormalization group for SU(2)," *Phys. Lett. B*, 172:77–80, 1986. Caltech Report C3P-741.

[Stolorz:92a] Stolorz, P. "Merging optimization with deterministic annealing to solve combinatorally hard problems," in Moody, et al., editor, *Advances in Neural Information Processing Systems 4*, pages 1025–1032. Morgan Kaufmann, 1992.

[Stone:87a] Stone, H. S. *High-Performance Computer Architecture*. Addison-Wesley, Reading, MA, 1987.

[Stone:91a] Stone, H. S., and Cocke, J. "Computer architecture in the 1990s," *IEEE Computer*, pages 30–38, 1991.

[Stonebraker:91a] Stonebraker, J., and Dozier, J., "Large capacity object servers to support global change," 1991. Report #91/1, SEQUOIA 2000.

[Stuben:82a] Stüben, K., and Trottenberg, U. "Multigrid methods: Fundamental algorithms, model problem analysis and applications," in *Multigrid Methods Proc.*, pages 1–176. Springer-Verlag, Berlin, 1982.

[Su:93a] Su, A. *Hierarchical Algorithms—Theory and Applications*. PhD thesis, California Institute of Technology, 1993.

[Sun:92a] Sun, Q., Winstead, C., McKoy, V., and Lima, M. A. P. "Low-energy electron-impact excitation of the $\tilde{a}^3 B_{1u} (\pi \rightarrow \pi^*)$ state of ethylene," *Journal of Chemical Physics*, 1992. Submitted for publication.

[Sunderam:90a] Sunderam, V. S. "PVM: a framework for parallel distributed computing," *Concurrency: Practice and Experience*, 2(4):315–340, 1990.

[Susskind:70a] Susskind, L. "Structure of hadrons implied by duality," *Phys. Rev. D.*, 1:1182–1186, 1970.

[Sutherland:68a] Sutherland, I. E. "A head-mounted three-dimensional display," in *Proceedings of the Fall Joint Computer Conference.* AFIPS, 1968. 33–1.

[Swendsen:79a] Swendsen, R. H. "Monte Carlo renormalization group," *Phys. Rev. Lett.*, 42:859–861, 1979.

[Swendsen:87a] Swendsen, R. H., and Wang, J. "Nonuniversal critical dynamics in Monte Carlo simulations," *Phys. Rev. Lett.*, 58(2):86–88, 1987.

[Synnott:90a] Synnott, S., Riedel, J., Stuve, J., Halamek, P., and Lehr, W. "Three-dimensional geometry from image processing on the JPL/CIT hypercube," *Supercomputer 35*, VII(1):21–28, January 1990. Caltech Report C3P-763.

[Takatsuka:81a] Takatsuka, K., and McKoy, V. "Extension of the Schwinger variational principle beyond the static-exchange approximation," *Phys. Rev. A*, 24:2473–2480, 1981.

[Takatsuka:84a] Takatsuka, K., and McKoy, V. "Theory of electronically inelastic scattering of electrons by molecules," *Phys. Rev. A*, 30:1734–1740, 1984.

[Tanaka:88a] Tanaka, H., Boesten, L., Matsunaga, D., and Kudo, T. "Differential elastic electron scattering cross sections for ethane in the energy range from 2 to 100 eV," *J. Phys. B*, 21:1255–1263, 1988.

[Tanaka:89a] Tanaka, H., Boesten, L., Sato, H., Kimura, M., Dillon, M. A., and Spence, D., editors. *42nd Annual Gaseous Electronics Conference*, 1989. Held in Palo Alto, California.

[Teng:91a] Teng, S. *Points, Spheres, and Separators, A Unified Geometric Approach to Graph Partitioning*. PhD thesis, Carnegie Mellon University, August 1991. School of Computer Science.

[Terzopoulos:86a] Terzopoulos, D. "Image analysis using multigrid relaxation methods," *IEEE Trans. Pattern Analysis Machine Intelligence*, 8:129–139, 1986.

[Tevanian:89a] Tevanian, A., and Smith, B. "MACH—the model for future UNIX," *BYTE*, 14(12):411, 1989.

[Theiler:87a] Theiler, J. "An efficient algorithm for estimating correlation dimension from a set of discrete points," *Phys. Rev. A*, 36(9):4456–4462, 1987. Caltech Report C3P-734.

[Theiler:87b] Theiler, J. *Quantifying Chaos: Practical Estimation of the Correlation Dimension*. PhD thesis, California Institute of Technology, October 1987. Caltech Report C3P-474.

[Thompson:82a] Thompson, K. "Computer chess strength," in M. Clarke, editor, *Advances in Computer Chess*, pages 55–56. Pergamon Press, Oxford, England, 1982. Volume 3.

[Trew:91a] Trew, A., and Wilson, G. *Past, Present, Parallel: A Survey of Available Parallel Computing Systems*. Springer-Verlag, Berlin, 1991.

[Truhlar:78a] Truhlar, D. G., and Horowitz, C. J. "Functional representation of Liu and Siegbahn's accurate ab initio potential energy calculations for $H + H_2$," *J. Chem. Phys.*, 68:2466–2476, 1978.

[Truhlar:79a] Truhlar, D. G., and Horowitz, C. J. "Erratum," *J. Chem. Phys.*, 71:1514(E), 1979.

[TSP:90a] 1990. TSP Workshop, organized by W. Bixby and G. Fox, Rice University, April 22–24.

[Tuazon:85a] Tuazon, J. O., Peterson, J. C., Pniel, M., and Lieberman, M. "Caltech/JPL hypercube concurrent processor," in *IEEE 1985 Conference on Parallel Processing*, August 1985. St. Charles, Illinois. Caltech Report C3P-160.

[Tuzun:82a] Tuzun, U., and Nedderman, R. M. "An investigation of the flow boundary during steady-state discharge from a funnel-flow bunker," *Powder Technology*, 31:27–43, 1982.

[Usab:83a] Usab, W. J., and Murman, E. M. "Embedded mesh solution of the Euler equations using a multiple grid method." Technical Report AIAA Paper 83-1946-CP, American Institute of Aeronautics and Astronautics, 1983.

[Veen:76a] van Veen, E. H. "Low-energy electron-impact spectroscopy on ethylene," *Chemical Physics Letters*, 41:540–543, 1976.

[Velde:87a] Van de Velde, E. F., and Keller, H. B. "The design of a parallel multigrid algorithm," in L. Kartashev and S. Kartashev, editors, *Proceedings of the Second International Conference on Supercomputing at Santa Clara*, pages 76–83. International Supercomputing Institute, Inc., St. Petersburg, FL, May 1987. Caltech Report C3P-406.

[Velde:87b] Van de Velde, E. F., and Keller, H. B. "The parallel solution of nonlinear elliptic equations," in A. K. Noor, editor, *Parallel Computations and Their Impact on Mechanics*, pages 127–153. ASME, 1987. Caltech Report C3P-447.

[Velde:88a] Van de Velde, E. F. "A concurrent solver for sparse unstructured systems." Technical Report C3P-604, California Institute of Technology, Pasadena, CA, March 1988.

[Velde:89b] Van de Velde, E. F. "Multicomputer matrix computations: Theory and practice," in J. L. Gustafson, editor, *The Proceedings of the Fourth Conference on Hypercubes, Concurrent Computers and Applications*, pages 1303–1308. Golden Gate Enterprises, Los Altos, CA, March 1989. CRPC-TR89002 Technical Report. Caltech Report C3P-766.

[Velde:90a] Van de Velde, E. "Experiments with multicomputer LU decomposition," *Concurrency: Practice and Experience*, 2(1):1–26, 1990. Caltech Report C3P-725.

[Velde:90b] Van de Velde, E. F., and Lorenz, J. "Applications of adaptive data distributions," in D. W. Walker and Q. F. Stout, editors, *The Fifth Distributed Memory Computing Conference, Volume I*, pages 249–253. IEEE Computer Society Press, Los Alamitos, CA, 1990. Held April 9–12, Charleston, South Carolina. Caltech Report C3P-902.

[Velde:90c] Van de Velde, E. F. "Data redistribution and concurrency," *Parallel Computing*, 16:125–138, 1990. Caltech Report C3P-635.

[Venkatakrishnan:92a] Venkatakrishnan, V., Simon, H., and Barth, T. "A MIMD implementation of a parallel euler solver for unstructured grids," *The Journal of Supercomputing*, 6(2):117–127, 1992.

[Verghese:92a] Verghese, P., and Pelli, D. G. "The information capacity of visual attention," *Vision Research*, 32(5):983–995, 1992.

[Walker:88b] Walker, D. W., Fox, G. C., and Montry, G. R. "The flux-corrected transport algorithm on the nCUBE hypercube," in G. C. Fox, editor, *The Third Conference on Hypercube Concurrent Computers and Applications, Volume 2*, pages 1117–1126. ACM Press, New York, January 1988. Caltech Report C3P-495.

[Walker:90b] Walker, D. W. "Characterizing the parallel performance of a large-scale, particle-in-cell plasma simulation code," *Concurrency: Practice and Experience*, 2(4):257–288, 1990. Caltech Report C3P-912.

[Walker:94a] Walker, D. W. "The design of a message passing interface for distributed memory concurrent processors," *Parallel Computing*, 1994. Accepted for Publication.

[Wallace:84a] Wallace, D. J. "Numerical simulation on the ICL distributed array processor," *Phys. Rep.*, 103:191–201, 1984.

[Wallace:87a] Wallace, D. J., "Scientific computation on SIMD and MIMD machines," 1987. Invited talk at Royal Society Discussion, Edinburgh preprint 87/429.

[Wallace:88a] Wallace, D., Bowler, K., and Kenway, R. "The Edinburgh Concurrent Supercomputer: project and applications," in L. P. Kartashev and S. I. Kartashev, editors, *Proceedings of the Third International Conference on Supercomputing, Volume II*, page 200. International Supercomputing Institute, Inc., St. Petersburg, FL, 1988. held May 15–20, Boston, MA.

[Walton:83a] Walton, O. R. "Particle dynamics calculations of shear flow," in J. T. Jenkins and M. Satake, editors, *Mechanics of Granular Materials: New Models and Constitutive Relations*, pages 327–338. Elsevier Science Publishers, North-Holland, Amsterdam, 1983.

[Walton:84a] Walton, O. R. "Computer simulation of particulate flow," *Energy and Technology Review*, pages 24–36, May 1984. (Lawrence Livermore National Laboratory).

[Waltz:87a] Waltz, D., Stanfill, C., Smith, S., and Thau, R. "Very large database applications of the Connection Machine systems." Technical report, Thinking Machines Corporation, Cambridge, MA, 1987.

[Waltz:88a] Waltz, D. L., and Stanfill, C. "Artificial intelligence related research on the Connection Machine," in *Proceedings of the International Conference on Fifth Generation Computer Systems, Volume 3*, page 1010. OHMSHA, Ltd., Tokyo, Japan, 1988. November 28–December 2, Tokyo.

[Waltz:90a] Waltz, D. L. "Massively parallel AI." Technical report, Thinking Machines Corporation/Brandeis University, Cambridge, MA, 1990.

[Wang:91b] Wang, J. J. H. *Generalized Moment Methods in Electromagnetics*. John Wiley and Sons, Ltd., New York, 1991.

[Warren:88a] Warren, L. V. "Graphics techniques in concurrent simulation," in G. C. Fox, editor, *The Third Conference on Hypercube Concurrent Computers and Applications, Volume 1*, pages 772–785. ACM Press, New York, January 1988. Caltech Report C3P-600.

[Warren:92a] Warren, M. S., Quinn, P. J., Salmon, J. K., and Zurek, W. J. "Dark halos formed via dissipationless collapse: Shapes and alignment of angular momentum," *Astrophysical Journal*, 399:405–425, 1992.

[Warren:93a] Warren, M. S., and Salmon, J. K. "A parallel hashed oct-tree N-Body algorithm," in *Supercomputing '93*. IEEE Comp. Soc., Los Alamitos, CA, 1993.

[Wasson:87a] Wasson, D. A. "Nuclear hartree-fock calculations on the hypercube." Technical Report C3P-412, California Institute of Technology, Pasadena, CA, March 1987.

[Webb:92a] Webb, J. A. "Steps towards architecture independent image processing," *IEEE Computer*, pages 21–32, February 1992.

[Wehmeier:89a] Wehmeier, U., Dong, D., Koch, C., and Van Essen, D. "Modeling the mammalian visual system," in *Methods in Neuronal Modeling: From Synapses to Networks*, chapter 10, pages 335–359. MIT Press, Cambridge, MA, 1989.

[Weingarten:81a] Weingarten, D. H., and Petcher, D. N. "Monte Carlo integration for lattice gauge theories with Fermions," *Phys. Lett. B*, 99:333–338, 1981.

[Weingarten:90a] Weingarten, D. "The status of GF11," *Nucl. Phys. B. (Proc. Suppl.)*, 17:272–275, 1990. Proc. of the 1989 Symposium on Lattice Field Theory.

[Weingarten:92a] Weingarten, D. "Parallel QCD machines," *Nucl. Phys. B. (Proc. Suppl.)*, 26:126–136, 1990. Proc. of the 1991 Symposium on Lattice Field Theory.

[Welcome:92a] Welcome, T. "Programming in LMPS." Technical Report UCRL-MA-107031, Lawrence Livermore National Laboratory, Livermore, CA, March 1992.

[Welsh:85a] Welsh, D. E., and Baczynskyj, B. "Computer chess II,". Brown, W. E., Dubuque, Iowa, 1985. Chapter on Cray Blitz.

[Werner:87a] Werner, B. T. *A Physical Model of Wind-Blown Sand Transport*. PhD thesis, California Institute of Technology, 1987. Caltech Report C3P-425.

[Werner:88a] Werner, B. T., and Haff, P. K. "Dynamical simulations of granular materials using the Caltech hypercube," in G. C. Fox, editor, *The Third Conference on Hypercube Concurrent Computers and Applications, Volume 2*, pages 1313–1318. ACM Press, New York, January 1988. Caltech Report C3P-612.

[Werner:88b] Werner, B. T., and Haff, P. K. "The impact process in eolian saltation: Two-dimensional simulations," *Sedimentology*, 35:189–196, 1988. Caltech Report C3P-365b.

[Werner:90a] Werner, B. T. "A steady-state model of wind-blown sand transport," *J. Geology*, 98:1–17, 1990. Caltech Report C3P-971.

[Werner:91a] Werner, B. T. "Computer simulation of sand surface self-organization in wind-blown sand transport," *Sedimentology*, 1991. In press. Caltech Report C3P-972.

[Westerberg:79a] Westerberg, A. W., Hutchison, H. P., Motard, R. L., and Winter, P. *Process Flowsheeting*. Cambridge University Press, 1979.

[Wetherell:82a] Wetherell, C., "Language working group FORTRAN manual," June 1982. Collaborative Technical Report FORT-82-1. Available from the National Technical Information Services, U. S. Department of Commerce, Springfield, VA.

[Wexler:89a] "Developing transputer applications," in J. Wexler, editor, *Proceedings of the 11th Occam User Group Technical Meeting.* IOS, 1989. Amsterdam.

[Whiteside:88a] Whiteside, R. A., and Leichter, J. S. "Using Linda for supercomputing on a local area network," in *Proceedings of Supercomputing '88.* IEEE Computer Society Press, Washington, D.C., 1988. Held November 14–18, Orlando, FL.

[Wieland:89a] Wieland, F., Hawley, L., Feinberg, A., DiLoreto, M., Blume, L., Ruffles, J., Reiher, P., Beckman, B., Hontalas, P., Bellenot, S., and Jefferson, D. "The performance of a distributed combat simulation with the time warp operating system," *Concurrency: Practice and Experience,* 1(1):35–50, 1989. Caltech Report C3P-798.

[Wilkinson:71a] Wilkinson, J. H., and Reinsch, C. "Linear algebra," in *Handbook for Automatic Computation, Volume II,* pages 227–240. Springer-Verlag, New York, 1971.

[Williams:86b] Williams, R. D. "Minimization by simulated annealing: Is detailed balance necessary?." Technical Report C3P-354, California Institute of Technology, Pasadena, CA, September 1986. CALT-68-1407.

[Williams:87a] Williams, R. D. "Dynamical grid optimization for Lagrangian hydrodynamics." Technical Report C3P-424, California Institute of Technology, Pasadena, CA, April 1987.

[Williams:87b] Williams, R. D. "Finite elements for 2D elliptic equations with moving nodes." Technical Report C3P-423, California Institute of Technology, Pasadena, CA, April 1987.

[Williams:88a] Williams, R. D. "DIME: A programming environment for unstructured triangular meshes on a distributed-memory parallel processor," in G. C. Fox, editor, *The Third Conference on Hypercube Concurrent Computers and Applications, Volume 2,* pages 1770–1787. ACM Press, New York,, January 1988. Caltech Report C3P-502.

Index